In the PATH
of
DESTRUCTION

It's the mouth of a volcano. Yes, mouth; and lava tongue. A body, a monstrous living body, both male and female. It emits, ejects. It is also an interior, an abyss. Something alive, that can die. Something inert that becomes agitated, now and then. Existing only intermittently. A constant menace. If predictable, usually not predicted. Capricious, untamable, molodrous... The slumbering giant that wakes. The lumbering giant who turns his attentions to you . . . Vomiting destruction, and then sinking back into somnolence.

—Susan Sontag, *The Volcano Lover*

In the PATH of DESTRUCTION

Eyewitness Chronicles of Mount St. Helens

RICHARD WAITT

WSU
PRESS

Washington State University
Pullman, Washington

WASHINGTON STATE UNIVERSITY

Washington State University Press
PO Box 645910
Pullman, Washington 99164-5910
Phone: 800-354-7360
Fax: 509-335-8568
Email: wsupress@wsu.edu
Website: wsupress.wsu.edu

Library of Congress Cataloging-in-Publication Data

Waitt, Richard B.
  In the path of destruction : eyewitness chronicles of Mount St. Helens / Richard Waitt.
     pages cm
  Includes bibliographical references and index.
  ISBN 978-0-87422-323-1 (alk. paper)
  1. Saint Helens, Mount (Wash.)—Eruption, 1980. 2. Volcanoes—Washington (State)—Saint Helens, Mount. 3. Volcanic eruptions—Washington (State)—Saint Helens, Mount—Personal narratives. I. Title. II. Title: Eyewitness chronicles of Mount St. Helens.
  QE523.S23W35 2014
  551.2109797'84—dc23
                                                                    2014019566

The author and WSU Press thank the United States Geological Survey for their generous support of the research, writing, and production of *In the Path of Destruction.*

WSU PRESS

Contents

The Stick   vii

Before   ix

The Fuse Is Lit, But We Don't Know How Long It Is: Anatomy of Crisis   1

1. Seismograph (March 19–24)   3
2. Stage   11
3. Geyser   31
4. Bulge   59
5. You're Perfectly Safe Here, Aren't You?   89
6. Totally Clear, No Activity   111

Let's Get the Hell Out of Here!   117

    18 May 1980   119

7. Air   121
8. Cascade Peaks   141
9. Devastation   151
10. West   187
11. North   203
12. Northeast   213
13. East   225
14. South   235
15. Who's On First   241
16. Air Again   247
17. What's On Second   291
18. Plains   295
19. Valley   309

It's a Totally Different World: Aftermath   319

20. Land of Lost Content   321

Appendix I: Cast of Characters   361
Appendix II: Sources and Methods   365
Appendix III: Summary of Interviews 1980–2014   371
Notes   379
References   395
Index   403

The Stick

However I may shudder at the memory
And shrink again in grief, let me begin.
            —Virgil, *Aeneid*

The broken scrap of wood doesn't look like much—ten inches long and two wide, squared, its patina of brickred paint abraded and faded. But like Proust's madeleine, it evokes a past. I'm surprised to find so small a thing among the mammoth mounds of shattered rock on this north shore of Spirit Lake. Reading clues in the landscape, the geologist's eye sees the stick had come in a colossal wave— Spirit Lake hurled hundreds of feet above a level it had lain four hundred years. These rocky mounds had been the top of Mount St. Helens six miles south and a mile higher. The gigantic mass crashing through the lake had ousted the water. Gray grains shot into the stick hint of other brutish violence.

The stick evokes a deeper past. It's come a mile—a splinter off a great lodge that had stood by the lake forty years. In it I'd sipped beer with 83-year-old owner Harry Truman as he told of decades past. Over on that south shore, and here on the north, a damp forest of 120-foot firs had stood for centuries. Now the basin is treeless, a sun-blasted desert. The landscape suggests Mars. The past is vanished.

Or is it entirely so? Two and a half weeks after Mount St. Helens' cataclysm, I cross the Cascades to resume work at the volcano. The front page of Seattle's *Post-Intelligencer* tells how a man and woman speeding down the Spirit Lake highway barely outran a hot ash cloud. I meet them in a Seattle bar, a noisy Friday evening. Soon I know no geologist scrutinizing the deposits could glean what they had witnessed being almost in the eruption. Might this and other stories reveal this volcano's violence? Reveal what could happen at many a volcano? And so I interviewed several, then many, then hundreds of witnesses, recording what they saw and heard and felt those brutal minutes of May 1980.

Scientists come from around the world. I bring four Italian volcanologists to a view of twenty square miles of flattened forest. They stand too awed to speak. Had this been Vesuvius, these million dead would be not trees but people.

The 1980 interviews aided science. Arranging material two decades later for popular reading, I fished again for these witnesses, then many others. Some I found only after years. One I queried deep in a prison. A few I found too late, demented or dying.

Through people we see the weeks of crisis in spring 1980. Their words take us through the May 18 eruption in exquisite fidelity: what they saw, heard, and felt, the timing, the pace and sequence of events. But to reveal the cataclysm, the adventures themselves must be in order. My task resembles Stephen Ambrose's telling World War II through soldiers: "[I] let my characters speak for themselves. They were there.

I wasn't. They saw with their own eyes. They speak with an authenticity no one else can match."[1]

Like survivors of firebombed war cities, Mount St. Helens' witnesses lose family or friends. Some won't talk, not to a stranger. One burned victim refuses an interview for eighteen and a half years, another speaks after twenty. Helicopter pilots inured to blood in Vietnam choke as they tell of Mount St. Helens. During interviews I pause while a 49-year-old man weeps over a friend lost 23 years ago, a lady over her young husband killed 24 years ago, an old man over his son's demise 25 years ago. We may shrink in grief, but let us begin.

The interviews stretched across more than three decades. Meanwhile as a geologist I've documented the eruption's effects, published reports, collaborated with others. I quiz witnesses knowing the cataclysm's geography, details, and timing.

First-person stories anchor this book. Narrated parts too stem from interviews, though based also in 1980 notes, diaries, logbooks, photographs, maps. Parts of backstory draw from witnesses' earlier memories. Some dates and details draw from newspapers or TV or radio tapes of reporters I interview.[2] Reconstructed dialogue stems from witnesses' memories.

Is memory reliable two and three decades after an event? People who don't remember my 1980 interview speak similarly twenty-five years later. A field visit to a witness's site confirms its geography. The sheer number of compatible accounts from independent witnesses tested at length is some proof of reliability.

Science is the study of objects and phenomena. A scientist so controls an experiment that others may reproduce the result. A geologist describes fossils at a specified site where others may come to elaborate or refute. A failed test of repeatability shows something wrong with concept, data, or technique—sometimes revealing shoddy or even bogus science.[3]

Yet a conversation between people happens but once. Repeatability and verification are difficult in a scientific sense. An element of subjectivity pervades this type of evidence. Says Thucydides, fifth-century BC historian of the Peloponnesian War: "Either I was present myself at the events which I have described or else I heard them from eyewitnesses whose reports I have checked with as much thoroughness as possible. Not that even so the truth was easy to discover: different eyewitnesses give different accounts of the same events, speaking out of partiality for one side or the other or else from imperfect memories."[4]

Yet people remember decades later just where they were and with whom when they learned an atomic bomb had exploded on Hiroshima, a President had been shot, a jetliner had slammed into a Manhattan skyscraper. Those caught in the Mount St. Helens' eruption hold such vivid memories. For scientist and natural historian I capture details of phenomena at each place. For people living near Mount St. Helens, I try to draw an accurate portrait of human history. The stories are for everyone.

Historian David McCullough once told me he writes each book like *1776* as one he wishes to read. The book you hold is how I've wished to read Mount St. Helens' story.

Before

On his new beat east up Spirit Lake highway, State Trooper Ron Spahman comes behind an unmuffled white pickup. He flips on the flashers, and the truck pulls right. He studies the license. "Well," he smiles, "you any relation to *the* Harry Truman?"

The old man glares back. "Mister, I *am . . . THE* Harry Truman."

All summer loggers ride gravel roads into the woods. Thousands of visitors stream up the highway on weekends to camp by Spirit Lake or climb Mount St. Helens.

As Don Mullineaux's and Rocky Crandell's two-decades study of Mount St. Helens winds down, protégés Rick Hoblitt and Jim Vallance come to plumb the past five hundred years. Camped at Spirit Lake August 7, they sample Floating Island lava flow and giant boulders shed from Goat Rocks. They ferry across Spirit Lake in evening. Dining at Harmony Falls Lodge, they toast an alpenglow reddening the regal mountain.

Off east next morning, they watch a logger fell a 150-foot noble fir. The faller saws off a round. Measuring its growth rings, Hoblitt might pin down when pumice fell here in the early 1800s.

"So when'll the mountain erupt?" the logger asks.

Mount St. Helens from the Meehan cabin on Spirit Lake, late 1970s

"I don't know, maybe next year," laughs Hoblitt.

Labor Day weekend begins at Spirit Lake like so many earlier: campground full, a last dip in the lake. But rain pours down all Friday night, and next morning rangers Chuck Tonn and Jim Nieland hear a roar descending Dry Gulch. At Deadman's Curve they see boulders and sand have filled the gulch, its bed now only a yard below the highway, the stopped-up Toutle flooding back into trees. Another mudwave down the gulch laps onto the highway. The next slews gravel across. A third buries it a foot and a half. Toutle River chops through the pavement.

Among those now trapped at Spirit Lake is Dick Nesbit, supervisor of Weyerhaeuser's Camp Baker twenty miles west. Soon two company D8 Cats scrape off the highway and rechannel wet Dry Gulch. Tonn and Nieland hike upgully. The flood has gouged sapphire canyons into Forsyth Glacier.

By October the guests have left the lodges. The campground is chained, the youth camps closed like coffins, the docks vacant. A few hikers traipse trails past vine maples flaming by the shore. In each fall storm the snowline marches down Mount St. Helens. Loggers migrate to the low country, and the rasp of saws fades from the hills.

By Thanksgiving snow muffs the woods about Spirit Lake, and ice skims the shore. A late-December cold snap freezes the west arm over in one night. In mid-January seven feet of snow falls in seventy-two hours. Another cold spell freezes the east arm.

Now a lonely, lovely quiet.

The Fuse Is Lit, But We Don't Know How Long It Is

Anatomy of Crisis

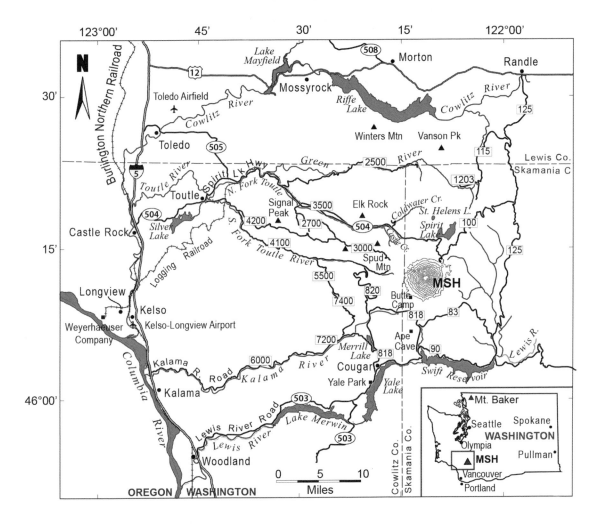

1
Seismograph (March 19–24)

Some say the earth
Was feverous and did shake.
　　　　　—Shakespeare, *Macbeth*

Headlamps reach into the twilight—a somber shadowed slot of highway through stately Douglas fir. The broken centerline flicks by like a strobe. Pale light lingers ahead on the ragged west brow of Elk Rock.

This March of 1980, young Sharon Burchard staffs the U.S. Forest Service's visitors' center on Spirit Lake at the north base of Mount St. Helens. Each Wednesday she drives the palegreen Forest Service pickup down Spirit Lake highway—state 504—to Longview for groceries, laundry, gas, and a dance class.

Before nine she'd logged the weather—temperature high and low, barometric pressure, humidity, snowfall. She'd driven four miles up to the loop at highway's end, an old climbing camp Timberline. A ten-foot snowpack draws cross-country skiers, snowmobilers, and climbers. Seeing no new avalanches, she'd radioed the District Ranger, who relayed to the Avalanche Center in Seattle. From data across the Cascades the Center forecasts today's avalanche hazard extreme.

Two students from Oregon State University pulled in. "Okay to climb Mount St. Helens?"

"It's ripe for avalanches," she says. "Not a great time."

"It's spring break. We climb soon or not at all."

All that was nine hours ago. Now she beats back up Toutle valley, a long climb toward Mount St. Helens and its secluded lake. From Longview, Interstate 5 ascends Cowlitz valley. At Castle Rock Burchard turns east up state highway 504. She skirts Silver Lake, threads through Toutle, passes Weyerhaeuser's 19-Mile Camp, and winds through Kid Valley village. She crosses Alder Creek and turns onto a green steel bridge across North Fork Toutle River that drains Spirit Lake and Mount St. Helens.

These western foothills of the Cascade Range are a magnificent land of tall, straight trees. Pacific storms ride up the mountains eight months of the year, dumping snow and rain. At low levels Douglas fir is king. The largest soaring 300 feet predate Columbus; young ones reach 150 feet. Hemlock, redcedar, grand fir, silver fir poke nearly as high. At higher levels noble fir is king. To a traveler from the east where oak and maple crown at 90 feet and white pine protrudes to 120, these northwest conifers are giants.

Burchard has the highway to herself and presses the pedal. She sweeps past Camp Baker, Weyerhaeuser's yard of logs, railroad, trucks, and shops, the road a half-lit slit through firs.

She rounds a curve into a straightaway. A dark clump ahead untangles into brown and beige hulks, ten big animals. *Elk!. . . but in the highway?* They graze all winter along the meadows by the river but don't stand in the highway. She slows. They mill in the middle, blotting the centerline. She crawls within fifty feet before they amble south, toward water. *This slowness strange too: they should startle, prance into the trees.* She's barely past when they clamber back to the center of pavement, away from trees. She pulls away, and the elk shrink into the backview mirror. Under Elk Rock she glances back the long straightaway. Dun dots dapple the road.

Past Elk Rock the road climbs and snow spreads like clouds. The valley fills with darkness. A ridge to the south by Jackson Creek is lit like a ballfield—a yarding tower with thousand-watt lamps, swing-shift logging for the Japanese market. Fifteen minutes later Burchard comes to the gabled Forest Service hut by Spirit Lake. Fir and hemlock stand like fluted columns of a weathered temple.

An hour ago daffodils and forsythia bloomed in Longview forty feet above sea level. Beyond Toutle at five hundred feet, alder catkins swelled dark red like drying blood. Under Elk Rock at 1500 feet leafless trees scratched the sky, fallen leaves beneath shriveled like old leather. Here at 3200 feet six-foot snowpack drapes the ground, Spirit Lake thick in ice.

Next morning the 20th, the Oregon State students stuff lunch into packs, tie on crampons, and palm ice-axes. From Timberline at 4400 feet they slog toward the summit at 9700. Sharon Burchard logs weather data at the hut, and drives up to Timberline. The climbers are gone, and no avalanches.

An hour later Duncan and Melonie Berry snowshoe in from Harmony Falls Lodge across the lake. "We're off to a music gig in Eugene this weekend," says Duncan. "Tenth anniversary of Earth Day. Back in a week."

The Oregon State climbers munch sandwiches atop rocky Dog's Head at 7600 feet, halfway up. They climb into the white sea of upper Forsyth Glacier—mushy snow, harder going. They stop, panting. They climb, stop, climb. They stop.

"Cripes! It's another 2000 feet up."

"Let's face it, we're out of shape."

"It's steep here, and she'd mentioned avalanches."

They glissade down the snowpack, plod to Timberline, and drive down to the Forest Service hut.

A horizontal drum a foot in diameter, a foot long, rotates so slowly you watch intently to see it move at all. The hot pen melts a black line through the waxy skin of clamped-on paper. Once a minute the pen offsets with a click, and in one second clicks back, a timing notch. In half an hour the drum turns once round, and the line has migrated a sixteenth inch right. Two and a half hours etch five parallel lines like music paper, the time-notches marking the measures. The hours tick by, and the paper fills with lines. It is really one continuous line the drum's rotation coils to a helix.

The pen jerks left, then right, left again, dodges back right, each stroke swinging wider. It snaps back, squeaking on the paper, *eeek*, sweeping back and forth now three quarters of an inch, *eeek, ee-eeek, eeek*. The skating pen etches black wisps across the parallel lines. The squeaks bring Linda Noson. She watches the ragged trace lengthen. The pen wobbles erratically—for a minute, now two—but the sweep narrowing. After three minutes it's down to a jittery line, after four to a straight one.

An earthquake. Not unusual on these recording drums in the University of Washington's seismology laboratory in Seattle. But this sweep is wider, its twitching tail much longer than the usual magnitude 1s and 2s in Puget Sound and the Cascades. The longer the jittery trace, the larger the quake. This one March 20 runs 3¾ minutes—roughly a magnitude 4.[1]

Of the three drums, the sweep is widest on the south seismic station, CPW south of Puget Sound.[2] On the middle station near Monroe it's much narrower and starts a little later. On the north station near Mount Baker it's narrower and later yet. The quake must be off south. Two Develocorders[3] in the lab record thirty-two seismic stations in western and central Washington. In ten minutes the film passes through developing fluid and scrolls past a viewscreen. The raggedest line is station SHW high on the west flank of Mount St. Helens.

In the Forest Service hut at Spirit Lake, the Oregon State students relate their climb. Sharon Burchard stands with an elbow on a wooden counter. A jolt! The hut shudders, cups rattle, a lantern wobbles. Burchard and the climbers fall silent. The hut sways. *As if suspended in air by loose springs with freedom to rock gently in all directions,* she will pencil to a notebook. The tremor lasts six seconds. "Earthquake!" she blurts. "Avalanche!" She snatches the microphone. A repeater relays the signal to Mount St. Helens District south of the mountain.

"You feel an earthquake?"

"No," says district ranger Ken Johnson. "And no one's called."

"We just had a good one. This hut shook so much it scared me. I'll see about avalanches."

Burchard and the students climb into the green pickup and in eight minutes swing around the Timberline loop. The surface of Forsyth Glacier is rumpled, a snow avalanche run down from 9000 to 5500 feet. Another has swept Nelson Glacier on the east. Snowdust floated out and settled on the road and four snowmobilers now loading onto trailers.

"Anyone missing?" Burchard calls to them.

"We're all here . . . But in a minute we're out of here!"

The students eye the slope. "Holy shit! If we hadn't come down we'd be in it!"

"We'd be dead!"

"Jesus! That'd be a cold grave."

"Not for long," Burchard says. "In two hours the sheriff would come to search. It'd be just my luck to stick you with an avalanche probe."

"Good thing we're out of shape, heh, heh."

"I said it wasn't a good day to climb," Burchard grins.

From the UW lab Linda Noson climbs to the office of 35-year-old seismologist Steve Malone. "There's been an earthquake," she says. "Fairly large, maybe Mount St. Helens." Malone charges downstairs. Craig Weaver of the U.S. Geological Survey crosses to the lab; grad student Elliot Endo comes.

Droning fans cool the computers. The Develocorders leak a sulfury odor of film-fixing fluid, this corner of the lab dim so not to spoil the film. The four squint at emerging traces. "Station SHW is usually quiet," Noson says. "But this week it's been alive with little quakes—magnitude 1s and less, but lots of them."

Most earthquakes start sharply, two spikes the first half minute, the pen tracing a pattern like a branching fir. This trace starts gradually and wobbles steadily like a swordfern. "This source looks shallow," Weaver says. "And must be somewhere south."

The quake struck just before 3:48 PM,[4] its 4.2 magnitude the strongest in the south Cascades in sixteen years. "Could it be Hood?" asks Weaver. "SHW is its closest station." Since 1969 many small earthquakes have jiggled Mount Hood 62 miles southeast of Mount St. Helens. In 1974 a magnitude 4 rattled Timberline Lodge on its south flank.[5] There'd been a few magnitude 3s a few miles northwest of Mount St. Helens, but all these years only a few little ones *at* the volcano.

In the Develocorder's magnifier Noson pinpoints the time the quake arrived at several seismic stations. She punches the data to IBM cards and feeds the deck to the reader. In ten minutes the computer calculates latitude, longitude, and depth. The quake plots only a mile deep beneath the north brow of Mount St. Helens.

Only a few seismologists watch this beginning. A few at Spirit Lake—Sharon Burchard, the climbers and snowmobilers, and the tetchy owner of Mount St. Helens Lodge, Harry Truman—have felt its reverberations. It's the opening curtain of a drama to play out over eight weeks. The cast will soon be thousands. (Appendix I lists characters in pre-eruption chapters 1–6.)

Unlike previous 4s in western Washington mostly deeper than nine miles, this one is *very* shallow. Sixteen minutes later another pops, only a magnitude 2. Thirty-one minutes later another, also a 2. In between lie several smaller. After a crustal magnitude 4 come aftershocks, and this is what they seem to be.

Dwight ('Rocky') Crandell and Donal Mullineaux of the USGS in Denver have studied the volcano since 1957 and assembled its history. In 1975 and 1978 they published reports on past eruptions and forecast a new one "perhaps before the end of this century."

Most public land around Mount St. Helens is Gifford Pinchot National Forest. Chuck Tonn—six-foot, muscular Forest Service recreation assistant for Spirit Lake—has known Crandell and Mullineaux fifteen years. Tonn telephones Mullineaux at Denver, who phones the USGS earthquake center at nearby Golden. Next morning Mullineaux calls Tonn: "Don't worry. It wasn't under the cone. Golden locates it ten miles northeast."

Early Friday the wiggles on UW's instruments reveal small overnight earthquakes, and they seem near Mount St. Helens. Aftershocks of crustal earthquakes soon taper off, but these persist. More seismometers would pinpoint them. By chance four instruments came to UW last evening. The scientists pack them into carryalls and install them around Mount St. Helens. At Spirit Lake it's in the only spot shoveled of snow: a Forest Service outhouse.

Malone and Endo drive up to Timberline. They're fiddling with cables when Forest ranger Chuck Tonn pulls in. It's dusk, the air still, the mountain clear, the low sun laying long shadows on snow.

"You guys came at a good time," Tonn says. "The mountain isn't often so beautiful and peaceful. What're you up to?"

"Installing seismometers," Malone says. "To catch aftershocks from yesterday's quake."

"Don Mullineaux says it was off north."

"Oh no, it was right here at Mount St. Helens. Definitely. There've been others since."

"What if they continue?"

"In Japan earthquakes sometimes precede eruptions."

"Could that happen here?"

"I doubt it … But if it does, it won't be beautiful and peaceful anymore."

Back to UW, Malone and Weaver scan the seismic drums: more wiggles. In Vancouver a *Columbian* headline sniggers "Quake Nothing to Get Shook Over."

Saturday the 22nd, Chuck Tonn marks out a trail near Spirit Lake. Skiing on a flat, he falls. Sharon Burchard radios, "An earthquake shook the hut like Thursday's."

Many seismometers record this one. UW registers a magnitude 4.2 at 2:23 PM and only a mile down. Smaller quakes persist. Maybe these aren't tectonic aftershocks, Malone and Weaver think. Maybe they're volcanic.

Malone telephones Gifford Pinchot National Forest at Vancouver. He calls District Ranger Ken Johnson. He calls the Avalanche Center in Seattle. Earthquakes could shake down snow avalanches. Five years ago one at Mount St. Helens trapped 26 college students and killed five.

At 7:23 Sunday morning, UW records a shallow magnitude 3.5. District Ranger Johnson calls Roland Emetaz at home. An expert in snow avalanches, Emetaz has climbed Mount St. Helens three dozen times since 1951 and knows its summit and gullies. In early afternoon he drives to Spirit Lake. It's snowing, the mountain fogged.

He meets rangers Tonn and Burchard at Timberline. "There're often avalanches here," Emetaz says, "and some have run down the gulch just west. Earthquakes have shaken down any snow primed to go. The hazard is now *less*. It's no big deal."

Reid and Fay Blackburn met as staffers at Vancouver's *Columbian* newspaper, dated, and married last August. They often visit Mount St. Helens and Spirit Lake—hiking in summer, cross-country skiing in winter. Sunday they pack the Volvo and with friends drive to Timberline. Reid shoots color Ektachrome and black-and-white negatives, aiming up the mountain he's climbed with photo editor Steve Small. The four clamp on skis and break trail through scattered small firs. It's tough going in soft snow, and the wind whips up clouds of icy crystals. They return to Timberline exhausted, another fine outing.

Thirty-year-old David A. Johnston, new-hire geologist with the USGS, had for three days attended a Geological Society of America meeting in Corvallis. Thursday evening news had grapevined about a magnitude 4 quake at Mount St. Helens. In Seattle over the weekend, Johnston hears radio news of more earthquakes. Two years ago he'd written his Ph.D. dissertation on the explosive 1976 eruption of Mount Augustine in Alaska. The early symptom had been earthquakes.

Monday the 24th he steps into UW's seismology lab and bedlam. The media sense something's up: telephones jangle incessantly. Elliot Endo and Linda Noson feverishly locate the weekend's earthquakes. Johnston no sooner arrives than pitches in—changing tapes now filling fast, answering telephones. He'll take night duty—Captain Midnight. It helps Noson and Endo catch up locating all the new quakes.

Rocky Crandell and Don Mullineaux find many messages in their Denver USGS offices. The Forest Service at Vancouver had telephoned, and District Ranger Ken Johnson. USGS headquarters in Virginia has rung.

Crandell telephones Steve Malone at UW: "What's going on?"

"We need help! Many earthquakes plot at Mount St. Helens."

"The seismologists at Golden said Thursday's was off north."

"Oh no, not at all. They calculate from a few distant stations. Those locations may be miles off. Our network across western Washington locates within half a mile. Thursday's was *at* Mount St. Helens!"

"You're sure?"

"No question. Many since then locate there. They're very shallow and coming more often. Something's up at the volcano."

Crandell heads USGS's volcano-hazards project. He and Don Mullineaux have worried about Mount St. Helens. Now comes one call after another from federal agencies, Washington State, and news reporters.

At Gifford Pinchot National Forest in Vancouver, Supervisor Bob Tokarczyk has read Crandell and Mullineaux's 1978 booklet. The 1974 Disaster Relief Act[6] designates the USGS to advise other agencies about restless volcanoes. Tokarczyk calls USGS headquarters.

Roland Emetaz meanwhile flies above Mount St. Helens: "I can't see the north flank through clouds. On the east big avalanches have come down into the Plains of Abraham, a usual place, so what? But on the south I see two big slab avalanches broken from a six-foot crown scarp. I've never seen one here."

Crandell and Mullineaux have known for years that if Mount St. Helens reawakened, they'd manage the crisis for the USGS. Bob Tilling, an office chief for the volcano program, calls.

"The Forest Service wants you or Mullineaux in Vancouver.

"Our project has $80 left in operating expenses," says Crandell.

"I'll find the money. One of you fly to Vancouver. It's urgent!"

All day Crandell and colleagues field calls from the USGS, from the Forest Service, from seismologists in Seattle, and as the day wears on from news reporters across the land.

Just before 1 PM the seismologists' press release notes the magnitude 4 earthquakes and "activity changed from an average two events an hour Friday to forty an hour this morning."

An hour later a shallow earthquake rolls from the mountain. This one's a 4.4—three times the energy of Thursday's. "This one's far too strong to be an aftershock,"

Elliot Endo says. "And now there've been enough of them to know this is no tectonic mainshock-aftershock sequence. It's a volcanic swarm."

Enough to know that after one hundred twenty-three years asleep, Mount St. Helens stirs.

Mount St. Helens as seen from the Cowlitz Farm, by Paul Kane. Cowlitz Farm, a Hudson's Bay Company facility, was located west of the mountain near present-day Toledo, Washington. Watercolor & graphite on paper, March 30–April 4, 1847.

2

Stage

Anyone can create the future, but only a wise man can create the past.
—Vladimir Nabokov, *Bend Sinister*

Before more 1980 drama, let us explore its stage set—bits of natural and human history that frame scenes to come. Why does a railroad own Mount St. Helens' summit 9600 feet above its track and dozens of miles away? Why private cabins inside a National Forest? Why thousands of miles of private road that law officers can't control? Why a volcano here at all?

A volcano sits atop a straw from deep in the earth. About sixty miles thick, earth's rigid crust floats on deformable mantle. Seven huge crustal plates and several smaller ones cover the earth, creeping in different directions. The plates rub at their margins—spreading here, colliding there, sliding past in other spots. Plates may separate an inch a year, the rate a toenail grows. Continued 200 million years, this slack pace opens an ocean.

Off America's northwest coast the oceanic Juan de Fuca plate collides with the continental North American plate. Heavier oceanic crust slides beneath the continental crust and drags down some ocean-floor sediment and water. The slab heats as it descends. Down 50 to 100 miles some of it melts, thanks partly to the water. Hot magma oozes up through the denser crust, eventually to the top of the straw, and voilà: a volcano.

A 25,000-mile volcanic 'ring of fire' rounds the Pacific Ocean. From New Zealand it reaches northwest through the New Hebrides and Solomon Islands; west across Papua New Guinea and Indonesia; north through the Philippines, Japan, the Kuriles, and Kamchatka; east through the Aleutian Islands into mainland Alaska; south down the west coasts of North, Central, and South America; and south into Antarctica. Cascade volcanoes are part of this ring.

Some volcanoes erupt every few years or decades. Kilauea or Mount Etna emit glowing basaltic lava that flows like syrup. It burns and buries buildings and trees but doesn't catch people. Volcanoes like Mount St. Helens erupt unpredictably. Periods between eruptions may span hundreds of years, thousands. Their dacitic or andesitic magma, stiff like putty, traps gas and over time builds pressure. It can explode and shoot miles skyward. Sometimes so much erupts so fast it spews sideways. Fiery ash hurricanes race out miles and flatten all in their paths. Let us recall how calamitous some eruptions have been.[1]

In about 1628 BCE Santorini in the Aegean Sea tossed out fifteen cubic miles of ash. The sea floor collapsed as a five-mile cauldron. Santorini's stratospheric eruption column may have been the pillar of smoke by day and fire by night of *Exodus*, the fallen island Plato's lost continent of Atlantis, and its tsunami crashing onto Crete what sank fleets and wounded Minoan civilization.[2]

In year 79 Mount Vesuvius erupted an enormous ash column for twelve hours. The cone then spewed a cubic mile of ash that raced off as incandescent flows. Miles away they buried Roman Pompeii and Herculaneum.[3]

In April 1815 Tambora in Indonesia coughed out a colossal twenty cubic miles of ash. It killed 10,000 people outright and starved 82,000. Ash injected to the stratosphere circled the globe. Fogs, rains, and frosts stunted crops across North America and Europe.[4]

Earthquakes beneath Krakatau in Indonesia began in May 1883; quakes and small eruptions continued three months. The vent vomited four cubic miles of ash August 26 and 27. A colossal burst the 27th propelled hot flows thirty miles across the sea to Sumatra, killing a thousand people. Krakatau collapsed into the sea floor, and its tsunami killed 35,500 more.[5]

Earthquakes rattled pointed Bezymianny in remote Kamchatka in late September 1955. They grew to hundreds a day by mid-October, then came a small eruption. Earthquakes and eruptions continued through November. Eruptions then tapered off but earthquakes persisted. On 30 March 1956 a huge explosion shot to 100,000 feet. An ash hurricane swept twenty miles southeast, devastating 180 square miles. The volcano lost its top thousand feet.[6]

Earthquakes rattled Hibok-Hibok in the Philippines all summer 1948, then a burst of mud buried a village. Oozing lava built a dome hundreds of feet high in three years. In December 1951 a great explosion spewed down through forests and villages. Its 1300° F killed 500 people and livestock. Gordon MacDonald's classic book *Volcanoes* opens with this eruption. It contrasts the chance jungle violence with lava flows off Kilauea—so Hollywood but predictable.

In eastern Papua tremors and steam disturbed Mount Lamington in January 1951. Earthquakes increased as ashy eruptions pulsed as high as 20,000 feet. Hot ash then burst eight miles through forest and villages, taking 2950 lives. The photos are unforgettable. Trees down, stumps splintered, torn-open houses filled with ash, a twisted jeep impaled atop snags, charred corpses littering a road. The devastation covered 90 square miles.[7]

On Martinique in the West Indies, Mont Pelée released ash bursts and many earthquakes in April 1902. A flood of mud and boulders swept down a valley, killing two dozen. Villagers fled into St. Pierre. Mont Pelée blanketed the city with inches of ash. Many prayed; few left.[8] The *Roraima* steamed in May 8.

> Our boat arrived at St. Pierre early morning. For hours before we entered the roadstead we could see flames and smoke rising from Mt. Pelée. Leaping red flames belched from the mountain. Enormous clouds of black smoke hung over the volcano.

Soon after we got in there was a tremendous explosion. There hurled towards us a solid wall of flame. It was like a hurricane of fire, which rolled down on St. Pierre and the shipping. The town vanished before our eyes, and the air grew stifling hot. Whenever the mass of fire struck the sea, the water boiled and sent up great clouds of steam. I ran to my stateroom and buried myself in the bedding. The blast of fire lasted only a few minutes. It shriveled and set fire to everything it touched. Burning rum ran in streams down every street and out into the sea. Before the volcano burst, the landings at St. Pierre were crowded with people. After the explosion, not one living being was seen on land. Only 25 of those in the *Roraima*, out of 68, were left after the first flash. The fire swept off the ship's masts and smokestacks as if they'd been cut by a knife. Of 18 vessels lying in the Roads, only the British steamship *Roddam* escaped, and she lost more than half on board. It was a dying crew that took her out.[9]

Twenty-five thousand died. Photographs of St. Pierre resemble later scenes of fire-bombed war cities—Dresden, Tokyo, Hiroshima.

Most Cascade volcanoes haven't erupted in historical time. But Mounts Baker, Rainier, St. Helens, and Hood have steamed in spots as if breathing. Mount Hood erupted twenty-four years before Lewis and Clark paddled past in 1805.

Lassen Peak in California rumbled to life 30 May 1914, jetting black ash. Some 180 explosions blasted out a summit crater. In May 1915 a lava dome grew over the vent and onto one flank. On May 22 ash burst to 30,000 feet and hot pumice ravaged the northeast flank. Sporadic bursts lasted two more years.[10]

Indians prowled the south Cascades for generations, hunting elk, gathering huckleberries. Upper Cowlitz (Sahaptin) people called the smooth, snowy cone Lawilayt-łá, one who smokes.[11] They wouldn't take salmon at its north base, these spirits of dead warriors in spirit lake.[12]

Having in 1778 sailed on Capt. James Cook's third voyage, Captain George Vancouver mapped inlets of the northwest coast in 1792.[13] From Puget Sound he notes in mid-May: "[a] high mountain covered with snow several leagues to the south of mount Rainier." And five months later off the mouth of Columbia River: "the high round snowy mountain like Mount Rainier seemed covered with perpetual snow, as low down as the intervening country permitted it to be seen. This I have distinguished by the name of Mount St. Helens, in honor of His Britannic Majesty's ambassador at the court of Madrid."

In 1853 ethnologist George Gibbs recorded a characteristic tale of the Klickitat tribe about Mount St. Helens and Mount Hood sixty miles southeast: "[they] were man and wife; they quarrelled and threw fire at one another, and Mount St. Helens was the victor; since when Mount Hood has been afraid, while St. Helens, having a stout heart, still burns."[14] It's more than a tale. Unusually thin growth rings on old firs show mudflows swept off Mount Hood in late summer 1781.[15]

Lt. Robert Johnson of Charles Wilkes's United States Exploring Expedition met Silimxnotylmilakabok, a chief of the Spokane tribe in 1841. Long ago "he was sleeping in a lodge and was . . . awakened by his mother, who called out to him that the world was falling to pieces. Then he heard a great noise of thunder . . . and all the people crying out in great terror. Something was falling very thick, which they at first took for snow but . . . it proved to be ashes, which fell to a depth of six inches, and . . . caus[ed] them to suppose the end of the world was at hand."[16]

This and other accounts by Indians in northeast Washington and north Idaho suggest a late spring or summer eruption. Tree rings show that a lava flow erupted on Mount St. Helens' north flank in 1799 or 1800 and pumice fell thickly in late spring 1800.[17]

Five and a half years later Lewis and Clark paddled down lower Columbia River. Camped ten miles below present Vancouver 4 November 1805, Clark writes: "Mount Hellen bears N. 25° E about 80 miles. it is emensely high and covered with Snow, riseing in a kind of Cone . . . perhaps the highest pinecal from the common leavel in america. it rises . . . in the form of a Sugar lofe."[18]

So unlike his Mount Hood description a day earlier: "This mtn . . . is of a conical form but rugid." Pulling upriver early next spring, Lewis pens to his March 30 journal: "we had a view of mount St. helines and Mount Hood. the 1st is the most noble looking object of its kind in nature. its figure is a regular cone. both these mountains are perfectly covered with snow."

David Thompson had mapped the headwaters of Columbia River for the North West (fur) Company. In 1811 he mapped the river by canoe all the way down. Coming and going past Cowlitz River in July he thrice pens: a simple conical Mountain buried under snow.[19]

By 1818 treaty, British and Americans would occupy the Columbia region jointly. The Hudson's Bay Company absorbed the North West Company and in 1821 built Fort Vancouver a hundred miles above the river's mouth.[20] An 1812 fur party had discovered South Pass across the Rockies. Trappers then trudged this way, and a few adventurers.[21] In 1841 a wagon train of several families struggled up Platte River, over South Pass, and down Snake River plain, from then on called the Oregon Trail. More than fifty thousand came across by 1859.[22]

Mount St. Helens' ash had fallen hundreds of miles east in 1800—but then no reported eruption for three decades. Lewis and Clark in 1805–1806 and David Thompson in 1811 noting Mount St. Helens' snowy whiteness shows it hadn't erupted in months. Nor in the 1820s is eruption or ashfall noted on the lower Columbia by fur traders or David Douglas.

Mount St. Helens erupted many times 1831 to 1857. Meredith Gairdner, physician at Fort Vancouver, wrote of darkness and haze from Mount St. Helens in August 1831 and August 1835.[23] In November and December 1842, two eruptions deposited half an inch of ash at The Dalles 62 miles southeast.[24] A summit red glow was seen from Oregon City and Champoeg 60 and 75 miles south. Ejecta heated Toutle River enough to kill fish. An Indian hunting at the mountain's base burned his leg after a February 1843 burst and came moaning into Fort Vancouver. Explorers, Hudson Bay traders, Oregon Trail pioneers, missionaries, and sailors speak of smoke and cinders in 1841–1845 vented north of the summit.[25] But no mention for months at a time by John Townsend, Rev. Samuel Parker, the Wilkes' expedition, Frémont, and James Clyman. Several isolated bursts occurred between 1847 and April 1857.

Two artists, Henry Warre[26] in September 1845 and Paul Kane[27] in March 1847, sketched plumes rising from Goat Rocks grown midlevel on the north flank by mid-1840s. Kane journals:

> March 26th—When we arrived at the mouth of the Kattlepoutal [Lewis] River, twenty-six miles from Fort Vancouver, I stopped to make a sketch of the volcano Mount St. Helen's, distant thirty or forty miles. This mountain has never been visited by either Whites or Indians; the latter assert that it is inhabited by a race of beings of a different species, who are cannibals, and whom they hold in great dread; they also say that there is a lake at its base with a very extraordinary fish in it, with a head . . . resembling that of a bear . . . These superstitions are taken from . . . a man who, they say, went to the mountain with another, and escaped the fate of his companion, who was eaten by the "Skoocooms" . . . I offered a considerable bribe to any Indian who would accompany me in its exploration, but could not find one hardy enough to venture. It is of very great height, and being eternally covered with snow, is seen at a great distance. There is not a cloud visible in the sky at the time I commenced my sketch, and not a breath of air was perceptible; suddenly a stream of white smoke shot up from the crater of the mountain, and hovered a short time over its summit; it then settled down like a cap. This shape it retained for about an hour and a half, and then gradually disappeared. About three years before this the mountain was in a violent state of eruption for three or four days, and threw up burning stones and lava to an immense height, which ran in burning torrents down its snow-clad sides.

While traveling by land farther north he sketched another burst.

In the thousands of new settlers, Americans had won the lasting foothold. With beaver hats out and silk in, the fur trade was done for anyway. Treaty with Britain in 1846 made south of latitude 49° the United States. The Oregon Donation Act of 1850 granted settlers 160 to 640 acres of land, mostly in northern Willamette Valley but many also north of Columbia River.[28]

Congress authorized regular surveying of the expanding United States. By the 1840s sixteen cadastral surveys had divided land into square-mile sections as far west as the Missouri River.[29] Now emigrants had leapfrogged to the Pacific. The Donation Act authorized the survey of Oregon Territory. In summer 1851 surveyors ran the Willamette Meridian north to Puget Sound and Base Line east to the Cascades. Over many decades, surveyors reached northeast into the Cascades, each township holding 36 square-mile sections.

Congress formalized north of Columbia River as Washington Territory in 1853. That summer governor Isaac Stevens and survey parties explored a Pacific railway route across the Rockies to central Washington.[30] Stevens appointed Captain George McClellan to find a pass over the Cascades. McClellan, 65 other men, and 173 horses and mules axed out an Indian trail from Fort Vancouver north to Lewis River and

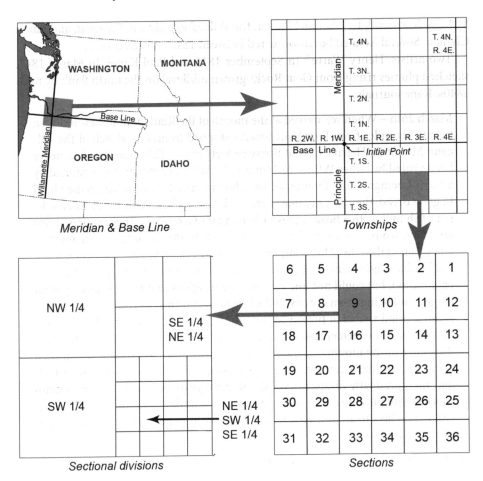

Cadastral land survey.

turned east. George Gibbs describes a great lava flow they skirted south of Mount St. Helens and writes of the cone:

> The crater of Mount St. Helens [is] on the northwest. Smoke was distinctly seen issuing from St. Helens during our journey... It's last considerable eruption was in 1842. The Indians have no tradition of an eruption of lava; they have only seen smoke and ashes come out of the mountain. They add that a bad smell came from it and that the fish in the streams died. Around the foot of St. Helens, they say, the ashes lie so deep and soft that horses cannot travel.

A few weeks later four men including Thomas Jefferson Dryer, editor of the *Oregonian*, followed McClellan's track. They climbed Mount St. Helens August 26. Down northeast a crater vented steam.[31] It was the first ascent of any major peak in the far West. Another party climbed in 1860.[32]

Governor Stevens hastened treaties with tribes that ended their rights to land except reservations. By 1864 Congress and Presidential executive order extinguished the rights of other tribes.[33] In November 1889 Washington became the forty-second state. Congress granted it three million acres, a third of it forest land. In the 1930s the state added 620,000 acres—land logged and abandoned.[34] Some seventy square miles of state forest lay west of Mount St. Helens.

Many people homesteaded in lower Cowlitz and Toutle valleys in the 1860s to 1890s. Men felled and bucked redcedar at Silver Lake, skidded bolts to the river, and floated them down to Castle Rock for milling to shingles. Villages sprang up: Silver Lake, Tower, Toutle, and farther up Kid Valley and St. Helens.[35]

In the 1820s to 1840s the federal government had granted land to states to aid the building of canals.[36] The state of Illinois then chartered the Illinois Central Railroad subsidized by 2½ million acres of federal land. The IC sold the land to settlers and loggers, generated capital and freight for the railroad—and populated Illinois. One IC lawyer was Abraham Lincoln.

In 1862 the war was going poorly for the Union.[37] To thwart talk of secession in the West, Congress and the President sped its growth. In May 1862 the Homestead Act offered 160 acres to anyone who would put the plow to it. In July President Lincoln signed the Pacific Railway Act. It granted the Union and Central Pacific a cash subsidy and ten square miles of land for each mile of railroad—later amended to twenty square miles. The second Pacific Railway Act in July 1864 chartered the Northern Pacific Railroad from Lake Superior to Puget Sound.[38] No cash this time, but the NP could claim forty square miles of land for each mile of road built. The NP built from Portland to Puget Sound in 1870–72 and crossed the Cascades at Stampede Pass in 1887.[39]

In February 1893 James J. Hill pounded the last spike into his Great Northern Railway built without land grants. A hundred miles shorter to Puget Sound than the Northern Pacific, its gentle grades bristling with branches, the Great Northern was profitable. The NP, built with an eye on the grant lands, had steeper grades, few branches, and staggering debt. Panic swept the financial markets in spring, and by August the Northern Pacific was bankrupt.

Hill and financier J. P. Morgan reorganized the NP as Northern Pacific Railway and by 1901 controlled the NP.[40] They bought the Burlington and access to the east. Hill ran a road down Columbia River and bought the line to Astoria. His rail empire laced the land from Lake Michigan to the western sea.

Land survey was far enough along for the Northern Pacific to claim grants for the Portland–Tacoma road. Three great claims in 1894 to 1896 patented 234 square miles reaching twenty-five miles east of the rails. The NP patented other big claims 1901 to 1908. Later grants patented 50 square miles around the volcano, section nine holding the summit. *To have and to hold . . . forever* reads the document signed by President Wilson in 1917. The last claim in January 1923 held the southwest of Spirit Lake. The grant land reached to six miles east of Mount St. Helens. The railroad held every odd-numbered section excepting prior claims like mines and Donation grants.

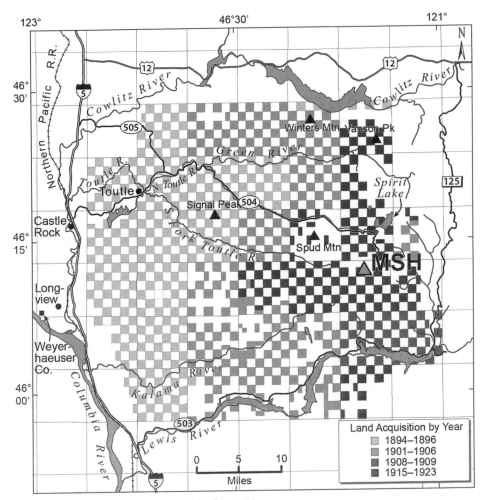

Land withdrawn from Public Domain for the NPRR

Hill had built a mansion on Summit Avenue in St. Paul, a gloomy pile of dark stone like a railway station. In a bright white wooden house just west lived Frederick Weyerhaeuser, lumberman since the 1850s and now a Great Northern board-member. Hill offered him freight rates less than half what the Northern Pacific had demanded. Douglas fir could compete in Chicago with southern pine. In January 1900 Weyerhaeuser and partners bought 900,000 acres of forest from the NP's grants at six dollars an acre. Next year they bought 261,000 acres. By 1905 Weyerhaeuser Timber Company held 2350 square miles of western Washington forests.[41]

In September 1902 the Yacolt Burn torched 390 square miles south of Mount St. Helens, taking dozens of farms and 38 human lives. Its huge updraft drew in a surface draft that bent small trees almost to the ground.[42] Weyerhaeuser staged hundreds of men in camps to salvage. Double-bit axes thunked into blackened snags. Two-man crosscut saws ten feet long hissed through logs bucked to 24 feet. A Northern Pacific spur hauled them down to Columbia River. In April 1906 earthquake and fire consumed San Francisco. Weyerhaeuser shipped logs and lumber south to rebuild the city.

In 1929 Weyerhaeuser built a railroad up Ostrander Creek and powered up gigantic sawmills at Longview. Mill One cut oldgrowth yellow fir, Mill Two smaller red fir, Mill Three cedar and white fir. Soon came shingle mill, pulp mill, and Presto-Log mill. They staged logging camps 1, 2, 3, 4, and 5 up the railroad into this big land of big trees.[43] The company broke with a cut-and-run logging culture. It would keep these lands, cut and reseed—a mammoth tree farm.

Major John Wesley Powell had explored a great unknown—the canyons of Green and Colorado Rivers—then led the Geographical and Geological Survey of the Rocky Mountain Region. Partly by his persuading, Congress authorized the U.S. Geological Survey in 1879 to classify public lands and examine their geological structure and mineral resources. As USGS's second director, Powell in 1881 to 1894 built it to a broadly scientific bureau.[44]

Congress formed the U.S. Forest Service in 1905. Columbia National Forest soon surrounded Mount St. Helens, and a district ranger stationed at Spirit Lake.[45] After gigantic fires swept north Idaho and Montana in 1910, suppressing them became a mission.[46] A lookout soon capped Red Mountain. Al Robbins and three others backpacked lumber up Mount St. Helens in summer 1921. They'd start at four in the morning, bake eggs in a steam crack at 8000 feet, and summit by nine.[47] Next year a fire lookout crowned the summit.

Lookout atop Mount St. Helens mid-1920s

COURTESY GIFFORD PINCHOT NATIONAL FOREST

Prospectors had probed around Mount St. Helens since the 1850s.[48] In 1891 some reported minerals near Spirit Lake. Scores swarmed in with inflated imaginations of wealth—more gusto than gold, more credulity than copper, grubstaked on borrowed money. They organized the St. Helens Mining District. Scattered mines drilled 11,000 feet of tunnel into low-grade copper.

Robert Lange built a cabin west of the lake and became district recorder. In 1901–02 he forged a road for the county from Toutle over Green Mountain, up the North Fork, and on to Spirit Lake. Up it the mines wagoned everything from pliers to engines.

Headed by Dr. Henry Coe,[49] Consolidated Mining Company in 1901 to 1905 surveyed sixty-four lode claims in the hills and six millsites on Spirit Lake. Their claims included the Norway, Sweden, United, Chicago, and Mary.[50] They drilled a 75-foot tunnel on the Mary-6 in Florence Creek and 2900 feet of tunnel in the Norway and Sweden in Spirit Lake's northeast cove. Headquarters sat off south among cedars by idyllic Harmony Falls. In 1907 Coe's miners built a log dam in the lake's outlet, raised its level five feet, and barged across tools, rails, and a steam engine.[51]

But by 1911 most of the lowgrade, hardluck mines had closed.[52] Of 27 groups of claims about Spirit Lake and Green River, only Sweden Mine took ore to a mill. Two

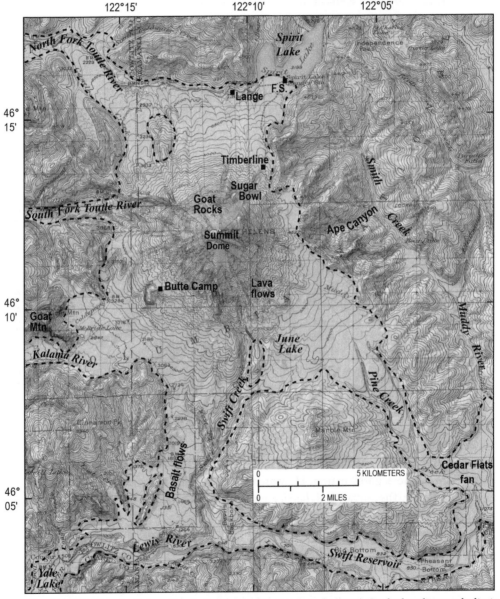

Base from USGS Mount St. Helens 30-minute topographic quadrangle (1919). Dashed outline marks limit of Mount St. Helens' pre-1980 debris. Rubble and hot-ash flows from the ovlcano reach farther down valleys off map boundaries. Swift and Yale Lake reservoirs now fill parts of Lewis valley floor. Hillslope shading as if illuminated from northwest by D.W. Ramsey. Modified from Clynne and others (2008, fig. 2).

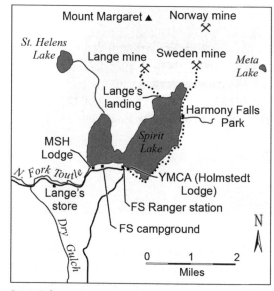

Spirit Lake 1890s–1930s

tons of its copper stand in Alice Cooper's 1905 bronze 'Sacajawea' in Portland. The patented claims owned not just mining rights but the land and timber, 1080 acres of them Coe's. They left the wagon road and a network of trails up Toutle and Green Rivers.

The Oregon Alpine Club placed a register atop Mount St. Helens in July 1889. Over the years scores of climbers wrote their names and routes and views.[53] On 17 August 1890 four men and two women climbed, L.A. McBride's eighth ascent, George Merrill's fourth. Their names linger on the land: from the southwest climbers hiked past Merrill Lake and McBride Lake. Mazamas club climbed in large parties from Butte Camp in 1898 and Spirit Lake in 1908. In late summer firesmoke often veiled Mount Adams and Mount Hood.

South of the mountain, Ole Peterson had homesteaded on Lewis River at the front of rough lava where McClellan's party had stumbled half a century earlier. On a high lava flat Peterson found a great underground tube running downslope. Lighting lanterns, he guided visitors through Ole's Cave.

But the north was the beauty spot. In 1911 the Forest Service permitted the Portland YMCA a camp on Spirit Lake where they built a gabled bunkhouse. Boys came by boat and rail to Castle Rock, then a three-day hike to 'Camp Blister.' John Williams' 1912 photo folio *Guardians of the Columbia* vaunted Mount St. Helens. In August 1908 an automobile came up the dirt track, winding between trees, crossing streams at fords. The upper twenty miles of pumice banks and boulders kept "mattocks in almost constant use." Dry Gulch often ran so heavy from Mount St. Helens' melting glaciers you waited till morning to cross.[54]

When cadastral survey finally reached the upper Toutle, Lange's place lay in section 16, a state school section. He was contested: *United States v. Robert Lange* in 1911, *State of Washington v. Robert Lange* in 1912. But Lange had settled before the survey, and before the National Forest. He prevailed, and in March 1914 President Wilson signed his 160-acre homestead patent.[55]

Jack Nelson opened a fishing camp on Spirit Lake in summer 1926—Nelson's Boat House. Harry Truman snowshoed in next winter on the run from rival bootleggers.[56] Nelson renamed his place Mount St. Helens Lodge in 1929, added a store, and took on Truman as a partner. After a dispute Nelson sold out to Truman, packed uplake, and leased Henry Coe's rotting cabins by the tall waterfall: Harmony Falls Park.

Mount St. Helens Lodge, summer 1939.

The county rebuilt the Spirit Lake road in 1929. They abandoned Green Mountain for a grade by the river bridged at Toutle. Robert Lange built a gabled store that held the Spirit Lake post office. Up at the lake Portland YMCA built majestic Holmstedt Lodge.

A 1933 flood swept away bridges and parts of the road. The state took over in 1936 and rebuilt it to highway 1-R. Above Coldwater Creek they rerouted it to north of the river and paved to the county line. Robert Lange had died, his store now isolated. By the new highway son-in-law Harry Gustafson built stone-faced Spirit Lake Lodge. A week with meals and horse riding cost $35. The Civilian Conservation Corps doubled the Forest Service campground, built a boat landing, and hacked out a trail network.

Ray Atkeson's exquisite photographs advertised Mount St. Helens' smooth crown of snow—America's Fujiyama.[57] But as if to remind she's volcanic, the mountain occasionally hiccupped steam—April 1898, September 1903, March 1921. Climbers up the north stopped by sulfurous steam jets on The Boot.

South Shore YMCA camp, 1938.

Truman's place burned. In 1939 he and Harry Gardner built three-story Mount St. Helens Lodge. Truman flew a Taylorcraft float plane off Spirit Lake running booze from Canada. He rented out rowboats, sold fishing licenses. Across the lake beneath the waterfall, Jack Nelson built cabins Harmony Hums and Shangri-La and a two-story lodge electrified by pelton wheel. Harmony Falls Lodge, he now called it.

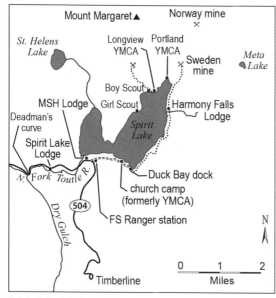

Spirit Lake 1930s–1970s

Automobiles and people having invaded Portland YMCA's isolation, they bought 80 acres of Coe mine lands on the northeast cove. Across a dozen years they built Camp Meehan and plumbed with creek water. Longview YMCA, Boy Scouts, Girl Scouts also moved north. But the mines lay moribund. Even during World War II the Sweden couldn't muster a road up the lake's east side to tap copper, gold, and silver.

After the war the state paved the highway to the lake. The Forest Service campground spread to twenty acres, and hundreds of people a week ferried to the far shore. Truman's snazzy Chris Craft slit the surface of the lake. Jack Nelson bought two steel-hulled Coast Guard boats for Harmony Falls Lodge that he named the *Tressa* and the *Ruby*. In 1954 Henry Coe's son sold Harmony Falls to a partnership. But then Jack Nelson died. The Gillises ran it two years, the Mietzkes fourteen. Lange's family divided his 160-acre homestead, and by the 1970s dozens of lots near Spirit Lake Lodge held cabins.

Harry Truman married pretty Edna—Eddie—in 1946. To Mount St. Helens Lodge they added cabins, restaurant, boat dock, scores of boats and Johnson

Eddie and Harry Truman at Mount St. Helens Lodge, early 1970s.

motors, a Century launch. One summer day in 1953 Truman didn't like the looks of a rumpled stranger and refused him a cabin. "You know who you turned away?" said a man at the bar. "Supreme Court Justice William O. Douglas!" Truman shot down the highway and brought him back. They mounted horses for the backcountry—one mule packing food, one booze.[58] Each summer Truman horsepacked Northern Pacific brass to Deadman's Lake. Forest Ranger Bill Reese then brought in an extra mule to pack out dead soldiers.

Heart attack took Eddie in 1975.[59] Truman left bedroom and bar untouched, admitted fewer summer guests to the cabins, and the lodge housed ever-more cats. Liquor had always lubricated the lodge but now he laced his Coke more with Schenley's. One winter weekend Roy Ford and Ray King set heaters to thaw their cabins and walked to Spirit Lake Lodge. "Truman sat at the bar yacking," says King, "fingers bandaged from a bout with a snowblower. A yellow stream from his pantleg pooled on the floor. He just jabbered on, tossing back whiskey."

Harmony Falls Lodge had run down when Dave and Laura Berry took over in 1973. They rebuilt dock, boat house, cabins, and the lodge nestled under cedars. Sometimes Dave fired up old *Ruby* but now met guests in aluminum *Loon*. And Spirit Lake Lodge got new owners, Dave and Mariam Smith. Son Rob reversed the handiwork of carpenter ants and dryrot, replaced ambiguous plumbing and heating, and added a deck. By fall 1979 the lodge stood fit.

Two young men with a long task shoveling a toilet pit at the Forest Service campground soon broke into circular blackness. They stood the outhouse over the rotted-out fir, and went hiking. The Forest Service built a long dock and boat

GOODWIN HARDING

Harmony Falls Lodge, late 1970s.

ramp on Duck Bay. Tollycraft donated 28-foot fiberglass *White Eagle* to ferry the Boy Scouts. Portland Y's Coast Guard lifeboat *Big Red* thundered up and down the lake plowing a great wake. Jim Nugent fished the North Fork behind his Kid Valley home. In July up came sockeye toward the lake, in August eight-pound cohos. In September fat chinooks, and in 1979 Nugent pulled in a 63-pounder.

On the lava plain south of the mountain, logger Lawrence Johnson in 1951 spotted a fir tilting into a sinkhole. Harry Reese and his sons roped down into an underground tube. Reese trooped in Explorer Post 348 who called it Ape Cave. The Forest Service built stairs. Ole's Cave may be forgotten, but thousands of visitors learned Mount St. Helens erupts lava.

High and cloudy, Mount St. Helens' fire lookout was abandoned in 1928. By the 1940s other lookouts surrounded the volcano—Mount Mitchell, Strawberry Mountain, Coldwater Peak, Vanson Peak, Smith Creek Butte, French Butte. State towers stood to the west atop Signal Peak and Elk Rock—Elk replaced in 1963 by Gilbert Ridge.

The lumber business picked up in the late 1930s. Weyerhaeuser's rails reached up South Toutle to Camp 6 and wound up Green River past Camps 7, 8, 9, and 10. By 1945 the railroad's 150 miles laced 31 staged camps. World War II brought demand for straight-grained, lightweight noble fir—for drydocks, minesweeper keels, and framing spars in RAF Mosquito bombers. Great stands of nobles furred higher levels above the North Fork. Weyerhaeuser ran a rail spur upvalley and built Camp Baker. Bulldozers carved road 2700 up Alder Creek. Nobles with basal diameters of six and seven feet soared 150 feet before the first branch. Bucked to 32 and 40 feet, logs went to Camp Baker by truck.

New tools invaded the woods. Seventy-pound power saws—Malls, Kiekhaefers with Mercury engines, Stihls—replaced axe, crosscut saw, and crochety drag saws. And now came diesels. Wartime proved the economy of trucks, and bulldozers could push into any corner of forest. Men bused to Camp Baker and 12 Road Camp, and rode 'crummies' out to the woods. Logs trucked to the camps rolled as gigantic loads down the rails to Longview.

Weyerhaeuser added a plywood mill at Longview in 1947 and now peeled some giant logs for veneer. They added a Kraft pulpmill, Kraft paper mill, fine-paper mill, milkcarton mill. Weyerhaeuser grew to the largest enterprise in southwest Washington.[60]

In the late 1950s road 3000 climbed from the North Fork up south, road 3100 up north. The 3500 worked east in the 1960s, branching into Jackson Creek (road 3600), Castle Creek (road 3800), and Coldwater Creek (road 4000). Open to hunting and fishing, the labyrinth made fine PR. The company built parks by the highway: Harry Morgan, Kid Valley, Al Raught, Hoffstadt Creek, Maratta Creek, and in 1978 Toutle River Park with trailer hookups.

A remnant of Typhoon Freda swept ashore 12 October 1962. Its 80–150 mph winds toppled millions of conifers. Famous in Weyerhaeuser lore had been a largest tree harvested, a 284-foot yellow fir felled in 1944 along Green River near Camp 9. It scaled to 71,550 board feet.[61] In 1965 Ted Sturgeon and Jim Nugent bucked an immense yellow fir felled by the 1962 storm—a 300-footer on lower 3000 road. It scaled to 80,000 board feet.

New sawmills stormed in. Weyerhaeuser built Green Mountain Mill for second-growth hemlock and Douglas fir, and at Longview computerized Hycom Mill while converting from oldgrowth to smaller logs. The 1929 triad—Mills One, Two, and Three—closed by 1979. Huge newsprint-paper mills rose in their stead.

Chessboarded with eastern Weyerhaeuser lands are timber lands of Gifford Pinchot National Forest (renamed in 1949). From the Washington state timber lands west of Mount St. Helens logging revenue reached $153 million—for schools, universities, Capitol buildings, and libraries.

But most of the roads were Weyerhaeuser's. By 1979 some four thousand seven hundred miles of roads laced the hills and valleys west of Mount St. Helens. Laid in straight lines this private road would run from Mount St. Helens to Manhattan to Miami to Memphis.[62]

A few geologists and botanists had poked around Mount St. Helens 1895 to 1915. They found charred logs in deposits 120 feet above Kalama River and the molds of burned-out firs riddling lava flows. They found the northeast flank blanketed in pumice.[63] Mature trees in these materials told they'd erupted hundreds of years ago.

Jean Verhoogen's 1937 report lays out the structure of the volcano and in microscopic detail its lava flows, broken debris, great lava domes, and outpourings from the 1800s. Mount St. Helens is younger than other Cascade cones, he writes, and built more of explosive deposits than Mount Shasta or Lassen Peak.[64]

In summers 1938 and 1939 young botanist Donald Lawrence cored trees and measured growth rings. Firs on Spirit Lake's south shore told that not long before 1550 the volcano had shed debris and dammed the lake sixty feet above an earlier level. Between mature firs lay cylindrical wells three feet wide and fifteen deep—firs drowned in debris long ago now rotted out. Tree rings told Lawrence that thick pumice fell northeast in about 1800. A lava flow then oozing down north rafted 40-acre tracts of rocky debris. Floating Island Lava Flow, he called it.[65]

Donal Mullineaux and Dwight ('Rocky') Crandell became the new experts. Mullineaux fought fires for the Forest Service in 1942. After a stint as a Navy officer on a destroyer, he entered University of Washington in 1946. He climbed Mount St. Helens often. Crandell had commanded an Army mortar platoon across France and Germany in 1944–45, emerged from Yale in 1951, and by summer 1953 was mapping for the USGS in southeast Puget lowland. For decades geologists thought a broad rocky deposit there had been dumped by an ancient Cascade glacier. Crandell found it had instead come from Mount Rainier. Seven thousand years ago, he inferred, Mount Rainier's summit had slid off and flowed fifty miles to Puget Sound.[66] Today it would be an immense catastrophe.

At Mount Rainier he found avalanches had swept south down Nisqually valley and rocky mudflows down several valleys these past 5000 years. Mullineaux meanwhile diagnosed ash layers. They wrote a hazards report with colored map.[67] In the late 1960s they surveyed Lassen Peak. They and protégés surveyed Mounts Shasta, Baker, and Hood, and Glacier Peak, writing of hazards in plain English.[68]

They pecked away at isolated Mount St. Helens. They found Toutle built on ancient mudflows that had dammed Silver Lake eighty feet above the river. Some flows reached beyond the Pacific Highway. The new radiocarbon method dated charred wood near Spirit Lake Lodge to 2000 years old. So the volcano had been long violent and its debris reached towns.[69] They sounded Spirit Lake. Shoal on the south, it deepened north into holes—175 feet in the east arm, 125 feet in the west. As Lawrence had surmised two decades earlier, prehistoric eruptions must have dammed the lake. Two ash layers at Mount Rainier had been thought erupted there. In 1961 Mullineaux found they thickened and coarsened southwest. So it wasn't hulks like Mounts Rainier and Adams who threw the worst tantrums but delicate Mount St. Helens.

Analyzing layer by prehistoric layer, Crandell and Mullineaux found Mount St. Helens only 40,000 years old. It erupts for years or decades, then goes quiet for centuries and more. Scorching ashflows had raced down all flanks, mudflows down every valley, and ash had fallen far north, east, and south. Pumice spewed out profusely 36,000, 13,000, 3500, and 500 years ago. The volcano's violent eruption 3500 years ago ejected a cubic mile. A yard thick at Spirit Lake, the pumice traces north and east 150 miles. Lava flows poured south 2600 to 1900 years ago. Sugarbowl dome exploded 1200 years ago. Pumice fell north and east in the 1400s while a lava dome built the summit.[70]

They published in arcane bulletins and journals. But if Mount St. Helens sprang to life again it could reach thousands of people and properties. Few living in the towns seemed to know. So they wrote for everyday readers. In *Science* magazine February 1975: "Mount St. Helens has been. . .more violent during the last few thousand years. . . Most of its upper part [formed] within the last few hundred years. Mount St. Helens probably has included. . .violent eruptions like Vesuvius in AD 79. An eruption is likely within the next hundred years." Longview's *Daily News* reprinted the piece. Seattle's *Times* and *Post-Intelligencer* and Oregon newspapers in Corvallis and Salem ran stories, and the *New York Times*.

Increased steaming and icemelt atop Mount Baker in 1975–1976 showed Cascade cones aren't all dead. From Crandell and Mullineaux's December 1978 USGS Bulletin *Potential Hazards from Future Eruptions of Mount St. Helens*: "Mount St. Helens we believe to be an especially dangerous volcano. . . In the future Mount St. Helens probably will erupt violently and affect human life, property, and economic welfare over a broad area. An eruption [may] occur before the end of the century."

In January 1979 regional newspapers ran articles, in March the *Los Angeles Times* a long one. But some scoffed, like Knight Ridder's Jim Dance:

> Specialists with the U.S. Geological Survey—a little gleefully, it seems to us—
> figure the eruption is due because there hasn't been one from Mount St. Helens
> since 1857 and the records show that it rather dependably goes off every 100 to
> 150 years. It is understandable that a volcano expert would welcome an occa-
> sional eruption. . .he could spend his whole adult life as a volcano expert and
> never see [one].[71]

And Ted Natt, frontpage in Longview's *Daily News*:

> One sure way for geologists to make the news is to predict one of the Cascade Range volcanoes is going to erupt again. One of the periodic predictions that Mount St. Helens is going to fizzle, pop or erupt is in print today. Two experts say St. Helens could erupt before the end of the century. They're right. It could erupt next week or wait 500 years.

A thermal survey of Mount St. Helens' summit in August 1979 recorded no more snowmelt or higher temperature than thirteen years earlier.[72] But bothered by USGS's slow reply in 1975 to Mount Baker, Robert Christiansen writes his office chief in February 1980. He suggests the Survey prepare to "get people thinking about. . . another Cascade eruption." Crandell and Mullineaux now think beyond forecasting to an actual burst. Their March 10 memo recommends that in a crisis the USGS appoint one person to command. They know any time soon it would be one of them. Ten days later an earthquake agitates Mount St. Helens.

Washington's 1980 governor, Dixy Lee Ray, is a scientist. A Stanford Ph.D., she'd taught zoology at the University of Washington in the 1940s to early 1970s. She urged UW's Friday Harbor Laboratories toward international stature, fostering visits by eminent researchers. She developed popular Zoology 330, Natural History of Marine Invertebrates, full of fieldtrips and labs. Her monthly KCTS-TV show *Animals of the Sea* popularized marine biology. Her research showed gribbles of genus *Limnoria* lived by digesting wood. She patented a method to retard their destruction of pilings and docks. She ran a symposium *Marine Boring and Fouling Organisms*, edited a book. Her research spared the Navy millions of dollars in damage and saved coastal towns millions more.

But she published little in reviewed journals. Some of her colleagues—males in a male profession—deemed her a lightweight. Promotion at UW was like academic Darwinism across the land: publish or perish. Ray said the system advanced careers more than science. She'd teach and research the practical. The department couldn't muster the nearly unanimous vote to promote to full professor. Activists who jilted science but embraced politics she came to hate and often said so. She took leaves of absence to the National Science Foundation and became its voice on Capitol Hill. After the 1962 Seattle World's Fair the Science Center languished. As its new director she turned it into a practical museum—installing laboratories, hosting symposia. She coauthored a 1970 biology report to the legislature that helped defeat a corporate plan to develop Nisqually delta into an industrial port. *Animals of the Sea* still ran on KCTS. The genial purveyor of biology became a household name. *Seattle Times*'s science reporter Lou Guzzo—later managing editor of the *Seattle P. I.*—says, "She was a brilliant and articulate woman. I've never seen her equal."

President Nixon appointed Dr. Ray to the U.S. Atomic Energy Commission. He wanted a woman with environmental credentials. Commission chair James Schlesinger wanted an articulate scientist to counteract Ralph Nader's antinuclear rhetoric. She took office in August 1972. Schlesinger moved over to head the CIA, and soon Dixy Lee Ray chaired the Atomic Emergy Commission. A Watergated year and a half later, Nixon himself was gone.

In 1975 Lou Guzzo, now counselor to Ray, found she'd be a viable Washington governor's candidate for either party. Her political sympathies were Republican, but three-term Governor Dan Evans wouldn't declare whether he'd run. "My father was a Democrat," Ray reasoned. "I might as well be one too." In Watergate's wake, the outsider won. But to Democrat loyalists she'd shanghaied the party. As her right-field politics grew clear, friends in the press became critics. Not that she didn't pass the ammunition. On election night she crowed: "The [press] backed the wrong horse. You think I'll forget that?" She called reporters "odd humanoid types."

Guzzo cringed. "Dixy! You need them on your side."

"I'm running this show. I'll do as I please."

Governor Ray and her staff hardly knew how state government works. She appointed amateurs qualified by loyalty to her. "The spoils system," Guzzo explained to news colleagues, "has as much going for it as against." She demanded scores of agency heads resign, offending Democrats and Republicans. She steered an ARCO supertanker down Rosario Channel in Puget Sound and championed a great oilport for single-hulled behemoths—this former defender of Nisqually delta. She advocated a fleet of nuclear-power plants across the state. She called for a state income tax, anathema to citizens since the 1930s. She tried to gut the Parks commission.

Her bills to the Legislature came with a message: do not tamper with. "She tried to bludgeon rather than persuade," says former House Energy Committee chair Donn Charnley. She sought to alter agencies to give the governor more power—invading legislative turf. When the House shot down one of her bills she blamed Speaker John Bagnariol. She summoned liason Jerry Hanna—former district court judge, former state legislator, urbane former state senator.

"You go up there and tell Baggie to shove it! " Ray snapped.

"You want *me*, to tell the Speaker of the *House*, to *shove* it?"

"Yes."

"I'll deliver your message, but not with that verb."

The urban press ridiculed. She cut off press conferences. They called her administration "the least accessible in twenty years," tagged her "Dixy Lee Radiation." She called nuclear skeptics "obstructionists," oilport opponents "zealots." She accused the press of inventing controversy. When a sow on her Fox Island farm dropped a litter, she at last held a conference. Each muddy pig, she said, is named for one of you, the Capitol press corps. The feud dragged on, even after she learned how Olympia works. But should a reporter ask about science, the governor softened to entertaining, erudite, professor Dixy.[73]

Washington's constitution was written when distrust ran high against railroad and timber trusts. The governor appoints the heads of but half the state agencies, others being elected or appointed by commissioners with long terms.[74] The elected Commissioner of Public Lands heads the Department of Natural Resources. In 1980 he is liberal Bert Cole with whom the conservative Ray doesn't get along. DNR generates

revenue through grazing and timber fees, a kingdom aloof from governor *and* legislature. Governor Ray ignores DNR. A commission also insulates the Game Department, who generates revenue through hunting and fishing licenses, another kingdom.

Department of Emergency Services originated in civil defense against nuclear
attack—building air-raid shelters, drilling civilians, stashing Geiger counters—but
had gradually shrunk to twenty-one. DES formed an emergency center in 1979 but
got no more staff or budget. Governor Ray had appointed young Edward Chow to
DES, an election debt to his mother Ruby of the King County Council. In December
Ray appointed him DES director though he's inexperienced in disaster readiness.
By early 1980 the Legislative Budget Committee charges that many in DES wouldn't
know what to in a disaster.[75]

Many volcanoes erupt that haven't before, not in anyone's memory. Paricutín spurted
up through a Mexico cornfield in 1943. At Heimay in Iceland in 1973 lava arced up
five hundred feet along a five-thousand-foot line where there'd been no eruption in
five thousand years. "Forecasts are difficult," quipped Samuel Goldwyn, "particularly
those about the future." In the volcano business, Crandell and Mullineaux's forecast
that Mount St. Helens could erupt before the end of the century is all the long-term
warning you can ask for.

In March 1980 twenty volcanoes around the globe spew ash or lava. Aso, On-take,
and Sakurajima in Japan, Arenal in Costa Rica, Bulusan in the Philippines, Ruapehu
in New Zealand, Kliuchevskoi in Kamchatka, Krafla in Iceland, Etna in Italy. And
now Mount St. Helens blinks awake. She may confound the natives but chants from
an old script.

3

Geyser

It's early afternoon Monday, March 24 in the University of Washington seismology laboratory in Seattle. Steve Malone, Craig Weaver, and Elliot Endo contemplate a magnitude-4.4 earthquake too large for an aftershock of the March 20 quake. They now see the many earthquakes at Mount St. Helens these four days aren't tectonic but volcanic.[1] Longview *Daily News* reporter Donna duBeth telephones Malone. "Mount St. Helens has erupted often in the past," he says, "and will again. The only question is when."

USGS's Rocky Crandell and Don Mullineaux in Denver now know the quakes plot beneath Mount St. Helens, not off north. Mullineaux calls Washington Department of Emergency Services. DES calls a meeting. Visiting Cowlitz County deputy Ben Bena attends, and a State Patrol lieutenant from next door. Terry Simmonds quotes from Crandell and Mullineaux's USGS bulletin and shows its map depicting ashflows out miles and mudflows far down valleys. The lieutenant marches off to brief his major. DES starts a telephone calldown. Deputy Bena dials his sheriff: "Don't rush home at five: I've something to discuss." By evening many bureaus know that something stews at Mount St. Helens.[2]

Over the next two days a dozen earthquakes magnitude 4.0 to 4.4 roll in from Mount St. Helens, most of them shallow. The seismologists watch their size and frequency climb. Quakes above magnitude 2.5 averaged four per day through the 24th, but next day come 152. Seismometer SHW high on the west flank records five small quakes per hour the 22nd but twenty five per hour the 24th. The paper goes dark noon the 25th—so many quakes they overlie each other's traces, many above magnitude 3. Then from 4 to 10 PM *another* threefold increase in seismic energy: twenty-four magnitude 4s in eight hours!

This swarm more intense than any ever recorded in the United States alarms the seismologists. An earthquake means rock shattering beneath Mount St. Helens. "Yet we're too busy counting and locating them," says Elliot Endo, "to think just what they mean."

George Theisen runs a meeting in Kelso for Gifford Pinchot National Forest. District officers have come as far as 130 miles. Forest Supervisor Bob Tokarczyk telephones in early afternoon.

"The mountain's full of earthquakes," he says. "You must organize a campaign."

"We've not done the budget. I'll be back tomorrow."

"That'll have to wait. I need you *now*!"

The Forest Service and geologists craft a news release, but USGS protocol takes all afternoon and three telephone calls to Crandell and Mullineaux to approve a few simple sentences.

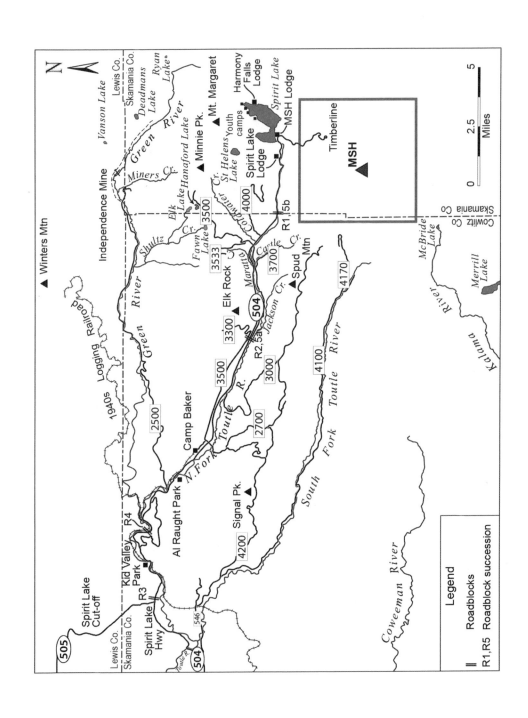

Harry Truman presides over Mount St. Helens Lodge on Spirit Lake's southwest bay. These years since wife Eddie died Truman's fire has cooled. He rents out a few cabins and boats in summer, sells kerosene and beer, but the lodge is going seedy, the man lonely and frayed.[3] Now media crews invade his snowbound peace.

Reporter Donna duBeth and photographer Roger Werth of Longview's *Daily News* drive up Spirit Lake Highway Tuesday morning and stop by the great green lodge. Its craggy proprietor beckons them in and unfolds his fifty years at Spirit Lake.[4]

"A UW seismologist says earthquakes can lead to eruption," says duBeth.

"I've felt no earthquakes and there'll be no eruption. I'm gonna stay till hell freezes over."

But earthquakes escalate in afternoon, and the Forest Service frets about avalanches. *Oregon Journal* reporter Don Hamilton interviews rangers Chuck Tonn and Sharon Burchard at Timberline. Photographer Steve Nehl watches the open door of Tonn's pickup swing to and fro—another earthquake. Tonn's radio crackles: "Close the mountain!"

Hamilton and Nehl stop at Mount St. Helens lodge. Truman pours Coca-Cola and Schenley's—Coke high. He pumps the old player piano, and out pours *Paper Doll*. Hamilton reads a framed letter about a horse trip, signed William O. Douglas. "Old Bill could hold his scotch all right," says Truman.

"What you think of the earthquakes?" asks Hamilton.

"Haven't felt a quiver. Wouldn't even know if I weren't asked to yak to TV cameras."

"The Forest Service just shut the mountain. You going to leave?"

"Naw. I've got the best little resort in the whole U-S-A. They're not gonna get me off this mountain. And if the sonofabitch blows, I'm the only one up here."

In next day's *Daily News* under headline GIVE 'EM HELL, HARRY, duBeth sketches Truman's decades at the lodge, fierce windstorms, a secret cave stocked with food and whiskey. "I'm king of Spirit Lake," he says. "I stuck it out fifty-four years. I'm gonna stay."[5] In a Werth portrait Truman hugs Old Red, his favorite of sixteen cats.

ROGER WERTH

A magnitude-4.3 earthquake strikes midafternoon the 25th. From the highway snowplow, Joe Gallow watches the heavy blade sway left and right, left-right. A pencil hangs on a string from a rafter in the Forest Service hut at Spirit Lake. "The hut shudders, and dust drops," says *Columbian* reporter Bill Stewart. "The pencil swings back and forth, a makeshift seismometer." Ranger Ken Johnson radios Tonn and Burchard: "Leave by dark. Tell everyone there to leave."

At Timberline Tonn watches dead snags sway like grass in wind. USGS's Elliot Endo pulls in and swaps a seismometer tape. "This is *not* a place to be," he says. But down at Kid Valley store Stan Lee growls, "It's just a crock of shit cooked up by the Forest Service and them environmentalists to delay development at Spirit Lake."

Sheriff Bill Closner preserves safety in Skamania County. His westside deputy George Barker has driven his new Porsche 924 east across the Cascades to Ellensburg. The campus police at Central Washington University find him. Barker telephones.

"How soon can you be back?" Closner asks.

"Four hours."

"Good. I'll expect you in three."

Barker slides behind the wheel. And does he ever enjoy driving the Porsche back at a comfortable pace. He clocks on at 9:20 PM and drives the county Blazer up Toutle valley. He finds the Forest Service gone from Spirit Lake, the only vehicle Harry Truman's white pickup.

Next morning at the *Oregon Journal*, Don Hamilton scans wire copy on Mount St. Helens—too bland to run. He telephones the geology department at Portland State University. Professor Leonard Palmer says, "Earthquakes are the birth pains of a volcano." In the background Hamilton hears shouting. "Tremors six miles down have climbed to the surface. An eruption seems imminent!"

At city desk Hamilton reads back the quotes—so intense compared to any news in two days. "Write it up," says the editor. When the *Journal* hits the street, its headline bellows.

USGS's Donal Mullineaux briefs a Vancouver meeting of thirty from agencies and companies—Forest Service, sheriffs of Skamania and Cowlitz Counties, State Patrol, state departments of emergency services, natural resources, game, transportation, Army Engineers, Weyerhaeuser, Pacific Power and Light, news reporters.[6] Mullineaux hangs a map and explains 4500 years of sporadic volcanic violence—eruptions large and small, ashfall, hot ashflows, mudflows down the valleys. An eruption could in days or years. Eruptions 3000 years ago suggest a long siege—months or decades. But recent history suggests small or moderate eruption. At a distance expect mudflows in the valleys and ashfall downwind.

The mountain looks pretty and has forever, thinks Cowlitz Sheriff Les Nelson. This will be interesting, at least. Weyerhaeuser's Jim Rombach asks about logging northwest of Mount St. Helens. "Eruptions will probably come slowly," Mullineaux says. "Mud could drown valley floors. Go uphill."

"How far?"

"Thirty feet above the river. Mud can flow faster than people walk. But with radios you'll know."

Mullineaux has described events that could be violent miles out, but his soft voice makes them seem only a nuisance. Many entered the room with no idea Mount St. Helens could erupt. Now they want certainty.

"Let's not beat around the bush," one says. "When'll it blow? How bad?"

"I can't tell *if* it will erupt," Mullineaux says, "let alone how or when."

"This nation can put a man on the moon, but *you* can't tell us if the volcano will erupt?"

"That's right!"

Lawmen brood. *Any* activity seems far–fetched on a mountain so long quiet. "Tell me the situation and I'll deal with it," one says. "I can't manage the indefinite." "We don't know what can happen in our county," Skamania sheriff Closner complains. "Mullineaux describes a whole range of activity. We're used to death, destruction, body parts. We need from him the worst."

"Mullineaux says the volcano could erupt almost any size in weeks or years," says John DeMeyer of Washington DNR. "He's vague about the near future. Expect mud-flows, but it could be worse. He can't say when. The man-on-moon taunt shows the frustration in the room."

The Forest Service hear more. "I understand but have heard him before," George Theisen says. "Many here yawn and mutter 'This can't happen.' But it *can*." Ed Osmond says, "Mullineaux is thorough. No one leaves ignorant of Mount St. Helens' past. We don't know just what's coming, but it could be bad."

A breakout group discusses how to coordinate. "Who'll take charge?" asks Cowlitz sheriff's deputy Ben Bena. "If something big happens and we've no agreed command, there'll be chaos." They deem Gifford Pinchot National Forest large and funded enough to coordinate. Here at Vancouver will be the radio hub.

Another group discusses how to communicate. From a few seismic swiggles a Portland State professor predicts Mount St. Helens "could blow in days." Or so shouts this afternoon's *Oregon Journal*. But here we can't be alarmists, Mullineaux says. Our forecasts must reflect all we know of the volcano's past. We'll report data but not speculate about the future.

"We don't want *this* to be another Three-Mile Island," says one. A year ago the core of a nuclear reactor in Pennsylvania partly melted. The accident began at 4 AM and continued all day, but few knew until Walter Cronkite's CBS evening news. Radio-active steam then drifted across towns. It took days to pry information from contra-dictory authorities. It's brought lawsuits. Today's team agrees they'll inform about Mount St. Helens quickly, directly, fully.

Sheriff Closner orders highway 504 blocked at the county line, barely beyond mountain's base. In ear-flapped cap, deputy George Barker stands by sandwich–board signs: ROAD CLOSED.

A Spirit Lake cabin owner drives up. "I need things from my place."

"It's too dangerous."

"Well, I'm going."

"If you do I'll have to write a citation."

"You block me from my own property? You're asking for a lawsuit!"

"The road's closed."

Responsibility for protecting life and property lies with the sheriffs. Skamania County contains Mount St. Helens and the cabins, lodges, and youth camps about Spirit Lake. Cowlitz County to the west holds highway 504 and villages like Kid Valley and Toutle. The two sheriffs have collaborated on searching for lost hunters but have no plan to deal with major disruption. Who now sets roadblocks? Who pays for them? Who's in charge? As Sheriff Nelson puts it, "We build a boat while rowing it."

The Forest Service administers 2050 square miles of Gifford Pinchot National Forest. But Forest squares alternate like a giant chessboard with state and private lands. Burlington Northern Railroad holds scores of square miles including the volcano's summit. To the west lie hundreds of Weyerhaeuser square miles. The National Forest can activate a command system quickly, as when Ruth fire burned 3000 acres south of Mount St. Helens in October. A fire boss coordinates radio, aircraft, county sheriffs, state timber, and large landowners. Forest Supervisor Tokarczyk is an old hand. In the late 1940s he'd fought fires at Spirit Lake, led climbs of Mount St. Helens. In 1950 he helped mop up a C-54 crash.[7] He's headed the Forest four years. He designates veteran Paul Stenkamp as crisis coordinator and George Theisen as acting fire boss.

The Seattle seismologists fret. Seismic energy accelerated the 25th and by afternoon eruption seemed imminent. The USGS Director in Virginia issues alerts, but many scientists, office chiefs, and media officers contribute. Crafting words to paper takes days. But the seismic energy beneath Mount St. Helens builds swiftly. Craig Weaver calls a deputy chief: "We *must* get off our butts, issue a statement! It can't wait!" But it waits.

Newspapers report that scorching ash clouds could sweep off the volcano seventy miles an hour, bouldery floods flush down valleys. Stan Lee scoffs from Kid Valley store: "I'd like to ask people who say they've felt the earthquake what they been drinkin.'" But Harry Truman, now spooked by the shaking, finds his booze running low. His pickup sprints downvalley to restock.

Three to five centuries ago hot flows and muddy floods swept all volcano flanks. A big flow into the reservoir on the south could spill water over Swift Dam. Overtopped dams have ravaged downstream—Wyoming in 1925, Italy in 1964. Crandell and Mullineaux's booklet calls Swift Reservoir a public threat. Might its failure breach lower reservoirs? Wipe away Woodland? Pacific Power and Light opens Swift's gates to draw down another 160 million cubic yards—enough to hold a large flow off Mount St. Helens.

In three quarters of a century the St. Helens mining district has yielded little ore. But prospecting in 1975 along Green River northeast of Spirit Lake, Jay Parker found white and green 'peacock' stones. He and Lindsey Thomas followed them upstream to a vein high on the west ridge and an old mine tunnel. They and Martin Remmen blasted rocks from it, and assay revealed copper, silver, and gold. After the Great War and influenza scythed through the worker pool in Butte, Remmen had at age 14 mined copper and gold at Black Rock Mine. He so named this new venture: Black Rock Mining Company. The partners staked two twenty-acre claims. Black Rock 1 and 2 lie, they think, just south of Coe's 1907 Mary 5 and 6. The ore vein having come from depth, they reason it'll be richer deeper. They'll bore in below the old tunnel.

Remmen and Parker dig through snow March 27 to relocate their claim stake when two loud explosions rattle the hills like artillery. Sonic booms of aircraft, they think. In late afternoon they snowmobile nine miles out past Meta Lake.

A new swarm of earthquakes begins morning the 27th. Nine quakes above magnitude 3 pummel per hour. News reporters interview ranger Jim Nieland at Timberline when at 12:36 PM a loud explosion from high on Mount St. Helens "reverberates like a quarry blast," says Nieland, "deep and echoing." Everyone freezes, listens, peers into the clouds. Nieland radios Vancouver, where Ed Osmond pencils the first paragraph of a contingency plan.

Radio-KGW's airplane flies off Vancouver's Pearson Airpark at 12:35. "We break up through clouds at 6700 feet and see Mount St. Helens' upper 3000 feet," reporter Mike Beard says. "The summit is oddly dark. As we draw near I see a crater two hundred feet across—a hole in the ice, black ash around it. It's clearly new: ice and snow cave from the rim. A small black plume drifts up like a smoking chimney. I radio the station. A disc jockey spins the *Beach Boys*. 'Stop the music! Put me on the air!' But he won't interrupt."

KGW plays top-forty music; even this crack news crew fights for air time. Paged at lunch, news director John Erickson charges up to the studio. Beard radios, "*John! This son of a bitch is erupting!*" Erickson dials the USGS. Don Mullineaux there wants to know: Is there a crater? At the summit or off one side? Any ash? These can be Erickson's prompts. He punches the dialer to Associated Press, "This is Erickson. Listen to KGW!"

A platter ends, the *Eagles* singing "I Can't Tell You Why." Erickson switches Beard to the airwaves. At 12:50 he squeezes the microphone. The aircraft engine drones in the background. Bass-voiced Beard broadcasts: "We are directly over Mount St. Helens at the ten-thousand-foot level, and there is no question at all that the volcanic activity has begun. You can see smoke and ash pouring from the top of the mountain. The ash is going down along the slope a thousand feet or so very evident beside the stark white snow. There is a crater. It's a large hole a little to the north, almost on top."

Erickson had called the Skamania County sheriff, but it's too soon for word to get around. The Cowlitz sheriff telephones KGW: "You're creating panic in southwest Washington!" A call from Washington Emergency Services: "The volcano's not *erupting*! It's a minor explosion."[8]

Cripes! thinks Erickson. Beard reports facts. He's calm and eloquent. The plane has turned from the volcano, but Erickson toggles Beard back on the air: "We could see the volcanic activity beginning. There was no question at all. A hole in the top of the mountain is spewing some smoke and a lot of ash." As KGW's plane nears Vancouver, a flotilla of small planes and helicopters climbs toward the volcano. The pilot threads his way through them and waves.

Forest Service press spokesman Jim Unterwegner steps into the control room, the whole bank of telephone lines lit. John Erickson plays back Beard. The room fills with people, radios squawk. Unterwegner takes one call after another. "It's like someone threw a pebble into a quiet pond," he says, "ripples spreading farther and wider. The first calls are from Vancouver and Portland. Soon Seattle and San Francisco. Then Denver and Cleveland. Finally New York and Miami."

The Forest's St. Helens District at Pine Creek sits on the volcano's south flank. "After lunch we hear a sonic boom," says Ranger Ken Johnson. "Soon the back door flies open and Dave Seesholtz strides in: 'I heard a reporter flying say the mountain's erupting!'" Johnson calls headquarters. "Pine Creek's too close!" Ed Osmond barks. "You get the hell out of there!"

Johnson flips on the siren at 1:20. In half an hour they close up, cross Eagle Creek bridge, and block road 90. A Skamania deputy evacuates the cabins at North Woods. Several dozen people caravan over the mountains forty miles south to Carson.

Rob Smith maintains Spirit Lake Lodge, cleans the rooms, cuts firewood, cooks meals. In winter only he and Truman live up here. Kathy Paulson helps March 27: "After lunch while making beds I hear a sonic boom. I think nothing of it."

Three deputies man the county-line roadblock. Their radios crackle about an eruption. "Now it seems dangerous at the lake," says George Barker. "None of us

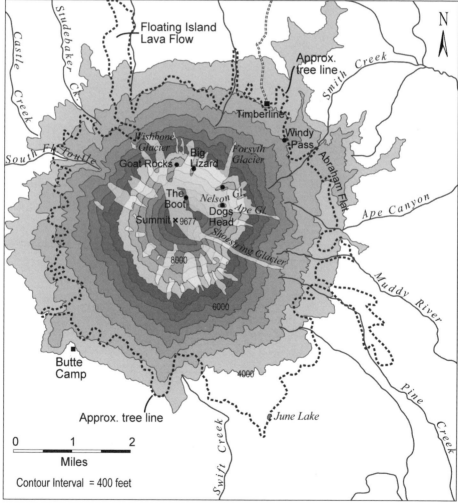

Pre-eruption detail.

wants to go, but it's my county. I race up the highway and turn in to Spirit Lake Lodge."

"An hour after the boom Barker pulls up," says Paulson. "He says the mountain's blown a hole in its top and he's evacuating Spirit Lake."

Barker speeds up the highway and whips around Timberline loop. Fifteen news folk cluster about rangers Jim Nieland and Chuck Tonn. Barker flips on the high-low siren and barks into the hailer: "I'm going to say it once and only once: You've got to go!"

Nieland and USGS's Rick Hoblitt motor down to the Forest hut and step out. A strong shock sways the firs. They shed snow that floats down like a cloud of feathers. In neutral and brake off, Hoblitt's Blazer rolls a foot back, a foot forward, back and forth, back and forth. The ground rises, falls, rises, falls. Waves roll down the road toward Truman's lodge.

Rob Smith and Kathy Paulson lock Spirit Lake Lodge, drive east, and step into Truman's. Half a century ago today, 27 March 1930, Truman got sole ownership of Mount St. Helens Lodge. He built this grand structure nine years later. Since wife Eddie died, Rob is the closest he has to a friend. He pours three Coke-and-Schenley's.

"The mountain's erupted and George Barker's evacuating Spirit Lake," Paulson says. "You going to leave?"

"Oh, I don't know. Where'd I go?"

"Come with us. Stay at my mother's at Silver Lake."

"Well, no. If anything happens I'll go across the ice."

Paulson hears in each reply Truman making up his mind to stay.

A sharp earthquake! "The walls sway as if it were a cardboard box," Paulson says. "Dishes rattle, pans clank. The lodge shudders and creaks. Much bigger than others, it scares me. 'Let's get out of here!' Harry's startled too but isn't coming." They tramp to the porch.

The UW seismic lab records many earthquakes today, five magnitude 4s since morning. At two a 4.7, largest yet—that oscillates the Blazer and troubles Truman's lodge.

Among those chased from Timberline are *Oregon Journal*'s Don Hamilton and Robert Bach. Hamilton recalls his Tuesday interview. "Stop! I want to see Harry again."

"I'll stay," says Bach. "But another boom and I'm out of here!"

Hamilton steps to the wide porch boarded against winter, Truman jabbing with a visitor. An earthquake! The wall lurches out and back some inches. Truman goes silent, and Hamilton sees the ruddy color drain from his cheeks.[9]

Herding cars down the highway, deputy Barker brakes at Mount St. Helens Lodge. He dashes to the porch, a radio blaring from his belt.

"Harry, the mountain's blown. I'm clearing Spirit Lake. Let me drive you out."

"This is my home."

"It's not safe."

"I'm okay. I've had earthquakes before."

"It's your choice, Harry," Barker outshouts the radio. "You coming?"

"Hell *no*! I ain't leaving!"

But in Truman's eyes Hamilton sees no bravery, his pale face contradicting the tough words. He's bluffing, Hamilton sees. His bluster to us reporters puts him in a box.

Barker knows he can't force a citizen from his home who breaks no law. It would violate his Fourteenth Amendment rights. "I've known Truman since I came here to Y camp as a boy. In summer I'm a neighbor. He's given no trouble, and I've never ordered him to do anything. He doesn't now refuse a command, only my offer of a ride."

"Let's get moving!" Barker calls to the reporters. About 2:15 he drives down the highway behind the last of them. Only Truman remains.

The Forest Service orders up an aircraft. With the USGS they'll watch the volcano day and night. Clouds dissipate in midafternoon. The crater has caved out a hundred yards, haloed by black ash. Just north and south fissures rip east-west across the snow and arc down northeast and northwest. Snow and the crater between the fissures have sunk like a grave. Just north cracks cleave snow like broken glass.

By late afternoon dozens of airplanes and helicopters cut this way and that at different levels. The Federal Aviation Administration takes control of airspace. Traffic will circle counterclockwise at three miles, summit runs one at a time, Forest Service coordinating.

The USGS director this morning finally issued a bland hazard watch: "earthquakes do not necessarily mean there will be an eruption." Mount St. Helens then spews forth. A hasty news release has the USGS "conducting observations [on] . . . volcanic activity that has been reported."

Governor Dixy Lee Ray addresses Superior Court judges at Port Ludlow in early afternoon. State Patrol sergeant Ron Walcker stands nearby. His pager rings: Emergency Services Director Ed Chow. Walcker slips a note to the lectern.

"Well," says the grinning governor, "I've just learned Mount St. Helens has blown it's *top!*"

Walcker chauffeurs the governor to the airfield, and they climb into a Beechcraft King-Air 200. An hour later they gawk into the soot-rimmed hole. "I hoped to live to see one of our volcanoes erupt," she says. "Yet . . . the whole thing may be over."

Longview's *Daily News* had been 'put to bed' when at lunch Donna duBeth is paged. It's managing editor Bob Gaston: "The mountain's erupted!" DuBeth and photographer Brian Drake race up the Spirit Lake highway behind a State Patrol cruiser. The trooper stops and won't let them pass. But loggers at Kid Valley explain Weyerhaeuser roads. The reporters bounce east along gravel roads [1910 and 2400 system] and return to the highway.

At Timberline an earthquake sways the car left-right-left-right. "Jeeze!" cries Drake. "Let's get out of here." But duBeth has come for a story. Others pull in—from *The Columbian*, *The Oregonian*, a Portland radio station, Associated Press. An earthquake pitches *Columbian* reporter Thomas Ryll against the van that shakes "as if buffeted by a gust of wind." AP's Les Blumenthal hears a *crack!* "We're nervous about this place," he says, "tension in the air."

PHOTOS BY DAVID A. JOHNSTON

First 1980 eruption

Seattle's KING5-TV calls Steve Malone at UW. "Will you fly with us to Mount St. Helens?"

"Too busy. How about a *real* volcanologist from the USGS? He's David Johnston."

The Hughes 500 has circled the summit for the cameras and now lands at Timberline. Pilot Bob Wright cuts the engine, brakes the spinning rotor. Out steps Johnston in a blue-plaid woolen mackinaw. KING Reporter Jeff Renner and cameraman Mark

Anderson set up. DuBeth and other reporters point microphones and cameras, scribble in notebooks. An earthquake, and from the helicopter Wright watches the rotor blades flop up and down.

"The more earthquakes," Johnston says, "the more I worry about this place. I'm genuinely afraid of it." He nods toward the mountain. "There's a new crater and cracks across the summit. That blast today is just the beginning of the fireworks. It was only a steam explosion, no magma at the surface. But the volcano *is* heating up. In 1976 Augustine in Alaska exploded steam like this in morning, then a real eruption in evening. Next day, big ones.

"We stand at a dangerous place, on deposits of earlier eruptions. A glowing avalanche could flow down here a hundred miles an hour." Another earthquake, and from high on the mountain a muffled roar of avalanche. The reporters glance up, shift feet. "We stand next to a keg of dynamite. The fuse is lit, but we don't know how long it is." Johnston eyes Renner. "If it were to explode now, we would die."

The KING crew climb into the helicopter. Wright powers up and lifts off.[10]

"None of us knows about volcanoes," says AP's Blumenthal. "Johnston says it's dangerous and flies off. So we pile into our cars and are out of here too." As they motor down, young Donna duBeth molds tomorrow's story. Smitten by the blue-eyed young man with a light fuzz of beard who speaks bluntly of danger, she plots another interview with David Johnston.

The deputies fret about the close roadblock. Sightseers would retard an escape on the narrow stretch of road. George Barker moves the barricade twenty miles down to Maple Flats.[11] Sheriff Bill Closner and a sergeant attend a police-academy graduation in Seattle when called about the eruption. From I-5 they turn east and come to the block at Maple Flats. Reporters close in. Closner will soon run for re-election, and a block so far down won't win votes. He orders it back to the county line. Closner hears an Air Force 304th helicopter on the police radio. He calls, and it lands on the highway. Above the summit the huey banks left and the doors roll back. Closner gapes down his pantleg into the vent.

National Forest spokesman Jim Unterwegner steps into a room of reporters, the front table bristling microphones. "Holy smokes!" he says, "you'd think the *President's* coming!" He summarizes today's eruption and roadblocks. USGS's Don Mullineaux lays out what could happen—mudflows down the valleys, ashfall downwind, might last years.

"Wouldn't melting snow extinguish the volcano?" asks a buck reporter.

Mullineaux stifles a guffaw. "Well, no . . . heh, heh . . . surely not."

Short and quiet, Mullineaux is a field geologist meticulous at gathering and analyzing data, his papers anchored in facts. His and Crandell's reports forecast across centuries, but now people ask about tomorrow. In the glare of lights, weary from three sleepless nights, he fidgets, pauses, qualifies. Privately he says, "I'd rather do *anything* but this."

His pale fire is any scientist's caution against pronouncing upon the unknown. Forecasting the near future is itself a hazard. In 1975–1976 snow and ice had melted near the summit of Mount Baker in northern Washington. When avalanche seemed likely the USGS issued warnings. A power company drew down a reservoir, flushing away revenues. Little happened. Yet even little bursts manage to damage. A year ago Dieng volcano in Indonesia burped carbon dioxide gas. Flowing invisible and odorless through a village, it asphyxiated cattle and 115 people.

Earthquakes and small eruptions at a volcano can herald disaster or nothing. In 1902 people at St. Pierre weathered two weeks of earthquakes and explosions at Mont Pelée thinking they'd die down. But a scorching cloud then swallowed the city and thirty thousand lives. In 1976 earthquakes and small eruptions rattled La Soufrière on nearby Guadaloupe. French scientists debated the danger: *Oui! Non!* Mindful of St. Pierre, authorities evacuated 73,600 people, the social cost enormous. La Soufrière didn't erupt. Scientists and authorities looked like fools and were loudly criticized.[12]

Mount Vesuvius had spewed violently in 79 and 1631 but in 1751, 1763, and 1944 erupted only lava and grit. In 1906 a great steam jet shot up eight miles and roared on twelve hours. Mount St. Helens, Mullineaux knows by its deposits, has been as temperamental and hardly predictable now. Today's symptoms could end with whimper or bang.

Half an hour past midnight the 28th, UW's seismometers record a magnitude 4.9 earthquake—largest yet. Spotters in aircraft radio observations, and in Vancouver they're entered into a Forest Service logbook. A USGS geologist in the plane scribbles notes. Through clouds and darkness, a black column jets up at 3:15 and burns on 50 minutes. Its plume rises two miles and drifts east-southeast, smelling of sulfur. At 10:04 a sulfury black plume shoots through clouds, rises a mile, and drifts southeast. A dozen more eruptions burst for minutes or hours.[13]

Seattle's KING5-TV televised their Timberline interview with David Johnston and fed it to NBC network. Les Blumenthal's story raced over AP wires. The *Oregonian*, *Columbian*, and *Daily News* run stories. Johnston's words leap from televisions and newspapers across the land. The volcano clouded the 28th, KING5's Jeff Renner and Mark Anderson interview from Hoffstadt Mountain seventeen miles northwest. Johnston says a big eruption could shoot ash up ten miles and send big mudflows down valleys. KING's "live from Mount St. Helens" relays to Seattle and is fed to NBC.

Johnston's spirited spoutings alarm USGS management. "He says this," a reporter tells Mullineaux, "so what do *you* say?" Office chief Robert Tilling recalls the fiasco at La Soufrière four years ago. The French scientists had few data, inconsistent stories, some 'experts' far from the scene. The USGS would avoid such errors at Mount St. Helens. "We don't know how this will play out," an elder tells Johnston. "We don't want people in harm's way but can't be fright merchants. We can't broadcast conflicting stories." The official voice will be discreet and at Vancouver.

Though only thirty and a term employee, Johnston does know about exploding volcanoes. After Augustine in Alaska erupted in winter 1976, a windstorm and helicopter crash stranded him and six others on the island. With scant food, three blankets, and a little jet fuel for heat, they huddled in a hut three days and nights. A week earlier a scorching flow had blown out windows, torn off a wall, and burned things inside. "Another would've cooked us," Johnston says. Filmmaker Bill Bacon says,

"The geologists were in a sweat to get the hell off." The storm abated, and a helicopter plucked them off. Twelve hours later scorching ash flowed to the sea.[14]

Reporters swoop in after Mount St. Helens' explosions. Don Mullineaux tells them the volcano is only "clearing its throat." Flows will likely be small. Cynthia Gorney writes for the *Washington Post*, "The national press corps descended on Vancouver smelling disaster, braced for Pompeii. Atlantis. The lava that ate Portland. But this apocalypse refuses to cooperate. The situation will worsen, improve, or stay about the same."

She mocks the ambiguous news briefings. Don't speculate beyond your data—not to reporters. Don't cry 'wolf.' Issue false alarms and you won't be heeded later. Or so goes USGS culture. Mullineaux is the very model of meticulous, quiet science.

Sightseers obstruct any quick escape from the highway 504 roadblock in Skamania County. The highway west is Cowlitz County. "Well, if we can't get out of it," says Sheriff Les Nelson, "we better get into it." The block moves down to mile 33¼. Weyerhaeuser's road crossing forms a wide flat to turn trucks. Deputies George Barker and Bob Nix staff the block in midafternoon the 28th. A clutch of national media stand below—NBC, CBS, *Time* magazine, two in jackets stenciled 'War Correspondent.' Donna duBeth and Roger Werth of the *Daily News* drive up.

"No one passes," says Barker. "You can join the big boys over there."

Petite duBeth flicks her brunette mane. "And *you* can step aside," she chirps. "Here's a note from the sheriff." Haughtily she hands it.

Barker and Nix think it a forgery—not typed on letterhead, only pencil scribbles to paper torn from a notebook. "I don't care where you got this," Barker says. "You're not going through."

"Like hell." DuBeth races to Camp Baker and a telephone. When she returns to the block the sheriff has radioed. "So there!" she hisses. The network reporters smirk and cheer.

"You go at your own risk," Barker growls. "Don't expect us to come for a rescue."

"As if I give a rip," DuBeth laughs and accelerates up the highway.

"That damned smart-ass," mutters Barker, who can only glare at the shrinking car.

Harry Truman ranted Tuesday he'd felt no earthquakes and there'll be no eruption. Now after two days of both he quietly strokes a cat. "I wish the shaking would stop," he says. "It scares me to hell. If water off the mountain takes out the road and I get marooned, I want to be at home with my cats. I've got enough food and liquor to stand a hell of a siege."

From Kid Valley store Stan Lee croaks, "There's no smoke coming out of the mountain, just bullshit." But all night and day Mount St. Helens lofts dark ash several thousand feet, a gigantic gray geyser. News briefings in Vancouver are up to three a day. The *Washington Post* and *Los Angeles Times* run features on Mount St. Helens' past violence.

Rocky Crandell joins Mullineaux in Vancouver. The sheriffs and Forest Service complain of puny and generalized maps. Crandell selects a large prehistoric ashflow on the southeast, enlarges it as a margin of safety, and projects it down each valley on a three-foot map. He then projects a medium-sized flow down each valley. He depicts incinerating ashflows, dense mudflows, and ashfalls from Mount St. Helens. A central red splotch depicts likely small flows. Green reaches farther. Orange octopus arms depict unlikely large flows many miles out. Red threads predict mudflows dozens of miles farther down the valleys.

Geologists collect all kinds of data, but what do they imply? Just gas steaming up? Hot magma rising into lower pressure where its trapped gas can explode? A team from Dartmouth College flies a correlation spectrometer (COSPEC)[15] to measure sulfur-dioxide gas from the crater. But they barely detect SO_2. A second crater blows out the 29th. For five nights a blue flame floods them both. Hydrogen sulfide? It ignites only above 260 degrees Fahrenheit. Is the top of the cone heating?

USGS's Robert Christiansen comes from Menlo Park to coordinate science and interpret data for Crandell and Mullineaux. Beside the Forest Service, the USGS seems anarchic. A hazards team comes from Denver, those shooting instruments from Hawaii, Menlo Park, and Flagstaff. The seismic network is run from Seattle. Few have worked together. "The USGS may seem a thousand-pound gorilla," says Steve Malone, "but it's really a thousand one-pound gorillas."

Clouds veil Saturday's views "like a miniskirt," a photographer tells reporters, "teasing and appealing but not quite revealing." The summit clears Sunday. A black column jets up and drifts downwind. Then another puff, and another, like a lumbering locomotive. A 7:40 AM burst shoots up a mile, and a dark anvil drifts southeast. Two hours later it powders Bend 150 miles away, like the 1842 eruptions. The *Columbian* runs photographs. The *Oregonian* explains hot-ash hurricanes and ravaging mudflows Mount St. Helens could unleash. The UW seismic lab records six more earthquakes between 4.5 and 4.7—the big ones now more often.

Andrei Sarna-Wojcicki and I map the newfallen ash. Under a microscope it seems all mineral grains and pulverized summit rock, no frothy pumice. The geyserlike bursts may rivet all eyes, but their ejecta brings no proof of new magma.

Surveying in Hawaii has shown the ground at Kilauea swelling some inches. Then as lava erupts the swell subsides—like a skin boil draining pus. Jim Moore and Don Swanson resurvey a triangle ten yards on a side at Timberline. The south rising would show the mountain flank swelling. But a week of leveling shows only tiny and inconsistent changes—no dangerous swell.

They nail yardsticks to logs, stumps, and docks in open leads around Spirit Lake. If the northern sticks sink and the southern shoal, they'd record the mountain flank rising. Two and a quarter miles long, Spirit Lake is now a great spirit level. They helicopter around the ice and measure waterline to a sixteenth inch. Moore reads the north shore 9:55 AM the 30th when an earthquake cracks the ice.[16] But by early April the sticks register no tilt of the lake. No evidence an intrusion beneath Mount St. Helens is big or broad.

The sheriffs have blocked highway 504 up Toutle valley from the west, highway 503 from the southwest, and Forest road 73 from the southeast. Snow fills others. Deputy George Barker tows his trailer at Spirit Lake down to the 504 block. Ray and Linda King use their cabin near Spirit Lake year-round. Saturday they come to sandwichboard signs.

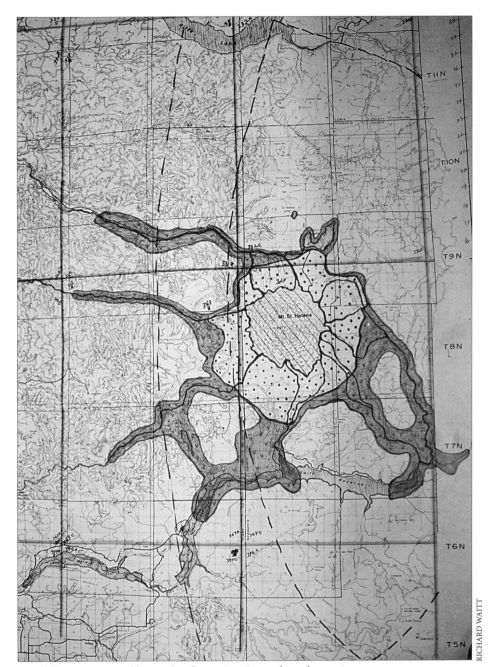

Crandell's map, as copied by Cowlitz deputy Ben Benna, legend opposite

"The highway's closed," says Barker. "Too risky up there."

"It's our property," says Ray King. "You know you've no legal right to stop us."

Barker lets them by. Finding nothing shifted at the cabin, they drive up to Timberline. The mountain's clouded but nothing different here either, no ash atop snow. "No reason not to be here," Ray says.

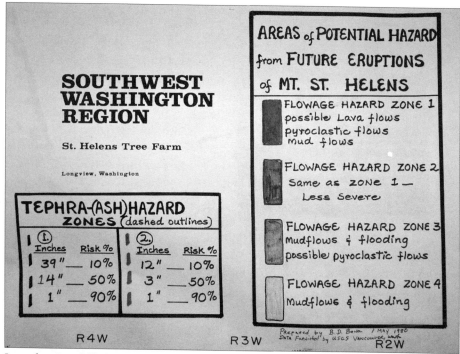

SOUTHWEST
WASHINGTON
REGION

St. Helens Tree Farm

Longview, Washington

TEPHRA-(ASH)HAZARD ZONES (dashed outlines)

① Inches	Risk %	② Inches	Risk %
39"	10%	12"	10%
14"	50%	3"	50%
1"	90%	1"	90%

AREAS of POTENTIAL HAZARD from FUTURE ERUPTIONS of MT. ST. HELENS

FLOWAGE HAZARD ZONE 1
possible lava flows
pyroclastic flows
mud flows

FLOWAGE HAZARD ZONE 2
Same as Zone 1 —
Less Severe

FLOWAGE HAZARD ZONE 3
Mudflows & flooding
possible pyroclastic flows

FLOWAGE HAZARD ZONE 4
Mudflows & flooding

Prepared by B.D. Benn / MAY 1980
Data Furnished by USGS Vancouver, Wash

R4W   R3W   R2W

Legend to Crandell's map

USGS's Susan and Hugh Kieffer drive up highway 504, turn into Coldwater, follow road 3500 up to snow, and pitch a tent in a hailstorm. Thunder awakens them in morning. Out the tent flap Sue watches black jet from Mount St. Helens. She films a 6:04 burst on super-8. Another starts 7:36 and in four minutes builds a massy outburst; lightning forks through. It ends abruptly at 7:55. An 11:29 burst lasts a minute. "Hey, here's another," she says two minutes past noon. She films at 2:10, 2:30, and 3:31. Erupt and stop, erupt and stop—as if gigantic Old Faithful geyser she's studied for years. Magma below maybe heats a water-filled chimney in the volcano, she thinks. It heats and boils, again and again.

The USGS seeks an observation post. Midday the 30th a Forest ranger snowcats Rick Hoblitt up roads 3490 and 3533 to a logging platform a thousand feet above Maratta Creek. They pitch an army tent in the snow, and the ranger showshoes out. Hoblitt records an ash burst as a full moon rises at 6:25. But clouds drift in at midnight, snow falling by

Early eruption, 10 April

RICHARD WAITT

2:30. Cold in the tent, Hoblitt finds the snowcat icy too. At dawn it's still snowing, the mountain invisible. The ranger comes and snowcats Hoblitt down. When the storm clears in late afternoon, the ranger motors Sue Kieffer up. She films a burst at 7:15, ash drifting north. Between clouds and hail, she films sporadic bursts for two days—the volcano a gushing geyser. There *must* be new heat inside, she thinks. She snowshoes off early the 3rd with frosted fingers.

DuBeth and Werth had visited Harry Truman again Friday, their story the *Daily News*'s front page. "If I left this place it'd worry me to death," Truman says. "If it's gonna go I wanna go with it." Many itch to interview him, but the sheriff won't risk them above the roadblock. Deputies drive Truman Sunday afternoon down to Toutle Lake High School. In green-plaid jacket and red cap he glad-hands Sheriff Nelson and fortifies forty reporters. "The mountain put on a show this morning," he laughs. "An earthquake walked my bed across the room before five. I decided it was time to get up." Lenses zoom. "But I think it's shot its wad. Those goddam geologists with hair down to their butts know no more about the mountain than I do. I've a supply of whiskey and rum and today got reinforcements. You couldn't pull me out with a mule team."

Since wife Eddie died, Truman has been a bleak recluse, the winters especially lonely. But into today's limelight steps a blustery performer. He's on the front page of the *San Francisco Examiner*. From the *New York Times* he nuzzles Old Red in Roger Werth's endearing shot. Two days later Truman drives down to reporters at the roadblock: "I'm gonna stay regardless of the volcano." Yet a quieter Truman putters around Mount St. Helens lodge where he lets Moore and Swanson (goddam geologists) place a barograph to record pressure spikes—eruptions.

It's one meeting after another for the nervous authorities—sheriffs, State Patrol and DES, Forest Service, USGS, Weyerhaeuser. Skamania Sheriff Closner says our small staff is fatigued, and so's our budget. We need help manning roadblocks. USGS's Crandell says hot ash on the mountain's snow could trigger mudflows that'd reach the 504 roadblock—mile 33¼—too fast to evacuate people. Before magmatic eruptions the block should go down to mile 15. He points to his map. Orange tentacles depict unlikely dangerous flows ten to fifteen miles down valleys. Green fingers depict plausible smaller flows. Ash could fall a foot thick fifty miles out, day go black.

USGS managers consider its Hawaiian Volcano Observatory 'graduates' like Moore, Lipman, and Swanson an elite corps—PhDs from top universities plying cutting-edge science. "We measure with instruments what's happening now," says Dan Dzurisin, "take Kilauea's pulse through eruptions." Some HVO grads think Crandell and Mullineaux obsolete. "What they do is hardly rocket science," smirks one.

Aero-Copters pilot Lon Stickney has trouble getting off Vancouver's morning fog. He and the geodetic field crew—now Swanson and Moore—move forty miles north to Kelso. Less fog, shorter flights to Mount St. Helens—and far from meetings.

The UW seismologists by March 30 installed ten new instruments near Mount St. Helens. The large quakes continue—nine above 4.5 March 31 to April 2. The energy of seven large ones, 4.8s and 4.9s, is twice that of earlier big ones. A few locate thirteen miles down—magma feeding from that deep.

Having monitored central-American eruptions, David Harlow now aids UW's seismology lab. Dan Miller calls his old friend. "What d'you make of the earthquakes?"

"Boy, all these magnitude 4s, their energy's huge. If magma isn't already under the volcano, it soon will be."

"You think *magmatic* eruption soon?"

"I've a bad feeling about this one."

Low-frequency 'harmonic tremor' appears during some eruptions of Kilauea. Seismologists think it caused by magma flowing through underground cracks. Just after noon March 31 a weak tremor beneath Mount St. Helens lasts two minutes. In evening April 1, tremor rolls on five minutes. Next morning a bout lasts three. Then starting 7:35 a fifteen-minute burst records mightily on seismometer CPW seventy miles north and shows on MBW 180 miles north.[17] "Strong all across the seismic network," says Harlow. "In Guatamala tremor not even this strong emerged *only* when Fuego erupted." But an aircraft circling Mount St. Helens sees no action.

Rocky Crandell fields a call from Steve Malone. Elegant at 58, Crandell seems a father to us much younger. A man who's studied volcanoes for decades might be forgiven some exhilaration. But the taut face of this former artillery officer exudes a touch of fear. "How can all this tremor *not* lead to eruption?" he mutters.

On earthquakey April 2 the Forest Service evacuates Pine Creek ranger station. They empty cabins of beds and clothes, offices of desks and files. Seventeen moving vans haul it to Cougar. Two hours past midnight a magnitude 5 earthquake rattles the new ranger station.

Two bursts of tremor the 4th each run half an hour. "Tremor being so strong on distant stations, it must originate down ten miles," says Dave Harlow. "Magma *must* be pouring up. To us in Seattle, magmatic eruption seems inevitable." *Oregon Journal*'s April 3 headline quotes Steve Malone: ALL SIGNS INDICATE MAJOR ERUPTION.

Cowlitz and Skamania Counties have asked the state for help in keeping sightseers from danger. They'd handed the 504 roadblock to the State Patrol. Now April 3, Governor Dixy Lee Ray signs a Declaration:

> Volcanic activity at Mount St. Helens has created conditions that may threaten life and may result in widespread destruction to . . . property . . . The . . . potential destruction and . . . need for rapid evacuation would be beyond the capabilities of [sheriffs] . . . A State of Emergency exists in Washington State . . . All resources of the State are authorized to be employed . . .[18]

The governor forms a Mount St. Helens Watch Group headed by State Patrol Chief Robert Landon. They will, she directs, develop plans to deal with eruptions and evacuations and to coordinate local governments.[19] Its first meeting brings the heads of Departments of Agriculture, Ecology, Financial Management, Transportation, Emergency Services, Social and Health Services, State Patrol, National Guard.

But no Game Department, who map which lakes near Mount St. Helens to open for fishing. And no Department of Natural Resources. DNR manages state timber lands and roads near the volcano; its State Geologist knows how big eruptions may be. But the governor allows only cabinet departments she controls. None whose chief is elected or appointed by commission.

The crisis turns the offices of Gifford Pinchot National Forest into a whirlwind. The nerve center is the radio room. Into an adjacent room have crowded twenty USGS scientists. Another room wired with hot-line telephones holds desks for sheriffs, state Emergency Services, State Patrol, the FAA. The parking lot sprouts pay-telephone trailers; a rented ballroom holds burgeoning press conferences.

A state snowplow clears Weyerhaeuser roads 3490 and 3533 up to the logging platform above Maratta Creek. Hoblitt now drives to 'Coldwater' post, as he calls it. He scribbles April 3rd to a notebook at 5:16, but then clouds blot the mountain.

Driving down the highway, he stops for a longhair in beret and backpack—young Fred Miller caked in ash. April Fool's Day he'd hitchhiked from Snohomish, yesterday thumbed a ride up the South Fork and climbed to treeline. Today he's trudged a long spiral to the summit. Still two craters, he says, ice at their rims capped by fifteen feet of new rocks. Rotten-egg gas wafts up crevasses. Ash douses him on Dog's Head. He's hiked thirteen miles down from Timberline. In Castle Rock Hoblitt buys him dinner and jots the details. He drops him at I-5 and turns south.

Flying this April 3 over gentle slopes below Goat Rocks, Swanson and Moore spot horizontal fissures crossing snow and bare ground. Goat Rocks punching up from the mountain? But riveted to the summit spectacle, other scientists shrug.[20]

Closed roads have idled scores of loggers. "The roadblock business is tough," says State Patrol Capt. Bullock. "Our troopers live in towns with loggers. I stand in a blue uniform with a guaranteed job. But when you block a highway you're telling a logger: 'You've no job today.' Many loggers can't work winters when the woods are full of snow. They can't now take a day off. Work puts food on the family table. 'We've been in the woods all our lives,' they say. 'We *live* with danger. We know to take care.'

"We officers block people from jobs because something might happen. *Might.* Facing them at a roadgate, you can't but empathize. Yet Rocky Crandell tells me the earthquakes and harmonic tremor mean it's dangerous up there, and I believe him."

A hundred loggers, contractors, mill owners, and attorneys meet April 4 in Vancouver with county commissioners, sheriffs, State Patrol, the USGS, and *Daily News* and *Columbian* reporters. Crandell points to his map, reviews Mount St. Helens's past, and suggests what could come soon: mudflows and ashfalls, maybe hot ashflows, maybe no warning. George Theisen says the Forest Service will keep closed the roads toward risk.

Crandell has said a big ashfall comes once every 3000 years. "Good odds," a logger growls. "I'll work under them." Another says, "We're treated like children. We're used to the woods." A timber attorney says, "I doubt a clear and present danger exists. I doubt the Forest Service and county have authority to close roads." Grouses Crandell, "They can't visualize the dangerous events I describe. But restrictions might cost them income. That they *do* understand."

In the ninety square miles of state lands west of Mount St. Helens, timber sales are legal contracts. Once timber is sold the contractor owns it. Except for fire risk, DNR can't stop logging. DNR Supervisor Ralph Beswick stops new timber sales but honors existing ones.

Skirting the roadblock, *Columbian*'s Ralph Perry photographs Harry Truman skipoleing down an ash-gray snowpath to his restaurant on Spirit Lake.[21] Robert Kaseweter climbs snowy steps to his A-frame near Spirit Lake Lodge. In 1966 he'd graduated in geology and chemistry from Portland State University and is now analytical geochemist for Portland General Electric. He focuses a long lens on fissures that rake grayed glaciers.

Mukilteo school-bus driver Brad Backstrom buys a Ricoh camera, 200-mm telephoto lens, and film. A dollar buys him a Metzger map. A Toutle clerk fingers the logging-road maze on Green Mountain. Backstrom drives up roads 4100 and 4200, works east on the 4250 past Signal Peak, and on to crest road 3000. He passes no roadblock, no gate, no sign. At noon he sits in a high clearcut west of Spud Mountain. The volcano spurts gray ash that fluffs into white cauliflowers and drifts southwest. Next morning Backstrom photographs a black jet that rolls down the north flank, backlit by sun.

Eruptions forceful for 10 to 50 minutes now come hours apart, former little ones gone. Unlike late March's black wet bursts, ash now erupts gray. Andrei Sarna and I sample at dusk April 4th near Spirit Lake Lodge when a dark curtain drops below rain clouds. We speed west and pull underneath. Ash falls gray and dry despite wet air. The volcano's top must be drying.

Rocky Crandell sites a USGS post atop Mount Mitchell south of Mount St. Helens. Sandia Laboratories brings two $25,000 Milliken 16-mm movie cameras that in New Mexico monitor missile tests at 400 pin-registered frames a second. Photographer Terry Leighley has modified them for time-lapse. He sets one atop Mount Mitchell, the other at Coldwater. They shoot Mount St. Helens twice a minute. The USGS changes batteries and the 400-foot film rolls.

National Geographic editor Rowe Findley and photographer Jim Sugar can't linger at Mount St. Helens. Unemployed house painter Fred Stocker telephones *National Geographic* and sells photo editor Bob Gilka a glib line he's a photographer. Gilka grants him an advance and expenses. Stocker borrows a snapshot camera, and a buddy drives him to Lone Fir Inn at Cougar. "I'm from *National Geographic*," he crows, strutting to the Wildwood, building a tab at the bar.[22]

Portland State University geology prof Leonard Palmer has flown to Mount St. Helens in KOIN-TV's helicopter but can't match one photo through clouds to another. A radio ham, he imagines a network of fixed cameras fired by radio. In Cougar he runs into a man with a big smile. "Hi, I'm from *National Geographic*." Over beer in the Wildwood, Palmer talks of radio-controlled cameras. "If you do the electronics," says Stocker, "*Geographic* can supply cameras."

Tektronix engineers by day, Roger McCoy and Tom Hill are Tektronix' Employees Radio Amateur Club by night. Palmer maps out an array of five cameras and triggering transmitter. Hill and McCoy calculate they need a 35-watt signal and engineer a system.[23]

Late April 4 Washington State Patrol shifts the 504 roadblock eighteen miles down to an old log-scaling siding at mile 15. "It's well beyond the reach of hot flows Crandell describes," Captain Bullock says, "and high above any mudflow." It's a game

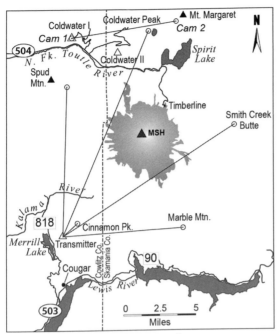

Len Palmer's early April concept for remote cameras (south array) and the eventual setup (north array) in early May.

checkpoint with AC power, wide enough to turn trucks. Deputy Barker tows his trailer down and plugs in. Weyerhaeuser foreman Ralph Killian donates a barrel stove and firewood.

But people live and loggers work above the block. Trapped in a queue, a gyppo log-truck driver paid by the load comments on a trooper's ancestry. Customers now blocked below his store, Stan Lee plows through traffic cones shouting obscenities.

The counties' pleas bring reinforcements. The governor occasionally authorizes the National Guard to dig out avalanches, sandbag against flood, cut fire lines.[24] They now assist at roadblocks.[25] Sixty Guardsmen in combat fatigues and helmets shoulder M-16 rifles. They defend against a straggly Easter army of curious citizens.

Dave Berry, manager of Harmony Falls Lodge, comes Saturday in his 1967 pickup, toboggans in the back, with him brother-in-law and brother Duncan. A nervous Guardsman fingers his rifle sling.

"I'm visiting my property," says Berry.

"I'm ordered to let no one pass."

Berry pulls over to a state trooper and deputy Barker, who radio the sheriff. Berry approaches the Guardsman.

"You can't stop me."

"My orders are—"

"I *am* going through, son. You could shoot me, but I think we both know what you'll not do."

Berry crawls past and accelerates. In thirty miles they stop by the Forest Service hut, strap on snowshoes, and tow the toboggans down east. Ash has painted the snow an eerie charcoal. Full of cars and kids in summer, Duck Bay now sits silent in snow, dock frozen in.

They tramp across snowy lake ice. Fat white flakes drop from drooping clouds. In an hour and a half they come to Harmony Falls. 'Shangri-La' cabin looks ransacked—but burgled by a pine marten. They load a hundred pounds to each toboggan: Duncan's and Melonie's belongings: clothes, wedding quilt, goldsmithing tools, enameling kiln, chain saw.

"Isn't this enough?"

"It's a piece of cake across flat snow."

They pile on another seventy pounds and climb into the traces. Berry strains, nose nearly to the snow before the load breaks loose and he staggers five feet. Ash has sanded the snow. The empty sleds had skidded easily. Loaded, they grip.

The ice is thin and watery in spots. A month ago Duncan and three others fell through into freezing water half a mile out.[26] The men tow the bogging toboggans south around mushy leads. Ash occasionally sifts down from dense clouds. In two exhausting hours they're back to icy Duck Bay. From the shrouded volcano a loud pop, and a roar like a distant jet.

"Christ, listen to that!"

"And this is the lowest spot."

"Let's get the hell out."

They pant up the snowroad, pausing every fifty yards for breath. They drive past Truman's Lodge in twilight, its windows twinkling Christmas lights.

Sightseers clog highway 503 south of Mount St. Helens. Sheriff Nelson deems Cougar's evacuation plan invalid and moves the roadblock downvalley. Rifle-toting Guardsmen patrol here too, a camouflage truck jutting a .50-caliber machine gun. The Cougar merchants dial the governor. By Tuesday the roadblock is back above town. The Guard and the guns are gone.

By moving to Kelso the geodetic crew—now Moore, Swanson, and Peter Lipman—separate from the USGS team and hog the helicopter, Crandell fumes. "The Three Musketeers," Dan Miller calls them. Crandell demands they come to staff meetings.

"That wastes time," the musketeers grumble. "And it's *we* who ordered the helicopter."

David Johnston tells reporters the mountain will "just go *Bang!* Magma will come up from however deep, maybe no warning before big eruption." But Mullineaux says, "The probability of big eruption is low. The 1840s' eruptions [wouldn't] cause much damage even today.".

Flamboyant 66-year-old Haroun Tazieff—volcano aficionado, maker of books and films, politician—had been director of research of France's Global Physics Institute. Fingerpointing after the La Soufrière debacle had ended his job. En route to Eugene April 5, he diverts into Vancouver. Tazieff takes a volcano's pulse by sampling gas at the vent. He demands the Forest Service fly him; George Theisen says "No." Tazieff gathers reporters: "Harmonic tremor means *nothing* at a Cascade volcano, significant eruption unlikely."[27] Alexander McBirney, head of University of Oregon volcanology, tells Don Mullineaux, "Don't worry, *this* volcano won't do anything." Three days later McBirney's colleague Brian Baker tells a reporter, "Mount St. Helens is a warmed-over minor affair." Stanford University volcanologist Gail Mahood chimes in: "Predictions of major eruption are overreaction. This sort of eruption happens every week in Guatamala and Japan."[28]

As earthquakes rumble through Mount St. Helens Lodge Sunday, Harry Truman pumps his player piano for tomorrow's *Today* show. Asked about David Johnston calling Mount St. Helens a fused bomb, he says, "That's just poop."

The USGS seems officially to agree. Sunday Don Mullineaux tells the press a big eruption is unlikely. "I don't think even a big one will take lives." But in the Seattle seismology lab Craig Weaver tells a reporter harmonic tremor may be the *only* warning of major eruption. A tremor episode yesterday lasted 35 minutes.

An *Oregonian* story tells how fiery flows off Vesuvius buried Pompeii and entombed people and dogs. And hot flows ran twenty miles from Crater Lake six thousand years ago. Ashflows populate the prehistory of Mount St. Helens, new ones quite possible.

Logger Gary Roggenback escorts *Oregonian* reporter Sue Hobart and photographer Randy Wood up the South Fork Sunday on gravel roads 4100 and 4200 past Signal Peak over Green Mountain and down Alder Creek on the 2700 to the highway nine miles above the roadblock.

They step out at Timberline, the upper mountain clouded. "I've never felt an earthquake," says Hobart. USGS's Don Swanson squints through a survey level, calling off numbers to Jim Moore. Still no hint of north-flank tilt.[29] Moore remeasures one of the yardsticks on Spirit Lake: no change in level. At two the reporters hear a rumble from above, and gray ash sifts through the clouds. A smart shock pitches the ground at 3:26. Firs sway. From the mountain a *crack!* and deep rumble: an avalanche. All

Blister on north (arrow), Mount Hood on horizon.

RICHARD WAITT

eyes question the inscrutable clouds. "Okay, I've felt one!" Hobart cries. "Now get me out of here!" The UW lab pegs the quake a shallow 4.4.

A magnitude 5.1 next morning the 7th swings chandeliers in Kelso 34 miles west. During a surveillance flight I photograph a large cracked blister on the upper north flank. The two craters have merged into one chasm 550 yards long, 350 wide, 150 deep. Across 2½ hours we record seven bursts, two of them strong, and downwind smell sulfur dioxide. A strong burst next morning at 8:22 burns on 5½ hours. But through a microscope its ash seems all crystals and pulverized rock, no pumice.

The Federal Aviation Administration meets with state Emergency Services, State Patrol, National Guard, Air Force Reserve, Cowlitz County sheriff.[30] "Who coordinates aircraft during an eruption?" asks the FAA. "The governor's declaration suggests it's Emergency Services."

"Not us," says Rick LaValla. "We support local government when they ask."

"Who clears requests for aircraft evacuations? Should National Guard and Air Force pilots just *assume* command?"

"Local authority would control, the Cowlitz County sheriff."

"We're one county," says sheriff Nelson, "the volcano's in another."

"Well I don't know," sighs LaValla. "Maybe the Coast Guard . . ."

In two meetings of local and state authorities, USGS's Mullineaux reports no detectable swelling of the mountain's lower flanks. A pond in the crater means the summit isn't hot. We've now many instruments in place and flights continue, he says. We should detect signs hours or days before anything big. Our worry has been large eruption, but now it's the unstable north. An avalanche could take out highway 504. Sheriffs Nelson and Closner say money's so drained they need more state help at roadblocks. Much of Skamania County is National Forest, Closner says, but we get no timber revenue. Department of Transportation will explore gating highway 504.[31]

Only the mountain above timberline is closed. For a week the Forest Service has discussed shutting some of the National Forest. But on the accessible northwest the Forest ends on the volcano's base. Beyond lie state and Weyerhaeuser lands. Theisen asks DES Director Chow to review his map of land closure. "I've got problems with this," he shrugs and moves off.[32]

Washington Department of Labor & Industries calls Emergency Services the 8th. Loggers have complained that if the county and state block Mount St. Helens to tourists, it's also unsafe for workers. Other loggers have called L&I who don't know the complaint process.

Washington Game Commission announces fishing season. They'll open five lakes near Mount St. Helens the 20th. Hoo Hoo Lake lies deep in a canyon, a floodpath on Crandell's map. They'll open Swift Reservoir on the south flank May 24 and a dozen high lakes north of the volcano. It would all but invite people past roadblocks.

Martin Remmen urges his aged bulldozer onto snow. Claims allow a right to prospect and mine, but the trees are National Forest. Until the Black Rock can prove commercial viability, equipment must come in over snow. Remmen has logged for decades and maintained a permit to blast. In Butte he bought jack-leg drills and ore cars and has stockpiled compressors, hoses, generators, blasting powder, and steel rails. He has serviced his 1945 D7 Caterpillar and bought lumber and dynamite. Now he throttles over snowpack, towing a twenty-foot sled groaning with lumber and mine equipment. His grandson Tim Grose and Rick Parker behind persuade a snowmobile through deep slush.

From Meta Lake Remmen plows a snowroad a mile northwest through firs and over a low divide to a bench by Florence Creek. He pushes ten feet of snow into the ravine. Here the Black Rock will base operations. Late the 10th, Grose wades west half a mile through snow and up 700 feet to a crest. He peers through a 50-power telescope. "Mount St. Helens reminds me of a huge nuclear power plant," he scratches to a diary .

The USGS geologists and UW seismologists now fax a report daily.[33] Dozens of government agencies, news agencies, and companies get identical information. The update for April 8 reports an hours-long eruption, a hole in a glacier that filled with water and broke to widen the crater 350 feet, and four earthquakes above magnitude 4.

Forest Service, sheriffs, Department of Emergency Services, Portland General Electric, and Pacific Power and Light sign a Mount St. Helens Contingency Plan. It lists roles and actions so far. The main hazards are mudflows and ashfall, and in close incinerating flows down to Spirit Lake. But it's mute on how to cooperate should disaster be large, who's in charge, where to base operations. Nothing on coordinating large search and rescue.

For a week Bob Tokarczyk, Paul Stenkamp, and George Theisen have discussed how to close parts of the National Forest to tourists but permit daytime logging. April 10 they permit loggers into the south and east—if they sign liability waivers and carry radios.

State Geologist Ted Livingston dials the governor. The Mount St. Helens Watch Group lacks the Department of Natural Resources, he complains, and so "has no geological expertise. It's a dangerous volcano. Serious mistakes could be made." But Governor Ray will stay with her cabinet heads. A secretary jots to the phone memo: "DNR has the same [non]status as Fisheries, Game, and Parks."[34]

The red-brick yellow-trim governor's mansion nests among firs on an Olympia hillock. A State Patrol guard always attends the governor, but occasionally Chief Landon walks her to her office and transacts business informally. Governor Ray steps from the Mansion, wolfhound Gillie and poodle Jacques tugging at leashes. She and Landon stroll down past cropped lawn, pink-budded rhododendrons, and gray-granite capitol steps. They enter the Legislative Building, climb to second floor, and walk the marble cavern to the governor's suite.

Rocky Crandell briefs Governor Ray April 10. Pointing to his map, he describes possible hot flows in the upper North Fork and flood down the Toutle. Orange fingers show a worst case, he says. An actual eruption will likely affect only green or red areas. Ash would fall far east. We can't predict when. Maybe months away, could last years. Flying to Goldendale next morning, the governor gawks down at Mount St. Helens' ash-black crater and cracked north flank.

Don Swanson had laser-ranged from Smith Creek Butte to East Dome on Mount St. Helens in 1972. He and Moore dig through snow April 10, find the benchmarks, and reshoot. Across 4½ miles the line reads only ⅔ inch longer—within the error of measurement. No change in eight years. Like other data, this shot detects no swelling of the volcano's lower flanks. Under a microscope ash erupted the 11th shows no new glass—still no sign of new magma.

Dartmouth College's Larry Malinconico has trained David Johnston to measure sulfur-dioxide output by correlation spectrometer. Dartmouth scientists have shown volcanoes in central America, Sicily, and Hawaii vent much SO_2 just before eruption. Mount St. Helens' output so far has been trivial. But the profs can't linger this spring term. They loan the instrument, and Johnston will watch for a sulfur spike.

The geologists sup April 12 at restaurant Casa Grande. Dave Johnston fakes a signature in the guest register: Haroun Tazieff saying *No it won't!* Tom Casadevall fakes Johnston's signature: *Yes it will!* But chewing an enchilada, Johnston says, "We do take risks working so close. It could surprise us. And this wasn't a great year to hang around volcanoes. Dieng gassed a village; Karkar killed Robin Cooke. Mount St. Helens will likely erupt magma, but it may take time. Bezymianny had months of minor action like this before its 1956 burst."

Weyerhaeuser has stopped logging on valley floors, mapped out high escape roads, and handed the evacuation plan to camp superintendents. Sheriff Nelson meets the 11th with company officers. "Tourists on our roads don't know logging," complains Jack Schoening. "They stop in the roads and block log trucks. They must be stopped."

"You'll have to do it," says Nelson. "I've a few deputies for the whole county. We can't patrol vast private roads."

Agencies swiftly run out of money. To staff roadblocks, Cowlitz and Skamania Counties, the State Patrol, and the National Guard have spent more than $35,000. The Forest Service spends $7500 a day on Mount St. Helens, in three weeks nearly $160,000. On the 10th they close the rented ballroom. They scale back surveillance flights costing $2500 a day. Department of Emergency Services lays out $750 a day in travel and overtime. The USGS shells out $2000 a day for room and perdiem, $300 an hour for the helicopter. Bob Tilling stews over the deepening red ink, nothing to tap for an unbudgeted emergency.

Mount St. Helens groans on immensely indifferent. By April 10 flurries of earthquakes as large as magnitude 4.7 are routine, a 5 almost every day. Moore and Swanson record Timberline tilting up and down as if the mountain breathes. UW records two bursts of harmonic tremor the 10th—one twenty-two minutes, the other sixteen. Two days later seventeen minutes of tremor end with a 4.8 earthquake.

4

Bulge

Confusion now hath made his masterpiece.
—Shakespeare, *Macbeth II,iii*

Barry Voight, landslide expert from Pennsylvania State University, comes to assess the north flank. Voight and I share a helicopter April 11. From Timberline the Bell Jet Ranger whines up more than a mile. Pilot Lon Stickney loops above crater and north flank for our photographs. The common head of Forsyth, Leschi, and Loowit Glaciers is now a big split blister, the ash-black snow lashed by gashes. Fissures that bound the sunken crater arc down three thousand feet. Snow has avalanched far down to west of Timberline. How fearful indeed to cast one's eyes so low.

A Vietnam pilot, Stickney noses north, picks up airspeed, skims down the cracked black slope, and drops into a gully. We careen down left, right, left as if a bobsled. Boulders above whisk by 120 miles an hour. If anything goes wrong it's curtains, but a thrill this once. Beneath us appear rumpled, dirty avalanches. Stickney nudges back the cyclic and we pop into sunlight, bank right, and land at Timberline. Swanson and Moore survey near eight-foot ashy snowbanks. Had we been hurtling hot pumice, they'd have had but a minute to live.

I'm jotting notes when eight minutes before 4 PM the Ford Bronco bucks. Voight shoots a puzzled glance. "Earthquake!" I say. The car shudders. Tall firs lurch, bushes sway, rocks tumble to the snow. Waves roll down the road like swells on a sea. We wobble north-south, north-south five seconds. "The crater walls slough!" Moore radios from the helicopter. Seismometers speed the signal to UW.[1]

Two miles down we stop by the palegreen, redtrim lodge. Harry Truman wears a faded Deere hat, frayed green sweatshirt, floppy shoes. "Come in," he beckons. We cross a red-planked porch paneled against winter. A sign points lakeward:

←BOATS   MOTORS   CABINS

Inside stinks of catpiss. Painted plywood walls sprout tremendous trout, an elk rack, above the stone fireplace a majestic photograph of Mount St. Helens. Antique player piano, old nickelodeon. A hanging Rainier sign: ICE-COLD BEER. Cats stretch on the floor, chairs, the bar. We follow Truman left.

Shelves line the long kitchen groaning with food, cooking oil, towels. Cluttered countertops carry plates, silverware, screwdriver, wrenches, buttered bread, peanut butter, Dutch Cleanser, motor oil, newspapers, tape recorder, unopened mail. More cats—in a box, on the TV. In the windows dangle carmine Christmas balls, an Olympia beersign. Truman pulls two brown bottles from a roundshoulder refrigerator as I study dozens of black-and-white photos. The lodge, dock, motorboat, a jaunty Truman in yachting cap, pretty wife Eddie, float plane, horses, dog, cat. Truman now looks old and tattered, but the framed photos show a young man's vitality, decades of work and guests. I ask about the lady, the lake, the lodge; he answers of Eddie and boats and old friends. "I'm part of this lake," he says. The lodge and all this stuff seem to prove it.

In the big room Truman foot-pumps an open-front player piano: *Blue Tango*. He pulls a long box from a cabinet, clips on a punctured paper roll, and pumps: *Lazy River*. We sit at the bar, and Truman tumbles to an overstuffed. He sips from a Coca-Cola glass—mostly Coke but he's not omitted some Schenley's.

You don't so much converse with Harry Truman as listen, amused, to a raspy monologue, his arms waving and poking. "That earthquake's the granddaddy of them all," he says. "*That's* the one everyone will talk about. Couldn't stand in the sonofabitch. Thought the goddam building would come down."

"On our radio we heard it's a four point eight," says Voight.

"Oh balls, it ain't no such thing! It's the worst yet—five point five. Scared me to hell." He waves toward a basement. "I go down to my bunker in these big ones. Got a bed there."

He flicks a crooked finger toward a corner. "That goddam beer sign banged the wall. Everything in this place swung east-west, then went north-south. The quakes always go east-west, but twice the big ones switched to north-south."

Our language heads south. Barry laughs, "To measure earthquakes we can just sit at the bar and watch the fucking beer sign."

"Big quakes bother us too," I say. "Crap could come down from up there."

"Geologists and reporters come and go but don't know *shit*!" Truman says. "Except those two in the chopper [Moore and Swanson]. They keep coming back. They know what's going on."

"I've been here fifty-four years. This is my life. It scares me sometimes now, but I couldn't leave this place." Sip. "I'm never sick." He raises the whiskey'd Coke. "A bug gets in me, he leaves my asshole barking."

"And if things get really nasty?" asks Voight.

"It's all big trees above me. They'll stop anything the mountain throws this way." He waves across the bay. "I've a cave stocked with food, whiskey, catfood, generator, Christmas lights."[2] Sip. "If anything big happens I'll go across, ride out any trouble. Hell, I've lived life clean as an angel's drawers."

An hour gone, the beers down. He won't let us pay. "Good-bye, Harry." He follows us out.[3]

Swanson and Moore report north-flank cracks wider, new ones lower. But the real action is the high welt. Stickney flies them to set targets on Sugarbowl and Goat Rocks.

RICHARD WAITT

Harry Truman at Mount St. Helens Lodge minutes after magnitude 4.8 earthquake, 11 April 1980.

Sunday the 13th at Timberline they turn a theodolite atop a tripod. It reads angles vertical and horizontal to one 500th of a degree. A slightly different angle from one reading to the next measures the motion of a point of rock. These two have gauged fire fountains at Kilauea, shots across a quarter mile. Can it work at Mount St. Helens across three miles? Through the sighting telescope the orange boards flutter in sun's heat. The angles show Sugarbowl stationary. Yet over an hour and a half Goat Rocks seems to move from Sugarbowl by a foot. *These numbers can't be real*, thinks Swanson, *our first shots with this instrument. Volcanoes don't move this much.*

Several earthquakes twitch Timberline, at 10:58 a horrendous one. Moore cradles the tripod and reels to the asphalt. UW seismology registers it a 4.9.

Rocky Crandell and Don Mullineaux have cooped in Vancouver with the agencies and press, no recent photos. Crandell drives up the Toutle this Sunday, swings around Timberline loop, and steps out by snowbanks black from last night's ash. He studies the mountain's brow ballooned like a bad tire. Forest ranger Chuck Tonn drives in with girlfriend Karen Jacobsen.

"I'd no idea how the mountain's changed," says Crandell.

"Been swelling two weeks," says Tonn.

"This side's so steep! Some could slide off. Spirit Lake's no longer safe."

Down at the Forest Service hut Tonn rescues avalanche gear, then on to Mount St. Helens Lodge. In summer Harry Truman is a neighbor. A back-country ranger, Jacobsen had met Tonn here, danced evenings. Truman sums her up as a badge and a bikini.

"I cooked you these apple pies," says Karen.

"But shouldn't you leave?" Tonn says.

"Oh, it'll take more than a few earthquakes to chase me out."

Don Mullineaux drives USGS Director William Menard and entourage up the Toutle to Timberline. Familiar with the mountain's profile since the 1940s, Mullineaux stares at the fissured slope. *So appallingly sheer,* he thinks. *No one should be here.*

Austin Post steps toward Crandell sweeping his arms palms up toward the volcano. "You've noticed *this*?"

"It's way too steep."

"I've photographed these glaciers twenty years. I hardly recognize this side now."

"It could slide into Spirit Lake."

The director's group climb the knoll where Swanson sights the theodolite. "Strange," he says, excitement in his voice. "I'd set the crosshairs on a rock point. Two minutes ago it seemed a bit higher, now a bit lower—like it's moving up and down. Yet maybe it's just light distorting as the sun comes in and out." Only later will he know that even as the USGS director gawks and talks at Timberline, the blackened slope inches out above.

Later Moore and Swanson fly over a gentle slope below Goat Rocks. Cracks they'd measured April 3 now gape twice as wide. Goat Rocks punching up?

Next morning Mullineaux telephones Forest Service snow expert Roland Emetaz. "The north's so steep it could shed huge avalanches. What about the cabins around Spirit Lake Lodge?"

Snow avalanches have never come within two miles of the highway. But big ones full of rock and glacier ice . . . "The cabins," Emetaz says. "I think they're in trouble."

Yet the volcano has settled into a pattern of earthquakes and ashy bursts. The eruptions have declined from one an hour in late March to one a day April 11. Says a *Columbian* editorial:

Excuse us, mountain

Mount St. Helens' celebrity is beginning to wane. The once-in-a-lifetime experience [for] geologists has become a bureaucratic problem how to pay for [it]. The press offices are closed. The briefings have ended. None of us can afford . . . much longer . . . attention to the tantrum. Thanks for the show, St. Helens. But . . . we've other business to attend to . . . Do keep in touch.

"How long can a curious public be kept from the puffing dragon?" the *Oregonian* asks. Don Mullineaux tells a reporter the USGS now has enough instruments to warn of a major event hours or days ahead. UW calls the earthquakes 'moderate.' Weekend tourists flood the roads to Mount St. Helens, hawking coffee mugs, bumper stickers (*Lava or Leave It*), T-shirts (*Helen is Hot*).

Weyerhaeuser forester Bob Dieter and family drive the ridge between the Toutle rivers. East on road 3000, down 3800 to the 3840, blocked at last by snow. From this crest east of Castle swamp they photograph Mount St. Helens just five miles away.

National Geographic freelance photographers seek a volcano story. Late afternoon April 11, Columbia Helicopters' pilot Dwight Reber lands Michael Lawton and John Marshall at YMCA Camp Meehan at the north end of Spirit Lake. Next morning they snowshoe a mile back and 1800 feet up to a perch overlooking iced-over Spirit Lake and ashgray Mount St. Helens. Overcast washes out evening's shots. They camp, then awaken in a crystalline dawn. Ash spurts from the crater at 6:30, and they shoot long-shadowed photographs, Lawton's a panorama.[4] In afternoon they snowshoe down, and Reber lifts them out.

An *Oregonian* reporter pries details about the ashy climber from Rick Hoblitt. The *Columbian*, *Seattle Times*, and *Seattle Post-Intelligencer* run stories. So now a parade of climbers. Dr. Peter Reagan, photographer Ancil Nance, and another park at Merrill Lake, ski five miles to treeline, and start up at midnight. At 6:30 AM the 12th, they pant up 800 feet below the summit when a cloud roils out upslope.[5] At eight they stand at crater's edge, the grayed snow pocked by hundreds of cobbles. It's Reagan's 13th ascent.

"I hardly recognize the place," he says. "The crater's half a mile long!"

"If it erupts now these helmets won't do us much good."

On Seattle's TV airwaves, KIRO-7 competes with KING-5 for news of Mount St. Helens. Chuck Sicotte, former Vietnam Army pilot, flies KIRO's cream-and-copper Bell 206 this morning carrying reporter Brooks Burford, cameraman Steve Baxter, and UW grad student Lee Fairchild. They know the summit is railroad land. Baxter zooms on three figures at the crater. Chopper 7 closes, and the men disappear. "If they can be here," Burford says, "why not us?" Sicotte circles, tests the wind, and lands sixty yards back from the summit. Fairchild is astonished: he holds no scientist's permit. "You got ten minutes," barks Sicotte. Eyeing the hundreds of cobbles in craters, he holds rpms for a getaway. The men climb out.

"You think we should be here?" asks Burford.

"Hell no," says Fairchild, "look at the rocks. But let's make the most of it."

From crater's edge Baxter films "thirteen adrenaline-filled minutes." Sicotte punches the siren. The men scramble back, and Sicotte lifts off.

Below thickening clouds Friday evening, a Hiller 12E helicopter ferries filmmaker Otto Sieber and young mountaineers Brian Witt and Andy Sterne to the southwest flank. They land at treeline and overnight in a snowstorm. Saturday they steal upslope in white camouflage, heavy with Arriflex 16-mm film cameras, a Hasselblad for stills, sound gear, and batteries. "I don't consider this illegal," says Sieber. "We're documenting natural history, now or never." In afternoon sun they bog in mushy snow and runny mud. A sunset-red cloud rises upslope, builds to a roar, and stops. They huddle the night in a snow cave, the mountain shaking.[6]

They stand west of the summit early Sunday when a gray column boils up, whooshing like tires on pavement. The jet builds to a roar, climbs 2000 feet, and arcs like a fountain. Rocks drop silently into the snow. An earthquake shakes down ice and rock; the vent vomits them back up. Sieber sees it all through the Arriflex. Another earthquake, and more ice rattles down.

Brian Witt pulls the tab off a beer, blows off foam, tips it back. Sieber zooms on the label: Olympia. Take two zooms on Budweiser. Sell a commercial and it'll cover the helicopter. As they tramp down through altitude 8500 feet, the crater bursts. Boulders thud upslope, and the cone shudders.[7] Descending through 7000 feet, they wave to a climber. Robert Rodgers too blends in, gray parka against gray ash, climbing the tracks of bounced rocks. At the crater he shoots two rolls of Kodachrome.

Overnight the 13th, eight quakes above magnitude 4 agitate the volcano. Monday morning from his snowcamp, Barry Voight eyes Mount St. Helens in binoculars. Cracks now look wider and reach farther down than on aerial photos shot two weeks ago. And why the subsided graben in between? For it to sink like a keystone, Voight thinks, the north welt must have moved out a hundred yards. The north is *still* deforming.

Voight decamps from clouds and rain. He comes to Vancouver unshowered, bearded, in muddy rubber boots, woodsmoked wool shirt. Fresh-shaved Rocky Crandell in buttoned-down collar and pressed slacks briefs a meeting of Forest Service, sheriffs, State Patrol, DOT, and DNR timber. During a break he chats with Voight.

"You think a landslide could trigger *magmatic* eruption?" Crandell says. "Ash flows?"

"Yeah. A slide could be gigantic. When that much rock goes, the pressure drop on magma below is huge. Two hundred bars maybe. *That* could trigger eruption."

"*That* eruption gives no warning."

"No."

The meeting resumes. Crandell says the mountains' north slope is unstable, parts of it moving. Massive landslide could remove half, maybe trigger large eruption. The slide could sweep down to Spirit Lake, dam it to a high level. Mudflows would sluice downvalley. The North Fork should be free of sightseers down to the roadblock.[8] Voight graphs a cross section. The whole cracked north flank could slide. He calculates its volume: a quarter cubic mile!

"In our many meetings," says Skamania Sheriff Bill Closner, "Mullineaux and Crandell have been so guarded—maybe this, maybe not. Perhaps big, probably not. Only now have we an idea how bad it could be. The whole Spirit Lake basin, all the lodges and cabins, could be destroyed. Why didn't they say so? We've squandered weeks of preparation."

"Well, it's hard to get through to Skamania County," Mullineaux says privately. "They listen but don't hear. One of them dwells on what a psychic tells him about Mount St. Helens."

"After lots of coffee and talk," says Cowlitz Sheriff Nelson. "we see a grimmer picture." He asks county Emergency Services to craft evacuation plans for Toutle valley. "No," says its director, "it'd waste our time. The mountain's going back to sleep." So in the sheriff's office deputy Bena drafts a plan.

After complaints about the militarized roadblocks, the National Guard are cut to ten. Forest Supervisor Bob Tokarczyk attends a meeting afternoon the 14th. Skamania County moans of $12,000 spent on the blocks. The Guard saved us nothing. As snow melts back, it'll be impossible to staff all roads. "The only impending disaster bleeds us financially," Sheriff Closner says. "We don't qualify for aid we'd have if it blew. We're tired of abuse at roadblocks. I'll cut back deputies tomorrow." Tokarczyk orders Forest rangers to staff two roads and gate others.

Mullineaux's quiet ambiguity may bore the spotlit meetings, but behind scenes the Forest Service—Tokarczyk, Theisen, Osmond—rely on him. A chat with Mullineaux reassures them it's prudent to block roads into the threatened National Forest.

KIRO's helicopter summit landing sans permit has televised. The Forest Service and Skamania sheriff try to fine the pilot but find their jurisdiction murky. Most of the mountain is National Forest but summit land-section 9 is Burlington Northern's. Each year they pay county tax on it. But the railroad now cedes administration of section 9 to the Forest Service, stiffening the closure.

Mount St. Helens' virginal beauty has been debauched in just a month. Filthy in ash, craters and cracks furrowing her brow, now a swelling tumor. But the bursts dwindle, and the USGS and UW reduce their updates to twice weekly. Some staff return to home offices, and the north flank goes unmeasured. USGS's official statement reads, "no indication [of] major eruption. . . in the near future." Yet the earthquakes persist. A magnitude 5 jiggles Longview 37 miles west midmorning the 17th.

For weeks I've plotted the time each Mount St. Helens burst starts and stops, how high it jets, direction ash drifts—culling from logbooks and geologists' fieldnotes. Seismologists note the number of earthquakes dwindle but large ones persist—still four a day above magnitude 4.3. Returning to Menlo Park, I scrutinize reports on Lassen Peak in 1914 and Bezymianny in 1955. David Johnston is right: their early symptoms resemble the pattern of bursts and earthquakes now at Mount St. Helens. G.S. Gorshkov's 1959 paper lists months of earthquakes and small bursts before Bezy's great 1956 explosion.

I call Vancouver; a senior scientist picks up the phone. Rather too excitedly I say how Mount St. Helens' data so far mimic Bezymianny's. "This could lead to *huge* eruption."

"*This* isn't Bezymianny."

"Yes, but the patterns—"

"This is *not* Bezymianny!"

The voice allows no argument. I've small experience with volcanoes; his papers stretch back two decades. Newspapers in Seattle and Longview have run pieces about Bezy, but my exuberance sounds naïve.

"Well, if that's what you think. I've mailed you copies of Gorshkov."

Seismic energy beneath Mount St. Helens stays high. Saturday a magnitude 5 quake trumps one that spooked Truman a week ago.

Newspapers report the Forest Service trying to nab the summiting climbers and helicopter pilot. "Until some new evidence of an emergency appears," the Eugene *Register-Guard* scoffs, "people ought to be able to travel roads near Mount St. Helens, fish the lakes, use their cabins, and even climb. . ." As if the volcano hasn't spilled such evidence for weeks.

But only the mountain above tree line is closed. The Forest Service has debated two weeks how to shield tourists from danger but allow loggers their felled timber. George Theisen and Gene Sloniker map a hypothetical restricted zone west to Maple Flats (mile 20). "But where's the scientific basis to block an area so big?" asks DES's Terry Simmonds. The next map restricts only down to mile 25. "We might close this ideally," Simmonds says, "but politics over jobs means we can't." Trial balloons float away.

Behind the D7 Cat April 12, Martin Remmen, Jay Parker, and other Black Rock miners skid a sled groaning with lumber and mine equipment over snow. At dusk an ash cloud spreads over from Mount St. Helens. Next day they clank west to Florence Creek. They build a 12-by-18-foot chalet and sleeping loft and lay in three cords of firewood. Late the 21st they ride the bulldozer out for fuel and equipment.

Those manning the roadblocks have no real authority to close a highway. "Bluff long as you can," Patrol Capt. Bullock counsels the troopers. "But if someone demands to go through and persists, you can't stop him."

"One day I stop by the 504 block," says Bullock. "I'm telling sightseers they can't pass because it's dangerous. But now *down* the highway comes a Weyerhaeuser truck with a load of logs. 'If it's really dangerous,' says the tourist, 'why're they up there? If it's safe for them, why isn't it safe for us?' I've no good answer to this."

The roadblock lies below Stan and Josephine Lee's store at Kid Valley. For years Josephine aided campaigns for Democrat state senator Don Talley and Julia Butler Hansen—state legislator, then U.S. Representative. The Lees protest to Hansen, Talley, and Governor Ray. From Olympia the State Patrol orders the block five miles up—above the store.

This gravel pad at Maple Flats (mile 20) turns traffic, but Capt. Bullock hates the place—dubious radio signal, by the floodable river. Under a bluff, it's sunless and cold. The troopers haven't thrown a hotdog on the barrel stove to make it a cooking fire. Department of Ecology stops by, writes a citation, and threatens daily fines.

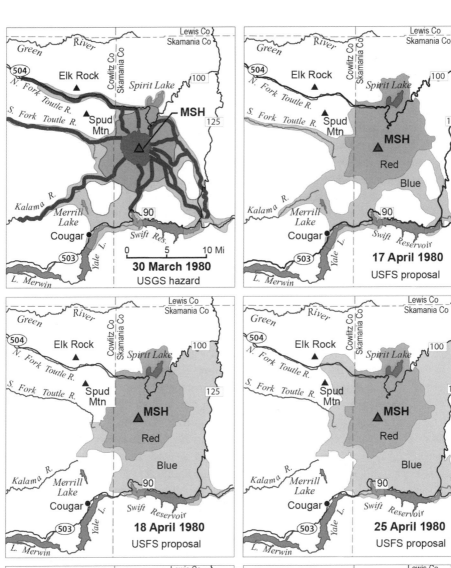
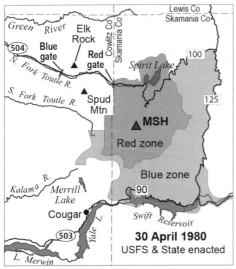
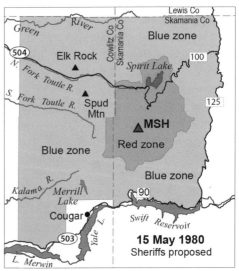

The Forest Service still seeks land restrictions. From Crandell's hazard map, Sloniker and Theisen sketch an inner zone of full closure, an outer zone that allows daytime logging. Next day they pull in the west and southwest, putting Cougar and state and private lands outside. They *add* a buffer on the east three to six miles wide. The Forest Service may close federal lands at once. But a closure west beyond the National Forest needs the governor and Weyerhaeuser.

Radio amateurs Roger McCoy and Tom Hill—Tektronix engineers by day—have camped nights and weekends in Hill's apartment. Tables groan with meters, batteries, soldering guns, pliers, circuit boards, chips, transistors, capacitors, oscilloscopes. With components donated by Tektronix, they've modified a GE transmitter and built encoders, decoders, amplifier, receivers, antennae, battery packs. A 35-watt signal on the 432 MHz amateur-radio band would trigger five remote cameras around Mount St. Helens. To exclude spurious radio signals, Hill has defined tone control precisely by quartz crystals and computer chips. Wires from a voltmeter lead into his freezer—testing stability in all weather.

Fred Stocker calls *National Geographic* and requests cameras and tripods. "Too much to risk," says photo editor Bob Gilka. "You're on your own." The *Columbian*'s photo editor Steve Small meets April 18 with collaborators. *National Geographic* won't supply cameras, Stocker says, but I'll charge them the helicopter. The *Columbian* can supply cameras and manpower, says Small. The transmitter, receivers, and batteries cost money, says McCoy. What if—? *Geographic* will reimburse losses, Stocker says. They need approval within the National Forest. Professor Len Palmer, licensed ham N7AQA, could transmit the signal. But his media antics offend the Forest Service. Photos would aid our monitoring, says USGS's Bob Christiansen. We'll help *National Geographic* and the *Columbian*—but not Palmer. But he's the one legal on the amateur band, says Small. Then we'll request the FCC allow a non-ham, Christiansen says.

River fishing opens Sunday the 20th. Sightseers and fishermen crowd toward Mount St. Helens. Tailgaters sell bumper stickers, T-shirts, coffeemugs, watercolor paintings, ash—a mountain carnival. Otto Sieber's climb adorns *Seattle Times'* front-page: "On Top of New Smokey." Seattle and Portland papers carry Peter Reagan's climb.

UW reports seismicity up—forty-seven quakes above magnitude 3, seven above 4. A 5 popped yesterday afternoon. Another this morning sheds debris off Goat Rocks.[9]

Harry Truman leases his Spirit Lake land from Burlington Northern Railroad. For decades BNR executives like John Garrity have saddle-horsed with Truman to beery camps among the mountains far from the glittering city. Sunday the 20th, Rob Smith drives Truman to Seattle and they fly to St. Paul for Garrity's retirement party. It's an all-nighter, Truman jabbering, waving a Coke and bourbon. But at dawn he frets about his unguarded lodge and all the sightseers. Smith returns him to Spirit Lake. "Look," points Truman, "my fireplace hasn't gone out."

Prehistoric ashflows have reached down the upper Toutle. Rocky Crandell and Rick Hoblitt scratch into roadcuts at Coldwater post. They find pumice dropped 3500 years ago but no fine ash to suggest a hot cloud has ever come this high. But Crandell mutters, "I fear there'll be a tragedy here."

The eruptions stop but earthquakes rumble on—four today above magnitude 4, one a 5. David Johnston lands on The Boot and samples a gas jet. At crater's edge he studies the chiseled chasm he'd seen as a puny pit four weeks ago.[10] Arnold Okamura had installed tiltmeters low on the north and south flanks. Measuring tiny changes in slope, tiltmeters on broad Kilauea anticipate eruptions.[11] But on steep Mount St. Helens the numbers are tiny and inconsistent.

The USGS–UW updates resume daily. Crandell writes Forest Supervisor Bob Tokarczyk:

> The highly fractured surface of Forsyth Glacier. . ., if triggered by an earthquake or volcanic explosion, could lead to a large avalanche of snow, ice, and possibly rock without warning. Avalanches like this move down steep slopes at a high velocity and. . . long distances. . .
>
> Such an avalanche into Spirit Lake [could] generate a large wave across the lake. The avalanche might extend up. . . the north side of the Toutle River.
>
> An avalanche could flood the North Fork Toutle valley. . . [Above] Camp Baker are 6 points [where] the highway is less than 10 feet above the river.

An aircraft above Mount St. Helens April 7 and 12 shot nine-inch vertical stereographic photos. Jim Moore and USGS topographers contour the changes. They find the top of the cracked blister 320 feet higher than the area had been in 1979. The north brow doesn't just sag: it swells. Aerial photographer Austin Post shoots again, the north flank now a hump. The *Daily News* runs Roger Werth photographs titled "Peak Bulges Ominously."

Werth and Donna duBeth drive up the Toutle afternoon the 24th, the roadblock at Maple Flats unstaffed, a ROAD CLOSED sandwichboard unconvincingly on the shoulder. How unlike the confrontation with deputies and sniggering audience four weeks ago. They hie up the highway to Timberline where two young men sweep up ash to sell. DuBeth scribbles, Werth shoots, and the shaggy men drive off.

"I've never felt an earthquake," says Werth framing a shot.

The ground shudders.[12] "Will that do?" she says. *But the bulge looks so big and steep. It could shake loose.*

They pull into Mount St. Helens Lodge. Since their story a month ago Harry Truman has adorned newspapers and television. A pile of letters includes two marriage proposals.

"You've become a legend." duBeth says.

"That's a bunch of hooey—except the kids. I'd like to visit the Oregon class who wrote."[13]

Robert Rogers starts up the west flank again. Exhausted at 4 A.M., he unrolls a bag and wraps on a gray poncho—camouflage against ashy snow. A helicopter's whine bolts him awake in dazzling sun. The Jet Ranger lands.

Rogers approaches, coiled for a swing of his ice axe and a dash downslope. "D'you arrest trespassers?" he calls.

"No, we're scientists. Come on up."

Peter Douglass and Mark Utting have staked black plywood ✚ targets about the mountain to control aerial photographs. This last one marks the summit. The men climb in, and Lon Stickney flies off. Rogers photographs great cracks and gaping crater. On its south wall five feet of layered snow and ash cap 170 feet of bluish ice and corn snow. The helicopter returns at noon; from it David Johnston photographs a climber on the summit. Rogers bolts down tracks of rolled rocks.

The Forest Service and USGS meet with Weyerhaeuser, sheriffs, and state DES, DNR, and Parks. Crandell reiterates the hazards. A magmatic eruption could burst with no warning, no time to evacuate, he says. Theisen shows his map: inner red-colored area to be closed, outer blue-colored area permitting logging. On the northwest the red zone stops at the National Forest boundary. This blue "dog's ear" beyond is bare minimal. But it's outside our jurisdiction and up to the sheriff and the state. What do you think?

To an afternoon meeting come Forest Service, Federal Emergency Management, State Patrol, DES, county sheriffs, and owners of cabins, lodges, and youth camps.

"Two women from Spirit Lake Lodge complain that government restricts business and property," says State Patrol Capt. Bullock. "They demand to go in: 'We'll open regardless.'"

Idiots! thinks *Daily News* reporter duBeth. After all we print, people *still* don't get it.

Rocky Crandell stands. "On the north flank of Mount St. Helens, Forsyth Glacier has humped into a big, black rock mass three hundred feet higher than it was two months ago. More than two thousand earthquakes...have cracked this area... A large quake or steam blast could send a 150-foot ice mass careening down at 180 mph. It would reach Spirit Lake in two minutes. There'll be no way to warn people. They won't be able to get out of the way.

"When speeding ice and rock hits Spirit Lake, it would raise a tidal wave twelve feet high. Mudslides could flood down Toutle valley to its mouth. A mass like wet concrete flowing 35 miles an hour carrying boulders would destroy all in its path... fifteen feet above the river.

"A cloud downwind will turn day to darker than night for hours. Pumice could fall forty inches deep. A magmatic eruption would propel an ash... cloud down the mountain at... 1000 degrees Celsius... 100 miles an hour. Nothing in its path would survive...

"I can't tell you when this might happen... Only it's a real possibility and a dangerous one."[14]

Crandell asks the lodges and youth camps to not open, recommends Forest Service and state close the area. George Thiesen says the Forest Service forbids its rangers near the mountain. He shows the map for closure—inner red zone including Spirit Lake, outer blue zone.

Dave and Laura Berry manage Harmony Falls Lodge. "I've read that Mount St. Helens erupts every century or so," Dave says. "The lodge is only three feet above the lake, all nine cabins no higher than fifteen feet. Crandell says an avalanche into Spirit Lake can throw a big wave. Well...we'll not open."

The meeting ends. The women from Spirit Lake Lodge come up and chat with Crandell. "Hearing this," Mariam Smith says, "maybe we don't need to go up there after all."

Next day the *Daily News* publishes duBeth's story and Crandell's letter to Tokarczyk.

The governor can order the National Guard to command if disaster overwhelms local authority.[15] The Guard's 21 hueys lie at Gray Field 65 miles north of Mount St. Helens. Guard operations study aeronautical charts and reconnoiter airfields—should Mount St. Helens erupt large. But they ignore the sheriffs, charged by statute with search and rescue. They ignore the Air Force Reserve 304th whose hoist-rigged hueys and trained jumpers assist the sheriffs in mountain rescues.

Brad Backstrom has sold thousands of color prints of erupting Mount St. Helens. He and his wife drive to Spud Mountain the 26th but find the volcano socked in. Retreating to the South Fork, they turn up roads 4100 and 4170 onto the mountain's flank. The low-clearance 1979 Toyota Celica makes it easily.

When a high wall collapsed at Questa open-pit mine in New Mexico, an immense block hung near the top. Cracks behind it widened faster and faster before it crashed to the mine floor. Engineers plotting the block's accelerating outward creep predicted when fall grew nigh. Here's a way, Peter Lipman sees, to forecast a collapse of Mount St. Helens' bulge.

A laser beam can measure the distance to a distant reflector to a quarter inch. Repeated shots recording a shrinking distance could measure the bulge's swelling. Don Swanson borrows a $30,000 Geodimeter Model-8 from the Smithsonian Institution. But its expensive cut-crystal reflectors would stand in risky spots. Will cheap ones work? Lipman and Ron Gordon paint boards orange, screw on plastic reflectors, and test these targets across miles. By helicopter they stake ten of them on Sugarbowl, Dogs Head, and Goat Rocks. They shoot from Timberline April 25, then shoot the theodolite, Lipman's first use in years.

Sunday the 27th, Lipman zeros the theodolite's telescopic sight on Windy Ridge target a mile east. He turns southwest to Goat Rocks, setting angles Gordon quotes from Friday's notes. The target should be centered, but it's not in the field of view. "Mygod, I've forgotten how to measure!" mutters Lipman. He nudges the telescope right for another yard of view: no target. Another nudge, and on the periphery there it is.

He centers the crosshairs and reads the angle. The target is 0.052726 degree of arc right of where recorded Friday.

He swings the instrument to the angle they'd shot to Dog's Head. That target is in the crosshairs where measured Friday. "So I've not forgotten how to measure," says Lipman. "In two days Goat Rocks must have moved three yards north. Incredible though it seems, it must be right." He shoots two targets on Sugarbowl: they too lie where measured Friday. He swings right and zeros on a second Goat Rocks target. Like the first, this one has moved three yards.

Lipman repeats the shots; the numbers verify. It's not just glacier ice sliding. A mile-wide face of rock bulges north. The great blister of 2½ weeks ago has swelled tall and wide. Goat Rocks pushes out one and a half yards a day. Even at fast spots on Kilauea the pace is inches per year. "This is the first time," says Lipman, "anyone has proven so fast an earth movement." It confirms the bloat gauged three days ago by aerial photographs. Theodolite shots April 29 verify the fast pace. "Amazing Rates," puns Don Swanson. "Bulge" is on all lips.

And now the tiltmeter concurs. Timberline on the northeast flank gradually tilts out—the volcano swells. It's as if a rod half a mile long were lifted on its volcano end four hundredths inch a day—so slight and slow as to be detected only over time.

Scientists' ruminations spill into the news. "The cause of the bulge is not known," Mullineaux says. Johnston tells the *Daily News*, "So much swelling shows drama inside the mountain, magma pushing Goat Rocks out. It may take days or weeks, but it *will* fall." Crandell had warned a landslide could smack Spirit Lake. But Christiansen tells the *Columbian* it's "inconceivable a mile-wide slab of mountain could slide into a lake six miles away."

Some reporters quest for controversy. "I telephone Crandell daily," says Steve Malone in Seattle. "We discuss what may be happening inside the volcano. Some reporters write as though we disagree. After Watergate, they imagine a cover-up. A *Seattle P.I.* reporter accuses us of conspiring with logging companies to limit restrictions. This is absurd and I say so. He demands to listen to my telephone calls. This is absurd and I refuse. We find him in the lab rummaging through our trash. A cover-up is nonsense but important to his story."

Reporters reply: we're assigned to the volcano we know little about. Scientists speak in jargon or bore with myriad qualifications. We translate, but they moan that we oversimplify. Some won't talk for fear of looking silly to colleagues. A news editor gives a deadline. We've little time to build a story and verify every fact.[16]

College profs and students clamor to pass the roadblocks. Prof. John Allen's committee at Portland State reviews their applications. Allen signs permit #1, and the Forest Service approves. PGE chemist Bob Kaseweter applies, and his former prof Allen signs permit #3 to "monitor a seismometer near Spirit Lake." Sunday the 27th, Kaseweter and fiancé Beverly Wetherald dig beside his cabin north of Spirit Lake Lodge and place his homebuilt seismometer—sensor, timer, pen, chart recorder, batteries. Through a telephoto the mountain looks close enough to touch. Cracks he'd photographed April 3 now reach far down.

Sheriff Les Nelson attended Friday's meeting and read Crandell's letter. He tells the *Daily News* the mountain is "extremely dangerous. Reading the daily USGS reports is like a scary story building to climax. It's a question only *when* that volcano goes up. People don't realize it because the mountain looks so beautiful. Can you imagine the speed of hundreds of tons of ice coming down? Anyone near Spirit Lake won't have time to get one pant leg on before it hits. And there won't be a road left to get out on. There can't be a worse place to be."

"Well, he may think the Toutle unsafe," complains State Patrol Capt. Bullock, "but doesn't push for closure. He won't offend Weyerhaeuser."

Crandell having heightened the hazards, Gifford Pinchot National Forest announces a closure—inner red zone, outer blue zone. Blue reaches out 14 miles east and south but on the northwest only four miles—the edge of the National Forest. "This closure is insufficient," says Paul Stenkamp, "but better than none."[17] The *Daily*

News prints Theisen's and Sloniker's latest map—its blue zone down the North Fork nearly to Elk Rock.

USGS topographers in Menlo Park contour new Mount St. Helens. Goat Rocks has bulged 250 feet north-northwest. An April 30 press release headlines: Bulge Newest Hazard at Mount St. Helens. An avalanche of it could drop tons of debris thousands of feet downslope at more than 100 miles an hour.

Having mustered out of the Marines, John Williams heard on Kansas City radio of Otto Sieber's climb. He buses to Kelso and hitchhikes to the south side. He pulls his pack from a car evening the 27th at the roadblock three miles east of Cougar. "I know why you're here," says a stonefaced deputy. "If I catch you in there I'll burn you." Williams returns to the car but steps out a mile west. He hikes up Dry Creek to a little falls, bathes in the frigid stream, bolts a can of Spam, and crawls into a sleeping bag. He wakes at 8:50 to rustling and cracking. Oh shit!—a bear smelling Spam? Tall firs sway, dead branches crack and thump down. The ground rises and sinks, Williams feeling he's riding an ocean swell. The stream surges and sloshes over the falls. UW's seismic lab registers the earthquake a magnitude 4.9.

He wakes in dawn's drizzle. He packs upslope on logging roads, climbs a rock knoll, drops into a gully—pushing northeast through snow. In evening he crawls into his bag. Next day he ambles six hours up snow to treeline and spreads his bag under a stunted fir.

He awakens after midnight, zips on a down jacket, and climbs under a full moon.[18] At 6:30 a helicopter flies over toward the summit. He stands by a rocky ridge at 8:08 when a balanced boulder clank-clank-clanks and the mountain slope squeak-squeak-squeaks: an earthquake. At 9 o'clock the helicopter hovers over, and Williams blends his brown jacket into rocks and ashy snow. He slogs up troughs boulders have plowed, then to the crater. Another helicopter nears; he dives into a six-foot trench. Its bounding cracks vent steam. Another earthquake: cracks in the snow open an inch and shut, open and shut. UW registers a magnitude 4 at 1:51. When the helicopter flies off he steps to crater's edge. This block will be next to slough in, he sees. Many fallen ones lie on the crater floor 500 feet down. He photographs gray crater and the bright scene north to Mount Rainier.

Portland State professor Leonard Palmer climbs into a helicopter predawn Wednesday with Allen permit #2. The *Oregonian* funds the flight to a unique news story. Reporter Sue Hobart and photographer Tim Jewett climb in, and pilot Dave Fabik lifts off Scappoose toward Mount St. Helens.[19] Fabik circles, scouts a landing, and lands on a rise. The passengers tramp north over ashy snow pocked by erupted boulders. At 25° Fahrenheit, wind whips rock chips that sting. Steam billows from the crater wall, sulfur in the air. An earthquake drops ice into the crater. *Jeepers!* thinks Hobart, *this place is the end of the earth!* Palmer ropes down, chops at icy ash layers, bags samples, and climbs back. Jewett clicks away. At 8:08 the ground jolts and the three scramble back, lurching into each other like drunks. Ice and rock roar to crater's floor.[20] They climb into the helicopter, and Fabik lifts off in buffeting wind. In next day's *Oregonian*, Palmer hangs off a rope as if staged for the camera.

The exclusive news interview violates his permit. "Front-Page Palmer," they sneer in Vancouver. "Oh c'mon," retorts the prof, "with no funds how else do I gain access?"

Nine earthquakes magnitude 4 and more these past two days but no new eruptions. Five days ago David Johnston had remeasured sulfur-dioxide fume: 10 tons a day. A smelter emits 22 tons a day, a coal-fired power plant 100. Kilauea volcano pumps out 150 tons a day, Mount Etna 1000 to 3000.[21] Mount St. Helens' output is barely a hundredth of Etna's.

Yet SO_2 dissolves in water. Is it disappearing in groundwater, snow, and ice? A sample of crater-pond water might tell. It's been more than a week since an eruption: Johnston thinks the risk worth it. At 10:20 the 30th, a helicopter lands him at the crater's west lip. It returns at noon with Rick Hoblitt. Johnston says he's felt nine earthquakes—edgy about them, Hoblitt sees.[22] Radio ready, he watches Johnston tramp into the crater at 12:28 toward ice blocks earthquakes have shaken from 500-foot cliffs. Rocks clatter down while Johnston kneels at the pond and fills three bottles. Gas bubbles through murky, sulfury water he measures at 63° F. He plods back up the ashy slope to crater rim at 12:57. The helicopter comes and lifts them off. Three-quarters hour later a magnitude 4 quake drops tons of ice to the pond.

The Forest Service fax state Emergency Services its land closure, recommending closure to the west. County commissioners and sheriffs urge the governor to close. Flanked by Chow and LaValla April 30, Dixy Lee Ray holds a felt-tipped pen over the document.

"Is this the reasonable thing to do?" says Ray.

"Yes, Ma'am."

"It's what the sheriffs want?"

"Yes, Ma'am."

"All right, then." The governor signs Executive Order 80–05.

It sets a red zone and blue zone around Mount St. Helens. Red is closed except to volcano monitoring, law enforcement, and search-and-rescue. Blue is open to daytime logging. DOT will gate highway 504 at mile 33¼ and mile 40. It's a misdemeanor to use the highway above 33¼. The red boundary on the northwest and west runs "south and west along Trail No. 208, and west to the county line at the west quarter corner of Section 7, T.9N, R.5E; then south along the county line to Section 6, T.8N, R.5E; then westerly to the northwest section corner of Section 1, T.8N, R.4E; then southerly . . ."

State Patrol Capt. Bullock plots the waypoints to a map and dials the National Forest. "The state's closure seems yours. Have I missed something?"

"I'm afraid you've got it right," says George Theisen.

"They're moving the roadblock *toward* the mountain."

"I see that."

"It makes no damned sense. I expected it go back down to mile 15. Why move closer? It's risky there. It's unenforceable with the logging roads open."

"And what happened to our blue zone on the west?" moans Theisen. "We'd whittled it back to just a few miles. Now they lop off even that."[23]

The state's county-line definition in the North Fork apes the Forest Service's—the limit of their jurisdiction. On the east, south, and southwest the blue zone is 2½ to 14 miles wide. On the threatened northwest and north there is no blue. The red zone lies just four miles from the great bulge. "Well, the idea of a blue zone is stupid," explains the governor. "It's dangerous or not: you're either pregnant or not."

The deputies and troopers have been bluffing at the roadblocks—no legal authority to close a highway. The governor's order closes highway 504 and authorizes fixed barriers—but shifts the block upvalley. "Each time in a big meeting Rocky Crandell shows the mountain growing dangerous," muses State Patrol Capt. Bullock, "Olympia moves the roadblock closer. Mile 15 was beyond all threat. Crandell announced the north flank unstable but the block flew five miles up. Crandell escalated the risks Friday and here we go again—this time *way* up. If this isn't Weyerhaeuser and county politics, it makes no sense at all."

The roadblock moves thirteen miles up to mile 33¼ where it sat a month ago. Seven miles outside the red zone, it's only a few feet above Toutle River. It's not far below the hot flows on Crandell's map. Bullock sees no safety in that arbitrary line. "Too risky," he says. "I'll not have troopers here." DOT's steel gate is locked, and a chain-link fence defends the shoulders. A trooper drives up dawn and dusk to check.

The legal description in Executive Order 80-05 is gibberish to most citizens, but only the *Columbian* prints a map. DES simplifies the red zone as about five-mile radius, blue zone about ten miles. Yet on the accessible northwest there is no blue zone. After signing the Mount St. Helens order, the governor signs EO 80-06 freezing state staff. Emergency Services director Chow asks $600 for red-zone signs. "Just find it in your budget," the governor says.

Two and a half hours after midnight May 2, a Grumman TC-4C turboprop lifts off Whidbey Naval Air Station for infrared training. Aboard is USGS's David Frank. "We fly the volcano before dawn when solar heating is least." Several warm spots show where seen ten days ago around the crater and fractured north. Today they're stronger.

At 6 AM a magnitude-4.8 earthquake rattles people out of bed in Toutle, a town built on mudflows from Mount St. Helens. The *Daily News* reports water wells bottom in logs fifty feet down. Most residents know of former big firs, buried in mud and now rotted out into wells.

From Coldwater Rick Hoblitt had eyed a ridge 900 feet higher four miles east. Friday Weyerhaeuser bulldozes snowbanks off road 4020. Hoblitt and a Forest ranger tow a camp trailer up to a clearcut and rock quarry atop the ridge. The new USGS post—Coldwater II—lies just 5½ miles from the north flank. Dave Johnston's assistant Harry Glicken comes to staff it. Hoblitt sets a time-lapse camera. Each Coldwater post now shoots the mountain every half minute.

Bea and Barry Johnston of Washington State University had photographed eruptions in early April. Now they encounter the highway 504 roadblock, retreat, turn up road 3000, and wind east to Spud Mountain.[24] Mount St. Helens looms seven miles southeast but Saturday offers no action. Unemployed millwright Don Selby has bought a used camera and telephoto, hoping to cash in like Brad Backstrom.

Backstrom and Selby watch too from Spud Mountain, but the volcano disappoints. Backstrom returns to his job; Selby camps and waits.

Yesterday USGS landslide expert David Varnes helicoptered to crater's rim to study the fissures and sunken graben. At staff meeting he sketches a graph from a Chilean open-pit mine. In 1968 one wall crept out over months, accelerated, and failed.[25] This graph, Varnes says, suggests Mount St. Helens' steady creep isn't near failure.

The Forest Service has denied access to students. "Too risky," says George Theisen. Ben Hurliman grants or denies permits. He's a stern enough excluder to earn a nickname: Hurl-a-man. "The mountain's red-zoned because it's dangerous," he says. "I won't permit students. And if I did, hundreds more would line up tomorrow."

Pilot Lon Stickney needs a day off from flying the USGS. But for the *Today* show NBC's David Burrington has huddled with Portland State's Leonard Palmer and Aero-Copters' owner Gerry Garbel. So May 4 Stickney flies Burrington, cameraman, PSU professors Palmer and Paul Hammond, four students, and climber Robert Rogers. At crater's west rim they bag samples and snap photos. Occasional earthquakes jump the ground. NBC films a sunny spectacle.

"I've flown geologists for weeks," fumes Stickney, "and *this* isn't science—Palmer dangling on a rope for the camera. In this wind I need them on the ridge for pickup. But they're down in a hole, and no radios. I must *back* down the crater's downdraft. If the wind picks up I may not get in there at all." But at 3:30 he lifts off with the last of them.[26]

Lipman and Moore shoot the EDM from Coldwater II. With each shot the five-mile distance to Goat Rocks shrinks two inches. The bulge creeps out steadily. The only earlier such record was the subsurface dome Showa Shin-zan at Usu volcano in Hokkaido in Japan. The Sobetsu postmaster had drawn a new welt in May 1944, then redrew the profile every few weeks. By September 1945 the ground had risen 1000 feet.[27] Mount St. Helens' bulge now swells a mile and a half long, a mile wide. The *Columbian* runs a Ralph Perry shot of Truman's place "below the ominously bulging north face." USGS's Dan Miller tells a reporter the bulge is like Goat Rocks, built slowly in lava-dome eruptions. "A highly explosive eruption is improbable, more likely a push like toothpaste from a tube."

Tailgate entrepreneurs this weekend hawk T-shirts, baseball caps, vials of ash, watercolor paintings. Kid Valley diner sells a Volcano Burger.

A 285-foot antenna at Headquarters Camp reaches all Weyerhaeuser radios—in foremen's pickups, in the crummies. Duane Wend of the Woodcutters union visits cutting and logging sides. "Some men worry about the volcano," he says, "others pay little attention." But Monday the loggers find many motorists on company roads.

Weyerhaeuser meets with county commissioners, Sheriff Nelson, Forest Service, Claire Jones of the governor's office, state Emergency Services, Natural Resources, State Patrol. The roadblock steers sightseers onto our one-lane roads around, says Jack Schoening. They don't know our big log trucks.[28] When school's out there'll be a huge influx. Shouldn't we clear viewpoints away from logging? asks Jim Rombach.[29]

The geologists discuss eruptions. After a week of earthquakes and small eruptions, Mount Lamington in New Guinea exploded in 1951. It killed 3000 people and devastated 90 square miles as far as eight miles. Long after small eruptions tapered off and stopped at Bezymianny, it exploded in 1956 and devastated 195 square miles. Bezymianny—its name means 'nameless'— lies in remote Kamchatka that also harbors cold-war aircraft and submarines. Not even Soviet geologists witnessed the big eruption. Just what happened there is mysterious.

In a meeting about May 6, David Johnston asks might the bulge burst like Bezy? We've studied deposits all around the mountain, Mullineaux says. Sugarbowl dome blasted a few miles out 1200 years ago. But we've no dome now. We see no evidence a flow has run far out.

State agencies remain ununited. "Emergency coordination is pathetic," says John DeMeyer, head of Natural Resources' southwest office. "Only Bob Tokarczyk [Forest Service] has emphasized risk. Sheriff Nelson now does. The Governor seems in charge but does nothing. Emergency Services coordinates nothing. They sit at meetings seeming not to comprehend. The Game Department won't close streams to fishing—the risky low areas. We've shut our campground on the river. The State Geologist says the volcano may erupt, maybe not. He can't say when. We rarely see geologists or Forest Service. We're on our own."

We're a tiny agency and don't know volcanoes, replies Emergency Service's Jim Thomas. Mount St. Helens needs several people, but we've no extra staff.

For weeks USGS's Bob Christainsen has interpreted the geodetic numbers for Mullineaux and Crandell. When he rotates out, the job falls to Jim Moore. New to the EDM, Moore needs hours to calculate its numbers.

"You're not interpreting your data," Mullineaux complains at staff meeting. "I don't understand them."

"Not my job," Moore says. "Take time to calculate and I'll get no numbers."

"We all need the pace of swelling. *That's* important, not just science!"

"Someone must measure! *That's* why I'm here."

Another flareup: the Denver folk cooped in Vancouver, the HVO grads in the field. Next day Bob Decker presents the two scientists Mount St. Helens T-shirts: *Even Saints Blow Their Tops*. But now he'll interpret for Mullineaux.

Fred Stocker has enticed the *Columbian* into Len Palmer's remote-camera plan, and photo editor Steve Small likes teaming with *National Geographic*. But the Forest Service refuses Palmer further entry to restricted areas, and the FCC refuses a non-ham on the amateur band.

Photographer Ralph Perry has dealt with Stocker enough to see through the mask. "The guy's a phony. He's using us."

"And we're using him," says Steve Small. "He's our *National Geographic* link."

Small lends tripods and from Nikon Professional Services borrows two Nikon F2A cameras—motordrives, 250-exposure filmbacks, autofocus and autoexposure lenses. Other Nikon loaners aren't back from Saturday's Kentucky Derby—won by the filly *Genuine Risk*. Palmer's five cameras are down to two.

As licensed ham KA7AMF, Reid Blackburn can punch the transmitter on the 432-MHz band. His wife Fay too works at the *Columbian*. "How d'you feel about Reid going to the mountain for a week?" Steve Small asks.

"Fine—for a week."

"The project needs a radioman and an outdoor photographer."

"And he can take care of himself in the woods."

Blackburn's colleagues speak of him.[30]

"Ready for anything. He risked ammonia gas to photograph a rescue from a train wreck."

"He reads people and lighting quickly."

"Creative with photographs, he tells a story in one shot."

"We're thrilled by Mount St. Helens, a national story brewing. I envy his field posting."

There's little to see from Cinnamon Peak on the southwest. The USGS having moved to Coldwater II, only a tent and camera remain at Coldwater I. Early the 7th, auburn-chinned Blackburn drives his 1969 Volvo sedan to the logging platform on road 3533. Perched a thousand feet above Maratta Creek, Coldwater I lies outside the red zone but only eight miles from Mount St. Helens. He stakes out a tent and unpacks cameras. Colleague Ralph Perry drives in. Jim McWhirter comes in his handicapped-fitted van. In 1975 this Air Force veteran had turned a .357 revolver to his chest and pulled the trigger—so he explained to the *Columbian*. The slug hit the spine, paralyzing his legs. From Florida he'd driven to Cougar. Fred Stocker soon emerged from the Wildwood to snag him as a driver.

Dwight Reber flies Fred Stocker, engineers Tom Hill and Roger McCoy, cameras, and batteries. He drops Hill and Stocker at Coldwater I and flies Perry and McCoy east to the south flank of Mount Margaret 2000 feet above Spirit Lake. They set the east camera.[31]

Dwight Reber and Ralph Perry set the east camera.

ROGER MCCOY

Ralph Perry overnights with Blackburn. After midnight they bolt awake to a loud roar "like an avalanche for fifteen seconds." A light blinks on in the USGS trailer four miles east.

Rob Smith skirts the roadgates to Spirit Lake Lodge and finds locks broken, beds slept in, kitchen soiled. He overnights in this home of six years among clothes, books, tools, furniture. Next evening he leaves the lodge tidy for visitors.

Eruptions resume late the 7th, jetting as dark and high as in early April. Next afternoon muddy rain smears Jim Moore and the theodolite at Timberline. After midnight a nearly magnitude 5 earthquake. Harmonic tremor resumes, first since April 12. At 10:30 PM the 8th, more tremor.

Lon Stickney helicopters USGS's Moore to the bulge May 9 and lands Norm Banks at Plains of Abraham by large snow avalanches. At 11:06 a sharp quake! Banks drops his pack, struggling to stand.

"Hey Norm, you feel that?" Moore radios.

"You kidding?—a real leg-spreader."

"Ha! Any avalanche?"

"Not here. I worried about it."

Glicken writes to the Coldwater-II log: "Strong quake rolling the trailer, and from the volcano a muffled roar." Half a mile north, Louie Fanony and other Weyerhaeuser cutters lunch in the crew bus. It sways some seconds. "Shit! You think it's okay here?"

State Patrol Troopers Ron Spahman and Glen Austin drive Spirit Lake highway toward Timberline. The cruiser lurches, Spahman steers for the shoulder. Cobbles roll down a bank onto the pavement. "I've felt other quakes, but this one scared me." It registers a shallow 5. The seismologists now think the huge creeping bulge itself causes some of the earthquakes.

A week ago Toutle residents asked to meet with scientists. Someone heard a hundred-foot wall of water could burst down the Toutle. Northbound on I-5 May 7, Don Mullineaux saw a black cloud spurt from the mountain—the first in weeks. Oboy, is this the *real* eruption? He'd zipped back to Vancouver. For two days Mount St. Helens has unleashed a barrage of earthquakes above magnitude 4.5.

Now Friday evening the 9th, the rescheduled meeting brings 130 residents to Toutle Lake High School ¾ mile back from the river and a hundred feet above. Years ago Mullineaux and Crandell had found that 3000 years ago several sandy mudflows had filled the valley this high. The river has since cut down and widened an inner valley. From study in Ecuador, Mullineaux knows that when Cotopaxi erupted a century ago and mudflows drowned thousands of people, many could have escaped by climbing upslope.

Scribbling on chalkboard, Mullineaux says it took many flows 500 years to bury the valley. One mudflow can't inundate this terrace. "The river should flood no more than in the last two eruptions." The volcano's north side will likely come off in several small slides. A flood would inch up, no wall of water, he says. At its peak expect no worse than a spring freshet. This school and most homes are high enough. Don't try to drive down the valley. People trying to outrun a Colorado flood got caught.

"Things could be worse!" someone shouts. "A landslide could send Spirit Lake water down!"

"It would dam the basin higher and hold water *in*. Past debris off the mountain is what formed Spirit Lake."[32]

Sheriff Nelson says to expect no more than a two-hour warning. A high-low siren means go to high ground. Tune to AM radio 1270 KBAM.

As the meeting ends a man asks about Maple Flats. "Well yes, mud could reach houses less than twenty feet above the river," Mullineaux says. "Be ready to leave."

Mullineaux quells the wall-of-water rumor, but his quiet voice and guarded words belie the ugly violence of a lahar. It may not suddenly glut the whole valley, but watery sand flowing thirty miles an hour, rising thirty feet, incorporating boulders and big logs . . . well, he speaks of a relentless flow few can picture. Can Mullineaux even?

Cowlitz deputy Ben Bena has planned how to warn and evacuate hundreds, held meetings and drills. He'd like people a little scared but hears Mullineaux reassure them. "This tonight," Bena sighs, "doesn't make my job easier."

Next day the *Daily News* headlines: GEOLOGIST CALMS TOUTLE. "In a soothing . . . voice, volcano expert Donal Mullineaux [says] risks from Mount St. Helens eruptions are something they can live with."

Some pages back is a Donna duBeth piece, GEOLOGISTS AT ODDS ON ERUPTION CHANCES. It seems not everyone agrees with smallness. Seismologist Steve Malone says, "We're in the ballpark for a magmatic eruption." Mullineaux replies, "Maybe, maybe not." PSU's Leonard Palmer says magma in the bulge "is very explosive and can cause fierce eruptions, fire avalanches" (yet he took students to the crater Sunday). Mullineaux tells the *Seattle Times* a magmatic eruption is "only slightly probable."

USGS headquarters in Virginia had in March found their public statements slow—that Mount St. Helens' voice must be at Vancouver. But now a Reston pressman muses: "It's we who find *them* cautious. It sounds like they think the volcano will blow. They should say so."

"Pinning scientists down is like trying to corner a rat in a roundhouse," mutters Cowlitz Sheriff Les Nelson. He scowls at the state's small closure. It's time he works on this. But to restrict land we need Weyerhaeuser. Having been their security chief, he knows his amiable way around. He and state DNR timber meet with them. Would a wider zone impede you much? He asks. How hard is it to block a few roads?

Well, we could close some by felling trees, says a foreman. Pull culverts. Maybe gate a few.

Pressured by timber attorneys, the Forest Service regional office calls Gifford Pinchot National Forest to complain of the restrictions. And recreation staff urges areas be reopened. George Theisen's face tightens: "You need to get *me* fired. Long as it seems dangerous, I won't budge." Saturday he takes a telephone call from Washington D.C. It's Max Peterson, Chief of the U.S. Forest Service, calling from home. "Do what you must to keep your closure," he says. "Don't worry about the others." Theisen understands 'others' to include the regional office.

For weeks county deputies have tried to persuade Harry Truman to leave. Saturday the chiefs try. Cowlitz Sheriff Nelson and a sergeant, and Skamania Sheriff

Closner and deputy Barker drive up. "It's dead and silent," Nelson says. "No wind, no birds—eerie, ominous, like impending doom. I know it's dangerous. We park headed down the highway. We'll try to outrun anything off the mountain." The four walk into the lodge.

Truman has received a letter:[33]

> When everyone else involved in the . . . eruption appeared to be overcome by all the excitement, you stuck to what you knew and what common experience and sense told you. We could use a lot more of that kind of thinking . . . in politics . . .
>
>   As far as the Republicans being responsible for the activity of the mountain, you may well be right. Hot air, steam, [and] smoke seem . . . always . . . their trademark.
>
> —Dixy Lee Ray

"She needs me on her staff," says Truman. He passes the letter around. "How should I address the unmarried governor? Dear Madam? Dear Governor?" Barker sees their mission to take him out futile.

"We try to convince him for half an hour," Sheriff Nelson says. "But I respect his right to stay. He's been here every year since the 1920s. What would we arrest him for—being in his home? Yet he can't see the danger. 'There's a hump up there between me and the mountain,' he says. 'Anything coming off will go down the east side, or down the draw west of me. Me and my cats will be okay.' After all the press talk he thinks he'll look silly if he goes out and nothing happens. He's painted into a corner. He's only human."

Having asked the National Guard for mobile bunkers, Dan Miller relieves Harry Glicken at Coldwater II. He studies the geography next day. From the bulge a slope comes to the very base of this ridge. Ash flows could come this far, hot clouds drift up. This place isn't wholly safe. Glicken returns at 10 PM, and Miller rattles back down. The National Guard calls next day. "We've armored carriers for your posts. One next weekend."

Reid Blackburn at Coldwater I can barely radio a repeater in the Coast Range. From Tektronix' radio club, Dave Livesay drives in and swaps the short antenna on Blackburn's Volvo for a three-foot high-gainer. Sunday Blackburn calls the repeater, awakens the telephone patch, and chats with his mother this Mother's Day.

Martin Remmen and Tim Grose clank up to the chalet by Florence Creek—the D-7 Cat towing a sled of mine timbers and steel rails. Next day the Cat bogs in pumice. "From Mount St. Helens," Grose writes. "How could we survive hot volcanic foam?" They haul lumber, jack-leg drills, hoses, air compressor, and ore car up to the rock wall. They drill holes and blast a vertical face. They drill, blast, slush out the rock. Drill, blast, slush. They lay in wood crossties and spike down a set of rails. By the 30th Grose asks, "What kind of hard-labor camp have I gotten into?" He figures they'll run the drift 350 feet to ore. After two weeks they're in twenty feet.

Partner Jay Parker drives in and reports the geologists say the mountain might break off into Spirit Lake. He carries out Remmen's message to his wife Lucy: You go to the wedding the 17th. We've gotten the Black Rock this far and will stay to make it pay. May 12 the Forest Service runs a snowplow out road 100, and Jay Parker drives within a mile of the mine. He bears Lucy's reply: The mountain's going to blow! It's not safe! And about next weekend: she's *your* niece. You *are* coming to that wedding! Remmen and Grose drive out. A ranger gates the road at the blue zone.

For his film Otto Sieber charters an aircraft May 11 and brings Sacramento State prof Steve Harris. As they near the mountain 2:30 PM, a gray plume jets up. "Much bigger than I'd seen earlier," says Harris. Sieber films a sooty cloud pumping up and drifting west.

The USGS now shorthanded, David Johnston calls a friend, grad student Lee Fairchild at UW. "How about helping at Mount St. Helens?"

"Love to," says Fairchild, "but I'm teaching and can't leave."

"Well, it may be just as well. I do worry about working so close."

Mike Cooney of the Air Force Reserve 304th had in early April asked Johnston how eruptions might affect the helicopters, what jumpers should expect on the ground. He calls for an update.

"Well why don't I just fly with you?" Johnston asks.

"Okay. From a helicopter you can inform us while observing."

Dwight Reber flies *National Geographic* Sunday afternoon. He drops Rowe Findley at Coldwater I for an overnight. Next morning he takes on Ralph Perry, stops at Coldwater for Findley, and lands at Mount St. Helens Lodge. "My wife and I vowed we'd never leave Spirit Lake," Truman rasps. "She went down the road goddam feet first, and that's how I'll go."[34]

The volcano creeps and cracks on. The *Seattle Times* reports the geologists think a massive rock avalanche inevitable. Each morning the USGS and UW fax their summary to agencies, companies, and news bureaus, May 12 typical: "Steam and ash eruptions continue. . . The north flank moves outward at 5 feet a day, the. . . rate for three weeks. Over these 24 hours came 40 earthquakes magnitude 3 or larger, 10 of them magnitude 4 or larger."

A few magnitude 4s so alarmed seven weeks ago but now ten a day barely noteworthy. News is change, and now there isn't much.

As the snow melts, Weyerhaeuser moves east to higher country. Hook tender Ed Nugent and eight others start a logging side Monday seven miles northwest of the volcano. They turn up Coldwater Creek on road 4000 as a sedan comes out—USGS's Jim Moore and Bob Decker.

"It's safe to work here?"

"I don't know," Moore says. "We're glad to leave."

The loggers lowboy a D8 Cat and shovel loader to the ridgecrest 1900 feet above Coldwater valley. They park the Madill yarder and a water truck. They raise the 90-foot steel tower and guy out cables. It sways in a sharp earthquake.

Driving toward Duck Bay, Moore and Decker bog in a snowpatch. They dig out at 9:26.

"Quit rocking the car!" calls Decker from the right.

"I'm not! You are!" Moore shouts from the left.

A magnitude-5.2 earthquake agitates the car and harries the Harrys—Truman at Mount St. Helens Lodge, Glicken at Coldwater II. Lamps swing in Longview.[35]

Moore and Decker drive to Mount St. Helens Lodge. Truman says the Christmas balls swung one way, then another. They rent a boat and cross to the north but find no change in the great spirit level. Motoring back they see through clouds a gigantic avalanche off Goat Rocks has flowed far down. A black finger across Sugarbowl points down to Timberline as if to say 'you're next.'

Several ash eruptions shoot up next day. At Timberline at 1:34, Norm Banks reads the theodolite as Moore on a timber bench jots the numbers. Banks zeros on a target two miles away. The orange square blurs. He twists a focusing screw but at the telescope's periphery small firs whip a mile away. The ground jolts! An earthquake rolls off the mountain. Banks cradles the tripod and lurches to the bench. An avalanche roars a minute, stops, roars a half minute, slushes two minutes, and subsides.

"Another leg spreader?" grins Moore.

"Yeah. But y'know, a big slide could reach here."

At Coldwater II Harry Glicken steps from the swaying trailer. An avalanche roars off Mount St. Helens 1½ minutes, he jots to the logbook.

A mile north, Ed Nugent and three others on a pitch below the tower set chokers on logs felled across slope. The ground shudders, and several big logs roll.

"Dive! man. Find a hole!"

Nugent and another crouch behind a stump four feet across. A log thumps in from above. Another cascades overhead.

"Je-sus H. *Christ!*"

It's soon over. The men pick up the cables and resume work.

UW registers a 4.8. Banks relevels the theodolite. The bulge punches out 2½ inches an hour.

Since March 27 the seismologists have counted some 2550 earthquakes magnitude 3 and above. Steve Malone and a Seattle TV crew scout this morning's avalanche and land at Mount St. Helens Lodge. Truman ejaculates how big the quake was, lamps swinging this way and that. "He's *nuts* to stay," mutters Malone. "This place could be wiped. He acts for the press. Without their Harry hoopla he might leave."

Word reaches Sheriff Closner that Truman wants out. Deputy Barker sprints fifty miles upvalley. He comes to Mount St. Helens Lodge as a TV helicopter lands. Truman-upon-Lake salutes with a glass of Schenley's-upon-Coke. "Whoever said I'm coming out, is a *liar*."[36]

Washington Emergency Services calls a meeting Tuesday at Vancouver—sheriffs, Weyerhaeuser, State Patrol, state DNR, Game, and Commerce. Forest Service's George Theisen thinks the state has at last come to negotiate a western closure. USGS's Don Mullineaux says the volcano's erupting again, earthquakes persist, the bulge bulges. Avalanches could reach Spirit Lake, maybe no warning. Mudflows would flood the Toutle. George Theisen recaps closures of National Forest lands—red zone, blue zone.

But the Olympia entourage argues to *open* the upper Toutle valley. Tourist season starts Memorial Day, says DES's Terry Simmonds. Media want into the blue zone without a deputy escort, says Sheriff Closner, and some access to the red zone. Cabin owners want to remove things. The sheriff needs latitude to let people in. Game Department's Keith O'Neill says we need revenues from fishing licenses and want to open Merrill Lake. We'll open St. Helens Lake and Swift Reservoir the 24th. We'd like to open the upper Toutle and all lakes. Commissioner Walt Church says it's the county's economic interest to keep lakes and forests open. Commerce Department's Don Richardson says we need overlooks for sightseers, some in close. DES legal intern Fay Chu notes USGS hazards reach beyond the red zone. Why the discrepancy?[37]

Theisen and Dan Miller feel blindsided. It seems the state and counties have come to pressure the feds. Miller points to an orange finger down the North Fork. "Look folks, hot flows have swept this area in the past and could again. We've used this map for weeks. The state's closure doesn't acknowledge miles of real hazards. You treat them as an inconvenience to tourism and fishing. You're not listening. The volcano's dangerous!"

"National Forest lands will not reopen," says George Theisen. "Any area the state opens to fishing and sightseeing *stops* at the Forest boundary."

"Who will take charge?" a law officer had asked seven weeks ago. There's still no answer. Whatever happened to the governor's Watch Group—to develop plans to deal with eruptions, coordinate local governments? The governor claims to heed Crandell,[38] but DES won't lead. Its director has irritated many in other agencies. "Little Eddie," sneers one. "Department of Everlasting Screwups," mutters another.

"Emergency Services partners with the counties," says Rick LaValla. "In a big crisis the governor activates the National Guard. The U.S. Forest Service?—that's not how the system works. Our contacts are the sheriffs who enforce the laws."

Yet two weeks ago Cowlitz Sheriff Nelson had written DES: "Having watched the . . . deterioration of stability on Mt. St. Helens . . . I am convinced [it's reached] . . . the point of imminent peril . . . This dangerous area [being] under the jurisdiction of several units of government, the governor's action is needed to establish one set of rules . . . "

"Spirit Lake's dangerous," Sheriff Nelson now says. "I like the red zone kept closed."

"Easy for you to say in my county," says Sheriff Closner. "Nothing's closed in yours."

Weyerhaeuser's Jack Schoening complains of tourists slipping past the roadblock onto company roads used by big trucks.

"We can't staff that block," says State Patrol Lt. Don Mason. "The captain thinks it risky."

"Then shouldn't we move it down?" asks Nelson.

"The Executive Order doesn't allow law enforcement to alter boundaries or move the roadblock," says Simmonds. "That needs new legal authority."

"People can park at the gate and walk upriver, to fish," says Game Department's O'Neill. "If the Toutle's risky . . ."

"So how about a wider blue zone?" George Theisen asks.

Nelson with Weyerhaeuser and DNR will map out a new closure. "Deliver us a proposal by five Thursday," Simmonds says, "and we'll have it to the governor noon Friday."

The meeting breaks up. Sheriff Closner eyes a map where Mullineaux points to Coldwater and Castle Creeks. "This area seems risky. You and sheriff Nelson might get it closed." Across the room Don Richardson buttonholes Schoening. What about overlooks on Weyerhaeuser land? Schoening fingers road 3810 east of Castle Creek, a crest only six miles from the summit. This, says Richardson, is just what we need.

Information pours into the Forest Service radio room day and night from surveillance aircraft, rangers, USGS, deputies. Nearby desks hold emergency telephones for sheriffs, State Patrol, DES, FAA. Nearby the USGS faxes the daily update.

"But the Forest Service has no legal obligation to DES," says Rick LaValla. "We need our own system." Emergency Services has used radio-amateur spotters during fires and floods. They now authorize Radio Amateur Civil Emergency Service to station hams with mobile rigs near the mountain. The state's eyes at Mount St. Helens will be volunteers.

This afternoon the 13th, Mazamas mountaineers Ty and Marianna Kearney, W7WFP and W7WFO, drive up Forest road 8117 west of the mountain to Weyerhaeuser's 5700. They park their 1965 Dodge van on a rise seven miles from the summit.[39] They call on the 2-meter amateur band, and a repeater near Centralia bounces the signal to Olympia.

Ralph Perry tapes cameras to the skids of the Hughes 500 and strings control cords inside. Aloft, he shoots telephotos as the outside cameras click wide-angles. He photographs Dwight Reber at 9000 feet—eyes riveted to the instruments, arched arm pulling full power.[40] They land at Mount St. Helens Lodge. Perry frames Truman by budding bushes that only weeks ago lay beneath snow.

Carl Berg, volunteer for county emergency services, drives Toutle valley daily. Tuesday afternoon he asks Truman if he feels safe and pokes on a recorder.

> The worst [the mountain] can do is pour something down Dry Gulch . . . Then the whole goddam road is going out . . . But . . . it can't do a damn thing [to me]. If it rolled hot lava out, it . . . runs slow. And hell, a glacier [avalanche] . . . will go [east] down Ape Canyon . . . [or] down Dry Gulch . . .
>
> How's it feel to be a hero?
>
> I didn't ask for that. This is the goddam truth. If anything comes down it'd take the road out. I didn't want to be on the lower side . . . Those earthquakes scare the living hell out of me, but I'm gonna stay. Jesus Christ, I'm . . . going on 84. This is my home. I've got a huge spread here . . . If you've lived 54 years in one place, you don't just walk off and leave it. If an earthquake got this place I'd rather go here with it.
>
> If anything happens there'd be the damnedest line of copters. They'd jerk me off here in three minutes.[41]

Wednesday morning Reber flies *National Geographic*'s Rowe Findley and Fred Stocker to Mount St. Helens Lodge. A 5th-grade class at Brooks, Oregon, had written Truman. "He's nervous about his first helicopter ride," says Reber, "but on the intercom talks of flying biplanes in World War I and floatplanes off Spirit Lake."

They land at Clear Lake Elementary, the whole school outside. Dapper in a leisure suit, Truman thanks the students for the letters: "What a hit they made in my kitchen." To a reporter he whispers, "Quakes every damn minute, never a dull moment." Soon Reber lifts off north.

Columbian's Steve Small flies a Cessna turbo-210 to check Mount St. Helens and radio Reid Blackburn. He photographs a Jet Ranger landing between parallel fissures—a block fated to fall. David Johnston steps to crater's edge. A gray burst spurts up, he sprints back, and the helicopter powers off. Small lands at Pearson, Dwight Reber from Brooks. Small climbs into the Hughes and flies to Coldwater I. Reid Blackburn has been here a week.

"You okay till the weekend?"

"It's cold and cloudy," says Blackburn. "I thought camping would be more fun."

"Any photographs?"

"Not the shots I'd like. But I can't leave this transmitter."

"Come in whenever you wish."

"I think something'll happen. I'll stay."

"Okay, but in another week I'll pull the cameras."

Reber flies the east camera back to Coldwater I. Blackburn checks connectors, punches the transmitter twice, and jots to his log:

2:05 P.M. ② BOTH CAMERAS AT BASE CAMP.

Fathom 36 company brings video cameras to Coldwater II—Hoblitt's idea to replace USGS people in close. "But they bring eight people and four vehicles," complains Dan Miller. Images telemeter from post to post. Very nice, says Miller—but we haven't the $40 thousand for this system. Then we'll loan it, Fathom says—and come back for advertising. "They don't give a shit if we buy or not," mutters Miller. "They just want a junket."

Lon Stickney lands Miller at Coldwater I. "The *Columbian's* supposed to have one photographer here," Miller gripes. "But here are *seven* people and a helicopter![42] We facilitate their permit, then they risk many people."

For a week Norm Banks has clambered about Mount St. Helens experiencing 'leg-spreader' earthquakes, avalanches, and small eruptions. Now he glimpses the mountain from an airliner climbing out of Portland. *I've made it! But one of these days it'll erupt. The way we hang around the north side, someone could be nailed.*

One scientist backfills for another. Joe Rosenbaum programs a computer to plot how Mount St. Helens' ash would distribute in National Weather Service's winds-aloft forecasts. Harry Glicken must leave Coldwater II for a week. Hoblitt dials a former field assistant.

"I'll take it," says Jim Vallance, ecstatic at this posting.

"Coldwater II *is* a ringside seat," says Hoblitt. "I just hope it isn't ... ah ... *too* close."

Sheriff Nelson calls a meeting to widen the blue zone. Closing land won't work if landowners don't buy in. "Only the highway's closed in our county," Nelson says. "Shouldn't we shut more?"

"The roadblock puts motorists into our logging," Jack Schoening says, "Let's move it west."

"Weyerhaeuser's concern isn't public safety but self interest," says Capt. Bullock. "The State Patrol can't close a public highway just to keep sightseers off private roads."

"Our concern *is* safety on our roads. We can now agree to restrict land."

To the roadblock in afternoon come the sheriff and deputy Bena, DNR's John DeMeyer, and Weyerhaeuser's Schoening and Dick Nesbit. A mile above Camp Baker the highway is straight, and a flat just north could be a turnaround. The sheriff will request the governor declare a western blue zone and move the block down.

The Portland Boy Scouts' camp on Spirit Lake holds 28-foot fiberglass launch *White Eagle* Tollycraft had donated to ferry boys to the north shore. For summer camp the Scouts need the boat and $30,000 in gear now trapped in the red zone. Portland YMCA's Camp Meeham a mile northeast holds $40,000 in gear. Paul Hathaway, vice president of Northwest Natural Gas, sits on the boards of the YMCA and Boy Scouts. His neighbor, Jim Lematta, flies logging helicopters. "Most neighbors come over to borrow a lawnmower," says Lematta. "Paul comes to borrow a helicopter." Hathaway has organized an expedition of donated equipment and time. Governor's press secretary Ray Walters has written an exception to the executive order and yesterday handed Hathaway the authorizing letter, signed Dixy Lee Ray.

Columbia Helicopters donates *two* ships. "We understand the risk is landslide off the mountain," says Lematta. "We'd have a couple minutes to fly off."

Dwight Reber lands the Hughes in the sandpit by the roadgate. In climb Hathaway, Jack Wolff (YMCA), and Duane Rhodes (Boy Scouts). Reber flies under clouds dripping sleet and drops Wolff at Mount St. Helens Lodge, flies across to the Scout camp, and hovers over the dock to drop Hathaway and Rhodes. He flies to the Y camp past firs far taller than on the south shore.

Wolff hands Truman a bottle of bourbon, unties his 14-foot Starcraft from the boathouse, and guns over to the Scout camp. Into *White Eagle* the men pile 35 tents, 119 life jackets, trading-post goods, fire pumps, climbing ropes, generator, CO_2 rifles, tools, aluminum skiffs, canoes. They winch the launch down to the water, and Hathaway and Rhodes climb in. Wolff tows *White Eagle* up Coe's cove. They unload skiffs and canoes onto the YMCA beach and wrap slings to *White Eagle*.

A 22-cubic-yard dumpster has been lowboyed to the sandpit. Jerry Koschnick hovers down in a big two-rotor Vertol 107. Lematta sets the slings, and Koschnick lifts the dumpster—15 by 7 by 6 feet—to the beach. He hovers above *White Eagle*, and Hathaway and Wolff clip on the slings. Koschnick lifts the loaded launch west—four tons. From the Y camp the men pile tents, tools, backpacks, lifejackets, kitchen gear, canoes, sailboats into the dumpster and top off with the Scouts' canoes and skiffs. The Vertol dangles the dumpster's six tons down to the pit.

Wolff stops by his own cabin before throttling across to the boathouse. Reber lands and Harry Truman ambles out.

"The earthquakes scare me," Truman says. "But if I left this place it'd be vandalized."

Having kept the books and repaired motors here, Wolff knows Truman as a robust man, shrinking from nothing. But now he's quiet, reserved. On Truman's face Wolff reads fear. "If it get's *too* scarey here, my boat's in the water. Take it over to our place."

Reber flies the men back to the sandpit.[43] To credit Columbia Helicopters, Hathaway invites reporters. Network news air stories; Associated Press wires off one; the *Oregonian* and *Daily News* run pieces. Owners trying to visit their cabins had been threatened by fines. Now one group is allowed to retrieve gear. Cabin owners dial the sheriffs.

Steve Small radios Reid Blackburn from the Cessna. "The Tektronix hams will back up a sheriff this weekend. They can't spell you."

"I'm okay here but can't stand Stocker hanging around."

"Rowe Findley likes the camera project. With this quality *National Geographic* link, we don't need Stocker."

"Well *I'm* staying and need Ektachrome."

"I'll send it up."

In evening Blackburn radios an autopatch home. "He saw an eruption this week but only clouds today," says Fay Blackburn. "He'll stay the weekend."

Martin Remmen and Tim Grose drive in road 100, and Forest ranger Dave Purcell snaps their lock to the gate. They haul timber to Meta Lake and hike to Black Rock mine. "Lucky we're in the blue zone," Grose writes. "We can hit that big copper lead. I'm pumped about getting rich." Driving out in evening, Remmen and Grose meet a limegreen 1971 Pontiac Grand Prix coming in—Don and Natalie Parker and nephew Rick. A gash on Rick's knee from the snowmobile five weeks ago has healed. Purcell hands Grose a children's book he's written, *Cascade Volcanoes*. "He tells me how dangerous they can be," Grose says.

Weyerhaeuser scrapes out a highway turnaround above their 2700 road. "On our own land we act quickly, no permits," says construction foreman Dexter Salsman. "D8 Cats, quarry, and trucks sit a mile away. Dick Nesbit calls, 'Get your ass over there.' In five hours we clear trees, bulldoze a circle, and rock it."

Cowlitz deputy Ben Bena plots the proposed blue zone. The west boundary runs between land Ranges 2 and 3 across highway 504 a mile above Camp Baker. On the north it follows the county line east to the blue zone on Forest road 125. The south boundary follows highway 503 and Forest road 90 east to road 125. A reentrant leaves Cougar outside.[44] The zone twelve miles west and eight miles north of the red zone would exclude sightseers but permit logging.

Bena telexes the legal description to DES where Terry Simmonds drafts a packet for the governor. Bena telephones.

"Wow! That's a big closure," says Simmonds

"We've a big problem."

At Pennsylvania State University, Barry Voight has drafted a report: *Slope Stability Hazards, Mount St. Helens Volcano.* It exudes Newton's Second Law, equations, and long clauses:

> . . . wide variety of settings, in heterogeneous or relatively homogeneous ground, and with or without the influence of anisotropy . . .
>
> . . . intergranular horizontal compressional stresses arise in the edifice, normal to the strike of the ridge top depressions during periods of deflation—inasmuch as the stretched 'surface length' of the edifice cannot now fully decompress . . . .

. . . In the absence of reliable site specific measurement procedures it is appropriate to use apparent friction values back-calculated from published slide profiles.

The arcane language of specialists. One section suggests a gigantic landslide, half a cubic mile. It could trigger explosions: "Near-boiling groundwater inside the volcano could flash to steam and propel a hot fragmental flow down the flanks." As had devastated 27 square miles at Bandai-san in Japan in 1888. But this section ends: "the bulge may lead only to increased rockfall, snow avalanche, and glacier fall."

Voight advocates his former student continue geodetic monitoring that "should be not by scientists . . . compromised by . . . tasks of greater interest to them." So he dismisses USGS monitoring. No plain summary, no telephone call to explain. The report contains vibrant ideas—gigantic landslide, ensuing magmatic eruption. But "like a ghost," wrote Charles Dickens, "an idea must be spoken to a little before it will explain itself."

Dated May 1, the report doesn't arrive in Vancouver for more than two weeks. "It wasn't in Vancouver when I left midday the 16th," says Don Mullineaux. Rocky Crandell saw it only after May 18. Bob Christiansen says, "As science coordinator I got all important documents. I didn't see the report until the 19th." Arnold Okamura says, "I didn't hear of it in any of our meetings."[45]

But May 16 Dan Miller walks it to the Forest Supervisor Bob Tokarczyk, who faxes it to the governor. Don Swanson bristles at its insult to USGS monitoring. Since April he and others have worked 14-hour days in bad weather at personal risk.

Jim Moore calculates from new topographic contours. By April 12 the bulge held 104 million cubic meters, the sagged crater 24 million. One minus the other means 80 million cubic meters [100 million cubic yards] added to Mount St. Helens. Surely it's intruded magma.

David Johnston worries about Harry Glicken at Coldwater II. Johnston has advised the Air Force Reserve 304th squadron at Portland and would fly in their hueys in a big eruption. At 5:30 PM the 15th a telephone rings at the 304th. Reservist pilot Bill Hewes picks it up.

"We've a man on a ridge near Mount St. Helens," Johnston says. "If flood blocks the highway, could you fly in and lift him out?"

"Of course. You call, we haul."

Next morning at Coldwater II, Glicken writes to the May 16 logbook:

5:35   Quake—shakes bed slightly.[46]   *ARISE!*

5

You're Perfectly Safe Here, Aren't You?

Thinning snow opens roads usually shut into June. The gate on the Spirit Lake highway is easily skirted on logging roads.

FRIDAY, MAY 16

Loggers head up the South Fork and North Fork the last workday this week. This morning UW records seven earthquakes magnitude 4 and up. A 4.7 twitters Coldwater II and Longview at 5:35. A predawn aerial infrared survey shows two dozen hot areas about the crater and bulge. But it'll take three days to compute and plot the data.

Weyerhaeuser safety officer George Steig and Woodworkers union rep Joel Hembree visit field crews Fridays, today up the South Fork. Men cutting on road 5710 worry about the close mountain. "What if it erupts?" Steig and Hembree tell them to stay off low roads like 4100. They point to high roads 4250 and 5500. "Your foreman will know any change by radio."

Last season cutters felled fir, hemlock, and cedar on road 4170 high in the South Fork. Now to fetch them. A crew lowboys a D8 Cat, sets a diesel yarder, raises the steel tower, and guys out cables. Driving out at 4 PM, they stop to chat with a man by a pickup and a man by a station wagon. Early Monday Hugh McCully will haul in a loader and by eight be down in the volcano's shadow setting chokers.[1]

Bill LeMonds—32-year-old cutter whose family tree holds two dozen loggers—leaves Castle Rock at 5:30. Usually he boards a Weyerhaeuser bus but today drives his 1968 pickup. For volcano news the FM radio dial sits at 94.5, Longview's KUKN. Past Camp Baker he turns north up gravel road 3300 and snakes up the 3340. On an overlook his boss, bull buck Bob Booth, sits in a company pickup eyeing Mount St. Helens ten miles away. A Weyerhaeuser crummie comes, and Booth and LeMonds climb in. From thermos jugs the twelve men pour coffee against morning's chill. Cutters in Coldwater have lunched with the USGS guy on the ridge. If it's safe for him round the clock, it must be okay farther out.

Booth says no change at the volcano but the sheriff worries about this north flank. "Aw shit," one says, "it ain't gonna do nuthin but put a little mud in Spirit Lake."

"The guys don't worry much," says LeMonds. "Most think the Forest Service overreacts. You hear such different stories from experts on radio and TV. Almost anything could happen. But we've work to do."

They wind a mile north to where they've worked a month. The crummie drops a quarry crew, then the fallers. From Elk Rock they look west to Camp Baker seven miles away. "You guys better work like hell up there," supervisor Dick Nesbit had laughed. "I can watch from here."

At 7:30 LeMonds yanks the cord of a Stihl 051, and it coughs to life. They cut Douglas fir—red fir and a few fat yellow fir—and some hemlock and cedar. They cut by union schedule: 7:30 to 9:30, break half an hour, cut 10 to 11, break an hour for lunch. In afternoon LeMonds saws steadily three hours, the air sweet with sawdust, pitch, and bruised needles.

Grimey at 3:15, he stashes saws, wedge belt, and gas can beneath a log and tosses a dull chain into the crummie. He drops gloves and toolkit into his pickup, climbs behind the wheel, and bumps down the gravel road. Many cars fill the old sandpit by the roadblock, and people traipse up to an old platform to watch the volcano. He turns down the highway. At 3:30 the other cutters stow their saws among the stumps, and the crewbus jolts toward Camp Baker.

High on the southeast of Elk Rock a crew logs trees from the path of a new spur off road 3330. Turn hooker John Killian has felt earthquakes this week—even behind the thundering Cat.

Louie Fanony walks to the highway and a Weyerhaeuser bus. At Camp Baker he and other cutters board a crummie. It rattles east up into South Coldwater Creek and switches up the 4020 onto south Coldwater ridge. Fanony powers up the Stihl 041. In this stand of red fir and hemlock, he cuts alone, a single jack. The men lunch in the crummie an earthquake had bounced a week ago. Fanony has felt the ground quiver this week even through a vibrating saw.

Bull buck Jim Pluard often drives half a mile up to the USGS trailer for coffee with the skinny guy, and Harry Glicken likes the company. At lunch the crummie sometimes brings the whole crew. Pluard doesn't fear the mountain, Glicken sees, but some of the men do. Last week Fanony saw in the spotting scope a great knob of rock. This week it had fallen.

"You're not afraid to stay here night and day?"

"I'm okay and *like* it here," says Glicken. "Many in the USGS would love this job."

"What if it blows?"

"Oh, I'll scoot down in the quarry behind one those rocks."

"We can't see the mountain. If something makes you leave, blow your horn on your way by!"

Camp Baker superintendent Dick Nesbit stops by. "Tuesday we'll set a yarder below you to pull in the logs," he says. "It'll block the road two weeks."

"The volcano's erupting!" says Glicken. "If it blows and the road's blocked, I can't escape."

"It's *our* road. We must log."

Fanony thumbs off his saw at three and changes a worn chain. The men scan the brush: no fires from the saws. They step onto the crummie, and it creeps toward Camp Baker.

A Weyerhaeuser bus up the highway stops for Ed Nugent. From Camp Baker a crummie rattles twelve miles east and up roads 4000 and 4040 to the ridge between the forks of Coldwater Creek. Since Monday this crew has cabled logs up to the tower. Though clouds Mount St. Helens looms seven miles southeast.

The choker setters trudge downslope, calked boots biting into bark. The yarder rumbles, an air whistle shrieks, black diesel exhaust jets. Two logs at a time wind up to the landing. The loader's claw sorts them by type and size. A truck pulls in, and the claw lifts off its piggyback trailer. It stacks on 40-foot logs one by one. The driver cinches the chains, steps into the cab, and grinds toward Camp Baker.

"Working so close, we keep an eye on the mountain," says Nugent. "The north side's changed just this week, and I've felt earthquakes. We're nervous enough to knock off early today and bring the crummie down behind the ridge, ready to go." At 3:40 the bus lurches west.

Ed's father Jim Nugent boards a Weyerhaeuser bus at Kid Valley. From Camp Baker he drives a crummie twenty miles up road 2500, down into Green River, and up Elk Creek to a cut on road 2618. Ten men step out and eye the swelled hulk fifteen miles away. "Many of the guys worry about the north even this far out," says Nugent. "Some haven't shown up—on what they call 'sick leave.' Them that are here . . . well, they talk."

"Christ! What're we gonna do if that thing blows straight at us?"

"Stick your head between your legs and kiss your ass goodbye."

"No shit."

The men walk down to their lines and rev the saws. They fell big straight firs for the Asian market, bucking them to 32 and 40-foot lengths. At 3:30 they stow saws beneath downed limbs, pile in the crummie, and Nugent grinds south. Weyerhaeuser's workers being unioned, the hills will rest till Monday.

Gyppo cutters are bound by no union. Thirty-six-year-old logger James Scymanky has worked before with Leonty Skorohodoff and Evlanty Sharipoff, and now for a month on a Weyerhaeuser contract. José Dias joined a few days ago. Where they turn onto road 3100 above Camp Baker, Mount St. Helens looks a long ways off. Camped in a quarry on road 3208, the men thin 45 acres of fir where oldgrowth had been logged two decades ago. They hardly think of the mountain thirteen miles away behind ridges.

Sheriff Nelson yesterday asked the governor to move the roadblock west. Weyerhaeuser has bulldozed and rocked a circle by the highway a mile above Camp Baker. Finish work awaits the governor's signature. State Patrol Capt. Dick Bullock studies the new turnaround. But this cobbled turn around a stump is absurd, he muses—one trailer could block it. Its hardly above the river, and trees screen the mountain. I won't sign off on *this* as part of a state highway.

Having for years studied glaciers for the USGS, Milinda Brugman now surveys Shoestring Glacier atop Mount St. Helens. At 8:11 AM at Coldwater II, she beams a Laser Ranger to Goat Rocks, the first shot clouds have allowed in twelve days. The line measures fifty-three feet shorter. "Hard to believe such growth, she says. "But it must be right: I've used this instrument for years." The volcano's north flank still bulges—4⅓ feet *per day!*

Bob Decker and Jim Moore rotate off the geodetic team, Don Swanson on. Swanson entices grad student Gerhard Wörner. By a visa glitch he's an illegal alien but now aids the USGS. Lon Stickney lands Swanson and Wörner at Timberline at 9:30 then flies Dave Johnston and Dan Miller beneath clouds. They measure a Goat Rocks crack at 56°F but only trifling sulfur dioxide.

Dwight Reber flies Rowe Findley to Coldwater I. He flies eight miles east to the spur of Mount Margaret where Ralph Perry resets the east camera. Reid Blackburn punches the transmitter and in a neat hand writes: 11:30 AM ① TEST, #2 BACK IN POSITION. A helicopter crosses the mountain's flank [Johnston and Miller]. Blackburn punches the transmitter twice: 11:47 AM ② TEST w/ CHOPPER IN PIC?

Reber lands at Mount St. Helens Lodge, Truman now a comfortable acquaintance. "People think the mountain may erupt, Harry. I've a deal with Rowe Findley. If anything happens I'll fly in for Reid Blackburn and *National Geographic* pays."

"Ah . . . would I be included in an evacuation?"

"That's what you want?"

Truman nods.

"All right. If I come for Reid, I'll stop here too."

The *Columbian*'s Steve Small flies again in a Cessna. "Since the Tek guy can't spell you," he radios Blackburn, "you want to come in the weekend?"

"If the project's ending Wednesday, I'll just stick it out."

Mindy Brugman and an assistant drive to Timberline. "The bulge looks *huge*," she says, "inflated like a balloon." Stickney lifts them to Shoestring Glacier. But Timberline operations grow contentious, many geologists thinking the bulge could shed a big avalanche. Stickney flies Swanson and Wörner to a new site on road 100. They turn angles by theodolite.

KGW-radio reporter Mike Beard drives up the Toutle in afternoon, now seven weeks since he announced the first eruption from the air. At Timberline his car door wobbles on its hinges. "Hey look," he calls, "another earthquake." He stops at Mount St. Helens Lodge. Ice tinkles in Harry Truman's Coke and Schenley's.

"What about the earthquakes?" asks Beard.

"I'm not worried. One shook my chimney off thirty years ago. Six years ago a good one shook me out of bed one night. The goddam bed was walkin all around. Thought I'd drank too much. Then I heard the damnedest noise down here. It shook all them dishes—the whole goddam lot—down on the floor."

"And if Mount St. Helens erupts?"

"Oh, I'd stay here and watch."

"You're not worried?"

"Nooooo. It's too far away. It's a mile through here all heavily timbered. I'm down at 32 hundred feet; the mountain's almost ten thousand. If it spurted it wouldn't hurt a damn thing here. And hell, I'm the only one here."

At Camp Baker Bud Tippery keeps Weyerhaeuser's saws running, more than a hundred of them. On good days he sees Mount St. Helens from the shop. He'd traced the profile on the window glass in March. He's redrawn from time to time, each line a touch left or higher, tracing the north flank's swelling across seven weeks. He has rustically mimicked the Japanese postmaster who'd redrawn a strange welt rising by Usu volcano in Hokkaido in 1944–45. Tippery draws another line, humped a bit more. He locks the shop and steps into his pickup.

KING5 news has televised from Spud Mountain for days. Mount St. Helens is clouded the 16th when two seedy men drive up with rifles, hunting out of season.

"What're you doing?" one grunts.

"Waiting for an eruption."

The other lofts a handful of rocks that crash onto their car. "There's an eruption," he leers.

Cameraman Mark Anderson eyes these armed wierdos, thinking of his $120,000 in equipment. They radio Seattle, and KING recalls their crew.

Robert Landsburg drives his green 1969 Dodge Coronet wagon up the South Fork for a weekend of photography. On the 4170 he stops 300 feet above the river just three miles west of the mountain.

DES packages a proposal for Governor Ray that "would place the governor's Executive Order in realistic alignment with existing geologic conditions," Sheriff Nelson telexes. Its blue zone reaches 12 miles west and 7½ miles north of the red zone. News media, loggers, and Harry Truman could be within by permit. Sheriffs could allow others. Offices in Kelso and Vancouver expect the order this afternoon. But DES's Rick LaValla found the draft rough. This first restriction of land by the state must be done with care. When a staffer at last delivers the packet, the governor is on her way to a luncheon, then an ROTC graduation at University of Washington.

Having worked 52 days straight, Forest Services's George Theisen packs for a weekend home in Trout Lake he's not seen in two months. "The State Patrol called saying they may take people to Spirit Lake tomorrow," he says. "It only increases pressure to reopen the Forest." All afternoon he's expected a telex announcing a state closure. Fire Staff Paul Stenkamp steps in at 5:30. "You go home, George. I've got it this weekend."

Cowlitz Deputy Ben Bena too awaits the governor's telex. "When we have it," he says, "we'll move the roadblock and shut surrounding areas. We and Weyerhaeuser can have it done tomorrow morning." He stops by his boss at five.

"You heard?"

"Nothing." The sheriff Nelson dials DES: "What's up?"

"The governor will think this closure too big for Weyerhaeuser," says Rick LaValla.

"They planned it with us! When she signs they'll finish the turnaround. DOT stands by to move the gate."

"Well, she's gone. We'll have to work it out Monday."

An hour later Bena drives up the highway. He's run evacuation drills in Castle Rock, Tower, and Toutle. This evening's the last, Maple Flats. Twenty people come to the DOT shed. Have a suitcase packed, he says. A high-low siren means evacuate to high ground. Kid Valley store's a place to congregate. Here's the call-down tree.

Since his covert climb April 13, Otto Sieber has filmed from the air and from the ground beyond roadblocks. He's stood today by a tripod above Coldwater Creek. He retreats downvalley at dusk. After a Seattle film run, back to this perch Sunday.

Catherine and Paul Hickson drive from University of British Columbia this Victoria Day weekend and turn east into the mountains. Paul an astrophysicist, Cathy a geology student, they grope in clouds up gravel roads and pitch a tent among firs.

It's evening when young Bruce Nelson and Sue Ruff, Terry Crall and Karen Varner leave Longview in Nelson's Blazer. They drive highway 504 and road 2500 to Green River. From the east bridge they hike the trail by flashlight two hundred fifty yards through second-growth fir. They pitch tents on a terrace back from the river.

Harry Glicken has seen little through clouds from Coldwater II. Just before dark he notes Mount St. Helens eighty percent clear. USGS–UW's May 16 report lists no eruptions. The summit steams, the north flank grows outward, five earthquakes above magnitude 4. Too routine to be news.

Owners have for weeks agitated to visit their Spirit Lake cabins. The airlift from the youth camps opens a way. Friday afternoon Sheriff Nelson telephones State Patrol Chief Landon. "A crowd's gathering at Toutle School tomorrow, maybe a mob. They threaten to force the roadblock. The state caused this, you come deal with it."

Landon calls Governor Ray, saying he'd okayed a request for the airlift.

"As a Scoutmaster you've a soft spot for them," she fumes. "Now we've little choice but to let people in.[2] But when you come out, have Harry Truman with you."

The governor's in a trap she helped make. Landon calls Skamania Sheriff Bill Closner. "We may escort people to Spirit Lake tomorrow."

"That sounds risky."

"If we can't talk them out of it, we *will* go. I'd rather you be there."

"See you at noon."

Daily News's Donna duBeth has avoided Spirit Lake for two weeks.

"I've got weekend duty," says Rick Seifert. "You want to go tomorrow?"

"No. The mountain's a monster."

"Metaphors like that exaggerate. No one knows what'll happen."

"It'll be *terrible*!" DuBeth drives off to Seattle.

With cabin owners agitating, the State Patrol guards the upper roadgate. Signs glare back: HAZARDOUS AREA   ROAD CLOSED   DO NOT ENTER. From his cruiser trooper Ron Spahman sees an orange Volkswagon fly up the highway and dodge off south. He corrals it on a dirt track skirting the gate. It's Bob Kaseweter and Bev Wetherald.

"The red zone's closed."

"I'm doing geology at my cabin. This is my secretary."

Secretary my ass: this is his girlfriend. Spahman radios Kelso.

Down the highway comes the white pickup Spahman had pulled over months ago. It stops on the shoulder and Truman shambles to the gate.

"Well, Harry, everyone says you know about the volcano."

"Oh hell, I've no idea what the damn thing will do."

They chat until a sergeant radios back: "Vancouver says they're okay, but no car."

"You can drive around *this* gate."

"The highway's closed."

"Okay to pedal up?" asks Kaseweter, lifting a bicycle from the rack.

"I don't see why not," says Spahman.

"How'm I going?" says Wetherald

Truman looks her up and down. "Hell, I'll give you a ride. Jump in."

Spahman watches Kaseweter pump up the blacktop, bike tilting left, right, left, falling farther behind the old pickup and his young lady.

Chris Carlson, David Johnston's sometimes girlfriend, is now a Stanford student working at the USGS in Menlo Park. "Dave's called every night this week and calls this evening," she says. "From all the work and late nights he's almost too tired to drive to the mountain. 'I think it's near eruption,' he says. 'It scares me. Yet the state will let people up the valley—loosening when they should tighten.' He's pissed at the press for painting Harry Truman a colorful character. 'The old fart acts defiant, scoffing nothing'll happen. Others then dismiss an eruption,' Dave says.

"He worries," Carlson says, "that Harry Glicken—young and keen about the volcano—doesn't know the risks. He doesn't like him alone so much at Coldwater II. More than once Dave's told me, 'If I die young, I hope it's in an eruption.'"

SATURDAY, MAY 17

Harry Glicken has staffed Coldwater II two weeks but tomorrow starts a California visit. When USGS staff meeting opens, no one's volunteered to spell him.

"Maybe I'll go up for a couple days," says Bob Christiansen.

"That won't work," says Don Swanson, "you're needed here. We'll cover till he's back. I've fieldwork with Wörner today but could go up Sunday."

"I'll take Coldwater tonight," says Dave Johnston.

Thirteen miles northwest of Mount St. Helens, Jim Scymanky and his companions gas their saws for another day thinning Douglas fir. They do need the cash: Scymanky's share supports a wife and four kids. The men cut all day, then camp in the quarry.

From Butte Camp Lon Stickney helicopters Swanson to get a reflector. The helicopter's bleed valve sticks from ingested ash, the compressor pulling only eighty percent power. He lands and shuts down, and the men traipse to the crater. It gapes 1550 yards long, 660 wide, 220 deep. Ice rattles down from the rim, then a seraphic serenity.

At 10:45 a laser from Butte Camp reflects off the new target. Stickney flies Swanson and Wörner to Toutle site, and by theodolite they remeasure the creep of Goat Rocks.

Harry Glicken at Coldwater II can't reflect the laser off the Goat Rocks prism. At five miles his aim must be exact, but he doesn't quite know the site. Stickney hovers over the target. But squinting into the sun, Glicken can't see white helicopter against the snow. Stickney flies to Coldwater II. Still no reflection.

It's training weekend for reservists. The National Guard 116th Air Cavalry has twenty-five hueys at the Firing Center a hundred miles east of Mount St. Helens. Gunships bristling rockets skim the barren hills and blast derelict dumpsters. The Air

Force Reserve 304th squadron trains near Mount Hood. Cowlitz search-and-rescue drills with the Civil Air Patrol at Chehalis airport.

Dan Balch and Brian Thomas, co-workers at Longview Fiber, will share a weekend at Green River with friends Terry Crall, Karen Varner, Bruce Nelson, and Sue Ruff. In Balch's Ford pickup at Silver Lake they watch the sun rise behind Mount St. Helens. They turn onto road 2500, follow Green River east, and park by the bridge. A hike through second-growth fir and alder brings them to a decrepit ranger cabin. They pitch a tent facing upriver, the other four tenting seventy yards east.

The six hike up the trail into big oldgrowth—"here for the wilderness," says Thomas. They crawl into Independence mine's blackness. Just upriver three prospectors shovel gravel into a sluicebox. It's oddly quiet, no birds, Thomas thinks while lying on a log over the river. They roast backstrap elk, bake potatoes in the coals, sip beer into the night. Thomas crawls into his bag in long underwear. Balch stays by the fire till 3 AM.

In Vader, Weyerhaeuser logger John Killian and wife Christy have planned a weekend fishing. At 9:30 he stops by sister Charlene's place.

"You're off to Cispus?"

"Well, they've opened Fawn Lake. We're going there."

"Isn't it a bit close?"

"It's okay, Char."

They drive up the Toutle and Green, cross on the 2800, weave south to the 3900. A pitch on 3920 through big firs brings them to Fawn Lake where John has fished since a child. They step out with three dogs. Snowbanks linger on the south headwall. It could be any pretty Cascade cirque.

Young Bruce Faddis has driven his sister's 1975 Subaru station wagon across the Cascades, through Portland to Castle Rock, stopped to call his boss, and driven up the Toutle. Bill and Susan Tilton have driven their brown pickup from Seattle. From the roadgate they turn east through a sandpit onto a gravel road. A hiker ahead drops his pack behind a tree. They stop.

"He's a ranger."

"No, he's spooked like us. He thinks *we're* patrolling."

They crawl ahead. "Want a lift?"

Bruce Faddis retrieves his pack and climbs in. "Are we legal?"

"We hear it's a $500 fine. We're looking for a view."

"Well, I'm going up to meet Harry Truman."

But in two miles road 3310 ends at an old logging platform. They photograph Mount St. Helens. Faddis is peering through binoculars when the Tiltons turn west at 12:30.[3]

Near Spud Mountain this week, Brad Backstrom and Don Selby have photographed a backlit plume, sunset-red summit clouds, yesterday morning a plume dusting the south flank. "They're logging and planting nearby," says Backstrom. "People fish the rivers. If it's really dangerous they'd stop the logging and fishing. The worst up here would be ashfall." For that Selby's camper holds Army gas masks and cylinders of oxygen.

From Pullman, Bea and Barry Johnston drive their 1978 Jeep, Jim Fitzgerald his 1972 Datsun. Three miles west of the roadblock they turn up road 3000 and east to Spud Mountain. These geology students discuss the risks.

"The bulge could slide off and the Toutle flood."

"Any ashflow should stay in the valley."

"The ridges would stop it coming up."

They train binoculars on a helicopter at the crater [Stickney and Swanson]. A curley-redhaired guy with a black dog strolls up the road from a pickup.

"I'm here often," says Don Selby. "Here's my photos."

Bea flips through dark eruptions, red sunsets. "Beautiful," she says, "just why we've come."

The Johnstons hibachi hamburgers. Selby has one, and the dog. They open beers. But no action. At dusk Fitzgerald and the Johnstons drive to Silver Lake—Jim to camp, Barry and Bea to a motel. They'll meet early tomorrow at Spud Mountain.

Helicopter pilot Chuck Wolfe lands Portland General Electric's twin-turbine Messerschmitt-Bolkow MB-105 on Smith Creek Butte six miles east of Mount St. Helens. PGE engineer Ray Halicki and geologist Rick Kienle step to a plastic pool set out to trap ash. For PGE to operate Trojan nuclear plant on Columbia River, the Nuclear Regulatory Commission requires they monitor the volcano's ashfall. Glass in it could herald magmatic eruption. Major eruption could imperil the plant's cooling water. In PGE's chem lab it's Bob Kaseweter who studies the samples. The men bag the ash and climb into the ship, and Wolfe lifts off. One more sample—at the Forest Service campground at Spirit Lake.

They circle crater and bulge, snap photos. A civil engineer grounded in mechanics, Halicki stares at the steepness. So many wet spots, so many sloughs, far more broken than earlier. They descend toward the clearing.

"We'll not land," Halicki says over the intercom.

"Why not?" says Kienle.

"That bulge is too damn active and steep. It could break off at any time."

"This helicopter has guts. We'd just fly away."

"It'd come too fast for us to get off."

"But—"

"No! No landing."

Wolfe twists the throttle, pulls the collective, nudges the cyclic, and gains airspeed.

State Patrol Chief Landon in Olympia calls Capt. Bullock in Vancouver. "We may escort cabin owners to Spirit Lake today."

"That's not a good idea. Something'll happen there, and we don't know when."

"We *will* go if we need to, Dick. I'll need a few troopers."

"Well, we shouldn't order anyone. I'll ask for volunteers." Bullock dials Sgt. Elder in Kelso.

"Yeah, 'volunteers,'" says Russ Cavens. "Here's how it works. The sergeant calls in us troopers. 'We need three volunteers,' he says, pointing, 'You, You, and You.'" So troopers Cavens, Danny O'Neill, and Ron Spahman cruise toward the roadblock.

Chief Landon fetches Jim Hall at Emergency Services and heads south. At 11:30 Bullock's cruiser from Vancouver and Sgt. Elder's suburban from Kelso pull in at Toutle Lake High School. Cowlitz Sheriff Nelson comes in street jacket and cowboy hat, Skamania Sheriff Closner in pressed brown uniform. Chief Landon pulls in with Hall clutching liability forms. A few dozen people mill about. Pale-blue sweatshirts in Mount St. Helens' profile proclaim *I Own a Piece of the Rock*. Landon eyes the crowd. "Yesterday some said they'd pull down the roadgate," he says, "be armed. I see they've brought the worst of all weapons: TV news cameras."

The crowd doubles. Bud Will tells the *Columbian*, "I worry more of vandals at my cabin than the volcano." Another says, "They let the Boy Scouts in, now they're gonna let us in." World-War-II vet Chuck Williams barks, "We're going through the gate come hell or high water." Says Landon: "I've dealt with mobs—the Vietnam-war protests at University of Washington. You can lose control quickly. I'll have no such disorder here."

Commanding in starched blue uniform and campaign hat with gold braids, Landon argues a trip to Spirit Lake isn't worth the risk. Many glare back unpersuaded. If we don't take them in now, Landon sees, there'll be an unruly entry later. "If you insist," he says, "the governor has directed us to assist. But at your own risk: no one passes the gate without signing a waiver holding state and counties harmless if you're injured."

Seattle's KING-5 reporter Jeff Renner and a cameraman duck into a carryall for a story with Sandy Ford and Linda King. Cars head east. Two months ago Sharon Burchard drove the chilly valley under sullen skies and barren trees. In today's sun, maples leaf full, alders fledge light green, dogwoods dilate white, fir buds burst. Emerald bushes screen fall's umber. Fiddleheads unroll twenty to a clump. Broom yellows the roadbanks. Beneath the green bridge Toutle River flows clear and cold from melting snow.

Bob Kaseweter's sister Connie Pullen and family reach the empty roadblock before noon and turn up Weyerhaeuser's road. They rejoin the blacktop to the upper gate: ROAD CLOSED. Down comes a white camper-backed pickup. Harry Truman steps out in frayed green sweatshirt.

"I'm cutting firewood," he says.

"So you're staying. Y'know the geologists say—"

"Those longhairs don't know the mountain as I do. Why . . ." Truman rattles on, waving three stamped letters. At last he stoops and hands them to five-year-old Chris Pullen. "You'll mail these for me?"

"Sure," grins the blonde boy.

The Kaseweters stop at Coldwater to hike. Trooper O'Neill sends them down to sign in. Rob Smith and Kathy Paulson emerge from a logging road, and O'Neill sends them back.

A Patrol cruiser sits by the locked gate when *Daily News* reporters drive up at noon. They pull behind a 26-foot motorhome. A silverhair waves Roger Werth inside.

"I'm spotting for the state," says Gerry Martin. "Any way for my rig around this gate?"

"Red" gate, Truman's pickup beyond

As a college student Werth had worked summers as a Weyerhaeuser ranger. "Veer right onto road 3500. In five miles it crosses the highway. The 4000 line then takes you up a ridge." Werth steps out, and Martin drives his Dodge Superior up the gravel.

Of the crowd at Toutle only three dozen cars queue below the gate. George Bowers' van wears American flags and sprayed-on slogans: U.S. ALL THE WAY and DIXY OPEN THE GATE. Newsmen thumb on microphones.

"You've no right to keep us from our property!" a man growls at a Patrol trooper.

"Oh don't listen to him," a woman murmurs. "You're doing a good job." She passes oatmeal cookies the officers soon scarf down.

"We pay taxes!" says Sandy Ford. "We want to use our property."

"We've a right to go," says Linda King. "How'd Dixy like being locked off Fox Island?"

Jim and Pauline Lund occupied their cabin in the red zone until threatened with arrest. "It's our home, and we've a right to stay," Pauline says.

KIRO's Chopper 7 lands, and Brooks Burford and a cameraman amble to a red pickup for a story. The KOIN-6 chopper lands on a log road, and reporters emerge.

Down in Kelso, Cowlitz Sheriff Les Nelson mutters, "It's asinine to let in all those people ill equipped for disaster." Skamania Sheriff Bill Closner by the gate says, "Common sense says it's dangerous, like playing Russian roulette with the volcano. But some allege vandalism up there. It's my county, and we'll check it out."

"This is a beautiful Saturday assignment, and our job is to go behind the curtain," says *Seattle Times* reporter Suki Dardarian. "People scoff at what seems an absurd rule to keep them out. Yet the officers worry. Anything from the mountain and they'll shoo us out."

Thirty-five people sign the liability waivers on the hood of a State Patrol cruiser. "We'll stand by in case anything happens," Chief Landon announces. "Everyone out by six." Just after two o'clock a trooper swings open the gate. A few vehicles pass, then Landon and Closner in the brown Mercury. More cars and pickups, and a State Patrol Suburban and cruiser. Reporters of the *Daily News*, *Oregonian*, and *Seattle Times*, *Oregon Journal* reporter Don Hamilton in opentop MGB. Deputy Bob Dieter drives a county Plymouth, deputy Barker a brown Blazer. KIRO's chopper lifts Patrol Sgt. Bob Johnson upvalley. From a Patrol Cessna, Dave Gardner and Bob Cory monitor mountain and convoy. Cars turn left and right off onto gravel roads. Police vehicles drive on to Truman's Mount St. Helens Lodge.

From Coldwater I photographer Reid Blackburn watches cars round a highway turn, cross Coldwater bridge, and crawl like ants up a straightaway. He's thrice punched the transmitter and the cameras shot serene Mount St. Helens.

In Olympia, DES Director Chow signs a cover letter for yesterday's proposal for a western blue zone. "Put it there with the rest," says a governor's office aide. In Port Townsend, Governor Ray watches the Rhododendron Festival Parade. A rogue truck cuts in from the side and crawls past the reviewing stand. On its flatbed lies a fat dead hog lettered in red: **Dixy**.

Former Navy buddies Charles McNerney and John Smart now work in Seattle, McNerney at SeaFirst Bank, Smart in a steel mill. In McNerney's Honda Prelude they cruise up the Toutle to a State Patrol car at the roadgate.[4] But a gravel way right has no cops. McNerney turns up road 3500. They cross Castle Creek and branch south up the 3800 to a logging platform. Smart sets camp; McNerney shoots the sundrenched mountain seven miles away. After dark McNerney trips on a log, and his cigarette lighter lobs into alder blackness.

Edward "Buzz" Smith, a Weyerhaeuser logger who's often hiked the backcountry, packs his 1976 Chevy pickup for a campout with his boys—Eric 10, Adam 7. They're bound for Island Lake in mountains eleven miles north of Mount St. Helens. They motor up the highway and road 2500 east and park by other cars at a bridge. They hike up Green River past a campsite, cross Green River on a log bridge, hike Miners Creek up to a bluff, and tent in big firs.[5]

From Silver Lake, Mike and Lu Moore with Bonnie Lu (four years) and Terra Dawn (three months) drive up the North Fork. They wind up roads 3100 and 3130 and hike to old Gilbert Ridge lookout. A geology graduate, Mike photographs Mount St. Helens ten miles southeast. They drive down Shultz Creek, up Green River, and park at a bridge by other rigs.

Up the trail they pass a shack and small tent, and by farther tents chat with two young couples. They amble through fragrant firs, pass Miners Creek fork, cross some windfall, and set camp among oldgrowth by defunct Independence Mine.

Five miles southwest, contract logger Keith Ross yards timber on an east tributary of Shultz Creek, his 110-foot tower dragging in a half million board feet in logs felled by road 3922. Don Crick and Ken McCarthy fell trees nearby on the 3921. During a break tomorrow Crick's son-in-law Tom Gadwa and Wally Bowers will fill in.

William and Jean Parker of Portland, Mazamas clubbers often in the mountains, crawl up road 3500 in their palegreen GMC pickup and camper full of outdoor gear. A spiral spur brings them to a clearcut knoll above Hanaford Lake. Three deep valleys separate them from Mount St. Helens nine miles south. Mount Rainier's white bulk looms farther north. From a wide stump Bill in blue flannel shirt smiles into Jean's photo.

Blackbearded Vietnam-vet Clyde Croft drives a borrowed brown pickup south up Quartz Creek road to Ryan Lake 12½ miles northeast of Mount St. Helens. He and Alan Handy untrailer horses, cinch the saddles, lash on packs, and turn the nickering noses west. They ride down Forest Road 1203 toward Green River. By abandoned Polar Star Mine they drop the saddles and kindle a fire.

Four miles southeast, campers among bulldozed stumps watch the volcano from the high log landing off road 100. Geophysics grad student Keith Ronnholm comes in his Toyota pickup, Viola and Wendell Johnson in their Ranchero and trailer. Gary Rosenquist and Joel and Linda Harvey drive in at dusk. They laugh and sip beer by a fire far into the night.

Catherine and Paul Hickson tent by road 125 east of the volcano. Their sunset photograph shows in silhouette the north punched far out. Opposite on the west, Ty and Marianna Kearney, spotters for the state, have since Tuesday parked their Dodge campervan on the height of road 5700. Marianna scans the northwest flank she'd climbed with the Mazamas 35 years ago.[6]

Seven miles northeast, Gerry Martin steers his Dodge Superior up road 4040 past a logging tower and loader. He parks in a saddle facing the volcano. A man moves by a trailer and tan car a mile south—Coldwater II. Martin and the Kearneys radio on the two-meter amateur band.

Francisco Valenzuela starts his summer job with Gifford Pinchot National Forest tomorrow. Today he explores Forest road 8117 on the volcano's west in his Ford Pinto. Robert Rogers has twice climbed to the crater since the mountain's closure. Today he stops his 1965 Simca at a saddle near Goat Mountain and scouts a new route. Valenzuela climbs in. They wind gravel roads down into the South Fork and east to the red zone. Valenzuela won't risk a trespass, and they retreat. Across the valley an orange tent stands by a palegreen pickup in a clearcut.

Robert Landsburg is camped just west. Camera tripoded at 7:45 AM, he'd scribbled to a notebook: *a lot of people. . . would. . . enjoy being here, but everything considered, it's better. . . I'm alone.*

And at 12:15: *It's almost like waiting for a salmon to hit. Feel right on the verge of something.*

Young Roald Reitan and Venus Dergan drive from Tacoma to Jericho Hole on the South Fork. On this inside bend they cast all afternoon for steelhead, the air hot, river frigid. They tent five feet above the river and thirty feet back.

USGS's David Johnston drives a Ford Pinto up the North Fork past road 4000, unsure where Coldwater II lies. The highway takes him to Timberline. Lon Stickney lands for him, then at Coldwater II for Harry Glicken. Stickney drops Johnston at

9200 feet on The Boot to resample steam vents. After a stop by Toutle site for Swanson and Wörner, Stickney returns Glicken to Coldwater II.

A strong earthquake shakes Coldwater II, Glicken writes at 2:42. Wörner stands with the theodolite at Toutle site when the ground sways. He cradles the tripod as rocks tumble past. At Timberline the helicopter's twirling blades warp up and down. The slopes come alive.

"Big avalanche!" Stickney radios. "Coming down all over the place! Dave, you okay?"

"Come get me."

"Quick as I can."

The helicopter climbs, slowly—*that damn sticky valve*. Stickney touches skids, Johnston jumps in, and they're off three minutes after the quake.

From Timberline Johnston drives ten miles west, turns onto road 4000, and grinds up the 4020. He steps into cool air at Coldwater II. It's barely spring at altitude 4500 feet—lingering snowbanks, barely budded aldersticks.

David Johnston at Coldwater II

Having no time together these two weeks, Glicken and Johnston chat. "Why's a trailer on the north ridge?" Johnston asks. "Is it official?"[7]

"Who knows? It came this afternoon."

"How'd it get in?"

"I don't know . . . Say, what about the earthquake at 2:42?"

"The Boot kicked me on my ass. Cracks opened and closed."

"And two weeks ago you went to the base of the crater."

"That was scary too. But let's keep quiet. I don't want the press to think me a show-off."

"You do it for science."

"The risks are real. We can't encourage others."

"Well, I'm off to Long Valley tomorrow. Back here next weekend."

"Ah . . . we've arranged others to cover Coldwater. I need you in Menlo Park with these gas samples."

"Well, maybe it's best," grins Glicken. "If I die here, no one'll remember an assistant. If *you* get nailed they might name it for you."[8]

At the base of this ridge *Oregonian* reporter Les Zaitz watches people load a Foosball machine from a cabin into a pickup. Into others go leather chair, piano, fishing poles, framed photos, barbecue grill. "They're quick," Zaitz says. "Throw a few things in and get the hell out."

Pauline Lund eyes the ash around her home. "When the weather's clear like today the mountain sleeps," she tells reporter Don Hamilton. "But when it's cloudy she shakes down her skirt and goes wild." Chased out a week ago, the Lunds had left food for the cat. Pauline refills the bowl—meaning to return, Zaitz sees.

"I only came to visit," laughs Linda King. "In Kelso my husband said, 'Now don't bring down a bunch of shit we'll have to haul back in a month.' Climbing the stairs you feel this place shake. I thought earthquakes would break things. But nothing's amiss—not even the stemmed glasses on that wobbly crate. There's no proof of shaking here. I'd stay the night."

Sandy Ford steps from her cabin with a box of liquor as *Seattle Times*'s Geoff Manasse frames a shot, the volcano poking above firs. "Nice," says Manasse, "—if only I had an explosion."

King and Ford stop at Spirit Lake Lodge where Rob Smith (King's brother) and Kathy Paulson spruce up. "The mountain's quiet," says Smith, "the bulge dark and ominous like something about to happen. People have slipped around the roadblocks, and today I found the lodge broken into *again*, the front door kicked in."

"They dirtied the kitchen," says Paulson, "slept in beds. Today we wash dishes, make beds—get ready for the next visitor."

Smith cooks burgers and fries for neighbors. Young brother Mark comes with friends. They open beers and flip through photos. "The threat here's vandals, not the volcano."

Pat and Chuck Long check the cabin they'd built last summer, its deck ash-dusted. "It's so quiet," says Pat, "no wind, no birds." A small earthquake. "Like many earlier I suppose—yet nothing's dislodged." KOIN's helicopter lands in the meadow. As the cameraman sets up on the deck, Pat dashes down and charms the pilot into a tour. Driving west, the Longs pause at Deadman's curve. "A terrible rotten-egg sulfur stink comes down Dry Gulch," Pat says. "Still no birds." A trooper escorts them to the gate.

Connie Pullen climbs to the south deck of her brother's A-frame. Bob Kaseweter and Bev Wetherald peer through tripoded cameras, another weekend here with the seismometer.

Daily News reporters come. Bob and Bev grin into Roger Werth's lens. "Nice view," says Rick Seifert.

CONNIE PULLEN

Bev Wetherald and Bob Kaseweter

"People by the river laughed when I built this high," Kaseweter says. "Now when a flood comes those cabins will float up here."

"There *is* a bit of danger here," smiles Wetherald.

"I don't think it all that dangerous," says Kaseweter. "Any lava would be thick and slow."[9]

"What'd happen here in an eruption?" Pullen says.

"Some ash. Mud could hit cabins by the river but not up here. In a worst case rocks could fly everywhere. But first I think my seismometer would show something, and we'd leave."

Oregon Journal reporter Don Hamilton trails officers into Mount St. Helens Lodge. A sergeant introduces Patrol Chief Landon to Truman. So commanding at Toutle, Landon's deferential here, Hamilton sees. Lawmen and reporters and cabin owners mill about, some new to Truman, others old friends.

"This place is filthy. It reeks of cats."

"It was spotless while Eddie lived."

"*He's* dirty, and his clothes."

"He charms the press now but for years has been an arrogant butthead."

"A foulmouthed old drunk three sheets to the wind."

"Only one. He keeps an even keel."

Christmas balls dangle in the kitchen window. A Coca-Cola promo bottle hangs on a nail, and a wooden sign. An earthquake: the balls tinkle on glass, the bottle sways, the sign thumps. "My seismometer," laughs Truman. "That's a four-point-two."

A quarter hour later another shudder, less clattering. "And that's a three-point-six. It's like this every goddam day."

"The lodge is full of cats and smells of it," says Sgt. Elder. "And Truman's so profane—goddam this, sonofabitch that. Chief Landon takes just so much then steps out."

Up here at 3200 feet it's early spring. Noble firs drape pollen sacs like old blood, buds swell the spiky tops. Cottonwoods fledge yellow, alders palegreen. Coltsfoot blooms underfoot, and Indian plum. Dandelions spread over midweek's gray ash in Truman's spare lawn. "I stroll by the lake, this sunny afternoon," says Landon. "Snowbanks melt, trilliums bloom, a trout follows at the edge of the water."

"Truman walks us down to the lounge," says Sgt. Elder. "He'd made the bar from one piece of myrtle, polished and shellacked, a fine piece of work." Truman sits in a redvinyl booth, kerosene lamp on the table. He looks through binoculars up the arm of lake. "That swelled area keeps growing," he points, "and I'm filming it."

"We walk to the boathouse," says Sgt. Johnson. "It's quiet: no birds, no wind. At the end of the dock the lake bottom's clear seven feet down."

"The boathouse is full of canoes and dinghies," says Trooper Russ Cavens. "An old wooden Chris Craft sits on blocks—6 cylinders, dual carbs, a cherry."

"A boat in the water with supplies is ready to go" says Sgt. Johnson. "Up in a shed he stores all kinds of old stuff—a 1956 Cadillac."

Daily News reporters tramp into the lodge at 3:30. "Everybody in the goddam country's up here," Truman growls.

"Oh c'mon, Harry," says Roger Werth coaxing him toward sunlight. "How about a photo?"

Landon and Truman at Mount St. Helens Lodge

SGT. 'WICK' ELDER

Truman sits on red-cement steps and squints into sun. Werth punches the shutter. In worn blue denim and greasy high-laced shoes, Truman looks isolated and vulnerable—so unlike the dapper leisure suit and broad smile at Brooks school Wednesday. "As I shoot this photograph," Werth says, "Harry's pissed at me for dragging him outside. He scowls as if to say, 'I'll go along with this but let's get it over.' But I also think he's scared. With all the people and news he's boxed in. I think he feels if he goes out now and nothing happens, he couldn't save face."

Landon sits beside Truman and Sgt. Elder clicks off two, Truman allowing a faint smile. "This place is spectacular," says Elder, "sun, bumblebees, hummingbirds." He zooms on Mount St. Helens, summit hidden by the ashy bulge. "You can't see it all from here," Truman says. "A few days ago I canoed over to Bear Cove. There it looks much bigger."

"Isn't staying here risky?" Rick Seifert asks.

"I flew biwings in World-War One," glares Truman. "*That* was risk. I flew a Taylorcraft in and out of here for years. You go in a circle and watch for logs until a pontoon lifts off. That's how you get off the goddam lake. I know about risk."

Truman tugs Don Hamilton's sleeve. "You want to stay the night?"

"Y'know, I'd like to but must file a report."

Hamilton climbs into his MGB, his passenger Steve Meredith, news director of Vancouver radio KGAR. Meredith plays back his Truman tape—in every sentence a goddam, a hell, a sonofabitch, a shit. "Jeeze," says Meredith, "I don't think I can put any of this on the air."

Thursday's Spirit Lake airlift left four long canoes on the Boy Scout beach. Larry Thomas and four others drive to the dock east of Truman's and motor across. They tip the canoes into the water and tow them south. Beneath beautiful firs they pull out sleeping bags and a stove. A deputy drives in. "You guys looking to stay?"

"Just the night."

"No you're not. Everyone goes out."

Down at the roadgate State Patrol Capt. Bullock and Lt. Don Mason have checked people back out. They stroll about the two dozen cars in the sandpit, chatting with Eleanor and Ed Murphy by their motorhome and with a young couple. From a tape Jimmy Buffett wails: *I don't know where I'm a-gonna go, When the volcano blows . . .*"

Lon Stickney lands USGS's Swanson and Wörner at Timberline. Despite yesterday's new site on road 100, Swanson is loathe to stop the measurements here. "I'd abandon an old friend," he says. They shoot Goat Rocks through the theodolite. The brown Mercury swings into Timberline and Landon and Closner step out. The uniforms climb the knoll. Swanson looks up from the tripod: "What're *you* guys doing here? Don't you know it's *dangerous*?"

"He explains the surveying," says Landon, "the cracked area ballooned out 500 feet." A county Blazer drives in. Deputy Barker photographs the two chiefs before the black bulge. The officers drive off.

Landon and Closner stand outside Mount St. Helens Lodge, Barker a pace behind. Truman's presence encourages others, but Closner isn't keen on moving him from his only home. A week ago Truman showed Closner the governor's letter: "your independence a fine example for all of us." Yet neighbors complain of the inconsistency. Days ago Closner said only voting residents could stay. Rob Smith then complained he and the Lunds lived here until being chased out.

The sheriff fishes from his pocket a commission card inked in the name of Harry Truman. "If I deputize him," he says, "it solves our problem."

"Er . . . two weeks ago he waved a gun at reporters," murmurs Barker. "If you commission him, what if they print *that*?"

Closner pauses. He slips the card back to his pocket.

"The governor asked me to bring Truman out with us," Landon says. "I'll give him no choice."[10]

"I wish you'd not do that," says Closner. "Cabin owners alleged vandalism, but we've found nothing. Truman's a reason."

"Well . . . It's your jurisdiction."

"You *can* support my request to exempt him from the closure."

Landon and Closner drive downvalley. Most people have signed out the gate, but one car is missing. The Patrol had handed David Johnston a police Motorola.

"We're looking for two newsmen," Landon radios. "It's past time."

"They're here," says Johnston, "reporter and photographer."

"Send them down! If I have to come up I'll put them in jail."

At Mount St. Helens Lodge, Sgt. Johnson pulls a satchel from a patrol car and hands it to Truman: letters from schoolkids in Woodland. The old man's eyes water over. He's sentimental, Johnson sees, worried about this place and now weeping that children think of him. He's trapped by the publicity. He may *want* us to take him.

"Why don't you come down with us?" asks Johnson. "I've a seat for you."

"Well, thanks. But I'll stay here at home."

"It's up to you. Here's my card. Call if you need anything. We'll be back tomorrow."

A mile west, Rob Smith and Kathy Paulson finish at Spirit Lake Lodge. "Earthquakes today shook the place and rattled dishes," Paulson says. "Rob talks of staying the night but I say 'No way.' We cleaned today, then friends came. No time for Rob's things. His truck's empty"

"Spirit Lake Lodge is my home," says Smith, "all my clothes, furniture, and tools here. We'll load them tomorrow."

"We drive up to Mount St. Helens Lodge, " Paulson says, "and Truman comes out with our cat! It had wandered the mile up here."

Smith steps out. "Harry, can I bring your mail tomorrow?"

"Don't bother. I'll drive down in a couple days for supplies and primroses."

"Truman's not at all his press image," Paulson says. "He's lonely, quiet, apprehensive."

"Time to go," Sgt. Elder calls.

"Truman grips my arm tightly," Smith says. "His eyes tear up—and mine."

"Oh c'mon," whispers Truman, "let's keep a stiff upper lip."

"He wants us to stay, but we can't," Paulson says. Smith hands Paulson the cat and slides behind the wheel. They drive out the hollow highway. By the river among firs where it's stood four decades, tidy stone-faced Spirit Lake Lodge awaits its next visitor.

Sergeants Elder and Johnson and deputy Barker search for stragglers. Elder tracks an aroma of barbecue to an A-frame. But Bob Kaseweter and Bev Wetherald hold a permit. The sun sinks below trees when troopers shut the upper gate and snap the lock. By 7:45 all have signed out the lower gate. A trooper swings it shut. The officers will return tomorrow for people who couldn't come today. On a police radio, DES's Jim Hall summons Coldwater II.

"We'll be back in morning. Anything new about the mountain?"

"No," says David Johnston, "and no reason to think it'll be different tomorrow."[11]

In Seattle the seismologists watch round the clock—Captain Twilight, Captain Midnight, Captain Daylight. "We seek a spike in seismicity or a cessation," says Steve Malone.

The Forest Service radio log is uneventful. Surveillance plane four-niner-golf radios 10:37 to 10:57 of steam venting from high on the bulge and Shoestring Glacier. An afternoon sortie reports "very little change," a 3:50 photo showing the familiar cracked bulge.

Hot weather and low humidity forecast for Sunday evoke fire hazard. East-flank tree planters must move higher. In evening Forest Service's Kathy Anderson calls the USGS. "We'll watch from Coldwater tomorrow," Dan Miller says, "and watch the seismograph in Vancouver. We can probably give a few-hour's warning."

The KING5 crew files a story. On NBC news a Florida family sees cousin Linda King kiss her Spirit Lake cabin goodbye.

Radio friends come to the Kearney's camp potlucking soup, hamburgers, baked beans, and cocoa, then leave. Robert Rogers and Francisco Valenzuela climb from the South Fork. Finding the van on the high spot of the 5700, they camp just west. Marianna Kearney sits under the amber mountain and a sky full of stars—another fine night like so many others.

Don and Natalie Parker and nephew Rick bed down in the chalet by Florence Creek. Lindsey Thomas gripes at buying a blue-zone pass he'll not use: he'll spend tomorrow at the racetrack.

Larry McCulley, Joe Findley, and four others drive road 125 south and camp on Clear Creek. About 11:20 PM McCulley sees an orange glow near the volcano's top and hears a hiss of pressured steam. Findley fishes in dark off a jam of logs. They shift in an earthquake at 11:30. He folds his pole and heads for camp.

Coldwater I

Fred Stocker wearies of Reid Blackburn. "How about a steak dinner?" he asks. Jim McWhirter's van bumps down gravel toward pavement and Tumwater.

On the platform above Maratta Creek, Blackburn punches the transmitter and the two Nikon cameras snap a frame of Mount St. Helens: 6:41 PM ① CLEAR W/ THIN CLOUD. He radios a phone patch to Fay in Vancouver but talks to the message tape.

Steve Small flies again. "Ralph Perry would give teeth to be in your place," he radios.

"Nice I'm the radio ham," says Blackburn.

"I see steam vents in this low light."

"I got some in a morning shot."

"Below I see our old route up Dog's Head."

"Bring your backpack tomorrow and we'll climb."

Columbian reporter Bill Stewart drives the empty highway and turns onto the gravel way. Blackburn drives down.

Stewart hands a 20-roll brick of Ektachrome.[12] "A lot of film, so you're staying."

"I don't want to miss anything. Come up for the night: there's a spare tent."

"But no one'd know where I am."

Stewart turns west. Blackburn grinds up the graying valley.

Coldwater II

USGS's Mindy Brugman and Carolyn Driedger find the helicopter at Timberline. They want a lift to Shoestring Glacier, but it's late and pilot Lon Stickney tired. Swanson rushes theodolite shots. The helicopter with a stuck valve is going to the shop, so he'll cache the Geodimeter for tomorrow. Stickney flies to Vancouver with Swanson and Wörner, then to Seattle at dusk.

Brugman and Driedger haul the Geodimeter down the highway and up the gravel way to Coldwater II. David Johnston and Harry Glicken discuss today's adventures. "That earthquake was *spectacular* on The Boot," Johnston says. The four take turns in a director's chair trying to raise a hand just before the next steam puff—directing the enduring pageant of Mount St. Helens.

A trailer atop the north ridge faces the mountain. "It's crazy to watch so close," Brugman says—from this spot even closer. "But I've known Mount St. Helens since a kid—swam in Spirit Lake, climbed the summit, fondue-partied, watched elk there cross the crater, skied down Forsyth Glacier."

The women pull out sleeping bags. "You're perfectly safe here, aren't you?"

"I'm not sure," Johnston says. The mood sombers. He tells of being trapped on Augustine during eruptions, almost not getting off. "This place may be dangerous."

As Driedger remembers he goes on to say: "See that bulge? A landslide could cross the valley and ride up this ridge."

As Brugman remembers, Johnston goes on to say: "A landslide off the bulge could uncork a hot flow across the valley and up this ridge."[13]

"That's hard to believe."

"Oh yes, it could."

"We want to camp."

"No, too risky. Only one's needed here."

Brugman and Driedger bounce down 4020, then the 3500 past elk. Under Elk Rock they turn onto pavement, down the shadowed slot where Sharon Burchard crept up past confused elk two months ago. Light bleeds from the valley.

Johnston and Glicken laser the Goat Rocks prism. The bulge has swelled 2¾ feet since Brugman's shot yesterday morning.

The last entry to Coldwater book B in Glicken's hand reads: *21:00 Harry Glicken leaves, Dave takes over using log book A.*

In the gloaming David Johnston radios Dan Miller in Vancouver. "The earthquake at 14:42—what was its magnitude? I was sampling fumaroles, and it rolled me."

"The record here shows a good-sized one, a four-point-five or five."[14]

"Lon says it shook slides down the north side. It *really* got me on The Boot. Cracks opened and rocks fell all around."

"I'd like to hear more next time you're back. By the way, the National Guard will bring up an armored personnel carrier tomorrow."

"You're *serious*?[15]

"We're serious."

Don Swanson radios. At Coldwater II tomorrow, Swanson will shoot the Geodimeter, Johnston the Laser Ranger. They'll compare numbers from the two instruments measuring the contracting distance to Goat Rocks.

Assuming there'll be a tomorrow.

6

Totally Clear, No Activity

Have you not heard of them that were made to err? Those you see in
pieces at the bottom of this mountain are an example to others to take
heed how they clamber too high.

—John Bunyan, *Pilgrim's Progress* (condensed)

Sunday morning the 18th, USGS's Bob Christiansen in Vancouver radios Coldwater
II. David Johnston quotes three laser measurements to Goat Rocks since 5:50.

"What's it like up there, Dave?"

"Very nice, totally clear. You can see the mountain entirely. About ten degrees C."

"A little brisk. Any S-O-2 this morning?"

"No, heh, heh, but a little H-2-S from here."

At USGS staff meeting the bulge still bulges, Swanson says. Shoestring Glacier
moves as earlier, Brugman says. A fumarole on The Boot measured 87°C yesterday,
Johnston had radioed. Two armored vehicles coming, one today for Coldwater II,
Miller says.

If the geologists sense eruption draws near, radio and meeting exude no urgency
an hour before horror. Nor do anyone's field notes, the logbooks, or flight talk. It
seems the volcano's earthquakey bulging could continue weeks.

Reporter Hugh Clark interviews USGS's Robert Decker in Hawaii. Will Mount St.
Helens blow? How big?

"If I thought it'd erupt soon I'd not have come back," says Decker. "In the past it's
had many small eruptions, few large ones. It could be big this time—the symptoms
are unusual. But if I were a gambling man I'd bet this eruption small."

The *Honolulu Advertiser* runs the piece Sunday.

Bob Tokarczyk, supervisor of Gifford Pinchot National Forest, had on Friday sent
Barry Voight's report with its idea of giant landslide to state Emergency Services. It
lies in the office of Dixy Lee Ray by the sheriffs' urgent proposal for a northwest blue
zone. But the governor at Fox Island feeds pigs and rakes turds. State Patrol Sgt. Ron
Walcker stands by the shining limo to chauffeur her to a Seattle meeting with the
Teamsters.

David Crockett of KOMO television awakes at three-thirty. He packs betacam,
still camera, and lenses into a white company Mercury. From Bellevue he drives to
Toutle and bounces up the South Fork on road 4100. At 8:32 he steps out and focuses
a lens on Mount St. Helens.

Having felt several overnight earthquakes, Robert Rogers and Francisco Valenzuela drive down into the South Fork again and east to the logging platform. They
hike up Sheep Canyon trail to a meadow by Forest road 859. Rogers climbs above

scrub firs, photographs the mountain about 7:45, and scouts a climbing route. Valenzuela lies on a twelve-foot log. It twitches—a small earthquake he couldn't feel standing. Another jiggle. These and the illegality of being in the red zone sum to clarity. Rogers returns. "It's too damned uncomfortable here," Valenzuela says. "We've gotta go." They hike back down.

Through binoculars they see no one at an orange tent the north valley side, but Valenzuela glimpses a sleeping bag in the pickup bed. Fifty yards west a green station wagon pointed downvalley is ready to go. A tripod holds a camera aimed at the volcano. The men drive back to camp. Soft air floats from the west. A canopied pickup creeps near Spud Mountain.

From his Dodge van on road 5700, Ty Kearney radios Gerry Martin north of Mount St. Helens. They discuss steam wafting from the crater. A tan cloud drifts by Wishbone Glacier. Marianna Kearney sketches the shadowed mountain. I've all day, she thinks, to paint a watercolor. Valenzuela sits on a stump ten yards back, peels an orange, and eyes the summit.

Across the valley at the station wagon Robert Landsburg had mounted a camera at five and scribbled of calm weather. At eight he notes his viewframe. Then these:

8:20 The road is part of it now…in this morning back light. I like my composition… [obliterated] better.

[obliterated lines]

8:25 From the crater steam is spilling lightly down the north flank, falling silently through the Goat Rocks. The sun…

[obliterated lines]

Oh God, it is exciting. ☺

He shoots six photographs.

Higher and three miles west, Brad Backstrom and Don Selby

AUTHOR COLLECTION

awake in the pickup. Backstrom eyes a two-day residue: two dozen dead soldiers.

"I'm going to Toutle for a couple six-packs," he says.

"A long way just for beer."

"I'll bring some food."

Backstrom steers his Celica down the South Fork to the highway. He gasses the car at Drew's and steps into the store.

Jim Fitzgerald stops his Datsun at yesterday's spot a little above Selby. He screws his camera to a tripod. Mount St. Helens fills the lens in backlit shadow.

Four miles north at Coldwater I, Reid Blackburn stabs the transmitter. The two cameras snap another frame of Mount St. Helens. He jots in a notebook:

7:11 AM ① TOTALLY CLEAR, NO ACTIVITY.

Two miles west, Arlene Edwards and daughter Jolene stand atop Elk Rock. They'd left home in Portland at five, driven to the roadblock, and apparently took on Bruce Faddis.[1] Arlene snaked her white 1978 Dodge pickup up the 3300 west of Elk Rock, across Hoffstadt basin on the 3340, up the 3130 to Gilbert Ridge and the 3540 south to Elk Rock. They'd tailgated a snack, then with two dogs scrambled up 90 feet. At 8:30 they stand on two summit knobs and aim cameras to backlit Mount St. Helens ten miles southeast.

Ed and Eleanor Murphy awake in their Southwind motorhome by the roadblock. Ed climbs into the little Plymouth Cricket, towbar folded up, and turns onto the pavement. He waves to two young men tossing a Frisbee and drives to Kid Valley. Cruising back with breakfast, he nears Camp Baker at 8:32.

From their Silver Lake motel, Bea and Barry Johnston had driven their CJ-7 Jeep past Camp Baker toward Spud Mountain.

"Y'know I don't want to sit up there all day without breakfast," Barry said.

"You never want breakfast."

"I do now."

They'd turned back. Now full of toast and eggs, they motor southeast, Bea smouldering: they should be up with Jim Fitzgerald this crystalline morning. They pass Camp Baker at 8:31.

Jim Scymanky, Leonty Skorohodoff, Evlanty Sharipoff, and José Dias wake in the Hoffstadt quarry. Frying eggs on a camp stove, they give no thought to hidden Mount St. Helens.

"Let's go to town," says Dias.

"No. We can finish the cut today."

But Dias, a Catholic, won't work Sunday. He stays at Leonty's pickup on upper road 3200. The other three walk half a mile down to the lower 3200, cross a clear brook, and scramble upslope. They pull saws from the brush and power up. They thin six- to ten-inch firs, leaving bigger ones, working upslope.

Dias ambles down, and the cutters quiet the saws. They shout in Spanish.

"Grab a saw!" Scymanky calls. "Ten acres left. You help and we'll finish."

"Not on Sunday." He trudges back to the truck.

Ron and Barbara Seibold climb into their red Chevy Blazer with Michelle and Kevin, 11 and 9, and motor south. Ron—DOT engineer, outdoorsman, president of the Olympia Mountaineers—has often brought family to the hills near Elk Rock. From the Spirit Lake highway they turn up road 2500, the fast gravel way up the Green. They turn south onto the 2800, cross a bridge, and wind up the 2530, 2336, and 3545 to the head of Shultz Creek. They turn west up the 3540 under Gilbert lookout. Longshadowed Mount St. Helens lies ten miles away.

From Toledo 35-year-old Tom Gadwa drives his red 1972 Chevy pickup south to Winlock, and in climbs 41-year-old Wally Bowers. One of Jim Pluard's men cutting below Coldwater II, Bowers has two kids, and wife LaVada fights cancer. With his own swelling mountain of unpaid bills, he moonlights weekends. They drive up road 2500, the 2800 across Green River, and the 3900. The 3921 spur ends ten miles northwest of Mount St. Helens.[2] Bowers stuffs wallet and thermos into a pack. Gadwa throttles his saw into a 150-foot yellow cedar. Bowers trims the flared base of a cedar and starts his undercut.

Weyerhaeuser's foremen patrol the woods against vandalism. Jim Pluard will show wife Kathleen she shouldn't worry about his cutting sides farther out than the USGS post. They scribble a note in their kitchen: "7:30. Gone to the mountain. Back in two hours." Pluard drives the yellow company pickup up the highway, skirts the gate, and on to Coldwater. He turns up roads 4000 onto the 4020.

Atop this ridge David Johnston scribbles in a fieldbook at Coldwater II. The Laser Ranger awaits another shot on Goat Rocks.

In his Dodge motorhome a mile north, Gerry Martin chats by ham radio with Ty Kearney. Through the repeater state agent Reade Apgar listens in Olympia.

John Killian casts for a trout from his rubber raft on Fawn Lake. Wrapped in a blanket and holding her white poodle, wife Christy watches from the pickup at the outlet brook.

Five miles northwest, Dale and Leslie Davis and Al Brooks in a Ford pickup climb road 2810 up Shultz Creek toward a pass and view of Mount St. Helens.

Six miles west, Mike Hubbard, Keith Moore, and Robert Payne fish for steelhead on muttering Green River.

Nine miles upriver Bruce Nelson and Sue Ruff stoke a fire. Terry Crall hooks a big steelhead, loses it, climbs to the terrace, and tugs at the snarled line. Dan Balch and Brian Thomas doze in their tent sixty yards west.

Ten miles southeast on road 100 above Bear Meadow, Keith Ronnholm awakes and glances out his Toyota pickup: no summit steam. Gary Rosenquist has been up all night at the fire with Linda and Joel Harvey, licking lager, swapping lies. He screws a camera to a tripod, frames the ashy pyramid in cerulean sky, and punches the shutter.

Ten miles south, Cathy and Paul Hickson strike camp, drive road 125 south, fill a water jug at a culvert, drive back north, and turn up into a rock quarry. At 8:30 Mount St. Helens in full east sun is asymmetric, a great bump on the north. From the crater notch a wisp of steam.

Planting crews drive into clearcuts south-southeast of Mount St. Helens. Forest Service supervisors Kathy Anderson and Kran Kilpatrick approach Forest road 71.

Climbers pant up Mount Rainier 50 miles northeast of Mount St. Helens, Mount Adams 33 miles east, and Mount Hood 60 miles southeast.

From home above Columbia River at Rainier, Jim Rombach eyes Mount St. Helens 38 miles east. This Weyerhaeuser engineer packs his family for a drive up road 1600 to Hemlock Pass overlook, then down to the South Fork. Finding an easy loop for sightseers might keep hundreds off roads near logging. Driving his 1976 Chevy will show the way isn't too rough.

State Patrol officers ready for another convoy to Spirit Lake. Thinking the upper valley risky, Capt. Dick Bullock had pondered retirement this morning. "I had a hard time getting my uniform on," he says. "But maybe no one'll come." At 8:32 he pumps petrol into his patrol car.

Mary and Harold Whitney breakfast in Portland thinking of the cabin they'd built in 1952 on a half acre Mary inherited near grandpa Lange's old store. On television men had said they'd force the roadblock Saturday with pickups and rifles. The Whitneys want no part in a mob. After church today they'll go in quietly—if the State Patrol allows.

At 8:18 a United Airlines Boeing 727 lifts off Sea-Tac south toward San Francisco. Another flies north toward Seattle. A Northwest Airlines DC-10 takes off north at 8:23.

From Yakima, Keith and Dorothy Stoffel fly in a Cessna 182 with pilot Bruce Judson. They circle Mount St. Helens thrice. From the north at 8:20 they look across dark forest and glassy Spirit Lake to Truman's spread in the south-shore clearing. A red pickup ambles up the highway toward Timberline.[3] Now one last eastward pass by the summit. At altitude 9900 feet, they near the gaping crater at 8:32. All is calm, all is bright.

From afternoon March 20 to morning May 18, Mount St. Helens released more than 10,000 earthquakes, 7000 of them magnitude 2 and larger, at least 289 magnitudes 4 and 5.[4] Within this ashen elevation the next will be no larger.

Let's Get the Hell Out of Here!

Bulge

Goat Rocks

Stoffels' air view of the summit about 8:00 AM, May 18

18 May 1980

Vancouver!   Vancouver!   This is it!
—David Johnston

An Auroral dawn opens Sunday May 18. Around Mount St. Helens and in communities beyond, people stretch, ignite a flame for coffee . . .

"It's a beautiful day here. Everything's quiet, no activity at all . . . Oh wait!"
"Earthquake . . . shakin' . . . there's a whole . . ."
"Holy shit!"

People across hundreds of square miles speak at once. To take in the coming details, let us survey the whole. Mount St. Helens' eruption was savage even by volcano standards. Two catastrophes—colossal landslides, forest-flattening hot surge—were almost new to science. Each witness experiences parts of different phenomena. A synopsis anchors each description within an order assembled from airborne observers, instruments, photographs, accounts of witnesses, and geologic fieldwork.[1]

First our journey so far. Earthquakes beneath Mount St. Helens began March 20 and jumped in number and size, by March 25, to some thirty magnitude 3 or larger a day. A small March 27 burst blasted out a crater, and cracks unzipped north of the summit. Earthquakes continued seven weeks, several magnitude 4s a day. Small black eruptions shot up intermittently until April 22, stopped, resumed May 7, stopped again the 15th. The summit craters widened and subsided to a gigantic sloping ditch. The north brow bulged a phenomenal five feet a day.

At 8:32:11 AM May 18th another magnitude-5.1 earthquake. The fractured bulge starts down as two colossal landslides. They accelerate, divide into fragments larger than skyscrapers, break into houses and sheds, shatter into boulders and sand. The sliding, pulverizing rock flows off the volcano and seventeen miles down the North Fork. The great avalanche buries the valley floor in huge rocky mounds.

The slides remove a quarter-mile slab of rock. The gassy magma and hot fluids below, now suddenly lower in pressure, explode. Gas and rock loft thousands of feet. It's silent to watchers, but people hundreds of miles away hear distant explosions.

The suspended mixture falls back. It accelerates down the flanks to more than three hundred miles an hour. The scorching current surges north, east, and west as a hot hurricane, hugging the landscape. It speeds beyond the landslides. It rides up a near ridge, boils over its top, flows down into the next valley. It rides up and over another ridge, spreading outward.

Two minutes after the first earthquake, a third great landslide takes the summit. An even larger hot ashy surge rolls across the rumpled land. The searing surges of doom reach out ten to eighteen miles, mowing down forest, killing all in the way. Within six minutes 234 square miles—ten Manhattans—are barren, scorched waste.

As the surge flows out and slows, it deposits most of its hot rocks and coarse ash. Now lighter than surrounding air, it rises from the huge, hot devastation. In three minutes the column punches through 35,000 feet, three minutes later through 60,000 feet. By 8:50 the top is at 80,000 feet. It spreads into a mushroom bigger than Hiroshima's that fearful morning in 1945. The uprush carries millions of tons of the surge's sand, silt, and tree litter above 40,000 feet. The mushroom dumps ash densely west, north, and east. Winds spread a gigantic ash anvil east. Blackened fir debris litters the white snows of Mount Adams and Mount Rainier. Steetlamps blink on in Yakima and Moses Lake. Brave day sinks in hideous night.

High on the volcano's flanks the hot, turbulent current melts snowpack. Slush-flows converge as muddy floods. They pour off the volcano into the heads of South Fork Toutle, Smith Creek, and Muddy River. Flushing down valleys, they strip away bridges, buildings, trees, all else.

Besides rock, the landslides carry off the volcano's groundwater and glaciers. This water leaks from the lumpy deposit in the upper North Fork. A muddy flood rages down Toutle and lower Cowlitz valleys to the Columbia, smashing bridges, logging camps, and houses.

After great surge and mushroom, only a weak plume drifts from the new crater. It grows to a strong, dark column, and by 9:25 widens and straightens to a black jet convecting up six miles. Winds carry its ash hundreds of miles east, keeping day night. In afternoon the column widens, goes turbulent, and feeds fiery ashflows down to Spirit Lake. The column increases and at 5 PM again reaches 63,000 feet. But then subsides—by 8:10 down to 17,500 feet.

People near the eruption report from different heights, distances, and directions. Exact places and times are vital to knowing the pace of an event, the sequence of many. Italics and curly brackets *{Ward}* signal one account crossing another. Chapters 7–15 describe morning, chapters 16–19 afternoon and evening. Stories lasting some days end in chapter 20.

Let us return to Mount St. Helens. It's 8:32 AM, Sunday, 18 May 1980.

7

Air

*Here's **another** asshole telling us the mountain has erupted.*
—Air-traffic controller

At 8:30 AM on 18 May 1980, a Cessna nears the summit of Mount St. Helens. Airliners fly to and from Sea-Tac airport. By 9:30 several small aircraft fly south and west of the erupting volcano. A surveillance flight and three to follow—radio-linked to a logbook—record details.

Keith Stoffel, Dorothy Stoffel, and pilot Bruce Judson

[Dorothy B. and Keith L. Stoffel were geologists in Spokane—Keith for Washington Department of Natural Resources, Dorothy for Department of Ecology.[1]]

Keith: We had some hours before a minerals show in Yakima. My birthday present to Dorothy was a Mount St. Helens flight. We took off from Yakima in a Cessna 182 with pilot Bruce Judson at 7:15 AM and neared Mount St. Helens about 7:50. From 11,000 feet the mountain looked serene, only wisps of steam. But the swollen north face looked wet. We circuited the mountain's east and south.

Dorothy: The snow wasn't wet on the southeast despite sun.

Keith: We continued clockwise around the base of the cone. On the north, huge wet areas glistened around Goat Rocks and Sugarbowl.

Dorothy: A *lot* of water oozed out.

Keith: Many long, open fractures ran upslope across glaciers draping the north side—unlike normal curved and contouring crevasses. Dark red-brown debris flows, wet and recent, lay around Goat Rocks, and fresh white-snow avalanches around Sugarbowl.

We turned west and flew over south of the summit. The crater was serene, only a steam vent at the bottom and a steaming hole 70 yards wide southeast of the rim. Water seeped from the north wall toward a crater-floor pond. Just under the summit, many open east-west cracks seemed poised to peel into the crater.

We looped north and east, then flew again over the summit photographing the open north-south cracks and the east-west ones bounding the crater.

Dorothy: We arced widely northwest, north, then southeast over Spirit Lake. Two miles across the lake sat Harry Truman's lodge and cabins. A red pickup truck crawled up the straight highway above Truman's. The north face looked *so* wet and unstable.

We circled the mountain clockwise a few miles out. At 8:30 we turned east for a last pass. We approached the crater a thousand feet up.

Suddenly ice and rock dropped from the south wall into the crater.[2] Bruce dipped the right wing for a view.

Keith: A mile-long east-west fracture popped open just north of the crater. The whole mass north of it began to vibrate, ripple, and churn. Huge east-west waves undulated like agitated jello. Ten seconds later the great bulge north of the fracture sank north—a *gigantic* mass detaching from the mountain. The steep scarp grew taller by the second.

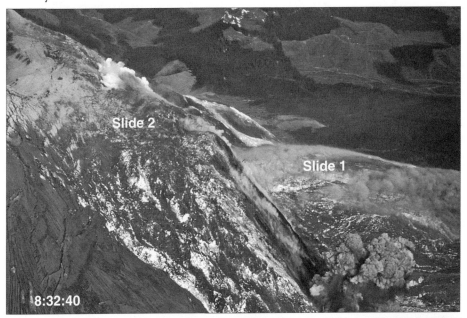

Start of two landslides and initial explosions.

PHOTOS BY KEITH STOFFEL

Dorothy: The fissures on the crater's south now crumbled and began sliding north. A *second* gigantic landslide gliding on a second detachment plane. This slide took the crater. The summit just south didn't move.

Keith: I slid across the back seat to the north side. A thousand feet below the airplane the mile-wide face of the mountain was flowing, picking up speed. How spectacular it will be plowing into Spirit Lake, serene and blue down in the trees.

We were now just east of the sliding bulge. Below us a huge explosion blasted up out of the slip plane, but I felt and heard nothing. Its gray and frothy cloud billowed beneath us and plunged north. Within seconds it blocked my view of Spirit Lake.

The cloud grew huge just behind. "We gotta get out of here!" I yelled to Bruce. He opened throttle and dove to gain speed. The cloud swelled fast, chasing us. In a few more seconds it grew to a mile and more.

Bruce: I pitched the nose down, the airspeed indicator redlined at 180 knots (205 mph). Dorothy pushed the front panel, urging us on. She glanced behind. "Shit!" she screamed, pounding on the panel. "Go faster! . . . *Shit!*" I nudged the throttle, pitched the nose down more, and we flew 190 knots (220 mph), beyond redline. Any faster and I could rip a wing off.

Keith: The boiling gray cloud closed on us! It billowed fastest north. "Turn right!" I yelled. Bruce banked south.

Dorothy: Bruce dove for a minute or two. The trees grew larger and larger.

Bruce: I leveled off a thousand feet above them. The ground sloped south, so we still descended, airspeed 180 knots.

Keith: On the radio Bruce tried to tell Seattle Center [traffic control].
"The whole north side of the mountain went! It's erupting!"
"What level?"
"The whole mountain!"

Bruce: Nonchalance at Seattle Center. They thought me overexcited.
"Well, how large is it?"
"Fucking *big!*" I screamed.

Keith: In another two minutes we outran the clouds. They grew and grew, spreading north. The edge rolled over the summit and down the south, soon only the low flanks visible. We flew low southeast of the mountain. Bruce turned west. But the cloud billowed west even faster.

Dorothy: Seven minutes after the eruption began, the low billowing gray clouds east of the mountain remained, but an overhung stratus layer poked far east as an anvil, ash falling from it. Lightning bolts thirty thousand feet high shot through the clouds.

Keith: About 8:45 Seattle Center asked for the cloud's size. Bruce said it topped above 50,000 feet.

Dorothy: Bruce turned east toward Yakima but couldn't beat the cloud. He turned south. We landed at Portland airport about 9:10.

Keith: Bruce later met the air-traffic controller at Seattle Center. At the first radio call he'd leaned toward a colleague: "Here's *another* asshole telling us the mountain's erupted."

Northwest Airlines

Jim Davidson, Glen Bowers, Rich Ryan, and Bob Bioren

[James M. Davidson was a passenger on Northwest Airlines flight 78, Seattle to Washington, D.C. Flight crew: Glen Bowers (Captain), Rich Ryan (copilot), Bob Bioren (engineer).]

Davidson: I was a nuclear engineer at Hanford in charge of fuels and materials for the Fast Flux Breeder Reactor. Three of us from Battelle Northwest Laboratories had flown in a Cessna to Mount St. Helens March 27, six hours after that first eruption. I flew April 3 and in early May and photographed black eruptions. For decades I'd hiked and packed between Mount Adams and Mount Rainier. I'd flown flight 78 often and knew its path.

Early May 18th I flew from Pasco to Seattle. Mounts Adams, Rainier, and St. Helens stood in sun beneath wispy clouds above 20,000 feet. The Seattle terminal was almost empty. *Seattle Times* ran an article on Saturday's caravan to Spirit Lake. People angry about being kept from their cabins had forced authorities to let them retrieve goods.

I boarded Northwest flight 78 and sat in first class six rows back. The captain announced all passengers were aboard and pushed back early, about 8:10. We taxied out, rolled onto the runway, and took off north before 8:25.

Bowers: I was Captain in the left seat of flight 78, a DC-10, to Washington DC. We pushed back from the gate at 8:15.

Ryan: It was my turn to fly. From push-back at South Terminal it was eight minutes or so to the south end of the runway. We took off north [8:23] at about 150 knots, climbed out three or four minutes increasing to 160 and 200 knots [8:27], and turned east across Lake Washington. We climbed through 3000 feet and I increased airspeed to 250 knots.

Bowers said, "I wonder what Mount St. Helens is doing." From my right seat, I glanced right and saw some steam. But I was flying and returned to the instruments.

Bioren: As flight engineer I sat on the right, a tight view behind Ryan. Over Bellevue we talked of Mount St. Helens erupting in past weeks. A hundred miles to the south, it only steamed.

Bowers: Our Sea-Tac tower communications turned over to Seattle Center. I asked for a deviation to view of Mount St. Helens. They gave permission.

Ryan: We climbed through 10,000 feet and I increased airspeed to 300 knots.

Davidson: The Captain said with a tailwind to Dulles we'd divert nearer Mount St. Helens. After we turned south I saw Mount Rainier ahead out my left side, Mount Adams farther, and high up thin stratus cloud.

The plane being only a quarter full—three in first class—I switched to a right window near the front. Mount St. Helens lay ahead on the right. When the pilot announced we may change to the right side, others moved over. We flew west of Mount Rainier and veered southeast over highway 910 at Ashford. Now Mount Adams was far ahead on the right.

Ryan: We climbed through 12 and 14 thousand feet. I leveled off around 16,500 feet flying about 325 knots [497 miles an hour ground speed].[3]

Davidson: Several plumes shot up from Mount St. Helens, seeming to ring its top.[4] They looked like earlier eruptions, but these grew big and poured north off the mountain. A turbulent, vertically striated wall of gray ash flowed out from Mount St. Helens thirty miles south. It looked slow, but realizing the enormous scale I knew it came fast. The mountain disappeared as the cloud expanded out a few minutes. Dozens of lightning bolts ran around the cloud's edge. The pilot slowed the DC-10. I looked down a slant to others at windows farther back. The mountain-diameter cloud now shot up into the stratus layer above 20,000 feet. We flew southeast over US highway 12 east of Randle.

Ryan: My eyes had been on the instruments. "Holy shit!" Bowers blurted. "Look at that!" A big column climbed toward 25,000 feet.

Bioren: A wide gray cylinder. Lightning flashed up and down through it.

Ryan: The column went higher and spread out into an anvil above 25,000 feet. It drifted fast northeast but spread in all directions. Lightning shot down from it like a gun.

Bowers: The mountain had disappeared in the cloud. The smoke and ash rising in the brownish stalk pushed the top higher.

Davidson: As we neared Goat Rocks the dark clouds around Mount St. Helens were several times the basal diameter of Mount Adams. Wind brought the overhead cloud toward us. The pilot opened the throttle, the plane's tail came up, and we flew out of there.

Bowers: We'd had our show. I didn't want to arrive late at Dulles.

Ryan: I increased speed and climbed east.

Bioren: I called the tower at McChord Air Force Base. "You see the smoke to the south?"

"It's the military at Yakima firing range."

"It's Mount St. Helens, and it's huge. People will need help!"

"Roger."

Ryan: A United pilot coming toward Sea-Tac said: "That's no eruption, it's a thunderstorm!"

Yeah, right, west of the Cascades, at 8:45 in the morning.

United Airlines

Captain Joseph H. Mathes

May 1980 was a period of turbulence at our cruising altitude. To avoid it I flew high, 37,000 feet. From the Captain's left seat I flew United Airlines flight 274, a Boeing 727, north from San Francisco in Airway V-23. We began descent toward Sea-Tac airport. About 8:37 we were 24 miles west-southwest of Mount St. Helens descending north through 36,000 feet. An Air Canada flight above the mountain caught turbulence and was assigned a new vector. We couldn't see through haze a layer below us at 33,000 feet and another down at 25,000 feet.

At 8:38 the co-pilot on the right saw a tremendous column poke up through the clouds at 25,000 feet ahead to the right. I banked the plane right to see. It's enormous energy boiled up to our altitude of 35,000 feet in two minutes [8:40]. I grabbed the camera from my flight bag and snapped one photo—end of the film. In two more minutes the column had shot to 60,000 feet. From about 8:43 to 8:47 the top spread into a mushroom 35 miles in diameter—its underside about 49,000 feet and top above 60,000. A thistle-like spike projected up from the mushroom. The column feeding up into the mushroom was 15 miles wide.[5]

As we came around the west side the column was so dense it blocked the sun—no light came through. The spiked top dissipated in a few minutes. Bolt after bolt of lightning shot steeply within the column at 25,000–30,000 feet, some single strands, some branched. It lasted the five or six minutes we were deep in shadow.

The top of the mushroom expanded so fast we were soon under its west edge. I veered the aircraft west. When we were well northwest of it I veered back north. A pilot flying at 9000 feet on the east side radioed about pelting rocks.

At Sea-Tac we touched down northward at 8:54 and blocked at 8:58.

We took off north at 9:52, climbed, and circled south. Near Mount St. Helens at about 10:12, we saw the column still boiling up to 40,000 or 45,000 feet, but the huge dense mushroom top above 50,000 feet had blown off east.

Captain William L. Airis

I flew Boeing 727s between Seattle and San Francisco and had watched Mount St. Helens on many flights. Sunday morning planes were taking off and landing northward. But traffic and winds were light, and from our north terminal the tower set us up southward. We took off about 8:18, I as Captain flying from the left. I climbed slowly so we'd pass Mount St. Helens low enough for passengers to see.

From the northwest in Airway V-23 at about 10,000 feet the volcano looked quiet. As we pulled opposite 25 miles west, a huge cloud enveloped the mountain.

"You see anything unusual?" air-traffic control radioed.

"Yeah. The mountain just disappeared."

Three minutes later I said, "Streams of lava are flowing down the mountain's west side."

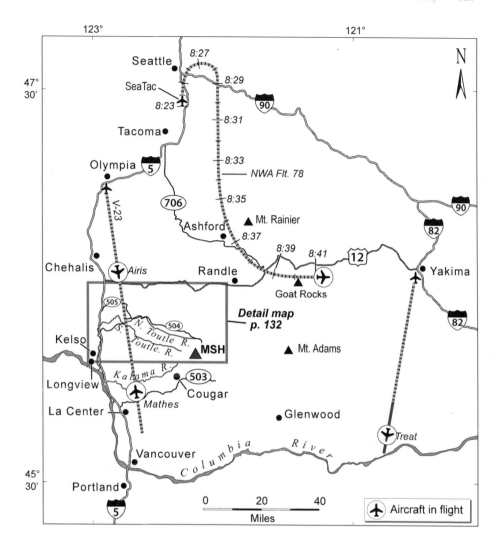

They were almost black against the volcano's light gray. Several dark tongues reached lower and lower down different gullies. At this distance they looked like lava. I later realized they were mudflows.

Captain Peter Gallant

A former World-War-II Navy flier, I was a veteran United pilot flying the Seattle-Chicago route. I flew a Boeing-747 May 18th, as Captain from the left. About 8:40 AM we took off north and banked east. From a tall cloud out the right, bolt after bolt of lightning struck the ground.

"You've got one hell of a storm to the south," I radioed.

"Mount St. Helens just blew up!" the tower guy screamed.

I made ninety-degree turns right and left for passengers on both sides. Cloud-to-ground lightning continued five minutes as we climbed through six, eight, ten thousand feet. As we reached cruising altitude 35,000 feet 150 miles northeast of the mountain, the cloud expanded east at 60,000 feet, way above us.

Ronald Purdum and Joan Kropf

[Purdum flew his hot-air balloon at a rally near La Center 31 miles southwest of Mount St. Helens. Kropf was staff writer for the *Albany Democrat-Herald*.[6]]

Purdum: We launched *Chinook* about 8:10 and drifted east-northeast two or three miles an hour.

Kropf: From the wicker gondola we gazed down on greening fields, new-planted gardens, backyard junk.

Purdum: After fifteen minutes I climbed to 1000 feet. Mount St. Helens looked calm.

Kropf: I scouted the ground, then glanced at the mountain: "Look! It's erupting!" A puff of light-gray ash grew fast. I steadied my lens on the gondola's padded edge.

Purdum: This cloud expanded much bigger than earlier ones. And so fast I worried a shock wave might strike the balloon. But I saw no wind in trees nearer the mountain. A cloud flowed northwest from the mountain's base, turning dark gray as it sped along the ground.

Kropf: I heard and felt nothing—a violent movie with the sound off. Cloud soon cloaked the peak. Boiling clouds crept down the west flank.

Purdum: The silence seemed odd. Lightning appeared across the expanding ash-cloud. In a few minutes a column of light-brown ash climbed miles and spread as a mushroom. Its top disappeared in moisture clouds. Lightning bolts came ten a minute but after six minutes diminished and almost stopped.

Gary Treat

[Treat flew his wife and two sons in a Cessna 182 south from Yakima. They were at 10,000 feet over Columbia River at Biggs 75 miles southeast of Mount. St. Helens.[7]]

We noticed the eruption at 8:35—a gigantic billowing cloud racing out from the mountain. In two minutes it engulfed the mountain and within three minutes had grown ten miles wide. Then no more outward billowing. A vertical tube of ash rose into a haze layer thousands of feet up.

As the cloud expanded about 8:40, a group of ball forms connected neither with cloud nor ground made a very impressive shower of light. They streaked much too fast to be projectiles. They dove east at a low angle and seemed to spray the base of Mount Adams.

We took four pictures. The last shows a high cloud far northeast, its leading edge behind Mount Adams. Seattle air-traffic control said their radar tracked it at 50 mph.

Andre Stepankowsky and Roger Werth

[Stepankowsky was a reporter and Werth a photographer for the *Daily News* at Longview.]

Stepankowsky: Reporter Jay McIntosh and I were eating breakfast when out the east windows a black cloud billowed above the horizon. Just another eruption, we thought. But this one grew fast and huge. We wolfed down omelets, hash browns, bacon, toast and sped to the office.

Werth: The *News* telephoned me at home: "The mountain blew!"

Stepankowsky: Managing editor Bob Gaston said there'd be a flight with Werth. Jay and I flipped a coin: I won. We took off in a low-wing Beechcraft around 9:30 and turned east.[8]

Werth: After 15 minutes we saw through clouds the mountain erupting.

Stepankowsky: It pumped out a column of soot towering tens of thousands of feet, laced with lightning bolts. We flew over the south flank several miles out. The summit was gone, the air too ashy to see farther north.

Werth: It was hazy. After half an hour it cleared and I shot many color and black-and-white photographs. The pilot flew rim-height only ¾ mile away. Out the small open window I got several tight shots showing the power of the jetting plume. I heard nothing from huge lightning bolts in the column.[9]

Stepankowsky: After more than two hours we flew west. Weyerhaeuser's camp in the South Fork had been flooded and many logs swept downvalley.

Werth: I photographed the wreck of 12-Road Camp.

Stepankowsky: Farther down Weyerhaeuser's railroad bridge was gone. We flew down over Toutle and caught up with the front of the flood at Hollywood Gorge—a jam several hundred feet long of reddish-brown logs filling the valley side to side. Where the canyon turned sharp left, the front ran 25 feet up the right bank, stripped off brush and small trees, and fell back into the canyon. At the next sharp right bend the flood rode high up the left bank and stripped off brush and trees. Some logs were trees off the banks, but many were cut, from the camp. Ahead of this muddy brown water the river ran clear, no logs. We circled as the front worked down beneath bridges to Cowlitz River.

We landed at Kelso-Longview airport. Governor Dixy Lee Ray stood in the main building. I asked questions, but she brushed me off.[10] We left the airport behind an unmarked State Patrol car holding the governor.

Chuck Rosenfeld

[Charles L. (Chuck) Rosenfeld was associate professor at Oregon State University.[11]]

From March 27 our Oregon National Guard unit had monitored Mount St. Helens from an OV-1 Mohawk—a twin-engine turboprop cruising at 210 knots. We shot thermal-infrared and radar images with mounted instruments. From a helicopter we'd measured hot spots along the south crater wall by hand-held thermal radiometer. Since April 30 we'd watched spots on the bulge around Goat Rocks, Wishbone Glacier, and a crack near the summit. Our May 16 and 17 images showed them hotter.

A predawn May 18 flight took a thermal-infrared image at 5:51 and I got it about 7 o'clock. It showed a huge thermal output from the bulge and some new spots below Goat Rocks. I wanted a photograph.

Pilot John Sedey and I took off in the Mohawk from Salem about 8:40. In a few minutes we heard the mountain was erupting. Over Newberg Hills we saw a black curtain stretching from Mount St. Helens far east. From south of the mountain at 9:10, we saw a hell of a big plume churning up, its cap swelled out south and west above 30,000 feet.

We flew at 8300 feet to the west side. A few lapilli clicked on the skin of the plane. The stem of the dark-gray column sucked in clouds, yet flying just half a mile away was strangely calm. Dense haze covered valley and ridges to the north. From near Spirit Lake an odd white-steam plume poked up through this haze to 7000–8000 feet. I took many photos around 9:15. We neared Coldwater Creek, but gray murk ahead and a big ashy mushroom unfurling overhead stopped us. We turned east toward the plume, then south. Through haze I saw an earlier big flood had flowed down the west flank and converged into the South Fork. We flew downvalley. I didn't notice the front of the flood, and in the lower South Fork trees stood along the river.

We turned around over Silver Lake and flew back east upvalley, still no mudflow. We turned over the ridge into the North Fork and up to Camp Baker, nothing unusual.

Two miles above Camp Baker we came to the end of an enormous new avalanche, its steep dark-gray front 50 feet high, and behind it rocky mounds 100–200 feet across in shades of gray and brown. I shot a photo northeast about 9:35. Gray ash coated everything on the north valley side but little on the avalanche. The debris was dry except spots oozing dark-gray mud that crept as rivulets into lows.

We flew east under ashcloud. The ground came up fast toward a haze curtain near Elk Rock. The thick hummocky debris filling the valley reached up farther. Trees lay down on both valley sides, the forest gone, nothing green anymore, a landscape like the moon. We turned around.

We turned south into the South Fork. A dark ribbon down the valley center marked where a flood had swept out trees. We dropped to 5500 feet, ridgecrest level. Downvalley we came to 12 Road Camp, and I photographed [about 10:30]. The flood had just gone through and strewn sawlogs everywhere. A yellow bus stuck endwise out of the mud. A big reddish pool of fluid had spilled from the sheds.

We climbed north through 15,000 feet almost to 25,000. The dense cloud north of the mountain topped about 15,000 feet, and an atmospheric cloud layer bottomed up at 35,000. In between we flew in clear air. A plume blew east-northeast from the column. Heavy mammatus drools hung from its base about 22,000 feet. It disappeared into haze toward Mount Adams.

Back south we passed within 1000 feet of the plume, a gray-brown wall swirling off our wingtip. We flew away some miles and saw it topped above 50,000 feet. A small ash flow descended over Toutle Glacier leaving a light-gray trail [12:17].[12] A mudflow from it dropped into the South Fork.

The column churned more convulsively, morning's cool-looking black now hot-looking light gray. It billowed sideways as it cleared the rim and pushed the remaining black ash up fast. At 20,000 feet it swelled a fresh mushroom. Ash flows boiled down the north flank toward Spirit Lake. A dense plume from it rose and drifted northeast. We turned west down Toutle valley.

The jam of logs from the South Fork flood had worked down the lower Toutle to the Pacific Highway bridge. I photographed it flowing under the I-5 and railroad bridges. Reaching the Cowlitz, the flood ran downriver but also backed upriver a quarter mile before current began moving the logs down. We left about 12:35.

View northeast (upriver) of lower Toutle River

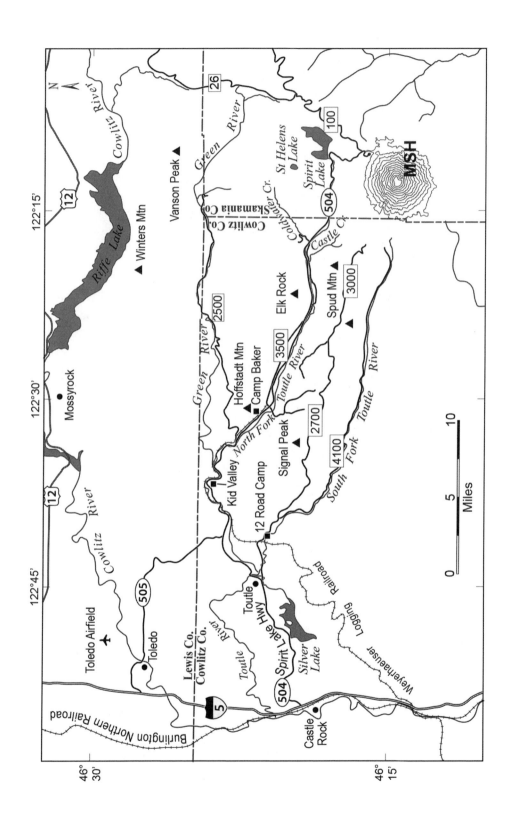

Dave Gardner

[Washington State Patrol pilots David Gardner and Robert Cory had orbited the upper North Fork yesterday during the convoy to Spirit Lake.]

Sunday I was to fly for a second convoy. At 8:50 Captain Swier called me at home saying Chief Landon had reported a big eruption. From Olympia I'd fly down and radio what's going on.

With Bob Cory as copilot I took off in our 1969 Cessna 182. A huge dark cloud filled the southeast. We flew south to the North Fork and turned upvalley about 9:45. The ceiling lowered and we entered thick haze. I throttled back to 90 mph. Even down at 500 feet we couldn't see far. Near Camp Baker gray ash coated everything—this far west! Fading into view ahead trees lay down across the mile-wide valley.

"Wow! Look at that clearcut!" I said. "I didn't see *that* yesterday."

"No. It's new."

Something had leveled the forest way out here, all trees down parallel like hair on a dog's back. We circled above Camp Baker in air too ashy to fly east. We flew downvalley, crossed the ridge south, and angled up the South Fork. Clouds ahead obscured Mount St. Helens, but here the river flowed clear in the sun. We came to a chocolate wall of mud, boulders, and logs plowing down the valley. It flowed twenty miles an hour, filling the inner valley. It pounded trees on both sides, dust shook off, and they fell. We circled as it flowed down a few miles. It swept past 12-Road Camp on the right bank [10:05].[13] The mud rose fast and poured in. It smashed buildings. It pushed big trucks and tipped them over. It stripped hundreds of logs that floated as a great raft below camp.

Two miles down, the logs piled behind Weyerhaeuser's railroad bridge. The mud rose and logjam lengthened. The bridge lifted off its footings and pushed downriver [10:15]. The jam of logs and mud poured down behind.

This sunny Sunday fishermen and boaters would be on the lower river. We radioed our Patrol office at Kelso it was coming toward I-5. I opened throttle and flew down. We saw a boat on the Cowlitz, two guys fishing. I throttled back, descended to 300 feet, and lowered the landing flaps to slow to 75 knots. I switched on the loud hailer: *This is a State Patrol aircraft. You need to get off the river. Mount St. Helens has blown. A wall of logs and mud is coming!*

The men waved, reeled in their lines, and sped toward the boat ramp. We hailed five other boats, and they hurried off the river.

Our radios reached our tower in Olympia, so the governor soon knew. We landed at Kelso 1:00 PM to refuel.

Mark Anderson, Jeff Renner, Bob Wright

[For KING5 Seattle, Anderson was cameraman, Renner science reporter, Wright pilot.]

Anderson: The phone rang, my wife picked it up, and my mother near Mount Rainier blurted, "Where's Mark? I heard a 'bang' from the south. I think it's Mount St.

Helens." I called the station and got an assignment. I drove there for gear and on to Boeing Field.

Renner: At home in Redmond, my wife and I awoke hearing a 'thud.' "What was that?" I asked, and drifted back to sleep.

Carl Berg telephoned from Kid Valley. "The mountain's erupted a big cloud."

I imagined it like past little eruptions. "Call if it gets bigger."

He called. "This cloud's huge and black, and full of lightning."

Wright: KING5 called me at Federal Way: "The mountain's erupted. Come to Seattle!" I flew my white-and-blue Hughes 500A to Boeing Field. Reporter Jeff Renner and cameraman Mark Anderson loaded gear and got in. We took off south [~10:35].

Anderson: Past Olympia we saw a big dark cloud in the southeast.

Wright: Near Riffe Lake in Cowlitz valley I flew into snowlike flakes of ash and turned southwest. Twenty miles down the Cowlitz I crossed the divide south. The FAA now put a wide exclusion around Mount St. Helens.

Anderson: But everyone wanted to see what's happening, and it's our job to get in. We flew up the Toutle below radar. The river was clear.

We came to muddy water, then a few floating logs and limbs, then a mass of logs. Bob circled and I filmed. The river was clear to the west, but to the east bank-to-bank logs. Lots of cut sawlogs but also many whole trees with roots [11:25].[14] They jammed on bends but flowed on.

Wright: I circled and followed it down.

Anderson: We then flew 18 miles upriver past Kid Valley to Camp Baker.

Renner: The light grew dim as we went under heavy cloud.

[Continues chap 16]

Chuck Sicotte

[KIRO's Chopper-7, a Bell-206B Jet Ranger, had flown from Seattle to Mount St. Helens many times since 27 March, Sicotte landing on the summit April 12.]

Sunday I was home with the family when KIRO called. Chopper-7 sat on their roof. I drove in and preflighted. A reporter and cameraman got in and we took off about 10:20.

We flew south over Orting and Morton. The cloud towered over the mountain, the sky growing darker and darker. It was wide and high and awesome. An ashy haze thickened beyond Riffe Lake. I turned southwest, staying beyond FAA's twenty-mile restricted airspace.

About 11:45 we came to Toutle River nine miles east of I-5. The cameraman filmed a logjam sweeping down the canyon. The river below was clear and serene. The abrupt front of the jam stood twenty feet, and logs reached back more than a quarter mile. Most were forty-foot sawlogs, some whole trees with limbs. Down the curvy canyon the log flood ran up high on the outside of a right bend, slopped down in, and ran up on the outside of a left bend, stripping away trees. Standing firs shook back and forth, then fell. We followed the log front a mile or so, then sprinted down and landed half a mile ahead on a sloping bank.

The cameraman got out and trotted down to the bank. The front twenty feet high swung around a bend, the logs higher farther back. The front swept by and the cameraman dashed upslope. From the banks the log flood rose fast onto the gentler slope, coming higher and higher.

We took off and circled above the flood around meanders and under the Pacific Highway bridge. The sheriff had stopped traffic on I-5. Below the railroad bridge I landed on the south gravel bar at the Cowlitz junction ten feet above water. I kept the throttle up. The cameraman stood on the skid. The water quickened and rose onto the lower part of the bar. He filmed a big log front sweeping under the railroad bridge [12:45]. The logs neared, he ducked in, and I took off. The flood covered the bar.[15]

We flew to Kelso, landed about 1:15, and refueled. One huey after another flew in, the place now a military staging area.

[Continues chap 16]

Dwight Reber

[For Columbia Helicopters, Dwight Reber had flown *National Geographic* and *Columbian* photographers since early April.]

May 18 was a day off from *National Geographic* but we had a television contract. I took off from Aurora, Oregon, in the Hughes 500C about 8:15 AM under 25,000-foot overcast, winds 270° at 5 knots, temperature 58°F, Mount St. Helens veiled by haze. I landed at Pearson Airpark in Vancouver. The rotor blades were still turning down when the TV crew ran out.

"The mountain's blown! Let's go!"

I had a standing order with *National Geographic*'s Rowe Findley to evacuate Reid Blackburn from Coldwater in a big eruption, and Friday I included Harry Truman. I dashed into the flight office and telephoned the Forest Service. Since Blackburn had radio and vehicle, they said I wasn't permitted to fly in during eruption.

The TV crew boarded, and we flew toward the mountain. Soon we saw the cloud was a great mushroom, and Portland radar reported it up 55,000 feet. I flew back and forth south of the volcano as they filmed. We landed at Pearson about 10:45.

My blades still turned when Rowe Findley dashed out. He and photographer John Marshall had come for me, agitated that Reid Blackburn hadn't called since the eruption. Stocker and McWhirter might still be at Coldwater I. Findley said at *National Geographic* expense I was to fetch Blackburn and Truman. I'd fly alone with room in the Hughes for four.

I took off after 11. An ash curtain fell east. I flew north toward Coldwater but came to a dust cloud miles wide. I worked under it just above the trees past Merrill Lake and miles north. In the South Fork there was too much windshield glare and falling ash to see. I turned back south.

Coming low over a ridgecrest I saw two cars stranded on a road. Maybe I could help. But fifteen feet from the ground a huge ashcloud came up and I pulled off [~11:45] *{Rogers & Valenzuela}*. Yet this wasn't my mission to Reid Blackburn.

I worked south of the cloud, climbed, and flew north over it. After flying miles above 9000 feet, I saw it a continuous dense stratum of suspended ash. I saw no hole to sneak down through. I retreated south.

I flew northwest nearly redlined about 125 knots and crossed into the South Fork Toutle and over the next ridge into the North Fork. I turned east and above Kid Valley went under cloud.

[Continues chap 16]

Ray Pleasant and Jack Schoening

[Clyde Ray Pleasant Jr. was a pilot for Weyerhaeuser Aviation, Jack Schoening oversaw logging in St. Helens Tree Farm.]

Pleasant: Sunday I was home in Kelso, my usual helicopter number 62W in Tacoma for a new engine. Woods Manager Jack Schoening called that the mountain had erupted. A pilot flew our Bell 206B Jet Ranger 28W down from Chehalis. I lifted it off Kelso airport about 10:45 with Schoening and stopped in Castle Rock for Ren Broomhead (contract supervisor of 12 Road Camp).[16] Up the lower Toutle we passed the front of a huge log-laden flood coming down.

Schoening: The logs flowed down three to five miles below the highway bridge [~11:00].[17]

Pleasant: We flew up the South Fork. Our railroad bridge over the river was gone. Two miles upvalley our big log-loading facility, 12 Road Camp, had been wrecked. The flood had passed and subsided. A *National Geographic* [January 1981, p. 34] photograph shows trucks and hundreds of large logs thrown like toys, and red transmission fluid leaking from maintenance sheds. Many of the logs had been stripped off loaded rail cars now wrecked along the river.

Schoening: We assessed damage [11:05–11:10], then flew up the South Fork. In twelve miles [Herrington Place] we ran into heavy ash in the air and veered south.

Pleasant: By radio I heard the Forest Service had pulled our clearance to fly near the mountain. I landed while they sorted it out. We got permission to fly [11:37].

Schoening: We waited on road 1151 high in Disappointment Creek. The air cleared enough that we followed this valley down to the South Fork.

Pleasant: Lightning flashed in the big ash cloud toward the mountain. I flew northeast to the cloud. The edge lifted a little and we glimpsed beneath. Here eight miles from the mountain all trees were down! Dozens of fires smoldered in this one area [11:55].[18]

Our dispatcher radioed a request from the sheriff [12:07] to help people stranded below the South Fork road bridge. We flew down but saw no one *{Dergan & Reitan}*.

[Continues chap 16]

Don Swanson

[Swanson is the first of four USGS scientists who from the air systematically document and photograph the eruption.]

At 8:30 AM in Forest Service headquarters in Vancouver, I readied to drive to Coldwater II. The seismograph went wild. I dashed up to the radio room and radioed Dave Johnston but got no response. By radio and telephone came reports of a huge eruption.

We radioed Coldwater II several times, but no answer. I sped to Pearson Airpark for a Forest Service observation flight with spotter Dave Gibney.

We took off at 9:20. A tremendous gray column stood above Mount St. Helens. We approached from the south-southwest at 11,000 feet at 9:34. A roiling, dark column pumped and convected up as a high cloud looking like dirty cauliflower but every knob moving. A little knob grew to a huge one, this all over the outside of the column that rotated up to the right, a twisting helix. It looked very slow, but from its enormous size I knew it must be very fast. Inside the droning airplane the show was silent. It towered miles above us, far larger than I'd imagined.

Clouds covered much of the mountain and I saw no details beyond the rim. Twice the clouds pulled back enough to see the column jetted from a great hole. "Incredible!" I said over the radio. "The top of the mountain's gone!" The views were so brief and fuzzy, a missing summit so unexpected, we were in denial about it. A quarter hour later came clearer views. The new hole was enormous!

Through dense ashy clouds the top of an isolated white steam plume puffed up several miles north from near Spirit Lake. It looked like steam and hadn't the cauliflower texture of the big column. But what caused it?

We flew west over the South Fork. All trees were gone along a wide dark-gray ribbon down the valley floor. A mud line ringed trees on the sides high above the floor. We'd seen no large flow off the volcano, so this big mudflow had gone down before 9:35. Now water only trickled down a swept-out valley.[19]

Dark-gray streaks down the upper west and south slopes of the volcano converged down gullies to below treeline—large mudflows before we'd come. We flew back over the south flank, and at 9:45 I saw a dark mudflow swath down Pine Creek and Muddy River.

Many lightning bolts struck at the mountain. At 9:55 we flew east and saw all trees down, everything coated in gray ash, many dispersed small fires—like ruins after a big bomb. How could ash falling through cool air set fires? Had lightning set them— but then why so many? This is four miles from the crater! Devastation to the north must be huge. Close people like David Johnston must be dead.

We flew west. The clouds cleared enough I saw a deep crater had replaced the summit. We again flew north but ran into ash and clouds and turned back.

We flew east as the column changed. Now it jetted up powerfully from the hidden vent, the volcano's gasses thrusting it straight up. Little cauliflower structure roiled in its lower 300 to 1000 yards. By 10:38 the lower part of the column had narrowed, and we saw the edges of a mile-wide crater where the summit had been.

9:50

Above and opposite: eruption column from surveillance aircraft

12:25

On the west side at 10:50, we saw the new crater wasn't circular. The north side had blown away, but I couldn't see how deep. At 11:04 I drew a sketch hardly believing what I saw. The rim was chopped off above Northwest dome, more than a thousand feet below yesterday's summit. To the west I saw ground as bare and gray as on the east. On the ridge between the South Fork and Castle Creek the trees were down, some burning.

All this time lightning flashed every few seconds within the ash column. Many blocks, some big boulders, dropped from the column onto the cone near the new rim. Gray ash sometimes boiled over the rim and flowed as a dirty cloud a couple hundred yards down. The flows looked slow—until I considered the large size of the mountain and knew they were fast.

At 11:19 dark-gray mud flowed down the southwest flank and by 11:40 fingered onto Butte Camp flat. Small mudflows crept down the south flanks. The hot blocks falling high on the cone must be melting snow.

I shot many photographs, recording times in a notebook. With an old Bell & Howell hand-wind 16-millimeter movie camera I shot at 24 frames a second.

By radio we heard law officers worry about flood taking out the I-5 bridge over Toutle River. How could something forty miles from the mountain be threatened? The flowpath down the South Fork Toutle didn't look so bad to make trouble far away.

[Continues chap 16]

8

Cascade Peaks

Climbers on Mount Rainier (50 miles north-northeast), Mount Adams (31 miles east), and Mount Hood (60 miles south-southeast) watch the eruption unfold.

MOUNT RAINIER

Clear weather drew climbers to Mount Rainier—summit 14,411 feet—many to the south side above Paradise.

John Downing and Mike Williamson

Williamson: Five of us had camped overnight below Nisqually icefalls. John Downing and I were the first rope, three on a second. John and I came to the bottom of Fueher's Finger at 10,500 feet, a mile west of Camp Muir. The sky was clear, the air still. The second party came up. One said, "Hey, Mount St. Helens is erupting!"

Downing: A small puff of smoke rose near the summit. Then it grew.

Williamson: So much it covered the mountain.

Downing: A distinct flow ran out northwest, and a bit later one east. They were 1000 to 1500 feet thick and hugged the ground. The head of a flow disappeared into a valley, hopped into view over a ridge, and disappeared again into a valley.

Williamson: Its leading edge flowed like water. It hit a ridge, poured up over, then dropped into the valley. It flowed over the next ridge, and down into the next valley, following the shape of the land. It looked slow. But we were fifty miles away and those ridges miles apart, so the clouds really sped. It lasted some minutes. I heard and felt no change.

Downing: Between the two big fast flows—one northwest, one east—another flowed over the ground north toward us. I heard nothing.

Williamson: I expected a concussion, and here we stood at the base of a rock wall. We dug foxholes in the snow while shooting photographs. The big gray cloud stopped flowing out. It climbed tens of thousands of feet through a cloud layer that wasn't there before. It boiled up turbulently like a thunderhead and mushroomed out.

Downing: The cloud billowed up in cauliflower texture, then mushroomed fifteen minutes. Long lightning bolts ran around its outside, and I heard thunder. Dark streamers dropped from the mushroom. The cloud grew bigger and darker, and the air below went hazy.

Williamson: I heard muffled thunder. The mushroom blew fastest east but also came toward us north-northeast. It was awesome: "Wow!" "Oh wow!" Faint shouts came from higher climbers.

Downing: The top of the mushroom top blew mostly east. Haze worked through the valleys north from Mount St. Helens like fog creeping into valleys in evenings. It approached us.

Williamson: The upper cloud came close. Now it was "Shit!" "Oh shit!" We roped up.

Downing: The cloud pulled overhead, and we headed down. My watch read 9:30 as we descended through 10,000 feet. Twigs from evergreen trees fell coated with ash. They were ¾ to 1 inch long, about the diameter of matchsticks, and charred.

Williamson: And fresh wood splinters like matchsticks and larger, pieces of tree bark, and green needles evident against the white snow. Ash sifted down lightly and the view south faded. It was eerie, like walking into fog. We followed our tracks down to base camp, the snow dusted in ash.

Downing: We reached camp more than an hour after eruption's start. The air was hazy and smelled earthy. Silt-sized ash veneered the tents. I saw Paradise a mile away.

Williamson: We rolled up the tents and they left white squares. As we hiked down, ashfall increased and visibility dropped. We had trouble navigating. We'd hiked up between dark rock ridges separated by white snow. Now in uniform gray you couldn't tell rock from snow. We followed our flags across Nisqually Glacier.

Downing: We came to Paradise parking lot about 10:45. A quarter inch of ash coated pavement and cars. Fine ash fell.

Williamson: Others had left, the lot nearly empty. The radio gave only static. Driving west, we met no vehicles.

Downing: As we reached the park's exit four miles west of Longmire, only very fine ash filtered down. Beyond Ashford, no ashfall.

Williamson: The sky turned sunny and blue.

Olaf von Michalofski[1]

Four of us would climb to Camp Muir at 10,000 feet, then to the summit Monday. From camp at Longmire we drove to Paradise and set out at 6:30 AM. The day was clear, the snow slope up Paradise Glacier inviting. We carried skis for the run down.

We climbed high enough to see Mount St. Helens in her gray coat. After we passed through 8500 feet, people below on Nisqually Glacier shouted. I turned and saw Mount St. Helens erupting a mighty and expanding plume. It had covered the volcano and was rising and drifting rapidly northeast and east. Spectacular lightning in it shot all directions.

A slight rumble, a small gust of wind. We shot many photos. The cloud turned Mount Adams black in half an hour. About 9:15 the cloud reached us, and we put on skis. But ash turned the snow gray and they didn't work. After a few hundred yards we strapped our now-dewaxed boards back on.

Lower it got darker and gloomier, the silence eerie. At Paradise our cars were covered with a quarter inch of fine ash like talcum powder.

We drove west in low visibility. Streetlights were on in Longmire, the only eastbound car a ranger's. The sky was light at Ashford, the fall barely noticeable.

William Halliday[2]

This clear morning four of us hiked Skyline Trail at Alta Vista Ridge. At 8:30 we paused at the 5800-foot level. We'd climbed high enough the upper few hundred feet of Mount St. Helens had come into view. How different with a crater on the north and snow streaked gray and black with ash. We plodded up in snow. I turned and saw a grayish-brown cloud around the Mount St. Helens summit. "Hold up!" I called ahead.

I shot photos. In a minute the cloud covered the mountain. A roiling gray wave washed over ridges toward us. It grew miles wide. I thought nothing could live in it. A high part intersected a barely visible moisture plane a few thousand feet up and instantly turned it milky.

After some minutes a wide column of dirty smoke shot up mile after mile. Lightning played in it, and thunder rolled. Gray cauliflowers poked from the west base but were swallowed by the giant cloud slanting up west. The low air went hazy miles out from the column.

We hiked a few hundred yards east to Alta Vista Point. The cauliflower heads of brown-gray ash continued up. Over minutes the top broadened and lost its cauliflowers and dirtiness. It grew to a magnificent thunderhead ten miles high, strung out east. From its base a dirty black curtain floated down, eclipsing Mount Adams. The top also came northeast.

We practiced ice-axe arrest, but by 9:30 a black downpour from the cloud's north edge looked like heavy rain. We hurried off the mountain. At Paradise, gray ash stained the snow.

We threw our packs in the car and sped away. We entered a rain of brown, dry ash that turned the snow black. A few more minutes down switchback curves and we could barely see. Visibility then improved, but an uphill car swirled dust and the air went dark for seconds. Ash covered the road at Longmire, but at 10:30 in Ashford ashfall was slight.

Jim and Greg Hill

Jim: From 1971 to 1979 I'd climbed Mount St. Helens fifteen times from the north in May or June when snow bridges crevasses. I'd climbed Mount Rainier six times, five from Paradise.

Greg: I'd climbed Mount St. Helens nine times with my dad.

Jim: Friday five of us climbed from Paradise up past McClure Rocks to Moon Rocks at 8000 feet and camped. Saturday dawned sunny, Mount St. Helens a large cone on the south horizon. We climbed through Camp Muir, up Cowlitz Glacier, past Cathedral Rocks, and camped on snow flats at Ingraham Glacier, 11,500 feet.

Sunday we set out in dark at 3:30 and climbed above Disappointment Cleaver to 13,000 feet. I'd neither slept nor eaten and felt ill. I gave my camera to my son Greg. Two of us descended to the top of Disappointment Cleaver [12,400 feet]. We'd summit later if I felt better. The sun rose in clear sky.

Greg: Three of us climbed on one rope. Below false summit at 14,000 feet, we dropped our packs. Another small party had stopped here. A couple minutes later I glanced at Mount St. Helens and saw a cloud growing on it. I fished out the camera and shot a photo. The dark cloud grew bigger, and half a minute later I shot another. Gray cloud rolled down the east side into Ape Canyon. It expanded rapidly east and northwest. Then part of it came northward. Something so huge must be wiping out Spirit Lake.

Two minutes later the cloud had spread many miles northeast and northwest. For several minutes the cloud expanded no more but rose into a white cloud that appeared suddenly above the eruption cloud. The top of the gray cloud rose higher and higher above the horizontal white cloud until it was up ten miles. The high cloud spread mostly east but also toward us. As the cloud approached the sky darkened.

Jim: Down at Disappointment Cleaver behind Gibraltar Rock we couldn't see southwest. I heard and felt nothing. When a big cloud with a scalloped bottom blew over from the southwest I knew Mount St. Helens had erupted. The cloud's bottom sagged in one area, then drew back up, this all over the cloud's bottom. Within minutes the cloud blotted the sun in the east, and the air grew darker. Down south through Cadaver Gap I saw an ashcloud turning upper Cowlitz valley near Packwood black, and lightning flashed there. We'd be an exposed target here. We started down. The cloud front pulled over us, and a hail of quarter-inch to half-inch mudballs fell thunk, thunk, thunk on the ice and snow for two or three minutes. It got darker, and fine ash began falling. Ash fell heavier and the sky darkened but stayed clear northeast. The snow turned gray. We tied bandanas over our noses.

Greg: Lightning flashed through the cloud sailing east toward Mount Adams and nearing us. It seemed risky here high and open. We pulled on our packs and started down. The other party followed. As the cloud came over, little rocks or mudballs pelted down. The mudballs ended in a few minutes, then fine ash fell. The air warmed 10 or 15 degrees, but no smell.

We descended Disappointment Cleaver fast. In the middle of the rope, I got tangled and fell. I slid but self-arrested. Ash was turning the snow gray. We climbed down to our camp.

Jim: From Ingraham Glacier we watched two parties climb down Disappointment Cleaver, and I saw Greg's spill. They soon arrived. All was pale gray, but when we pulled the tents each left a print of white snow. The air lightened but stayed heavy with haze.

Greg: The other party passed as we packed our tents. Now we were the high party.

Jim: Hiking toward Camp Muir we descended through an air layer we couldn't see but smelled of acrid sulfur.

Greg: An ashy, sulfury smell.

Jim: It got pretty bad, and Ron Fulton who'd had asthma as a kid had no bandana. Down another 300 vertical feet the sulfur smell ended. It was a distinct horizontal band. In the gray air and snow we followed the tracks of other climbers to find our way.

Below Camp Muir in the 9000–7000-foot level, lots of shriveled or blackened needles of fir and hemlock lay on the ash, and charred wood splinters up to three inches long and an eighth inch across. This litter hadn't landed higher—but now we were a mile lower and two miles closer to Mount St. Helens. By 'eruption' I'd imagined lava flows as in Hawaii. Now I thought it must have set a huge forest fire.

Greg: Charred needles and shreds of bark lay in the ash below Camp Muir.

Jim: I'd climbed to Camp Muir thirty times but had trouble navigating in the uniform gray.

Greg: Descending parties sometimes drift right and end up on Nisqually Glacier. Even knowing this tendency and guarding against it, we drifted right in the haze. But not so far as to miss Paradise.

Jim: Paradise parking lot was empty and coated a quarter-inch in gray ash. We drove the loopy road west to Longmire and the park entrance. Ash along the road grew thinner and the air lighter. A quarter mile west of Ashford the ash ended abruptly, like the edge of thunderstorm rain.

With no bandana during our descent, Ron Fulton breathed ashy, sulfury air. Next day he lay in a hospital with asthma for the first time since a boy.

Don Lund[3]

I'd hunted near Mount St. Helens since the 1960s, often to the northwest in Schultz Creek. May 17–18 had been long scheduled for the Olympia Mountaineers to practice on Mount St. Helens. We instead practiced at Nisqually Glacier Saturday, then camped.

Early Sunday four of us climbed in cross-country skiis. Atop McClure Rocks I shot a photo of two of my companions, Mount St. Helens gray and static on the distant skyline. Soon we saw it erupting! My next five photos show the cloud expanding out north and northwest, racing over the landscape. It blasted over ridges and poured north into Shultz Creek, covering almost everything. "Shit!" I murmured, "my colleague Ron Seibold and his family are right there, by Gilbert lookout! Across half an hour I shot fifty more photographs.

8:35:15

DONALD L. LUND

Eruption as seen from McClure Rock at 7345 feet level, Mount Rainier [including next 3 photos]

8:35:50

8:36:00

~8:39

After ten minutes a high cloud came east and also northeast toward us. In half an hour it pulled overhead and ash began falling. The snow grew dark. We tried to ski but the ash stuck. We strapped the skis to our packs and hiked down.

Snow should be white against darker surroundings, trees dark against lighter surroundings. But ash soon turned the snow dark and trees light. It was like walking through a film negative.

From Paradise we caravanned in darkness down the highway. The ash grew thinner and the air lightened toward Longmire.

Ron Seibold didn't come to work at DOT Monday. Something was badly wrong.

Mount Adams

8:33:45

Eruption as seen from false summit of Mount Adams at 11,800 feet.

8:34:59

8:36:00

PHOTOS BY JOHN V. CHRISTIANSEN

John V. (Jack) Christiansen

Saturday twelve of us from near Seattle hiked from Morrison Creek campground and in afternoon set camp about 7800 feet on the south slope of Mount Adams. Mount St. Helens was calm.

Sunday morning we started climbing by 4:30. We reached false summit, 11,800 feet, at 8:30. Shortly someone shouted, "Look at St. Helens!" I photographed the eruption at half-minute intervals, then every minute or two.[4]

A dark cloud rose from the summit and a light cloud from the lower north flank. Half a minute later the two clouds swelled and merged and flowed north off the mountain. A minute later dense black cloud swelling 2000 feet thick flowed fast many miles north, burying the landscape. Gray ash also billowed down the east and south mountain flanks. The wide gray cloud rose raggedly and formed a higher horizontal pale weather cloud not there earlier.

A few minutes later the dark-gray cloud now more than ten miles wide rose into the thickening weather cloud. The mountain's south side cleared as the low gray cloud drew into the rising big north column. The summit emerged planed off, nothing rising from it.

Ten minutes after the first eruption the air went still and a heat wave passed. Temperature rose 30–40 degrees for several minutes. Fifteen minutes into the eruption a high black cloud came northeast and east. A dark and dirty cloud pulled overhead. The air seemed charged. Holding up my metal ice ax, I was shocked through a woolen mitten. We couldn't summit. I called those ahead to descend.

The cloud darkened the sky and about 9 o'clock sand-sized ash rained down in a 20-mile-an-hour west wind. Stretching east, the cloud soon blocked the low sun. As we descended in ashfall, charred wood and cones fell, and branches up to 16 inches long. The ash storm lasted half an hour and coated Mount Adams a quarter inch in brown grit.

We got down to camp at 7800 feet about noon. We packed and descended, watching and photographing Mount St. Helens until trees and ridges blocked it.

About four we came to our cars veneered by an eighth inch of ash. Driving south, we left the ashfall five miles north of Trout Lake.

Dale L. Hanks

Sunday morning four of us from Yakima were climbing the northwest ridge of Mount Adams. The air was warm and dry in a slight breeze. Climbing at about 8000 feet, we noticed Mount St. Helens replaced by a large gray mound—a cloud had enveloped the mountain but now appeared still. In a few minutes the cloud went up, then spread northeast.

About fifteen minutes into the eruption a cold 25 mph wind blew west toward Mount St. Helens, and we put on jackets. The south side of Mount St. Helens cleared. As the vertical cloud continued to grow, lightning bolts seemed to strike the volcano every second or so.

In another quarter hour the cloud pulled overhead. First to fall were BB pellets dry enough they crunched between my fingers. Five minutes later, down came tree litter, a hundred pieces in view at any one time. Branches and tops of fir trees fell up to 16 inches long and ¾ inch diameter, singed on one side. Singed fir cones fell hot.

About ten minutes after the BBs fell, pellets up to ¾ inch fell, and lots of burned cinders. Within ten minutes it got almost too dark to see. We knelt to find our tracks. Lightning bolts struck, a great blast every fifteen seconds or so. The ash smelled like fresh-burned paper and strongly of sulfur.

We found our tent twenty minutes after the first BBs fell. We stayed half an hour in dark. When it began to clear we walked back up the ridge to retrieve film. More branches had fallen, for some lay atop the new ash. The high cloud blew off east. The air cleared at our level above 8000 feet but stayed dark lower.

We packed camp and hiked down. We re-entered the cloud at 5500 feet about 12:30. BBs rained dry, as earlier, and larger discs broke when picked up. It continued like this down to our truck we came to about 4 o'clock.

We drove down Forest road 123 [later, 23] north and northwest, and the ash deepened. It rained ash continually but tapered off as we neared Randle. We entered Randle at 6:30, the air murky but no more fall.

Darryl Lloyd

I'd been raised at Flying L Ranch in Glenwood sixteen miles southeast of Mount Adams. I'd climbed Mount Adams, Mount St. Helens, and Mount Hood many times since 1963. In April 1980 I flew in a small plane to Mount St. Helens and shot Kodachromes. Huge fractures north of summit suggested a coming collapse, so I stayed away.

Sunday we heard and felt nothing at the Flying L but about 9 o'clock saw what looked like a thunderstorm to the northwest nearing Mount Adams. I photographed from the deck. It was sunny here and miles north but farther north shady from the cloud. The upper part of Mount Adams was disappearing in the cloud, the white snow going dark gray above 8000 feet. I surmised Mount St. Helens had erupted. A friend called to say he'd heard so.

We drove ten miles southwest to the ridge above Diamond Gap where years earlier there'd been a fire tower (2900 feet). Here it was sunny, but to the north the big dark plume from Mount St. Helens drifted far east. From Lewis valley a white fog flowed southeast down Trout Creek valley. It gradually filled the valley a thousand feet, and when it thickened up to us smelled sulfury. The fog spilled over the divide into Camas Prairie and crept east through Glenwood.

The eruption cloud half-shrouded Mount Adams all day and the next day. When it cleared the 20th, Mount Adams was stained gray.

Next Saturday May 24, six of us climbed the south flank of Mount Adams and camped at 7800 feet. A new eruption the 25th blew northwest away from us. We climbed higher during the day. Atop old snow between 8000 and 9000 feet, singed Douglas fir branches up to three feet long that had fallen a week earlier smelled burnt. Countless fresh tree splinters up to eight inches long, the biggest 5 inches by 2 inches by 2 feet long.

Mount Hood

Steve Guthrie and Dave Rodeback

Guthrie: I'd climbed Mount St. Helens from the north in 1972 and 1974. In 1980 a mountaineering class I taught at the University of Oregon had an outing to Mount Hood. Friday the 16th, twelve of us stopped along the way for rock climbing then drove to Timberline on the south side of Mount Hood. Next day we practiced snow glissading and self-arrest and in late afternoon climbed to Silcox Hut [6900 feet].

Sunday we left Silcox at 4:15 AM and climbed the southwest flank, stopping at Illumination Saddle [9350 feet] about 8:15. Mount St. Helens to the north was quiet.

Rodeback: We dropped our packs. The west sky was clear but a bit hazy to the northwest under thin clouds. I photographed Mount St. Helens, its top blunt, no activity.

Guthrie: As we lunched facing south someone said, "Look at Mount St. Helens!" An eruption cloud over it looked small, like earlier photos. I stood and shot a frame. At this distance the cloud was unimpressive, but the photo shows a jagged smoke cloud much wider than the summit. A cloud flows down the south flank, and a big lump fattens the mountain's upper east.

The cloud grew fast. In my second shot a minute later the cloud was 2000 feet high, the east profile broad, and a large cloud rolls down the west.

Rodeback: My second photo caught a huge gray cloud flowing west off the mountain, an even larger one east. The eruption formed a high pancake cloud darkening the sky. In two more minutes the gray cloud grows gigantic, and the high white pancake cloud thick and wide.

Guthrie: In my third shot a huge smoke cloud shrouds the mountain. It has flowed many miles east, and a large bulb poofed up west of the mountain's base. The smoke rising a few thousand feet forms a white pancake cloud miles wide.

Rodeback: My third photo more than five minutes into the eruption shows a high gray column ten miles wide rising on two separate stalks, a sliver of blue sky between them. The column streams high into a new horizontal white-cloud layer that shadows a huge area.

Guthrie: In my fourth shot the low cloud has spread wider than twenty miles, enveloping Mount St. Helens. A broad gray smoke cloud rises into the horizontal white cloud the eruption has made. A window of light separates two wide stalks of the rising cloud. Lightning flashes across the clouds.

We descended west onto Reid Glacier and saw the eruption no more. In sun the students practiced ice climbing on a serac and rescue from a crevasse. In mid-afternoon we hiked west down the glacier, then in trees down to Ramona Falls, and on down to the road.

9

Devastation

A great and powerful wind tore the mountains and shattered rocks.
After the wind there was an earthquake.
After the earthquake came a fire.
And after the fire, a gentle voice.
                                        —1 Kings 19:11

It's gonna get me too. I can't get out of here.
                                        —Gerry Martin

Several inside what became devastated left accounts of some sort. Five got off radio messages or photographs before perishing. Some escaped in speeding automobiles. More than fifty die who leave no direct story.

RADIO

David Johnston

USGS's Coldwater II sat 1300 feet above the North Fork on South Coldwater ridge 5½ miles north-northwest of the volcano.[1] David Johnston took over from Harry Glicken evening May 17. Radio linked the post to the Forest Service and USGS in Vancouver.

Before 7 AM Johnston shot three laser measurements to the bulge and radioed the data to Vancouver. A ham operator records two transmissions by Johnston after 8:32.

Vancouver! Vancouver! This is *it*!
  (Hiatus, probably less than a minute)
  (Radio repeater clicks on)
Vancouver! Is the transmitter on?
  (Repeater clicks off)

Gerry Martin

Martin was two miles farther north on road 4000 atop the ridge between the forks of Coldwater Creek.[2] He is one of the Radio Amateur Civil Emergency Services group. "Camper and car to the south" is Coldwater II. The Kearneys' account is in chapter 10. This continuous tape records times during and between transmissions. His first utterance I register as time zero {0:00}. This corresponds to 8:32:20 PDT or some seconds later.

Radio hams: Gerry Martin, Ty Kearney, Marianna Kearney, Bob C. Clark, Reade Apgar (coordinator in Olympia), and Jim Carlson (18 miles north-northwest of Martin).[3]

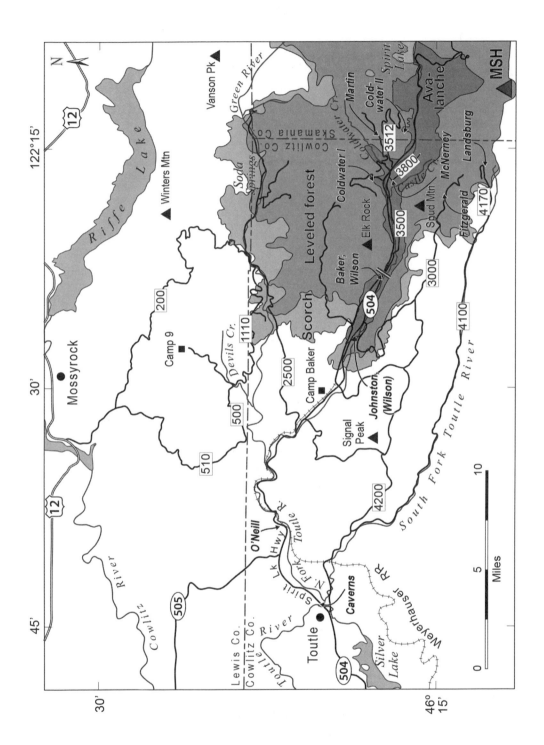

N

122°15'

30'

45'

U.S. 12

Riffle Lake

Mossyrock

Cowlitz River

Lewis Co.
Cowlitz Co.

505

O'Neill

Spirit Lk Hwy

N. Fork Toutle

Toutle River

Toutle

504

Caverns

Silver Lake

Weyerhaeuser RR

South Fork Toutle River

4100

4200

Signal
Peak

Johnston
(Wilson)

Camp Baker

500

510

2500

1110

Devils Cr.

Camp 9

200

Leveled forest

Scorch

3000

504

Baker,
Wilson

Elk Rock

3500

Coldwater I

Spud Mtn

McNerney

Fitzgerald

4170

Landsburg

3800

Castle Cr.

Coldwater Cr.

Soda
Springs

Green River

Winters Mtn

Vanson Pk

Cowlitz Co.
Skamania Co.

Martin

Cold-
water II

3512

Spirit Lake

Ava-
lanche

MSH

46°
15'

30'

0   5   10
Miles

Martin: {0:00} (08:32:20) Earthquake... shakin'... there a whole... northwest side {0:17}...

Ty Kearney: ...

Martin: {0:27}Now we've got an eruption down here... a big slide coming off... the west slope. Now we got a whole great big eruption out of the crater. And... another one opened up on the west side. The whole... northwest side is slidin' down.{0:46}

Apgar: Keep goin' Gerry.

Martin: ... {1:24}all right... the whole... north section blowing up, trying to... It's coming up over the ridge toward me. I'm going to back out of here.{1:40}

Martin: ... {1:50}down on the... camper and the car sittin' over to the south of me is covered. It's gonna get me too... I can't get out of here.{2:04} [~8:34:24]

Kearney: {2.33} ... We are leaving the area!

Clark: ... Which way you leaving Ty?

Marianna: {3:21}We're going south...

Apgar: ... I've reported this to the office [state DES]... I'd like more details.

Clark: {3:54}... It's... the biggest one yet. It's covered... clear over to the right side... of the mountain... It's obscured the whole mountain.

Apgar: Okay... what is taking place... a major slide...?

Clark: {4:15} A major eruption. Gerry was reporting slides. He reported an earthquake at 8:33 and then he saw the mountain sliding, then it started erupting and he was leaving.

Apgar: Any sign of lava flow?[4]

Clark: There's a great big cloud up there... going way high... It keeps piling up... {4:49}

Carlson: {4:59}... We're on highway 12... and Reade you wouldn't believe it, it's covering an area 15 or 20 miles in length and its going clean up in the clouds now. It's... black... it's unbelievable... It keeps boiling... at the bottom, boiling and boiling... The whole Green Mountain ridge is obscured.{5.38}

Apgar: You did say it was blowing north?

Clark: ... It's going... northeast.

Marianna: {5:56}... The cloud went northwest.

Clark: Well, it's going all directions now.

MUTE PHOTOGRAPHS

Three who perished got off photographs whose film survived. A shotbook survived.

Robert Landsburg

For two days Robert Landsburg has photographed from the west. He camped by road 4170 on a ridge above the South Fork four miles west of the summit.[5] He's shot six photographs today since 5 AM.

After the eruption begins Landsburg squeezes off eight shots, the last showing the billowing surge sweeping down on him. He tears the camera off the tripod and within a hot hell rewinds the film and stows the camera in a pack.[6]

8:32:11	Initial earthquake
8:32:20	Landslides start down north
8:32:41	First visible venting
8:32:57 to 8:34:12	Photos 7, 9, 12, 13

Jim Fitzgerald

8:33:05

8:33:23

By his blue Datsun B-210 coupe high on road 3000, 7½ miles west-northwest of the summit, geologist Jim Fitzgerald snaps six photographs as the gray cloud billows north and turns west toward him.[7] He shoots seven more. After his 13th he wrenches his camera from the tripod, shoots another frame, stuffs the camera into a bag, and slides it under a car seat.

8:33:47

PHOTOS BY JIM FITZGERALD

Reid Blackburn

Columbian photographer Reid Blackburn controls two remote cameras from Coldwater I. He keeps a cryptic log, circling the number of shots he's triggered by radio transmitter. After an entry at 7:11 come these:

    8:33 AM ②
    8:34 AM ②

The eruption is well underway when Blackburn punches off the cameras twice. Then twice more. Unlike earlier entries his handwriting is shaky, hurried, and no time to comment. He shuts the transmitter lid and snaps its latches—sealing in the notebook. He jumps into his Volvo and slams the door. The hot ashcloud smashes in its glass. Inhaling mouthfuls of ash, Blackburn soon dies of asphyxia. Nor does his film survive.[8]

Ron or Barbara Seibold (?)

Three mysterious photographs of the approaching surge taken—as relocated 25 years later—on road 3130 two miles northwest of Coldwater I. The Seibold vehicle ended a mile or so west with four fatalities. Photos show cloud piled over volcano, its north edge approaching Coldwater Peak, and nearest edge only three miles away (~8:34:20).

NORTH FORK TOUTLE ALONG HIGHWAY

The Spirit Lake highway was roadblocked eleven miles northwest of Mount St. Helens. After the eruption this spot lay two miles inside the downed-timber zone and deep beneath avalanche.

Barry and Bea Johnston

Barry: Jim Fitzgerald had driven in early. We drove up the highway to join him.

Bea: Above Camp Baker Barry said he wanted breakfast. I was angry. Jim at Spud Mountain would have fine sunrise pictures.

Barry: At Toutle café it was a breakfast from hell, Bea griping every minute what we're missing.

Bea: We started back up in our 1978 Jeep CJ7 about 8:15. Tall firs screened the upper valley. Two miles above Camp Baker we rounded a right bend into a southeast straight. A convoluting gray cloud had piled where Mount St. Helens should be.

Barry: I braked to the right shoulder and we jumped out.[9] Bea snapped a photo maybe twenty seconds after we first saw the cloud.

Bea: A pickup truck down the highway pulled to the other shoulder. Two guys got out to photograph {Wilson & King}. A car behind them drove on. I shot with two cameras. I've missed it, I thought. *Damn it!* On the ridge Jim's getting great shots. I'm not because of breakfast! The cloud grew bigger, much lightning flashed in it, but the show was silent. No noise with something so big: the brain can't comprehend what's happening.

I shot seven photos over about a minute. The gray cloud overtopped a distant high ridge [Elk Rock] and poured down the west side. Now *much* closer, looming huge, it sped downvalley toward us. "We've got to get out of here!" I yelled. The guys across the road climbed into their pickup and roared off.

Barry: "Yeah," I said. "Let's move!"

PHOTOS BY BEA JOHNSTON

From below highway 504 roadblock (northwest)

We jumped in. I turned across the pavement and mashed the pedal. With no traffic I was soon up to 75 miles an hour on straight stretches. Glancing in the mirrors and over my left shoulder, I saw the cloud coming closer—gaining!

"Ohmygod!" Bea cried. "Close the windows!"

Bea: Though scared, I crawled into the back and shot four photos out the back window. The cloud was coming fast, full of lightning, much too big to frame in one shot.

"We're gonna die!" I cried.

"Jesus!" Barry said. "I can't go faster."

It was going to get us. Or Barry would flip on a curve. This'll be the last thing I ever do. Maybe someone'll find the photos.

Barry: The speedometer pegged at 80, top of the gauge. I rounded some curves tipping onto two wheels. I sped around a right bend. A motorhome broadside to the road was turning around. I braked to a stop.

Bea: We'd run five miles and had gained on the cloud—until the motorhome blocked us. When Barry stopped I shot two more photos. The cloud seemed to start up. I glanced at the river below. The highway had been only a little above the river. But I saw no rising water.

The motorhome backed. Barry scooted around the front and accelerated. We drove on some miles, through Kid Valley.

Barry: We gained on the cloud: we'd made it! I stopped by the bridge below Kid Valley.

Bea: We got out here fairly high above the river. I shot two photos of the cloud going up, its edges backlit by the east sun. Another car stopped *{Wilson & King}*. The river

Mushroom cloud observed from Silver Creek in the Cowlitz valley (northwest)

looked normal, but this guy said mud may come. That was my worry. We drove on many miles to Silver Lake.

Barry: The cloud was swelling into a mushroom, looking like an atom bomb had gone off. The mountain had cleared. Nothing now rose from it.

Bea: About 9:10 the cloud still rose, and swelled. The air was quiet. Five or ten minutes later I shot a photo as the plume spread into a huge mushroom, its top backlit by sun, dark beneath. Except for Barry's breakfast we'd be up *in* that stuff.

Barry: We'd wait here for Jim Fitzgerald—hoping he was okay.

Bea: We told firemen that Jim might be trapped on the ridge, that the ashcloud down the North Fork would have buried roads he'd driven up. An hour later a fireman said flood had also cut the South Fork road.

Larry Wilson and Shawn King

King: My Datsun pickup towed a 4-by-8-foot wood-sided trailer.

Wilson: We slept in the trailer near Camp Baker and drove up the highway to the roadblock about 7:30.

King: Signs read of hazard area. "Let's drive to Spirit Lake." I said.
"No. Let's chill here," Larry said.

Wilson: A large motorhome sat in a gravel area just north. We turned around and parked on the shoulder just west.

King: Across the road we freshened in Toutle River and brushed teeth. At the truck we each drank a beer—all we had for food. Larry shot a couple photos.

Wilson: The air was cool and calm, the mountaintop venting a little steam, a beautiful picture. About 8 o'clock a man from the motorhome [Ed Murphy] drove past in a little gold car, its towbar folded in front. We waved. We walked around, threw a Frisbee. But we needed to leave. I got in to drive, Shawn in the right.

King: We headed down the highway a little after 8:30. After a ways two cars came up from the west—a Jeep, and behind it a 1972 Impala. Both cars braked onto the shoulder, the doors flew open, and people jumped out each side.

Wilson: "What're they doing?" Shawn asked.
A black cloud filled the mirror. "It's erupting!" I said.

King: Larry pulled to our shoulder, all three cars within fifty feet. A young couple by the Jeep aimed a single-lens reflex {Johnstons}, the older folk at the Impala an instant camera.

Wilson: I rummaged for my camera in the pickup bed. The cloud got bigger and darker and covered the mountain.

King: Larry fished his camera from an ammo box, mounted the lens, and leaned against the trailer. Half a minute had passed.

Wilson: The base of the cloud seemed to explode. A great black wall raced toward us. An arm shot north a couple miles and exploded up with a *whooom!* like a great rush of air.[10] I shot three photos. The huge cloud climbed over a far ridge fast, blotting it out. A thousand feet higher than the ridge, the cloud covered the land, coming fast.

King: I was jumping around: "Wow!"

Wilson: "We're seeing it!" Shawn shouted, waving his arms. "We're seeing it!"

"Hey man, that's what they said at Pompeii!"

We jumped into the pickup. Shawn drove, I held my camera. Many miles upvalley the cloud came fast. We gunned down a straight stretch of road.

King: A Datsun towing a trailer can't go 65 mph. The Jeep passed, and the Impala.

Wilson: The boiling gray cloud grew much too big to shoot without a wide angle. Shawn cut the next left curve as the little car with the towbar sped up toward his motorhome.

"Christ! He's gonna die!"

We raced down some miles and crossed a bridge. We sped around a right bend. A motorhome loomed broadside in both lanes, turning around. The lady passenger threw her hands over her face against the imminent impact.

King: Motorhome with a vanlike front.

Wilson: "What'll I do?" Shawn cried, braking hard.

"Don't stop!" I said.

Shawn veered around the front, skidding on the gravel shoulder.[11] I looked down into the river. He pulled back onto the pavement, and the trailer stayed on. He slowed a little. A two-ton flatbed truck roared up behind.

King: An old flatbed with dual wheels flew past doing 80, an old couple.

Wilson: On a curve it slewed two-foot firewood rounds onto the pavement.

The road turned west, and the big gray cloud started up. We sped on to a high bridge across the Toutle, two other cars here. We stopped and got out. The cloud was now rising, blue-green lightning in it.

A lady by a Jeep shouted, "Can you believe we're seeing this?" {Bea Johnston}.

"A lake at the volcano's base could send down a lot of water," I said. "We should go!"

No other car came down the highway.

King: We drove on to Toutle and stopped at a store [Drew's].

Washington State Patrol Troopers

Danny O'Neill: I was patrolling Spirit Lake highway below Kid Valley when down a straight stretch an old Datsun pickup came by 80 miles an hour. I turned around, flipped on the flashers, and chased him down. I walked to the driver's door. The truck was covered in ash.

"What's the rush?"

"The mountain!" he cried. The mountain!" He was incoherent. "The mountain!"

He cranked the window half-down. Inside was coated in gray ash. The lower half of his eyeglass lenses were frosted with ash, maybe pitted. In the pickup bed was a dog hutch three by four feet with side holes. The limp heads of three dogs stuck from the holes, nostrils and mouths stuffed with ash, dead. Over the hood was a plywood strike pad. This lead dog hung over the left fender from chain to his collar, dead. I unclipped the chain and lifted him to the pad.

My radio barked to close the highway. I let the man go.[12]

Russ Cavens: I'd been ordered to block the highway at the river bridge above Toutle. At its southwest end I stopped cars from going upvalley. An old small pickup came down across the bridge coated in ash. A dead dog lay on the strike pad, nostrils full of ash.

Kathleen (Kathie) O'Keefe and Gil Baker[13]

[Photographer Gil Baker and writer Kathie O'Keefe drove up highway 504. Baker's earlier photographs would exhibit at SeaFirst Bank in Seattle. O'Keefe has come to write captions.]

O'Keefe: About 8:25 we pulled into a gravel area on the left at the roadblock. Gil set his camera on a tripod and got back in his dark-green Oldsmobile Toronado.

All was still: no birds, no animals. Clear and sunny, the mountain looked more a mural than real. The gravel pit held several cars. A bearded guy stood on the hood of a small black car photographing the mountain [Joel Colten]. A station wagon pulled in—a middle-age couple, the driver large [Fred and Margery Rollins]. He killed the motor. I walked over and told him their lights were on. "Thanks," he said and switched them off. Gil was now snoozing in the car.

A guy outside a cream-colored motorhome on the west talked with a lady inside [Eleanor Murphy]. I walked over.

Baker: The shaking car woke me. I thought it was Kathie, but saw her by the motor-home. I got out. The volcano vented white steam.

O'Keefe: In the doorway of the motorhome, Mrs. Murphy faced the volcano. As we talked she looked away behind us and said: "Ooooh. Look at that!" I turned to see a black puff of ash shoot up from the crater. A couple seconds later a larger puff went up. A few seconds later an even larger black puff. "Oooo!" Mrs. Murphy said so casually, "the north side of the mountain fell off." A black ashcloud now covered the north flank.

I stood mesmerized. Soon the view was replaced by a big black inky waterfall a mile high and wide—a semicircular shroud.

Baker: The waterfall cloud speeding downvalley hit a ridge miles upvalley of us.

O'Keefe: "You sure we should be here?" I called to Gil. The guy who'd been by me with Mrs. Murphy had gotten into his car.

"Hey!" he yelled across the lot. "Time to get the hell out of here!"

"Kathie, he's right!" Gil called.

Baker: I'd seen earlier small eruptions. This was enormous. When the black cloud crossed the ridge, I knew we should leave fast.

O'Keefe: I ran to the car and got in. Gil threw his tripod and camera in the back window. Other cars had left—except for the motorhome and the guy still photographing from his hood.

Baker: I jumped into my Toronado.

O'Keefe: Gil backed but stalled the car. He cranked the engine several seconds . . . God, I thought, are we going to die because the car won't start? . . . Then it caught.

Baker: I spun gravel and sped onto the pavement. Soon the speedometer read 100 miles an hour. After a minute the black cloud almost caught us.

O'Keefe: The edge of the cloud was soon running beside us about a hundred yards to the right, a hundred yards to the left, and chasing us fifty yards back. The leading edge appeared all around as an inky waterfall. The advancing edge totally cut off the view. The front came down with much authority. It poured down with such force it bubbled back up.

Baker: It was like running out of a huge open shell with points right and left. To me—occasionally glancing in the mirror and back to the left—the cloud front looked like boiling oil coming fast. Like huge bubbles, black inside but a phosphorescent skin.

O'Keefe: The churning cloud was an incredible sight. I said nothing or this photographer might stop for a picture. Two cars came *up* the highway. Gil flashed headlights and blew the horn, but they whizzed past.

Baker: Two miles below our starting point, we came behind a car. I slowed and glanced at the speedometer.

O'Keefe: It was the station wagon that had pulled in behind us.

"He's only doing 80," Gil said. "What'll I do?"

"Pass him!"

Gil passed on a blind right curve. Anyone coming in the other lane . . . As we passed, I saw the large man and woman.

Baker: Our speed was then 80 to 105 miles an hour, depending on the road.

O'Keefe: We quickly outpaced this car and raced through a broad clearing on the left. As we got past I looked back and the car behind was just reaching it, headlights on again. It disappeared into the chasing cloud.

The cloud's high front now projected over our heads, moving faster than we were!

Baker: We were gaining on the one behind. I glanced up at the leading edge of the cloud slightly ahead of us. The top had a silver lining. But the obscured sun was behind: it wasn't backlighting. This edge was even, not boiling. About 2000 feet up a wide white contrail shot out—a projectile northwest away from our west direction. Lightning ran through the cloud.

O'Keefe: We gained on the cloud. Along a stretch five minutes from the roadblock where the trees opened, I got a view of the truly immense size of the cloud. A hole had formed through the rising inky cloud, and the sun beat down through it.

Baker: A mile past Kid Valley the road turns south. We saw the cloud now well back had lost its churning and looked like gray fog. The road turned west and we left it behind.

O'Keefe: We turned north [hwy 505] and didn't stop until Toledo.

Later we pulled onto a frontage road along I-5. The radio had news of ash falling lightly at Morton [23 miles north of Mount St. Helens].

"Listen to this! All we escaped is a little ash."

"For that we drove like maniacs. Risked our lives."

"Ha, ha."

Charles McNerney and John Smart

[McNerney and Smart overnighted on a log landing by road 3800 at Castle Creek eight miles northwest of the summit—six miles inside what will be leveled forest and buried by landslide.[14]]

McNerney: About 7:30 someone started a jeep and woke us. We struck camp and packed the car. It was calm, no wind.

Smart: An old A-frame log choker sat on this landing. My photos before the eruption show a ridge a mile closer to the mountain.

McNerney: I found my lighter in the alder where I'd tripped last night. John called. I jumped from the brush to see the mountain's north side collapsing. A black jet spurted up.

Smart: The slide came down and flattened out. An ash eruption started fifteen seconds later.

McNerney: A white ring looking like fog, or like a puffy white doughnut, descended fast as an expanding apron. Black ash shot from the top of the mountain. It didn't go up much, but started down the mountain flank. The white ring led the growing black cloud down to timberline where the black cloud seemed to catch up with it. I heard nothing.

Smart: There was no sound. A bright white cloud swept down, expanding and hugging the ground like fog, ahead of a big dark cloud still on the mountain.

McNerney: A warm wind picked up from the mountain. The cloud like black chalk dust climbed over a nearer ridge. I looked through the white haze to the black wall behind. The warm wind increased to forty miles an hour. Trees bent and branches fell. The only noise was wind in the trees.

Smart: "Let's get the hell out of here!" I yelled, and jumped in the car.

McNerney: My 1979 Honda Prelude sedan faced downvalley. We took off less than a minute after the first venting. We raced fast as I could down the gravel road. The wind blew very warm from behind and made pressure inside. "Y'have the heater on?" John asked. I closed the sunroof. When I drive this car at 70, the sunroof doesn't let in much air. The warm air behind had pushed in—the only time I've felt such pressure. We passed sprinting deer. At 65 miles an hour, we didn't gain on the cloud.

Smart: The cloud looked like lambswool. We averaged 60 miles an hour on the straight gravel, and the cloud stayed a few miles upvalley of us. We turned a sharp right and a sharp left onto pavement by the roadblock.

McNerney: Three cars sat on the north shoulder. Upvalley the white cloud still led the black chalky cloud. Here it was clear, no white haze. We sped down the highway

75 miles an hour and gained on the cloud. We raced through tall timber and got well ahead.

About 2½ miles below the roadblock we pulled onto a wide left shoulder by a clearcut planted in small firs. I got out.

Smart: I stood through the sunroof. The dark cloud was now a few thousand feet high. It came closer but also started up. It slowed and appeared to stop five miles upvalley.

McNerney: John took four pictures—I'm on the edge of one. Only a gentle breeze here.

But then the clouds came down the valley again. The white mist, the big black cloud behind, followed a clockwise bend in the valley [around Elk Rock]. The black cloud was really moving. The two clouds—white mist ahead of black—came 50 miles an hour. The front of the haze caught up with us. The base of the black chalk dust behind looked like creeping avalanches. One black part shot out in front, then another, then another like waves lapping up a beach. It didn't boil above this base, just a cumulus effect. I jumped back in.

Smart: The white cloud coming again was a thousand feet high leading the dark cloud. We'd stopped half a minute.

McNerney: Six cars zipped down the highway. We sped out behind the last one and caught up.

Smart: The straight road was too tree-lined to see upvalley. At a little clearing at the west end of the straightway we slowed toward the right shoulder, let a black Toronado pass {O'Keefe & Baker}, pulled back onto the pavement, and kept a fast clip.

McNerney: We followed this car downvalley 65 miles an hour. We passed a sign on the right: CA BAKER. I braked and the Toronado pulled away.

Smart: We stopped at a logging camp and got out. This clearing was too surrounded by trees to see the white cloud. The dark cloud now towered way up. I took four pictures as the top grew up and out. I saw lightning and heard faint thunder.

McNerney: An officer sped up the highway, siren blaring, ordering people to leave.

Smart: We drove downvalley to a store on the left [Kid Valley] and stopped five minutes. People talked about the cloud. A truck came by. It's megaphone told us to leave.

McNerney: Lightning shot horizontal in the cloud. Soon the growing gray cloud blotted out the sun, and the sky went dark.

Smart: We stopped at Drew's store in Toutle, emergency vehicles now everywhere.

HOFFSTADT CREEK

Jim Scymanky

[James (Jim) Scymanky, Leonty Skorohodoff, Evlanty Sharipoff, and José Dias y Miranda thinned small firs 12½ miles northwest of the volcano on a north slope above Hoffstadt Creek off lower road 3200.[15] Skorohodoff's pickup sat on upper road

3200. After eruption the area lay a mile inside downed timber and 2–2½ miles inside the edge of standing scorched trees.]

We started cutting about seven on the south side of Hoffstadt valley, Mount St. Helens invisible behind the ridge. Dias wouldn't work on Sunday and stayed up at the pickup. We thinned up into a wall of second-growth Douglas fir six to twelve inches diameter, leaving a tangle of downed trees behind. I was in the middle, Evlanty sixty yards east, Leonty sixty yards west. Upslope I could see only fifty yards into the trees, the upper road and truck much higher. Cutting with chain saws, we heard and felt nothing.

I heard screeching or screaming. I shut off the saw thinking one of my companions was hurt. I started toward Evlanty. He'd stopped his saw and started toward me. He was okay but had heard screeching. We turned toward Leonty, who'd shut off his saw. We'd gotten within twenty yards when Dias—a short, compact soccer player—came running down through the trees, hurtling over a fallen one, waving his arms and shouting. We couldn't understand until he got near. "*El volcán esta explotando!*" he screamed. He'd left the truck without shoes, sprinting down through the forest barefoot. Even now didn't stop but screamed and ran between us and fell into our jumble of felled trees. It was like he'd gone nuts, was being chased. But behind him up through the trees I saw nothing.

Then up in the trees I saw the top of a tall one jiggle and fall, and another nearer, then another. Rocks zinged through the woods, bouncing off trees, then the tops of trees snapped off. *What the hell. . . ?* Ten seconds later a horrible snapping, crashing, crunching, grinding came down through the forest from the southeast. It grew louder, like a gigantic locomotive, or like ocean waves but very loud. I hurled my saw away and scrambled down into the jumble of trees we'd cut.

Suddenly I could see nothing. I'd been knocked down and my hard hat blown off. It got hot right away, then scorching hot and impossible to breathe. The air had no oxygen, like being trapped underwater. I gasped for breath for a minute, and the inside of my throat got very hot. I felt I was being burned, thought even I was being covered by lava. I was being cremated, the pain unbearable.

After a minute I got up, my back to a searing, painful heat coming down from the south. It was hell, the noise deafening, like standing next to screaming jet engines. I don't remember rocks or other projectiles, just this very hot gas for about two minutes. It was completely black, and deafening noise, as I gulped ashy air.

I thought I was dying. I thought of my wife and kids. *God damn! How can you do this to me?* I yelled a stream of phrases that are unrepeatable—pissed to be going out like this.

Some minutes—maybe three to five—after being enveloped I saw dim shadows. All the trees were down, except a few small ones standing as eerie silhouettes. Everything was drab gray and covered in a foot of ash. The trees had blown down northwestward but none fell on us. My clothes didn't burn, but my skin had badly burned through my clothes—arms, legs, back, chest, and the inside of my mouth burned. My gloves were welded—burned—onto my hands. Pain from the burns was excruciating. I gasped for air, coughing and spitting out ash, which was thick in the air.

My friends stood slowly down near a huge boulder I'd not seen before in the trees. It had been a beautiful green forest, clear air. Now the trees are down, covered in gray, the air itself heavy with dust. All landmarks are gone. I can't tell where the hell I am. I knew the roads and streams, but now I see no water, no roads. It's a wholly different world.

I stumbled twenty yards down to the others. They were pathetic, badly burned and caked in ash. I must look the same. They too had been burned beneath their clothes. Each of us in pain, we said little. We hiked down through warm ashy, jumbled timber toward the lower road. The creek was oozing warm sludge, no longer freezing cold. We rolled in it and threw the mud-water over us to soothe our burns. My hands were especially badly burned. Looking at the others covered in mud, I saw what I looked like. It was awful.

We left the mud and started up the road. The truck was the only shelter. The road was thick in ash, almost obliterated in spots, crossed by many downed trees. We climbed over and under them, each in pain, saying nothing. The truck had blown west along the road and north into a ditch but was upright. The glass was out of the passenger door but the rest intact. The back camper door was bent shut. Both cab doors were a little bent, but we pried them open.

It was getting dark again now forty minutes after we'd been burned. We got in the pickup cab for shelter—four of us onto the one bench seat. We hollered at each other, for it hurt to be touched. Ash fell thick and dry. It went pitch black again, but this time no heat and we breathed easily. Our burns hurt, yet we're wedged into one cab. We couldn't stand the agony but stayed in the truck forty minutes. Soon as it cleared a bit we got out.

We'd get no help here. We had to try to get the hell out. When it lightened a little we started back on foot down the logging roads [road 3208] toward Camp Baker. Dust-sized ash still rained too dense to see through. Ashfall decreased gradually, then stopped, and the air lightened. Trees were down everywhere, many across the road. We climbed over, under, and around them. Ash lay on the logs and all over, in the air a stench like a burnt building or burnt forest.

We walked and stumbled along, climbing over and under downed trees, in pain, hardly speaking, Dias without boots. We were getting cold, maybe from our burns. We sat awhile back-to-back to warm up, but it hurt. We gradually got down three or so miles [road 3100] to a sharp curve where a cold spring trickled from a rock face three feet above the road, the only clear water we'd seen.[16] We stayed ten minutes and drank.

Thirty yards beyond the spring a side road went down west. Seventy yards farther we came to a huge mound of debris. An avalanche had buried the 3100 and all beyond. This debris more than a hundred feet high held giant rocks. We were trapped.

Now two and a half hours after the eruption [about 11:00], we were cold. Some trees here were green—some standing, some pushed over by the avalanche. We lay on green branches back-to-back to warm up. But our burns hurt too much to lie for long. For an hour we alternated between standing and lying. Needing water, we turned back toward the spring.

Evlanty Sharipoff decided to take the west road. He was in much pain from burns. I pleaded with him, "We need to stay together. Camp Baker's too far. Here we have water. The roads are gone." He argued angrily. He walked unsteadily, stumbled. I tugged his shirt to urge him back, "You'll die!" He threw my arm aside yelling, "Don't touch me!" My touch hurt his burns. And it hurt my fingers. He walked down the road.

Three of us plodded back in ash to the spring. A little powder still fell. A quarter hour later Dias said, "I'm not staying." We argued with him, but he walked down the road, up the mountain of debris, and over its crest.

About five hours after the eruption [1:40 PM], a reddish-brown gooey mudflow from the main valley oozed up the tributary below us—its edge a hundred yards away and a hundred feet down. Many huge trees and rocks churned on top. It carried a trailer, logging truck, car, other junk, flowing less than a hundred feet a minute. It buried the road west and widened to a huge sea of mud. "Evlanty's gone," Leonty said. Afraid of this flow, he wanted to go back up to the truck. "No," I said. "Here we have water and can be seen. If it rises we'll move up."

Several helicopters flew around far downvalley, occasionally one over the Toutle but none closer than a mile. From our burns we were in great pain and cold as hell. Leonty hurt when he lay down, hurt when he got up. He lay down again. Up and down, up and down. Gradually he grew too weak to stand. How can I make it through the night? I thought. How long does it take to die? The pain is so great, to die would be nice.

Eight hours after the eruption [~4:30] two National Guard helicopters flew over following our tracks. Leonty barely moved, and I couldn't stand much. They hovered down several times, blowing great clouds of ash. One landed above us in a huge dust-cloud {*Hagerman*}. A guy walked down. "You have anything for pain?" I asked. Two guys walked up from below. One carried Leonty to the ship, and two helped me walk up. The pilot took off in dust. I was so damn glad to be out of there.

They flew us to St. Johns Hospital in Longview. Nurses wheeled me in on a gurney. My hands were black and swollen, and they said my head was black and swollen. A circle of doctors and nurses looked down on me.

"Oh God, we can't do anything for *this*, not here."

"He needs the burn center, in San Antonio."

The pain is killing me. "For chrissake do *something*!" I groaned. They went to work.

Within an hour they put Leonty and me in a life-flight helicopter that flew fifty miles south to Emanuel Hospital's new burn center in Portland [7:00 PM].[17]

José Dias, who'd left us and walked onto the avalanche, was rescued, brought to Longview {*Stebner and Wedding*}, and life-flighted to Emanuel [9:30].

GREEN RIVER

The Davis and Brooks party were the closest to the mountain to survive inside devastated area. From Shultz Creek the surge fanned into Green River—downvalley toward Payne and Hubbard, upvalley toward Nelson, Ruff, and others.

Dale Davis, Leslie Davis, Albert Brooks

[The Davises and Brooks drove up Shultz Creek 13 miles north-northwest of Mount St. Helens.[18]]

Dale: I'd hunted here eighteen years. In my old red Ford pickup we were showing Al Brooks around and photographing wildlife. From Winters Mountain [4½ miles north of Green River], Mount St. Helens looked peaceful.

Leslie: We set a spotting scope on the hood to watch the mountain. We tried to photograph a rare albino deer.

Dale: We drove down to Green River and crossed the bridge.

Leslie: Dale was driving, Al on the right. The mountain lay behind ridges. We'd go to Gilbert lookout for a view. A mile beyond Green River on road 2810 we drove south through a clearcut, only brush and very small trees.[19] We rounded a bend and started up a steep hill.

Dale: A plume rose from behind the ridge. Then east toward Hanaford and Fawn Lakes the cloud rose all at once. It looked like that range exploded.

Leslie: Dale stopped the truck, got out, and took a photo.

Dale: The cloud then rolled over from Coldwater drainage toward us. There was no wind. It looked like a boiling mass of rock. It threw trees out at the front. The front came to a little valley and followed the contour of the ground. It flowed over and down a stump like water.

Leslie: The high billowy cloud had been far back behind the ridge. It now rolled over hill and valley, and so fast, the front only sixty feet high. "Dale!" I hollered, "It's coming fast!"

Brooks: It looked like the ocean rolling, huge and fantastic, following every wrinkle in the ground. "We better get the hell out of here!" Dale said.

Dale: I jumped in the pickup and backed into an old spur but jammed against a bank and stuck [truck facing east]. "Roll up the windows!" I said. In thirty seconds the cloud was on us— simultaneously a blast of wind, noise, heat, and total darkness.

Leslie: When it hit the right wing window broke in. The heat was intense.

Brooks: I wore short sleeves. Pain slapped my bare right arm. I stuffed a rag into the broken window, but ash blowing through it burned my right arm. The pickup rocked like it was balsa.

Dale: We yelled through the roar. A sound like large hailstones beat on the pickup some minutes. Later I saw it melted the pickup's grille, ripped a chrome strip and mirror from the right side, and sandblasted the windows.

A minute after it hit, the air lightened a little for ten seconds, then total darkness again. I saw no lightning but very loud thunder crashed for half an hour.

Brooks: Heat neared the unbearable. Would the gas tank explode and the pickup be our coffin?

Leslie: Ash piled on us. I felt I'd suffocate.

Dale: I was choking, the way ammonia shuts your wind off. Dust like talcum powder stuck in your mouth and couldn't be spat out. We rinsed our mouths with coffee from the thermos. Chunks pounded the side and top of the pickup.

Leslie: It hit on the right side five minutes. Some was ice, for the windshield felt wet despite the heat. I rubbed some of the moisture on my face. The noise dropped off. "Let's drive!" I said.

Dale: I got out and wiped off windows and headlights. With headlights I saw only a dull glare—barely saw the hood. Ash still fell steeply from the south.

Leslie: But the truck was stuck.

Brooks: Worried about a gastank explosion, we left the vehicle. We brought the thermos.

Dale: The air was warm. I held a flashlight low to see the road edge.

Leslie: The ash fell warm. The five inches of ash on the ground was hot but not scalding. Dale and I had on only tennis shoes and socks.

Dale: Particles peppered hard from the southeast. In the dark and blowing ash we veered off the road. We came to Schultz Creek. I fell into hot mud, but Al pulled me out. Beneath a crust it was hot as hell and blistered my leg.

Leslie: Al and I waited on the road while Dale looked for the bridge. Now around ten o'clock, still dark, Al was getting weak. "You two go on," he said.

"No way," I said. "Three of us came in, and three are going out."

Dale: I stumbled down through smashed brush to Shultz Creek and followed a rock bar toward Green River. I heard mud in the creek running fast, but it was too dark to see. I jumped from rock to rock. I fell into hot ash again but it didn't burn through tennis shoes. The air lightened a little: I was under the edge of the concrete bridge.

We crossed the bridge. I heard the water rolling and rocks rumbling.

Leslie: We turned west onto road 2500, and the air lightened more. This had been a forest, but now the trees were down.

Dale: Les stepped into a pocket of hot ash. We tried walking on logs to stay above it.

Leslie: Ash was thicker here—a foot deep in spots and hot.

Dale: On logs upslope from the road the ash was only six inches deep. We walked up one log, stepped to another.

Leslie: It was tough going—steep and scary, some logs twenty feet from the ground.

Dale: About 10:30 it grew light enough to see twenty feet. "We should be on the road in case someone's looking for us." We climbed down, still a foot of ash there.

Leslie: This finer ash blew and hurt our eyes.

Dale: The mountain rumbled at times. I tried to drink from Green River but it was hot enough to scald hogs. Deer lay in the road, noses full of ash, eyes matted, hair burnt.

Leslie: Alive but didn't move. A burn on my backside broke open and ran down my leg. Searching for water we found only mud. At 3:30 we came to a watertank. It too was muddy water, but we rinsed our faces and Al's burnt arm.

Dale knew the roads. From road 2500, we turned up the 2566 a few miles north to roads 1100 and 1130. We heard aircraft but the air was too ashy to see far. The top of Winters Mountain was thick in ash.

We walked west down roads 555, 553, and 550, then northwest on Winston Creek road 200. Ash on the ground got thinner. Around six two guys drove up in a pickup but went on to Winters Mountain. We hiked farther down, and they came back about seven. From the truck we'd walked seventeen miles. They drove us home to Mossyrock.

Our son Tom said our son-in-law Keith Moore was missing at Green River *{Payne & Hubbard}*. An ambulance took us to St. Helen's Hospital in Chehalis. They treated our burns and released us.

Brooks: Stopping on Winters Mountain to photograph deer spared our lives. Otherwise we'd have been up on the ridge when it erupted.

Bob Payne and Mike Hubbard

[Robert Payne, Mike Hubbard, and Keith Moore stood along Green River sixteen miles northwest of Mount St. Helens,[20] Payne's truck on road 1113.]

Hubbard: Three of us went fishing on Green River. We felt no risk from Mount St. Helens so far away. Bob's truck was two hundred feet up and two hundred yards back from the river.

We stood on the north bank on an inside bend where current eddied slowly upriver. Along the banks stood partly leafed maple, alder, and cottonwood, and farther back tall firs. I worked upriver toward Bob, then we worked up toward Keith fishing a hole.

Payne: It was sunny, calm, the water clear and cold. Not fishing, I stood between Keith upstream with a fish basket over his shoulder and Mike just downstream fishing off rocks. Down in a steep part of valley among trees, we could see up but only partly south.

Hubbard: We were now eight yards apart—Keith on a point at the top of the hole, I near the lower end casting a lure past a steelhead I saw.

Keith hollered and pointed south: "Goddam! Look at *that!*" A huge, churning cloud billowed a mile south of the ridge, really moving, dark gray at the center, lighter at the edges.

Payne: The big cloud, black and billowy, rolled toward us making no sound.

Hubbard: We could see half a mile of ridge line. The cloud suddenly loomed over the ridge as a wall. It didn't continue up but flowed down through the forest toward us. The front was a thousand feet high—boiling, gray, turbulent, coming very fast.

I dropped my pole and ran down the bank. I looked back and already it was almost on us, a hundred yards back. Bob ran just behind me, and I glimpsed Keith forty yards back running from the river into taller timber. Just ahead of me was a huge maple tree, four feet in diameter. I dove in behind it, Bob dove in, and it turned black.

Payne: It enveloped us, pitch black and indescribably hot. Thunder like heavy artillery close by lasted ten seconds—trees coming down, I think. Then came heavy rumbling and thunder from the mountain, and lightning in the cloud. A fierce wind knocked me back onto Mike. It lasted half a minute. It was like Navy boot camp when we jumped into water with fire on it, but this much hotter and longer.

Hubbard: Ripping hot. I heard breaking trees like a timber operation for many seconds. It was hard to breathe, my mouth hot and full of dust. I was on my knees, my back to the hot wind. It blew me along, lifting my rear so I was up on my hands. Then I came up and bounced along a couple times. It pushed Bob along too, and we stayed together bumping each other. It was hot but I didn't feel burned—until I felt my ears curl. After half a minute the wind slackened.

"Dive in the river!" I yelled. The icy water ended the burning. The hot and dry dust in my mouth was now mud. I fingered it out.

Payne: The wind stopped, and we rolled into cold water up to our armpits. I pulled my wet shirt over my head to breathe through—a Navy bootcamp trick.

Hubbard: Bob yelled, "Unbutton your shirt! Pull it up and rebutton!"

Payne: I helped pull Mike's shirt up. It was too hot to stay above water. We bobbed down and up. Without my Navy training we'd be dead. For an inch above the water it wasn't quite as dark.

Hubbard: We stood submerged, only nostrils and head out, wet shirts buttoned around our heads. We ducked then bobbed up. We could talk only by shouting.

Things fell in the black that felt like pumice but may have been pieces of tree. It stayed hot but not as bad. We bobbed up and down in the water a quarter hour.

Payne: The water grew thicker and warmer but didn't rise. The air lightened: I could see two inches, then four. Then the black cloud pulled back east upriver. I smelled sulfur.

Hubbard: A slight breeze came upriver, and a patch of light appeared to the west. It grew and grew. Within a minute wind sucked the ash off us. Now at the base of a huge plume, we looked up forty thousand feet, fifty. The billowy cloud racing down the ridge had been big, but this wall was mighty. It didn't churn like that other. It was like a great column of smoke going up. It mushroomed way up. Huge lightning bolts ran around its edge.

Most trees were down! Heat had shriveled maple and cottonwood leaves. We climbed onto the bank and walked up where Keith had been. Hundreds of big trees were down. Could he be pinned by one?

Payne: We searched and hollered for Keith but got no answer. Mike's throat was so burned he whispered. We could see eight feet through talcum-powder ash in the air. On the ground the ash was over my eight-inch boot tops and hot. I found Keith's fish basket and pole fifteen feet north of the bank where he'd fished. I hung them on a snag by the river. The big black cloud stood in a north-south line and curved far east, full of lightning and thunder.

Hubbard: We yelled for Keith and watched for any movement. My burned throat and vocal cords hurt. I called hoarsely enough to be heard. Warm ash lay eight inches thick over everything. For five minutes we searched and called and made noise he might hear. We found only his fishing gear. The air stayed fairly clear, but only 500 to 1000 yards away the vertical gray wall went up fifty thousand feet—so huge and powerful I felt tiny.

The base of the wall widened and came back downriver. When the edge was fifty feet away we worried of heat again and got back in the river.

Payne: The cloud came back and the air went dark again. The river was now warm and thick. The air was hot but not like earlier.

Hubbard: The river was full of grit and fifteen degrees warmer. The air blacked out again, this time not so hot. We got cold.

Payne: We began to shake—going into shock or hypothermia. Moving and talking, we stayed in the water another 45 minutes.

Hubbard: We climbed out and sat on the bank, air temperature about 100°F. It grew lighter over an hour and a half until like night. The mountain growled and ground shook. Shook 10 to 15 seconds and subsided. Fifteen minutes later another growl and shake. It died away as the air lightened.

We had to get out. My voice was much hoarser, and I might be going into shock. I suggested going downriver. I didn't want to leave what had saved us. If another blast comes when we're away from water, we're cooked. But Bob said "No."

We called for Keith, but again nothing. I thought him dead under a tree.

Payne: We couldn't go downriver through a rocky canyon in hot ash across downed trees. We hiked toward the truck in hot ash many inches deep, stirring up clouds of powder.

Hubbard: We climbed steeply in semidark over and under many downed trees.

Payne: Trees had blown down both sides of the truck. About 11 o'clock I snapped a photo of Mike and he one of me. I hung the camera on the steering wheel: someone would know we'd come this far. Lightning flashed in the black cloud overhead. The mountain rumbled.

Hubbard: Eight inches of ash covered everything. We walked up road 1113. In cuts we went under downed trees, on fills over them. The mountain rumbled from time to time. The air lightened and ash on the ground thinned. We were in and out of down timber. After a mile we got beyond the down. The ash grew thinner but coated standing trees.

Payne: We walked north to road 1110, west to the 1100, and on west. Every creek ran thick with mud. I heard helicopters far south. We walked to Devil's Creek, six road miles from our start.

Hubbard: The ash thinned to an inch as we walked another two miles. Two dark-green military hueys flew by, but we were in standing trees.[21] At clearer water I went down to rinse off and Bob stayed. After a couple minutes he called, "Someone's coming."

Payne: A Bronco came by, two half-drunk teenagers. Mike came and we got in.

The best way was road 500 northeast toward Camp 9. But we drove into the ash cloud before Camp 9.[22] Back west after many miles we turned north on road 510. We drank two of their beers.

We merged north with Salmon Creek road. After many miles the road crossed the divide and wound down to Winston Creek road. Miles farther we joined highway 12. From EJ's store about 4:30 I called a friend, Mike Mulligan, and told him about missing Keith.

Hubbard: The kids drove us to Mossyrock. An ambulance moved us to the Morton hospital.

Payne: I was dehydrated by eight pounds, Mike—a tall, large man—by fifteen. They gave us shots and cleaned us but weren't equipped for extensive burns. An ambulance took us to a burn center at St. Joseph's Hospital in Tacoma.

Bruce Nelson and Sue Ruff

[Bruce Nelson (age 22) and Sue Ruff (21) with a dog were camped thirteen miles north of Mount St. Helens among firs just north of Green River.[23] Terry Crall and Karen Varner (both 21) camped yards west with a dog and puppies. Dan Balch and Brian Thomas tented seventy yards west. Green River is twenty feet down a steep bank.]

Nelson: I got up about 7:30 and lit a fire. Terry and Karen woke at eight but Karen stayed dozing in the tent. By 8:15 Sue and I were dressed and boots on.

Ruff: I put the coffeepot on the fire. Toting his fishing pole Terry said, "I'll try my hand before sun hits the pool." I climbed down to the river, washed my face, and put in contact lenses. Terry fished fifteen yards upstream.

Nelson: A little before 8:30 he hooked one that broke his line.

Ruff: "I can't believe how big it is!" Terry hollered. He scrambled up the bank.

Nelson: He sat on a log in front of his tent facing south, winding line onto a stick. I stood farther back from the river behind the tents.

Ruff: I returned to the firepit. Terry's hands shook, excited by the fish.

Nelson: "Mygod!" Terry then said. "There must be a fire!" A tall black cloud stood to the south over the trees and ridge between the canyons of Miners Creek and Green River.

Ruff: A little black cloud grew taller like a rising fire plume. But in fifteen seconds it spread not just up but far west into upper Shultz Creek and filled a quarter of the sky south of us. It was silent. Terry and Bruce together shouted, "That's no fire!"

Nelson: It could only be Mount St. Helens—an ash cloud at tremendous speed.

Ruff: I wanted my camera in the tent but couldn't leave my cigarettes behind. I stepped to the firepit for them. Suddenly wind roared through the trees from the south. The flames shot out two feet along the ground. The black cloud sped from the south. Arms of it spurted out in front a hundred to few hundred feet, boiling and branching, the black wall quickly caught up, then other arms shot out. The fire's flames were now out three feet flat to the ground, the roar of wind horrendous. With my back to the wind, my hair braids blew straight out in front. I glanced back. The cloud had grown big so fast and was racing straight toward us. "Holy shit!" I called. Behind our tent, Bruce held a bag of marshmallows, popping them one after another in his mouth staring, backing slowly away.

Nelson: For fifteen seconds the wind blew hard from the southwest where the dark cloud was coming. "Karen!" Terry yelled and dove in the tent.

Ruff: Terry's three puppies scurried between the fire and our tent, scared by the roaring wind. I ran through. I glanced behind and the cloud was now at the river, coming fast and black. I ran to Bruce, not wanting to see my killer. I hurtled over our tent ropes as my dog Cody ran beneath.

Nelson: I stood northeast of a fir, opposite the cloud. Sue got to me, I put my arms around her, and everything went black. I could see nothing. I heard trees boom down all at once.

Ruff: I got thrown onto my back in utter blackness but heard tremendous *boom! boom! boom!* My mouth filled with ash I tried to spit out but it clung.

Nelson: I smelled fresh dirt. We must be in the hole of an uprooted tree, buried in fallen trees.

Ruff: It was totally black. "Are you here?" I called.

"I'm here," Bruce said.

"What happened?"

"The trees came down."

Nelson: I was standing. Sue got back up. We couldn't see but were alive.

Ruff: I held Bruce's back and with my other hand dug ash from my mouth. I felt his back go up.

Nelson: I started to climb through fallen trees. But it got extremely hot. My hair sizzled. I'm a baker who works with huge ovens. This was five or six hundred degrees Fahrenheit. Sue was farther down in our tree-cave.

Ruff: It burned the top of my hair. I felt hot pitch boil out of a tree.

Nelson: "We're dead!" I screamed and dropped back. I knelt and dug with my hands.

Ruff: Bruce fell back in crying, "Omygod, we're gonna die, we're gonna die." I was pissed he'd caved in so fast. "We're not dead yet," I said. "Let's try to get out."

Nelson: The heat stopped. Ash sifting between the logs and limbs burned our fingers. I burned my legs climbing out. I pulled Sue out. It was like walking into a cooler but dark as a cave.

Ruff: Dark as shutting your eyes. Ash behind my contacts was excruciating.

Nelson: It had been sunny, and now it cleared enough to see blue sky to the north— and a hillslope. We could see enough for Sue to get her contacts out.

Ruff: Only for a couple minutes. "Hurry!" he said. "Hurry up!" as I picked them out. The air was hazy with fine ash, but I saw blue sky beyond.

"Terry!" we called. "Karen!" They had to be close, but no answer. Around us was no green, every needle gone. No sign of our green tent or Terry and Karen's red one.

Nelson: Black was coming again—straight down and thick, like a blanket falling. I dropped Sue's contacts in a cigarette-pack cellophane. Ten minutes after the start, thick, warm ash fell and we couldn't see again. This time there was no wind. It fell densely, like somebody pouring a bag of fine sand over your head.

Ruff: It went totally black again.

We hollered: "Karen!" "Terry!"

"I don't know," Bruce said. "I don't think they made it."

"We *must* find them."

"They're on their own for now. We gotta get out of here."

Nelson: The air was so bad here we'd climb to find better. I'd seen the hill. We felt our way in blackness. Climbing mostly on logs, we felt the ground tremble.

Ruff: It was totally black. You felt for a tree, and pulled up. An earthquake pitched me off; Bruce pulled me back. A leaning tree fell—I heard its scrape and thud. Ash fell thickly: breathing hard I got a mouthful too dry to spit out. We pulled shirts over our heads.

Nelson: For twenty minutes we climbed onto logs, groping in the dark. Earthquakes shook us off twice. The air smelled of sulfur like Yellowstone.

Ruff: The rotten-egg smell of hot springs where I grew up in Thermopolis, Wyoming, but stronger here.

Nelson: My feet got hot through boots. The mountain boomed. We saw only when lightning flashed but climbed a hundred feet. Some large things thudded down. One hit Sue in the head and left a knot.

Ruff: In blackness the lightning weirdly went horizontally. To a loud *crack!* it flashed pinkish and bluish. Some stuff fell wet. I felt wet enough on my arms to think it was raining. Larger sharp things stung my arms. After some big thumps we crawled under a fat log.

Nelson: From beneath the log I heard more chunks hit. Trees still up and branches falling? But then we felt wet: chunks of ice? The lightning quit. Ash had fallen heavily about fifteen minutes. It tapered off but the air stayed dark.

Ruff: I got nauseous and cold, started falling asleep.

Nelson: We talked to stay awake. Sulfur smell lingered in the dark.

Ruff: Under the log with shirts over our heads, I thought of Mount Lassen in 1915—stories in the *Oregonian* and *Daily News* in past weeks. "This could go on for days."

Nelson: "Sue, if we get out of this, will you marry me?" I couldn't even see her.

Ruff: "Yes," I said.

Nelson: After an hour it began to clear. After many more minutes we could see ten feet.

Ruff: We pulled our shirts down. Most trees were down, and ash now covered them. The beautiful green forest was gone and gray. We were in hell.

I heard a long moan like a foghorn. Then again. There'd been a log skidder across the valley. Had someone gotten to it and was calling by horn? We climbed down. "Karen!" we yelled. "Terry!" No reply. "Brian! Dan!"

Nelson: We got down near our campsite. Now two hours or so after the start I could see fifty feet, but my eyes burned. Down west Balch and Thomas yelled for help.

Ruff: I called my dog: "Cody! Come on Cody!"

"Forget the dog," Bruce said. "People need our help."

Nelson: Cody whined and emerged from fallen debris. So this was our camp.

Ruff: I checked her. Eyes caked in ash, but nothing broken.

Nelson: Trees had piled everywhere. I couldn't tell where the tents had been. We yelled "Karen!" and "Terry!" but heard nothing. A big pile of trees lay about where I thought their tent had been. It didn't look good.

Ruff: I recognized nothing. Terry's puppies whimpered faintly but I couldn't tell where.

Nelson: Balch and Thomas called again. We hiked west to them through a tangle of downed trees.

Ruff: "Was there a horn?" I asked Dan.

"It was me calling 'Hellllp!'"

"Where're Terry and Karen?" Brian asked. I turned away, not wanting to hear Bruce's answer. The air still stank of rotten eggs.

Nelson: Dan had been in the open during the heat. He said he held a tree at first and felt it falling. His arms were burned elbows to fingertips, fingers black, swollen, cracked open, raw flesh showing.

Ruff: Skin hung off like a marshmallow left in the fire too long. Swollen fingers had fused together and looked like burnt and split hot dogs. I'd had nothing to eat since last evening. Gross as this was it made me hungry.

Nelson: Brian said a tree had rolled on his leg and broke his hip. Dan had pulled him from a tangle of logs. We tried to carry him, but he screamed in pain. We carried him, lifted him onto a log, but he screamed with every jolt. It took half an hour to go ten yards to an old shack.

Ruff: Trees lay on it; we couldn't get inside.

Nelson: We sat Brian on the porch. He begged us not to leave. "There'll be more heat," he said. "I'll die." But someone had to get out for help before nightfall. All our clothes, gear, food, water lay beneath trees and ash. The flattened forest stretched hundreds of yards at least. It would take hours to get him to the trucks. We built a lean-to with wood and long cedar shakes from the porch. He could crawl behind it if another ash cloud.

Dan went down to the river and stuck his arms in. He came back with some skin sloughed off—open meat. It freaked him out.

Ruff: "Look at this!" he moaned. "Just look at my arms!"

Nelson: Without shoes his wet socks filled with ash. He walked off toward the road. Brian wore only long underwear. I gave him a shirt. He again begged us not to leave. I promised I'd be back. I didn't think he'd last the night. *Someone* had to get out. That meant us.

We met Dan down at the trucks. Trees had fallen on one. The mountain boomed and quit, boomed again. Dan hurt from burns. We hiked with him down road 2500, climbing over many downed trees up to two feet across.

Ruff: A few were five feet, others piled together. I lifted Cody onto a log. She walked it down and jumped off the west side. I lifted her onto another.

Nelson: Ash on the road was warm. But slopes above and below the road were too steep. Ash had slid off high banks and pooled on the road almost too deep to walk in, the bottom six inches hot as hell. In boots we waded through quickly, and the dog ran through okay.

Dan ran through barefoot and hopped onto a log to cool. It burned him. We hiked with him an hour and a half but made only two miles. At this pace none of us would be out by dark. I didn't think either Brian or Dan would last overnight out here. To find help before dark, I said, we had to hike fast.

Ruff: "Can't *you* stay with me?" he begged.

"No!" Bruce barked. "We must reach help. Brian'll *die!* For all to get out, we have to go."

Nelson: "I'll be back," I said. "If something happens, get in the water." We left him by the river.

Ruff: It was hard to leave a friend.

Nelson: Down the road we encountered a dozen elk, then two dozen. Hair and skin had burned off one side, noses plugged with ash. They stood but wouldn't make it. We saw lizards, porcupine, grouse, other birds. Many birds lay dead on the ash; others alive but couldn't fly.

Ruff: I washed one in a puddle. Everything was dead or dying. I set it in a bush. But it fell and lay on the ash gasping. I couldn't save even one little bird.

Nelson: We walked two more miles, blinding fine ash blowing up at times, the air lightening.

Ruff: The mountain rumbled a little. The rotten-egg smell ebbed. Ash in the air lightened, sun almost breaking through. We came to standing trees. But what if another cloud? We scooted through to the next clearing.

Nelson: Green River was gritty and tasted of sulfur. Three hours into our walk, some puddles had settled enough we got water that was sulfury but not grainy. I dipped plastic from a cigarette pack to get a little. Finally we found a clear spring.

Ruff: Many little animal tracks ran in circles.

Nelson: Spiders scurried in the ash. A long ways farther on road 2500 we came to an old man and small dog walking what seemed the wrong way, *up* Green River. He'd driven in from Morton trying to reach Camp Baker for tools, but his car had shorted out. On the CB he'd talked to people on road 1100 who'd wait for him. That sounded pretty good.

We hiked four miles, but found no one. We turned west on the 1100.

Ruff: To us in our early 20s, Grant Christiansen in his 60s with leathery dark skin seemed old. He told of being a survivor of Guadalcanal in 1942—at sea in a lifeboat two days before rescue.

Nelson: The old man's glass eye kept getting ashy. He popped it out several times to wipe off.

Three hours after we left the spring, not long before dusk, a huey helicopter flew near. The air was still dusty. Covered in ash, we blended into the gray road. They turned away.

Ruff: We shed our outer shirts and beat them on the ground. It raised the dust.

Nelson: The helicopter turned back. But the road here was narrow.

Ruff: They landed a few hundred yards west and walked back to us.

Nelson: This National Guard helicopter held a news photographer [*Seattle Times*'s Rick Perry] who shot as we approached. My singed hair is fluffed into an "afro."

RICK PERRY, *SEATTLE TIMES*

Ruff: Pilot Mike Cairnes and copilot Mike Samuelson had been searching for someone to rescue. Cairnes hugged me and said, "We're *so* glad to see you!"

"Not half as glad as I am," I said.

Nelson: They'd tracked our footprints until the ash thinned. We reached the helicopter about 8:30. The dogs had made it. We'd hiked fifteen miles. We told of Dan and Brian.

Ruff: They'd gotten Dan {*Kolb & Frishman*}.

Nelson: I asked them to fly up to the hut for Brian. They were low on fuel and said their orders were to take rescued people to Kelso.

"It's late," I said, "Brian won't last the night. I promised both injured guys we'd come back."

"No one could be alive that far up," they said.

"*We* came that far!"

We didn't need a hospital. "Okay," Cairnes said, "we'll go."

Ruff: I sat in a jump seat behind the pilots and through a headset heard their talk.

Nelson: They flew east. But at the hut no Brian! The only place to land was on the Green River bridge, too small for our huey. They radioed a small chopper nearby and showed him the place *{Hagerman}*.

Ruff: The helicopter raised a huge dustcloud and pulled off. It went down into another cloud but landed on the bridge. We circled while they searched. I told our pilots of others we'd seen yesterday—the bearded man, a woman, and little girl [Moores]; a man and two boys [Smiths]; the two miners. After ten minutes a pilot said, "We're too low on fuel." As we turned away, Cairnes grabbed my arm: "They got him!" They'd found Brian.

Nelson: I saw the cloud had run down Green River three miles, but timber stood farther west. When we landed at Kelso the pilot said we had five minutes' fuel left.

Dan Balch and Brian Thomas

[Balch and Thomas were camped by Green River by a decrepit Forest Service cabin seventy yards west of Nelson and Ruff.]

Thomas: Something woke me.

Balch: "What was that?" I asked. Out the tent's back window, I saw white clouds on the distant southwest ridge.

Thomas: I looked out.

Balch: Brian stared. I looked again and the white clouds had turned black and expanded very fast toward us. "Let's get the hell out!" I yelled.

Thomas: I shot out of the tent wearing a watch and long underwear. I sprinted toward a down oldgrowth tree four feet in diameter fifteen feet away. I dove into a two-foot space beneath.

Balch: I heard faint rumbling like a truck on gravel. Some wind came through. Then three pops like gunshots in the distance, each one quieter. Behind Brian I ran from the tent in blue jeans, long-sleeved shirt, and wool socks. In the few seconds of semi-light I got ten feet to a tall fir.

A wind blast hit. The tree I held tilted, and two others just beyond leaned. Within a couple seconds it got darker, then pitch black. The ground vibrated as if many trees came down all at once. The blast knocked me face-down and pushed the air out of me—I couldn't breathe. Mud and ice rained down. I tried to get up, but the air was gone. There was enough down at the surface to breathe. Heavy chunks of mud and ice hit my back and melted. I grew cold. I could see nothing. I heard something like mud slopping down.

Thomas: As I rolled beneath the big log, something made a big muffled rumble. Trees fell onto my big log with enough force to roll it. A branch spur caught my right leg and hip, and with great leverage turned me into the ground and out sideways. A sharp pain meant my hip was broken. In darkness I couldn't tell which way was up. I knew this was an eruption. It seemed the end.

Balch: Air pressure suddenly rose: my ears popped like coming down fast in a plane. Only seconds after the cold mud, everything burned. The wet and icy mud coating me baked to clay. Many dirt clods fell and thumped on the ground. I put my hands behind my head to guard it. They began burning. I'd been wet and freezing but seconds later felt dried as a prune. Ahead I felt a log. The tree I'd stood against was down! My fingers burned on it. Heavy chunks falling on me hurt. A big one hit my lower back. A hot one hit my left leg and burned. The heat and thumping lasted ten seconds, tapered off over ten, and stopped.

Thomas: Even down in branches I got warm. I smelled sulfur, burned fir needles, and dirt—or like the pitch, sulfur, and steam of pulping liquor in the paper mill where I work. I groped out of my hole onto the trees but felt the heat and fell back.

Balch: A minute after the heat wave it lightened enough to see a few feet. I pulled up against two big logs, grabbed another on top, and stood. Three logs had piled on top of each other, three more stacked just beyond. Brian was farther. Bark on the trees had blistered. "Brian!" I yelled. No answer. The air cleared rapidly. Almost every tree lay on the ground! From the north they pointed south toward me, across the river they pointed north, on the west they pointed east. A huge swirl. Only a few stood. "Brian!" I yelled. Silence.

My burned hands felt on fire. I climbed over trees down to Green River. The air smelled of burnt needles. A few inches of mud had set up like concrete; on top lay four inches of dry powder. The air was hazy. A big ash cloud way up flashed hundreds of red lightning bolts.

I got in the river. Yesterday's icy clear water was now warm and thick with black mud and tree limbs. Even so it felt good on my burned hands. I stayed in a couple minutes. I tried to wash my hands, but the mud made them worse. They were badly burned but the skin on.

Thomas: I was in pain and disoriented but realized I was buried. Trees had fallen all around, at least four big ones and their branches. In a pocket between fallen logs I could only stand on my good leg. I tried to move branches above. Some light showed that was the way out. But the logs were too big to climb with my broken hip. I yelled, but into lightning thunder.

Balch: I got out of the water, scrambled up the bank, and climbed onto a downed tree. "Brian!" I yelled. No answer. The thunder wasn't loud. I yelled again. "Can *anyone* hear me?" I screamed. Brian called faintly, like he was a far uphill. I walked a log north above the ash.

Twenty yards from the riverbank near where the tent had been I walked the top of a stack of three big downed trees. I slipped off and stuck out my elbows. One caught the log I'd fallen from, the other the top of trees piled just east. As I hung between them a hand grabbed my foot! I looked down to Brian! —on the ground reaching up through limbs. His voice had been faint from down here.

Thomas: As I groped up through broken limbs Dan's foot stepped through.

Balch: I got down, broke off limbs, and grabbed his hands to pull him up.

"My leg! My leg!" He screamed. "I think it's broken!"

"I gotta get you up," I said. I pulled again, but skin on my hands pulled down to my fingers.

Thomas: Dan tried to pull me up, but when skin peeled off his hands I let go.

Balch: I reached down, this time around both his wrists. I pulled and he stood, screaming in pain. A five-inch limb helped me push him to the top log six feet up.

Thomas: Dan was in horrible pain from burns. I was barefoot, but down in the hole the ash and branches were only warm.

A patch of blue sky was closing. We sat atop logs. Warm ash fell heavier and heavier. The air grew dark, the thunder loud. I held my undershirt over my head and spit out ash.

Balch: The light after the heat wave lasted about seven minutes. The air went black again, ashfall so thick I could see only inches. I screamed from my burns: "It hurts!" Ash poured down intensely from the southwest for a half an hour. My nose clogged with ash; I breathed through my shirt. This powder hit like snow with no sound. Lightning flashed a few times. Temperature should have been 50 degrees but stayed 100. Ash fell thickly an hour and a quarter.

Thomas: The fall tapered off, thunder and lightning quit, and the west grew lighter. Over some minutes it cleared. I saw the trees all down.

Balch: I got down and walked, yelling in pain.

Thomas: Bruce Nelson and Sue Ruff came from upriver.

Balch: They climbed through the trees but in ashy air we didn't see until they were close {Nelson & Ruff}. Others were alive! It had been two hours since the blast. I could see ten yards.

"Where's Terry and Karen?" Brian asked.

"Trees fell on them," Bruce said. "I think they're dead."

Thomas: Moving was like walking in a slash pile. I couldn't walk on my hip.

Balch: We carried Brian to the demolished cabin. The south front stood but other walls had fallen and roof collapsed. We set him on the porch and built a cover of cedar shakes. I left him my long-sleeve shirt. He begged us not to leave, but we couldn't get him past all the trees to the trucks. I threw up what seemed a gallon of ash.

Thomas: It was all they could do to get me those ten yards. They left.

Dan Balch

I had only socks on my feet but had to try to walk out. I climbed to the south valley side on a big downed tree. Then west along big logs as much as twenty feet above the ground. I screamed from my burns. At the road my truck and Bruce's were okay, the car between [Smith's] smashed by fallen trees, and one across the road [Moore's] covered by them. Ten minutes later Bruce and Sue came climbing over trees by the riverbank where the trail had been.

About 11:00 the three of us started down road 2500. In ashy air we could see twenty yards. Some spots were clear, but trees had fallen in piles. We climbed over and through them. Wind stirred up clouds of ash. The air cleared a little, and we stopped at the river to cool.

Two miles down at Soda Spring flat[24] the ash was a foot deep here and hot. My socks filled with hot ash. It was cooler barefoot. I walked on downed trees where I could, but clearcuts had none. We came to 200-foot stretch with no logs.

"The ash is too hot for me," I said.

"We'll go on. Someone's got to get out for help."

They hiked away along the bank above the road where ash wasn't as deep. I scrambled to the river and walked down its gravel. Twenty burned elk lay along the river. They barely moved as I walked through them in mud-water. They were dying.

Half an hour later, a man and two boys walked down the road {Smith}. I climbed the bank. Buzz Smith gave me tennis shoes from his pack. We walked on many miles. A deer lay by a water hole, alive but burned and dying. We sat under the bridge where the road crosses Green River [6 miles west of Soda Spring] and I cooled my burns in the water. Buzz gave us red licorice.

Back up on the bridge were foot tracks! Someone had crossed north while we sat below, ash muffling the sound. Farther down road 2500 a logger stood by his stalled pickup. His partner [Grant Christiansen] was walking out toward Toledo. Now five of us hiked west in air clear enough to see a hundred yards.

Two National Guard hueys flew over, saw us, and landed a quarter mile west. We hiked to them {Kolb & Frishman}. The pilot said they'd been flying in the North Fork and tried Green River this last trip out.

I pointed on the pilots' map where Brian was.

"No way you walked that far," one said.

"That's where we started too," Buzz said. "My truck's there."

We told about Bruce and Sue, and the other logger walking out toward Toledo. The other helicopter went to scout the road along the north side of the river. After awhile the pilot radioed, "I see survivors!"

We got into the helicopter. They flew us to St. John's Hospital in Longview. I gave Buzz back his shoes. The nurses gave me morphine and put me out.

Brian Thomas

I sat on the porch of the smashed cabin an hour. But I'd die here in the open. At the cars I could last the night. The air cleared some, and the sun returned through haze. I left the porch before noon.

I couldn't walk on a broken hip, and a cedar crutch didn't work in downed trees. No sign of the trail. At a down tree I crawled under if I could. If the space was too small I dragged myself up and flopped to the other side. It took eight hours until dusk to crawl and flop two hundred yards almost to the road. Ahead was a tall roadbank.

A helicopter landed on the bridge and they started toward me *{Hagerman}*. I'm covered by ash, my long underwear filthy gray. When I stuck my head up it startled the pilot. They must have carried me to the helicopter and flew me to Longview hospital.

Edward ("Buzz") Smith

[The Smiths had camped eleven miles north of Mount St. Helens.]

A Weyerhaeuser logger, I took my boys—Eric age 10 and Adam 7—for a campout. We'd be in high country many miles from the mountain, so I wasn't worried about an eruption. From home on Tower Road I drove my Chevy pickup up Spirit Lake highway and road 2500 and parked at the east bridge over Green River. We hiked up the Green and up Miners Creek to a bluff where the trail steepens [2370 feet] and tented among oldgrowth firs.[25]

Sunday I got up, built a fire, and cooked pancakes and eggs. We packed all but the drying tent. The trail ascends Miners Creek then climbs east to Island Lake. Snow was melting, many fresh streams, why carry water? I poured it out.

The air had been still but now I felt a few puffs of wind. That seemed odd—puffs instead of steady, and reaching us down in big trees. Seconds later came a loud *crack! crack! crack!* like rifle fire a mile off when sound carries in quiet air.

"What was that, Dad?" asked Eric.

"Must be someone shooting."

It came from the upvalley—this too odd. Someone wouldn't poach a deer miles from his rig. I thought of the mountain, but the sky was clear. I knelt to fold the tent. I got an uneasy feeling, that grew—like an air-pressure change.

Down in big trees, we could see up but not out. I glanced again. A black cloud billowed fast from the south a thousand feet above the trees. It quickly pulled overhead, and the day grew dim like approaching dusk. It had to be the mountain.

The boys looked scared. "Don't worry," I said. "Looks like we'll get a little ash." Actually it looked like a *lot* of ash. "Let's pack our stuff up to the trail before it comes."

Light-gray rocks the size of marbles fell through the trees and onto the tent as I folded and rolled it. I stuffed it in a bag and strapped it to my pack. The rocks were hard but lightweight. They ricocheted off trees but didn't hurt when they hit. The air pressure grew noticeable. I felt as though being pushed to the ground. The dark cloud stayed high, only rocks coming down. Then the cloud pulled back quickly—as if a vacuum sucked it south. The sky above was blue.

We started up toward the trail, the cloud not out of sight. In another minute a loudening roar came like a low jet. I'd been a Marine and it sounded like an F-4. Now I really felt the air being compressed and knew something big was coming. I was at the north side of a big oldgrowth yellow fir, its base six feet across. When big trees fall as in the 1962 Columbus Day storm, your best chance is to ride the roots. They hold up the butt end and leave space beneath.

As the roar began Adam pointed south, "Dad, look!" I grabbed his arm and yanked him to me behind the big fir. "Eric!" I barked. "Get over here!" and he came. With my back to the trunk, I looked south and saw a huge dustcloud explode off the rock bluff through trees, felling some of them. A closer big cedar tilted toward us. I pulled my head back and within seconds could see nothing. The ground rumbled and shook—as when you fall a big tree. But there wasn't much noise. Down in a draw at the base of the bluff, I felt no wind. The cloud blew well over our heads. I held my boys but couldn't see. Ash fell damp and cool like mud. Coarse pellets seemed to come straight down.

I felt in the top of my pack for the flashlight. I turned it on but in black air could see but a few inches. I unstrapped a sleeping bag and held it over us. I felt a branch in front of us where there'd been none. The big fir we stood behind was up but another had come down. I felt my way out ten feet in air completely black. Now I was sep-arated from my boys and wasn't sure of their direction. I called but heard nothing. "Eric!" I yelled, "Adam!" I heard faintly "Dad! We're here!" Only three yards away, I hardly heard them. The densely falling ash absorbed sound. I groped back. We held each other. Feeling along the branch I pulled them along. We crawled beneath the big downed log. I felt a couple branches sticking out to hold the sleeping bag—better than holding it up, and safer if anything big fell.

Damp mud beneath the tree and bag felt cool. But out the edges the air felt hot, now a couple minutes after the trees fell. It grew uncomfortably warm in four minutes. The ground shook: rumble and stop a second. Rumble and stop. Rumble and stop. Was the whole mountain exploding? It rumbled ten minutes. Thunder seemed close but muffled, the air too black to see lightning.

The boys started going to sleep. I too felt peaceful, blasé, sleepy. Except for the cool mud, sleep would be easy. Adam asked, "Daddy, are we going to live with Jesus?"

"Well . . . maybe, but not now."

That woke me. I should be scared—not lying here sleepy. "We've got to get *out* of here!" I said and pushed up the bag. Inches of ash fell off, warm but not burning.

The air had lightened. I got out but with the flashlight could see only a few feet. The ash might be deep ahead. I was disoriented again and with ash falling in darkness couldn't see my tracks to go five yards back. I hollered; they yelled back. I saw the bag only when I reached it. I crawled back under. We stayed another hour.

The fall thinned, the air like a foggy night, and I could see fifteen feet. "C'mon, let's go," I said. I rolled the sleeping bag and strapped it to my pack.

"Can I have a drink?" Adam asked.

"Ahh . . . I poured it out. We'll get some along the creek."

In the dark I'd lost my wristwatch. I thought it about 10:30. Most of the trees in this canyon had stayed up but their tops sheared off. I don't know why we'd not been speared.

No sign of the trail. We walked north down the draw through many inches of fluffy ash, climbing over deadfalls. When we sank in a foot, the ash was hot. We'd been in a pocket of mostly standing trees and snags but now came to many newfallen trees. Miners Creek was gone in the ash. In a mile and a half we came to Green River. No water here either—just mud, nothing to drink. Pouring out the water had been a big mistake.

I found an oldgrowth log spanning the river. I've walked them often and now put one boy in front, the other behind, and we crept to the north bank. But the river could flood. We climbed forty feet back from the river over downed trees and turned west. In suspended ashdust like dense firesmoke I could see only 150 feet but knew the road lay downriver. We fought through fallen trees and debris, past where the camp had been but now no hint of it. Finally I saw the bridge. I heard someone toward the river screaming, but I couldn't leave my boys here. We stumbled through trees and ash and after another two hundred feet reached the road.

Now at maybe 2:30 PM, it had taken four hours to come this far. My pickup was mashed lengthwise by a tree. But with all the ash and downed trees there was no driving out. Tracks in the ash showed people had walked down the 2500 road {Nelson & Ruff; Balch}.

From upriver came a cry, "Hellllp!"—the guy I'd heard earlier. Another "Helllp!" I told my boys to stay with the pickup and scrambled east over fallen trees. Among them I came to Brian Thomas. He couldn't walk on one leg but had crawled some distance from his camp {Thomas}.

"Don't go," he begged. "Don't leave me here."

"It'll do no good to stay. I could only keep you company. I've got kids with me. We need to walk out and send someone back."

"Others have gone for help." These would be the tracks I saw on the road.

"I can't stay. We'll find someone to come back."

I thrashed back. The boys and I started down road 2500. This area had been logged, the trees smaller second growth, the road clearer and easier walking, only a few trees down across it. A burnt-wood odor hung in the air. The kids grew tired and thirsty, but Green River had no water. We sat to rest and I gave them pancake syrup and fruit rolls. We continued through very light-gray ash. Where deeper than a few inches it was hot. We had boots on, but after deeper pockets of hot ash we climbed on logs to cool our feet.

We came to deer with hair burned off in patches, eyes caked or gone, noses plugged with damp ash. They acted drugged. Their tracks led down to the river and back to the road. Like us they wanted water. I saw a hole where a field mouse had come up through the ash, left a circular track, and at its end lay dead. Yellowjackets had come up through little holes and walked in the ash. Birds lay half covered in ash, dead. Some had walked a track on the ash.

"Why didn't the birds fly away?" Eric asked.

"I don't know. But look: even birds and hornets are walking. That's how we'll get out."

The boys grew very tired. We walked a stretch, rested. Walked, rested. After an hour or so we reached the river flat. Still following foot tracks, we passed a pair of ashy socks hung on a branch. We came to Soda Spring, no water here either. This area had been logged twenty or thirty years earlier: occasional downed trees were small.

Down the road one set of tracks diverged to the river. A guy sat sixty yards away where the river should be but was just mud. Weeks ago I'd seen T-shirts printed I SURVIVED MOUNT ST. HELENS. "Hey!" I yelled, "Hey! Survivor!"

He turned and called, "Come down here. I don't have shoes."

He mistook my red pack for rescuers. I was tired and had kids. "No. You come here."

He walked up slowly, filthy in ash, arms and shirt caked gray. We were all gray— Adam with streaks down his cheeks where tears had run and dried. The guy was Dan Balch *{Balch}*.

"My hands are burned," he said. "Would you button my pants?"

I did. He was barefoot. I pulled tennis shoes from my pack, slid them on his feet, and laced them. I gave him syrup and a fruit roll, now perhaps 4 o'clock.

This far out the ash was fluffy, and every step stirred it up. So we wouldn't breathe in so much, we walked a hundred feet apart—I leading, the kids, then Dan. We stopped twice looking for water but found none. About 4:30 a loud explosion came from the southeast and shook the ground way out here—like a big bomb in the distance. The mountain must've blown again. We picked up the pace. I was sure Elk Creek, a big stream from the north, would be flowing. But the ash had absorbed its water. It was chocolate-colored mud only foot wide and inches deep. A mile west we came to Cascade Creek, but ash had sucked up its water. Just beyond, the foot tracks we'd followed turned north onto the 2566 toward road 1100 *{Nelson and Ruff}*, the long way out. We stayed on the 2500.

From where we found Dan it took three hours to walk west five miles to the river crossing.[26] We were dehydrated, badly needing water. Green River was still mud. But I spotted a seep down a bank. I brushed away ash and groundwater trickled out. I dug in so a cup didn't fill with powder. I gave half a cup of water to Adam. Then one to Eric. Twice more and we'd all had some. Because of grit the kids wouldn't drink more.

"You want more?" I asked Dan.

"No."

He'd been walking behind and I hadn't seen him close. Now I saw water oozing from his neck, and no skin! I looked him over. No skin on parts of his arms—not much hide elbows to fingertips! He'd been so caked in ash I hadn't noticed this. Now I saw how bad off he was and realized I should've paid more attention.

"Man, you're hurt. You need to drink more water."

"It'll just make me throw up."

"You're burned. You need drink water even if you do throw up."

I got a big cupful, and he drank it all. "How'd you get so burned?" I asked.

"Didn't you feel the heat?"

"Not *that* hot. But we were in a hole under a bag."

It was toward evening but we had a long way to go. Here we had water, what we most needed to survive. Stay or go on? Our food would last two days, but that's no good without water. I knew of good water miles ahead—a hand-dug well at an old homestead. But it would be a long slog. I'd had a nosebleed off and on, the kids were very tired, Dan in terrible shape. Yet we'd be okay with good water. I stashed the kids' packs and things from mine under the bridge.

We started west. After a hundred yards a dark military huey flew over low. They must've followed our tracks in the ash. They waved us ahead where they could land *{Kolb}*. Two of the crew walked back to us. The kids were exhausted. Crewmen carried

Dan Balch with burned hands, "Buzz" Smith beyond

Eric and Adam. Dan and I trudged up *{Balch}*. We climbed in, and a newsman shot photos *{Frishman}*.

I told them about Brian Thomas badly injured up by a bridge they could land on. They said another helicopter would go. They shut the doors and tried to lift off but blew up a huge ashcloud. They shut down, got out, and cleaned ash from the airfilters. Again they tried to fly but a big dustcloud came up. Again they cleaned the filters.

"Listen, if you can't get this thing off, we'll get out. We don't want to crash."

"We're okay."

They tried again. It went white outside, but they climbed on instruments. We broke above the dust and the crew cheered. They'd been worried too. I realized this was the National Guard—weekend warriors—untrained for such conditions. The crew chief said it was 7:50.

They flew over the ridge southwest, came to Toutle River in flood, and followed it down. We flew over our house on Tower Road, the flood some distance away. They landed at the Longview hospital about 8:15.

Dan handed back my tennis shoes and walked into the hospital. We went in too. They cleaned and checked us.

10

West

Lord, Lord! methought what pain it was to drown;
What dreadful noise of water in mine ears!
—Shakespeare, *King Richard III*

For five chapters we circle Mount St. Helens clockwise outside the great surge.

Near Mount St. Helens

Ty Kearney and Marianna Kearney

[Marianna and Ty Kearney were radio amateur spotters for Washington Emergency Services. They've camped in their van 7½ miles west of the summit on road 5700.[1]]

Ty: We woke to a beautiful sunrise, chilly at 47°F, high overcast, slight west wind, Mount Rainier clear to the north.

Marianna: Ty in the van talked by radio with Gerry Martin. I sat in a folding chair sketching the mountain. I had all day for a good drawing.

Ty: Through binoculars I saw steam plumes from The Boot. Gerry and I discussed two white ones we'd seen Saturday. Gerry described a new dust-colored one drifting across Wishbone Glacier. I felt a solid jar to the van.

Marianna: I felt nothing. Ty called, "We're in an earthquake!"

Ty: Gerry radioed about it. I radioed it lasted four seconds.[2] {*Martin*}.

Marianna: I looked up from my sketch. A black jet shot from the crater. Then clouds boiled out round and black. Larger gray clouds boiled out lower on the north side. This is what we'd waited for. But the lower cloud grew and grew. In half a minute it spewed huge rocks and ice chunks up and north from Wishbone Glacier.

I stood and watched. Rogers and Valenzuela behind jumped and yelled, "This is *incredible!*" "It's *huge!*" I hadn't noticed them until now. The cloud grew fast. Billows like black velvet etched in silver and gray rolled west off the summit. It was terrible but beautiful. It should be loud, but I barely heard low rumbling. Inside the van, Ty listened to Martin. The boiling black cascade from the north grew bigger and bigger.

Ty: Rogers and Valenzuela outside were yelling. My windows were steamed. Fifteen seconds after the earthquake I grabbed my camera and stepped out. On the skyline ridge I saw the lower part of Goat Rocks *sliding!*

I shot four frames toward the mountain, then two toward Mount Rainier. A gap between my fourth and fifth pictures is Rogers driving away and I waiting for dust to settle {*Rogers & Valenzuela*}. An east wind now blew from the mountain. My next

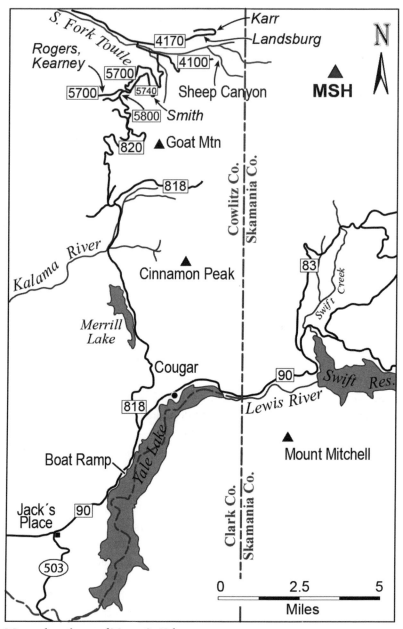

West and southwest of Mount St. Helens

photo shows the cloud coming over a ridge into South Fork valley. I called to Mari-anna, grabbed the tripod, and got in.

Marianna: As the cloud rolled into the South Fork, Ty yelled: "Let's get out of here!" He jumped into the van and radioed, "We are leaving the area!" [~8:34:53] *{Martin}.* I was in no hurry. I added touches to my pencil sketch, closed the pad, folded the chair. Our gas and propane tanks sat by the van. "What about the tanks?" I asked. "Forget 'em! Get in!" he said and slammed the top down.

Ty: I sped east toward the mountain. In half a mile I saw lightning. Everything in front and north was now black.

Marianna: I scrambled to the back and knelt to hold a radio on a table. A cupboard door flew open, and cups and stuff fell.

Ty: Part of the huge black cloud shot up like a poof from a steam locomotive starting from the station. It hit the high overcast cloud layer and flattened as a black disk. I turned south on road 820 [later part of 8117].

Marianna: As we sped south I saw out the east window only a huge gray cloud that looked like it would engulf us. Smaller columns churned up into it. The radio screamed with static, but I heard others call. I radioed we're driving south and the cloud's going northwest toward Martin. Lightning ripped the cloud. I was scared.

Ty: Several cars were at the gap.[3] I sped on behind the next ridge.

Marianna: The cloud was all shades of gray like a monstrous mural in pastels of swirling grays. Many columns churned up. Swipes of lighter gray—here vertical, there horizontal—crossed the cloud flashing with lightning.

Ty: Minutes later we neared Fossil Creek. A mushroom cloud swelled high over us; aspen blew in the wind. I felt better with a ridge between us and the mountain. The mushroom grew west beyond us and the sky went darker. Light remained southwest.

Marianna: Near Merrill Lake I got my first high look at the eruption cloud, a dramatic, huge cauliflower light gray against the deep gray gloom of the rest of the cloud, upper and south edges backlit against blue sky.

Ty: I drove into sunlight and stopped. The wind now [~9:00] blew *toward* the mountain. I shot another photo.

Marianna: It was serene, radio static gone, blue sky overhead. To the northeast all was dark. The west edge of the cloud towered like a fountain. The stalk below the scalloped top was circled by clouds stacked like saucers.

We passed the Forest Service roadblock at the end of road 818 [later, 81]. We drove southwest along Yale Lake, turned south at Jack's Place, and drove through Amboy. Church bells rang at View. I shot photos about 10:30.

Robert Rogers and Francisco Valenzuela

[Robert Rogers and Francisco Valenzuela had camped just west of the Kearneys on road 5700, later part of 8117.[4]]

Valenzuela: I felt several earthquakes overnight. After an early drive and hike in Sheep Canyon, we returned to camp about 8:20. Marianna Kearney sat sketching the mountain. Northwest across the South Fork a pickup with canopy crept near Spud Mountain [Selby].

Landslide

8:32:45

ROBERT ROGERS

8:32:56

ROBERT ROGERS

8:33:15

TY KEARNEY

8:34:05

TY KEARNEY

Rogers: Steam wafted from the south crater rim. I stood by the open door of the van. Ty Kearney inside listened by ham radio to Gerry Martin describing plumes in his view from the north. I told Ty details from my climbs. Martin talked on.

Valenzuela: Fog hung over the bulge. I sat on a stump ten yards behind Marianna, peeled an orange, and watched the peaceful mountain. A sharp earthquake rocked me north-south. The land rose and fell.

Rogers: The ground shook. A few seconds later dark-gray ash spurted from the crater, the first I'd seen in more than a week. I bolted toward my car twenty yards away.

Valenzuela: Just after the earthquake a white haze like thin ground fog flowed down the mountain. I could see through it. A sooty jet shot from the top of the sinking bulge. The north slope slid like pudding as a mass.

Rogers: I glanced back while running. Francisco pointed, "Look! The north is sliding!" I wrenched open the car door and snatched my camera. I shot six quick frames starting ten seconds after the earthquake. The film jammed and I shot a triple exposure. The plume had filled the north slope, billowing north.

Valenzuela: The summit was hazy like after an explosion. A light-gray opaque cloud like a duststorm flowed downslope fast, hugging the ground. Ty Kearney stepped out with a camera.

Rogers: Kearney shot several photos just after the last frame of my triple exposure. The cloud was now tremendous. The summit and lateral plumes merged and flowed off north as a dense cloud, orders of magnitude larger and faster than any I'd seen before. Part of the cloud flowed toward us down into the South Fork.

Valenzuela: The earthquake continued weakly. The lower cloud rolled over a ridge toward us—a swift, curling wave. It grew thicker, billowing up 500 feet. Half a minute after eruption's start the west breeze stopped. From the mountain came a tumbling, bubbling, increasing roar like many distant explosions. Ty Kearney shot pictures. I dashed to my car.

Rogers: I jumped into my old car, Francisco into his, and we raced off. Behind I saw the Kearneys climb into their van and pull out. We raced east.

Valenzuela: *Toward* the mountain. Rogers ahead raced 60 mph. The great cloud on the mountain flowed toward us like thick gray foam. Its base funneled down into the South Fork while its top billowed and rose. A light-gray cloud rolled south and west over the summit like fume from a beaker. It flowed down the flanks in puffs.

Rogers: We turned south by a bulldozer onto road 820 [later part of 8117]. The sky was clear above, the mountain now behind a ridge. At a triangle intersection I swerved onto the right fork.

Valenzuela: I drove off the road and stuck in mud. I dashed to Rogers' Simca.

Rogers: I swung east. The Kearney's van whipped past on the main road.

Valenzuela: We drove road 820 south to a sharp bend and stopped.

Rogers: Four minutes after leaving camp we hiked east sixty yards to the saddle.

Valenzuela: Warm wind whipped through the saddle *from* the mountain. Lightning flashed all over the dark plume. Three miles northeast a bolt hung on a tree that burst into flames. Ten minutes after the eruption's start the north clouds had pulled into a column. A huge mushroom top came high overhead.

Rogers: The hazy edge of the rising cloud blocked the sun, an ominous feeling like an eclipse. The air went cold. Mount St. Helens cleared: its top was gone! Hundreds of lightning bolts from the rising cloud struck Mount St. Helens. They hit the ridge north of the South Fork again and again. The forest there was *down!*

An appalling dust haze hung in the South Fork. Lateral movement had ceased. The wind reversed again, now a cool fifty mph *toward* the volcano. The mountain rumbled as if a freight train with a thousand square wheels—yet we're *up*wind in air roaring through the saddle. We shouted to each other.

I jogged down to the car and opened the door. Wind blew my map away. I realized in our haste from camp I'd dropped a roll of film. I rewound film, reloaded, and ran back to the saddle. Through a 50-mm lens I shot twenty-one overlapping frames of the swelling cloud. Five look straight up. The anvil edge five miles up is southwest of us. Orange lightning in it was silent. Many bolts to the north struck the ridge above the camps [Landsburg, Karr] and set fires.

A reddish pickup came down the road. Francisco dashed down.

Valenzuela: Loggers in a 4-wheel-drive pickup wouldn't help with my stuck car.[5] The mushroom cloud grew out horizontally, and dark ash streamed down.

Rogers: The wind toward the mountain weakened. I thought any ashfall wouldn't reach us: we could return to camp. We left the saddle after fifteen minutes. We came to Francisco's car and dug it out in ten minutes. We sped back north.

The overhead cloud grew west and north, the sky going dark. Ash fell lower: we'd soon be in it. At our camp I saw the film canister in the road. I opened the door and grabbed it—unexposed film, but I'd need it. The overhead cloud touched down to the west and migrated toward us.

We turned around east, I leading. The cloud descended on us.

Valenzuela: Ash streamers hit the ground. The air smelled sulfurous, acidic. Ash fell heavy like a curtain and covered the windshield. The air went dark and warm.

Rogers: Dry powder slanting down from the west turned the air dark in half a minute. Francisco dropped back from a cloud I raised. I could see little but headlights thirty yards back. I slowed to 5 mph. Ahead I could see only ten feet and missed the bulldozer and intersection.

Valenzuela: I didn't see the intersection or sign. The air smelled of sulfur; my eyes and throat burned. I rolled down the window. A few orange flakes like snowflakes fell. Glowing cinders?[6]

Rogers: I entered standing trees and realized we'd missed the turn. I got out and ran back to Francisco. I felt no extra warmth and smelled no sulfur. We turned around and drove slowly west. Again we missed the intersection and came to our camp.

Valenzuela: Six minutes to drive a mile. At the hilltop ash fell lighter and I could see a hundred yards. We parked next to each other. Every radio station broadcast music or talk—oblivious to this horrendous eruption. The ground steamed of heated moisture. A slight wind from the west like before the eruption cooled the air. Breathing got easier. Evidently in flood, the South Fork roared like a freight train.

Rogers: Big Bull Mountain appeared three miles west. Ashfall lightened and a patch of light approached. I got into Francisco's car. We drove west toward light to road's end. Ashfall tapered off. The light grew and reached south. To the northeast lay dense cloud. The mountain rumbled constantly. We drove east to the campsite.

Valenzuela: We were in cloud and haze more than two hours. A sixteenth inch of ash lay on the ground. I got out bread, lettuce, tomato, cheddar, mayonnaise for sandwiches.

Rogers: A brown Hughes 500 helicopter flew north through the haze. It soon returned. He saw our cars and hovered down. But at fifty feet he blew up a huge dustcloud and pulled off.[7]

Valenzuela: Ash-and-cheese sandwiches we had now.

Rogers: The mountain roared dully. The air lightened. Higher levels cleared, then gradually lower. About 12:30 I took twenty-six photos of the erupting column. A west bulge in the column detached and tumbled downslope. Several turbulent gray ash-clouds billowed over the west rim. One flowed down almost to timberline. Another descended a third the way in fifteen seconds. The flow stopped and its cloud blew away: a white trail marked the path.[8]

We returned to the saddle about 12:45. A slight breeze blew toward the volcano that still rumbled. The high mushroom had blown off east and we were in sun. But increasing low dust obscured the mountain. I shot photos of the rising plume.

About 1:20 we drove south. West of Goat Mountain about 1:50, I shot photo mosaics of the energetic plume.

South on Forest road 818 [later, 81] we came to a gate. About 3:15 I shot nine photos of the plume. We turned west on highway 503 and passed a roadblock at Jack's Place about four.

Dennis Smith

Saturday four of us fished our way up the South Fork and crossed to the south. Pat Sullivan set chokers for Weyerhaeuser. We camped near the end of road 5740 at the edge of trees near his yarder just outside the Red Zone.[9] Just north lay South Fork canyon. We cooked our trout and camped without tents.

Sunday morning we bitched about Mount St. Helens doing nothing. On a road across the South Fork a guy stood outside his car by a tripod [Robert Landsburg]. "The mountain's vibrating!" Pat blurted. A big landslide went down north. A huge explosion blasted up from the mountain and out north. Another shot up steeper. Then another even steeper. They merged into a roiling gray wall full of lightning. Through binoculars I saw the guy still standing at his tripod. With each explosion ripples like shock waves came out the edge of the cloud that soon covered the mountain. I heard nothing.

The cloud flowing out across the North Fork banked up a far ridge, and the near edge swelled into the South Fork. We sprinted to the cars—Pat and I to my Ford F150 pickup. We roared up road 5740, winding 1½ miles northwest and southwest. When we joined the 5700, down north the cloud running west was filling the South Fork. We turned uphill, hit road 5800, broke over the ridge, and raced south. It joined road 820 winding downhill.

A ways down a guy came running up. I slowed, and he grabbed my open window. "My car's in a ditch!" he said. "Help me pull it out!" {*Valenzuela*}.

"No time," I said. "We've gotta get out!" He walked holding the window as I crept along. "Just get in!"

"No. It's all right," he said and let go. I stepped on it.

We stopped at piney flats—Kalama River—then drove out past Merrill Lake and Yale Lake.

South Fork Toutle Valley

Annie Sullivan, Joe Sullivan, and Mark Dahl

[Joe Sullivan, Ann "Annie" Sullivan, her brothers Mark Dahl and Teek Moser, and infant daughter Addie drove up the South Fork. A timber faller, Joe knew the roads.]

Annie: We walked a logging road in the South Fork where Joe had been cutting timber. It was quiet—no breeze, no birdsong.

Joe: Near the old Herrington Place homestead. We got back in my 1974 Ford pickup, five of us on the bench seat.

Annie: We headed toward the mountain. A pancake of fog rose gradually up it.

Joe: I drove road 4100 east, the north valley side east of Trouble Creek.[10]

Annie: Deer jumped into the road, balked, and ran back.[11]

Joe: They seemed confused.

Mark: We rounded a curve and saw steam venting. We got out.

Annie: A black snake shot from the summit.

Joe: "Hey man, this is neat!"

Mark: "Yeah, cool!"

Annie: After a few seconds a gray jet shot up from lower, a mile north of the summit. More gray cloud rose from farther north, behind a spur a couple miles ahead of us. The north clouds grew to a gigantic expanding one that soon obscured the mountain.

Mark: The north flank seemed to explode north. Joe shot three photos. A big black cloud rolled over the northeast ridge toward us.

Joe: Now it's not so neat and cool. It's "Jesus!" and "Holy shit!"

Mark: Joe jumped in the truck and turned around.

Annie: A minute after the black snake, we four again squeezed onto the bench seat, little Addie on my lap, I 4½ months pregnant. Joe sped west. We skidded toward the road edge on curves.

Mark: He drove 60 mph. I knelt on the seat, slid open the back window, and shot photos of the swelling cloud. It was like an atom bomb had exploded. When we left, the cloud was miles away; in less than a minute it rolled from the northeast into the valley, chasing us. On a straighter stretch of road we gained on it.

Annie: After four miles [~8:38] a dark-gray cloud like cauliflower billowed above the ridge *ahead* of us! The cloud had run down the North Fork faster than we sped down the South!

Mark: How could it run down the North Fork so fast? It was like watching a TV adventure with the sound off.

Joe: The wall of billowing smoke and ash rose and poured over the high ridge five miles northwest of us. So big and fast so far down the North Fork! I drove very fast. Behind I saw only billowy black smoke.

After four miles I sped through Herrington Place and turned left across the South Fork bridge. A mile farther we passed Bear Creek turnoff [road 5500]. Weyerhaeuser had told us loggers to get out of the valley if the mountain erupts. The 4100 stays by the river another seventeen miles. I jammed the brakes, turned around, raced back, and turned up the 5500.[12]

Annie: "Joe! You're heading *toward* the mountain! You know what you're doing?"

Joe: "We've got to go *up*! This is the way!"

Annie: The mountain was behind a billowy gray cloud rising miles and spreading especially north [~8:43].

Mark: The front of the cloud had come down the valley to within a mile or so of us.

Annie: We drove up fifteen minutes toward the mountain we couldn't see.

Joe: A dozen deer ran down the road erratically, scared.

Mark: The clouds churned high, full of lightning. We came to the top [ten miles WSW of summit]. The cloud base pulled north. A thousand feet of the mountain was *gone!*

Joe: I drove fast, eyes on the road. Mark yelled, "The top of the mountain's gone!" I glanced and saw it cut off. Lightning bolts struck down to it. [~9:00]

Annie: Viewed across south of the mountain, Mount Adams was clear. Spectacular lightning shot from Mount St. Helens—some red, some white. And tremendous bolts laterally toward Mount Adams.

Mark: The churning big plume boiling up tilted north, lightning bolt after bolt from it. A few projectiles arced toward us trailing streamers. It was a silent movie. Mount Adams was white but the summit going behind the east cloud.

Joe: I sped some miles southeast. I turned down road 7400 into the Kalama.

Annie: We saw the mountain no more.

Joe: We paralleled Kalama River on roads 7400, 7200, and 6000. Heading on the mountain, the river might flood. Miles down, guys in driftboats fished for steelhead. I yelled down, "The mountain's erupted! The whole top's gone! Get off the river!" They kept fishing.

At Weyerhaeuser's Camp Kalama I ran into the office. "Hey, the mountain blew!"

"Yeah, we heard."

"No! It *really* blew!"

Annie: When we reached Castle Rock about 10:05 the eruption clouds were way up.

Mark: At a store we mentioned taking pictures of the eruption. Two guys heard.

"We're with Associated Press and can pay a thousand dollars for photos. You get any *lava*?"

"No, that's not what Mount St. Helens—"

"We're not interested."

David Crockett

[David Crockett had covered Mount St. Helens for KOMO-TV for weeks. He left Seattle at 4:30 AM in a KOMO car and drove up the South Fork.]

I'd driven up South Fork road 4100 to five miles west of Mount St. Helens. I got out of the car, focused on the mountain, and a black plume shot from the summit. I shot five photographs of the summit eruption and a huge dark-gray cloud boiling above the ridge to the north. There was no wind or sound. But now a huge cloud poofed above the north ridge downvalley *west* of me![13]

I jumped in, turned around, and roared down the road 60 mph. After five minutes, I saw in the rear-view mirror a horrible wall chasing me. It was like a tidal wave 20 feet high, tumbling trees and big rocks, burying the road a hundred yards back, gaining. I drove frantically. Two minutes later I came to a logging road. I turned left onto it to get out of the valley.

The road curved over a mound and turned down to a swale. As I raced downhill a huge mass of water, mud, trees, and rocks crashed across the road fifty feet in front of me. It had lots of water but wasn't a water flow. Some trees were many times the size of my car. It snapped off trees and seemed to explode when it hit lows, bursting up over obstacles. It struck the road embankment and burst up fifty feet. I jammed on the brakes and almost skidded into it. I backed uphill fast. Another flow bounced over the ridge and across road behind, full of trees and rocks. My car backed into the logs.

If I'd stayed in the main valley I'd be dead. If I'd reached the swale sooner I'd be dead. If I'd backed up faster I'd be dead here.[14]

31 May 1980

RICHARD WAITT

Crockett's KOMO-TV4 car backed against logs

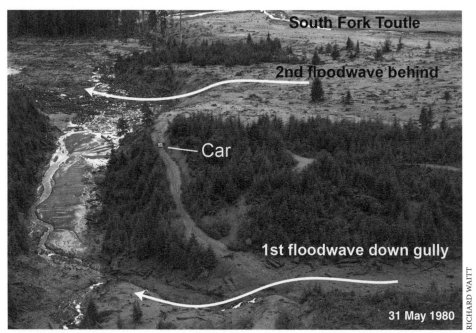

View northwest from the air, Crockett's car on road

I was on an island, surrounded. If these fast flows deepen I'll be buried. High ground lay south. From the mountain came growling and rumbling explosions and an east wind. Ash clouds to the north over the main valley flashed lightning. That big flow had subsided some—more watery now but still carrying trees and rocks. A thin light-gray dust settled on the car. I collected cameras and a radio. Shooting newsreel, I walked down the road to where the flood had burst in front of me. Now ten minutes later, my foot sank in quicksand but found hard bottom. I waded down through warm fluid brown concrete. I held the cameras above my head and did sink in once 2½ feet. I put the camera on my shoulder and shot as I crossed warm, muddy water.

I got out of the mire onto the other side thirty minutes after the eruption began. A dark cloud descended. The road curved up southwest. I walked up as sandy ash rained vertically. The sky got very dark except for a patch of light over a low part of the southwest ridge. I put the camera on my shoulder and shot—a record if I died.

I walked up toward this light. I felt pressure pulses on my face, and my ears popped. From the mountain came deep rumbles and a few deep explosions. I smelled burning wood. In occasional breezes from the mountain, ash slanted down from the east, falling denser when wind increased.

It grew exhausting to walk. Dry sand ash rained down heavily. I was suffocating not from dust but from oxygen-poor air. I stopped to rest every fifty feet or so. I don't smoke or drink; I run five miles a day, hike a lot. In strong condition, I carried only 42 pounds of camera gear. But I could only creep up this gentle hill. The patch of light got smaller, then just a sliver of light. I talked as the camera rolled: "I'm walking toward the only light I can see—on top of the ridge . . . The ash is in my eyes . . . it's . . . very hard to breath . . . hurts to talk . . . This is hell I'm walking through."

The patch of light closed. "I can't see . . . I'll . . . sit . . . and wait it out."

It turned black. I could see nothing, no sliver of light. The air was poor. I coughed and choked on ash. It was hell on earth. On my radio I called "Mayday! Mayday!" No response. I thought I wouldn't make it. The ash now fell so fast I'd be buried and not found. Complete pitch-blackness.

In half an hour it lightened slightly to the west. I trudged farther up the ashy road. After I climbed a few hundred feet, a breeze picked up from the west toward the mountain. The air grew more normal, and I walked up with reasonable speed.

An hour ago trees and bushes were green. Now ash covered road, trees, stumps, brush, rocks—everything drab gray far as I could see.

I'd lost my radio in the dark. I had no matches to light a fire. I turned back to the car. The film camera with sound had jammed in the ashfall, but I shot photos and silent film. In the car I found a signal flare. I wrote a message in ash on the hood.

I hiked up to a ridgecrest. I lit three fires in a triangle, international distress signal.

[Continues chap 16]

Carol Koon

Sunday morning one of our KOIN6 reporters was at air-traffic control at Portland airport when a pilot reported Mount St. Helens had erupted. Bruce Collins and I heard about 8:45 and drove to the station. We drove our microwave-transmitting van north up I-5 and 504. A big rising column like cauliflower disappeared up into high overcast. We talked our way past a roadblock.

Just above Toutle we stood on the bridge over the river. A deputy said a mass of logs had gone through not long ago [~10:50]. The subsided brown mudflow flowing beneath carried a few logs, some of them sawed. When one hit a pier, the bridge shook. The deputy got a radio call of a huge mudflow coming down.

We drove logging roads up the South Fork and up a ridge. Logs rode on the subsided mudflow. We stopped at Signal Peak to transmit to Portland. A Weyerhaeuser logger drove up and said, "Our 12-Road Camp is wiped out." We drove down and shot video of trucks strewn like toys in the logs and mud.[15]

[Continues chap 16]

Roald Reitan and Venus Dergan

[Roald Reitan and Venus Ann Dergan (ages 20 and 21) were camped on the South Fork half a mile above the South Fork bridge, 26 miles west of Mount St. Helens.]

Roald: Saturday we fished Jericho Hole, the South Fork about 42°F. We'd camped on the north bank five feet above the water and thirty feet back. My 1968 Oldsmobile was up a steep bank ten feet above the tent. We were on a gentle inside bend, the opposite bank high steep rock.

Sunday I got up at daybreak but went back in the tent and slept. I woke to a high-low siren in the distance. The river gurgled like yesterday. Five or ten minutes later I heard rapids and got out of the tent. The river looked like chocolate milk. Debris floated by—sticks, then branches, then limbs. "Venus!" I called. "Get up! Something's wrong with the river! We should get out of here!" She got up and we put on shoes.

Venus: The river rose slowly. Velocity picked up, and the water splashed. We ran our sleeping stuff up the bank to the car. The rising water turned to rapids.

Roald: Suddenly logs came down fast bank-to-bank. The muddy water rose two feet more. The logs were sawed, from a sorting yard upstream. The first were small—16 inches diameter, 20 feet long. They got larger and larger as the stream rose.

Two minutes after the first logs passed a structure came around a bend half a mile upstream. Trees on the south bank shook when hit hard. The structure came around end-on but swung broadside to the stream. It was a wooden railroad trestle 50 feet long, 15 high. Logs stacked behind it were huge as Greyhound buses. A few were in front, and the trestle floated on some.

Venus: The trestle came down slowly, a huge mass of logs pushing it along. Logs behind it were ten feet above those in front.

Roald: Sixty yards behind the trestle the spreading flood was snapping off trees like they were matchsticks for ten yards each side of the banks. Trees were hit hard, dust shook off, and they fell. The earth shook, the snapping grew loud, and the air stank of trees. The bridge came down across the stream about 25 mph.

We ripped up tent, poles, stakes, scrambled up the bank, threw them in the trunk, and got in the car. The trestle broke apart and released the logjam. It came down very fast, a spreading flood of logs and mud. The trestle went by in pieces, and the big logs rolled with high momentum up onto the road in front of the car. They jammed every which way, some sticking above the car. The trestle pieces disappeared.

Venus: As the bridge passed, the flood full of logs rose ten feet in fifteen seconds and spilled over our low inside bank. Most logs were sawed, from the camp. But the flood kept snapping off big trees that gave a strong smell of needles and wood.

Roald: Chocolate milk had become chocolate pudding.

Venus: Mud rose to the car. We got out, shut the doors, and climbed onto the trunk. The swelling flood pushed the logs and car slowly along the bank. We climbed to the roof. It had been serene; now it was the end of the world.

Roald: The mud and logs pushed my car into the flood. I jumped.

Venus: The car dropped off the bank into the river of logs. I landed in mud. I expected a cold-water shock, but it was warm like bathwater, perhaps 80°F. I keep my head up easily swimming in water, but it was very hard in this mud. Arms and legs felt as though I had weights on them. I kept afloat by holding logs as best I could.

Roald: I landed on a log and straddled it. But my right knee got pinned by a big log beside. We were swept along fast, 25 mph in mud thick and warm, 75 or 80° F. The logs were sawed fir two to five feet across, 40 feet long but also some alder. In places they piled one atop another among lots of small debris. The mud smelled like rich earth, but in the air a heavy stench of trees. I faced forward on a log parallel to the fast current bucking chaotically up and down. My pinned right knee was being crushed between the logs.

A branch underneath caught my left foot and held. My left leg slowly stretched back with force, while my right knee was being mashed between logs. The pain was intense. A smaller log rolled over from behind and knocked me flat. I slowly pushed back up, but another rolled over and flattened me. I lay face-down, the pain excruciating from my legs being mashed and stretched. I hoped the next log would kill me.

The debris released my left foot and I pulled it up. The press on my right knee lessened and I pulled it up. My log bucked wildly in the current. I crawled on hands and knees to its front. Down in the mud 15 feet ahead was Venus! She kept going under. I jumped to another log.

Venus: I was pulled along fast in the current down between logs. They squeezed together and caught the arm I was holding on with. It mashed my left wrist and tore skin away. Up on a big log Roald screamed "Hang on! Hang on!" We were fighting forces far beyond control. His screaming kept me going.

Roald: I grabbed her arm and pulled. The logs were rolling and bouncing, the mud slippery. The bouncing force tore her loose. I fell to the rolling, pitching log. This happened again. Twice I got her halfway up, twice I lost her.

Venus: Again I floated between big logs, grasping anything floating to stay up. The logs were far too big to hold much.

Roald: She floated down between the sawed ends of two big ones. I saw only her face covered in mud, and two eyes. If the logs came together they'd squish her. They separated a little. Her hand come up and I grabbed.

Venus: Roald grabbed my arm enough to pull me onto the log.

Roald: We rode down the mudflow on a big log—5 feet diameter, 40 feet long—on the fast right side of the current. Out in the middle my car went by even faster, riding high, only the tires submerged. We went under the South Fork road bridge.

Venus: Roald's car floated by like a boat. Kneeling on the log, we drifted another half mile. No one was on the South Fork bridge. The logs drifted to the north side and jammed up.

Roald: The valley widens beyond the bridge, and the current spread and slowed, near the bank even slower. We jumped from log to log toward shore. We rode a log six feet across, forty feet long going through the edge of timber smashing down trees. It was forty yards to the edge of mud creeping into trees at a park. Only two or three feet of a chemical toilet stuck above the mud: we couldn't get off here.

At the edge of mud the door of another chemical toilet was only a foot in mud. We waded toward shore through warm gooey mud like chocolate syrup.

Venus: Waist-deep, it got shallower the last few yards.

Roald: We came to a road at river's edge. We'd been in the river five minutes. It seemed like five hours.

Venus: I felt cold. The mud dried fast, caking up before Roald could pull it off. It was heavy like cement. We wore only jeans and T-shirts. The flood had taken shoes and socks. We needed rescue but no one knew we were here.

Roald: We were on a slight rise in a road in Harry Gardner Park. Rising mud crept toward us from both directions. We climbed the steep brushy slope.

Venus: It's surprising what you do when endangered. Though injured, we climbed.

Roald: At the top of the slope fifty feet above the road we rested. Picking our way barefoot through timber, we came to a jeep trail. But it petered out. We followed the trail in the other direction toward the bridge. I carried Venus partway. The jeep road led down into the mud. Logs at the edge now didn't move.

Venus: We left the track and stumbled through trees and brush up toward the bridge. People were now on it.

Roald: We'd come a quarter mile. The bridge was higher and 200 yards away. A sheriff's car sat there, and people watched the river. We yelled; they heard.

Venus: We had to go back down to where they could see us. Roald was adrenalized—pacing, pacing despite his injuries.

Roald: Two men waded through the mud. They hollered to the bridge for a rescue.

Venus: Mud at the edge neither rose nor fell. Through the trees we heard the main flood. Above us gray sky had replaced the blue.

Roald: A small helicopter came but had no place to land and flew away [~12:10] *{Pleasant}*. For a quarter hour the guys cut away brush. The helicopter came back and hovered down. Passengers got out and the guys loaded Venus *{Pleasant & Schoening}*, and the helicopter took off [12:35].

Another helicopter came, and I got in [~12:43] *{Erdelbrock & Schoening}*.

Venus: They flew us to Toutle high school fields.

Roald: Then ambulances took us to Longview hospital.

Venus: I was covered with mud dried like a cast. They said I looked like a mud statue. They put me on morphine, washed me three times, and found my wounds. In the mud the big logs had bruised and abraded my face.

Roald: Ripped skin off her cheeks.

Venus: My left arm had torn open knuckle to elbow. The left wrist was broken—the one Roald had pulled me up onto the log by.

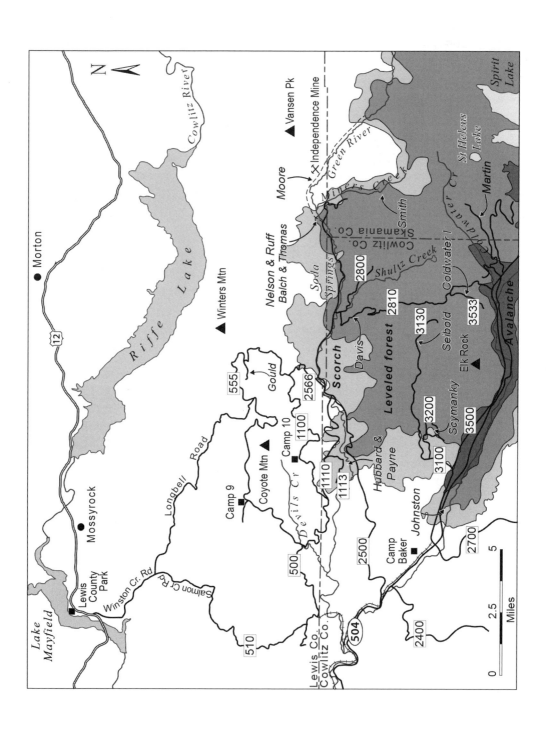

11
North

As things change to fire, and fire exhausted falls back into things.
— Heraclitus, 5th c. BCE

Near Devastated Area

Mike Moore and Lu Moore

[Mike and Lu Moore with 4-year-old Bonnie Lu and 3-month-old Terra Dawn camped by Green River.[1]]

Mike: In afternoon the 17th, we'd hiked up Green River 2½ miles to Independence Mine, fourteen miles north of Mount St. Helens. We tented among oldgrowth fir, one eight feet across. Upslope lay a collapsing elk-hunter's shack. Sunday dawned sunny, the air still.

Lu: We hardly thought of the mountain.

Mike: Lu made breakfast as I set up to photograph wildflowers. A low rumbling from the south like a distant aircraft lasted fifteen seconds. The ground vibrated. Seconds later air pressure rose rapidly. I swallowed to equalize my ears that popped repeatedly ten seconds.

Lu: Just after the rumble I felt a pressure as if someone were squeezing my body gently. My ears went pop-pop-pop-pop-pop, like never before.

Mike: We looked at each other puzzled. An eruption? But how could we feel effects so far out, across many 5000-foot peaks?

Lu: A huge gray cloud suddenly billowed above the timber to the south.

Mike: I dashed to an opening. My first photo looks up 40 degrees above the tops of trees taller than 200 feet. The cloud came as a wall and raced toward us. A major eruption: we'd get dirty.

Lu: I abandoned breakfast and tossed camp things into the tent.

Mike: I took twelve photos 15 to 20 seconds apart for 2½ minutes, the only sounds the camera click and Lu's rustling camp gear. The cloud was a turmoil of grays and yellows. The top pulled out overhead. The advancing lower billowy wall slowed and stalled. My last photo looks nearly straight up. Ash might be heavy, and the tent was flimsy. "Let's go to the shed!" I called. Lu moved the children and camping gear toward the tumbledown shack. The upper plume drew overhead like a thunderstorm but fast.

Lu: The air grew dark. We struck the tent and hustled gear and the children up to the shed. After we got there we still had light to pack a few minutes. A wind came up.

Mike: Ten minutes after we noticed the cloud, its upper edge had pushed well north of us. In twilight I pulled our packs and tent into the half-collapsed shed. Ash fell like large snowflakes and on the plastic roof sounded like big raindrops. I stuck my hand out. I found the ash warm, and small rocks bounced off. A few clumps fell. Under a flashlight I saw their outside ash dry but inside damp the diameter of a nickel. Ashfall increased rapidly. The air went completely dark twelve minutes after we first saw the cloud.

Lu: Black like inside a cave. Soon the ash penetrated the plastic roof and cracks in the walls. Terra Dawn was in a blanket. We now wrapped her in plastic, an open-ended cocoon. The rest of us breathed through dampened socks. It didn't get cold as at night.

Mike: It was too dark to tell your eyes are open. We fumbled to pack gear. We might be forced out if ash grew too heavy on the flimsy roof. Huge thunderclaps came every five to ten seconds for half an hour. We shouted to talk. Some strikes sounded very close, but no flash penetrated the ashy darkness. With the thunder came the sound of heavy drops on the plastic roof. Not rain—I stuck my hand out into dry ash. Is this what Pompeii was like?

Ten minutes after it went dark, several tremendous explosions from the mountain mingled with the thunder. Loud and sharp, they sounded like great dynamite blasts, as if the mountain were tearing apart. Ashfall was very heavy. This was Bonnie's first camp trip. Lu told her stories. After awhile I could see six inches with a flashlight.

Lu: It was dark more than an hour. Part of the plastic collapsed, and dry ash dropped inside into a pile. It slowly lightened, and Mike went outside.

Mike: The air was dark with dust but ash no longer fell. After ten minutes I saw the faint outline of a near tree. We pulled our packs outside. A little light to the west grew a bit larger and lighter. We'd be okay. Lu nursed the baby.

Lu: Hemlock cones were covered with ash—what we'd heard thumping on the plastic. Two large tree limbs cracked and fell.

Mike: In twenty minutes the air lightened to dense fog. I could see a hundred feet and see the trough of the trail. Gray ash like talcum powder covered everything. We weren't the first out: mouse tracks dimpled the ash. Cutting through I saw no layers of different color or grainsize. I measured it 1½ to 2 inches. I looked for pumice but found none.

We shouldered our packs about 10:45 and started down. In half a mile we crossed three windfall trees we'd crossed coming in. Then we came to ten or twenty large trees down I didn't remember. But if they were new, why hadn't we heard them fall? They lay across the trail, limbs covered in ash. Bonnie and I scouted around the north, Lu around the south. Ash off the limbs fell all over us. A branch snapped back in my face: I couldn't open my eyes. I called to Lu; she called she'd found the trail, Bonnie led me south, and Lu washed my eyes with canteen water. We worked across this new blowdown onto the trail. In the next quarter mile we crossed several more down trees we didn't remember.

In another quarter mile, past a sign for the fork south to Miners Creek, the trail disappeared into a huge clearing of down trees, only five percent standing. We'd seen nothing like this yesterday. Were we on the wrong trail? Or is this from the eruption? That seemed incredible. At least a hundred trees were down, many of them big old-growth. We walked atop one, but the next hung fifteen feet off the ground. Lu carried the pack holding Terra Dawn: "I'm not going up there with the kids."

We retreated through the small area of blowdown and turned north off the trail. We'd skirt this problem. We hiked uphill a quarter mile through oldgrowth and turned west along a contour on a 20-degree slope. With no trail it was slow with our heavy packs and 4-year-old Bonnie. The air stayed very hazy. After 150 yards on a steepening slope we came to a huge area of blowdown, half the trees down. Through standing ones I could see west only eighty yards but at least two dozen trees were down, some of them oldgrowth. They lay directly upslope, now thirty degrees, impossible to cross. This had to be new from the eruption. It seemed incredible so far out.

It was 3 PM, Bonnie getting tired. We'd have to camp the night. We retraced our tracks east and south. We came to an old down tree. We stopped and sat for the first time since leaving the mine. We snacked and sipped water, I took photos, Lu nursed Terra Dawn.

Three hours till dark. We hiked the trail back east and set camp among big oldgrowth.

Lu: Many tiny tracks marked the ash. Centipede tracks showed individual feet. About 5:30 Bonnie sat in a patch of sunlight, the first since the eruption.

Mike: I hiked west for water. All streams were mud, but I found a spring to fill canteens. Near the big clearing of blowdown lay a stack of cedar bolts I'd seen hiking in. So we'd been on the trail. The eruption had downed all these big trees. Just beyond where Miners Creek trail came in from the south I saw footprints! An adult and two kids headed out {Smith}. Others had survived.

I looked west scouting a way across the downed trees for tomorrow. A helicopter flew overhead about seven. I was under standing trees, wore a green jacket, no bright color to wave.

During the night explosions came from the volcano but not as loud as during the darkness. I smelled sulfur and smoke for the first time.

[Continues chap 20]

Whoop Gould and Dave Merzoian

[Alan "Whoop" Gould Jr., Dave Merzoian, and four other men were cutting timber west of Winters Mountain 18 miles north-northwest of Mount St. Helens.[2]]

Gould: Owning a logging company, I often work weekends. Six of us were felling and bucking timber south of road 1131. The clearcut gave us a wide view south.

Merzoian: Gould dropped Bob Vojanski and me. The other four drove away toward their cut a few hundred yards east. With Stihl 056 saws Bob and I cut a narrow remaining strip of trees. Our south slope looked toward Mount St. Helens and a nearer ridge above Fawn Lake, Mount Margaret southeast, Elk Rock southwest. I was 150 feet southeast of Bob. He felled trees west away from me, I felled mine east away from him.

Gould: I felt an earthquake. Bucked logs three feet across and forty feet long wobbled. A puff of white steam shot from Mount St. Helens, then a gob of dark ash. A big cloud from the rim came down into the North Fork like low fog but very fast. (Later I thought maybe dust off the big landslide I didn't see.)

A big blow above Goat Rocks soon covered the North Fork valley. Its light-colored ash cloud ran over Coldwater ridge like a surf wave rolling up a beach. Mount Margaret stood clear as this cloud rolled over the ridge like low fog.

Merzoian: In hard hats and ear plugs and cutting with vibrating saws, we weren't watching. I felled a fir east. Three logs 41 feet long well upslope of the tree I felled rolled that shouldn't.[3]

Bob yelled and I glanced south. An enormous black and gray cloud rolled toward us down upper Schutz Creek. It hid Mount St. Helens and even the closer ridge. Holy crap! My brother-in-law John Killian and his wife were at Fawn Lake. The swirling, boiling light-gray cloud came northwest down Schultz Creek, down the 3900 and 2800 road systems, in two waves. There was no sound.

Gould: The big cloud spread quickly miles north of Mount Margaret over the highland lakes. It poured down the 3900 road system and down Shultz Creek. The cloud's west arm split around Elk Rock. One gray wall climbed south toward us over Gilbert ridge, the other followed the North Fork west. I heard a gentle rumble.[4]

The cloud running down the North Fork west of Elk Rock crossed the ridge into the lower Green. Small jack fir [lodgepole pine] stood between the two V's of ash now coming toward us. This cloud only sixty feet or so high on the 3100 roads steamrollered over the jack fir, felling it to the ground.

Merzoian: Much of Shultz Creek had been logged within twenty years and grown back in jack fir. An upper part of the cloud curled forward 1000 feet off the ground, but I could see in under it. This back part of the cloud mowed the jack fir down like hay. Patches of red fir, hemlock, and cedar 100 to 140 feet tall left as seed trees were also laid flat by the cloud less than a mile behind the projecting high front. The base of this ash cloud felled them northwest then covered them [land sections 9, 10, 15, 16]. It was silent.

Gould: The west part of the cloud now rolled east *up* the Green toward the 1110–1100 road lines[5] faster than the big dark-gray cloud flowed north down Shultz Creek. Ahead of the cloud down Shultz Creek I saw for a few seconds a cloud of greenery a mile high in the air. The gray ash cloud pushed it on.

Ahead of the main ash wall coming down Schultz Creek, a big smooth cloud curled high over us—like being in front of a gigantic surf wave about to break. The main wall of cloud five miles from us flowing toward Green River laid down timber.

Great ball-like structures boiled everywhere in the big low cloud from the ground to its top across its ten-mile width. It wasn't straight. A front tongue lost intensity until the part behind caught up. One tongue after another, every fifteen seconds or so, pushed forward and stalled. The west end raced down Green River almost to Cascade Creek but then slowed.

Merzoian: "What're we gonna do?" Bob asked.

"Get the hell out of here."

The flow slowed and froze near Green River. Then the cloud stood up. Over some minutes we worked down the steep slope to the road.

Gould: The gray clouds stopped at Green River, as if the water acted as a firebreak. It stood like a picture. It boiled in place and climbed vertically on an east-west line. Miles back near Mount Margaret a huge cloud now rose quickly 40,000 feet.

All morning a gentle breeze drifted from the west. Now suddenly a wind blew fifty miles an hour south toward the mountain—the way a big forest fire makes its own backwind. Loose greenery blew south across the road.

The cloud drifted closer and the light dimmed. Lightning in it made little noise. Within a square mile ten balls of lightning the size of pickups formed, then rolled and bounced across the ground like tumbleweeds.[6]

Merzoian: When Bob and I reached the road the edge of the overhead cloud dimmed the air like dusk. Birds flew in to jack fir as before night. Lightning jumped within the cloud.

Gould: The four in our group jumped into my Chevy 'six-pack' [crew-cab pickup]. I bolted west on road 1131 toward our other group. Two of the tough woodsmen cried.

"Don't stop!" one said. "Just get outta here."

"Hell no! If anyone's to die, we'll all go together."

Merzoian: After some minutes the pickup came from the east and we climbed in.

Gould: The wall of ash a thousand feet high came over the ridge only a thousand feet back. I sped back east. A few globs of mud flattened on the windshield the width of a golfball, and steam rolled off. Some left chunks of ice but dried almost at once. The shower stopped in couple hundred feet. We ran through four or five mudball showers. Small rocks bounced off the ground.

Many dead branches had blown into the road at road 555A intersection. From the pass we drove down north and lost the roar of the backwind.

Merzoian: The overhead cloud pushed rapidly north, and the air beneath grew dark. Down on Riffe Lake people in a boat sat in sun. The cloud closed and squeezed off the view.

Gould: In half a mile we came to the 555. By mistake I turned east. The ashfall changed to drier and constant and the air went dark. It grew hot, forty degrees warmer than a few minutes earlier. I smelled sulfur. The guys ripped off shirt sleeves and wetted them to breathe through. The temperature gauge rose to red. I turned around.

Merzoian: I smelled the sulfur as some larger stuff fell.

Gould: Something like hail rattled on the pickup. The air was almost black. With headlights I could see 25 feet. Two got out with flashlights. They found roads 558 and 557, and we zig-zagged slowly down many miles. We found the old railroad grade, road 222. It was rough but took us down northwest. Ash floated on puddle water. Two poked with a stick to be sure there wasn't a deep ditch across the road. The pick-up's temperature gauge stayed in red 2½ hours. Lightning flashed. Finally on the 222 down Winston Creek we came to a pocket of daylight.

Next day I saw on the edge of our clearcut several trees a foot in diameter had blown down toward the mountain in that backwind.

Gene Palmer

[William (Gene) and Kathy Palmer were on road 2770, 16½ miles north-northwest of the volcano.[7] They shot nine photos of eruption clouds.]

We—Gene and Kathy Palmer in a Jeep, David Brewer in a car—had been photographing since six. We were two miles south of Winters Mountain when a couple of puffs of white steam rose from the volcano's summit. The crater filled with black ash. The mountain seemed to shudder, and a huge explosion blew upward northeast. In twenty seconds the gray cloud expanded hugely as we shot two pictures.

The cloud spread low. It overtopped the ridge at Fawn Lake [7½ miles south-southeast] but didn't loft. The base followed topography over the crest, no gap beneath. A muffled sound like distant cannon came, then a roar like a train going by. Brewer sped off, then we.

The dark cloud rode the slope down north to Green River. Then it built rapidly up as a wall of shining silver, a boiling cauliflower texture changing continuously.

We tried to keep up but lost him and missed the turn to Winters Mountain. [Brewer took the west fork of road 1100, drove his car off the road, and walked six miles northwest to Winston Creek.] I took the right fork of road 1100 but dead-ended overlooking Riffe Lake [road 1130A]. We met the Whitlocks who knew a way out. We drove a short way to a log pile in the road and stepped out.

The cloud had lots of strange lightning. A white dot appeared, then a bolt shot from it—mostly in the cloud but some to the ground. The mountain roared. We shot five pictures of a gray-ash wall rising from a huge area north of Mount St. Helens and spreading up into a dark mushroom. Low white clouds appeared in the valleys, drifting from the mountain. To the north on Riffe Lake two miles away, a sharp boundary separated wavy, rippled water behind from the calm in front—a wind front. Soon we were hit from the northwest by a 50-mph gust for a few seconds. Now seven minutes after eruption's start, it stalled the coming cloud.

A dark veil of ash we could see into approached from the southwest in an arc overhead. A wind now blew north forty miles an hour. A little ash blew past, like a truck down a dusty road. We got into the Jeep. Pea-sized clumps of wet ash fell. They stuck to the windshield in splatters the size of dimes and quarters. Something hard like little rocks pinged off the Jeep, but we couldn't see them. The clumps and rocks stopped in half a minute. Fine ash now fell, the air going darker. The wind stopped. Soon it got so dark we could see only five feet with headlights. Occasional muffled explosions punctuated the mountain's constant roar. Lightning ceased.

~8:45?

GENE PALMER

Ash starting to fall from overhung cloud.

After twenty minutes it grew lighter and we could see twenty feet. But in half a minute darkness closed and lasted more than 1½ hour. Ashfall was heavy, like having a giant sifter over you. Occasional larger ash clumps thumped down on the hood and canvas top.[8] It was still dark at 10:30 by a watch. The ash smelled acrid, dry, and slightly of sulfur.

About 11:00 it began to lighten. In fifteen minutes we saw stumps twenty feet away. The ashfall subsided. A steady wind blew ash off trees. Fine ash in the air blew more than fell. Many insects walked on the ash surface—apparently knocked out of the air.

After noon came a huge *boom*, loudest all day. The mountain roared louder, erupting again (*{Swanson}* chap 16). This persuaded us to leave. We drove with the Whitlocks to their camp a quarter mile away. Then crept east to road 1203 and wound down north, ash blowing off trees. Small trees and brush heavy with ash bent over the road. We reached highway 12 about 1:30.

Jack Whitlock

[Jack and Doreen Whitlock were on a ridge seventeen miles north-northwest of Mount St. Helens.]

We'd camped overnight. Our car radio suddenly filled with static. I got out and shot a photo of the eruption. I heard a rumble as I shot five more photos with two cameras. The cloud topped the ridge eight miles south and flowed down the side facing us very fast, hugging the ground.

We drove a short ways, and I shot more photographs. In the last the cloud has reached a ridge three miles to the south. Gene and Kathy Palmer drove up. We drove a short ways to a dead end. Ten minutes from the start a wind suddenly blew south toward Mount St. Helens 50 mph.

Muddy rain began to fall. Then dozens of hard pebbles pinging off the car. The cloud had a lot of lightning. Ash fell heavily and it went pitch black. We saw no more lightning but heard thunder, and the mountain rumbled.

It stayed black forty minutes, then for ten minutes we could see a short ways, then another hour and a quarter total darkness. About 11:30 it gradually lightened. Many insects were walking in the ash.

We drove back to camp. Wind had blown the fly off our tent.

Brian Cole

[Brian and David Cole and dog Bridgette were north of Green River near Deadman Lake, twelve miles north of Mount St. Helens.]

The north side of Green River valley was calm, no wind. We broke camp and about 8:30 began hiking trail 217 northwest along Goat Mountain ridge toward Vanson Peak.[9] A sudden pressure for half a minute made my ears pop a dozen times. Half a minute later we heard a rumbling like a jet that grew loud.

Walking ahead, Dave turned. "Hey! Look at *that*!" A giant plume filled the south sky.

The cloud grew terrifically, big expanding boily balls. It was four miles to the pickup, no way to outrun it. Its top edge came high overhead though its base hadn't reached Green River. We trotted up the trail. Lightning raked the cloud, faint thunder.

The mountain rumbling grew to a steady roar. As we hiked away the overhead cloud reached north of us. Streamers fell, and lightning flashed through them. Five minutes after we noticed the cloud the wind picked up, short gusts up to forty miles an hour *toward* Mount St. Helens. Dave—he fights forest fires—said it's like a big fire rising that sucks in wind from the sides.

Green River valley filled with ash like a dust storm—not the boily plume. Its dust blew over the ridge toward us. Half a minute later—fifteen minutes after the pressure change—ash began falling. It was gritty like sand but felt a little moist. Lightning bolts struck the ground all around, loud thunder with them. Dark gray closed in. We sat beneath a big tree in case pumice fell. Lightning struck everywhere, one bolt awfully close.

It turned utterly dark. Chunks fell through the trees and hit our packs. The wind toward the mountain lasted twenty minutes but dwindled. Fine ash fell. It and my pack felt moist. I draped a coat over me and Bridgette. A few chunks fell—apparently rocks from the way they hit the tree and bounced, sounding solid. After 45 minutes the bigger stuff quit, and no more lightning. As fine ash fell it stayed black dark. I smelled sulfur like a match. The dog fell asleep, and I felt sleepy. It grew warm. We sat beneath the tree 1½ hour.

A gentle wind came from the west and it grew lighter, visibility fifty feet. About 10:30 we brushed off the ash and started hiking. Two small ridges to climb, the rest downhill. The inch of ash didn't obliterate our old footprints in snow. Dust hung in the air despite a slight west wind. The mountain continued a dull roar—at times fairly loud. Fine ash still drifted down when we came to the truck about 12:45.

Don LaPlaunt

[Don LaPlaunt, his sons, Kathie Pierson, and Lynn and Julie Westlund were camped by a logging road a mile north of Green River fourteen miles north of Mount St. Helens.[10]]

The Westlunds slept in their pickup camper, my boys in my car, and my girlfriend Kathie and I in sleeping bags on the ground.

An earthquake shook the car and pickup, they said. I saw a small ash plume at the mountain's top. Then the mountain's front seemed to slide off—though I couldn't see well at this distance. Ash engulfed the mountain within seconds. The mountain had seemed the size of a baseball; the ash built to a grapefruit. It grew and grew. A second quake shook the truck and car. A deep roar grew louder and louder. In the vehicles they said the earthquake began 15–20 seconds before the roar, but sound coming this far takes time [1⅓ minute].

The spreading cloud hugged the ground like a D8 Cat. It came over a hill, then down following the land tight. The cloud came over another crest and rolled downslope. It came up the next ridgetop then down like a wave, engulfing trees. We looked over the top of this to the cloud piled over the mountain. It was clear to the east and in the canyons west around Coldwater.

West down Green River a little dark cloud poked up. Then southeast upriver another boiled up behind Mount Margaret. We couldn't see how close it was coming, hidden in valleys hugging the ground. Suddenly the cloud loomed up in one huge line, miles east and west. It rose like a giant wave two thousand feet high. It had to be traveling at a tremendous speed. Kathie shot a picture.

It happened so fast! We jumped in our car, the Westlunds into the back. Kathie had no boots, my boy no pants. We sped north. In three minutes we made the ridge. Mr. Westlund said he felt heat on his neck through the back window.

We broke over the crest and down toward Riffe Lake. The cloud torrent made a strong backwind across Riffe Lake. Trees whipped and limbs flew. When the wind met the cloud, hellacious lightning and thunder began. We wound north downhill and turned northeast. Way up, the cloud curled over us and toward the lake where it was still light. To the south I looked up a 50,000-foot gray wall.

I drove to the east end of Riffe Lake where campers sat drinking coffee.

"The mountain blew!"

"Yeah. We've seen it blow before."

We raced on. Down at the bridge at the head of Riffe Lake many people were camped, a motor home, someone putting a boat in.

"The mountain blew!" I said.

"Oh, we know," a lady said, like it was nothing.

Mudballs began falling, now twenty minutes after leaving camp. They splattered wet the size of half dollars. Soon they covered the windshield. I rolled down the window to see. They felt a little warm on my face. Mudballs and hard rocks came down a couple minutes. I drove down the flat on the east end of Riffe Lake in terrific lightning. We reached highway 12 as it was getting dark, mud slick on the road. The mud tapered off and turned to falling dry ash.

I drove west on the old north road—farther from the mountain. Ash fell heavily in Morton. I aimed for a patch of light in the west near Bear Canyon road. Five miles west of Morton—half an hour after the eruption—we outran the ash and hit wind coming in. The spreading cloud reached out to Mayfield Lake thirty miles northwest of the mountain.

COWLITZ VALLEY

Stan Rylee

[Stan Rylee, his wife, and several others were on east shore of Riffe Lake in Cowlitz valley nineteen miles north of Mount St. Helens.]

The morning was calm. We couldn't see Mount St. Helens far south behind ridges. I heard rumbling when a cloud in the south billowed like an oil fire up to 12,000 feet. A second billow appeared farther west, and then a third still farther west—along 120 degrees of horizon.

Five to seven minutes after the rumblings a cloud came over at 10,000 feet. A sudden wind blew forty knots toward the mountain for ten seconds and made the lake choppy. Then a fierce wind, perhaps eighty knots, blew from the mountain for ten seconds. We packed to leave.

Small rocks and clumps of damp ash fell ⅛ to ¼ inch in diameter. The ash became finer and smelled sulfury but didn't raise temperature. The mountain rumbled. The high cloud to the south reached above 20,000 feet full of cloud lightning and some thunder.

Jack and Audrey Joyce

[Jack and Audrey Joyce were at home three miles east-northeast of Glenoma with a view of Mount St. Helens 22 miles south. Jack shot 26 photos of the cloud over Cowlitz valley.[11]]

Around 8:40 we saw through our picture window a large cloud south toward the volcano. We went outside and Jack took pictures. A wind blew the flag stiff. [Five images show a light cloud near east horizon expanding in front of the advancing dark cloud.] As the cloud approached, lightning bolts flashed all over it, many fluorescent pink. It came overhead about 9:20, and the air grew dark and cool. Mudballs fell that felt warm. We went inside. By 9:35 it was too black outside to see beyond the windows. Ash fell and it stayed dark—until about 12:15 it lightened. The mountain roared and rumbled and the ground shook gently many times. Ash like cornstarch lay about, and the air smelled like fertilizer.

12

Northeast

But sometimes everything I write
with the threadbare art of my eye
seems a snapshot
. . .

Yet why not say what happened?
　　　　　　　　　　　　　—Robert Lowell, Epilogue

Several people camped at a high point of Forest road 100 [later, 99], an old log landing eleven miles northeast of the volcano near Bear Meadow.[1]

Gary Rosenquist, Joel Harvey, Linda Harvey, and William Dilly

[Gary Rosenquist, Joel and Linda Harvey, and the Harveys' neighbor William Dilly
camped on the landing. Rosenquist had studied photography and worked in film
processing. He shot an iconic set of photos of the landslide and initial eruption.[2]]

Rosenquist: I'd been up all night by the fire. About 8:25 I set my Minolta 35-mm
single-lens reflex on the tripod. I'd shot lots of film with this camera. It was loaded
with 36-exposure color-print film, 24 shots remaining. I framed the mountain and
shot one photo.

Dilly: Through binoculars I saw a little white steam from the mountaintop. Five
minutes later the ground shook. The mountain got fuzzy, like dust. The fuzz got bigger and bigger and went down the mountain. And part of the mountain was sliding!
"Hey Gary!" I yelled. "There it goes!"

Rosenquist: I turned and saw the whole side of the mountain sliding down. It's like
when you're a little drunk and things look blurry, seeing all that movement. But it
was really moving.

　　I dashed to the tripod, grabbed the camera with both hands, but accidently turned
it slightly right [that will center the eruption cloud] and punched the shutter. I looked
in the viewfinder but was too excited to adjust. I'd shot this camera often. I advanced
film and punched by reflex. And again. The first few photos are a few seconds apart.
I didn't want to shoot all my film on just a landslide. But then I saw its huge size and
shot quickly.

Dilly: The fast-sliding lower part hung up. An explosion rose from the summit,
another from the landslide. The cloud grew bigger and bigger. I ran to the car.

J. Harvey: I felt a minor pressure change and heard a big rumble.

Rosenquist: Too much was happening fast to adjust the camera. I shot barely watching. I looked over my shoulder to Dilly by the car, turned farther around to Joel

Landslides

8:32:42

8:32:49

8:32:55

08:33:11

08:34:06

08:34:28

behind me. I advanced the film and shot, advanced and shot, barely looking. A summit cloud appeared eight seconds after I'd started. A black cloud shot out the side and expanded. The dark north cloud really moved. Now it's only a second or so between shots. The film ran out. The cloud came over the first ridge, the pace really picking up. We had to get out of here.

Dilly: The cloud blotted the mountain and kept coming.

Rosenquist: The cloud hit a ridge and went up. It continued toward us.

J. Harvey: It hit a ridge and went up in the air, but it continued out. It hit another ridge, and went up. It hit a third ridge and went up. It was like bombs going off—wide divisions between the verticals in the cloud top. It came really fast, running low except when going over ridges. I heard a loud rumble.

We dashed to my car—a new Datsun. At lower level a mile to the south, the cloud front had flowed a mile east of us and flashed lightning.

Rosenquist: I unscrewed the camera, folded the tripod, and dashed to the car. I threw the tripod in back and climbed in as front passenger. We left tent and sleeping bags.

Joel backed the car. With a second camera I shot the approaching cloud out the window as a blue Ranchero starts from a camper *{Johnson}*.

J. Harvey: I turned onto the gravel road east but looked back. A low-level shock wave ran out, a blurry little wave like heat rising from something hot. It passed by fast but I didn't feel it. We drove road 100 southeast a mile. Here it was a sunny day. But after a right turn there was the cloud in front of us to the south—now five miles high, lightning all over. A wind kicked up, knocking down moss and green branches.

Dilly: Nothing had reached us but the blurry wave. The cloud came closer, and in it thunder and lightning. Wind now blew west toward the mountain. Dust shuffled on the road; tree debris fell. The black cloud behind swirled violently.

J. Harvey: I drove 45 miles an hour down the gravel road. I turned left on road 125 [now 25] and stepped on it. A mile north I saw over my shoulder the cloud behind. A patch of blue remained to the north. In another mile the cloud overtook us.

L. Harvey: It turned dark. For two or three minutes rocks fell sounding like hail.

Dilly: First came hard rocks. I heard them explode on the road like little bombs, and some bounced off the road. It started gradually, then a barrage.

Rosenquist: A mudball whacked the windshield.

J. Harvey: Then many. I rolled down the window and wiped some off—fairly warm, dry mud. It came down heavier. I could see nothing in front or behind. Twice I drove onto the shoulder.

Rosenquist: I could see only out the side. Suddenly a roadbank approached. "Hey! *Stop!*" We sat in the dark several minutes, too disoriented to continue.

J. Harvey: A pickup rolled by, and I followed it. The ash got deeper.

Dilly: It fell like dry snow. The air was a little yellowish and smelled like lighting a match.

J. Harvey: Smelled like chemistry lab, and a weak sulfuric acid stung my eyes.

Rosenquist: Ash fell all the way to Randle. After noon it let up and we drove west.

Keith Ronnholm

[Keith B. Ronnholm, graduate student at the University of Washington.[3]]

In the camper of my Toyota pickup I awoke at eight. The summit was quiet. Half an hour later I heard yelling and glanced at the mountain. The north bulge was sliding—a mile wide!

In five seconds a puff of ash rose from a cirquelike wall the landslide left. I dove to the front of my truck for my camera, jumped out the back, and stood in underwear. I shot a photo fourteen seconds after I saw the landslide. I shot more, adjusting shutter speed and focus.

A cloud had risen slowly from the summit. A huge light-gray one burst like a sphere north from the vacated area. Projectiles trailing ash arced up and out—must be large as houses. A gigantic block of mountain still slid. The gray cloud grew and grew. Awful but beautiful, it was silent. In twenty seconds the landslide went below the ridge except its tail.

The mountain disappeared in the gray cloud that swelled huge as it came out far more than rose. A ray of the cloud raced north into the upper Toutle much faster than the northeast part coming across Windy Ridge. Still no sound.

Half a minute after I first saw the slide the cloud hit a ridge and boiled upward. It crested the ridge and kept coming, like a huge sea wave crashing over a breakwater. Lightning in the cloud now was also a silent movie.

I shot more photos but saw it growing so gigantic so fast I might want to leave. Where're my pants? I reached in the back, found them, put one leg in, took a photo, put the other leg in, zipped up, shot a photo. Where're my shoes? the keys? I found the keys, unlocked the door, shot a photo. The flow had come over two closer ridges, each time crashing like a wave over a breakwater. It kept coming fast! Patches of white water-vapor clouds laced the edges of the huge gray cloud. I closed the back of the truck, ran to the front, got in, and turned around, stopped, and shot a few more frames.

The leading edge now came high overhead, projecting beyond the big cloud like an enormous breaking wave. The basal cloud climbed the ridge less than a mile away. I took a blurry one-hand shot over my shoulder as I drove off four minutes after I'd first noticed the landslide.

I drove 50 miles an hour down gravel road 100. Two minutes later a gust of wind blew tree branches and raised dust on the road. I heard thunder. Two miles down the road with clear air overhead, I stopped. Here it was serene and sunny—complete contrast with the violence to the west. The cloud must've stopped. I shot four photos about eight minutes into the eruption. The high part of the cloud, a great, gray breaking wave, now cast a shadow. The main cloud formed a charcoal-gray wall two miles southwest, churning like a thunderstorm. From high in the cloud a huge lightning bolt shot to the ground. My last photo looks south beneath the 20,000-foot base of a dark-gray anvil blowing fast east.

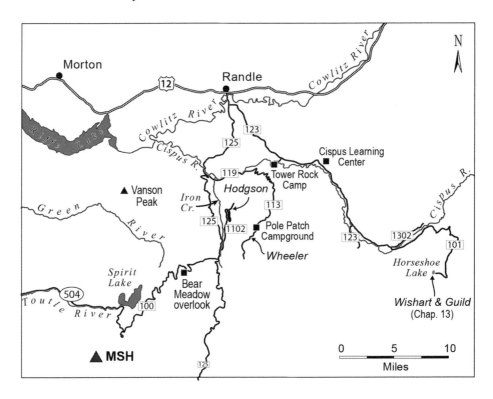

I heard noises like animals in the woods. A rock whizzed by and bounced in the road leaving a little crater in the dust. This dense rock the size of a golfball was coated in dried mud. Rocks zinged through the trees. More rocks hit the road. I picked up two and they weren't hot.[4] I got back in and drove on.

The infrequent falling rocks increased, beating on the truck at a roar. I pulled down the visor in case the windshield shattered. The rocks tapered off but big mud gobs increased. After a minute no more rocks, but mud drops fell on the windshield.

After two more minutes I reached road 125 [later, 25]. It was dark under the ash cloud but the sky blue north and east. As I drove north the blue narrowed, then was gone. Mud drops flattened on the windshield to ¾ inch in diameter but didn't splatter. The air seemed warmer.

The mud tapered off and fine dry ash fell thickly. I came behind a pickup truck going 30 mph and passed him. Thunder and reddish lightning continued. I slowed. The mud drops got suddenly intense but then dropped off as a lot of dry ash fell. I'd driven into and back out of a shower.

It went too hazy to see distant hills and grew dark. Dry ash fell thicker and thicker. I wet a handkerchief in the ice chest and held it over my mouth. It was hard to see in uniform gray. Bushes suddenly loomed in front! I was going off the road. I stopped 1½ miles north of road 100.

I sat in almost total darkness. I thought of Pompeii. If this ash fell a foot or two deep I was okay. I had food and water. If it got six feet deep I was in trouble. Ash sounded like soft snow on my cab. I heard distant thunder but saw no lightning. I sat five minutes.

Behind came a red glow. What's *that*... lava? But how absurd behind a ridge twelve miles from the mountain. The glow divided and grew yellow. A pair of head-lights crept closer. A flatbed crawled up behind me, two men walking ahead to show the road. Eight loggers huddled on the back and four inside the cab. The pickup I'd passed followed. I pulled in behind, visibility only a few feet.

After driving 5 mph fifteen minutes, it lightened some. The flatbed stopped and the men climbed in. Two Latinos got into the back of my pickup. A van went past {Hodgson}. We continued north. The air lightened and we rolled at 10 mph, then 15. In six miles we came to Randle about 10:15.

The town seemed deserted. I stood under the overhung roof of a restaurant at the main intersection. Against the traffic light it looked like a heavy snowstorm at night. But this is midmorning! Other cars came from the south.

Within an hour sixty people crowded into the downstairs of a church. Out in my truck only static on AM radio but FM played music. A song ended. The DJ said, "Mount St. Helens has exploded! All roads are closed! Yakima airport's closed! Now back to music."

I left Randle at 11:45 and drove highway 12 slowly west. I stopped in Morton. A sign in my photograph reads 12:28 PM. Farther west the ash thinned and disappeared.

Wendell Johnson

[Viola "Lou" and Wendell Johnson camped at the overlook with Barbara and Mike Erlenmeyer. Wendell had taken geology courses.]

We'd been to this overlook in earlier eruptions. We drove our camper in May 17th. We walked west down road 100 with the Erlenmeyers looking at old pumice layers in roadcuts. Only a couple small steam plumes rose from the crater.

Sunday we were in the camper when someone outside yelled, "There she goes." I bolted out. A big landslide moved slowly down the north. An eruption burst up behind the slide, and black ash shot from the summit. In fifteen seconds or so the slide dropped behind a ridge. Ash boiled up and north out of the maw, but no sound. The big cloud grew very fast. Within a minute it blocked the mountain. Gary Rosen-quist's photos from next to us shows its expansion.

A thin bluish color ran out from the mountain in front of the big swelling gray cloud—like a horizontal wave you see on atomic-bomb films. I felt a pressure increase for a few seconds. Now about 1½ minutes after the start of the landslide and three-quarters minute after the big horizontal explosion, I heard a noise like a thun-derclap, then for some time a quieter rumble like a distant freight train. Horizontal lightning flashed in the cloud.

The Erlenmeyers sped off, and someone yelled, "Let's get out of here!" I ran bare-foot to the trailer, got my boots, and Lou and I dashed to our Ford. Rosenquist's last photo while speeding away shows our Ranchero moving, last to leave. The coming cloud now built rapidly up.

We raced east down gravel road 100, the cloud gaining. After a few minutes lightning flashed many colors. We reached road 125—three miles—in five minutes.

A warm wind descended. Rocks up to an inch but mostly pea gravel pelted the car. I stopped to grab some; others landed in the back. Most rocks were angular black andesite but some round and smooth. They were warm—some very. Some dented the car. Sand ash began to fall.

The cloud followed topography downhill above the treetops. I drove north. Balls of slightly damp ash as large as five inches rained down and exploded upon impact. The cloud enveloped and the air went black. In twenty seconds it blotted out sunlight on the east. Ash balls fell about two minutes. Then very sticky mud fell in drops that splattered as discs one to three inches across, sticking like stiff mashed potatoes. Rocks and dry ash still fell. With my head out the side window the headlights lit only ten feet.

The warm-mud gobs diminished after some minutes, then dry ash fell heavily. Lightning struck all around. I could barely see—the road so obscure we veered up a logging road that stopped. I turned back. Our ears kept popping. In the headlights ash fell vertically. It smelled like burnt fireplace ashes or a forest fire, no sulfur. The mountain rumbled.

On lower road 125 we stopped by a young man stranded when his car stalled *{Wheeler}*. We stopped for an older man, who got in the back.

We crept on and came to Randle about 12:30 and went to a cafe. Outside it was still dark and three inches of ash lay on the ground,[5] an eerie silence punctuated by occasional rumbles from the mountain. By 1:00 the ashfall decreased and the sky lightened. Roosters crowed and dogs barked like before dawn.

About 2:30 we drove highway 12 west. The asphalt was scarcely visible in dry ash stirred up by passing vehicles.

Jerry Wheeler

[Wheeler had camped 17 miles northeast of Mount St. Helens on Forest road 113 [later 77] near French Butte a mile southwest of Pole Patch campground.]

I'd lived in Yakima since 1959, knew roads around Mount St. Helens, and in April and early May drove in several times to camp. The past weekend a friend and I camped at the 504 roadblock. It was rainy and cloudy, no one else there. I felt nervous in a valley close to an invisible volcano. A State Patrol officer drove up each evening. This weekend I camped northeast of Mount St. Helens. Vern Hodgson camped a mile away at Pole Patch, and Saturday we discussed cameras and photography.

Sunday I shot a photograph of Mount St. Helens about 8 o'clock—birds chirping, animals rustling. I visited a couple from California at their camper 75 yards southwest of me. Walking back up to my camp, I heard a rumbling. I turned and saw a big dark cloud growing near the mountain. I switched a telephoto off my camera for a 55 mm and shot a few photos. I ran down to the couple.

"Shouldn't we get the hell out of here?"

"No," he said. "If it gets bad we'll get in the camper."

But the cloud got big and came out fast. Soon he too cried, "Let's get out of here!"

I dashed to a lean-to I'd thrown up from timber scraps. The cloud reached overhead. I left sleeping bag and cooking gear and drove my 1972 Toyota northeast away from the cloud. A mile ahead at the ridgetop I stopped and shot more photographs.

Mudballs the size of golf balls thumped so loud on the car I thought they were rocks. But when one stuck it was a flattened lump of steaming mud—no rock inside. They fell a minute. The edge of the cloud passed overhead quickly, still light to the east.

I drove down north. But ash fell densely and the air went black. I could see almost nothing. I turned on the wipers and the ash smeared, still damp. I crept along five mph, my head out the window to see the road. Lightning struck repeatedly and thunder roared, more scary than the dark and ashfall. I crept down north into the valley. I ripped my shirt apart to cover my head and breathe through. After many miles I came to the bottom and Cispus River road (road 119; later 76). I crawled miles west. My car stalled. I got out and opened the hood but couldn't see. I got back in, and it started.

I crept another mile or so. The car stalled again and wouldn't restart. When I got out the door banged on metal. I was on a bridge [Iron Creek]. I walked west two hundred feet to road 125.

A faint glow appeared, headlights of a car creeping north. A man and wife in a Ranchero stopped *{Johnson}*. I walked back for my camera and got coated in ash, but they let me inside.

We crawled a few miles through woods. The driver said not a word. An older guy appeared. He'd driven his small pickup into a ditch. He climbed into the open back. We crept along several more miles as ashfall gradually lightened.

We came to Randle about 12:30. I could see a block. People stood around. Kids ran in dry-powder ash thinner than an inch, threw a football and frisbee, like Sunday in the park—this after our hours of worry about life and safety.

We turned east on highway 12 to a café. Inside it was full. The couple who drove were clean but the older guy and I filthy with ash. People stopped talking and stared. We cleaned up a bit in the restroom. The couple and I sat at a table, the driver for a long time saying nothing, stunned.

Stranded people were let into the school for the night. We overflowed to the principal's house. I slept on the floor.

Vern Hodgson and Bernadette Chaussee

[Vern Hodgson and Bernadette Chaussee watched from ¾ mile south of Iron Creek Butte, 17 miles northeast of the volcano.[6] Hodgson shot sixteen eruption photographs.]

Hodgson: This calm sunny day I removed the sunroof of my 1974 Ford van into the back. We stopped along a high part of gravel road 1102 [later, 7708]. I set the camera with a telephoto on a tripod and checked a light meter. Looking through binoculars, Bernadette said, "A puff of steam's coming!" I pushed the shutter but had set a ten-second delay. Before that elapsed, the white puff became large and a black eruption began to overwhelm the summit; a north promontory seemed to shatter and fall. A dark cloud blew out from that spot.

Chaussee: Through binoculars I saw the north bulge start down the mountain.

Hodgson: I watched the mountain sliding and took two more photos at ten-second intervals.

Chaussee: For seconds after I noticed the landslide, the clouds seemed like dust from the slide. A light-gray cloud then burst from the flank, then darker from the summit.

Hodgson: I heard no sound. The slide fell more than 2000 feet in half a minute and disappeared below a ridge. I changed to a 50-mm lens.

Chaussee: The eruption rose from different spots. A low column built over the mountain while a rounded part flowed down east.

Hodgson: The cloud front expanded north very fast. About when it reached Spirit Lake a big 'thump' built gradually and after a second stopped abruptly, like a van door sliding shut.[7]

Chaussee: White clouds grew along the edge of the cloud.

Hodgson: The cloud flowed out, rising only here and there. I changed to a wide-angle lens. Behind the ridge west of Iron Creek only the top of the cloud flowing north boiled above the crest. It raced at first, then slowed. It flowed east too, but slower. After some minutes the cloud rose.

Chaussee: As the cloud grew, lightning raced through it—blue, red, orange—but I heard nothing. Well north of the mountain a vertical column rose into clouds. The low cloud climbed over a ridge west of the valley before us. The boiling lower part continued out slower as an upper part grew out overhead. The sky filled with clouds and lightning.

Hodgson: The cloud drifted toward us with lots of texture. Still no noise except crackling and hissing thunder. The lower part boiled over Strawberry Mountain four miles southwest as the smooth upper concave part came out 40 mph and pulled nearly overhead.

Chaussee: The overhead cloud formed a smooth concave curve back to the vertical wall of clouds from the mountain. This upper cloud also arced east and north, but Mount Rainier showed beneath. There was no smell, no sound, no breeze.

Hodgson: Gray ash began coating trees in front of the ground cloud.

Chaussee: We left about eight minutes after the landslide.

Hodgson: I drove 30 mph two miles down two switchbacks, then three miles south on road 1102. I stopped at the edge of paved road 125 near people camped at Iron Creek.

Chaussee: We told them to leave; they said they weren't worried. It got darker and darker.

Hodgson: Clumps of ash and small cones began to fall.

Chaussee: Chunks of gray rock came through the open sun roof. A fir cone fell in, and balls of warm, slightly moist ash as large as an inch but mostly smaller. One hurt when it hit.

Hodgson: A wind blew, the air warmed, and the sky rained clumps of ash up to ¾ inch. They were damp enough to stick on the windshield and leave a cone an eighth inch high. On pavement they splattered into dust.

Chaussee: The air went dark as ashfall grew heavier and wetter.

Hodgson: The mud clumps lasted one or two minutes, then tapered off as the fall of dry ash increased. Then it showered heavily and visibility dropped to five feet. Ash coated the windshield—not entirely dry but not damp enough to stick to me when I got out. It built half an inch in two minutes. It smelled pungent.

I drew in a breath and ash stuck in my nose and mouth. With each breath a little more coated mouth and throat. I was starting to suffocate. Then more. A cold numbness crept up my body. This is it, I thought, we're dying.

"Here's some towels," Bernadette said.

Her calmness snapped me out of it. Better try to get out. We wrapped our faces in towels.

I crept north onto road 125 but couldn't see. The left tire dropped off onto gravel—the edge of pavement—and I veered right. I crept down in blackness two miles an hour. I felt the right tire drop and steered left. I got out and cleaned the windshield.

Chaussee: After five minutes a wind blew through the trees from the volcano, maybe down a creek valley. It lasted some minutes.

Hodgson: I pulled my hat low and drove with my head out the window to see the road edge. We idled downhill three miles an hour, stopping twice more to clean the windshield. Barely damp ash fell twenty minutes. It continued heavily but now dry enough it no longer stuck to the windshield. It fell through the absent sunroof.

The density of fall varied. I saw the road edge at times, then it disappeared. The air was still; ash fell in the trees quietly. I thought of Pompeii.

Chaussee: I saw only an occasional flash of lightning. It grew warm and stuffy. The air smelled of sulfur. The fall got finer and lighter.

Hodgson: Visibility increased slightly. I crept past a yellow pickup truck {*Ronnholm*} stopped in the road behind a logging truck and two men outside. We came to Randle about 10:15, visibility 300 feet. I turned west onto highway 12.

Ash still came in and the motor ran rough. I stopped and opened the hood. The air cleaner was choked in ash; I shook it out. We started west again, ash blowing up as we drove. The van ran rough; again I got out and tapped ash from the filter.

We came to Morton 11 o'clock or so. Ashfall tapered off, sunlight struggled through, but fine dust fell lightly. Farther west we left the ash behind.

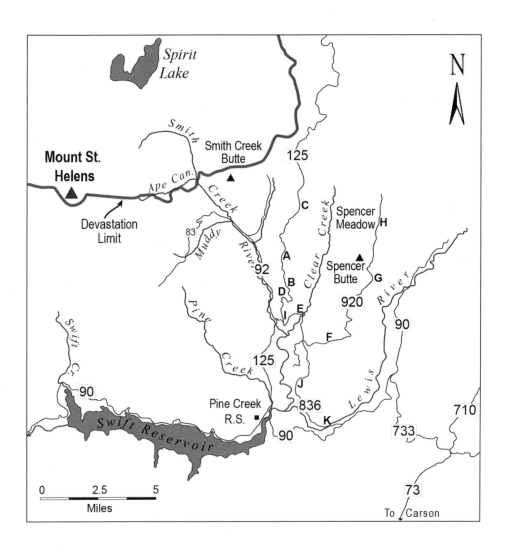

13

East

*Before us the thick dark current runs. It talks up to us in a murmur
become ceaseless and myriad, the yellow surface dimpled monstrously
into fading swirls travelling along the surface for an instant. . . as
though just beneath the surface something huge and alive waked. . . .*
—William Faulkner, *As I Lay Dying*

Cathie Hickson and Paul Hickson

[From Vancouver, B.C., Catherine and Paul Hickson camped the night. Paul was a postdoctoral astrophysicist, Cathie a geology student, at University of British Columbia.[1]]

Cathie: Early Sunday we and two dogs—big malamute 'Crystal,' black labrador 'Dawn'—were camped along road 125 [now 25] nine miles east-southeast of Mount St. Helens. We struck camp [Map, site A] and packed our green 1973 Renault wagon.

Paul: The mountain was quiet, just a hint of steam. The east profile of the mountain was asymmetric: the summit, a flat notch just north marking the crater, and farther north the bulge.

Cathie: We drove 1½ miles south, filled a water jug at a creek [site B], and drove back. Two miles beyond our campsite we turned up a gravel road into a quarry. Trees on its west above road 125 had been cut, a superb view of the mountain [site C].[2] We pulled out gear and about 7 o'clock set the spotting scope on a tripod to watch Mount St. Helens. A little steam wafted from a crack on Shoestring Glacier.

Paul searched across the quarry for discarded blasting wire. The dogs usually explore. But Dawn oddly paced between me and Paul. Crystal lay by the car. I checked her paws but found no thorn. I set up to cook breakfast, Crystal oddly glued to my leg as I moved between stove, water jug, pots, and spotting scope. Dawn came back with Paul. I checked her paws: no thorn.

Paul and I climbed into the car with bacon, eggs, and coffee watching the bright sunlit mountain and its bulged-out north.

Paul: We'd just finished when I noticed the shape of the mountain changed: the bulge was more! "Cathie! Look!" I didn't comprehend but then saw the large bump sliding down the north flank. There'd been no sound or vibration. I grabbed the camera and stepped out.

Cathie: A summit eruption began. We dashed to the berm just west. The dogs came with us. "Sit!" Paul said, and they sat.

We shot photographs, the first fifteen or twenty seconds after we'd noticed motion. The landslide was streamlined and had a beautiful internal bedding—orange on top and streaked white beneath. In silence it was hard to take in what was happening.

Paul: The landslide was halfway down when a dense, black cloud shot up near the summit. A billowy collar swelled slowly around its base. A separate dark-gray eruption shot up halfway down the north, behind the landslide going still lower.

Cathie: The flank cloud shot up a couple seconds and arced out laterally.

Paul: A bigger puff came up between the landslides closer to the summit. Half a minute later I heard a rumbling, maybe the slides. The big bulge neared the bottom of the mountain. The high smaller one slid slower.

PHOTOS BY PAUL HICKSON

Cathie: The upper landslide overrode the flank vent and shot like a fountain over the lower slide. The blocks arcing north during these fifteen or twenty seconds must have been huge.

The lower landslide and its streamlined top suddenly bunched up. The front steepened and the structure in its side folded up. A couple seconds later the swelling cloud covered both slides.

Paul: The enveloping cloud was long northward but not high. But within another fifteen seconds its top rose to much higher than the mountain. It now spread in all directions, fastest north. It reached many miles north in less than two minutes. It then flowed east off the mountain.

Cathie: The big cloud pushed far above the mountain many shades of gray, billowing, constantly changing. Its base spilled down east as a low wall. It hugged topography down the mountain, flowing almost like water, its rounded front 300 to 500 feet high.

The front disappeared into a valley, then rode up over a closer ridge. One lobe outdistanced the cloud flowing down the mountain. This lobe had topped the next ridge while the front of most of the cloud still flowed in the valley behind. The front was very thick, black, and rolling but had little height.

It looked like pictures of a nuée ardente [incandescent ashflow] at Mont Pelée—but no towering cloud above this flow. The cloud front was very sharp and opaque—no dust in front, no blocks shooting out.

The cloud coming much closer was *so* enormous. Yet still no sound. In silence it's hard to take in what's happening. So big, so silent, is surreal.

Paul: The initial cloud rose several thousand feet above the summit. This high flat pancake now spread down and out over everything. It rolled down the south volcano flank and we saw the mountain no more. I ran to the car, switched a wide-angle lens to the camera, and dashed back to the berm. The textured black curtain spread in all directions. Little white vapor clouds interlaced its upper edges. A continuous low rumbling gradually built louder.

The cloud much higher than the mountain reached north three times the mountain's basal width. The dense cloud rolling down the east side came down into another valley, up over the next ridge, huge and still expanding.

Cathie: We took our 7th photograph. Two minutes after the eruption's start the dense, dark cloud billowed out still larger, coming fast. It looked like nothing would stop it. Through all this the dogs had sat, Dawn staring at the eruption.

"This is *not* great," Paul said. Indeed our situation was perilous. We ran to the car and opened its doors. The dogs crammed in—70-pound Dawn on the passenger floor, 125-pound Crystal in the middle. We jumped in, leaving tent, stove, cooking gear, $600 telescope and tripod.

Paul: I sped down the quarry road and south on curvy gravel road 125.

Cathie: The black cloud front crossed a close ridge a mile northeast of Smith Creek Butte. I was terrified! The convex basal, leading part of the cloud was 500 feet high but the whole cloud flowing down the mountain 6000 feet high. The high gray cloud was now billowing and growing rapidly just behind the ground-hugging flow. The cloud filled my whole passenger-side view. I took more photos. It came within a couple miles.

Paul: After five minutes the cloud stopped spreading and started up. Lightning flashed in it.

Cathie: Paul sped down the gravel dodging boulders fallen from roadcuts. Elk and deer crashed out of the brush uphill from the west and across the road. One banged into us—more frightened by what's behind than by our car.

The dogs hadn't moved—Dawn on the floor at my feet. Crystal filled the seat between us facing back, paws gripping the seat top, butt on the stickshift. Paul shoved aside her 125 pounds to shift gears.

Paul: After we sped past our campsite and were three miles south of the quarry [site D], I saw more lightning in the column and a high anvil cloud poked out east. We turned east onto road 920 [later, 93]. In a mile it crossed Clear Creek on a bridge past two vehicles and people camped. We drove south uphill past road 836 [later, 9039] and the road turned east.

We got out at a high point that seemed safe, twelve miles southeast of the volcano [site F].[3] I changed film and shot more pictures, ten to fifteen minutes after the eruption's start. The plume at the mountain spiraled up 50,000 feet or more. It sucked up everything. Once the updraft started, nothing had come down the south or east flanks. The anvil cloud from the column's top swelled faster east than south, casting a dark shadow.

Cathie: The huge updraft cleared the mountain. Clouds that had flowed off lay low on the east flank. White condensation clouds and gray streamers encircled the dark column. A veil wavy with streamers hung from the dark anvil.

The summit remained during the first two minutes of eruption, only the bulge sliding. Then the cloud enveloped the mountain. When it cleared the summit was gone! It went between two and fifteen minutes after eruption's start.

Paul: The column moved up strongly, the high anvil jetting east. The summit was cut off, the east flank clear, nothing flowing down. There'd been lightning since before the cloud started up, but now lots of it, mostly close to the column and striking down or angling back into it. Only segments of very long bolts showed in the overhead anvil.

The roiling south upwind wall of the column looked like a gray cauliflower. Ash rained out as a streaky curtain northeast that reached the ground toward Mount Adams.

Cathie: We shoved Crystal and Dawn into the back and now had some room.

Paul: We drove northeast on road 920 toward the black curtain. Near Breezy Point [site G] a dense, white fog had crossed the ridge and now twenty minutes into the eruption hung in the valleys to the east. The high east plume was obliterating the top of Mount Adams, its south flank white in sun.

Cathie: The fog in the east valleys may have been part of the lateral cloud that drifted over the ridges south. The air was clear and sunny above the fog. North was the way we knew out.

Paul: We drove road 920 north. Near Spencer Meadow gobs of mud fell from the south edge of the plume, the largest blobs like the big leading in a thunderstorm [site H]. Ahead an obscuring curtain hung from black clouds. The air smelled a little acrid.

Mud had been falling here some time, the road black and slippery. Black, muddy rain covered the windshield. Big opaque ash drops splattered with too little water to flow. I stuck my head out the window to see but got smeared with cool mud that stuck.

We turned around. Ten minutes after we'd driven into the mudfall we drove back out. No ash had fallen here to the south; just north it must have rained mud continuously. A few miles west we met the people by Clear Creek *{McCulley & Findley}* and studied their maps.

Cathie: They wanted to cross the Muddy and drive west down Lewis River. We thought that many miles across the volcano's south flank risky. My watch read 10:00. The volcano roared like a jetliner, punctuated by an occasional loud crack! Signs at the gate across road 125 (site I) read ROAD CLOSED and RED ZONE.

"Boy, if the Forest Service catches us taking the gate off . . . " one of them said.

"We've much bigger problems now," I said.

"They could put us in jail."

"We're Canadians. What can they do to us?"

Paul and I lifted the gate off the hinges. A roar coming down from the north grew louder, sounding like a big flood. Their cars disappeared down toward Muddy River a quarter mile away. In a few minutes they came racing back up.

"The valley's full of hot mud and water!"

"The bridge washed out before we got there!"

"Giant trees are coming down!"

Over maps we decided to try road 125 north, the way we'd come in. We'd started off when a small car came south. The driver said to the north they'd run into rocks falling. He was incoherent. Rocks from the sky? Rolling off roadbanks? Here the air was only hazy, visibility several miles. The vent roared and the plume rose, but no fallout here.

Paul: Our three vehicles headed north. A couple miles before the quarry fine ash veneered the ground and still fell.

Cathie: We dropped back from a cloud the Volkswagon van blew up. The Toyota Landcruiser behind us dropped back.

Paul: At the quarry turnoff we couldn't see far in gray haze and falling dry ash.

Cathie: Paul let me out to flag the Landcruiser and drove up for our gear. The van had gone ahead, the vehicle behind not in view, Paul's gone, we're close to the volcano roaring and rumbling. I felt alone and vulnerable—so near, unable to see in the dust, ash sifting down from the firs, a few lumps of pumice dropping. The inch of new material on the ground included ash spheres a tenth-inch across. An occasional *crack!* punctuated the mountain's roar. Hearing a tremendous crash, I thought large rocks could fall any time.

After some minutes the Landcruiser crept into view. They stopped, but then sped north. I was alone again. Another loud *crack!*—an unmuffled explosion. Paul finally came from the quarry.

Paul: I'd gotten our gear with its caked-on ash.

Cathie: The cooking pot held dry spherical BB pellets mixed in loose fine ash. As thick at the edges as in the middle, it'd fallen more or less vertically.

The van returned from the north about 10:20, headlights flashing, its top white with pumice. They said pumice fell so heavily they'd pressed their hands to the windshield thinking it might break. Fresh pumice fell here more now but not like that. They brought angular chunks as large as 2½ inch and said bigger ones lay on the road. We couldn't go north. The Landcruiser came back, and all three vehicles drove south.

Paul: We continued on our earlier route, but the other vehicles stopped. We turned onto road 836 [later 9039] and stopped to see Muddy River [site J]. A huge flood had gone down but little water remained now, about 11:00.

Cathie: Standing bankside trees were coated halfway up in mud; many others lay in the sludge.

Paul: Two miles south we came to Lewis River. The flood hadn't backed up here.

Cathie: Paul gunned across the bridge about 11:30. The eruption rumbled fifteen miles away.

Paul: The amplitude grew during the eruption. The first minutes only a muffled rumble. About 10:15 back at the quarry the rumbling was louder, plus sharp reports. Now it rumbled steadily like a jet aircraft at a distance—subdued but strong. The air was very hazy even this far south.

Cathie: We drove south to Carson, west to Vancouver, and north on I-5. In our photo from north of Castle Rock in late afternoon, the column looks twenty miles wide and up to 40,000 feet.

The cylindrical telescope from the quarry was covered by 4 mm of caked-on fine ash. Atop the water jug was gray fine ash and in it and on top the little spheres. There must have been two falls. The first ash stuck to horizontal and vertical surfaces, and perhaps fell moist. Then loose ash spheres that rolled off sloping surfaces. They had a crystal nucleus but broke upon touch. Under a binocular microscope I saw they consisted of two to three layers.

Larry McCulley and Joe Findley

[Larry McCulley, Joe Findley, and four others were camped by Clear Creek eleven miles east-southeast of Mount St. Helens (site E).]

McCulley: We got up about eight and made breakfast in a gentle breeze.

Findley: A pressure change popped my ears. Only patches of sky showed beneath a giant tree. I thought a rolling black cloud was a thunderhead. I dashed to the river and saw the volcano going off.

McCulley: An ash cloud half as high as the mountain moved away from us, soon turning all northwest of us black. A riverbed was no place to be. We started north up road 125.

Findley: We drove through trees. At an overlook we saw devastation below, trees blasted everywhere. The mountain sounded like a freight train. The top of a huge rising cloud mushroomed out. Lightning ran around its outside. We watched ten minutes as the mushroom spread, fastest northeast beyond us. It looked like an atomic-bomb cloud. As the mushroom grew, lightning shot from it down into the forest.

McCulley: It mushroomed up at 20,000 feet. A ground wind began to blow toward Mount St. Helens forty miles an hour, a draft bending trees and branches west. The updraft drew clouds toward the dark north. It cleared the volcano.

A roar of rolling and tumbling came down the mountain, the sounds of mudflows. A white vapor cloud near the volcano grew and came east toward us. Ash started to fall and visibility dropped. A few small birds fell.

Findley: Ravens flew in low from the east *toward* the mountain and landed in nearby trees.

McCulley: We drove south. A disoriented elk followed my van. The white vapor cloud stayed over us. We stopped at the junction of road 919 [site I] thinking to go out southwest. A Canadian couple came up the road *{Hickson}*. While talking we heard a flow coming down Muddy River sounding like a freight train.

The Canadians lifted off the gate, and we drove down to the river. A big flow had just taken the bridge and now watery mud flowing 35 miles an hour bubbled and steamed. Logs rammed into the bottom and spiraled up and out. The flood felled gigantic green trees from the banks. They bobbed along like corks, but some crammed onto the banks. We drove back up and put the gate on.

Our two vehicles and the Hickson's drove north up road 125. A man in a Subaru came south screaming "boulders! boulders!" In the distance I heard the mudflow ripping down Muddy River.

We drove in under a yellowish cloud. The Hicksons stopped but we went on. Ice chunks started to fall, some up to ¾ inch in diameter. Two or three minutes later, down came huge drops of cold mud damp enough to splatter up to three inches. Mud covered the windshield. We got out, wiped it off, and continued north. Now round BB pellets of ash fell. We got out and got some. Pumice rock came down, then very fine gray-powder ash.

Findley: First to fall on us was ice chunks, then mud. Later BB ash, then pumice rock. I was scooping BB ash into a Metzger-map envelope when pumice started to fall. We continued north. The pumice got bigger. I got out and grabbed some, and they were warm. A loud *crack!* came from the mountain.

McCulley: We turned back south. Ash covering the road was slippery. We drove out of falling ash and got back to the junction of 919. There'd been no fall here, fine ash just starting.

We drove east and south on road 836 to the junction of 836A [site J]. My van was low on gas, but Findley turned down 836A. The Hicksons continued on the main road.

Findley: We went down to find a bridge. We couldn't get past downed trees.

McCulley: They came back up in twenty minutes. I heard another mudflow coming. We drove to road 836 and turned south. We came to a high point across from Cedar Flats and got out, now two hours into the eruption. Mud the color of creamed coffee flowed through the flat below, branching into streams five feet wide and crossing the road. They seemed the consistency as up at Muddy River bridge but here only creeping.

Findley: From a quarter mile back we watched mud cover the flat and logging road we'd driven on fifteen minutes earlier.

McCulley: We drove on and came to our first clear water, Pepper Creek. We crossed on a bridge. We followed the road over Lewis River and out south through Wind River.

Larry Wishart and Irving Guild

[Irving R. Guild, Lawrence (Larry) Wishart, and twenty-one others of a 4-wheel-drive club had camped 31 miles east-northeast of Mount St. Helens by Horseshoe Lake.[4]]

Wishart: Horseshoe Lake was clear and cloudless. Someone yelled, "Hey, there she goes!" A dark-gray massive chimney came up over the trees, and its top spread toward us.

Guild: I hustled up to a clearing. The cloud was already large. Within ten minutes it filled the southwest sky. Light-gray rocks came pinging into the trees—up to half an inch but mostly pea gravel. It lasted five minutes.

Wishart: The air warmed as rocks ⅜ inch fell, then fell smaller and smaller. Lightning flashed over the cloud, mostly down toward the mountain. The underside of the coming cloud tumbled.

Guild: About nine the sky grew much darker and BB-sized pellets fell. They splattered on impact—moist but not wet mud. We packed our vehicles as gigantic lightning flashed through the cloud.

Wishart: Mud splats fell about five minutes, then fine ash.

Guild: Our eleven-vehicle caravan left about 9:10.

Wishart: We drove in ash falling like black fog. We crawled a few miles an hour with headlights on, barely seeing taillights just ahead. We talked on citizens-band radios. Even with windows up, ash like bath powder crept in. People joined us from stalled vehicles.

Guild: Coarse-sand ash fell as we crept in dark north and west on Forest roads 101, 1302, and 123. There were two great lightning flashes—one a ball of fire at 30 degrees struck trees with a crash that shook the vehicle. We passed more abandoned cars.

Wishart: The air grew lighter. After many miles we passed through a roadblock near Randle.

Guild: Ashfall stopped before Randle where the sky was light yellow.

Wishart: We got to town after 12:30, the air like light fog. We drove highway 12 west. Ash on the ground thinned and was gone before Ethel. At an I-5 rest area I talked to a reporter.[5]

Guild: We crossed Toutle River flooding with logs.

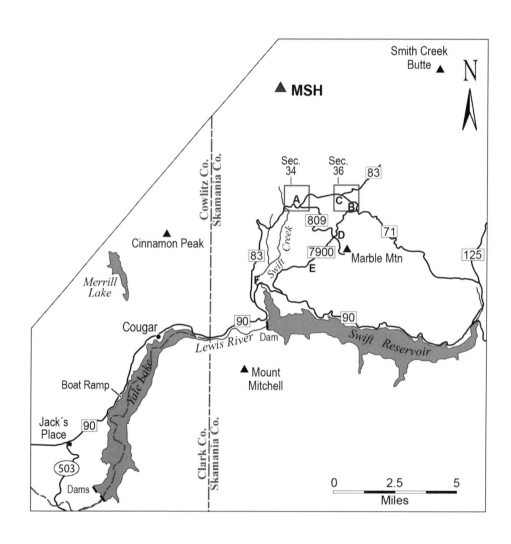

Smith Creek
Butte ▲

N

▲ **MSH**

Sec.
34

Sec.
36

83

A

C B

809

D

71

83

Swift Creek

7900

▲ Marble Mtn

E

125

Cinnamon Peak ▲

F

Cowlitz Co.
Skamania Co.

Merrill
Lake

90

90

Cougar

Lewis River

Dam

Swift Reservoir

Boat Ramp

Yale Lake

▲ Mount
Mitchell

Jack's
Place

90

503

Clark Co.
Skamania Co.

Dams

0   2.5   5
Miles

14

South

Animals, as they pass through the landscape, leave their tracks behind.
Stories are the tracks we leave.

—Salman Rushdie, *Step Across This Line*

Kathy Anderson, Kran Kilpatrick, Valerie Sigfridson, Kate Brennan, John Morris

[Anderson was Forest Service officer for tree planting 5½ miles south of the summit. Kilpatrick and Morris were inspectors in southeast of land section 34 [T8R5], Brennan and Sigfridson inspectors in southeast of section 36.[1]]

Anderson: In 1978 I'd helped collect noble fir cones above Spirit Lake now grown to seedlings we'd plant today. I contracted crews that for ten days had planted eight miles east-northeast of the mountain. This would be our first day south—on the north slope of Marble Mountain. Barely off the volcano's base, we'd watch the mountain and radio the ranger in Cougar.

Sigfridson: I worried about being so close, but each truck had five gallons of water, 48 meals, filter masks, tools, and radio.

Kilpatrick: We drove up roads 90 and 83 to 809 to where Morris and I would inspect planting in section 34 [site A].[2] Kate and Valerie went on east to section 36. It was a clear day, birds chirping, a huge view of the dust-covered volcano.

Anderson: I reached the section-34 unit about 7:10 and stayed half an hour.

Kilpatrick: The crew began planting seedlings. Kathy and I drove east toward section 36, and she showed me the escape route.

Brennan: In section 36 [site B][3] each of the eleven planters bagged 300 noble-fir seedlings, and from the road we trudged 500 feet down north.

Anderson: I drove with Kran up road 809 southeast. We stopped and by binoculars I watched steam near the top of Shoestring Glacier. We drove northeast to section 36.

Kilpatrick: From the ridge road we walked north down to the plantings Kate and Valerie inspected. We returned to the road and drove off.

Anderson: At 8:30 we drove north toward Forest road 71 [site C].

Sigfridson: Standing on a log in section 36, I felt it move.

Morris: In section 34, I felt a tremor and saw logs move.

Kilpatrick: As Kathy turned right onto road 71, trees swayed back and forth.

Anderson: A small black two-headed column rose from the north behind the mountain summit. I radioed Cougar that it's erupting and we'll leave. The black cloud rose quickly 1500 feet, foaming and flowing. From the hidden north a huge dark-gray cloud shot up northeast.

Kilpatrick: It was silent. The cloud grew suddenly to bigger and more intense than several I'd seen earlier. "Let's get the hell out of here!" I said.

Sigfridson: I glanced at the mountain. A plume billowed out near Shoestring Glacier on the east side. I heard Kathy radio Cougar. I yelled to the planters below, "Get up to the rigs!"

Anderson: I radioed Morris and Brennan to leave and we'd meet at road 809 junction.

Morris: We dropped tree bags and hoedads and ran toward the rigs.

Brennan: Black billows replaced blue sky. "Evacuate!" I yelled. The foreman screamed, "Run for your lives! We're gonna get burnt up!" They dropped shovels, hoes, and bags and hoofed up.

Anderson: Billowy clouds shot also from the mountain's west side 60 degrees up northwest.

Kilpatrick: The mountain's west base sent a huge cloud up, its downward flow terrifying. I told Kathy what I saw; she radioed Cougar while driving. Huge billowing clouds throwing rocks ahead rolled down the west and southeast sides at fantastic speed.

A minute and a half after the beginning, three explosions on the south blew in tight succession east to west, like primer cord—tan plumes unlike the dark-gray ones. They burst up 60 degrees from the 8500-foot level, arced out like a spout, and landed at about 6500 feet. They slung rock ahead while racing down toward us.

Sigfridson: We scrambled up south, backs to the mountain. The eruption was silent. "Hurry!" I urged the planters, "Hurry up!"

Anderson: After two minutes ash clouds obscured the mountain above 6500 feet. A flow came down Shoestring Glacier, many light-colored ones down the south like whipped milk from the rim, but narrowing downward. A white cloud billowed up behind the nose of each descending flow. A flow came down Swift Creek to timberline. Clouds soon covered the low flanks.

Kilpatrick: Down to timberline in a minute or so.

Anderson: Driving southeast from the mountain, I glanced back. The eruption was now going way up, tilted northeast. We reached the section-36 unit six minutes after eruption's start. The pale clouds at the mountain rose and joined a main column to the north.

Kilpatrick: Just before we got there two plumes punched up 20,000 feet in a minute. Two wide, dark columns, blue sky between.

Anderson: Billowy clouds east and west rose thousands of feet into one column. Blue sky showed through a vertical gap between the unjoined lower many thousand feet.[4] A dark horizontal cloud now stretched east, 800 feet thick near the mountain tapering to nothing beyond Smith Creek Butte. Above and below this band the sky was clear.

Morris radioed: his planting crew had reached the vehicles.

Kilpatrick: We came to Kate and Valerie's rig [site B]. I found the keys and started it up.

Brennan: Valerie and I reached the hilltop road in five minutes. The last of the planting crew were a few minutes behind.

Kilpatrick: The planting crew ran up, and I handed them masks. They were screaming, scared, as dark clouds billowed up fast. They jumped in their rigs and we started up the road. Huge bolts of lightning flashed, and thunder roared. Wind picked up and swirled the trees.

Morris: In section 34 the planters climbed into their van, and we raced east on the 809.

Anderson: Now one dark, wide column rose from north of the mountain—no gap between clouds. Trees shielded the mountain, but the clouds were full of lightning.

Kilpatrick: Morris and his crew were out watching the mountain when we came to the junction of road 809 and a private road [site D].[5]

Morris: The others arrived five minutes after us. Our caravan now had three vans and three pickups.

Anderson: We drove road 7900 1½ miles southwest diagonally through section 11, then stopped ten minutes [site E]. The dark column north of the mountain mushroomed out south high over us, a new gray billowy ceiling. Wind swirled the trees. Much cloud-to-cloud lightning. Static blocked the radio. The air smelled of sulfur like a match.

Sigfridson: Which way to go? West we'd cross Swift Creek from the volcano. East was farther and we'd cross two low valleys from the volcano. West seemed better.

Morris: Planters in one van panicked, and the foreman broke up a fight. Two others walked to my pickup and said they were going into the woods. "You'll die," I said. "Let's stay together." They returned to their van.

Anderson: We drove southwest on the 7900 and turned west onto Forest Service road 90. The dark cloud drew over us like a tent, lightning all around. We reached the bridge over Swift Creek.

Kilpatrick: The radio worked again. We asked for the plane to verify no mud was coming down Swift Creek. Forest headquarters said the plane wasn't up yet. A USGS geologist radioed us to evacuate. So much for their two-hour warning.

Anderson: Last night Dan Miller had warned a hot flow could follow Swift Creek. Kran walked onto the bridge. He waved us by. He waved each vehicle across and climbed into the last. We shot photographs.

Kilpatrick: I smelled sulfur and tasted acid. A little fine dust settled on the rigs.

Anderson: We drove southwest as the dark-gray cloud mushroomed south over Swift Reservoir. We reached Cougar about 9:40.

Kilpatrick: For all the monitoring around the mountain, the geologists didn't radio us until 25 minutes after the eruption's start—long after we'd left.

Brennan: How often had we been assured of a warning, that it's safe to work near mountain, that they'd watch when we were close? None of us wanted to be so close. Then they forget us.

Anderson: I took it as a hope of warning *if* they detected something. Our warning was our eyes.

Ernst Hoger and Vern Putrow

[Ernst Hoger, Vern Putrow, and Vern's brother Harold fished on Yale Lake 12½ miles south-southwest of Mount St. Helens.]

Ernst Hoger: We trolled two hours, the fishing good until 7:30. The mountain was quiet, wind calm. By 8:30 we were near the lake's southeast side.

Vern Putrow: A puff rose from the mountain like ones I'd seen earlier. But this one grew, and ash rolled down the northwest flank. In about two minutes the mountain seemed to explode, more horizontal than up. Ash clouds rolled down all sides, smaller down the south.

Hoger: The ash plume got huge fast, but we heard and felt nothing. The summit was there when ashclouds enshrouded it.

Putrow: We kept trolling. Harold and I shot 14 photos. Our last two show a second eruption cloud flowing northwest a minute after the explosion. It flowed steadily many miles northwest over three or four minutes to beyond our view. We caught one more fish.

The cloud then rose very fast. In a few more minutes it mushroomed out, its south overhang coming overhead. We pulled in our lines.

Hoger: Lightning started, no thunder. We gunned across the lake in wind still gentle from the southwest

Putrow: Fifteen minutes after the start of the eruption lots of lightning in the mushroom cloud struck back toward the mountain.

Hoger: In twenty minutes we came to the landing. We took the boat out onto the trailer like several others. One idiot in everyone's way put a boat *in* the water. The sky got darker overhead and I smelled sulfur.

We drove southwest three miles to Jack's Place and on to a viewpoint to the south an hour after the first venting. The eruption was vertical, the sky dark at the mountain.

Steve Terrill

I knew Mount St. Helens as a landscape photographer. The nearest good site from Portland was a point of land between dams on Lewis River that impound Yale Lake.[6]

I camped with my son May 17 and we watched the mountain. Sunday we were eating breakfast when I heard a muffled report from the north like a distant quarry blast. A dark cloud appeared around Mount St. Helens, then covered it, then rose high. I started shooting but the air grew hazy. We drove to the south end of Yale Lake. I framed shots for a 4x5-inch camera, a tree on the right as in 1979 shots. The summit was gone!—the mountain hundreds of feet lower. Gray cloud grew like an animal, and blossomed like a giant cauliflower. The scale was absolutely huge—a mile wide and many miles high, as if the Dawn of Man. But it was silent.

Mute Photographs

Two sets of eruption photographs from the south help reconstruct the great surge and rise of ash columns. Encountering Harold Fosterman in Cougar, USGS's Dick Janda thought him uneducated until he asked, "These lahars you're researching: they are non-Newtonian fluids?" In 1984 we measured by theodolite the surge cloud expanding on Siebert's photos.

Harold Fosterman. From twelve miles south-southwest of Mount St. Helens Fosterman shot twelve photos, nine of the developing cloud ½ to 2½ minutes into eruption. His 9th and 10th show a south eruption developing perhaps as the summit fails, this cloud then expanding and flowing broadly down the south flank.

Ken Seibert. From a high site twenty miles south-southeast of Mount St. Helens, Seibert shot 45 photos 8:32 to 11 AM showing the early cloud flowing out low north and east, then a double-stalked rising black column showing sky between, then a planed-off summit issuing a feeble pale plume slanted northeast, then building to a strong dark jetting column.

Kerri Altom

We lived on Lingle Hill a mile southeast of Dollars Corner, 34 miles southwest of Mount St. Helens. Sunday I left home about 8:20 on an Appaloosa mare I'd ridden for years and knew her habits. I glimpsed Mount Hood, Mount St. Helens, and the Cascades through meadows this sunny day. For weeks we'd seen occasional puffs from Mount St. Helens.

On the northeast of the hill on a stretch of trail through trees, the mare suddenly pranced. She lifted in succession all four feet as horses may when entering a trailer. Prance, stop, prance again. Had she seen a snake? But still she pranced well beyond this spot. I tried to comfort her but she was skittish. Something lodged in a hoof? I got off and checked but found nothing.

I glanced toward a distant noise. Mount St. Helens billowed a gray and black cloud. It was much broader than other eruptions and not shooting up. A low gray pillow of sooty smoke obscured the top of the mountain, billowing out low. After a couple of minutes it built some height, the gray cloud swelling bigger and bigger. I held the horse by the reins but she'd calmed down. Maybe she'd felt an earthquake I couldn't riding.

The gray cloud now rose tens of thousands of feet and its top spread to a huge mushroom. Minutes later its top began drifting rapidly east as an anvil.

15

Who's On First

Verification is the only scientific criterion of reality.
—John Fowles, *The Magus*, 1977

People beyond a hundred miles hear eruption's start. Agencies hear in fits and starts.

BIG LAKE

Bruce Stoker: In Walker Valley near Big Lake, rumbling thunder approached from the south, grew louder and louder to like a sonic boom, then diminished northward, lasting fifteen seconds. It echoed off hills just east and west. Friends darted from their cabin and said windows had rattled and a door slammed. "Mount St. Helens," we joked.[1]

VANCOUVER

In the Forest Service basement, USGS's Don Swanson chats with Joe Rosenbaum by a drum playing out the seismic signal of station LVP southwest of the volcano. The pen rattles, jumps to and fro, tracing a signal like none before.

"Joe! look at *this*!"

"What the hell? The amplitude's huge."

"That's no glitch. It's real!"

Swanson sprints up two storys to the radio.

"Coldwater! Vancouver." Silence.

"Coldwater-two, this is Vancouver. Dave, d'ya hear?" Nothing, not even the repeater's click.

SEATTLE, OLYMPIA

In the UW seismic lab the recording pens rattle at 8:32:15. Overnight officer Steve Bryant—Captain Midnight—telephones Steve Malone.

"A huge signal's coming in on many stations."

"Mount St. Helens?"

"Must be, biggest by far."

Malone races to the lab. The Forest Service in Vancouver reports a high eruption cloud. The USGS calls: "Dave Johnston doesn't answer the radio!"

Had Captains Twilight or Midnight missed something? Malone scans the records. "I see no change in earthquakes," he says. "No buildup in size or frequency, no long stoppage. The 8:32 signal starts abruptly. All our counting and locating to detect a warning is for nought."

At Department of Emergency Services, Jim Hall awaits State Patrol Chief Landon, his ride to Toutle valley. He dials the Forest Service in Vancouver.

"We'll escort cabin owners to Spirit Lake again today. What's the mountain's status?"

"It's a beautiful day, everything quiet, no activity . . . Oh wait! . . . Hold on . . ."

"What's up?"

"Something at the mountain."

Reade Apgar, coordinator of radio spotters, telephones DES. Hams near the mountain report a gigantic explosion spreading way out, he says.

Hall had seen houses by Toutle River yesterday, boats on the water. "Now we've no way to warn these people," he moans to a colleague. "We're in a world of hurt."

Lou Guzzo steps from the governor's suite in the Legislative Building.

Two staffers scurry past. "Come up to the dome," one calls. "You can see the eruption."

"What eruption?"

They crowd up the narrow stairway. A dark column pokes above haze far south.

"Well it's big," says Guzzo, "but I've an 11 o'clock in Seattle."

Driving I-5 ten minutes later, he sees the cloud mushroom higher and higher above trees.

State Patrol Chief Landon calls Capt. Dick Swier, commander of Patrol aircraft. "Mount St. Helens has blown. I've cancelled the convoy. Be ready for the governor."

Swier drives to the Patrol's hanger. Dave Gardner readies a Cessna, Bob Cory rolls back another.

"Where're you going, Bob?"

"Moses Lake."

"You've not seen the sky?"

The three step outside. A gray cloud blots out the southeast.

At the farm on Fox Island, Sergeant Ron Walcker stands by to chauffeur Dixy Lee Ray to a Seattle meeting with the Teamsters. She steps in from feeding the pigs.

The telephone rings. "Oh? . . . Yes? . . . Uh-huh . . . Okay." She hangs up.

"That's Ed Chow. Mount St. Helens has blown. A hundred times bigger than earlier."

In the blue Chrysler, Walcker drives the governor to Emergency Services in Lacey. The whole bank of telephones is lit, only two staffers answering. She sits and punches a button.

"Governor Dixy Lee Ray speaking."

She leans to Terry Simmonds. "Hey, listen to this one," she grins and pokes on the speaker.

"To stop the eruption sacrifice a virgin," says the caller. "You're it, Governor."

Sgt. Walcker chauffeurs Governor Ray to Olympia airport. They climb into the Beechcraft King-Air 200, and Capt. Swier accelerates south.

LONGVIEW AND KELSO

At 8:37 the dispatcher at Cowlitz County sheriff's office in Kelso takes a telephone call, Sheriff Nelson himself: "You getting any calls?"

"No."

"That mountain has really coughed up a bunch. The chandeliers here are swinging. Biggest cloud I've seen up there"

"For heavens sake."

The sheriff hangs up.

"When the goddam chandeliers shake here," a sergeant says, "then we'll worry about it."

Another call. "This is Department of Emergency Services. There's a big black cloud up—"

"Yeah, we had a call on it."

"Our radio amateurs near the mountain report a big eruption. The northwest side is gone."

Jim Nugent telephones. "What the heck's going on with the mountain?"

"There's a major cloud."

"I live in Kid Valley and it's rolling toward us, an awesome-looking thing."

"Far as we know it's just a cloud."

"Everyone here's getting the hell out." Nugent hangs up.

"I'm trying to get through to the goddam Forest Service," the dispatcher says. "How the hell do you dial them?

"9 first," the sergeant says.

"9, then the number?"

"Yeah."

"Nobody answers."

"Maybe nobody's there."

"Well shit, there oughta be. . ."[2]

At the State Patrol office Wick Elder washes a Suburban for today's convoy up the Toutle. The dispatcher bolts from the back door.

"Sergeant! Sergeant! The mountain blew up. It disappeared!"

"How in hell can a mountain disappear?"

Elder strides to the radio room. In a distant view from I-5, Mount St. Helens had 'disappeared' into an ash cloud. From Vancouver Dick Bullock pulls in to gas for the convoy.

Sgt. Elder sprints out waving an arm. "Captain! Captain! The volcano's blown up!"

Skamania County Deputy George Barker: I would breakfast with Cowlitz deputy Bob Nix, then assist the convoy to Spirit Lake. As I gassed the county Blazer in Kelso a dark cloud rose in the east. A big slash burn, I thought.

I drove north on I-5. Nix radioed from Toutle, "You better step on it. Something's up at the mountain." I sped in hammer lane running code-3 (left lane, lights and siren). On 504 I saw the huge cloud miles up and full of lightning. Sergeant Doug Mayfield radioed Nix to run high-low siren in Toutle—signal to evacuate—and ordered me up to watch for flood. From a hill I saw the cloud's base: ten miles wide! Its top had mushroomed out west. I sped east; it loomed larger and darker. I drove under falling ash at Kid Valley and turned on wipers and washers. In three miles I was out of fluid. I turned back to Maple Flats and parked well above the river.

A car came up the highway. It stirred up such an ashcloud I couldn't get close, and they couldn't see my flashers. I broke the chase. I stopped some cars, but some got by. The North Fork ran normal. A deputy radioed of a flood coming down the South Fork and he's clearing people from houses by the river.

Vancouver and Portland

USGS's Dan Miller drives I-5 north toward Mount St. Helens. A wide gray cylinder in the northeast climbs through twenty thousand feet. He turns back across the median. At the Forest Service in Vancouver he steps into pandamonium. The skeleton staff takes one telephone call after another. At 10:30 Miller dials the Air Force 304th. They'll search for David Johnston.

A transistor radio to his ear, Bob Decker strolls into USGS's Hawaiian Volcano Observatory and eyes Tom Casadevall. "You heard about Mount St. Helens?"

They and Norm Banks dial Vancouver.

"We lose anyone?" blurts Banks.

"Well . . . ah . . . Dave Johnston was at Coldwater II," Arnold Okamura quavers. "We've heard nothing from him. Swanson's flying and says the eruption's huge."

"*Damn!* Anything else?"

"We know nothing about Reid Blackburn and a *National Geographic* crew at Coldwater I."

By afternoon a score of geologists from Hawaii, Menlo Park, and Denver converge on Portland, some packing thermocouples and temperature probes.

The *Columbian*

Greg Herrington: The radio reported the mountain had blown, and I drove to the *Columbian*. Reporters and photographers came in, and we dispatched them to Toutle and to Cougar. Photo editor Steve Small fretted that Reid Blackburn hadn't radioed.

"He's okay," I said, "just hasn't called." But we were too busy to worry. The eruption would bring national media, and we can't be scooped.

The *Oregonian*

Les Zaitz: My Spirit Lake report ran in the *Sunday Oregonian*. Assistant City Desk called me in Salem: "Mount St. Helens is erupting!"

"Today's for my wife and kids. Call back if I'm really needed."

The phone soon rings. "Come now! This is the big one!"

Mount St. Helens lies a hundred miles away, but crossing Willamette River on the hump of Marion Street bridge about 9:50, I see in the north a huge plume. *Holy shit!*

I speed north and dash into *Oregonian* offices. They've called all hands, and I'm on re-write. Reporters bring me stories and AP script; TV screens flash live footage. My desk fills with paper. After noon we learn people have died.

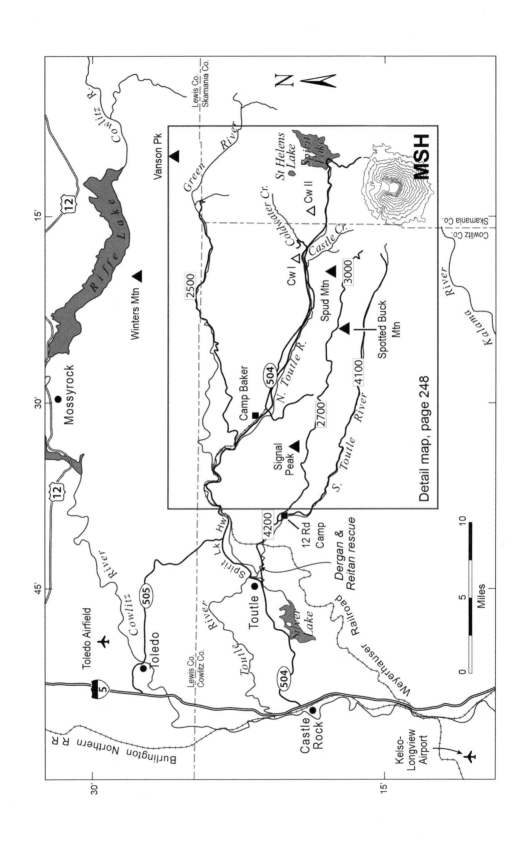

Detail map, page 248

16
Air Again

His flight was madness.
  —Shakespeare, *Macbeth*

The Forest Service surveillance flight continues and three more follow whose observers record and time the eruption. An Oregon National Guard Mohawk still flies.

Helicopters of the Air Force Reserve, Washington National Guard, and Coast Guard reach into ruin. News photographers board National Guard hueys. A Forest Service aircraft aids search communications; an Air Force C-141 flies control 4:25 to 7:20.[1] Pilots for Weyerhaeuser, *National Geographic*, and the USGS fly in deep.

USGS

Don Swanson

[USGS's Swanson still watches from a Forest Service flight since morning (chap 7).]

All morning the dark-gray base of the eruption column filled the new crater. By 12:17 the column had gone lighter gray and much wider, slopping over the crater rim. Two small hot avalanches, light gray and cauliflower textured, swept down west. The column roiled high as we could see. Even its lower thousand yards boiled—so different from morning's fast jet. It was far more turbulent by 12:26—yet no sound pierced the drone of our plane. We circled just southwest of the mountain while relaying radio messages from rescue helicopters. At 12:30 a large ashflow boiled down the mountain's north. I shot movies of it and others. Small flows down the west flank didn't drop from the column but rolled over the crater rim. Big ashflows poured north. A huge new trough must channel them that way.

I still couldn't see Spirit Lake or Coldwater ridge through ashclouds, but Harry Truman's chances seemed zero. We flew only a mile or so off the column, and ash pelted us twice. But we were observers, not participants.

I'd been measuring the mountain for weeks. We thought increased swelling and seismicity would herald a big event. Now just outside the airplane I see the result of all the earthquakes and bulging: gigantic eruption. Yesterday we'd measured from a ridge just below and landed on the summit. Had it erupted then we'd be dead. Had Gerhard Wörner left earlier I'd have been at Coldwater II. It could be Dave Johnston flying here now worried about me down there.

We left the mountain at 1:25.

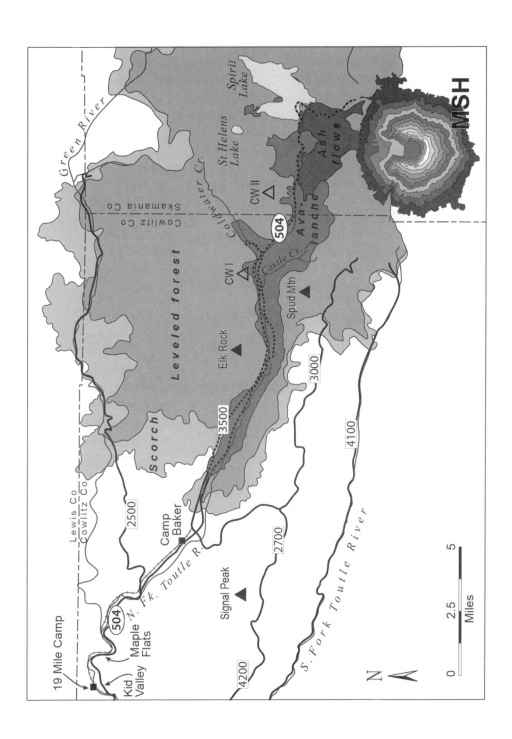

Joe Rosenbaum, Bob Christiansen, Rick Hoblitt

[Forest Service surveillance flights continue, each with a geologist.]

Joe Rosenbaum: A second flight left Pearson Airpark at 1:00, a Cessna 340. A dark-gray column was boiling up thousands of feet into clouds, and ash falling northeast. A cloud churning up from the north looked like a tail draped down from the big column. The summit was gone, a new rim more or less horizontal. The pilot said wind blew strongly from west, southwest, and south—feeding the big column. White weather clouds formed near the new summit, another layer higher.

I shot 250 photographs from 1:20 to 4:20. Early the column occasionally slopped over the west rim, and a few small ash flows ran partway down. The column rose slower and less turbulently 1:40 to 3:00 but increased greatly 3:00 to 3:30. A big ash-flow ran north into the east side of Spirit Lake at 3:01, small flows down the outer cone. A big ashflow began 3:48 from Shoestring notch and flowed fast down the east flank—the only outer-flank flow to reach the volcano's base {*Rooth and Giesbrecht; Rosenfeld*}. At 3:55 its white deposit reached miles east onto Plains of Abraham. The eruption peaked about 4:00: a wide, gray convoluting column boiled up into clouds and ashflows descended the west and southwest flanks. We left at 4:21.

2:44

JOSEPH ROSENBAUM

Bob Christiansen: Pilot, Forest Service spotter, and I left Pearson in a Cessna 310 at 4:17. A gray cauliflower-structured cloud over Mount St. Helens rose convectively and drifted northeast. A brownish ashcloud rose off ashflows on the north plain. An odd white steam cloud poked up a few miles north of the mountain. The North Fork had filled with debris. But dust shrouded a wide area north-northwest of the mountain including Coldwater II.

At 4:32 a strong vertical blast rose, gray and cauliflower-structured. By 4:39 it mushroomed out in the stratosphere. Another strong upburst at 4:45. At 4:53 another cauliflower cloud burst, and I estimated its rise at 4000 feet a minute. A burst at 5:12 rose 4000 to 5000 feet a minute. It formed a mudflow down Toutle Glacier into the South Fork. At 5:20 an ash column only 2000 feet wide rose 4000 feet a minute, leaning northeast. The vent cleared to show a deep crater breached on its north. The ashflows had poured through this new gap. At 5:32 a column burst that drifted over all rims, and a beige cloud rose from an ashflow down the north. Several little columns rose from the lower plain near Spirit Lake, apparently large fumaroles bursting through new ashflows. Several ashflows ran down the north 5:34 to 5:47, and each time beige clouds rose from them.

Large ashflow

Pale ash blanketed the ridge between the North and South Forks like dirty snow. Thousands of trees lay down northwestward. On both sides of the North Fork all the trees were down and covered in ash. Many small fires smoldered.[2]

By 5:53 the plume topped only 4000 feet above the crater rim. But at six another strong column rose 5000 feet a minute, and at 6:10 another big ashflow poured down the north. Three minutes later another ashflow ran north.

In the upper North Fork below Coldwater II, dark areas looked flooded. At 6:36 a hot mudflow rolled down west into the upper South Fork. A brownish cloud rose northeast—another big ashflow from the crater. At 6:49 a big white cloud billowed up through ashclouds near Spirit Lake. A few minutes later a big gray fumarole burst from this north plain.

Our helicopter pilot radioed he was flying to Coldwater II {*Stickney*}. He described eruptions from where Toutle River had been—the ashy fumaroles I'd seen at a distance. At 7:10 another ash column rose above rim. Seven minutes later a cloud filled the crater, then a column rose. We turned south at 7:24.

Rick Hoblitt: Pilot and Forest Service spotter in front, I in the back, left Vancouver in Cessna 5GM and neared Mount St. Helens at 8:02. A turbulent eruption plume rolled up and drifted east, topping only 9000 feet above the volcano's new rim. The North Fork and beyond lay under dense haze. A small pale-gray plume near Spirit Lake stood above the haze, hardly moving.

The eruption waned and clouds pulled back at 8:10 to reveal a steep east wall bounding a new crater half a mile wide. Only hours ago this hole had been the volcano's interior! I photographed the crater and roiling gray plume.

Wind was clearing the air. We flew northwest. Between the South and North Forks the forest had been toppled like grain in a summer storm. Coated in gray ash, it disappeared north under dense haze. Such destruction so wide so far out! I couldn't see Coldwater II, but it seemed impossible Dave Johnston had survived.

Hummocky debris buried the North Fork, its toe a few miles above Camp Baker. The whole top of Mount St. Helens must have failed, left the crater there, and strewn debris fifteen miles downvalley. It must have released a giant explosion.

We stayed west to relay radio calls from search helicopters. A helicopter hovered near a red truck in Hoffstadt Creek at 8:45 *{Walters}*. It kicked up a huge cloud of powdery ash and disappeared down into it. We radioed them to collect an ash sample. "You can take it from my lungs," their pilot called.

Where Maratta Creek had met the Toutle, muddy water welled from hummocky debris—a giant, dark spring boiling up and flowing west. It seemed the source of mudflows downvalley. A levee of hummocky debris had blocked Castle valley. The plane's altimeter read 8400 feet as we flew near at the level of the crater rim. At 9:35 the helicopter radioed they'd found three bodies at the red truck: two adults, one child *{Walters}*.

After dark I saw hundreds of small fires in downed trees. We watched till 11:50.

OTHER FLIGHTS

United Airlines' Captain Bill Airis

[Captain Airis' morning flight from Seattle had passed about 8:35 (chap 7).]

After seeing flows off Mount St. Helens we flew the Boeing 727 to San Francisco. The return flight north in airway V-23 pulled west of Mount St. Helens around noon. Mud had flowed down the Toutle into Cowlitz River. Nine miles west off my left side a sharp line in the Cowlitz separated brown flood from clear water to the south. Fifteen minutes later we landed at Seattle.

Our flight south passed Mount St. Helens about two. The line between muddy-brown flood above and clear water below had pushed into the Columbia.

Guy Rooth and Roland Giesbrecht

[Guy Rooth, geology professor at Western Oregon State College, and Roland Giesbrecht photographing for the Salem *Statesman Journal*, flew in a Cessna 182. Rooth published two brief pieces.[3]]

Giesbrecht: The *Journal* called asking me to photograph the eruption. It took hours to find a plane and get in the air with Guy Rooth and Cheryl Guggenheim. I shot with several cameras and different lenses, and Cheryl changed the film.

We flew along the Columbia and lower Cowlitz. I shot many photos where a flood had carried thousands of logs down the Toutle and Cowlitz.

Rooth: We arrived after two. Turbid floodwater was down into Columbia River but the flood was subsiding. Many logs had stranded along the rivers and piled behind bridges. Several houses off their foundations showed a brown mudline four feet up.

From 11,000 feet we watched and photographed the mountain from the west and south, beyond the FAA's 20-mile limit. A huge gray column poured up and disappeared into stratus clouds at 16,000 feet. From our distance it looked motionless, but watching carefully I saw turbulence. A bit of cauliflower texture rose and turned over as the cloud expanded, the whole column alive like this. Lightning shot through. Its ash drifted northeast. We descended west over flooded areas.

Giesbrecht: About 2:30 I photographed the wreckage of Weyerhaeuser's 12-Road Camp in the South Fork—cut logs and trucks thrown about and a large red spill of fluid.[4] Miles downvalley thousands of logs had jammed in valley reentrants and in channels behind islands.

Rooth: The flood had taken a railroad bridge below 12-Road Camp but had subsided fifteen feet. Mudflats a hundred feet wide and wet sandbars held lots of stranded logs. Turbid water now within the banks rafted few logs.

Giesbrecht: Many logs had stranded behind bridge piers. Hundreds jammed the confluence of the South and North Fork. Miles downstream the Toutle makes a big right turn then a left. The submerging flood had cut across the bends. We flew back east.

Rooth: Weather clouds obscured the mountain top. Small ashflows descended the northwest flank. Almost all ash went up and east, but low-level wind brought fine dust west and made low levels hazy.

Giesbrecht: We turned south low on fuel.

Rooth: Giesbrecht then said, "It's different." We turned. A cloud fell onto the upper southeast slope. A flow charged out of the bottom, a round white bulge a few hundred feet high racing down Shoestring trough. The bulge seemed a basal avalanche of a nuée ardente in textbook pictures. It went much faster than the turbulent cloud above also drifting southeast. At 3:52 by my watch the flow neared the volcano's base {*Rosenbaum; Rosenfeld*}.

Giesbrecht: It ran into the forest at the base of the cone. Through a 230-mm telephoto lens I saw several trees fly up in flames and tumble just ahead of the front.

Rooth: The front ran from crater to hills 2½ miles out in two minutes—80 miles an hour. Debris poured down this track another two minutes and its cloud rose thousands of feet. At 3:56 the material settled and clear sky replaced the cloud {*Rosenbaum*}. We turned south.

Chuck Rosenfeld

After our morning flight we rigged an OV-1 Mohawk with side-looking radar to see through ash and dust. We launched from National Guard base at Salem about two and flew north. Morning's big mudflows down Pine and Smith Creeks had entered Swift reservoir.

Flying over the volcano's west flank at 8500 feet, I watched a small ashflow slop over the crater rim and flow down Toutle glacier. Its low, white edge hugged the slope, and a cloud billowed behind. It flowed beneath the aircraft 100 mph, but we felt no turbulence. Enormous ashflows raced down the north flank. Later as we flew on the south, a big ashflow swept 100 mph down the southeast flank [3:55] *{Rooth and Geisbrecht; Rosenbaum}.*

In late afternoon we got a radar image of Mount St. Helens. Shooting microwaves through the erupting plume, we imaged a new crater 2.2 miles long north-south and 1.1 mile wide at the top—nearly a cubic mile of mountain gone!

We didn't detect Spirit Lake. Later we saw its surface was all floating logs and debris that reflected the radar to show no water. The channel distinguishing moving from fixed objects showed mud flowing down the North Fork below Jackson Creek—a large flow down the left valley side, a smaller one down the right. They merged two miles above Camp Baker.

Northwest of the mountain lay miles of blown-down forests! Debris had flowed a mile wide far down the North Fork. Below Camp Baker it floated a steel bridge off its piers that now stuck up through the mud. We turned south.

Ashflow viewed close from Oregon National Guard Mohawk

KING5 TV (Seattle)

[Mark Anderson, camera; Jeff Renner, reporter; Bob Wright, helicopter pilot]

Anderson: After filming a log flood on the lower Toutle (chap 7), we flew up the North Fork [11:55].

Renner: The light grew dim under heavy cloud. The forest was gone, the valley full of mounds covered in ash, unimaginable violence.

Anderson: I also shot stills. But my color shot of the avalanche is gray.

Wright: We flew under cloud up the south side of gray debris—miles up to where the valley steepens and turns southeast [Maratta Creek]. The air beyond far too ashy.

Anderson: Starting down, we saw a chocolate flood running over the new mounds.

Renner: A mud river like hot fudge—roiling, plunging, boiling back up, steaming.

Wright: It flowed many feet deep over the debris, tumbling a few huge ice blocks, covering much of the valley center. I radioed a Forest Service aircraft.

"How bad is it?" they asked.

"It could take out everything from here to the Columbia."

We followed it down. Renner and Anderson wanted to cross to the north. We had no radio flight-following, the valley full of unstable debris, flood coming. But I flew across. I dropped them at Hoffstadt Mountain [12:30] and flew off to refuel.

Anderson: We'd do a newscast here as weeks ago. Wright returned and we flew again [2:00]. I filmed the broad flood curling around trees and below Camp Baker filmed the steel highway bridge now stranded downstream in deep mud [3:30].

Wright dropped me again at Hoffstadt and lifted off with Renner. A Coast Guard Sikorsky appeared. I filmed their landing in dust [3:40] {Walters}. Two crew got out.

"You seem okay," they said.

"We're from KING5 and come often."

"You're in the way of search-and-rescue. You've got to go."

"Our helicopter's coming back."

"You'll come with us. Willingly, or we'll arrest you."

Wright landed with Renner. The Coast Guard were pissed having to deal with us.

Wright: Their taking our cameraman guaranteed we'd leave.

Anderson: We landed at Toutle school fields, and Wright landed Renner. Medics took an old guy from a military huey and put him on a gurney and oxygen [~4:00] {Cooney}.

Roger Werth and Donna duBeth. *The Daily News*

Werth: In midafternoon reporter Donna duBeth and I chartered a small helicopter and flew up the North Fork [~2:30]. Above Camp Baker I photographed the valley full of new debris. A National Guard helicopter flew over a hundred yards up and hovered down, forcing us away. We landed on a north ridge.

duBeth: A churning wall of mud, trees, and debris swallowed Camp Baker, overturning bulldozers and trucks like toys.[5] Why such destruction so many hours after the eruption? His eye to the viewfinder, Roger shot frame after fame saying, "Ohmygod! Ohmygod!"

Werth: We flew downvalley a few miles. Flowing mud engulfed the green-steel highway bridge, and it lifted. I photographed as it crept down half buried in mud and turned lengthwise. It bumped along a hundred yards and lodged [~3:00].[6]

duBeth: We flew down over houses and gardens by the calm river. The muddy debris came and devoured them.

Werth: At Maple Flats I photographed mud surrounding houses and barns, moving some. Farther down I photographed people on a bridge as the chocolate flood churned beneath.

We flew ahead of the flood and landed. I ran to the bank five feet lower and clamped the camera to a tripod. I was composing a shot when I saw my feet *in* the mud! I grabbed the tripod and jumped back. The mud rose. I dashed to the helicopter.

duBeth: He dove onto the seat, and I pulled him in by the belt. The mud came within a few feet before we got off.

Werth: After refueling we flew up to concrete-slab Coal Bank Bridge. The rising mudflow stacked logs against it. I photographed mud surrounding a house on the river's east bank. Rising mud piled more logs against the bridge. A loud squeal of steel eeeeeeeeeeee!, a white puff of pulverizing concrete, and the deck broke loose. I shot a black-and-white of the north end turning into the flow.

The pilot gunned south, a white puff rose from that end, and I shot an Ektachrome northward, the bridge now off its piers. This end hung in trees as the north swung down the current. One end dipped, and the whole span sank beneath the mud [6:05–6:10].

duBeth: The 500-foot span floated like a surfboard. One end shot up, the other slid back, and it vanished into the mud.

Werth: We landed at Kelso about 6:30.

~6:10 p.m.

ROGER WERTH

Search and Rescue

Weyerhaeuser helicopters make the first aerial rescues. Weyerhaeuser helicopters fly to assess company camps, roads, and railroad. These pilots also fly for the National Guard. One of them appears in military role. Air Force Reserve 304th hueys begin search about 11:50, National Guard hueys about 1:20. A Coast Guard Sikorsky flies in.

Weyerhauser: Ray Pleasant (and passengers John Keatley and Dave Merzoian)

[Pleasant continues from morning (chap 7). Keatley was Weyerhaeuser's regional forester, Merzoian an independent tree faller.]

Pleasant: I flew Jack Schoening and Ren Broomhead in Bell Jet Ranger 28W to check our camps. The sheriff radioed of people stranded below the South Fork road bridge [12:07].[7] We flew down but saw no one. I turned toward our logging camps [12:19]. The North Fork wasn't flooding at the green-steel highway bridge near Alder Creek [12:25]. Radioed again to rescue people on the South Fork, we flew back down.

Someone had waded to them through the mud. He waved from the north valley side by a mudflat a quarter mile below the bridge [12:30]. Covered with mud, the people had blended into the gray [{Reitan & Dergan} chap 10]. No room to land. I toed down the skids and held power—flying the helicopter. Schoening and Broomhead climbed out. They brought a mud-caked girl over and put her in the back. One of the men signaled thumbs up, and I pulled up [12:35]. Dale Erdelbrock in Jet Ranger 62W went down for the injured guy {Erdelbrock}.

I flew to the high-school fields and helped my passenger out. Venus Dergan looked miserable—small, caked in mud, cold, shaking [12:45]. I flew to Kelso to refuel. Erdelbrock would retrieve my passengers.

The dispatcher asked me to check a rumored mudflow down Kalama River [1:07]. Flying alone up the lower South Fork, I saw that flood subsiding. Farther up the flood had subsided at Herrington Place[8] [1:11]. I flew toward Mount St. Helens, erupting straight up. On its flank just above timberline, altitude 4800 feet, my airspeed read zero but the ship moved *toward* the mountain! I turned around and airspeed shot to 80 mph yet the ship slowly *backed* toward the mountain! A huge draft up the South Fork as if feeding a gigantic forest fire swept the helicopter backwards *up* the mountain. I put the nose down and flew out of there.

I flew south into the Kalama, then downvalley. No flood, only muddy water from a landslide [1:35]. I refueled at our 10,000-gallon tank at Headquarters Camp.

Flood had been reported in North Fork. At Longview forester John Keatley and two others boarded [2:25]. I dropped the two at their house at Maple Flats below the coming flood. We flew upvalley. Mud flowed under the highway bridge three miles below Camp Baker [2:40]. Mud poured through Camp Baker. I flew down to 19-Mile and dropped Keatley.

Keatley: I and men who'd driven up moved many log trucks and shop trucks to higher ground [2:45–3:00].

Pleasant: Up at Camp Baker the mud had taken logs, many buses, and trucks *{Erdel-brock & Schoening}*. Mud spread through higher parts of camp. It rafted a pickup truck forward like someone driving it. It pushed a yellow crew bus end-on into a four-foot fir. The bus folded like tinfoil. The flow had crushed in the back doors of our maintenance shops and burst out the front—through all nine equipment bays, the saw shop, and tire shop. I flew two miles upvalley, visibility only a few hundred feet through fog. A station wagon sat on the road among downed trees, beside it a large body. I hovered down but ash blew up. The air was too dusty to fly farther.

Flying back down I saw the highway bridge had floated off its foundation and grounded 75 yards down [3:01]. I retrieved Keatley, circled until the others drove away, and flew upvalley.

Keatley: The bridge was gone, and at Camp Baker [3:25] mud flowed through the shops. Three miles farther we came to a big landslide. Its dry high parts caved into creeping mudflows like dry rock mixing into wet concrete. We turned west.

Pleasant: Logs floated down from Camp Baker. Unlike morning's South Fork flood, this dense mud coated them. Down at Green River our railroad bridge was gone [3:27].

Keatley: A west breeze was clearing clouds. We flew up Green River. All trees lay down across thousands of acres—here fifteen miles out! Nothing looked familiar.

"This *has* to be the Green," Ray said, "so that south road must be the 2500."

"Then that's the 1000 line," I pointed, "and there the 1100."

Pleasant: The blowdown seemed incredible, far more of it farther out than seen earlier.

Keatley: Downvalley the mud wasn't creeping overland as at Camp Baker but running fast in the channel. Logs pounded the piers of the highway bridge at Toutle [~3:40].

Pleasant: At Toutle I traded helicopters with Dale Erdelbrock and now had my usual 62W. I refueled at our Headquarters tank. National Guard hueys were fueling here.

Down at Longview we identified areas far up I'd search for our people reported missing. I took off with Vern Zilliet, maintenance foreman at Camp Baker who knew each piece of logging equipment in the woods. I landed at Vader for a Killian relative (Merzoian) [6:50]. We flew over Camp Baker [7:03], the mud now higher. I worked north up the valley side in murky air, trees and landmarks gone. In Hoffstadt Creek Zilliet identified a smashed yarder by number, and that told us the road.

We came to an ash-coated red Blazer, its top blown off. Adults and a kid lay covered in gray ash, dead. An Air Force control ship[9] radioed me to "squawk"; I hovered over the vehicle and punched the transponder. "Got it," they called and now had its coordinates. There were no foot tracks here, and no helicopter had landed.

We flew east to Fawn Lake for missing John Killian. Visibility through haze was a quarter mile. We saw no vehicle or tracks in the foot or two of ash [7:25].

Merzoian: Through haze I saw most trees in the basin down and buried in ash drifted like snow. A few snags burned on the south headwall. The lake was several feet too low, the outlet dry. Water must've *blown* from the lake! No sign of John and Christy. No one could survive this.

Pleasant: We flew north to look for fallers on road 3920 [Wally Bowers and Tom Gadwa]. We found logs felled across slope and bucked. All others had upturned root-balls—mowed down by the eruption. No men or vehicle. Down at Coldwater ridge we looked for our missing bull buck, Jim Pluard. On road 4020 where they'd cut Friday, all remaining trees were down and covered in ash. No pickup, no tire tracks, no footprints [7:47].

I flew north to Green River. We spotted foot tracks on road 2500 and followed them west [8:20]. It was growing dark. Out of the west haze a Coast Guard Sikorsky came low up the valley at 40 knots {*Walters*}. I radioed but got no response and he kept coming. I flipped on my lights and turned toward him, but he came big and fast. I hovered down into an opening in trees, and the Sikorsky flew over 200 feet up.

In lower Hoffstadt Creek we looked for a thinning crew on road 3128 {*Scymancky*} but in dim light saw no sign of them [8:35]. I flew south into the North Fork and over Camp Baker [8:45]. I dropped a passenger at Vader, and down at Kelso landed in dark with lights on.

Weyerhauser: Dale Erdelbrock (and passenger Jack Schoening)

[Erdelbrock headed the aviation division. A National Guard pilot, he'd recruited Ray Pleasant and Jess Hagerman as Weyerhaeuser pilots. Schoening was Woods Manager of Longview operations.]

Erdelbrock: In Tacoma we'd changed the engine of our Jet Ranger 62W. Called about the eruption, I pre-flighted at Tacoma Narrows airport and took off about 11:15. I flew south to our fuel tank at Headquarters Camp. The sheriff radioed us to medivac people below the South Toutle bridge. Ray Pleasant had dropped Jack Schoening and Ren Broomhead and was flying the injured girl [12:40] {*Pleasant*}.

Schoening: Three guys had waded through the mud. After Pleasant flew off, Erdelbrock flew in.

Erdelbrock: I hovered down on the north side of the South Fork. I flew the ship with the toes of the skids touching while the men got the guy in the back [12:43]. I pulled up and shouted to get him talking—a military technique to help an injured man not go into shock

"What the hell happened?" he asked.

I turned the helicopter so he saw the big gray ash column boiling up from Mount St. Helens. "*That's* what happened!"

At Toutle high-school fields, medics put him in an ambulance.

Schoening: Erdelbrock returned, flew the three guys out, and came back for Broomhead and me [12:53]. As we flew up the North Fork very little water ran in the river. No damage at our 19-Mile Camp.

Erdelbrock: We continued up under an ash cloud. At Camp Baker visibility was half a mile, the camp okay.

Schoening: But two miles farther east, timber was blown down across our big logging roads and the Spirit Lake Highway!

Erdelbrock: A military huey hovered here for a rescue [1:00][10] *{Peters et al.; Weed et al.; Cooney; Ward}.* The pilot saw me and on the radio growled, "Get the hell out of here!" He thought we were a news crew about to get in the way.

"We're Weyerhaeuser and own this land," I barked back. "We're checking our property."

Schoening: We flew down to Camp Baker [1:04] but the radio reported a "wall of water" coming down the upper North Fork. We crept five miles upvalley in haze.

A wide mudflow followed the river on the south valley side and a smaller one down Hoffstadt Creek on the north [1:25].

Erdelbrock: We flew down to Headquarters Camp and refueled. We flew back just as the mud reached Camp Baker [1:57].

Schoening: The big mudflow down the river passed on the south. The smaller flow down Hoffstadt Creek crashed into camp. A car had stopped by the shops. He got to a log bridge over Hoffstadt as the front of mud hit. He gunned across, and the mud pushed the bridge off. The car sped west through the sorting yards to higher ground.

Erdelbrock: The mud front a few feet high flowed fast as a man walks [1:58]. It oozed around buildings. It came up around logging trucks in low areas.

Schoening: It pushed them west. Fifteen crew buses parked by the office began to move.

Erdelbrock: Highway log trucks went with their piggybacked trailers; huge off-highway trucks with ten-foot bunks filled with forty-foot logs six feet in diameter; log stackers, pickup trucks, crummie buses, logs. The mud pushed them all slowly west.

Schoening: Mud crunched the buses together and swept them along. It pushed many log trucks west as a clump. We radioed for people to move equipment from 19-Mile Camp. Ray Pleasant in helicopter 28W said he'd land someone *{Pleasant & Keatley, Reitan & Dergan}.*

Erdelbrock: Half Camp Baker went in half an hour [2:30]. I flew back downvalley for a meeting.

Schoening: I allowed military hueys at Toutle school fields to refuel at our Headquarters tank. We flew to Longview [2:45], and I telephoned our vice president in Boston.

Erdelbrock: At Toutle I swapped helicopters with Ray Pleasant and now flew my 28W [~3:45]. Camp Baker supervisor Dick Nesbit had returned from the coast. I fetched Schoening and Broomhead at Longview, Nesbit at Castle Rock [4:40], and we flew up the Toutle.

Schoening: A massive muddy flood down the North Fork rose behind the highway bridge above Toutle. Up at 19-Mile Camp rising mud had stripped some logs from the yard. At Camp Baker [5:00] the mud was higher, buildings and equipment a total wreck. The sort yard remained except logs stripped from the south.

Erdelbrock: The sheds were now half full of rising mud. Log trucks, buses, and pickups lay where I'd watched them pile earlier. Nesbit surveyed his drowned domain. We took in the vast wreckage—railroad, trucks, shops, office, logs—saying nothing. Camp Baker had built over four decades, thousands of men in and out. Now in three hours most of it gone.

Schoening: We flew slowly upvalley five miles. Through ashy fog we saw more timber down than we had earlier [5:10–5:15]. We flew back downvalley. Rising mud had stripped more logs from 19-Mile's sort yard [5:20].

Erdelbrock: The wall of mud rafting long logs also tumbled stumps and trees with root balls and limbs, dense gray mud coating them all. I dropped Nesbit and Broomhead at Castle Rock and Schoening at Longview [5:50].

Later I flew two company managers downriver. Hundreds of sawlogs six feet in diameter and forty long, and thousands of smaller logs, floated in muddy water [8:26]. Trees with root balls had ripped from the river banks. From the Cowlitz our logs entered the Columbia, a million dollars drifting downriver.

Washington State Patrol: Dick Swier and Ron Walcker

[Capt. Swier commanded the Aircraft Division of the Washington State Patrol. Sgt. Walcker was the governor's security.]

Swier: Governor Dixy Lee Ray and Patrol guard Ron Walcker came to the hanger at Olympia airport. We flew south in our Beechcraft King Air 200. Beneath overcast we flew back and forth around the west side of Mount St. Helens—out 15 miles and up 8000 feet—watching the volcano's column rise into the clouds [12:30–1:00].

Walcker: The copilot climbed back, Dixy to the front, and she shot dozens of photographs. Watching the big ash column going up gave a sensation the plane was falling. At times the air smelled of fireplace ashes, and sulfur tingled the sides of my tongue [SO_2]. Roiling mud in the Toutle looked like Yellowstone's Fountain Paint Pots.

Swier: A flood of muddy logs came down the lower Toutle [South Fork flood]. Its steep head was dark mud full of trees, felling more along the banks. It rafted part of a house. We followed it half a mile down under the Pacific Highway bridge. In another half mile the massed logs passed beneath the I-5 bridge, where the sheriff had stopped traffic {Gardner}.

On the radio I heard Air Force Reserve helicopters coming down discussing the valley {Peters; Weed; Cooney}. I asked a pilot to brief the governor.

We flew to Kelso. Two hueys landed [~1:30] {Peters}. Major Mike Peters told the governor of the North Fork above Camp Baker—wide devastation, trees blown down over huge areas fifteen miles from the volcano even on the lee side of ridges. "I can't believe it," he said, his voice clipped. His hands shook though he'd just been flying. "When we hover, blinding ash comes up. We got jumpers down only by dropping them in the river. They crawled over logs to a car and found people so cooked their skin slid off. We barely retrieved our jumpers. A big flood's coming down."

AIR FORCE RESERVE 304TH AEROSPACE RESCUE AND RECOVERY SQUADRON

That day was white-knuckle flying. I had a real grip on the cyclic. So many things could go wrong, and you can't control what's outside.
—Capt. Tom Nolan

The Air Force Reserve 304th squadron at Portland flew mostly one-engine H-model (HH-1H) hueys in dark-green and tan camouflage. A power hoist with 250 feet of ⅜-inch steel cable can lower and retrieve pararescue jumpers (PJs). A full crew is a pilot, copilot, flight engineer who operates the hoist, and two jumpers. Many had been Vietnam flyers. Passengers Harry Glicken (USGS) and Bob Dieter (Cowlitz County sheriff's office) knew the terrain.

Bob Weed, Tom Nolan, Joe Zink, Charlie Ek

[Captains Robert Weed and Tom Nolan were pilots, Joe Zink flight engineer, Charles Ek a PJ.]

Weed: I flew a training exercise when a radio call returned us to base [10:50].[11] We refueled and learned the volcano had erupted.

Nolan: My crew was on alert status at base. Squadron commanders Maj. Peters and Col. Schroeder flew off in aircraft Save 82 without their PJs. Capt. Weed and I flew the second aircraft (Save 80). Mike Cooney and Charlie Ek were our PJs. PJs Dave Ward and Garvin Williams boarded. We flew [11:10] to Vancouver. Ward and Williams went to Save 82.

Weed: We were to rescue people north of the mountain—David Johnston of the USGS, and at another post Reid Blackburn affiliated with *National Geographic*. Our PJ Cooney—in civilian life a surveyor—knew the terrain. From Vancouver [11:28] we flew up the Columbia.

Nolan: We flew north to Woodland, cut northeast across hills, and turned east up the North Fork Toutle. Cooney sat behind me on the left. We passed Camp Baker. Then over a mile the trees went grayer, then abruptly only gray. Beyond that trees were down [~11:58].

"Wow!" I said, "look how they did that clearcut"... but then saw the logs had roots.

"Holy shit!" Cooney said. "What happened here?"

They lay parallel, almost all down across the half mile we glimpsed through haze. They must have *blown* down! A *huge* event. Could it happen again?

Weed: The trees were down northwestward. No green foliage or brush, just gray logs, an amazing destructive force. A car on the road two hundred yards inside the downed timber had run down the highway but not made it.

Nolan: Its headlights were on, trees fallen around it.

Ek: A body lay on the road beside it.

Nolan: Save 82 tried to hover, but fine ash blew up and they pulled off.

Weed: We descended to look but dust blew up thickly into our airflow.

Nolan: Save 82 flew south to a wet area—what was left of Toutle River—and hovered where damp ash didn't fly. They put two PJs down who started north to the car {Peters, Ward}. Nearby twenty elk walked slowly, heads down as if drugged.

Weed: One stood upright unmoving, seemingly dead.

Nolan: The PJs radioed of the huge logs they climbed over. This would take awhile {Ward}.

Weed: Save 82 would stay. We in Save 80 pushed east on our original mission—up into dense ash and scary lightning.

Nolan: The valley had so changed we could hardly navigate. Ashy air covered the ridgecrests, and we couldn't see the mountain. Twenty-foot ice chunks lay in craters. I watched the exhaust-gas temperature gauge. If it read hotter as we flew, it'd indicate engine damage.

Weed: Many huge craters in the debris held big rocks I thought the volcano had thrown out. Could more fly here? Steam rose from many little craters. The whole valley had no trees, everything gray like black-and-white film.

In ashy air we descended to 200 feet. "Keep going," Cooney said, "its on the left." When we got up there, the ridges were bare. The trees had blown down and ash thick on top, no roads. Cooney said we were near both sites.

Ek: Hardly a distinguishing thing remained. The ridges where men had stationed were wiped clean. No trees, no roads, no vehicles. A barren gray moonscape. Nothing could have survived.

Nolan: We neared where Spirit Lake should be.

Weed: Suddenly in the dust we were over a huge flat. No water, all horizontal logs and thick debris on them. The lake had filled with logs. Thick haze made all color gray.

Zink: Just south lay a mudfield of boiling water and whirlpools. We flew north over the big flat.

Ek: It didn't look like a lake—all logs, no water.

Nolan: We turned around [12:10] and flew back downvalley. A few miles above the PJs we spotted two cars on a stretch of highway.

Zink: A car on its side and another nearby with one lit headlight pointed up thirty degrees {Cooney}. I clamped the hoist to the penetrator, and Charlie Ek belted on. I rolled back the door.

Nolan: We hovered down. Suddenly a dark flow loomed out of the haze ahead. "What's that?" I asked over the intercom. A mudflow poured down the rubble onto the highway. I pulled up. Just south, dark mud trickled down the valley. It soon pooled and flowed faster.

Weed: A huge boulder floated on top. Why's the valley being engulfed now by an eruption hours ago?

Nolan: We radioed the PJs [~12:40]. They said they'd reached the car and people were dead—skin slid off when touched.

We flew down and spotted a small car that had come up the highway. A guy stood at the edge of devastation. The PJs hurtled down the road over trees and in two minutes reached this guy.

Weed: One of our helicopters had to land to retrieve them. I hovered at 200 feet, but our downwash swirled ash up, and I pulled off. Next time I just took it in.

Ek: The pilot commits and settle the bird fast.

Zink: We all agree to this by saying nothing. As we land, everyone watches for obstacles.

Weed: Whipped-up ash browned us out. I flew the last twenty feet down on instruments, and the engineer cleared us. Ash from the rear doors flooded the cockpit.

Zink: My head out the right door in thick dust, I talked the pilot down, calling on the intercom our height in feet: "Ten. Five. Two. One. Contact!" If an obstacle's under my right skid, I tell the pilot to move left or back [~12:50].

The PJs got out, Cooney running up the road. I stayed by the ship on the intercom.

Nolan: Our guys threw the reporter into the helicopter.

Zink: I assisted him.

Weed: The PJs climbed in and shut the doors. I took off in dust on instruments [12:55].

Nolan: We'd barely cleared the ash when the mudflow hit the reporter's car. We turned west.

Zink: We landed at Kelso to refuel [1:20]. National Guard helicopters had landed.

Weed: Both our helicopters started back upvalley [2:40] but stopped by Toutle.

Ek: The plume's base no longer flared gently up. Now it bulged sideways.

Nolan: We again flew under thick cloud. We'd gone far upvalley when a Forest Service plane radioed it seemed the mountain would blow [3:20] *{Rosenbaum}*.

Ek: They suggested we "get the hell out of there." In a force like this morning's, a huey would be like a ping pong ball in a hurricane.

Nolan: We turned back miles short of Spirit Lake. I took over flying. I move my hands visibly down to my controls and say, "I've got it." Weed raises his hands from his controls and says, "You've got it." We worked upvalley again but couldn't go far. An ash cloud blocked flying over the ridge north. We turned back.

Weed: Mud flowed faster now [3:45]. It had swirled earth-moving equipment and log trucks at Camp Baker like toys.

Nolan: Mud had pushed buses and trucks from low areas. Downstream it was full of logs. The valley narrowed, and the front grew twenty feet high. The logs knocked down standing trees.

Weed: We orbited the wall of logs and rocks coming down. It hit a bridge above Kid Valley. The concrete held, then cracked, then broke. Half the slab floated down atop dense mud.

Nolan: The deck floated sideways in the fast flow. Farther down the flood took another bridge and an A-frame cabin.

Weed: Now people were stranded. Our hueys separated toward targets of opportunity.

Nolan: Among scattered homes we saw a white **X** and people with suitcases [3½ miles east-northeast of Toutle]. We landed, and Mike Cooney put an oxygen mask on an old man.

Weed: We radio-beaconed other 304th helicopters here.

Nolan: We landed at the Toutle fields, and our PJ's got out [4:00]. In the next hour, 304th helicopters ferried sixty people.

Ek: Cooney and I got off to help. We flew people from several houses and farms. The mudflow down the Toutle kept growing.

Nolan: It took an hour to refuel at Kelso behind many National Guard hueys. Base ordered us back to ready for next morning. We flew to Portland [6:15].

Michael Cooney

Since 1966 I'd been an instructor, flight examiner, then pararescueman. I flew to Mount St. Helens just after the small March 27 eruption.

Sunday half our pararescue jumpers (PJs) are searching for a lost climber at Mount Hood. Late morning we're called that Mount St. Helens has erupted. Commanders Peters and Schroeder take off in Save 82. We leave base in Save 80 [11:10] with four PJs and cross to Pearson Airpark, where two PJs switch to Save 82. I think the USGS geologist we'll pick up is Dave Johnston whom I'd arranged to fly with us in an eruption. But it's Harry Glicken, and he boards the commanders' huey. Our mission is to find Johnston.

Behind Save 82 we leave Pearson—pilots Weed and Nolan, flight engineer Zink, PJs Charlie Ek and me, and a flight surgeon. I'm at the left window behind the pilots. In twenty minutes we cross the ridge into the North Fork above Kid Valley and follow the ashy highway east. The mountain's tremendous eruption column flashes lightning. Two miles above Camp Baker the trees turn gray with ash. Then suddenly ahead the trees down—across a mile at least!

A station wagon sits diagonal in the highway[12] trapped by fallen trees not far from the edge of standing ones [12:03]. A body lies by the driver's door. We descend, but a huge dust cloud comes up. Save 82 hovers at 200 feet, but the rotor wash brings a dust plume up and the rotors draw it down, whipping it past the ship like an egg beater. They climb out and try at 250 feet but again brown out [12:10]. Cable drop won't work. They turn south to what's left of Toutle River where the wet ash doesn't blow. They drop Ward and Williams a quarter mile from the car [12:15]. They won't need us for awhile.

We fly east alone. New rocky debris fills the valley floor, and all trees are down on both sides. I'd worked here as a surveyor and can't get lost. But the valley is so devastated there'll be no one to rescue. On my north side just below Maratta valley, debris had sloshed 400 feet up the valley side and scraped it clean. We fly upvalley to about where Johnston should be. The air is murky but I see the sides of ridges wiped clean. There's nothing we can do for him.

We fly east under dark clouds. Spirit Lake is all debris, the forested ridge just west now barren. Truman's lodge and cabins among firs are gone. Only horizontal logs and gray debris. We fly northeast. I see patches of water ahead: the lake's here, just covered. At Harmony Falls the big trees are gone, the area scraped clean [12:20]. The tall lower falls are gone; the upper ones now drop near the lake. No Harmony Falls Lodge. Flying back south I see wet ash in spots.[13]

We fly west. Rock rubble in the valley is a wild area of mounds, craters twenty feet deep holding glacier ice, pools of boiling sludge. Debris across Studebaker Creek dams a pond. Water runs over the debris on the south valley edge. Out the right I see again where debris had sloshed high near Maratta Creek.

We fly miles downvalley near the south side. We come to a Plymouth Road Runner and 300 feet upvalley maybe a Peugeot station wagon with one headlight on.[14] The Peugeot is on a short window of highway by a 150-foot rubble mound southeast [12:35].[15] Just west another arm of rubble has curled across the valley, surrounding a low pocket of the old valley floor. Rubble had pushed the Road Runner downvalley, raised it forty feet, and tipped it on its side.

The pilot hovers back and left, putting the dented car on my side. The windows are gone, no one in it. The pilot hovers toward the Peugeot. It's pointed down the ashy highway that disappears east and west under rubble 40 to 150 feet high. It seems someone sits in the front. Charlie and I look at each other. Lucky for me he's nearer the hoist. We move to the right side and move the doctor away—shift the 'ballast' aside. We roll back the right door. Charlie opens a seat of the penetrator, straddles and straps to it, and the engineer clips on the hoist cable.

We're hovering north below the top of a 150-foot wall of debris on the right in fog-like cloud, visibility 150 feet and going bad from ash our rotors stir up. As Zink starts to deploy Charlie, dark gray-brown mud pours from the north out of the haze over the rubble. It cascades thirty feet down and spreads across the flat. In ten seconds it covers the piece of highway. It flows around the car, slops onto its hood. *Shit!* Had we deployed a minute ago, one of us would be on the ground. There'd be no escaping this mud.

"Holy shit!" I say on the intercom. "We've PJs below here." The pilots turn west, gain airspeed, and climb a few hundred feet [12:40].

"Where're Dave and Garvin?" our pilot radios.

"On the ground," says Save 82.

We haul ass downvalley, jabbering on the radio. I thumb the switch.

"Everyone quiet! I need the radio!" "Dave, how close is your objective? A wall of mud is coming down the valley. Can you go back?"

"We'll go to the car." *{Ward}*.

We fly down. The PJs say they're at the car. Ward says they've found a guy and woman 'microwaved' that don't need help. Both helicopters circle. I spot a car and a guy standing at the edge of trees. On our hailer we call, "Don't move! We've people on the ground." Wanting him to stay, we don't mention the mudflow.

Save 82 didn't get down, but one of us must land. Pilot Weed tries but thirty feet from ground ash whirls up. He climbs out.

We were close that last try. "I'll just put it down," Weed says. He picks a spot on the ashy highway. We descend fast to a clearing below a bend in the road. Joe Zink sticks his head out the right and I mine out the left, doors rolled to our shoulders. Weed drops toward the pavement. Twenty feet up dust envelops us. On the intercom Joe talks the pilot down. "Clear left!" I call, and they know nothing lies near the left skid. Weed lands in a great dustcloud facing down the highway [12:45].[16]

We pile out, and I dash up the road. We've raised so much ash a speeding car could run into us. I run back a few hundred feet, and here they come 70 miles an hour around the dusty curve. But I get them stopped. Garvin jumps out and runs to the helicopter.

Soon Dave and I have the guy—a radio reporter—and his camera gear heading toward the helicopter, I with an armload. The reporter turns back. Dave runs back and grabs more of his stuff. "Get moving!" he yells. We head for the helicopter. As team leader I'm farthest out to see others to the ship. The engineer now runs toward me. "Go back!" I yell, "We're coming!" But the reporter has *again* turned to his car. Joe Zink is also a cop. He grabs the reporter, marches him to the helicopter, and throws him in the right door. I climb in the left, and we slam the doors. Weed climbs out in a dustcloud [12:50].[17]

We turn and look back. The mudflow has reached the road, the reporter's car gone!

Now we've all these people. The doctor, who's ballast; the reporter and all his gear, ballast; two extra PJs. I want a lighter helicopter, the pilots want a lighter helicopter. We fly west.

We land at Toutle [1:00]. Dave Ward says the couple at the station wagon had outlived the heat and dust, for he saw they'd breathed awhile. He has their wallet and purse. He and Garvin return to Save 82, Glicken climbs into ours, and we fly to Kelso [1:15].

In the operator's room where Weed telephones our base [2 PM], Ward waves me over to another phone.

"Look at *this*!" he says and opens the purse.

I paw through many bags of white powder and *lots* of loose paper money.

He snaps it shut.

A deputy comes, and Ward hands him the purse. "*You* inventory this stuff!" he says.

Refueled, we fly to Toutle. From here we launch our second upvalley sortie, Save 82 leading, Peters with Glicken back in determined to fly up to Johnston [2:50]. The mountain's vertical eruption column now bulges out more than jets up, bowing over the rim. Mud flows under the highway bridge at Alder Creek. Camp Baker has been hit hard.

We in Save 80 who'd been upvalley radio it's no use, the area's wiped out, we're just burning fuel. But Peters flies many miles up through devastation. Under cloud we lose sight of the mountain. The air gets murkier; we fly lower. "This is stupid!" we mutter over the intercom, "nothing to save." Save 82 pushes on. The Forest Service plane now radios: "The eruption has doubled, going nuts! If I were you I'd get those helicopters out of there!" [3:20] *{Rosenbaum}*. It has scared them. Since we can't see, it should scare us. Save 82 turns around near Coldwater.

We fly down several miles. Frightening as the mudflow had been earlier, it's far bigger now. It flows turbulent and chaotic down both valley sides and in the middle— huge, chocolate-gray *raging* rivers of mud. Downvalley we find its front a mass of logs. The highway bridge is gone. Farther down near Kid Valley people stand next to a concrete bridge about to go. On our hailer we call, "Get back! Get back!" The coming mudflow will drown this whole area. From the bridge the front flows downvalley fast. We fly down, turn, and here it comes.

At 19-Mile Camp a loaded log truck comes down a gravel road from the north. It stops, the driver gets out and shouts to men down at pickups below, and he drives down. Mud will drown this flat, but we can't stop this. The men race their pickups up north [~3:50].[18]

People are out in a yard three miles northeast of Toutle. Severed roads have stranded them. We fly them to Toutle [4:00]. The ambulance crew can't handle all the people coming in. I get out to help an 80-year-old with emphysema. While upvalley in a helmet in the loud helicopter, I've heard nothing outside. Now bareheaded I hear the mountain roar and rumble—though we're 28 miles upwind.

Later I get on Save 79 that Bill Peden flies *{Peden}*. People between the forks of the Toutle are trapped behind washed-out bridges and roads. They congregate; we land and haul them down to the school field. In three flights we ferry a couple dozen people. Two flights are *way* overweight, one with 17 people, luggage, and dogs. At 5:00, 19-Mile Camp is a raging torrent, the log truck in the flat carried away.

We fly to Portland [6:15] and refuel. A C-130 from the 303rd hasn't come. We take off [6:50], fly up southwest of Mount St. Helens, and pick up Pacific Power & Light guys at Merwin Dam. We fly east to Swift Dam and help them open flood gates to lower this reservoir. We fly back to Portland and land after dark. The C-130 is here.

On my way home I stop by the Federal Building in Vancouver, Forest Service and USGS here and a few news reporters. On a map the USGS had drawn [Crandell's of March 30], colored areas radiate from Mount St. Helens. It *predicts* what's happening in the valleys *now*. Orange reaches down the North Fork to yesterday's roadblock. Why was it so close to predicted danger?

David Ward and Garvin Williams

Ward: A small airplane had crashed on Mount Adams April 1. We flew next morning and found the wreck in the south snowbowl. As we flew back to base, a small burst from Mount St. Helens drifted ash north—our image of "eruption."

Four of us PJs—Cooney, Ek, Ward, Williams—are at base May 18th when we hear Mount St. Helens has erupted.

Williams: One huey sits fueled and loaded. The alert team could be off in eight minutes.

Ward: We're to rescue two men off "the mountain"—off Mount St. Helens, we think, where we'd done snow-and-ice rescues. We pack ropes, ice axes, crampons, pickets. Save 82 flies off. Save 80 carries four of us jumpers to Pearson Airpark. Williams and I move to the other bird. USGS's Harry Glicken climbs in—he knows the sites. Behind pilot Mike Peters and copilot Deon Schroeder, Glicken and a retired colonel sit on a jump seat. Garvin and I are on the floor on the left, flight engineer Don Schaefer on the right.

We fly down the Columbia and up the Toutle. At Kid Valley the highway is coated by ash—this far out! The eruption must be *big*, not just a bit of ash.

Williams: The column above Mount St. Helens is really cooking.

Ward: We fly east, the air goes hazy, and we go in under low clouds. Flying at 400 feet, we pass Camp Baker, then ashy trees. Now we come to an awesome sight: all the trees down! Big old-growth down like matchsticks and covered in brown-gray dust, hard to believe [11:58].

A tan station wagon sits on the ashy highway. The pilot pulls pitch, the rotors wop-wop-wop. A body lies beside the car. We discuss whether to proceed upvalley. If *these* people aren't alive in this huge destruction far out, how could our close mission succeed? We agree to examine this.

Engineer Schaefer opens the right door and pulls in the hoist cable. Williams lowers a seat of the penetrator and straps on. The engineer snaps the cable to its top. The helicopter hovers at 150 feet. Garvin steps out, suspended. But pilot Peters calls, "We're going IFR!" Instrument flight rules: they can't see. Our rotor wash has blown up ash, outside only the inside of a cloud. The engineer pulls in the cable and the pilot flies out.

Williams: The pilots hover at 200 feet, but again ash blows up. We set up to deploy "hard-fast-low": PJs stand on the skids in open doors and the pilot angles down fast. A few feet above the ground he pulls pitch and we jump off.

Ward: But off south I see a broad damp stretch—what's left of Toutle River. We hustle away the mountain-snow gear and pull medical packs over our orange vests that hold gloves, food, flares, radio. The helicopter hovers, and we drop from the skids into thigh-deep water. We wade to shore and switch on radios [12:15].

Williams: The ash is a foot thick and hot, the logs hot too. "If we're going to hell, Dave, we'll know what it's like."

Ward: Our helicopter will stay, but Save 80 says instead of just boring a hole in the sky they'll fly east {*Cooney, Nolan, Weed*}.

Four to six inches of very warm ash cover everything. We start north diagonally across trees felled northwest, the biggest eight feet diameter, small ones three feet. We go under some, over big ones, around root balls. We climb onto a fat tree, walk it 150 feet, jump down, climb onto another and walk it down.

Williams: We're soon soaked in sweat. We're strong, but it takes awhile to move a few tens of yards. The volcano grumbles like a distant thunderstorm. What's now coming down? And what if someone's alive at the car?—we can't move anyone through this.

Ward: It's hard climbing onto an ashy log seven feet high. "You look like rats crawling in dust," the pilot radios. Warm fluffy ash coats the root balls and their holes like snow. So the trees fell, then ash settled. Out twenty minutes, we're going hard but moving slow.

Williams: I hear radio talk between the pilots: "Save 82 this is Save 80. You want to get those PJs out of there! A wall of water's coming down!"

"Dave, d'ya hear that?"

"Yeah."

We pick up the pace.

Ward: Now we get a cryptic radio call—from Mike Cooney in the other helicopter.

"PJ ground, this is Save eight-zero. Where're you guys?"

"More than halfway to the car," I say.

"How long'll it take to go back?"

"What it took to get here."

"A mudflow's coming, covering the valley. You should go to high ground" [12:40].

"Well! . . . How long we got?"

"Twenty minutes, thirty tops."

"Stand by." I thumb off the radio.

"Garvin, if we go back and aren't picked up in time, we're in a low. Ahead is higher. We may not make it either way. But odds are better ahead."

"Go for it."

I thumb on the radio: "We'll go to the car and a hill beyond."

We double our efforts and in five minutes come to the station wagon. It's thirty degrees to the highway, trees down behind and in front, glass intact, everything ashy.

Station wagon on Spirit Lake Highway, 16 miles out

RICK HOBLITT

A guy lies on the left. We roll him and Garvin feels for a pulse. Someone had shut the car door.

I open it. Gray ash coats all inside.[19] A lady sits on the front seat slumped left. I pull her up, hold her head, listen for respiration. She's covered with a pall of whitish dust that's moist on her lip. She'd breathed awhile after the ashcloud. Her face looks sunburned but hard to see beneath the dust. When I touch it, the skin is loose and moves. Her pupils are dilated and don't react to my light. No respiration, no pulse.

I ask Garvin outside, "What's he doing?"

"No pulse or respiration."

Williams: I go around and open the passenger's door. I gently shake the right arm of a large woman in front. Through my gloves I feel skin and flesh slough.

Ward: They could be a family. The back is deep in camp gear, grocery bags, newspapers. "Let's look for kids." We paw through, Garvin at one back door, I at the other. In twenty seconds we're down to the floor. We rummage in the cargo back. No kids. The coming flood could bury this place. We grab ID—Garvin his wallet, I the purse at her feet. Garvin drops the wallet in the purse. We've been here three minutes.

Williams: Downed trees stretch north. It'd take twenty minutes to reach the hill.

Ward: The highway west is best. We jump over trees by the car. A little red Chevette comes up the highway and stops at the edge of standing trees two hundred yards away.

"You see that?"

"Yeah."

We book down the road hurdling branches, climbing over down trees. It takes some minutes. We dash to a guy with a camera talking to a tape recorder. He's Jim Reed, reporter for KOMO Radio in Tacoma. We're filthy with ash and sweaty. It's been a quarter hour since the radio call about mudflow.

"What's behind you?" he asks. "Anyone alive up there?"

"No, only destruction. We've got to get out of here."

"Where'd you come from? What're you doing?"

"We came by helicopter. We gotta go!"

"I need photographs. When'd this happen?"

"We're getting the hell out of here!"

We walk him to the car and shove him in the driver's seat. I climb into the cramped back, Garvin into the passenger seat.

"Drive!" I say. "A big mudflow's coming down!"

He steps on it. He says he skirted a roadblock to come for a story. Now he's speeding on four inches of fluffy ash.

"Drive," I say—"but we don't want a wreck."

Our dust billows behind. We enter a clearing in standing trees. Suddenly in the middle of the road in a big dust cloud is one of our hueys!

"Stop!" we yell, "*Stop!*"

He stops.

"We're getting into that helicopter."

I climb from the back with my medical gear and the purse. He gathers some stuff. The helicopter's tail is toward us—not ours but Save 80. Out on the road Mike Cooney beckons and shouts: "Come on! Come on!"

Williams: We get the guy running with us toward the ship. As I pass Mike he throws up his hands. The reporter has turned back. Cooney yells, "Go on! I'll get him."

Ward: We dash to the open left door and throw our stuff in. I dash back and grab the reporter.

"What're you doing?"

"Getting my stuff."

"Too late! We're out of here!"

I drag him back. Joe Zink hurls him into the helicopter. We all pile in, slam the doors, and the helicopter lifts off in a cloud. *{Cooney; Weed et al.}*

Williams: We made it! The pilot turns. Mud around the car pushes it into standing trees.

Ward: Seven of us are stuffed in the back with all our gear and the reporter's. We turn west.

At Kelso airport I telephone the sheriff. "Destruction is down to mile 28," I tell a deputy. "We found people there dead. Probably no survivors above. I have their ID."

"Leave it with the attendant," he says. "Well . . . give me their names."

I open the purse and wallet and read their names, a husband and wife. But the purse is full of little plastic bags of white powder, and *wads* of money!

I pick up the phone. "I can't leave this. You must take possession."

In my notebook I jot a receipt for the identity of the people and the stuff. A deputy comes, signs the receipt, and takes the purse.

An hour later we fly upvalley but see National Guard hueys at Toutle fields. We land and meet these guys. "Who's in charge?" our pilot Mike Peters asks. They hem and haw. "Fine," Peters says, "I'm in charge. Get out your maps. Let's not run into each other." They divide the area—who'll search where. Peters says we should search the edges of destruction for survivors. Others will fly down and move people below the mudflow.

We fly Save 82 east, our second sortie. Glicken's back in. We'll pursue our mission to Johnston and Blackburn. The other ship who'd gone up argue there's no point, no survivors. But our pilots, the commanders, are bent on going.

The mudflow front is now down in the narrows below Camp Baker, filling the valley. Its head, twenty feet high, churns many long logs. At Camp Baker log trucks turn in a big stew, a log trailer rolls end over end. Road graders have overturned in mud, D8 Cats moved. Why so much water so long after the eruption? We come to the huge area of downed trees.

Williams: "Dave, look!" I say pointing. Mudflows sweeping around north and south have missed the station wagon!

"Man! We'd have been okay there."

Ward: Upvalley we spot two cars. Save 80 radios they'd been there so we don't stop. We lose even the mowed-down trees: deep rubble covers the valley floor! Wet mud flows over it.

Visibility worsens, and we fly down at 300 feet, lightning all around. Eastward the valley broadens to a plain. The rubble vents up steam. Water flows downvalley here but curls east there. Gas bubbles from brown mud that swirls huge chunks of earth and ice, a stew in shades of orange and brown. A big lump bobs up, and the brown flows off: bluish ice. Low cloud thickens and darkens. We descend to 200 feet. Through my helmet above the jet-engine scream I hear a roar from the mountain we can't see. A high aircraft radios, "In the last few minutes the mountain has tripled its output. If I were you I'd get those helicopters out of there!" [~3:20] {Rosenbaum}

"That's my vote," we say on the intercom. "I've had enough." Save 80 radios. Both ships turn a sweeping left over the valley and fly back down.

The mudflow has grown huge in the valley. Just ahead of its front near Kid Valley we hail people to get off a bridge. South of the river we land where people stand in yards with suitcases. We fly them to Toutle, then make several runs. Others of our hueys have come. Base orders us back to ready for tomorrow.

Mike Peters, Don Schaefer, Harry Glicken

[Major Peters was aircraft commander (pilot), Deon Schroeder copilot, technical sgt. Schaefer flight engineer. USGS assistant Glicken knew Coldwater II.]

Peters: I was flying a training exercise, escorting retired Col. Mike Walker and a flight surgeon, when radioed back to base. Our task was to find a USGS guy.

Helicopters Save 82 (ours) and Save 80 launched, Walker on mine, the surgeon on the other. We landed at Vancouver. USGS's Harry Glicken boarded, who knew the site. Our PJs Dave Ward and Garvin Williams climbed in.

Glicken: We left Pearson [11:28] for Dave Johnston at Coldwater II and a crew at Coldwater I.

Schaefer: We flew down Columbia valley and up the Toutle and North Fork.

Glicken: I shot photos of the eruption column, Mount St. Helens's top gone.

Peters: Beyond Camp Baker we passed from the green world abruptly to a gray one.

Glicken: Heavy ash coated the trees [~11:58].

Schaefer: A mile farther all the trees were down. Among them on the road sat a tan station wagon, and by it a red barrel. Flying lower, we saw it was a large man in a red sweatshirt.

Peters: But ash blew up. As we hovered higher, a dark Hughes 500 helicopter flew past a hundred feet away—so sudden and close it startled me {Reber}.[20] In this low visibility he could have flown into our cable with a PJ on.

We moved to a wet area that had been Toutle River where our rotors didn't blow much ash.

Schaefer: The river was only a creek. We hovered a foot above the water, and Ward and Williams jumped off the skids.

Peters: Gray ash covered everything. Many elk carcasses lay nearby coated by ash. One stunned cow walked an endless forty-foot oval tramped in six inches of ash.[21]

Schaefer: Elk stood with burnt hair on one side. Ward and Williams radioed that the downed trees they crossed were hot beneath the ash.

Peters: We watched them climb over logs. They radioed it was hot on boot soles, ash on the logs hot through gloves. We flew away with our noise.

Glicken: Most trees were down parallel to the river but a few crossed. An elk coated in gray ash stood like a cement statue. We circled east over a huge avalanche [12:18]. Plumes of gray dust and steam rose. Smoke rose from burning timber on the valley sides. We flew a mile east over the avalanche [12:25]. No trees, no roads.

Peters: We flew back down and landed in damp ash.

Glicken: I got out [12:30] and photographed boulders and branches in the dried-up river bed coated in ash.

Peters: Save 80 radioed of a flood coming downvalley.

Glicken: We took off at 12:40. Major Peters said the paramedics found people at the car fried: "touch them and their skin falls off."

Schaefer: We flew up two miles to water working down the valley.

Glicken: Thin mudflows crept ten to twenty miles an hour, braiding around mounds in the avalanche [12:44].

Peters: We flew west. Save 80 managed to get down for our PJs.

Glicken: The helicopter blew ash off trees, and it fell like a blizzard.

Peters: Save 80 lifted off just as mud spread across the flat. It surrounded the small car and pushed it into trees. We flew downvalley.

Glicken: We landed at Toutle high school [~1:00] but took off again [1:15].[22]

Peters: Both aircraft flew to Kelso airfield.

Schaefer: We'd flown 1.9 hours since launch. I refueled.

Peters: The governor had landed and we'd been requested to brief her {Swier}. Col. Walker and I went to a room at base operations. I summarized what we'd seen—the devastation, people dead. The governor was upset.

"Everyone's evacuated from Toutle, aren't they?" she asked.

"No," I said, "no evacuation."

She said she'd allowed people up to Spirit Lake yesterday and worried people might be now. "Can you confirm nobody's up there?"

"I can't do that," I said. "And a big flood is coming down the valley."

After an hour at Kelso we flew up to Toutle. Two National Guard hueys were here, and a Coast Guard H-3 Sikorsky. Guys in flight suits stood on the ball field. Visibility was bad upvalley, and we'd almost been hit by a news helicopter.[23] I walked to these men. "Who's in charge?" I asked. They said nothing. "Okay, I'm in charge. Let's not fly into each other." We divided the valleys. The 304th with other helicopters en route took the North Fork. The National Guard and Coast Guard took the South Fork.[24]

We took off with our PJs Ward and Williams and USGS's Glicken [2:40].

Glicken: We'd attempt Coldwater. Below Camp Baker mud flowed within the banks [2:56].

Peters: We again passed from the green world into a gray one. The station wagon was still on the highway among fallen trees: mudflow hadn't reached it.

Glicken: At 3:05 an upvalley aircraft radioed there's no sign of life, only the top of a car visible [Coldwater I] *{Reber}*. Three miles above Camp Baker the valley was buried by mounds tens of yards high holding a few glacier-ice blocks, all coated in light-gray ash. Small brown mudflows laced between mounds. All trees were down on both valley sides at least up to cloud base.

Peters: Visibility grew terrible. We sought Johnston on a ridge. Ash covered everything like a plush carpet. Toutle River had been a hundred feet wide, and two-hundred-foot trees covered the valley floor. Now no trees, no river. Debris fills the valley. We felt our way at 15 knots searching for landmarks.

Glicken: The light-gray ash thickened eastward, obscuring all features. I'd not have known there'd been a forest. The crew said it looks like a nuclear blast. The valley was

Hummocky debris avalanche

First foggy glimpses of upper North Fork mudflows from rescue helicopters

full of gray mounds ten yards high. Dark-brown mud braided through them fifteen miles an hour, past occasional ice blocks. Three feet of ash covered downed trees on valley sides.

Schaefer: The terrain was a moonscape, craters 100–200 feet across of churning water and mud that boiled out in places and flowed away. "If our engine coughs," someone said, "we're dead. We should get the hell out of here."

Peters: A Forest Service pilot radioed the mountain might blow. He urged we leave.

Glicken: We turned back at 3:20. Mike Cooney later said we'd reached Coldwater Creek.

Schaefer: Mud flowed through Camp Baker—in one end of a building, out the other. It pitched trucks and rafted timber. At Kid Valley it was almost up to a bridge people stood on.

Glicken: At 3:52 the mud flowed within its high banks at Kid Valley. We landed at Toutle high school [4:00]. Mike Cooney said on his first sortie he'd flown by Coldwater and all the trees were down and deep in ash even up on ridges.

Major Peters said it's too dangerous to go again. I suggested they try Coldwater II from the north. "Dave's gone," he said. "*Gone!*" [4:31].

The river was swollen when we flew off Toutle at 5:45.

Peters: We landed at Pearson in Vancouver [6:15].

Fred Stovel, Dave Mullen, Bob Dieter

[Capt. Stovel and Maj. Mullen were pilots. Weyerhaeuser forester and Cowlitz County reserve deputy Dieter knew Toutle Valley.]

Mullen: While flying I heard a light aircraft pilot radio Portland about Mount St. Helens erupting—its top gone, looks bad *{Swanson}*. At base we assembled: Fred Stovel (pilot), Dave Mullen (copilot), Bill Miller (engineer), Rich Harder and Dave Olsen (PJs).

Stovel: We left Portland in Save 81 [12:40], flew north, and landed at Toutle fields [~1:25].

Dieter: I encountered pararescueman Rich Harder with whom I'd flown search missions. We boarded a 304th huey.[25]

Mullen: We took off to find a geologist and a photographer near Coldwater Creek.

Dieter: We flew up the South Fork, I in the back with sidedoors open. There'd been a rumor of flood and someone trapped on an island, but we found neither.[26] We crossed into the North Fork above Kid Valley. The highway bridge near Alder Creek stood.

Mullen: But the dark river raged full of debris.

Stovel: At Camp Baker logging trucks were strewn like toys.

Dieter: Mud had flooded the shops.

Mullen: We crossed into ashfall, the landscape shades of gray like a black-and-white movie.

Dieter: Beyond that all trees were down! Mostly northwestward but swirled in places. With everything coated in gray ash, the sky overcast, the air ashy, my color photos look like mud. Falling trees had trapped a station wagon on the highway. Just south mud flowed several miles an hour like fluid concrete.

Stovel: We discussed cabling Harder down, but Major Peters radioed they'd been here and the people were dead *{Peters et al; Ward & Williams}*.

Dieter: Trees were down on both valley sides. Debris full of rocks buried the wide valley floor—its rough surface pocked with holes half full of water. Out in the valley no trees at all: the new debris must be hundreds of feet deep. Farther up, wide holes between hummocks held water and big blocks of glacier ice. We came to the Coldwater valley reentrant. No streams now, the area filled by lumpy debris, ponds all over, debris stranded high on the ridges. Over south in Castle valley all trees were down and covered in gray ash.

Stovel: Little light came through the ash cloud. Visibility was half a mile but dark like twilight. Chunks of bluish ice were huge. Out my right side one covered by gray but blue in spots Harder called "a two-story house."

Mullen: Several steaming craters could hold a house. A huge ice chunk lay in each crater—miles from Mount St. Helens. We crept east, but I knew we'd not find the men.

Dieter: Flying at 200 feet, we came to many fumaroles in a flat part of the valley. A hundred yards away ash burst up a few hundred feet. Up came another from a different spot. Ahead out my open left door lay a huge flat of logs covered with gray ash. There's no level land up here: it had to be Spirit Lake.[27] No trees left, no roads, nothing of Harry Truman's lodge or cabins. We circled the southwest corner of Spirit Lake. Three more ashy bursts shot up. One of them 300 yards away punched up 500 feet—way above our level, clearly a danger.

Stovel: The air smelled bad. Visibility was poor and we were too close to the ground to turn sharply if we had to. It was unsafe. We couldn't see through clouds up to ridgecrests, but with the valley all hot debris, nothing could survive.

Dieter: We flew back down.

Stovel: A mudflow high in the valley looked like chocolate milk, much bigger than what had wrecked Camp Baker. It would take out bridges. Below Camp Baker the flood was full of logs.

Dieter: I got out at Toutle high school.

Stovel: We flew to Kelso and refueled. National Guard helicopters were here, and reporters. The sheriff wanted evacuations. We landed east of Toutle. Harder told people of a big flood coming. Some came aboard; others didn't believe him. After three flights, we flew to Portland. [6:15]

The *Oregonian* telephoned. My story ran on next-day's front page [*{Zaitz}* chap 17].

Bill Peden

[Major Peden was Operations Officer and a pilot.]

We launched Save 79 at 12:40 and reached Toutle about 1:25. We saw Mount St. Helens erupting a cloud to 50,000 feet. Every five or ten seconds a big lightning bolt spiked down it. We evacuated more than fifty people stranded by washed-out roads and bridges. One flight had 13 people in the helicopter whose top load should be about ten.

A great muddy flood poured down the North Fork into Toutle gorge after five. The mud flowed fast down the curves, banking high on the outside of one bend, then high on the opposite side at the next bend.

Columbia Helicopters

Dwight Reber

After trying for Coldwater I from the south but running into cloud [chap 7], I flew the Hughes 500C northwest. I turned east up the North Fork under thickening cloud. The ground turned gray with ash. And ahead the trees were down! I angled south of a big blow of dust. I made out two military hueys, one higher, the other hovering at 200 feet churning up a huge cloud of ash trying to cable down a jumper [~12:10].[28] *{Peters, Ward, Cooney, Glicken}* "Well clear on the right," I radioed. They didn't answer—maybe on a different frequency. I kept forty feet below, passing them by a hundred feet *{Peters}*. Visibility dropped upvalley and I flew slower and lower, down to twelve to fifteen knots but keeping behind ash my rotors stirred up. I felt lost in milk soup, forest and other landmarks gone. I couldn't fly so slow to Coldwater and have fuel to return. I flew back west.

I landed at Kelso airport by eight National Guard hueys, most of them just arrived, blades spinning. A general had commandeered the fuel truck. I had a specific rescue mission and had been a fuel customer for weeks. But my little Hughes had to wait for all these new guys with big tanks.

I took off about 2:15 and flew upvalley, my mission still to Reid Blackburn at Coldwater I. Visibility dropped to a hundred feet. Suddenly in the haze appeared the outline of a hovering big Coast Guard Sikorsky *{Walters}*. I didn't see this white ship in white fog until I was on him. It scared me. I radioed into the blind, "Well clear on the left" and passed him widely. A flood had swept Camp Baker. Log trucks, buses, and a bulldozer had turned over among logs like a Tonka Toy crash [2:28].[29] Mud was drowning the shops. Two miles upvalley I again came to devastation, all trees laid down northwest.

The ceiling lowered, and under thick ashcloud the air went as dark as during a total solar eclipse. I again slowed to fifteen knots. In poor visibility, all landmarks gone, I turned back west.

I turned and crept east again. The valley floor was all huge mounds of rocky debris, the forest buried. What else could the volcano send down? What if I had to land in this wild place? There was almost no definition of the valley floor, everything gray through milky air, no landmarks. Lost, I turned west again.

The forest on the south valley side was flattened. Through haze I spotted a yarding tower wrenched from its cables among down trees. It had stood by the edge of standing trees, and I'd used it in foul weather as a landmark for Jackson Creek. Now I knew

Coldwater I lay diagonally across the valley. Fine ash seeping through the door seals had dusted the cockpit. I turned on the bleed air heater, and it pressurized the cabin enough to keep ash out.

I flew a compass heading, my skids fifteen feet above the bumps. A vent ten feet across pumped up white steam: poof! a pause, another poof! I got across to the north. In fog I worked into the reentrant of Maratta Creek, now a wild deposit of dunes, gorges, craters, and rising steam. It looked like the aftermath of an atomic explosion. I smelled sulfur.

I crawled up the steep valley side, my skids almost on it. I came to what seemed an ash-covered logging road. But I couldn't be so soon up to Coldwater I. I crept higher but came to a ridgecrest! That road must be the right one. Visibility was so low—thirty feet—the only way to see ground while descending was to back down. My rotor wash in the ash uncovered cut-off stumps, a clearcut. In my backward descent a familiar log landing faded into view. In my right peripheral vision I saw the roof of Blackburn's Volvo. This was Coldwater I. The landing was gray and barren, only the top of the car sticking up. Reid's tent was gone, and the army tent. The cameras on tripods at the east edge were gone—the *Columbian*'s and the USGS's.

I hovered my left side down to the Volvo. It was buried four feet in ash. I circled the car, straining through blowing dust to see inside. It was full of ash up to the blown-out windows. No sign of Reid. No way could anyone survive here. I made three passes over the landing. Nothing alive. I again radioed the Forest plane [2:59].[30]

I backed slowly downslope and in 600 feet came to the wild lumpy deposit with craters. How can my altitude reading make sense? Coldwater I had been a thousand feet above the forested valley. This new debris must be hundreds of feet thick, the valley bottom now much higher. I couldn't take my eyes off the ground without risking vertigo but swept my eyes across the instruments. They were in green, and enough fuel for twenty more minutes here. Friday I'd promised Harry Truman if I flew to rescue Blackburn I'd include him. I turned east.

A seething, bubbling flow filled the valley floor. It held big chunks of muddy glacier ice but vented steam. I crept along the base of a steep ridge on the north. Blue lightning arced all around. In three miles I came to a big step in topography, a huge new bank where the river had flowed. I climbed this rise. I talked to myself to keep from being too scared. Ahead a boiling cloud rose like a miniature volcano. It spewed ash up twenty feet, blowing out a hole twenty feet across. It quit and ash flowed back in and closed the hole. Ten seconds later it blew again—pulsing again and again.[31] I crept between it and the north ridge. These hills had been forested; they're now scoured to rock. Near here Spirit Lake Lodge and many cabins had stood. They're buried. I gasped and choked on a strong smell of sulfur. I could see seventy feet.

If I followed the ridge on my left east up the former course of Toutle River I'd come to Spirit Lake. Topography didn't rise above the debris step. I'm flying *way* below weather minimums, and if the FAA learns they could pull my license. Yet it's a life-or-death emergency.

A mile past the little volcano I came to a wide flat where the lake had been. All around its south and southwest was a hellish boiling of ash and gas and a heavy stench of sulfur. Blue lightning arced just above the ground. Most of my flying has been in mountains, thus lots of lightning. But on this one flight I'd seen more lightning than in all my years of flying. Truman's lodge should be here, but it's swept away or buried. The forest is gone, not one remaining tree. Harry Truman is gone. No civilization here. Spirit Lake is no longer as we knew it.

Visibility was really on the edge now. I flew almost on the deck but kept airspeed ten knots to stay ahead of the ashstorm my rotors stirred up. I couldn't take my eyes off the ground or I'd go into vertigo, my big threat. Every so often I glanced at the gauges but had relied on the sound of the engine. Now my elevated arm told me I was pulling the collective to 95% torque—a hell of a lot just to hover. At this altitude it should be *far* less. Engine damage? I sweated profusely, shook fiercely. I glanced at the OAT (outside-air temperature) gauge. It read 60°C (140°F). I'd gone from 20° downvalley to 60° here! With each 2°C increase in OAT, the helicopter has about 33 pounds less lift. So 20 times 33 . . . the 40° rise in air temperature has lost me 660 pounds of lift. At 60°C my 3400-foot pressure altitude has risen to density altitude 9000 feet![32]—almost max for a Hughes 500C. But now I had reason for all the torque I was pulling. In these weird conditions the ship was flying well.

I could see only thirty yards but flew north over the flat. Spirit Lake was gone, all gray sand. My altimeter still read high. The whole lake seemed filled by mudflow. Then farther north in haze I saw a hole of open water five yards across. This seemed all that remained of Spirit Lake. I radioed the aircraft again [3:08].[33]

My fuel reserve was low. I turned west and flew slowly down the valley using the barren ridge and other landmarks I'd seen coming up. Knowing distance out, I was no longer frightened. Five miles below Camp Baker I came to a concrete bridge with a pier in the middle. Logs in the muddy flood crashed and jammed against the deck about to be swept away. A pickup stopped on the north [~3:30].

I emerged from under the cloud. Except for the Sikorsky early in the flight, I'd seen no other aircraft. At Kid Valley I was pushing fuel reserve but flew fifty miles south to Pearson at Vancouver and landed about 4:15.

WASHINGTON NATIONAL GUARD

The great devastation and strangeness made flying more frightening than in Vietnam. I felt small.

—Capt. Darald Stebner

The Washington Army National Guard 116th Armored Cavalry were training at Yakima Firing Center, most of their hueys olive-drab gunships.

Capt. Mark Edelbrock

The 116th had planned to respond to a large eruption. As ash began falling at Yakima Firing Center May 18, we jumped in and took off in order. Fifteen hueys launched before ashfall got too heavy. We flew north, washed off at Wenatchee, and flew west across the Cascades to Gray Field.

The M-model gunships dropped off hardware. But we flew our H models to Toutle high school and set up forward operations.

We returned to Gray Field at dark. Jess Hagerman flew an OH-58 for our 81st Brigade. Twenty-one National Guard aircraft flew 142 hours. The National Guard, Air Force Reserve 304th, and Coast Guard extracted 137 people, 8 dogs, and a boa constrictor.

Jess Hagerman

[Capt. Hagerman had been a Marine, then flown helicopters with Air America in Vietnam. He flew helicopters for the National Guard since 1976 and for Weyerhaeuser since 1978.]

Flying for Weyerhaeuser, I knew the land near Mount St. Helens. Since March 27 I'd flown often while the crater vented. I commanded the Guard's 81st Brigade. Our OH-58s—military versions of a Bell 206 Jet Ranger—had a small engine and only two seats in back.

I was home with family when called that the I-5 bridge over Toutle River had been closed and I was to fly someone at Department of Emergency Services. With crew chief Randy Fontz I lifted off Gray Field in an OH-58 [1:00].[34] We picked up Lora Murphey at Chehalis and crossed flooded Toutle River choked with logs and flotsam [1:50]. We dropped her in Vancouver, refueled, and flew north.

Four Guard hueys were at Kelso airport when I landed [3:45]. An Air Force Reserve huey landed. They told our pilots they'd been up to a blast area and their jumpers found people cooked. No reason to fly up, they said, everyone's dead. Yet somebody could have hidden in a cave or behind a hill. "Flying for Weyerhaeuser, Jess, you know this area," Col. Bob Watling said. "Do what you can with these hueys."

Two hueys went up the Green, the other two followed my OH-58 toward the mountain's plume [4:15]. A mudflow down the South Fork had ripped out trees. We crossed to the North Fork and turned east under cloud. A relay aircraft reported two vehicles on a road farther south.[35] The ash grew thick upvalley. I radioed the hueys to stay while we fly up for a look. We saw the south valley side clobbered—trees down, roads gone, mud creeping down.

Sky and ground were the same pale gray, like flying in a milk bottle. When we flew close to ground, ash billowed up and we couldn't see. How long we can breathe this stuff? Will the engine last? But with all roads buried a helicopter's the only way out.

The air got too milky. Before Elk Rock we turned north over the ridge. Thick ash covered downed trees and stumps. We spotted a pickup, and circling in we saw footprints! We followed them west down road 3100. In a few miles we came to two guys lying in ash on the road.[36] One stood a bit and slowly waved his arms; the other just lay there. If I flew down the ash would stir up. Wind was coming from the south; these guys lay 200 yards up from flowing mud.

"I'll hover over the edge of mud," I told crew chief Randy. "You'll have to jump in and wade. Then bring these guys down to load here."

"No problem."

I hovered close to the bank, and Randy dropped from the skid into knee-deep mud. I radioed the hueys. They dropped their crew chiefs this way. While they hiked up I saw again one of the guys lying prone. The other stood, staggered, and fell *{Scymanky}*. They're too injured and feeble to bring down the road and load over the mud. Somehow I *must* land.

I circled down to the road, raised a great cloud, but got a feeling for the ash: several inches. I went down and blew off more. Next time I'd land. I came down steadily. I lost sight of the ground but was close enough to hold power and pitch. I glimpsed something, pulled pitch, and cushioned the landing [~5:00].

I frictioned the controls and trotted down.

You got anything for pain?" Jim Scymanky asked.

"No. But we'll have you to a hospital soon. How many of you?"

"Four."

Scymancky was standing, the other [Leonty Skorohodoff] down. Two other sets of footprints led down the road—one barefoot! Someone without shoes in eight inches of hot ash? Scymancky's hands were black, gloves baked on. Open sores marked his face, big welts his forehead. I tugged his shirt, and it tore as if scorched.

The two mechanics slogged up out of breath. I fireman-carried the guy on the ground up to the helicopter. He was conscious enough to sit. The mechanics helped Scymancky walk up and sit in the back. Randy got in the left. I throttled up, pulled pitch, and a dustcloud enveloped us. I flew up on instruments. I radioed the hueys: "Get your crew somehow. Two more two sets of prints lead down the road."

I flew the guys to Longview hospital. We refueled at Kelso and started back up [6:00]. By radio we heard one of the hueys had plucked the barefoot guy from the mud and were headed to the hospital *{Stebner & Wedding}*.

I landed again in the ash. We followed the fourth set of tracks down to the mud-flow. No one nearby: the mud must've got him. We flew to Kelso. By radio we heard two of our hueys had picked up people and dogs in Green River *{Kolb; Nelson & Ruff; Balch; Smith}*. An injured guy lay far upriver.

We took off and flew up. One of the hueys radioed they'd left a guy with a broken hip at a shed above a bridge *{Nelson & Ruff}*. The bridge was high enough less ash would blow. I hovered down; Randy jumped off and moved logs and branches. I landed with the tail hung over the river [~8:30].

The huey is gone, our ship quiet. The sun's nearly down, long shadows. No sound from mountain or river. Fine powder floats in the calm air. We're alone. An eerie stone silence.

To the north sit four ashy cars, trees on two. It's eerie looking in these derelicts. Now for the guy. We shuffle down the roadbank. We crawl under a log, over another, working toward a shack where the he'd been left. Most trees are down and coated in gray-powder ash. It's getting dark. It's spooky too by a few snags looming up into ash hanging in the air. Suddenly a guy jumps up! It scares me. His hair is wide like an afro and orange—did heat do that? We're already spooked when this big-haired apparition pops up.

Brian Thomas had crawled on a broken hip two hundred yards through this mess nearly to the roadbank. We chair-carry him over trees to the bridge and lift him into the helicopter. It's almost dark when we blast out [~9:00] toward Longview hospital. We refuel at Kelso and land back at Gray field [10:35].

All day I felt it was like flying inside a milk bottle. When I could see I felt like a gnat in a universe. A speck next to the gigantic rising column. Our helicopter so tiny in the huge ruin.

Darald Stebner and George Wedding

[Capt. Stebner was a National Guard pilot, Wedding a photographer for the *San Jose Mercury* and *San Jose News*.]

Stebner: At Yakima Firing Center we always park our M-model hueys fueled to launch quickly, mine number 15150. We were being briefed when at 8:50 word came of the eruption. Outside dark marshmallow-like clouds filled the west sky. As first platoon leader in the front row I was first to go. Ash began falling damp and sticky [9:00]. Fifteen helicopters got off before ashfall grew too thick. We flew north to Wenatchee airport, and fire trucks hosed off our ships. We flew west. Spectacular cloud filled the south sky in many hues of black, gray, and blue. It trailed far east like a huge thunderhead with rain falling from it. We landed at Gray Army Airfield about 1:15, detached military hardware, and refueled.

Eight of our hueys flew south to Kelso airfield. From there [3:00] we flew northeast into the North Fork near Camp Baker, copilot Frank Shipton flying. We passed from green standing forest into shades of gray, and just beyond all trees down! Beyond this an alien terrain of huge lumps and roiling mud! The great devastation and strangeness made flying more frightening than in Vietnam. I felt small. Hazards we deal with are at a site—a firefight here, or a forest fire there—but most of the area okay. Today the whole region grew alien, then more so. Debris and mud filled the valley. Chunks of ice big as automobiles lay among fallen trees. After more than an hour we found no one and flew back to Kelso.

Wedding: From Everett I'd flown to Kelso airport. I hung around National Guard Capt. Stebner and his crew: "If you *do* go out, I'd like news photographs." In late afternoon Stebner invited me into the helicopter.

Stebner: Our crew included flight surgeon Maj. Bob Williams and crewchief Sgt. Bob Williams. It was my turn as pilot. We took off [~5:15] and flew up the Toutle alone. By radio we knew Jess Hagerman had rescued two badly injured guys above Camp Baker {*Hagerman; Scymancky*}. Other footprints led down to the valley now full of flowing mud.

Wedding: I sat in the back with two cameras loaded with black-and-white film. We flew beneath ashfog, and gray ash shrouded the ground. It was frightening not seeing Mount St. Helens from where trouble might come. They slid a door back and flew low. I was belted in, but ruined gray forest passed just yards away. We flew 45 minutes through haze, the crew discouraged they'd find nobody to rescue.

Stebner: About 6:30 we found foot tracks, one barefoot.

Wedding: They snaked down an ash-draped road. One set disappeared on an embankment at swollen, creeping mud. We circled with the rear doors back.

Stebner: "There he is!" copilot Shipton said. A log with upturned roots bobbed in the mud a hundred yards from the valley side. A man crouched at the roots, a tree three feet across more than thirty long. Mud working on the buried top rocked it. A roll would tumble him in.

Wedding: From 500 feet I shot a telephoto of a bedraggled guy crouched by the roots.

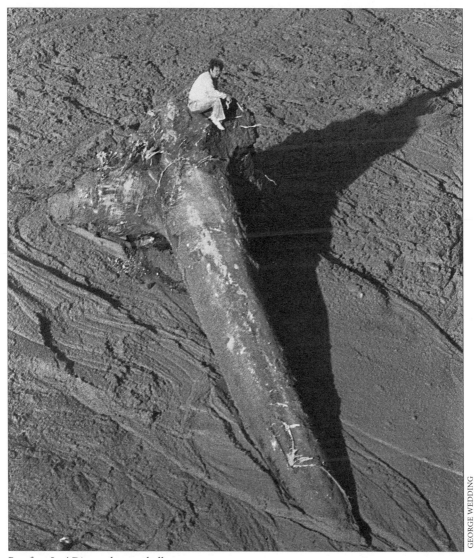

Barefoot José Dias on log rootball

Stebner: Hovering low here didn't blow up ash, but we couldn't land in deep mud.

Wedding: We flew lower. The man looked petrified, eyes fixed on the helicopter, caked in gray ash—and barefoot! We circled thinking how to get him. "I'll put one skid down," Stebner said. "Crew must pull him in." The guy sat on his haunches, glass-eyed.

Stebner: I could only hover my left skid high on the root disk nine feet above the mud. The man hardly moved, clearly injured. I held it more than a minute, watching the mud.

Wedding: The forlorn guy finally stood, and two crewmen reached out. Their hands jerked back.

Stebner: A flying huey builds up static electricity that discharges when you land. The skid wasn't down enough for that. When the men touched, the discharge zapped them.

Wedding: The man sat back on the log. We flew up, back down, pulled off again, hovered down a third time. The crew waved him forward. The guy stood afraid. The crew urged him closer.

Stebner: The charge was spent, but he didn't know. I hovered two more minutes.

Wedding: Finally he reached out quickly.

Stebner: The crew chief pulled him in. I turned downvalley.

Wedding: On the bench seat he slumped glassy-eyed against the left side. Through a wide-angle lens I focused his face, then a hand stretched toward me. How will they get that glove off? I lowered the camera. It was no glove. Ash-caked skin hung off the swollen hand. I focused the hand and snapped a photo, hoping depth-of-field enough for the face. I crawled forward and snapped another.

Stebner: He barely moved and didn't talk. The surgeon shook his head, saying he had burns, brutalized skin, open sores, bulging eyes. We radioed Longview hospital.

Wedding: He looked at everyone, pausing at each face, stopping on mine. We landed at the hospital, and emergency-room people rushed out with a gurney. He gave what proved to be a fictitious name [7:20].[37]

Stebner: We flew to Kelso airfield, refueled, and flew on to Gray airfield [10:45].

Wedding: I developed and printed my film and sent off photos by AP facsimile. The *San Jose Mercury* and the *San Jose News* ran many photos the 19th.

Hal Kolb and Rich Frishman

[Chief Warrant Officer Harold ("Hal") Kolb was a National Guard pilot, Frishman a photographer for the *Everett Herald*.]

Kolb: M-model hueys are military gunships—shorter body, larger rotor blades than H models—mine this weekend number 196.

Operations interrupted a briefing to say Mount St. Helens had erupted, ash coming east. We pre-flighted as the cloud came over high. "Crank," we were told when ash began falling from the west. I was back in second platoon. Half the hueys got off before ground people ceased launches. We lifted and climbed northeast—last to leave. I held control while co-pilot Bob Bryant mopped off his windscreen. He took control while I wiped mine—wiper blades would have scratched. We flew to Wenatchee and hosed off. We flew west through Snoqualmie Pass to Gray Field and dropped our rocket pods.

We and five other hueys flew to Kelso airfield. We flew alone up the Toutle that had flooded earlier and past Camp Baker just hit by mudflows. We crept up the North Fork. Ashy air stopped us west of Spirit Lake about 3:30. Geysers popped up just north, and glacier ice rolled in steaming craters. We flew down to Kelso and refueled.

A news photographer boarded, and we flew up to Toutle school field [5:40].[38] We flew to Camp Baker, then turned north.

Frishman: Newsmen expected flowing red lava as at Kilauea. But we came to an incredible scene: far as I could see trees laid down in one direction from the volcano. We flew over a gigantic new landscape of flattened trees piled with gray dust—massive utter destruction. My naïveté had been total.

Kolb: We found tire tracks in ash on a road by Green River. They led to a stranded pickup [Grant Christiansen's]. Following footprints west, we came to five people walking a road. I hovered down to a wide spot a quarter mile west. But ash shrouded us and I climbed up. I did five approaches to blow away ash. On the sixth we landed in a cloud.

Frishman: I couldn't tell which way was up. Branches dropped onto us and pinged off rotors. The pilots said the helicopter slid forward as we landed.

The dust settled, doors opened, and I jumped out. Ash fine as flour clung.

Kolb: A man walked down, then four people together. A father and two young boys covered in ash {Smith} seemed okay. A guy with badly burned hands moaned in pain {Balch} [photo page 186].

Frishman: A middle-age logger in bib overalls came, then the others. I shot many photos, some of the burned young man.

It was a difficult takeoff up backwards while enveloped in ash. More branches hit.

Kolb: We flew our passengers to Longview hospital. Refueled at Kelso [9:50], we took off for Gray Field.[39]

Rick Perry

[Paired with Kolb's G-196 was G-080, pilot Lt. Mike Cairnes and crewchief Mike Samuelson. *Seattle Times* photographer Perry flew on its last May 18 sortie.]

A *Seattle Times* reporter flew me to Kelso. National Guard hueys landed in late afternoon. California photographer George Wedding got on one, *Everett Herald* photographer Rich Frishman on another, I on a third.

We flew east. Above Toutle I shot photos of a huge flood about to take a bridge. Up the North Fork the ground went gray, and beyond that all timber down! Wow!

We circled down toward a station wagon among fallen trees. A body lay by the car. Now it's not "wow" but human tragedy. By radio the pilots knew of the car and didn't try to land.

We flew north and found forest down across miles. Trees lay on exposed hillsides as if someone combed them down. Broken trees stood behind cliffs. A tremendous blast had wiped the hills—powerful in the open, less so behind cliffs.

The crew found footprints and followed them west. We came to people hiking. We descended into a huge ash cloud we stirred up, only fog outside. Would we hit something? The pilots know where the ground is? They got us down.

Two of the crew hiked up the road. After many minutes they returned with three people and two dogs. I photographed them approaching, kicking up ash *{Nelson & Ruff}* [photo page 177]. They looked hot and beat, shocked and numbed. An older guy dragged an ashy sleeping bag.

We took off in a huge ash cloud, all outside light gray. I photographed the survivors—a young couple [Bruce Nelson, Sue Ruff], an old logger (Grant Christiansen). We flew miles east over downed forest. I photographed them realizing the huge devastation and photographed the pilot assuring Ruff about their friends. I shot the sea of downed forest—across the grain, parallel, in one view another huey.

Chuck Nole

[Chief Warrant Officer Charles ("Chuck") Nole piloted helicopters.]

Most of our 25 helicopters training at Yakima were M-model hueys. My H-model, tailnumber 22374, was a VIP ship—black-and-white, finer interior. We took off in falling ash, flew north, and turned west across the Cascades, the south sky black with eruption clouds.

We took off from Gray Field southward. Halfway down, an immense cloud of rising ash showed through the haze—so massive we didn't at first know what we saw. We landed at Toutle about one. Our operations team came [1:20], then other hueys.

The South Fork flood had trapped people. We flew some to the high school at Toutle, but some who worried about looting wouldn't leave.

We flew east over Silver Lake in late afternoon. Four miles ahead along the North Fork a tall fir shook violently and threw dust. Then another. As we drew closer others snapped and fell. A huge flood poured down the North Fork, its surface covered with long trees—some cut logs, some with rootballs. In fast mud they rammed trees on the banks. A few more fell. Rising mud surrounded houses; a piece of one drifted by among logs. We flew down looking for anyone on the river or on logs. We ferried more people from between the forks of the Toutle. With the mudflood snapping off big trees, they came willingly, in one batch a German shepherd.

We refueled about 6:30 and explored the South Fork. Wind had cleared the dust. Far up I spotted a white car in the valley marked KOMO. Footsteps west up a logging road led to a guy slogging through ash toward a platform where I might land.

I approached over mudflow. But I paused, and ash enveloped. I pulled up. I browned out twice *{Crockett}*. A big Coast Guard H-3 Sikorsky came upvalley. "You have a hoist?" I radioed.

"Yup," he said, "and a basket!" *{Walters}*.

He flew down to fifty feet but his rotors billowed up the ash. He hovered higher and got the basket down. Though enveloped in dust, the guy got in. They winched him up, pulled the basket into the helicopter, and flew west.

On the way we landed for a stranded KOIN news crew. At Toutle our medic helped the guy from the Sikorsky into our huey. He was David Crockett from KOMO news. The KOIN crew filmed *{Koon}*. We landed him at Longview hospital.

We refueled at Kelso, took off at 9:45, and flew in dark to Gray Field.

U.S. Coast Guard

Capt. Tom Walters

[Walters had been an Air Force helicopter pilot since 1972, for years flying an HH-3E Sikorsky in Iceland. In 1980 he was an Air Force exchange pilot flying for the Coast Guard.]

I flew a white-and-orange Coast Guard Sikorsky H-3 (HH-3E), aboard a copilot, flight mechanic, and radioman. We were called after noon that timber flooding down Cowlitz River might impede navigation in the Columbia. We flew up from Astoria. Thousands of logs were in the rivers and stranded on banks [~1:30].

The Cowlitz County sheriff called us to aid rescues near Mount St. Helens. We flew up the Toutle and North Fork and into ashfog where we could see only 200 feet, then 100. A small helicopter radioed past [~2:30] *{Reber}*, but I didn't see him.

People had been cut off by flooded roads and bridges. We landed in yards and flew people to Toutle Lake High School. I saw a Hughes 500 land a TV crew on the north valley side *{Wright, Anderson, Renner}*. In bad visibility extra aircraft endanger search and rescue, and the volcano could send down more ash. We landed [~3:40] and ordered them out—taking one with us to make sure. We refueled at Kelso and did two more rescues in the lower Toutle.

Flying up the South Fork about 7:00, we saw three fires on the south side. Someone stranded had lit a triangle to attract attention. There wasn't room to land, and our big rotor blades would stir up ash. We radioed and a National Guard huey appeared. He tried to land but raised a dust cloud and pulled off. He tried again, same result *{Nole}*.

Our hoist has 200 feet of ⅜-inch steel cable. In sea rescues we hover 25 to 50 feet above highest ocean waves. The mechanic opened the door, hooked on the basket, and wound down 50 feet of cable. I hovered down. We got the basket down and the mechanic saw the guy start to climb in, but ash came up. "We're IFR," I called, and flew up on instruments. The basket rose empty. Dust had poured into the cockpit.

The mechanic wound the cable down 150 feet and we tried again. I said if we go IFR I'll hold a hover six more seconds before pulling up. We flew down and put the basket on the ground. The guy came toward it, but the ash obliterated the ground. In a few seconds it billowed up and we went IFR. I held cyclic, collective, and pedals steady, keeping level by the instruments—holding what seems a hover though without visual reference I can't tell if we're moving a little or not. The cockpit again filled with white powder. I pulled up slowly. The basket emerged from the cloud with the guy in it. The mechanic winched it up and pulled it in *{Crockett}*.

I turned west. The guy coughed and gasped from all the ash, and they put him on oxygen. He sucked it empty and they gave him another. Then another. On one 24-mile flight to Toutle he used all three oxygen bottles. Once landed he wouldn't leave the basket, and the mechanic and radioman couldn't pry off his grip. They tipped the basket up on the field until he fell out. A National Guard helicopter flew him to a hospital *{Nole; Koon}*. I learned he was David Crockett when later he went on ABC's program *That's Incredible!*

We rescued 28 people in all. We were asked to check a Blazer far up. We flew low up Green River in a hurry in twilight. I saw no other helicopter *{Pleasant}*. We found the vehicle on a ridge, the ash much thicker here. I lowered the landing tires and descended toward the buried road. Twenty feet up we stirred up a huge cloud. We went IFR but I held pitch and power and eased down for a soft landing. After several seconds I'd felt nothing and was about to pull pitch when a slight lurch told me we were down [8:45] *{Hoblitt}*. So much powder had drawn through the door seals I couldn't see my copilot. After cooldown I shut down and sat five minutes. The dust settled some. From where I'd landed we'd slid down a slight slope of road a hundred feet into a little gully! The tires project almost two feet below the H-3's pontoons, but the ash was so deep the tires hadn't touched. As I held pitch, the helicopter floated on its hull in the soft ash. In the throbbing machine and no visibility, indicator reading level, I couldn't know we were moving. The jolt was a tire bumping a downed tree. Had the rotors with all their momentum whacked a root or branch sticking up it'd have damaged them too much to fly.

The mechanic and radioman waded in thigh-deep ash up to the vehicle. The copilot and I sawed limbs off downed trees so when we cranked up they wouldn't be in the rotors. Our crewmen came back saying they'd found fatalities—two adults and a child [Seibold & Morris].

I took off in dust on instruments [~9:35].[40] We flew directly to Astoria and landed about 10:30 well after dark.

CIVILIANS

David Crockett

[KOMO-TV cameraman Crockett had been stranded.]

After the huge morning flood [*{Crockett}* chap 10], the South Fork returned to its ditch. It had swept all trees from the valley floor. I heard another flood coming about two. It spilled from the ditch and kicked up over obstacles but was much smaller. It subsided after twenty minutes. The air cleared about five. I panned around with silent film. The mountain looked flat, its summit gone.

In early evening a dark National Guard helicopter saw me or my fires. I walked up to a higher landing where there was more room. He tried to land but stirred up a big cloud. He tried again but couldn't *{Nole}*.

A big Coast Guard helicopter came by. They lowered a basket on a cable, but the rotors whipped up a huge cloud of ash *{Walters}*. He hovered higher and lowered the basket. It bumped down as their rotors whipped up another great cloud. It drove ash into my eyes, mouth, clothes, camera. I groped blindly forward until my hand found the metal rim. I placed my cameras in it. As I climbed in the basket jerked up and bashed my head. I blacked out.

I came to groggy. They were slowly winching up the basket swinging on the cable. I looked down eighty feet and it made me almost sick. Since my morning ordeal in the ashfall that really scared me, I've been okay. Now they've blown ash all over, given me a mouthful, and conked me in the head. They wound the basket up and pulled it into the helicopter. From all the inhaled and swallowed ash and from my banged head, I could hardly breathe. I coughed and gagged. They put me on oxygen. It smelled sweet and refreshing as we flew down to Toutle.

Someone put me in a National Guard helicopter and back on oxygen. They flew me to the hospital in Longview *{Nole; Koon}*.

Carol Koon

[Koon and two others of KOIN-6 TV had reported from Signal Peak.]

In afternoon we heard by radio that flood had swept out South Fork road. Trapped, we radioed the station. A dark helicopter landed late in the day and and flew us to Toutle *{Nole}*.

The medic got out to help a guy on the field coughing. They brought him into the helicopter, and we took off. I shot video of him in an oxygen mask gasping. The sun was low—maybe 7:45—when we landed at Longview hospital. He turned out to be David Crockett of KOMO-TV Seattle *{Crockett}*. His dramatic video later played on television.

Washington State Patrol

David Gardner

[State Troopers David Gardner and Robert Cory fly again.]

We refueled the Cessna 182 at Kelso and took off about three. A large flood down the North Fork had spread across the valley above Toutle. Up in the narrower valley it flowed full of logs, smashing down tall cottonwoods on the banks and firs farther back. Dark-chocolate mud crept up a flat to a house, rose another foot and surrounded it, rose another two to above the foundation. Nearby trees shook; some fell. The house shuddered, lifted a little, and turned slowly into the flood. It smashed against trees and fell apart. So other houses went.

A swarm of helicopters and airplanes followed the loggy front down. Logs piled up at the highway bridge above Toutle. It was combat flying among military hueys, news helicopters, and private airplanes. We stayed above the highest of them. The mud rose upstream of the bridge until there was little room beneath. More and more logs jammed. The concrete deck lurched, rotated into the current, and floated down a few hundred feet. The mud swallowed it [~6:10].

Over the next hour the flood worked down the gorge below, much denser mud than the morning flood. It smashed out trees higher and higher. It surrounded several houses. It took some a few miles above the I-5 bridge. A maroon van bobbed among the logs. We radioed Patrol officers of the flood's progress: "Half an hour." And later: "Two more bends, a quarter hour." Troopers stopped traffic before the head of flood reached the bridge.

We flew back to Olympia, landing at dark.

AERO-COPTERS

Lon Stickney

[USGS's contract pilot, Aero-Copters out of Seattle.]

Tired from several long days of flying, I slept nine hours. My friend woke me about television reports of Mount St. Helens erupting. "Oh yeah," I said, "it erupts every day." But live TV showed a gigantic cloud like none earlier.

I called the USGS in Vancouver. "Can you bring a helicopter?" Dan Miller fretted. "We've no contact with Dave Johnston." I drove to Aero-Copters. Jet Ranger 23J wasn't fixed, but I'm also a mechanic. It took hours to prepare Jet Ranger 004.

In late afternoon I took off south, flew maxed out, and angled up the Toutle. Alone with no passenger, I radioed the Forest Service plane [6:32].[41] The mountain pumped up a cloud bent northeast. Above Camp Baker trees were down over many square miles, nothing green left, the valley full of debris. Farther up little volcanoes burst from the valley floor. Having flown the USGS here in bad weather for weeks, I navigated the haze.

I flew directly to Coldwater II [7:02]. I saw where the trailer had been by the quarry, where I'd landed the afternoon before. I flew over the bare ridge half an hour. I called the Forest Service plane: "trailer gone, ridge swept clean, no David Johnston. Nothing lives here" [7:35].[42]

I flew west of Mount St. Helens to within fifty feet of the new rim, next to the ash column blowing off northeast [7:54]. My altimeter read the rim at 8200 feet—1500 feet below the summit I landed on yesterday!

I landed at Pearson Airpark in Vancouver at 8:25. The USGS drove me to the Federal Building. I told Don Swanson and others about Coldwater.

17
What's On Second

. . . Travellers tell
How those old – phlegmatic mountains
Usually so still –

Bear within – appalling Ordinance,
Fire, and smoke, and gun,
Taking Villages for breakfast,
                    —Emily Dickenson, *Poem 175*

Olympia

State Patrol pilot Dick Swier lands the King Air 200 at Olympia with Governor Dixy Lee Ray. Security guard Ron Walcker drives her to Emergency Services in midafternoon.

"It was most impressive," the governor says of her Mount St. Helens flight. "Have you read *The Fall of Pompeii*? That's all I could think of."[1]

Kelso: Cowlitz County Sheriff's office

Ben Bena: In late morning deputies reported a big flood, many logs ramming the highway bridge at Toutle. Sheriff Nelson called the Washington State Patrol district. "A flood full of logs is coming. Shouldn't we shut the I-5 bridge?"

"Oh no. It'd cost too much. We can't close for that."

"Well, just watch me," says Nelson.

He calls again. "Well, Captain, nothing moves across Toutle River bridge. But I need my deputies. How about the Patrol taking over?"

Vancouver: *The Columbian*

Greg Herrington: Our reporters and photographers called that the eruption was huge. In afternoon we heard searchers had found people dead *{Peters and others; Weed and others}*. Steve Small fretted about Reid Blackburn—*still* no radio call from him.

Tom Koenniger: In late afternoon Small and I drove to Pearson Airpark. A pilot had just landed from Mount St. Helens *{Reber}*. "I've flown there for weeks. Now nothing's left," he choked out, weeping. "Reid's gone."

Herrington: The pilot had seen Reid's car buried at Coldwater I. A pall settled over the *Columbian* office.

Bill Dietrich: Reporting Mount St. Helens had been a thrill. Now I wrote in gloom, tears in my eyes.

Vancouver: Columbia Helicopters

Dwight Reber: From Kid Valley I flew fifty miles to Vancouver and landed about 4:30. During cooldown I sat shaking in the helicopter. Pushing my limits in the new world had been tense.

National Geographic's Rowe Findley came out. "There's no Reid Blackburn, no Harry Truman," I choked out. "No Spirit Lake. They're all gone."

Inside stood John Marshall, a *Geographic* freelance photographer I'd flown in April. I told him what I'd seen.

Portland: *The Oregonian*

Les Zaitz: By afternoon reporters' stories, AP wire copy, and notes cover my desk. TVs flash images, phones ring. Reports pour in: summit gone, huge mudflows down valleys, people killed, many evacuated, ash falling far east, cars stalled. I'm digesting all this but need someone who had been to Mount St. Helens. In evening I call the Air Force Reserve 304th. Captain Fred Stovel has just landed. "Trees are down by a tremendous explosion," he says, "radiating like spokes from the mountain. Ash has kindled fires in them. It seems no one survived." I write tomorrow's front page.

Longview: *The Daily News*

Bob Gaston: The news office was empty early Sunday. Having seen the cloud, Andrei Stepankowski and Jay McIntosh rushed in. Photographer Roger Werth called to say he has hired an aircraft. Reporters and photographers went out; I assigned some to Toutle, Cowlitz, and Lewis valleys. Donna duBeth dashed in from Seattle. I granted her and Werth an afternoon helicopter.

Publisher Ted Natt came in. We allowed Monday's newspaper eight extra pages. We'd make Mount St. Helens *our* story—report in depth and breadth. Reporters and photographers returned and wrote and processed film into the night. Tomorrow we'd run 45 stories and dozens of photos.

Donna duBeth: An explosion awakened me in Seattle. Managing Editor Bob Gaston telephoned me to Longview. But mudflow had closed the I-5 bridge over Toutle River.[2] I drove the shoulder against traffic and crossed to a road to Kelso. By telephone I found a helicopter, and photographer Roger Werth and I flew up the Toutle. In evening we hammered out stories and processed pictures for Monday's paper.

Roger Werth: My Ektachrome was flown up to our sister newspaper in Bellevue, who made color separates. I worked all night editing and laying out photographs for Monday's *Daily News*.

Vancouver: U.S. Geological Survey

Rick Hoblitt: In Denver Rocky Crandell had said, "Probably just another phreatic eruption." Descending in an airliner toward Portland three hours later, we saw to the north a plume miles wide boiling up tens of thousands of feet. "Does that look phreatic?" I asked.

Richard Waitt: Flying into Portland at 3:30, I see in the north a pale-gray cauliflower cloud wider than the volcano's base. It boiled up through clouds to 50,000 feet. Later Don Swanson says from the air he'd seen downed forests and fires, and David Johnston was likely gone. I telephone towns north of Mount St. Helens. Ashfall has quit at Morton and Randle. There I might sample.

Don Swanson: Harry Glicken returned to the Federal Building about 6:30. To escape radio and telephones we ducked out onto the fire escape. I told what I'd seen from the air, of Dave's almost certain death. He said he'd gotten close to Coldwater II in an Air Force Reserve helicopter, but everything was too changed to know. Coldwater II must be destroyed, he said. He'd camped there two weeks but now said he felt responsible for Dave. He wept.

Aero-Copters pilot Lon Stickney came in. After many days flying he was exhausted last evening when he flew off to Seattle. I was surprised to see him back. He said an hour ago he'd flown over Coldwater II. It had been wiped clean.

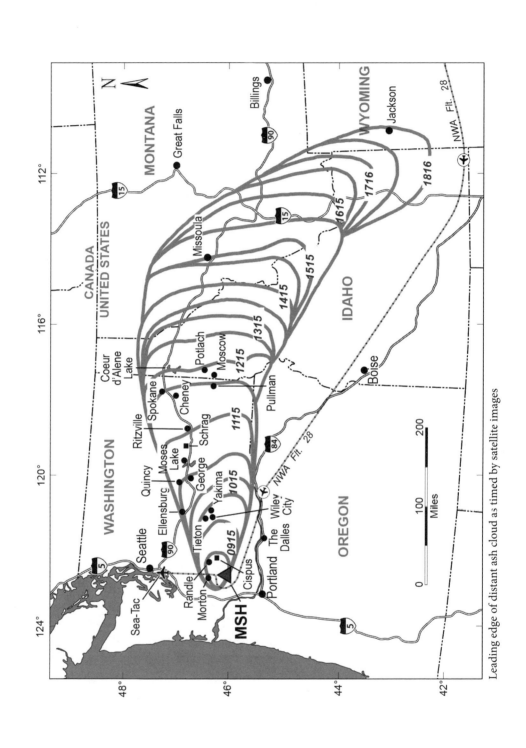

Leading edge of distant ash cloud as timed by satellite images

18
Plains

Damn stupid mountain went and dumped all that dirty gritty glassy gray ash that flies like flour and lies like cement . . . And the scientists are a real big help, all they'll say is we don't know, we can't tell, she might dump another load of ash on you just when you've got it all cleaned up. It's an outrage.

—Ursula Le Guin, *In the Red Zone*

Carried on west-southwest winds, ash fell far east, draping towns and cities, farms and highways in daytime darkness. First the Cascades, then Yakima (85 miles east), Moses Lake (150 miles), Spokane and Moscow (250 miles), Missoula (400 miles), and Billings (725 miles).

Kit Bakke and Billie Johnston

[Kit Bakke and teachers Billie Johnston and Sharon Wagner supervised children at Cispus Learning Center 23 miles northeast of Mount St. Helens.[1]]

Bakke: My daughter's primary school camped in green forest fifteen miles outside the blue zone. I helped two teachers care for thirty-six kids age 3 to 13. Sunday dawned sunny and cloudless. We packed gear into the cars, ate a pancake breakfast, and played in a field.

Johnston: It seemed *too* quiet—no birds. I noticed a big cloud in the southwest boiling gray and white. It could only be the volcano. I bolted across the field. "Mount St. Helens is erupting!" I yelled. "Let's go!"

Bakke: Black clouds boiled toward us like sped-up time-lapse film—much quicker than a thunderstorm. In less than a minute a dark curtain replaced crystal-blue sky.

Johnston: We threw the rest of our stuff in the cars.

Bakke: In a few minutes only a wedge of blue remained to the northeast. We hustled the kids to the cars. Five minutes after we first saw the cloud small rocks and cinders fell. The air grew warm, smelled hot, and turned dark with falling ash. We left in a caravan. Soon headlights barely penetrated a wooly blackness.

Johnston: In a Volkswagon minibus we teachers—Sharon driving—could see only the taillights of the car ahead. I watched for the road edge and said "steer left." Ash and mud pellets covered the windshield. We stuck our heads out the windows to see.

Bakke: The car ahead slowed onto the shoulder. The engine had died and wouldn't restart. They crowded in with us and another. The air smelled like a fire. Our air-cooled engine kept running. We crawled on. Afraid, some of the kids needed to pee. I told a girl to go in her sleeping roll.

295

Johnston: A sharp crack! and rolling thunder. Again and again. It scared us, not knowing if it was eruptions or lightning thunder.

Bakke: We crept through black ten miles northwest down gravel road 123 [later 23]. In an hour and three quarters we reached a paved road [125] south of Randle. A man in an ash-caked coat waved a flare, directing cars from the woods toward a church. By 10:45 the sky had lightened a little. Road, fields, trees, buildings were silted in light-gray powder, a lifeless landscape. Every footstep stirred up talcum ash.

Johnston: Not all our caravan arrived. We telephoned parents in Seattle: others had called from a home and a tavern.

Bakke: In the church basement colored paper, scissors, and glue occupied the kids. We argued what to do. Some didn't want to trade this inside haven for ash and stalling vehicles.

"If it gets worse the National Guard will come."

"No, we need to get out ourselves." This second group won.

Johnston: We tore up a bedsheet and tied a damp face mask on each kid.

Bakke: We bundled them into the cars and caravanned west on highway 12.

Johnston: Cars going east swirled up ash, visibility dropped to zero, and we stopped until it settled. One of our cars got rear-ended.

Bakke: Gradually we came to color. About 5:30 we had sandwiches at Morton fire station.

Richard Stearns

[Forest Service employee Stearns lived 95 miles northeast of the volcano.]

My wife Katharine and I lived on the west edge of Ellensburg. Sunday was sunny and windless. About 9:15 I saw a bulbous dark-gray cloud poke above Manastash Ridge thirteen miles south-southwest. I stretched my arm and it was two thumbs wide—beyond the ridge maybe a quarter mile wide. A hellacious storm brewing.

I joined an 80-year-old neighbor outside. We watched it grow taller and wider. It was almost black—not a gray weather storm or beige duststorm. Its base was several thousand feet above Manastash Ridge.

"Mount St. Helens has exploded," my neighbor grinned.

I laughed at his joke. "Well if it rains I won't have to mow the lawn."

The cloud grew in bulges—a big bulb on the east, then on the west, then on top, the middle pulling near. The cloud edge was sharp against blue sky. In fifteen minutes it swelled to a large pile over the ridge.

After 9:30 I went inside. An AM-radio talk show told of Mount St. Helens erupting: the cloud was no weather storm. Katharine worried about dust coming in through cracks in this old house to our three-week-old baby. We laid towels under doors and on windowsills.

I went back out. The cloud grew higher and wider, elongating northeast toward us. It spread over eastern Kittitas Valley. The line between black cloud and clear blue sky, now nearly overhead, stayed sharp. Spectacular bulbs sagged, enlarged, shrank, danced on the cloud's underside. I heard ash falling—too fine to see but felt it pepper my face. The cloud blotted out the east sky. The air darkened. Thunder rolled from the southwest but I saw no lightning. I later studied photos of drooping weather clouds. The sags in this ash cloud were much blacker and deeper.[2]

Blue sky narrowed to a sliver on the northwest horizon. Then it closed. Streetlights came on. They and neighbors' windows looked like they do at night. The ash was too fine to see. I heard a steady, soft *Shhhhhhhh* falling on street, sidewalks, roofs, and partly leafed trees. It felt like fine sand. It stayed dark two hours, ash accumulating like snow.

The sky lightened gradually, after an hour to like a cloudy day. In afternoon it gradually darkened again: another cloud coming over. This time outside I neither heard nor saw falling ash. It went entirely dark more than two hours.

The air lightened in evening but stayed hazy. Ash kicked up like silt but didn't billow like powder. It looked more than an inch thick, but on our outdoor table I measured ⅝ inch. Its basal quarter inch was dark gray, the top very light gray, the contact between layers sharp. Morning's cloud dropped the dark sand, afternoon's the fine gray.

In evening I saw in the ash a beetle's tracks, and two feet away a bird's. The bird had landed, hopped three times, and left a scuffed spot where it snatched up the bug. I saw many other tracks of insects and birds. During the ashfall people huddled inside. But outside the lives of birds and insects—eating and being eaten—went on.

John Snell

[Snell also lived in Kittitas Valley.]

I had sixty cows at my dairy on Tjossem Road five miles southeast of Ellensburg. I'd been up for hours, called the cows into the barn, milked and released them to the pasture, and needed to change for church. As I walked to the house about ten, I saw on the southwest horizon a small dark cloud like a distant thunderstorm. By 10:30 as I drove northwest to Ellensburg the sky was filling with the dark cloud. On the radio I heard Mount St. Helens had blown. Before mass at 11 o'clock I saw out the window Mount Stuart [9415 ft] standing in sun forty miles northwest but the valley from here to there shadowed.

Just past noon I drove in ash falling like light snow that blew on the road. At home it fell so heavily it turned the air black. Not like night when you can see, but black. I couldn't see car headlights on Tjossem Road until they got to my farm. It stayed black 12:30 to 3:30. At four it was time to milk, but now ash didn't fall much. I called the cows and all sixty came. When I finished at 4:30 the ashfall was done and the sky lightened.

Next day everything looked white, and every car blew up a rooster tail behind. Would the valley look like this forever?

John McCarty

[Wiley City in Ahtanum Creek valley near Yakima is 78 miles east-northeast of the volcano.]

Sunday was the annual rodeo in Wiley City—actually a village. My wife Shirley and I saddled our horses and rode a quarter mile south to the grounds. The rodeo would start at one but I rode in the early slack competition. After nine my partner and I sat on horses waiting our turn for roping. I noticed a dark cloud on the southwest horizon. Dark streaks fell from its base.

"Looks like rain," I said to Shirley. "Why don't you ride home for our coats?"

She soon rode back: "That's no rain. On a truck radio I heard Mount St. Helens erupted!"

The cloud grew, and they called off the rodeo. Ten minutes after I noticed the cloud everyone was loading horses into trailers. While the lot cleared I watched the dark cloud expand toward us. Its top was puffy, tumbling, rolling but dark streaks from its base looking like rain. Occasional lightning bolted in clusters. A bolt seemed to burn a hole into the gray cloud. The hole narrowed and within six seconds closed. Another bolt opened a hole in the cloud but over seconds closed. I was enamored of this display. The cloud booked downvalley toward us.

In ten more minutes everyone had cleared out, the air going dim as we rode our horses through the gate. Halfway home ash began to fall lightly. We got home five minutes later, ash falling steadily and the air going dark. The ash was fine sand but felt heavy. Though dry it stuck to everything it fell on. We put the horses in the barn and walked to the house. Not knowing if the stuff was harmful, we stayed inside. The radio was mostly static. The sky stayed quite dark until night.

Wayne Jones, Betty Jones, and Ken Sugarman

[Betty and Ted Jones and four children lived in Yakima 85 miles east-northeast. Sugarman taught Sunday school.]

Wayne: I was 13. We were at a Baptist church in west Yakima. Sunday-school class met outside this warm, sunny Sunday.

Betty: We went in to church about 9:40. I noticed a dark cloud on the west horizon.

Wayne: We kids sat on a west bank facing Mr. Sugarman. Mount Adams stood southwest, Mount Rainier northwest. A dark-gray cloud, just a point, appeared over the west horizon. It grew fast, coming toward us between Mount Adams and Mount Rainier and widening north and south. It looked dense except its feathery edges. As it neared, the black lightened to gun-metal gray. The center churned and rolled.

Sugarman: I faced the class. One of them said a big cloud's coming.

It came from the southwest, sharp at its leading edge, dense gray behind. Within a minute it pulled overhead like a widening arrowhead. I felt what seemed misty rain and heard it fall.

Wayne: He wiped his bald head, and his palm turned white like he'd rubbed a blackboard.

Sugarman: Someone heard on the radio that Mount St. Helens had erupted. The pastor cancelled classes.

Betty: Outside a big cloud pulled overhead from the west. I heard sand falling through a tree.

Wayne: My dad dropped a bandanna over my head and picked me up. "The volcano's blown," he said. I had asthma, and the bandanna would keep me from breathing ash. Mom and Dad hustled my sister and me to the car. I could see a hundred feet though haze like fire smoke.

Sugarman: The cloud was now miles wide, its edge pulled east, the air growing dark.

Wayne: We drove west toward the cloud. Through the radio's static I heard talk of Mount St. Helens. In three miles the sky turned black, and Dad slowed to a few miles an hour. Streetlights came on, and as we passed one I saw only an amber glow. Cars had stopped on the shoulder.

Sugarman: My wife and I drove toward Tieton fifteen miles northwest. Only five minutes since the kids mentioned the cloud, ash rained heavily, the sky so dark I had headlights on. Ash blew on the road.

Betty: The air smelled sulfury. We crept four miles home in twenty minutes.

Wayne: The warm air smelled like a fire. They wrapped my face and hustled us inside.

Sugarman: On Tieton road an eastbound car blew up an ash cloud I couldn't see in. I braked to a crawl. Lightning and thunder began. Another car went by and in its cloud I saw nothing for half a minute. It was a forty-minute drive to Tieton that should take twenty.

Wayne: Out our big window I couldn't see beyond twenty feet. I heard ash falling into the fireplace, and soon it piled up. Dad went up and covered the chimney. It stayed dark all day.

Sugarman: We got home in dark ashfall full of thunder and lightning. A radio reporter said: "Don't get ash on your skin. Don't wash off with water or it'll make acid. Acid will kill trees."

Ashfall tapered off in evening and the sky lightened. I went out and turned off overhead sprinklers in the apple orchard. Everything was one gray. The apple trees were thick in the ash, especially heavy where sprinklers had been on. Branches sagged to the ground and it seemed whole limbs would snap. We whacked ash off with poles to reduce the weight.

Conrad and Sandie Boccia

[The Boccias lived near Yakima, Conrad a telephone-line repairman.]

Conrad: We and our three kids lived twelve miles west of Yakima. Sandie went out to release the horses to the pasture. She came back saying, "It's strange. They won't leave the corral."

Sandie: They snorted and pranced and looked southwest. I opened the corral gate. They came out, but went back. Started out again, wheeled back. They're always eager to leave the corral in morning but now wouldn't. They seemed upset. They looked southwest, but I saw nothing.

Conrad: Ten minutes later a small black cloud appeared on the west horizon. It broadened north and south as it came closer fast. Lightning bolted from different spots, some cloud-to-cloud, others striking ground. The cloud grew and grew, its abrupt front north-south. The air grew dim. We and the kids got scared, not knowing what was happening. The radio reported this was Mount St. Helens. We weren't as worried—until a Yakima announcer shouted: "The whole Cascade Range is going out! Don't go outside! Don't breath this air!"

Telephone lines got so busy the company restricted them to emergency workers. Homes had no dial tone. The sky was very dark when I went out to the horses. They snorted, trotting with tails up as when upset, ready to run from danger. I could do nothing and went back in.

It went completely dark for hours. About three it gradually lightened. I went out and shoveled the roof—ash 1½ inch deep like coarse sand but felt heavier. Ash sagged the limbs of leafed-out trees and broke branches. With a broom I knocked some off the apple trees to lessen the weight.

Keith Graaff

[George, Washington, lies 131 miles northeast of Mount St. Helens.]

I was a young farmer working on the north flank of Frenchman Hills just south of West Canal ditch. Under a clear sky in a faint west breeze, I was setting a hundred siphon tubes on a field of dry red beans. Once the ditchrider releases water from the canal into our ditch we've paid for it. We use it or it flows away. The tubes siphon water from our ditch over its side to the field. You immerse a tube—four feet long, two inch diameter—and flip the outlet end lower while pumping the intake until water flows. I'd arrived about nine and had set twenty.

A little before ten I was bent over setting a siphon when over my shoulder I saw a broad gray cloud low in the southwest sky twenty miles away. A duststorm. I hustled to set tubes. A quarter hour later I felt sprinkles on my arms and hands, light-gray sand grains slanting down from the southwest. The coming cloud stretched from north horizon to south like someone drawing a gray woolen blanket over. It's base was up more than 3000 feet, its leading edge five miles west, the field growing dim. It came much faster than the faint ground breeze.

I set tubes fast as the darkgray blanket pulled over eastward. The sand sprinkled heavier. About 10:40 my cousin raced up in his pickup and said Mount St. Helens had erupted. This was no duststorm. We set tubes fast. The cloud moved farther east and the field grew dark. When we finished about eleven, the cloud edge was thirty miles east, only a crescent of blue sky to the northeast. Lightning bolt after bolt struck north in Quincy basin. They were abnormal magenta and fluorescent. The closest zapped eight miles away, and I heard faint thunder. Ash fell thicker but the grains seemed finer, for I no longer felt them.

Visibility dropped to a few hundred feet. We knew the roads but it took twenty minutes to drive our pickups eight miles northwest. We stopped at Martha's Inn at George. Many cars turned off I-90, and the place grew crowded.

After three hours there was no letup. Ash fell densely but fine as flour. I couldn't feel it or detect fall angle. There'd be few cars out. About 2:30 we climbed into my cousin's pickup and crept along four miles an hour, the road edge barely visible. We couldn't have seen a stalled vehicle until almost on it. We came to Quincy about 4:30, the air black. It stayed that way until night.

George Twigg

[Twigg was a Washington State Patrol Trooper at Moses Lake, 152 miles east-northeast.]

I had the 6 AM to 3 PM shift. Observing in my patrol car was Greg, a Boy Scout Explorer. About 9:45 we drove highway 17 northwest from Warden to Moses Lake. A radio call in Yakima ordered a patrol car to do something but there was too much static to hear. We drove to my house for lunch. I radioed off duty at ten. I noticed a dark cloud on the west horizon where storms come from.

We came back out about eleven. The cloud was huge and dark, its edge overhead. Its base 5000 feet up looked like dust balls—or like cotton but in shades of black to light gray. The west sky was dark as if someone was pulling a curtain over. Lightning shot across.

"We're in for a heck of a storm, Greg."

"Yeah, it'll be a buster."

I radioed back on duty and heard Mount St. Helens had blown, making problems everywhere to the west. So the cloud was ash. Its edge pulled east of us; birds had gone quiet to roost. We drove two miles downtown as it grew dim like dusk. In twenty minutes fine dark sand like pepper began falling.

State Patrol radios from Yakima were full of static. Our district office in Wenatchee said Yakima had heavy ashfall. They ordered me to the Vantage bridge forty miles west to stop freeway traffic from coming east.

We drove I-90 west. The cloud was very dark, rolling and billowing. Ashfall got heavier and I could see only a few hundred feet. The engine started missing. In ten miles we came to Winchester Wasteway and a car stopped on the shoulder. I pulled in behind and stepped out in my blue-felt brimmed Stetson. Their car was running rough. I explained this was Mount St. Helens ashfall, it might get worse, and they should leave the freeway. A radio call told us troopers outside to put on a gas mask we'd been issued. I handed mine to the Explorer. "You take it. I've been breathing this stuff and a little more won't matter." In the ten minutes outside, ash had coated my hat.

The air was dark, and I turned on headlights. Ash swirled in the road like cold snow. Near George 28 miles west of Moses Lake, ash fell like dumped flour. The cruiser now ran so rough and visibility down to two hundred feet it seemed we'd not make Vantage. If my car died, two of us would need rescue. Across I-90 people were pulling into the truck stop at George. I crossed the bridge to Martha's Inn.

People streamed off the freeway. A lady came over. "What'll I do, Trooper?"

"I don't know, this is my first volcano. But here you've got food, water, and restrooms. If you drive off and get stuck . . ."

About noon we drove I-90 east. In Moses Lake I drove a frontage road toward our Patrol office in the dark, streetlights on. Two forms loomed barely off my right fender. I'd nearly hit two people! Walking on the road with blankets over their heads covered in gray ash, they blended into the ashfall. This young couple's car had conked out. I got them into my sputtering patrol car and drove to the office.

Most of the motels in town had filled. My wife and kids were off to a reunion, so I took the couple home. "I'm going back out," I said. "I don't know you folks, but you can stay here. Take care of the place." I drove Greg home. Our patrol cars ran rough and radios crackled with static. I extended my shift five hours. Because of the car I patrolled only in Moses Lake. Ash fell heavily and darkness stayed into night.

We heard the eruption began 8:32 AM. But no one had called our office. We learned only when the cloud arrived 2½ hours later.

Next morning four inches of gray ash coated everything. It had three layers. First to fall was dark sand, then a lighter and finer layer, then a thick off-white layer fine like talcum powder.

Zilda Carlson

[Zilda and Melvin Carlson were 175 miles east-northeast.[3]]

About 9:45 Mel and I left the south end of Coeur d'Alene Lake in northern Idaho in our 1977 Volkswagon van, my 78-year-old mother a passenger. We meandered west through small Washington towns and gassed in Cheney. Tired from a late night, Mel crawled in the back to sleep. I entered I-90 about eleven.

Driving southwest near Ritzville, I saw a dark-gray cloud in the west. Over the next ten minutes it came closer and grew much wider.

"Looks like Mount St. Helens blew!" mother said.

"Nooo!" I laughed.

In February we'd seen a total solar eclipse from Hermiston, Oregon. Its dark shadow had swept up Columbia valley. The darkening now reminded me of that— but this was no eclipse. It looked like a hell of a storm. But why no wind? I drove west, the cloud came east, and when close it looked like hundreds of circular globs like dark-gray cabbages.

Mel woke thinking he'd slept till dark. I turned on headlights as stuff started falling heavy and dry. It dropped in front rather that veering up around the windshield like rain or snow. Soon it fell in sheets, visibility terrible. But stopping on the highway shoulder was risky. A sign read REST AREA 2 MILES. I crept along but in headlight reflection saw only fog. Around noon we pulled into Schrag Rest Area 22 miles west of Ritzville.

The radio in another car reported Mount St. Helens erupting. So this was its ash. The fine light-gray powder looked like fireplace ash but felt gritty like fine sand. It was dark, and overhead lights came on. Ash dropped past them like snow. Many other vehicles pulled in—a pickup towing a horse trailer, another camper-pickup. We set a stove in the restroom, cooked meals, and shared with everyone. Darkness lasted all day.

Ardis Bynum

[Ardis and Julie Bynum were at Ritzville 195 miles east-northeast.⁴]

My sister-in-law Julie and I were to drive from Spokane west to Seattle with a stop in Ellensburg. We turned my brother's BMW coupe onto I-90 just past noon, a sunny day. A radio station told of Mount St. Helens' ashfall in Yakima and Ellensburg. We'd gone a few dozen miles when a dark cloud appeared on the southwest horizon, apparently the ash. Over the next half hour we drove southwest, it came northeast, and the west sky filled with gray cloud. Its edge against blue was sharp. As we approached Ritzville before 1:45, light in the west dimmed rapidly. We exited, tanked up gas, and bought food and water. By two the cloud pulled overhead, and soon ashfall began. It fell heavier 2:15 to 2:30 and grew dark. We parked at Perkins Cake and Steak. Ash like gritty snow fell heavy enough to feel on face and arms. We stepped inside and tried to brush off, but it clung to clothes. We got a window table.

I could see a hundred feet or so to car headlights creeping off the freeway. People streamed into the restaurant, soon every seat taken. A lady at our table said they'd followed what seemed a stripe of road paint, but the car lurched down off the shoulder and they barely climbed back to the pavement. In less than an hour people standing were so packed in the waitresses stopped serving.

About 3:30 I walked out to the car. The air smelled dusty. Lightning in the dense ashcloud looked round—no visible bolts, only rolling quiet thunder.

About 4 o'clock sheriff's deputies came. They took older people and families with kids to a church. Outside was black. I'd no idea Mount St. Helens could affect places so far away. Deputies returned in evening. We caravanned in falling ash to an elementary school. Someone at the door vacuumed our clothes, but clinging ash spread inside.

The school's gymnasium held 160 of us. Spokane had hosted conventions, a parade, a tournament, and these acquaintances grouped. The school's cooks made soup, sandwiches, and coffee. The sheriff had closed a tavern: folk who'd thought to ride out the ashstorm on beer came in grumbling. The school had towels and we showered, but people climbed into ashy clothes. Radio news of Mount St. Helens was all western Washington, nothing about all us stranded in blackness in the east. It stayed dark into night. The Red Cross brought blankets, and we slept on gym mats.

Glen Lindeman

[Lindeman was a historian at Washington State University in Pullman, 245 miles east.]

By TV and newspapers I'd followed USGS and Forest Service reports of Mount St. Helens for two months—in recent weeks about a bulge swelling the north flank.

Sunday morning my wife Myrna and I were at home in southwest Pullman on a hill with views east, south, and west. It was cloudless and no wind. About 9:30 a friend telephoned about Mount St. Helens exploding. I turned on the TV. Three network stations from Spokane and PBS from Pullman carried nothing about Mount

St. Helens. Nothing on AM and FM radio. "Isn't this news?" I asked Myrna. I flipped around the dials twenty minutes but found nothing.

I went out to work but watched the west. About eleven the tip of what looked like a dark thunderhead but barely visible poked above the west-southwest horizon. I walked two houses down to friends washing cars. "Mount St. Helens has erupted," I said pointing west. "That little black thing is its cloud." They rolled their eyes as if I were crazy.

By noon the approaching cloud was far more than a thunderhead, and by one a broad gray blanket approached like a massive wave on the ocean. The edge of gray turmoil thirty miles away was sharp against blue sky. The cloud boiled tens of miles wide. It was the most spectacular natural phenomenon I'd ever seen. Wouldn't you know I was out of film.

My neighbors put their cars in the garage as the edge pulled over. It blotted out the sun and cast deep shadow. The air cooled. I put on a jean jacket, strung a hammock, and lay on it to watch. The front moved miles east, the remaining blue long and narrow. Sunlit thunderheads towered over mountains twenty miles east. It grew dusk like sunset—but light in the east!

By the door the cat looked to be let in as at dusk. I got up, let it in, and flipped on the porch light. I was powdered light gray—jeans, jacket, hands. As I lay in the hammock ash had been falling too finely to feel even in my eyes. The air smelled acidic. Streetlights came on at two. I went in again and checked TV news—*still* nothing.

The cloud moved east, and light narrowed to a sliver. The horizon went black—all light snuffed out. About three on what should be a sunny afternoon it was dark as cloudy night. In February 1979 it had been overcast here during a total eclipse of the sun. That dimness didn't approach today's darkness. I thought of Pliny the Younger's account of darkness during Vesuvius' AD 79 eruption.

In late afternoon we drove to friends' house. Ash fell like mist through the cones of light from streetlamps. Pale gray draped leafed trees.

Donald P. Hanley

[A forester with the University of Idaho Extension Service, Hanley lived in Moscow, Idaho, 252 miles east of Mount St. Helens.]

My wife Kris and I were digging shrubs west of St. Joe National Forest eighteen miles northeast of Moscow. We were in woods among sounds of birds this sunny day. About 1:30 or so it grew suddenly still and quiet, not one bird chirping. Up through the trees I saw to the southwest a dark-gray cloud up 10,000 feet, its east edge perhaps twenty miles away. It looked like a big thunderstorm—but no preceding wind. It must be Mount St. Helens.

Beyond its sharp north-south front it filled the west sky horizon to horizon. Its edge blotted out the sun in the south. It came so fast the winds aloft must've been strong, though on the ground among trees the air was still. We worked twenty more minutes as the edge of the cloud pulled overhead. Its base lowered, the sky darkened.

Having thirty road miles to Moscow, we packed the dug plants into our Buick's trunk. Ash fell lightly as we drove the gravel road north. In four miles we turned west on highway 6 into the gray cloud. The air grew dark as dusk, headlights reflecting off falling ash like driving on a foggy night. I could see only a hundred feet and drove 35 mph. Fine light-gray ash like dry cement fell vertically in still air, as if we were under a flour sifter. Each coming car stirred up a cloud, and for a quarter minute I slowed to a crawl or stopped. In eight miles we came to Potlach and turned south on US 95, ash sifting down quietly. Kris said the air smelled burnt. We drove south sixteen miles to Moscow and got home about 2:15.

Radio and TV ran conflicting reports on how much ash would fall and whether it was toxic. The shrub roots in the car trunk would dry in the warm air. I lit a two-mantle lantern and about three went out into black midafternoon. Fine ash fell densely: the lantern lit only three feet. A quarter inch of ash lay on the ground like cement powder. I heeled in the seedlings and went back in. It stayed dark into night.

Next morning was blue and sunny.

Eugene Kiver

[Kiver was a geology professor at Eastern Washington University at Cheney, 235 miles northeast.]

My wife Barbara and I were home five miles south of Cheney. University colleague Bill Steele telephoned around nine.

"Anything happen at Mount St. Helens?" he asked

"Not that I know of. Nothing on the radio."

"Outside a couple minutes ago I heard a boom from the west like blasting for the road. But they're not working on Sunday."

A neighbor later said that about nine he'd heard four or five rumbles from the west.[5]

A dark cloud like a distant thunderstorm appeared on the west horizon about eleven. The gray cloud came east. About noon a radio station reported ashfall in Yakima. The cloud came closer and filled the west sky.

In past weeks I'd been interviewed by Spokane television about Mount St. Helens and now got calls from network news. ABC and NBC interviewed me by telephone. Barbara saw the underside of the approaching cloud hanging down in gray bulbs. By two the light dimmed and birdsong stopped. By 2:30 it was dark.

As I drove 24 miles northeast to Spokane for a CBS studio interview, the sky lightened a bit to like dusk. Television reports on Mount St. Helens weeks earlier ran footage of molten lava in Hawaii. I'd discussed with students how Mount St. Helens usually doesn't erupt lava but explodes. TV kept running footage of flowing lava. Now with the mountain's ash overhead, here's the same thought.

"When's the lava coming?" the reporter asked.

"Maybe never. It's not that kind of volcano."

At 3:30 Spokane was dark. Ash fell like little dispersed snowflakes. I drove with headlights. Twelve miles south ash fell steadily like fine snow. At home about 4:15 the ground was lightly covered.

We had cows. Would ash harm their eyes? Bloat the gut? I herded them to the barn except one I couldn't find. She'd calve that night and they go off alone for this. Ash on our leafed-out fruit trees drooped almost to the ground. I shook off enough the branches wouldn't break. Heavy ashfall kept the sky dark past nightfall. Fine ash tapered off after 9:30 and stopped about ten.

Bill Steele drove over. He'd calculated the time for sound coming from Mount St. Helens. The boom he'd heard before 9 AM was right for an eruption after 8:30.

Captain Rick Myers

[Capt. Myers commanded the Washington State Patrol district office in Spokane.]

In early April a meeting of State Patrol district commanders heard Mount St. Helens could erupt. Just that. Out here in northeast Washington, so what? How could it affect us 250 miles away?

I was at home the 18th. In late morning our office radioed that Mount St. Helens had erupted. Again, so what? It had erupted off and on since March but hadn't come east of the Cascades, let alone out here.

In early afternoon I noticed a black cloud on the southwest horizon. A quarter hour later our dispatcher radioed that Fairchild Air Force Base west of Spokane was closing its air show. But why? Thinking of the cloud, I said to my wife, "Something's not right." I put on my uniform and drove east to our office at Dishman. A trooper radioed that ash was falling southwest of Spokane. This meant little until two troopers came in with uniforms dusted white. Soon ash fell at our office. I stepped outside. The dark cloud had pulled overhead.

I telephoned Yakima district, who said they'd had heavy sand ashfall since morning. We had no call from Patrol offices who'd known of the eruption's great size for hours. Nothing from headquarters, nothing from districts and detachments to the southwest, nothing from sheriffs. For all our statewide emergency communications—dedicated radios and telephones—the Spokane office learned the eruption was huge when ash fell here.

We called all troopers. FM radio stations scared people: The ash may be toxic, they said. It's acid could kill plants, take paint off cars. Late afternoon went dark as night. Our Ritzville detachment sixty miles southwest radioed of heavy ashfall and total darkness, people stranded along I-90. At the Spokane onramps we advised people not to go west on the Interstate.

Betty Dee Russ and Phil Russ

[Missoula, Montana, lies 400 miles east-northeast of Mount St. Helens.]

Betty Dee: We lived in a canyon five miles northeast of Missoula. Sunday was warm and sunny. In midafternoon our neighbor mowed his lawn and Phil washed the car.

Phil: A dark gray cloud came in high after four. It looked like a huge thunderstorm covering most of the west sky. I hurried to finish the car before rain. The cloud wasn't yet overhead when I noticed on the car black flecks like pepper. How strange: I'd just washed it.

Betty Dee: Phil came in and turned on the TV. We heard Mount St. Helens had erupted in the morning. This cloud was no thunderstorm.

Phil: I went out and told my neighbor. He stopped mowing and I put the car in. Over half an hour it grew dark and fine sand fell.

Betty Dee: It grew dark as night. Gray silt fell with heavier bits. Would it damage skin or lungs? We stayed indoors. Outside was silent and dark. The fall continued for hours, and it stayed dark until night. At dawn the air stayed hazy.

Phil: Ash covered everything an eighth inch in light gray.

Captain Paul A. Ludwig

[Capt. Ludwig flew a Northwest Airlines flight from Chicago, reported here in Pacific time.]

From NOTAMs [Notice to Airmen] in Chicago we knew Mount St. Helens had erupted and its ash drifted east. Flight 28 took off from O'Hare at 3:44 PM PDT. On our usual route over Pierre and Spokane at 35,000 feet, we flew into a yellowish cloud and the cockpit smelled of sulfur.[6] Through air-traffic control I diverted to a more southern course. We diverted south twice more.

Around 6:25 we crossed into southeast Idaho more than 350 miles south of our usual route over Great Falls. Over northeast Oregon we saw two hundred miles ahead a small gray pancake. As we approached around Earth's curvature, it appeared larger and higher. West of The Dalles we saw a heavy gray ash column way up from Mount St. Helens drifting east.

I requested a diversion for our descent. As we dropped through 25,000 and 20,000 feet, I flew clockwise on a right bank fifteen miles off Mount St. Helens around its southwest, west, and northwest. We watched its sooty dark gray plume pump up. Despite the diversions we chocked at Sea-Tac 7:54, only ten minutes late.

Joey Lekse

[Billings, Montana, is 725 miles from Mount St. Helens along the ashfall's curving path.]

I worked for UPS in Billings. Ash had fallen before dawn May 19. Several of our drivers called about stalled trucks that wouldn't restart. Our mechanics advised them to clean the air filter and tape pantyhose over the air intake to filter out ash. An eighth inch of ash fell, all day a thick haze.

Billings' schools don't close for the worst snowstorms, but they did this day. Through their Teamsters Union, some UPS drivers agitated not to drive, citing danger. Even this far away the volcano affected us several days.

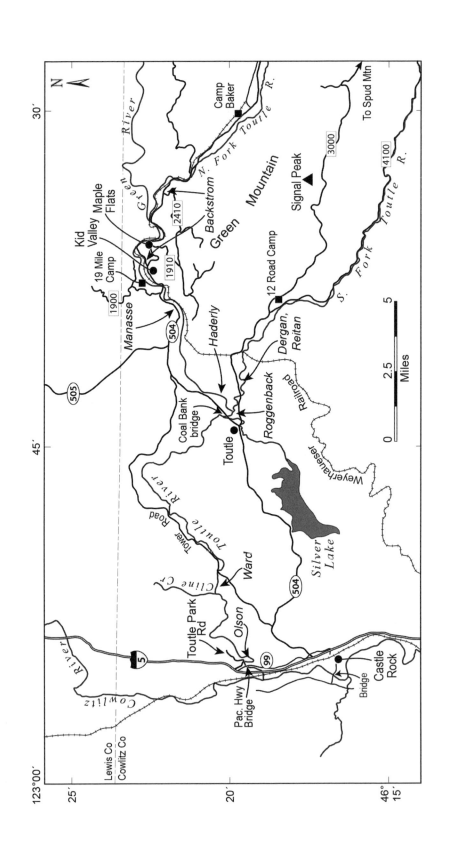

19
Valley

I am the daughter of earth and water.
—Percy Bysshe Shelley, *The Daemon of the World*

After the South Fork flood in late morning, a mud-flood emerges far up the North Fork.

Skamania Deputy George Barker

By 1 PM aircraft reported a big flood in the upper North Fork. Ordered out of Maple Flats, I took highway 505 out of Toutle valley. The State Patrol hadn't blocked this road, and cars were going by. People in Toledo ambled to grocery stores and church, oblivious to disaster in the Toutle. I sped south on I-5 and east up 504 to the Toutle bridge.

Brad Backstrom

[From his perch with Don Selby near Spud Mountain, Brad Backstrom has driven west to Toutle.]

I gassed my car at Drew's store. I paid for a case of Heidelberg about 8:45 when someone dashed in shouting, "A huge cloud's over Mount St. Helens!" Damn it! Selby's getting photos and I've missed it—for beer!

I sped east on road 4100 up the South Fork. Ahead a giant dark cloud broadened over the mountain. But I knew about flooding—and here I am by the river. I turned around and sped back.

I drove highway 504 up the North Fork, this road too low in spots. To reach Selby I had to find logging roads up to Spud Mountain. Lightning flashed through the mushrooming cloud. Near Kid Valley I turned off right—maybe road 1910. Several turns didn't work. Back near the highway I tried again but got lost. I was pissed at missing the eruption and now at wasting time hunting a way in. I opened the case on the seat and drank a beer. After more turns on logging roads I was really lost. I had a beer. I wound around some hours, dead-ending. I didn't know where the hell I was. I stopped for a beer.

In late afternoon I got back to the river now in flood. Trees along the banks were hit so hard dust shook off. Some fell. I photographed mud flowing beneath a concrete logging bridge. Mud, logs, and ice chunks smashed into the bridge; some covered the road beyond [road 2400?].[1] I climbed to a clearing.

Much later a National Guard helicopter landed. Roads were out, they said: I was trapped. I told of my friend Selby in a pickup near Spud Mountain. "We saw one on its side, no footprints," a crewman said. "If that's his, he didn't make it."

They dropped me at Kelso airfield before dark and flew off. A reporter from Port Angeles flew me in his Cessna to Boeing Field in Seattle. At 11 PM everything was closed. I walked eight miles north to the University District. I phoned my dad, and he drove down from Everett. We got home at 4:30 AM.

Paul Henderson and Geoff Manasse

[Henderson (reporter) and Manasse (photographer) were with the *Seattle Times*.[2]]

Manasse: The *Times* called me at home. It took awhile to learn how to approach the mountain and avoid ash. With Henderson I drove I-5 south, then state and county roads to Toledo. We talked our way past a roadblock on highway 505 and reached highway 504 in late afternoon.

Henderson: Manasse sped east, hunched over the wheel looking reptilian. Driving uphill through trees, we neared a left curve when a pickup wheeled around coming west. The guy waved his hands side to side. Manasse sped into the curve "Slow down, goddam it!" I barked. "The guy's telling us something!" Manasse eased off.

The river popped into view down on the right—a sea of mud and floating trees. Ahead the highway dipped into mud [~4:15].[3]

Manasse: We got out. Flowing mud had surrounded a Chevy Citation and a van.

Henderson: The mud lapped higher and higher, eating up the road.

Manasse: It rose a few inches deeper around the cars, then a few more. Three young men waded up to their thighs. Out of the river's roar came deep dynamite sounds— big trees bursting when rammed by logs. The ground shook.

Henderson: A vast expanse of mud raced through standing trees. It floated hundreds of logs, many of them sawed, others ripped from banks. Ten yards out in the current, forty-foot logs bucked on five-foot waves. Through the roar of raging mud came the crack! crack! of splintering trees. Powerlines sagged toward the mud as poles tilted. A police reporter, I'm used to the unusual. But this—so big and violent—seemed from Dante's *Inferno*.

Every few minutes the mud surged higher, drowning the little car six inches at a time. When it reached the windows, the car slid toward the river, turned slowly in the mud-current, and passed from view. KOMO-radio reporter Jim Reed said he'd rented it.[4]

Manasse: I photographed the river, the car, and men wading mud to the van. Twice I backed my car higher.

Henderson: The men still tried to free the van. A man on the pavement yelled, "Get the hell out of there, you fools." Mud flood rose to the van's windows. The men waded ashore.

Manasse: We started west in my car. I stopped to photograph an animal under a log—a bedraggled mountain beaver coated in mud. You rarely see these nocturnal animals. Flooded out, this one had crawled up in daylight.

Greg Drew

[Drew's store lies by highway 504 on the east edge of Toutle.]

The State Patrol blocked the highway below town about 9:45. I shut the store and walked a few hundred yards north to Coal Bank bridge. About 11:30 a flood full of logs swept down the South Fork and under the bridge but rapidly subsided.

By two the river seemed *too* low and over the next hour went very low. By 3:30 the North Fork—always the larger by far—dwindled to a trickle. Something above had stopped the river. The small flow beneath the bridge was all the South Fork, still muddy from its flood.

About 4:30 the North Fork rose and went muddy, and a few logs came down. The flow got gradually higher and faster, bringing more logs. Then came hundreds all coated in mud—sawed logs from the camps, and trees with rootwads off the banks. A garage floated by. By five, logs were stacking behind the bridge piers, one jam building near our south end. Some trees rammed in endwise, then bolted up. After the USGS's soothing talk nine days ago, none of us imagined a flood like this.

The mud and huge logjam rose to the bridge deck. A deputy {*Barker, Dieter*} hollered, "Get back! Get back!" Breaking concrete released a big white puff. The bridge swung into the river. The logs pushed the long deck a hundred yards downriver, and it sank. Logs and mud surged toward the canyon [6:05–6:10 PM].[5]

Deputies George Barker (Skamania Co.) and Bob Dieter (Cowlitz Co.)

Barker: I manned the south end of the highway bridge above Toutle. By radio we knew a big flood was coming down the North Fork. The river began rising in late afternoon.

Dieter: It rose gradually, bringing more and more logs.

Barker: Muddy water full of logs came up and up. It rose into a stand of large trees on the north and knocked many down at once. A military huey, tracking the main front, circled closer.

Dieter: Hundreds of sawlogs three to four feet in diameter, 42 feet long, came from 19 Mile Camp. Big trees with root wads had smashed off the banks. More and more logs jammed upstream of the bridge, and by six little space remained beneath. A few logs tumbled onto the bridge's deck.

Barker: I shooed back photographers, and the deck popped loose.

Dieter: From this south end came loud grinding, and pulverized concrete puffed up. The deck slowly pivoted downstream. Mud and logs poured through the gap ({*Werth*} chap 16).

Joyce and Floyd Haderly

We lived on 55 acres on the North Fork's east bank. An 1890s homestead there had rotted away until we took it down. In 1976 we built a one-story ranch at this north end of Fiest Road on a terrace 30 feet above and 300 yards back from the river. Just north stood our 24- by 36-foot shop-barn and a walnut orchard.

Many in town knew Silver Lake had been dammed by floods from Mount St. Helens and knew of tree wells high above the river. We understood them to have been standing trees killed by big ancient floods and since rotted out. One water well hit a horizontal log 40 feet down.

In April our neighbor, N.B. Gardner, brought us a police-radio scanner. He thought we were low enough to the river to need better warning of anything big from the mountain. How bad might the river be in a big eruption? We attended a meeting at the high school with the sheriff and USGS. What sticks in our minds 25 years later is an expert saying: "The worst to expect is no more than a spring freshet." The largest North Fork flood in memory had risen ten feet. The homestead had stood 80 years before we built. If we thought our house risky we'd have moved to our Toutle property.

We were eating breakfast Sunday when the scanner radio squawked, "Vancouver! This is it!" [Johnston at Coldwater II]. Then "Difficulty on the mountain!"[6] In five minutes a huge dark cloud broke above the trees in the east. In five more minutes Joyce's brother-in-law, Melvin Wheeler, raced up in his pickup. Cutting cedar bolts on Green Mountain, he'd seen the mountain go off. "It's huge," he said. "You gotta get out of here!"

Floods could take out roads and strand us. We had two boys, and Floyd's elderly mother might need help. We packed clothes and a cabinet of papers and about 9:30 drove our truck and car out. The cloud over Mount St. Helens looked like a gigantic slash burn—black, top at airliner height—but lightning flashing through it. Its top mushroomed west but mostly blew northeast. We drove to Floyd's mother's house in Toutle south of Coal Bank bridge.

Before noon a flood full of logs shot from the South Fork across the valley and under the bridge. From 300 yards away we heard the thump! thump! of big logs ramming bridge piers. We walked to the bridge where others watched. It was *much* higher than a spring freshet. "If anyone sees my moose head floating by," I (Floyd) joked, "grab it!" Big cut logs from the decks at 12-Road Camp rode the flood. Many logs and stumps thumped the bridge piers, shaking the ground. Cars lined the north side to cross. During a stretch with few logs, a deputy waved and one car sped across. Some logs passed, and he waved another car across. The flood subsided and we walked back to the house.

In midafternoon a deputy raced up the driveway. "A wall of water's coming down," he said. This house is 60 feet above the river and 300 yards back, but he urged us to higher ground. With kids and Floyd's mother to think of, we left for Castle Rock. The new flood sounded worse than the morning one. We worried about our house.

Neighbors who stayed in Toutle called. They said the evening North Fork flood rose way above morning's level. It couldn't pass the gorge below town fast enough. It backed up above the bridge, then took it. From a high spot before dark they saw our place flooded. Next day people who'd flown said our house was deep in mud.[7]

Gary and Brenda Roggenback

Gary: Our rented home was fifteen feet above the South Toutle and 200 feet back.

Brenda: After news in April about flood we'd taken away guns and family pictures.

Gary: We worried, living close to the river. At the May 9 meeting I listened closely to a USGS geologist and the sheriff. One said a flood would rise in Toutle, "no worse than a spring freshet." They tried to calm any worry we had. Some didn't believe them. "It can be worse!" one growled. "You're not telling the truth!" another said.

Brenda: We had a little daughter and I was eight months pregnant. I'd packed a suitcase in case we had to leave quickly.

Gary: I told Brenda what they'd said—don't worry—no worse than a spring freshet. We unpacked the suitcase.

Brenda: Saturday the 17th we planted potatoes and squash on the terrace toward the river six feet below the house. Sunday we'd plant spinach, beans, and carrots.

A neighbor telephoned about nine Sunday saying the mountain's erupting. Out the bedroom window I saw a huge dark cloud above the trees. On the radio, only static.

Gary: We drove to Drew's store. Melvin Wheeler said from Green Mountain he'd seen "the whole north side of Mount St. Helens blow to hell." We drove southeast up Sightly Hill and about 9:30 watched a high gray column full of lightning. We dropped our three-year-old at Brenda's mother's, drove home, and backed in the pickup.

Brenda: We were loading when a deputy hollered from the road: "Get ready to leave!"

Gary: I loaded an antique china closet and other furniture; Brenda packed a suitcase. The deputy came back down the road and yelled: "A four-foot wall of water's coming! Get out of here!" Four didn't seem much to a house fifteen feet above water.

Brenda: We drove to Drew's about 10:30. Firemen now said water's coming down the South Fork ten or twelve feet high. We fetched our daughter and drove to Gary's folks in Silver Lake.

Gary: In afternoon neighbors who'd stayed telephoned. A late-morning flood down the South Fork reached the garden we'd planted. Ten feet—much deeper than a spring flood we weren't supposed to worry about.

In late evening my brother called. A gigantic flood down the North Fork had backed up the South Fork. The mud got deeper and deeper. "The last time we saw the hill west of your house, the mud was halfway up the road." That meant it reached our house.

Brenda: I just knew our house and belongings were gone. Our second child was due in a month. What'll we *do*?

Gary: Brenda had packed for her, little Mandy, and the coming baby. For me, not even underwear.

Kyle Ward

[Ward, his wife, and three-month-old daughter lived on Toutle River's south bank ¾ mile below Tower Bridge.[8] Cline Creek joins just below from the north, where an uncle had a house.]

Roofing a house in Longview, I saw a big dark cloud building over Mount St. Helens. I drove home. A deputy drove near and bullhorned that a flood's coming and we should leave. Our rented A-frame was glassed on the north where a deck hung out toward the river. The water looked clear and normal. From measurements while fishing I know this time of year its temperature is about 62°F. We heard over police radio that a coming flood would rise ten or twelve feet. Water had been up twelve feet during our worst runoff last spring. I wasn't worried: we'd watch from the deck. But among trees we couldn't see upriver far.

About 11:45 we heard a big rumble like log trucks going by. The rumble grew, the ground shook more—like a coming flash flood. Helicopters closed from the east. The noise and shaking grew. From the deck we watched the front of the flow sweep by—abrupt and all logs, mostly sawed. You felt its force from the shaking and the roar. The water then rose twelve feet or so in half a minute. It came up within six inches of the house foundation, last winter's high. Cut logs streamed by half an hour. I moved most of our stuff out of the house to the driveway in case it came higher. But after 45 minutes the logs thinned and the flood began to subside. It dropped gradually eight feet and stayed there five feet above normal.

On the scanner radio the sheriff said a logjam had clogged Hollywood gorge three miles above us and ponded the river forty feet. For three hours the flow past us stayed the same. A deputy watching the gorge radioed he saw no change. I moved our stuff back inside.

About 4:30 the river began to rise and go muddy, a definite shift by 5 o'clock. This one looked heavy. Over the next hour it got thicker and thicker. By 6 o'clock I'd again unloaded most of our stuff from the house. The river got very thick, like wet concrete without aggregate, its height up to morning's level. The light-gray surface was flat, not rippling like water. I saw no water: it was like a sandy beach streaming by. Tree debris floated by. A car came by, strangely on the surface. A little steam rose. I watched fish struggle up through and flop on top.

It backed into the plain the house is on—like a series of little lava tongues, one every five or ten minutes. A six-inch tongue came in and the sand set up like cement. The next came farther and buried the earlier one. It kept building a deposit. I heard windows popping across the river—my uncle's place. The mud lapped high on the sides of our raised driveway. I drove out a load and stashed it.

When I got back, the low part of the drive was under the wet sandflow. I drove around on a farm road from higher ground. Now about 7:30, the rising flow licked the house foundation. We'd recently put in a new washer, dryer, and freezer. I waded through the mud to the house, the mud warm like our hot tub, 100 to 104°F. Many fish flopped on top—mostly steelhead, five to seven pounders, a good spring run. The laundry room had been added to the south side away from the river. I was pulling hoses off the washer and dryer when the house lifted a little, snapped wood, and ripped from the addition. Mud wasn't flowing into the house, but it lifted. I felt mud bump the floor beneath me. The house broke loose and drifted out ten feet. Now mud flowed just below, past the open wall, only this little addition left. It stayed because the freezer was heavy with a side of beef. On my back I carried the washer to the truck, then the dryer. The freezer was much too heavy. I wrestled it over, opened its door, and dumped the load of frozen beef through the open wall into the mud where the house had been. I dragged the freezer out through warm mud and pushed it onto the truck.

The house had stuck against trees by the river. Now it turned slowly out into the flow, sped up with the current, and was gone. Around 9 o'clock I drove the farm road out in dark.

Roger D. Olson and Erik Olson

[Roger and Susan Olson, sons Dale and Erik, and daughter Collette lived on lower Toutle River.]

Roger: We lived on Toutle Park Road ⅔ river mile above Pacific Highway bridge.[9] The three-bedroom ranch we'd had since 1976 faced the river. Farther back I'd built a barn with hayloft. A decades-old gabled cabin with a huge stone fireplace and chimney sat twenty-five yards upriver. To the north were three other houses, to the south two more. I was crushing rock at Lakeview in southern Oregon.

Erik: Mom and I were at home. In late morning our neighbor came and said a deputy had called from the road by bullhorn: Mount St. Helens has erupted, a flood's coming, evacuate!

Roger: The Lakeview radio operator heard of the eruption and called: "Big trouble, better call your wife." I couldn't get through by telephone. I hired a Cessna.

Erik: Mom walked our horse and towed our boat up, then we walked to a brick house on the hilltop. Many dispersed logs came downriver and gradually jammed up.

Roger: Approaching Portland, we saw a huge, billowy gray plume mushrooming above 30,000 feet. We landed at Kelso. A deputy had blocked Toutle Park Road, and it took an hour to argue past. I walked to the hilltop brick house and found my family and neighbors. Now about two, floodwater still flowed beneath Pacific Highway bridge 300 yards downstream. In half an hour it subsided. "Well, it's over," I said. At three we went down.

Our house stood twenty-five feet back from the bank, twelve feet above low water. Each spring runoff raised the river six feet. The flood had climbed three feet higher but didn't top the bank. A new sandbar against our west bank now held water's edge many yards east.

Toward evening the river started to rise and go muddy. A few logs came down, then more. The water rose muddier. Logs and stumps floated high, not mostly submerged. "Why's the river steaming?" Eric asked. Indeed the water looked hot! "Well, I guess it's not over." I moved tools from the yard to the deck. In an hour the water rose to bankfull.

Erik: I dropped my bike back from the edge. The mud inched up and topped the bank. It crept back onto the flat toward the house two or three feet a minute. I stuck my hand into warm mud. I turned and saw my bike tire in gray mud, and it scared me. I jumped on and tore out our driveway to the road top.

Roger: We threw some things in the car and drove north past two houses and up to the brick house, many neighbors here. Rising mud eddied slowly on an inside bend

150 yards upriver. It carried cut logs, whole trees, small buildings, parts of buildings, an eight-wheel log truck, another vehicle. Farther down the flood was only several feet below the bridge. A house floating high hit the bridge and smashed to smithereens. With every crash two beery teenagers yelled, "Yippee!" We adults were worried sick about our houses. A deputy came. "You'd better get those jerks out of here before someone pounds them," I said. It was nearly dark.

Some of us walked down east to the edge of the slow-rising mud. It had surrounded a neighbor's house. It flowed in the east and out the west through broken windows. Our house sat a hundred yards south behind trees. Lots of popping and snapping sounding like boards as well as trees told me the flood was taking our house. Nothing we could do. We walked up the road.

Randal Dinehart and Jack Doyle

Dinehart: In early afternoon Jack Doyle and I drove from the USGS in Tacoma south on I-5. The State Patrol let us through a roadblock, then to the east through another. Radio static coincided with lightning in a high ash cloud ahead. On one station Jimmy Buffett sang: *I don't know where I'm gonna go, when the volcano blows.* Water in the North Fork was half a foot below wet marks on trees [1:15 PM].[10]

People and a deputy watched the river from South Fork bridge. On the sheriff radio I heard a helicopter near the volcano call, "Looks like an atom-bomb blast."[11] Morning's flood had subsided, muddy water back within its banks.

Doyle: It was still thick. I tied a bottle with a weight and from the bridge dragged it through the flow. It took nine drags to sample the sediment.

Dinehart: On highway 504 we crossed Coal Bank bridge to Toutle River's north side, and drove 500 yards downriver to our gauge, blocked by debris. We measured the high mudline 21 feet above normal river level—highest since the first gauging here in 1909. Back on the south bank we found our overhead cableway fouled by morning's mud and tree litter.

About 3:15 a deputy at the bridge warned, "A hundred-foot wall of water's coming down." We walked from the gauge to the river on the morning's mud but didn't sink in much.

Doyle: We shoveled away mud and pulled tree branches from the gauge's fouled intakes but couldn't clear them. We propped open the well's door and set the gauge to record.

Dinehart: Back down in Castle Rock, people lined the banks. The flood some hours ago had subsided but the water still thick with mud, logs, and stumps.

Doyle: I reeled a calibrated cable down from the bridge to the water surface and read cable length. From this we'd compute discharge.

Dinehart: We checked into a motel. About 7:30 a Portland TV channel reported a big mudflow near Toutle. Most floods crest once, and one had passed. We'd dismissed rumors of a second. But now one's coming. We drove north toward the highway-99 bridge over the Toutle. A light-brown flat showed down behind trees.

"Jack! That's the river!"

"Can't be, just a field . . . Holy crap! Water's *that* high?"

At the bridge we found the river swollen in gray-brown mud. Logs smashed into trees along the banks. They shook, leaves quivered, branches snapped, and some toppled into flowing mud. A crack! crack! of falling trees punctuated a continual roar from the fast center. At one edge the flood crept into brush [8:30].

State troopers let us onto the bridge. We tied a bottle to a cable weighted with a ten pounds of lead. When the flow cleared of debris I swung the bottle upstream into the mud.

Doyle: We got the sample and measured down to mud surface. Four-foot waves stood in the middle of fast brown mud so dense trees floated high, a big one right on top. A pickup submerged only to the hubs swept under the bridge. Along came a house trailer.

Dinehart: About nine a lady asked, "The river's never been so high, has it? It's going higher?"

"I don't know."

"Mud's around my house," she said, weeping. "We got only a few things out."

Doyle: In Castle Rock about 9:30 we again cabled from the bridge. Logs and tree debris fouled the weight. Randy watched upstream for a clearer stretch, called "Now!" and I spun down the cable. The fast river flowed nine feet above normal, its discharge huge.

Dinehart: USGS's Richard Waitt was here, trapped behind the roadblocked bridge *{Waitt}*. We tracked the flood rising on a bridge pier.

Doyle: Once an hour we remeasured from the bridge—but quickly. After 11:30 tree debris declined and the weight fouled less. The mudflow now steamed.

Dinehart: We called our numbers to the National Weather Service, and they reported the rise and fall. About 1 AM floodlevel peaked at thirty feet—twenty above normal. From the bank we read mud temperature—85°F at 1:15 AM. By 1:30 the surface had dropped a few inches, by 2:00 inches more. The peak had passed.

Doyle: At 6 AM we returned to Castle Rock bridge. The flood, still muddy and warm, was falling. By cable off the bridge we found it subsided five feet.

Dinehart: Last night's mud had submerged our gauge, fairground buildings, and terrace beyond.

Doyle: At 8:50 AM the flow at Castle Rock had subsided four more feet and was now muddy water. But it measured 91.5°F. Only an occasional log floated by.

At our removed gauge below Coal Bank bridge we later surveyed peak mudline on trees 53 feet above datum. Thirty feet above the 70-year record. And *that* record was the South Fork flood just 7½ hours earlier!

Richard Waitt

By telephone I find ashfall has ceased in Cowlitz valley and I might sample. From Ridgefield at 8 PM I watch planed-off Mount St. Helens erupt turbulent ash up to only 20,000 feet. An odd white column miles north tops at 9,000 feet.

Roadblocks stop me at Castle Rock. Between levees, swollen Cowlitz River rafts hundreds of logs. Many watch, and cheers encourage a huge log with roots as it rams a bridge pier. But it swings past. Police allow a USGS water crew onto the bridge to measure *{Dinehart & Doyle}*. Automobile lamps light the streaming flood. At 10:00 I time the fast center at 17 miles an hour.[12] The water should be cold, from mountain glaciers and snow, but it feels 60° F. Even this slow edge is dense with sand, pumice, and pebbles. By 10:30 the surface has risen five feet, and I judge the current at 27 miles an hour. It freights many sawed logs, some forty feet long, many whole trees with roots, and stumps with roots. They ride oddly on surface, not submerged. Steam rises faintly. Many logs jam behind the bridge piers. A wooden dock breaks loose upriver and whips past. At 11:52 the flood feels slightly warm, and the thermometer reads 68°F. By 12:30 floating debris is sparser but the thermometer reads 70°. At 12:47 the flood edges higher, almost to the bridge girders. The mud feels warm and measures 81°, steam rising distinctly. It's late, most watchers gone—and no police at the bridge! I gun across at 1 AM during flood's peak.

Along Cowlitz valley I collect ash under headlamps till four. At Randle ash measures only ⅔ inch. Sparse powder floats in still air like feather down. The air is silent, the powder soaking up sound. No other soul is about.

Before dawn I'm down at the Pacific Highway bridge over the lower Toutle. Peak mudline measures 2.4 feet below the girders. Mud and tree litter had splashed nine feet higher onto the deck. By 5:40 the flood has subsided fifteen feet but still a fast gray slurry. The contoured surface, smooth like velvet, is almost too dense to splash. Its hissing sand flows like overwet concrete, rafting rock chips and pumice. Turbulent spots roar like a waterfall, and pointed waves splash up eight feet. A log floats by covered in gray mud. Steam rises 200 feet. At 6:05 the flow is too hot to hold a hand in, about 120°F. So the North Fork flood has peaked thrice: first in logs, then in height and discharge, now in temperature.

At Castle Rock bridge at 7:50, daylight shows glistening mud spread two hundred yards across the Cowlitz floodplain around fairground buildings, but the flood now down within the banks. By nine I'm back to Vancouver. Our helicopter pilot had flown over barren Coldwater II last evening. All hope for David Johnston has vanished.

It's a Totally Different World

Aftermath

20

Land of Lost Content

That is the land of lost content,
I see it shining plain,
The happy highways where I went
And cannot come again.
                    —A.E. Housman, *A Shropshire Lad*

MAY 19

Mount St. Helens spews a puffy pale plume without yesterday's enthusiasm. The lower Toutle runs like hot wet concrete. Fliers squint through dust to a smouldering ruin of forest. People lie burned and bruised in hospitals from Portland to Tacoma.

Governor

Many who died yesterday, says Governor Dixy Lee Ray on television, "deliberately ignored the warnings" and "willfully violated . . . restricted zones. You can't protect people from themselves."

Columbia River

The hot sand flood raged down the Toutle and lower Cowlitz all night and dumped 36 million cubic yards of sand and gravel—four times the concrete in Grand Coulee Dam. It enters the mile-wide Columbia at 4 AM on a rising tide. A sand delta spreading 7½ miles *up*river shoals the channel from 40 feet to 14.[1] Portland is portless.

Survivors

Brad Backstrom: I got home in Everett 4:30 AM the 19th. I called the sheriff for two days but learned nothing about my friend Don Selby. He must be dead. Governor Ray said people died because they violated the red zone. But we drove past no roadblock or sign. Men logged state timber nearby. We were *way* outside restricted zones.

Kathy Anderson: For ten days we'd planted seedlings near Clearwater Creek 8½ miles northeast of Mount St. Helens.[2] Now it's a mile inside devastation. If warm temperatures hadn't driven us higher and south, all 25 of us would be dead.

USGS

Don Swanson: Lon Stickney flew three of us about the northwest where we mapped the edge of tree blowdown. Fires smouldered in downed trees. Near Spud Mountain

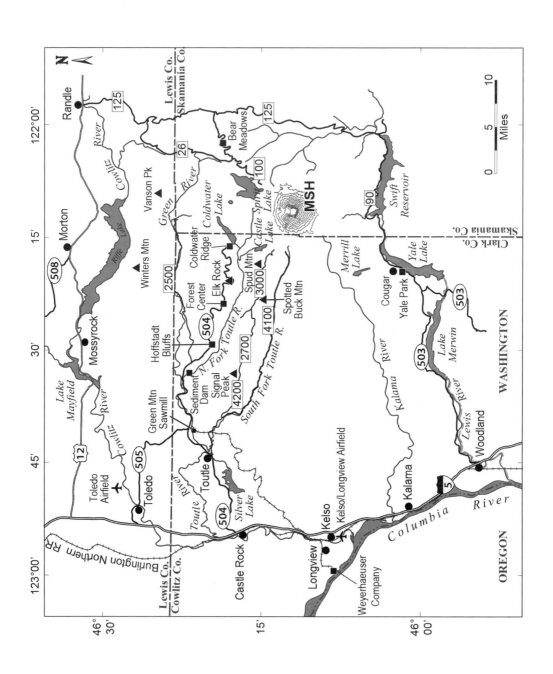

August 1980

RICHARD WAITT

Fitzgerald's Datsun near Spud Mountain, 7 miles out

we came to a burned Datsun. Footprints in the ash led from the driver's door up the road west. Returning prints were wider, someone running. We tried to land but ash blew up. A military huey came by and lowered a guy by cable *{Peters, Mullen, Williams}*. He looked the car over and tied on colored tape. Later I learned the body was my friend Jim Fitzgerald, geology grad student at the University of Idaho.

We flew in air so ashy we didn't know just where we were. In fifty-foot visibility we crept above new hummocks down the North Fork, we thought, where altitude should drop. "We're climbing!" the pilot said. "What's going on?" We climbed higher and higher just above rubble. The ground suddenly dropped away. We'd flown up Coldwater ridge. Debris had flowed a thousand feet *up*! We began to grasp how gigantic the changes are.

We tried to land by a buried car at Coldwater I but blew ash. Miles north we landed at a pickup [Parker's]. Animal trails dimpled the ash, and an elk walked with a deep chest wound it couldn't survive. We flew over what should've been Spirit Lake. It was all logs coated in gray ash. But flat and dark in spots, thus wet. It must be the lake thoroughly covered.

In late afternoon the eruption paused, dust cleared, and we saw a mile-wide crater. Despite skimpy views we realized Mount St. Helens had shed a great avalanche.

UW Seismology laboratory

Steve Malone: We'd failed. For two months we'd counted and located thousands of earthquakes, looked for changes to anticipate an eruption. Then it just happened. It killed many people. It killed David Johnston. We could hardly work.

Weyerhaeuser

Ray Pleasant: I flew company men up the South Fork where flood had buried roads and stripped out bridges. On the north side, square miles of timber lay flat. The air was hazy, the volcano still erupting. Viewing all this Jim Rombach said, "It wouldn't surprise me to see a dinosaur walk out of the woods."

Near Spirit Lake a vent a few hundred feet across erupted at times like a volcano. Dark ash burst up a hundred feet, then white steam billowed up a few thousand.

SEARCH AND RESCUE

By federal law, civil authority like county sheriffs controls military units aiding search and rescue. The Air Force Reserve 304th squadron at Portland and the Washington Army National Guard deploy many helicopters. The Air Force Reserve 303rd aids tracking and communications.

Air Force Reserve 303rd and 304th Squadrons

Lt. Col. Charles ("Bud") Weidman: HC-130 Hercules 14862 holds sixteen hours of fuel and nine radio systems, mostly VHF and UHF. We began orbiting Mount St. Helens May 19th. From 20,000 feet we assigned each military and civilian aircraft a transponder code. Our down-looking radar tracked them, and our radios linked them to each other and their bases.

Dave Mullen: Mike Peters and I flew a huey with Pat Riggs as engineer, Garvin Williams and Scott Denton as PJs. In the upper South Fork Williams cabled down to a pickup with the dead boy in back [Karr vehicle]. All around flattened trees pointed away from the volcano. Riggs said it resembled the aftermath of a 1950s atom-bomb test he'd witnessed in Nevada.

Garvin Williams: I cabled down to the pickup. I found a second dead boy in front. Scotty went down to the Datsun.

Dave Mullen: We came to a Datsun on a ridgetop, its glass gone. Footprints in the ash led fifty yards west, then back to the car. The driver now slumped in the front had outlived the ashfall [Fitzgerald vehicle].

Mike Peters: A PJ went down the cable and found him dead {Williams; Swanson}. His Air Force Reserve uniform in the back had captain's bars.

Dave Wendt: Yesterday some of our ships had flown in deep but found no survivors. Today we'd scour the edges. I flew a huey up Green River over standing green trees. We passed standing scorched trees, then *no* trees—the forest down and covered in ash. Mount St. Helens fifteen miles south lacked its top! For years I'd landed and deployed jumpers on the summit. Now the scene is beyond awesome. My choir had rehearsed Gabriel Fauré's *Requiem* for weeks and sung it Mother's Day. In the throbbing helicopter my bass line ran through my mind: *Dies illa, dies irae, calamitatis, et miseriae* [That day, day of wrath, doom, and misery].

We spotted cars and pickups covered in ash, trees on one. People had been here. Flying east, I spotted orange jackets among big downed trees. We descended but ash blew up. We cabled "Bagger" Harder down to a bridge.[3] He hiked half a mile over logs to them. Another huey cabled down Charlie Ek. Other helicopters retrieved them while we refueled {*Hagerman, Moore, Ek*}.

Charlie Ek: We hovered, and a hydraulic hoist dropped the cable from above the right door. The penetrator I ride down has three folding seats. I clipped on. In the stirred-up ash we used all 230 feet of cable. The engineer couldn't see through the ashcloud and dropped me into downed trees.

I scrambled to the family—Mike and Lu Moore, a little daughter, and an infant. For cable pickup we needed them on the bridge. We'd gone partway when a spotter aircraft radioed Mount St. Helens was acting up and we should move them pronto. A small National Guard helicopter came by and hovered down by the river. A deputy got out, the family got in, and they took off {*Moore; Dieter; Hagerman*}. Sergeant Harder and I in our medical packs, the deputy with Moore's huge pack, fought downriver through downed trees and ashy brush to the bridge.

A bird lowered the hoist. The rescuee sits across two seats of the penetrator. The PJ on the third seat crosses his legs over and straps both on. Once winched up, the PJ faces the bird, ducks through the door, and walk the penetrator in as the engineer slacks the cable. Harder and the deputy went up, and the cable came back. As I started up they dragged me into a snag.

Mike Cooney: We flew over Spirit Lake Monday. Some debris on the logs had sunk revealing water in spots. Pits still steamed off southwest. Yesterday's ice chunks had melted and ash caved in as big craters. Hundreds of little ponds remained. Miles west, Toutle River had cut a canyon eighty feet deep.

We flew off east in afternoon. From Clear Creek we followed tracks a mile down east of Muddy River to where mudflow had caved a fifteen-foot wall. No one there. A giant logjam lay below Pine Creek. Up that creek we found no one at a car trapped between washouts.

Dave Ward: The mountain still erupted in afternoon when we flew up the east side to falling ash. Mount St. Helens didn't stop other missions. We flew to Hillsboro where the sheriff thought a missing boy a crime scene. Flying a search, we spotted a boy sitting in an alfalfa field. We landed, and this was the one. We flew to Mount Hood for a fallen climber, found nothing, and they dropped me at Cloud Cap Chalet. Next morning I climbed a treacherous route to the summit past crevasses and zinging rocks. No sign of the climber, but sixty miles north Mount St. Helens had stopped.

Washington Army National Guard

[The Washington National Guard flew hueys and an occasional OH-58.]

Capt. Mark Edelbrock: Monday we again set operations at Toutle. We divided the search into eight sectors. Media flew with us when they wouldn't interfere. Looking for live rescues, we only tagged bodies. Rumor of big flood drove operations down to Kelso. Twenty-two National Guard helicopters flew 101 sorties and 143 hours, and the Wyoming Guard with us 15 hours. By day's end we and the Air Force Reserve 304th cleared five sectors.

Jess Hagerman: I flew with crewchief Randy Fontz in an OH-58. It blows less ash than a huey and I can land its short rotors in smaller spots. As a Weyerhaeuser pilot I knew the area. Still, we often crept along in ashfog seeking something familiar.

At Toutle deputy Bob Dieter climbed in the back and we flew to a red Chevy Blazer among downed timber on road 3130 high in Hoffstadt Creek.[4] We landed and got the plate number—two adults and a child dead in the front [Seibold and Morris].

A few miles east I landed at a pickup on a ridge south of Hanaford Lake. Photographers shot me circling, landing in dust, then jotting notes by the truck {Wedding; Reber}.[5] Window glass had blown out. Two people inside sat upright [Bill and Jean Parker], the guy's hands on the wheel as if driving, the lady's hands in her lap and head turned as if watching the volcano. Their deaths seemed sudden.

We refueled and searched up Green River, I leading a Wyoming Guard OH-58. Through haze people appeared on the ground—Air Force Reserve jumpers with a family.[6]

"You need help?" I radioed.

"Our hueys blow too much ash," they said. "If you land we can get these people out."

I had Dieter in back. "If they're coming in, Bob, you must get out."

"No problem."

On an ashy gravel bar by the river I touched my right skid to a log, floating the other. Fontz and Dieter got out and helped a mother, father, and small girl in {Moore; Ek}. Ash poured in the open doors, but I saw enough ground to hover. The Wyoming OH-58 now radioed the mountain is blowing ash and he'd punch out on instruments. He climbed and radioed when he broke out at 7000 feet. Now in came a big pack and frame. The OH-58 has a small engine, and all these people scared me.

"Leave that damn thing!" I shout. "We're grossed on weight!" Dieter tries to haul it out, the mother pulls it back—a tug-of-war and yelling.

"There's a *baby* in it!" she screams loud enough I hear.

"Okay!" I call, "Keep the baby."

I've been pulling power five minutes in heavy dust. Fontz gets back in, six people in the little helicopter. We're far too heavy to maneuver in a valley in ashfog among trees. The Wyoming ship had climbed out, so I pull up steeply on instruments.

In the fog I get vertigo. The helicopter seems on it side! I put both hands on the cyclic and force myself to fly the instruments. In a minute we break out at 7200 feet. We fly to Longview.

After refueling I heard Air Force Reserve hueys had cabled up their PJs and Dieter. I landed at Gray Field at dark with ten hours flight time.

Deputy Bob Dieter: We flew up Green River to a bridge where Jess had rescued someone yesterday *{Hagerman; Thomas}*. Just east the 304th had jumpers down helping a family *{Moore; Ek}*. It was too far to the bridge where they could cable them up.

Jess held power with one skid down, and I got out. Mike and Lu Moore and a child climbed in, then pulled in a big pack. I yanked back. We couldn't hear through the scream of engine and roar of downdraft. Jess fought to fly the heavy ship stationary. Above the racket I heard Lu scream: "A baby's in the pack." I let her have it. We clamped the doors, and Jess flew off.

We clambered across trees, I with Moore's big pack. Each log crawled under dropped ash. An hour's hard going brought us to the bridge. A 304th huey hovered high but stirred up a cloud. It took a minute to wind Harder and me on a penetrator up 200 feet through dust.

Mike Moore: We awoke to a sunny morning but everything coated in gray. We made breakfast, struck camp, hiked down west, and came to the huge area of fallen old-growth. We inched through ash atop big logs over gullies ten and twenty feet down.

About noon an Air Force Reserve helicopter spotted Lu's and Bonnie's orange coats *{Wendt}*. Paramedic Rick Harder came down on a cable, then another *{Ek}*. They were surprised we were alive—and with a three-month old! A huey trying to lower a cable raised too much ash. It was too slow across trees to the bridge, so we hiked south to Green River.

A small Guard helicopter hovered down *{Hagerman, Dieter}*. A deputy climbed out, we got in, and in came Lu's pack. In the engine's scream an argument erupted until the deputy realized the pack held Terra Dawn.

I donned a headset, and we started up in ashfog. The pilot told his crewchief he didn't know which way was up but trusted the gauges. We broke above cloud. Out the left, Mount St. Helens had no top! And a huge crater opened north!

Charlie Ek took photos with my camera. They show Rich Harder and Bob Dieter, legs out in opposite directions, riding the cable up to the helicopter *{Ek, Dieter}*.

Deputy Bob Dieter: Later from the OH-58 I photographed two Catepillar D8 bulldozers tipped on their sides on the southeast of Elk Rock. A D8 weighs 70,000 pounds, center of gravity low. Yet ten miles out the eruption tipped over two of them. We landed near the summit by an overturned truck on road 3540 [Arlene Edwards']. We found no one and no tracks.

George Wedding: I again boarded Capt. Stebner's huey, paired with a small helicopter. In haze we came to a pickup on a ridge. Out an open door I looked through a telephoto lens, monotone gray floating by. The lens landed on the truck and maybe the forms of people. Good god, did I just see bodies? The other helicopter landed in a dust cloud *{Hagerman}*. I photographed the pilot dashing to the truck. Two dead in the cab, he radioed.

That night I developed film in an AP lab and sent facsimile prints. The *San Jose Mercury* and *San Jose News* ran front-page photos.

Jess Hagerman in National Guard OH-58 at Parker pickup on ridge above Hanaford Lake

Cowlitz County Sheriff

Deputy Ben Bena: The Air Force Reserve 304th telephoned. "We're pulling out," Major Mike Peters said. "The National Guard tries to boss everyone. They've too many helicopters in the valley in fog. There'll be a collision."

"But you're the ones we know."

"We could stay in some capacity, but not if run like yesterday."

The 304th flew from south of Mount St. Helens—away from the National Guard.

I taped mylar to my copy of Crandell's map. People came with imagined locations of missing friends. State DES and the US Forest Service called in locations, our deputies some from the Guard and the 304th. I plotted the most certain on the map.

Columbia Helicopters

Dwight Reber: *National Geographic's* Rowe Findley and photographer Ralph Perry climbed into the Hughes, and I flew up the North Fork in haze. We came to a National Guard OH-58 and huey flying near a pickup [Parkers] with a ripped-open camper *{Hagerman; Wedding}.* Ralph photographed the landing in dust, then the pilot by the pickup.

We flew to Kelso. A National Guard huey readied to fly the governor. But they'd not flown to Spirit Lake and worried about flying her in fog. Findley convinced her about a pilot who'd flown *National Geographic* for weeks in bad weather and was just now back from Spirit Lake.

Dixy Lee Ray climbed into the front of my Hughes, her State Patrol guard into the back. I flew up the Cowlitz, Toutle, and North Fork, keeping the mud destruction to their right. Then over downed forest. On the intercom all their talk was about politics and money. How bad it would be *politically,* the governor said, to restrict Kelso or Longview. "The people would never forgive me. I won't have their votes in fall." I heard every word.

I flew them past Coldwater I and its buried car and to filled Spirit Lake. Visibility was far below FAA minimums, yet I flew the governor! Several times I radioed the control C-130. I dropped them back at Kelso.

Olympia

In evening the governor receives a telegram from the fire department of Noonan in North Dakota:

```
we have ash falling on us from your mount saint helen
will extinguish the fire for you when visibility improves
```

MAY 20

. . . how paradoxical it is to seek in reality for the pictures that are
stored in one's memory. The reality I had known no longer existed.
—Marcel Proust, *Swann's Way*

Flying

Richard Waitt: A dawn surveillance flight finds the eruption over and dust cleared, a first view of the whole devastation. Barren gray ash in place of darkgreen forest. Flattened conifers radiate from north of the volcano as if by a nuclear bomb. I map the east edge of blowdown running miles across ridge and valley and turning north—mirror-image of the west edge Swanson and Moore mapped yesterday. Coldwater II looks absurdly close, a shorn ridge not even halfway to the edge of desolation. David Johnston had no chance.

In the terrible panorama the geologist in me sees raw beauty. Millions of big trees are down; behind cliffs stand broken snags. A lumpy landslide reaches far down the North Fork. Ashy logs cover Spirit Lake. On a topographic map I sketch its new shoreline: two hundred feet above the old. Truman's lodge and Harmony Falls Lodge lie submerged. Realities we'd known no longer exist.

Dwight Reber: I flew Rowe Findley and Ralph Perry in clear air. Ralph photographed the Volvo at Coldwater I.[7]

George Wedding: The media had organized: pool people would share photos. But National Guard Captain Stebner was comfortable with me. We were about to fly when a media army marched onto the field.

"There's trouble," I said. "I'll get out."

"No no," he said. "You stay."

Someone outside shouted, "We agreed a pool guy'd go."

"As aircraft commander I determine who's on," Stebner said. "Wedding stays." *National Geographic* freelancer Jim Sugar then boarded.

We flew miles over leveled forest and came to a pickup covered with gray ash. In its bed lay a young boy face up, perhaps naked, certainly dead. The intercom went quiet, everyone shocked by the scene. Unlike Dias crouched on the log, unlike the couple inside the pickup, this kid was in the open, coated in ash. Yet it looked serene, like a boy sleeping.

The rear doors rolled back and the pilots put the truck on one side for Jim Sugar, then on the other for me. I shot through a 300-mm telephoto, hard to align and focus, most shots a little unfocused or blurred by motion. But one looking steeply down I thought steady with spot-on focus. The top of the photo shows violence, big trees down and splintered. The lower half seems a contrast, a boy peacefully asleep. But when you realize he's dead, the two halves converge and correlate. I'll never forget this scene.

We turned west. Our standard was not to publish an image of an identifiable body—especially not without calling kin. I had a powerful shot but an ethical dilemma. I called my office. They tried to track down who it might be.

I developed the film in AP's lab and sent prints by facsimile. The *San Jose Mercury* and *San Jose News* made a hard decision and ran a front-page graphic of death. The boy's grandparents near Santa Clara saw our newspaper. They telephoned their daughter Barbara Karr, and now she knew about her family.[8]

Air Force Reserve Squadrons

Master Sgt. Bill Kratch (303rd): I'd converted a 1978 CJ5 Jeep to a command-and-control platform, callsign Rescue 621. Its trailer held generators, gasoline, a spare of every radio, tools, tents and sleeping gear, food and water to sustain two people ten days. The Jeep's mast raised two Yagi satellite antennae 24 feet. A bracket held a 32-foot HF whip antenna, the roof several VHF and UHF antennae. Inside were eleven radio systems: UHF, low-band VHF-FM, high-band VHF-FM, HF, Civil Air Patrol and amateur-radio transceivers, and channels 3 and 4 on military ATS-3 satellite that could patch to telephones. I controlled them by console on a 211-foot cable. I could connect any radio system to any other or a telephone. A C-130 flew the Jeep to Portland. Early the 20th I set up at Yale Lake near Mount St. Helens with Maj. Bill Peden of the 304th.

Local sheriffs task us military units to assist. Our orbiting HC-130 Hercules controlled air traffic *{Weidman}*. Through the national coordinator in Illinois, the state requested deputy Ben Bena as overall search-and-rescue coordinator. He came to Yale Lake. Through the Hercules, Rescue 621 reached all military and civilian units near Mount St. Helens.

Mike Peters (304th): I copiloted a huey returning to cars we'd searched yesterday. The best landing site was a wide switchback. A spring wetting the road should keep ash down. As the pilot hovered down I held my left door ajar to watch for obstacles, and the PJs rolled back the big doors. Ash poured in suddenly too thick to see the instruments. The pilot dumped us twenty feet to the ground, a very hard landing that spread the skids. The transmission is held on by only four bolts, and the PJs didn't want to fly. But the engineer checked it, and we flew back to base.

Washington Army National Guard

Chuck Nole: In my VIP huey I flew press people from Kelso [7:30 AM][9] to Spirit Lake and back. Paired with a gunship, we then flew via Green River to Camp Murray for the Guard's Adjutant, Lt. General Bob Collins, then to Olympia for Governor Ray.

From Kelso [1:55 PM] the helicopters flew over Toutle and up the South Fork 2500 feet above terrain. We turned north across the divide. The governor saw the stunted mountain and crater, Spirit Lake full of logs, bare ridges and moonscape in the upper North Fork. We flew down over the havoc from Sunday's flood.

When the governor got out at Kelso the other huey landed so close it dusted her. General Collins raged and swore how he'd fire the pilot—this former Air Force pilot chewing out the Army.

Cowlitz Deputy Bob Dieter: I flew with Hagerman in an OH-58. We again landed by the Blazer trapped in falling trees in Hoffstadt Creek where two adults and a child had been found dead *{Walters; Hoblitt; Hagerman}*. The detachable top was blown off, the glass gone. The guy sat left as if driving—arm on the door, right hand on the wheel. The woman was turned back pointing toward the volcano. Behind a folded-down rear seat we found a second child. So four fatalities here [Seibold-Morris].

Jess Hagerman: In evening I flew up Green River to Ryan Lake, to a van and a pickup coated in ash.[10] Footprints and an empty beer can showed that after the ashfall someone hiked to the pickup then continued east. I wiped off an ashy license plate and wrote the number. We took off, but now it was dark. I later learned someone found the other end of the prints: the guy lay on the road in a sleeping bag, dead [Clyde Croft].

Capt. Mark Edelbrock: By day's end all leads had been checked and six of eight search sectors cleared. Ten National Guard helicopters flew 139 sorties and 51 hours, and Wyoming Guard helicopters flew 20 hours. Eighteen known bodies to extract.

Cowlitz County Sheriff

Deputy Ben Bena: The Air Force Reserve flew from Yale Lake on the south, and hueys of the Army 3rd Squadron of the 5th Cavalry assisted Lewis County on the north. The sheriffs needed overall control. I joined Bill Kratch at Yale Lake. Through the C-130 his high-tech Jeep reached all Air Force Reserve, Army, and National Guard aircraft near Mount St. Helens. I unrolled my big map on a park bench and plotted sites of victims radioed in. Yale Lake couldn't be a base, Kelso airfield also too small. A Lewis County deputy came and we decided on Toledo airfield in his county. Sheriffs Wiester, Nelson, and Closner concurred.

The Governor

Governor Ray steps off the National Guard helicopter from Mount St. Helens. "I feel like I'm back from the moon," she says, "hundreds of homes off their foundations and crushed."[11]

MAY 21–24

Cowlitz County Sheriff and Air Force Reserve 303rd

Ben Bena (Cowlitz County): Rainy May 21 three counties combine operations at Toledo airfield. When I arrive 7 AM, a National Guard sergeant holds the suitable space on the end of a hanger.

"I secured this for the Guard," he declares, squaring his shoulders.

"Look, sonny, it's *we*, civil authority, who are in charge. This is where we set up."

He backs off: "Ah . . . can we have a desk?"

"Take that one by the door. But this operation is civilian."

April's contingency plan charged the Forest Service with operations. But they'll not come to Toledo. The sheriffs take control. The President's declaration of disaster gives the U.S. Army authority. An Army colonel flies in wanting a large area away from the National Guard. It'll be south of the runway by their morgue and refrigerator trucks. The FAA hauls a mobile control tower from Boeing field. The Red Cross erects a Quonset hut for meals. The Salvation Army brings a trailer to serve lunches. The Grange and other volunteers staff them. I hang the big map and plot missing-person data. An Army major deals with media and families of victims. Joint press releases continue through the Forest Service.

Bill Kratch (AFR 303rd): Ben Bena delegated me aerial operations. I raised the mast on the command Jeep, aimed the ATS satellite antennae, and mounted the HF antenna. I powered up the radios and I strung the console cable into the hanger.

At 10:30 PM a phone call came through the ATS satellite. White House communications said the President would fly at Mount St. Helens tomorrow. "Can you support him?"

"Well, here's what I have," I said, and explained Rescue 621's eleven interconnected radios and satellite communications. "Want a demonstration?"

"Yes."

"How about the FAA tower?"

I set switches in the Jeep. From the tower the signal went by UHF radio to Rescue 621, switched through the transmitting Yagi antenna to ATS-3 satellite, bounced to GE-1 Research in Schenectady, and on by priority telephone to the White House. The return path is the same except through the receiving Yagi. White House communications and FAA's remote tower talked back and forth clearly. So with Rescue 621 and the orbiting Hercules, the President could communicate tomorrow while flying.

President Jimmy Carter

In the primaries President Carter and Ronald Reagan emerge as shoo-in candidates for November. But several disasters have beleaguered the President. In March 1979 radioactive steam drifted from a partial meltdown of Three Mile Island nuclear plant in Pennsylvania and for months came outcry against federal regulators. Islamic revolutionists stormed the American embassy in Iran in November. Critical of the President's risky plan to rescue hostage diplomats, Secretary of State Cyrus Vance resigned a month ago. During the attempt three days later a sandstorm crashed helicopters and killed eight servicemen. Race riots in Miami last weekend left 14 dead and 200 injured. This morning the President declares a state of emergency at PCB-contaminated Love Canal at Niagara Falls and orders its residents evacuated. In afternoon he declares Washington State a disaster area and boards Air Force One for Mount St. Helens.

Washington State Patrol

Capt. Dick Swier: I flew Governor Ray from Olympia. President Carter landed at the National Guard Air Base at Portland. He stepped onto the tarmac and shook hands with Oregon Governor Vic Atiyeh and Governor Ray [6:35 PM].[12] A motorcade took them to Vancouver [6:47].

Vancouver

President Carter and entourage—17 cars, 14 motorcycles—come to the Federal Building [7:04]. Uniformed and plainclothes officers galore: Secret Service, Washington State Patrol, Oregon State Police, Vancouver and Portland city police, Clark County sheriff's deputies, SWAT teams atop buildings. U.S. Marine helicopters circle.

At Forest Service headquarters USGS's Rocky Crandell briefs the President and his science advisor, Frank Press [7:10]. In Sunday's eruption the mountain summit gone, forests flattened, people dead and missing, an explosion equating to 10 million tons of TNT.

The President eyes a map. "I'm aghast at the devastation."

"The most violent Cascade eruption in thousands of years," says Bob Christiansen.

The President steps into a room where rotating drums play out seismic and tilt signals from Mount St. Helens. Arnold Okamura and Bob Decker explain how volcanic earthquakes are symptoms of injecting magma breaking rock, how an increase in seismicity should precede any new eruption, how harmonic tremor means magma flowing into the volcano, how tilt instruments detect any swelling of the volcano. The President, a nuclear engineer, grasps each concept.

Then a briefing of law enforcement—Forest Supervisor, FBI, Secretary of the Army, Skamania and Cowlitz County sheriffs. "How can we help?" President Carter asks.

"National rules allow military helicopters to carry live but not dead victims," Sheriff Closner says. "I've authority to move the dead, but only helicopters can retrieve bodies. It's nearly four days now, and relatives grumble."

"See what you can do about this," Carter tells the Army Secretary.

Into the conference room that comfortably holds thirty people have crowded 75: President's security, Press Secretary Jody Powell, Agriculture Secretary Bergland, Interior Secretary Andrus, Governors of Washington, Oregon, and Idaho, US Senator Warren Magnusson, several Congressmen, aides, Army Corps of Engineers, mayors of Vancouver and Spokane, national media. Many have traveled hours. The air grows stale and humid, "worse than a locker room," says *Columbian* reporter Bill Stewart. President Carter steps in [7:40].

The Corps of Engineers outlines dredging the Columbia so shipping can resume. President Carter asks how $500 million in dead timber will be harvested—

"This is all interesting," interrupts Govenor Ray, "but I'm concerned about the living."

"What do you need specifically?" asks the President.

"M-O-N-E-Y," spells the governor.

"The federal government can't afford limitless assistance," says Senator Magnuson, chair of Senate Appropriations Committee. "Our object is to balance the budget."

"The state has paid its way!" Governor Ray glares.

President Carter leans back as two Democrats conduct a new skirmish in their old war.

Washington National Guard

Chief Warrant Officer Chuck Nole: President Carter came on short notice, little time to prepare his flight to Mount St. Helens. The U.S. Army 10th Aviation Division at Fort Lewis hadn't flown at Mount St. Helens since the eruption. I'd flown often for the National Guard, a flight instructor with 6000 flight hours. Midmorning the 21st the commanding colonel asked me to fly and loaned two H-model Army hueys. We flew them to Portland. That evening behind Air-Force One a C-5A landed with limos and three Marine Corps twin-engine N-model hueys.

The National Guard allowed us long hair, and with all the volcano flying I'd slept at base. I'd no warning before the colonel's call. So now in Portland stands a 36-year-old unshaven woolly-headed Guardsman in wrinkled flight suit and scuffed boots. I face a cadre of handsome, young Marine officers—the President's elite fliers: close-cropped, fresh-shaved, immaculate in tailored flight suits, spit-shined boots. I briefed them that their maps won't work in the changed valleys, and rain will continue. Guard pilots familiar with new Mount St. Helens should lead the aerial convoy.

The Marines didn't buy this: the President's ship leads. We flew a test in evening. The President's flight coordinator, a Marine captain, stepped into my helicopter. We flew down the Columbia, up the lower Cowlitz valley, and turned up the Toutle in rain beneath low clouds. We'd gone a few miles over the flood-mangled valley when the Marine said over the intercom: "You're right. Our maps won't do. The clouds make it worse. You will lead."

State Patrol

Dick Swier: The motorcade returned to Portland [9:00], and I flew Governor Ray to Olympia. Early the 22nd, I flew her to Portland. The President, Secret Service, and others emerged from black limos onto the tarmac. President Carter invited Governor Ray into his Marine Corps huey [7:16 AM]. A flight of military helicopters flew off north.

National Guard

Chuck Nole: Flight crews were briefed at 5:30. At 7:20 the Marine captain in his tailored flightsuit stepped into my ship and sat just behind us pilots. The last man in wore a long coat and carried a small suitcase.

"Who's that?" I asked.

"The guy with the football."[13]

We lifted off Portland Air Base at 7:30. I led two Army hueys, then came three Marine hueys. The first carried President Carter and Governor Ray. The next two held Senators Magnuson, Hatfield, and Packwood and the Secret Service. Behind them three Army chinooks full of local dignitaries and reporters. We flew north down the Columbia and up Cowlitz valley under clouds and rain.

In Marine One: President Carter, Washington Governor Ray, Idaho Governor John Evans, and Forest Supervisor Bob Tokarczyk wear headsets. Governor Ray demands federal funds. She says so again and again. Carter taps Tokarczyk's knee. "My headphones don't work," he grins.

Glancing out the window he says, "I'm amazed at all this destruction."

"Ah . . . we're not there yet, Mr. President. Those are clearcuts."

Chuck Nole: We flew up the Toutle under an 800-foot ceiling going ragged. Visibility usually worsens into the mountains. I lead all these helicopters, just two back is the President of the United States, and visibility deteriorating in a narrow valley. I ordered the chinooks to wait. They went into a slow orbit over the lower Toutle.

The five hueys crept up the Toutle in rain under a 600-foot ceiling. The President saw shattered houses along the floodswept lower valley, the downed forest farther east, then the moonscape of debris, craters, and icebergs in the upper North Fork. Where the valley widens at Coldwater the ceiling went much lower, ragged with rainfall. We flew only 300 then 200 feet above desolate ground. It began snowing! Within close mountains five helicopters including Marine One were about to go IFR. "This is far as we go," I called on the radio. "Coming left." In a wide left arc we turned five miles short of Spirit Lake [~8:20]. You could see the mountain's base but not the crater or the lake.[14] We flew slowly back down.

One of the chinooks landed early. The other helicopters now landed in order. The President held a press briefing.

KGW radio

Reporter Mike Beard: Our chinook sprang a hydraulic leak, and we hustled down to Kelso. We came in fast, touched down, and the rear hinged down as a ramp. I jogged across the tarmac to a prepared spot [8:45]. Marine One landed and the President walked over [8:47].

Beard: "Mr. President, could you describe your impressions as you flew?"

President Carter: "I've never seen or heard of anything like this before. Somebody said it looked like a moonscape. But the moon looks like a golf course compared to what's up there. It is a horrible-looking sight. Mountains are... completely devastated. You can't see where the ground was, formerly. The ash is several hundred feet deep. There are tremendous clouds of steam coming up. There are enormous icebergs, big as a mobile home. A lot of them are melting, and as the icebergs melt... the ash caves in and creates enormous craters. There are a few fires about, on the edge of the ash flow, where logs are still exposed... But there's... nothing to burn... The ash has covered the [logs] thoroughly... It's an unbelievable sight."[15]

Beard: As Carter spoke a Secret Service agent thought me too close and tried to push me back. But I couldn't move: the President stood on my foot! I'd not interrupt him [8:53].

After a motorcade to an evacuation shelter the limos return to Kelso airfield, and the helicopters fly to Portland [9:53–10:18].

State Patrol

Dick Swier: The President wanted to visit Spokane, caked in ash. The governor had said she'd fly over in the state's King-Air 200 to visit with the President. I thought the ash would damage the prop-jet engines.

At Portland Air Base I overheard an Air Force major, the flight engineer of Air Force One, argue by telephone with Andrews Air Force Base. How stupid it would be, the major said, to fly Air Force One and backup Boeing 707 into the ash. He got overruled. I radioed our sergeant at Spokane airport. He described the fluffy ash, calling flying conditions *very* bad. The helicopters returned to Portland [10:18]. Governor Ray still wanted to visit Spokane.

"Governor, it's just not smart to fly our airplane over there."

She argued fiercely. I said the ash could damage the aircraft: it's not worth it. She was so angry I thought I'd lose my job. But the President invited her into Air Force One. And so she flew to Spokane [12:14–12:55 PM].

In midafternoon she returned in the backup 707 with the Secret Service. "Everything over there's deep in ash," she said. "When we landed it blew up and visibility went to zero, like inside a duststorm. Your decision not to risk our airplane was good." I still had my job.

Lt. Darrel Bailey: The President and governor met state and local officials at Spokane Airport terminal, then held a press conference [1:13–2:05]. Air Force One raised a huge ashcloud down the runway [2:17].

SURVIVORS

James Scymanky: Emanuel Hospital's burn center mapped third-degree burns over half my body. In high fever I puked gobs of gray ash for days. I saw Leonty Skorohodoff and José Dias once each as I was wheeled past. Third-degree burns covered a third to half their bodies. Leonty died May 28, José June 3, from burns and inhaled hot ash.[16] Why do I live and they don't? I did drink a lot of water at the spring.

I had weeks of skin grafts to my burns. Emanuel discharged me June 26. Our partner Evlanty Sharipoff who'd left us was found July 9, dead in a tree where he'd climbed above the mudflow *{Dieter}*. Governor Ray said on television that people died because they ignored warnings. We were miles outside restricted areas and carried Weyerhaeuser permits.

It took months of therapy to recover from my burns as much as I can. I'll keep forever the brutalized skin and scars on my neck, back, arms, legs—skin that can't sweat. I could no longer straighten my arms fully. No way could I return to logging.

Leslie Davis: Our grandsons and son Tom went to Green River May 19 looking for our missing son-in-law Keith Moore. Next day Tom helped the county search. A day later he and Dale went in for our pickup. Someone had pilfered from it. Dale and Tom sawed trees off the road, filtered ash from the engine with nylon stockings, and drove the truck out. It was sandblasted on the right and front where the ash cloud bore down on us. Some front plastic melted, but no sandblasting or melting in back. Keith wasn't found. I think he's in the river.

Bob Paine: Mike Hubbard and I were in the hospital a few days, I burned on back, face, and hands. Bone showed through knuckles on both hands. Blisters erupted on my face and back. Being on top, I got more burned than he.

I'd known Keith Moore since 1962. We'd worked several jobs, hunted together. My brother and friends went to Green River the 19th. They found the fishing pole and basket I'd hung by the river where Keith dropped them but nothing of him. County searchers went in with dogs but found nothing. Later our construction buddies from Satsop plant cut away every downed tree. *Still* no Keith. Even after twenty years I'm not over losing such a friend.

Mike Hubbard: My throat and vocal cords had been burned, voice gone. Bob Paine had shielded me some from direct heat.

Fifteen of us from Satsop went in the 23rd. We cut trees off the road down to Bob's truck and climbed down to the river. The huge maple trunk had snapped 2½ feet up and fell just beyond where Bob and I had crouched. We cut trees from a 60-foot radius where I'd last seen Keith running but found nothing. Ash had built ten feet out into the river. Maybe in the heat Keith went to the river as we did and is now beneath the ash. We climbed to the road and drove Bob's truck out. I got married as planned June 7, my face still a little red in the pictures.

I'd gotten my father's old Illinois Central pocket watch repaired and cleaned. The guy said it was valuable and I should put it away. On May 18 it was in my pocket in the ashy water. I took it back to the shop. He found it caked in mud but got it running. This time I put it away.

Sue Ruff: A doctor treated my eyes seared by ash. I feared for my friends Karen Varner and Terry Crall. Bruce and I described our camp to the Cowlitz County sheriff. They knew nothing about our friends.

Tuesday we went to three sheriffs—Cowlitz, Skamania, Lewis—with Karen and Terry's location. The National Guard had known the site since Sunday but hadn't been back. Wednesday NBC televised part of *Today* show from Benson Hotel in Portland. David Burrington had Bruce and me as guests. We'd still heard nothing about our friends.

Thursday Burrington hired two helicopters to fly an NBC crew, Bruce and me, and Karen's and Terry's relatives with saws and cable rigging. A sheriff ordered us to land at Toledo. They wouldn't allow civilian helicopters in. We stood in an Army morgue tent while they argued. Soldiers walked in and unzipped body bags. The eruption had turned a young boy's hair orange.

Bruce flew off in a National Guard helicopter.

Bruce Nelson: Governor Ray on TV accused people killed of violating restricted zones. But Green River lay way north, and going in we passed no sign. Loggers worked miles closer.

On NBC's *Today* show, Sue and I mentioned our missing friends and a runaround from authorities who'd not searched. David Burrington hired two helicopters, but the sheriff made us land at Toledo. An Army huey there wouldn't take civilians— yet only Sue and I knew the site. We stood in the Army's morgue tent some time, getting nowhere. Burrington suddenly stalked toward the uniforms, the cameraman shooting.

"I want to speak with whoever's in charge!" he shouted.

Deputies from two counties and a National Guard officer stepped forward. After four days they'd still not settled who's in charge.[17]

"If you don't let these kids look for their friends," Burrington bellowed, "we'll put you on national television and make you look like the assholes that you *are!*"

A small Guard helicopter landed and let me in *{Hagerman}*. During our rescue late Sunday this is the pilot we'd seen land near our smashed camp. We landed on the bridge and hiked 200 yards up across fallen, ashy trees, I with a pack and chainsaw.

Terry's three puppies ran around in ash at a jumble of down trees. A small tree pinned the bitch. We sawed it off and she walked. When we'd escaped this devastation I thought every breathing thing dead. Now here are four dogs! Could Terry and Karen have lived?

We sawed off more trees. I'd seen Terry dive in the tent as the cloud bore down. He'd put his arm around Karen, and that's how we found them now. A falling tree had crushed them. They'd been here four days, all the more awful. The Guard crewman threw up. An Air Force Reserve huey lowered a cable, in blowing ash we hooked on the body bags, and they lifted them over to the Army huey. We put the puppies in my pack and hiked down *{Hagerman}*.

People criticized our being up Green River May 18.

"You nuts? What were you thinking going so close?"

"It was stupid running roadblocks."

We weren't close. We skirted no roadblocks. Green River was many miles outside any restriction. We came to hike in the forest. Our friends who died did nothing wrong.

Joann Wolff: Jack and I wanted to drive up in the May 18 caravan and from Truman's motor across to our cabin. Had the eruption held off a few hours we'd have died. None of us on Spirit Lake—YMCA, the Berrys at Harmony Falls, Harry Truman, Jack and I—understood 'pyroclastic flow.' I thought it a geology term for a type of lava flow. Newpapers said lava rising toward Mount St. Helens might break out. TV showed flowing lava in Hawaii. But you'd walk away from lava. Truman expected to be flown out before lava came. Landslide or mudflow seemed nothing you couldn't drive from.

But May 18 television showed a gigantic cloud going way up. Wow!—that's not lava. The press then showed the whole huge top of Mount St. Helens gone, trees laid down miles out. They described earlier lethal eruptions in Japan. Now we knew how powerful and fast pyroclastic flows are, and there's no escape. I'd thought myself well educated. Now I felt naïve.

NATIONAL GUARD, COWLITZ SHERIFF, AIR FORCE RESERVE

Jess Hagerman (National Guard): Thursday I flew with Mike Cairnes to Toledo. The sheriff wouldn't let people who'd come in helicopters look for missing friends. Guard operations asked me.

My little OH-58 could take only Bruce Nelson. We flew up Green River and landed on the bridge where we'd found Brian Thomas late Sunday. An Army huey landed a ways off. We crawled under and over fallen trees and got filthy with ash. Puppies marked the site. We cut off five trees. The lowest had crushed the couple. We pulled them into body bags and hooked them onto a lowered cable. We walked back down. A photograph shows the bitch in my helicopter, Bruce and me outside, and a brown puppy head sticking from Bruce's pack.

Ben Bena (Cowlitz deputy): The active Army came Thursday morning in two chinooks and many hueys—the 54th Medical Evacuation Detachment under a colonel. They arrived at eight, set up tents for operations, mess, and sleeping, and were operational by nine. Body retrieval would be mostly Army assisted by the Air Force Reserve 304th with their cable hoists. It began after President Carter's flight. The first bodies in were the conspicuous ones from Hoffstadt Creek, South Fork, North Fork, and Quartz Creek.

The National Guard finally acknowledged civilian authority. But a colonel—in civilian life he owned a radio station—made problems. One of his media buddies in military fatigues weaseled into the morgue tent. The Army caught him and we arrested him.

I telephoned the Guard's Brigadier General Coates. "If you don't get that colonel out of here," I said, "I'll put him in jail." A huey landed posting the general's star. The colonel climbed in, and that's the last we saw of him. This act reinforced the sheriff's authority.

Bill Kratch (Air Force Reserve 303rd): We excluded media from the morgue and from where we extracted bodies. Yet twice they'd asked us to confirm locations and names they shouldn't know. I planned a test with the HC-130. On our regular high-band VHF-FM frequency we held a bogus conversation about bogus bodies at a bogus site. We made it juicy. Within minutes reporters came asking us to confirm details. So they monitored our radios with a scanner. Now we used secure frequencies—HF, low-band VHF-FM, and UHF.

Jess Hagerman (National Guard): I flew to a car the North Fork mudflow had swept from the highway. Dick Latimer crawled in and retrieved a wallet: Tacoma radio reporter Jim Reed.[18]

SURVIVORS

Jerry Wheeler: A logger heading for Yakima gave me a ride the 19th, but thick ash east of Randle made us retreat. We drove I-5 north and I-90 east. The State Patrol stopped us at North Bend, the highway east too ashy. Next day we drove south to Vancouver then east. In Hood River the logger sat in a bar while I changed the water pump. We hit ash on US-97 as we neared Yakima. This south edge grew thick over just a few miles. The National Guard later took me to my truck on road 119. It had stalled when ash melted on the ignition points. I cleaned them and drove out.

Dan Balch: In the Longview hospital they'd put me out. I awoke six days later. Burns on my hands, arms, neck, and scalp took months to heal. I had months of burn therapy.

Brian Thomas: I spent two weeks in Longview's hospital, my right hip broken into fragments. It took years to return to normal.

People later asked, "Didn't you know you were playing with a gun?" We couldn't see the volcano and didn't think of it. We'd only camped in the woods by a pretty river.

Venus Dergan: After rescue from the horrendous log flood I was in the hospital a month. Then several reconstructive surgeries and two years of physical therapy. We survived by luck. We were far enough downriver to hear sirens that got us out of the tent. We need to understand the forces of nature. I'm completely humbled by them.

Roald Reitan: In June we dug mud from my car and retrieved Venus's purse, my gun, a bottle of champagne—we drank that soon. It took 2½ years to heal my injuries. I couldn't run for four years. Even twenty years later my knee sometimes hurts from that day.

We were fishing and enjoying the river. If we'd come for the mountain I'd have found a close spot and we'd not be here. There's no guarantee life won't be snatched from you.

USGS

Richard Waitt: In staff meeting the 21st we pass around the *Oregonian*. Vern Hodgson's photos show a landslide-and-explosion sequence we yet barely comprehend. In afternoon I drive to Cowlitz valley with young Harry Glicken. He'd manned Coldwater II and now mopes because of Dave Johnston's death there. We measure the mudline beneath Pacific Highway bridge: the flood had crested thirty feet.

People in Randle say when the cloud came over Sunday, five-foot branches of green fir fell. Then pea-sized mud pellets splattering the size of a quarter, then dry ash. Most ash fell 9:30 to 10:30 but it stayed dark till 1:30. A geologist studying the ash couldn't know such details, not without witnesses. A forest ranger points on a map where he'd found a man who'd walked down Quartz Creek road, staggered awhile, crawled into a sleeping bag, and died [Clyde Croft] *{Hagerman}*. This one outlived the cataclysm some hours.

We measure ash widely northeast of Mount St. Helens. Others fly into ravaged areas. So begins a gathering of geologic field data. A year and a half later, one hundred thirty scientists will dedicate USGS Professional Paper 1250—seven and a half pounds—to David Johnston.

Medical Examiners

Military helicopters retrieve twenty bodies May 22. Cowlitz County Coroner Dale Winebrenner presides over FBI fingerprinters and forensic odontologists W.E. Alexander and R.L. Shoemaker. The King County Medical Examiner's Office in Seattle and the Oregon State Medical Examiner's Office in Portland later do autopsies. John Eisele of the Seattle team coauthors a summary.[19]

Dr. Bill Alexander: By 1980 I'd identified bodies by dental forensics for 28 years. Identification means survivors can collect insurance, inherit estates, and legally remarry. Bodies were flown to the Army's refrigerator trucks and morgue at Toledo. Soldiers brought a few at a time to the tent. We had dental and medical records for all victims, a lead-lined box for x-rays, chemicals for developing film. Over several days we identified twenty victims, later ten more. Our task was to identify, not determine cause of death. Yet we found most victims died by asphyxia from inhaled ash, two by blunt trauma.

Dr. John Eisele: The uniqueness of volcano deaths begged for details. Medical offices in Seattle and Portland autopsied 25 bodies. Asphyxia by inhaled ash caused 17 deaths and contributed to two more. The gritty powder mixed with mucous to form a plug that filled the larynx and trachea. Two men died in the hospital of infection caused by inhaling ash. Thermal burns caused three deaths and partly two others. Three died by direct physical trauma to the head—two by a falling tree, one by a large rock. Asphyxiated victims may have lived some minutes after the ash arrived. The bodies of four victims buried in hot ash had disarticulated—cooked—after death.

Eastern Washington, Idaho, Montana

Ken Macdonald: I'd been the last to man the Forest Service lookout atop Mount St. Helens, July and August 1926 and 1927. I had a toilet there. Now I'm blown all over the country.

John Snell at Ellensburg: The Milky-Way truck drained my dairy tanks early May 18, then got stuck. When it didn't come for pickup the 20th, I dumped 25 gallons to make room for the next milking. In afternoon a Darigold truck from Seattle drained my tanks. For ten days business in the valley came almost to a halt.

My brother near Royal City [46 miles southeast] had cut and raked hay into windrows. Two inches of ash then fell. When he baled it, so much dust rose he couldn't see the baler behind the tractor. That hay was heavy, and white dust drifted up from the feed bunk when my cows ate. Years later when dust came up at feeding I knew I'd dumped in a bale of 1980 hay.

John McCarty at Wiley City: I swept ash off several roofs. It was heavy and the sharp grains stuck, hard to push with a broom. Our eighty acres of matted-down alfalfa grew for a good crop. Ash on the sprouted stalks wore out my sickle bar in one cutting.

Conrad Boccia at Yakima: Supervisors at Pacific Northwest Bell wouldn't let trucks out without extra air filters—but none could be had. Lines down all over town, but no vehicles. After many complaints we went out with pantyhose over the air intakes. Stuck ash sagged lines over roads, and trucks tore them out. It took days to get them up. We tilled a lot of ash into our vegetable garden and had good crops for years.

Keith Graaff at Quincy and George: The powder poofed like talcum with every step. By Friday I had a flu-like cold. Many here did—evidently from breathing dust. The ash bent the bean seedlings in the field, and rain then mashed them down. But they resprouted, and we had a great crop in July. We had good crops for years, the ash maybe a fertilizer.

Lt. Darrel Bailey, Washington State Patrol at Spokane: Air cleaners in our State Patrol cars soon clogged with ash. I bought canister air filters for diesel trucks, and a metal shop made brackets. I bolted them to the front pushers and ducted dryer hose through the grill to the air cleaner. I rigged four cruisers.

Trooper George Twigg, Washington State Patrol at Moses Lake: People were stranded along I-90, motels were full, people camped in schools. Powder blew everywhere. We wore jumpsuits and ball caps to spare our uniforms. Visibility stayed so low we closed I-90 several days except for food trucks crawling toward Spokane.

Our patrol cars quit running. We taped dryer hose to the air intake, ran it out the grill, back over fender and roof, and into a rear window, all held down by duct tape. It looked awful but now the engine breathed the inside air we did. Climbing in and out of the patrol cars, we trashed them all, dust even inside the gauges. The pool sent beaters as replacements. They'd bolted canister air filters between the pushbars.

Capt. Rick Myers, Washington State Patrol at Spokane: Blowing ash nearly locked down Spokane and towns to the south. We responded only to emergencies—traffic accidents, delivering medical supplies. Thick ash near Ritzville stranded many along I-90.

Zilda Carlson, at Schrag along I-90: Monday was a dim, gray world coated two inches in ash. Take a step and it poofed like dust. Gray birds huddled still and silent on the ground. State people brought a bus to ferry us to Ritzville. A dozen went, but 22 of us stayed another night.

A few trucks crept along I-90 Tuesday. In afternoon a State Patrol car raced in, braked hard, and raised a big cloud. The spooked trooper hollered, "You all must leave! Some of you won't make it!" If they're agitated for this, what'll happen in a real disaster? Cars must stay separated so dust settles, he said. Mel pulled onto the highway where semis had blown out a pair of tire lanes. We crept west 25 miles an hour. Tracks of snakes marked ash on the shoulders.

A trooper in the highway turned us off to Moses Lake. "Motels are full," he said.

"We're headed to Seattle."

"Go north and you'll make it."

Ash grew thinner northwest on highways 17 and 28 through Quincy. Wenatchee had none.

Ardis Bynum at Ritzville: Four inches of ash covered everything. It sagged leafed-out trees, broke hawthorne limbs, smashed tulips. Deputies came and said roads were closed and driving in ash had ruined their cars. We all spent another day and night at the school gym.

Tuesday morning the sheriff allowed us south on US 395. A breeze turned the air white, and we stopped. A Volkswagen hit us from behind. We bought food and crept back to the school.

In afternoon the sheriff let the eager drive I-90 west, semis having blown out a lane. They released a car every four minutes. Drive twenty miles an hour, they said, don't stop. The car ahead raised a big cloud, but when we arrived four minutes later most had settled. In 42 miles we came to highway 17. A trooper turned us toward Moses Lake. Some of the stranded had moved on and we got a motel room.

Wednesday we drove highways 17 and 28 northwest. Ash was thin at Quincy, gone by Wenatchee. On US 97 south we reentered ash near Ellensburg but it didn't blow much.

Andy Lefever at Ritzville: The fluffy ash flowed around our plow blades. So we wetted a street, plowed ash into windrows, and front loaders scooped it into dumptrucks. We filled an old gravel pit. Dust wore out machinery though we changed air filters often.

Glen Lindeman at Pullman: We woke to a land half an inch in ash like snow. Yet it's spring, trees leafed. I drove toward campus. A coming car raised a cloud and I couldn't see. I stopped, hoping not to be rear-ended. The university president didn't cancel classes till midday. Now everyone drove back in this stuff.

Tracks of beetles, other insects, fieldmice, songbirds, and pheasant marked the ash. Honeybees with one wing working left circular patterns and died. The ash recorded life you don't usually notice.

In April the USGS had explained past eruptions and predicted distant ashfall. Many here scoffed—"yeah, right." Archeologic digs in eastern Washington show ash layers from past eruptions, some from Mount St. Helens. After seeing effects of May 18's small ashfall, it's sobering to think of a big one like Mount Mazama's 7700 years ago.

Donald Hanley at Moscow: Half an inch of fine ash coated trees, bushes, and roofs. It looked like mortar-cement powder. A step left a perfect boot imprint. Afternoon wind turned the air milky. The air is often murky in this treeless, windy Palouse country where farmers plow silt—but this level of dust exceptional.

I hosed a planted lawn and saw green again. The grass grew, and the ash disappeared. The 1976 Buick driven May 18 wore out—alternator bearings, wheel bearings, differential.

In 1981 I sprayed herbicide on part of the lawn. The grass shriveled, and there again lay gray ash. Wind turned our air milky.

Eugene Kiver at Cheney: Ash Monday dawned calm and clear. Television and radio stations called for interviews; Channel 6 drove out from Spokane. Afternoon wind blew the ash into fog. Our missing cow had been out all night and dropped a calf. We called it 'Fallout.' The wife of one of my students gave birth late the 18th and named the girl 'Ashley.'

My students drove roads and measured the ash: ¼ inch at Spokane, ½ inch to the south at Cheney, 1½ inch at Spangle. The base was black fine sand, the thick upper part light-gray silt. Rain the 21st compressed the ash to half its thickness and then didn't blow as much.

Betty Dee and Phil Russ at Missoula: Missoula schools close only for the worst blizzards. But here, four hundred miles from Mount St. Helens, schools and businesses shut for a week. There's been no other such disruption in 25 years.

Trooper George Twigg, State Patrol at Moses Lake: Wind blew ash so much a week after eruption we closed the freeway again. I was stopping traffic on a ramp in Moses Lake, ashfog too thick to see the highway forty yards away. A rancher drove up.

"Sorry. The highway's dangerous."

"I've hundreds of cows to feed. I need the freeway."

"I can't let you out there."

"Well, I'm going."

"If you do, I'll have to arrest you."

From the invisible road came a metallic *crunch!*—vehicles colliding. "Okay, I see what you mean," he said. "Maybe the cows can wait."

For months visibility on the freeway dropped in brisk winds. Once when the air went white, I braked to the shoulder. Only when the car tipped right did I know I was off enough not to be rear-ended. At a wreck on highway 17, I was up on a bank with people when the wind came up. A tractor-trailer went by yards away I couldn't see. Blowing ash caused fatal crashes a year later.

LOWER TOUTLE VALLEY

Floyd and Joyce Haderly

ROGER WERTH

Floyd: Tuesday I flew with Portland's Channel 8. On the terrace above the Toutle mud buried our house up to the eaves— nine feet. Elk and horse carcasses lay on top. Big logs had bashed the north end of the house and top- pled the outside chim- ney. Mud had flowed in through northeast doors and windows and out southwest. Our stove lay ten yards away. A big hemlock had pushed the barn thirty yards east.

The mud top set up but you broke in to quicksand. We jumped log to log to the house. Bucked logs had stranded all over our property. In fall Weyerhaeuser collected twenty truckloads off our 55 acres. The upper part of the fill had set up, but the rolling trucks shook the land like jelly.

Joyce and Floyd: The house and barn and contents we valued at well over $100,000. Our insurance paid nothing. In April we'd taken out the maximum $35,000 in fed- eral flood insurance. We recouped only that. In early May we'd gone to a meeting to learn about flooding. The USGS and sheriff didn't tell what they knew—didn't want to scare us. How could the USGS *not* know?

We barely kept family together. On one modest salary—a shipper at Weyerhae- user mills—we put our lives back together and two kids through college. We've chased away many reporters. All these years later we don't talk about May 18th 1980.

Gary and Brenda Roggenback

Gary: South Fork road was blocked. I waded in hot mud from the south with neighbors and a reporter. Below a ten-inch damp crust lay quicksand. We walked on boards and plywood to stay up. The North Fork flood peaked 21 feet above river level. Its logs backing up the South Fork had rammed our house. Mud smashed in doors and windows and filled the inside by five feet.

Our east neighbor's house three feet higher was intact. Logs stacking against ours spared theirs. We drove out two loads of their things and loaded a third. Sirens down in Toutle screamed, and we bolted away. People at Drew's store said a 200-foot wall of water was coming down. We camped on a ridge.

Brenda: In Silver Lake we heard sirens. "Get out of here!" A deputy bullhorned from the driveway. Two hundred *more* feet!—Spirit Lake coming down? We drove to a friend on higher ground. When Gary didn't come I thought the flood had gotten him. I cried all night.

Gary: The flood had been a dumb rumor. Inside our house I dug into rocky sand that two feet down was nearly 100° F.[20] We salvaged the dryer, refrigerator, and a few pots.

Buzz Smith: The mud was soupy for days at our Toutle River house above Tower Bridge. Mud couldn't flow through Hollywood Gorge fast enough and backed into these flats. It filled the house to the ceilings and lifted the roof. As it drained, the roof lowered onto a Sampsonite suitcase that now held up one end. We salvaged little. Acid rusted the few tools I got from the shop. The fire insurance didn't pay, and we had little flood insurance.

Kyle Ward: We returned to where our rented house had stood below Tower Bridge. You shuffled on plywood or broke through into quicksand. Along our straight stretch the flood had been slow at its edges. It didn't fell firs but baked the bark. After I saw the house float away the flood rose another fifteen feet, taking the addition I moved appliances from. The mudline was up to a branch we saw out a second-story window 25 feet above the foundation—48 feet above normal water. My uncle's house across the river had floated back into Cline Creek.

The flood cut across river bends and stripped off every tree. It scoured away twenty-foot boulders from the channel below our place. Huge boulders just below Tower Bridge were gone.

Roger Olson: Our house and barn were gone from the flat on the lower Toutle. At the corral entrance I'd stood two logs, notched for a horizontal log nine feet up. One post now protruded four feet. Five feet of sand and mud buried the flat.

On a bend ¾ mile below—the big eddy we saw swirling at dusk May 18—I found the old cabin that had stood near our house. Its stone fireplace and chimney were still intact—five tons. Nearby lay a corner of our dining room with hutch and pictures. In summer someone found my gun cabinet in mud along the Cowlitz 2½ miles below our housesite. Nothing salvageable.

Five neighboring houses disappeared, others filled with mud. Within 1½ mile up our side of the Toutle two dozen other houses vanished or drowned.

A class-action lawsuit made the insurance company reimburse the house contents. The mortgage bank took back the absent building. The barn I'd built without permits didn't officially exist. FEMA bought our land so it wouldn't be built on. Dredging trucks piled gravel hundreds of feet long, 200 wide and 30 high where our house had stood.

John Keatley: From the Toutle, the May 18 flood backed two miles *up* the Cowlitz. The dense mud rafted steel from shredded Weyerhaeuser trucks onto my farm.

MAY 25 ERUPTION

[Filmmaker Otto Sieber, Michael Lineau, and Joel Turgeson slink toward havoc.]

Sieber: The eruption was a huge natural phenomenon. I'd show in a film what happened. Aerial views of downed forest were fantastic, but for a human scale we must shoot on foot. I chartered a Hughes 500, and late the 23rd five of us with camera gear flew into the devastation by Green River. We hiked south all night in a full moon.

Lineau: We'd film Spirit Lake at dawn and scoot out.

Sieber: We slogged with cameras and batteries across fallen trees. After rain the ash clung to our boots like cement. By late morning we were well short of a ridge where we might shoot. An Army huey landed and offered a ride. I said "no." All our efforts would be futile.

Turgeson: Some of us had had enough, but Otto insisted we're all needed.

Sieber: We reached the ridge and filmed about noon.

Turgeson: But the gray valley we shot into wasn't Spirit Lake.[21] Otto thought returning north too difficult, better west to highway 504. But hiking south, I saw the Toutle full of debris. "This is crazy!" I argued. "We can't we go through that." Otto pressed on.

Sieber: A small helicopter landed and two lawmen trudged up the buried road. A county deputy cited us for violating a restricted zone. We were fatigued, but he made us hike back north.

Skamania Deputy George Barker: We thought the governor had closed the area. Sheriff Closner wanted them cited. In a Weyerhaeuser helicopter the Cowlitz undersheriff and I followed tracks from Hanaford Lake to men hiking road 3500 southwest.[22] I wrote Otto Sieber and four others tickets. Our little Bell 206 was full, and I wouldn't divert a huey from real victims. "You seem fit," I said. "You can damn well hike out as you came in."

Turgeson: We had no overnight gear. When that helicopter flew off, I thought only of survival.

Sieber: We grew exhausted hiking uphill.

Turgeson: It had been an arduous day and a half without sleep. At dusk we stopped at a fallen tree and spread two small tarps. We got little sleep. About 3 AM a huge rumbling announced an eruption. A week ago one had killed everything here.

Sieber: Ash dumped heavily till dawn, then fell lightly.

Lineau: It rained—at higher levels snowed. We had little weather gear. Wet ash caked my shoes.

Turgeson: Ten hours slogging got us two miles. Otto and Michael grew cold. Two big parallel logs had space beneath. "I can't go on," Michael said. We spread a tarp over the logs, lit a fire, and dried a bit. It grew dark.

Sieber: We were cold and tired, one of us hypothermic and hallucinating.

Turgeson: Monday we slogged in rain but grew wet and exhausted and returned to shelter.

Mike Cooney: We (Air Force Reserve 304th) were pissed about having to retrieve this crew, diverting us from victims. Two hueys searched through clouds. After a long while we found tracks, then men bivouacked in downed trees.

We landed a hundred yards away, now low on fuel. Four jumpers waded down through mud. Ash had clotted Otto Sieber's eyes. We got them open with fluid. He and others trudged toward our ships.

The cameraman wouldn't budge, wanting help with equipment. "Get your ass up to the airplane!" Garvin Williams bellowed, a hand resting on his holstered forty-four. It echoed around the hills. "Your stuff's irrelevant! We're out of fuel!" I heard it sixty yards away though the helicopters' whine, through my flight helmet.

Sieber: They flew us to Toledo airfield.

25 May 1980 eruption at dawn from Mount Adams

A Transamerica cargo flight takes off south from McChord Air Force Base May 25th at 4:39 AM. Capt. Ernest Tripp with more than 24,000 flight hours sees the ashcloud but flies into it. One engine dies, then another. The C-130 returns to McChord needing half a million dollars in repairs.[23]

↜

Darryl Lloyd: Saturday the 24th, six of us backpacked up the south side of Mount Adams and camped in South Butte crater at 7800 feet, tents facing clouded Mount St. Helens.

About 2:30 AM huge lightning bolts raked the west. I woke my tentmates: "Hey! It's erupting!" Daybreak showed a huge cauliflower plume boiling through clouds and drifting northwest. I shot twenty photographs. A white lenticular cloud formed at 25,000 feet. Low-level wind drifted some ash south. It erupted most of the day as we climbed higher.

LATE MAY TO SUMMER

UW Seismology lab

Steve Malone: Seismicity increased May 24. Had we noticed, we'd have anticipated a second eruption. Harmonic tremor then rose midafternoon June 12. It strengthened, and we called the USGS. During a large rise at seven we telephoned the USGS and state Emergency Services that eruption is likely. Just after nine it happened! In late July we monitored another seismic buildup and warned of eruption. Hours later it came. Then again in early August.[24]

We scrutinized seismic records of May 15 to 18 but found nothing by which we might have "called" the May 18 eruption. The huge seismic buildup March 25 seemed a wad of magma intruding into the volcano. *That* was the big event. In time it caused all the others.

Weyerhaeuser Company

Hugh McCulley: Early the 19th I'd have been setting chokers on road 4170 west of the mountain. Blowing a day later, the mountain would've killed all seven of us. Hundreds more would be dead. The destruction killed logging for two weeks.

Bill LeMonds: Newspapers and television ran photos of flattened trees. Still I couldn't believe it when I returned to the hills June 2. Almost all trees were down at Miners Creek twelve miles away. It felt a little scary working even out there.

Cutting blowdown was miserable. The dust blew, grit got into eyes and clothes, saw chains wore out. Our heads baked in hard hats, no shade. Rain made slopes slick and treacherous.

I returned to Camp Baker in July. Through field glasses I spotted trees on Elk Rock we'd cut May, horizontal as we try to fall them. Over surrounding miles trees lay downslope, upslope, sideslope in smoothly curved patterns, like someone took a giant curry comb to the forest—a *beautiful* falling job. When roads reopened I drove the 3340. I recognized our cutting site only by the rock quarry.

Jim Nugent: The eruption crossed Green River to road 2618 and felled trees we hadn't. In June I cut standing dead trees east of Camp Baker. Rock chips had shot into the wood, and ash filled crevices in the bark—even sixteen miles out. The rocks dulled our saw chains, and ash heated and expanded them. I usually dull one or two chains a day and only minor wear. Now it's three to five dull chains daily, worn to boot.

Jack Schoening: May 26 USGS's Rocky Crandell briefed the state in Olympia, then came to Weyerhaeuser in Longview. He said to be safe from pyroclastic flow a man should be a thousand feet above the valley floor. This was a *major* revelation. He and Mullineaux had mentioned pyroclastic flow but not so we understood. Mostly they spoke of mudflow reaching 20 or 50 feet above the river. He said an armored personnel carrier had been en route May 18 to the USGS camp. This too was a revelation. Since they'd staffed Coldwater day and night, we thought our workers farther out safe. Now we hear they thought it risky enough to bring a bunker.

Search and Rescue

Robert Rogers: At the Portland lab where I developed film they'd tacked up an April Mount St. Helens shot. "I know that site," I said.

Janet at the counter teared up. "It's Robert Landsburg's," she sniffed. "We don't know where he took it. He went back before the eruption and didn't return."

"Drove a station wagon?"

"Yes."

"Used a tripod?"

"I loaned him mine," she wept.

This is the car Francisco and I saw across the valley half an hour before the eruption. "He was in the South Fork," I said, "very close." Next day I showed the township and quarter section on a map—as earlier to the Forest Service.

Maj. Bill Peden (AFR 304th): A brother thought Landsburg might be on the west near the pickup with the dead boy. In June we flew two helicopters to search. We brought a logger and walked the road to his bulldozer. Walking back, he spotted a tire a hundred yards below. We climbed down and found two tires on an axle attached to a frame, and nearby the crushed body of a station wagon upside down and half buried. We searched up northeast. We came to motor, transmission, battery, muffler. The car had dismembered while tumbling. Near the road lay clothes, camp gear, and Landsburg's body. On the road edge a bag coated in ash held his camera.

Capt. David Mullen (AFR 304th): The station wagon had scattered down from a road. *National Geographic* published Landsburg's blistered photographs[25] {*Landsburg*}.

Robert Rogers: In July I hiked to where we'd seen him before the eruption. Below the road I found his shredded car. A wooden tripod lay by the road. Scratches on his photos show he rewound the film *after* the ash arrived. The flashes on the film occurred *inside* the camera—electrical discharges maybe triggered by lightning we saw strike the ridge above him twenty minutes into the eruption. *In* the car he'd have disappeared. I think he stayed outside. As the cloud arrived he must have wrenched the camera from the tripod, then in hot ash and dark rewound the film and stuffed camera and wallet into a sack. Then he blew over the edge.

Jess Hagerman: In July a sheriff asked about a fourth still-missing cutter in the North Fork. I described the May 18 foot tracks west from road 3100 and which quarter-section.

Cowlitz Deputy Bob Dieter: I searched for victims for weeks. From road 3100 where cutters had been rescued, their partner had walked into the valley *{Scymancky; Hagerman}.* July 9 we searched below the road, a Lewis County deputy with German shepherd "Hauser." On the flat 400 yards west of the road we found Evlanty Sharipoff's body in a small hemlock four feet above the mudflow. His tucked-up unmuddy left boot showed he'd climbed up before the flood. Mud had reached the boot ankle on his hung-down right leg. He'd lain in the tree immobile, one foot dangling in flowing mud.

9 July 1980

BEN BENA

Next day we searched for Jerome and Shirley Moore at Tradedollar Lake 11 miles north-northwest of the volcano. Hauser found Shirley's body on road 2800 by a propane tank where their Toyota Dolphin motorhome must have sat. The eruption tumbled it 500 feet north, where it lay squashed atop big downed trees. Jerome had been at the lake. Hauser found his body a hundred yards north under downed trees, halfway to the tank.

Jeanette Killian: Our son John and wife Christy vanished at Fawn Lake. When Weyerhaeuser plowed open some roads in June, Ralph and I hiked in. Below the lake and bluff I spotted a tip of red metal. We dug and found the crushed cab of John's pickup. For weeks we dug out frame, steering, fenders, bumpers. A sheriff's team searched in July. Near the wreck they found remains of Christy holding her poodle. Nothing of John. At 8:30 that Sunday he'd have been on the lake.

The state had opened the lake to fishing. Governor Ray said and repeated that the victims had ignored restrictions. She just lied.

Jeffry Doran: I and others handling German shepherds that detect cadavers worked with Lewis County. May 28 an Army huey flew us to a pickup on its side near Spud Mountain. My dog Ben nosed into the ash by the truck bed like a rooting pig. Diggers recovered a chunk of meat later identified as human [Selby]. Ben then found a disintegrated dog. In mid-July we seached below Fawn Lake near a mangled pickup [Killian]. The dogs found an ashy human form.[26]

Deputy Bob Dieter: July 17 we searched Fawn Lake for John and Christy Killian. Blown-out lakewater had washed downhill. Six hundred feet down this swath the Killian family had found the crushed pickup among logs. Steering column stuck up from the half-buried frame. Hauser found part of Christy's body. No sign of John.

Below Hanaford Lake we found Robert Lynds' shredded tent, but even with dogs nothing of him or his pickup.

Searchers had found Jolene Edwards' body by a summit knob of Elk Rock. We surmised her missing mother had stood on a knob just south. Working below the west cliff July 18th, we noted an odor. Arlene's clothed body had wedged upright in the crotch of a hemlock. She'd blown 800 feet back from the summit and dropped 600 feet into the broken and scorched tree.

In late summer we trucked vehicles off road 3000. The guy in a blue Datsun [Fitzgerald] and part of a guy at a burned pickup [Selby] had been retrieved. The owner of a red Toyota Tercel on a nearby road remained missing [Paul Schmidt]. In July 1982 salvage cutters found his skeleton under a log on Spud Mountain's southwest.

USGS

Don Swanson: A month after the eruption helicopter pilot Mike Holtsclaw flew me to ashy vehicles by Ryan Lake, one with a horse trailer.

Holtsclaw: As we stood on a downed trunk I caught an odor. "There's a body here."

"A horse?"

"This one's human. From Vietnam I know the difference."

I tracked it south. Near a smashed outhouse, a swelled lump had broken the crust of the ash.

Swanson: It wasn't a round human form. But then I saw it looked flat because of the deep ash.

Holtsclaw: I radioed the Forest Service, and they recovered him [Ron Connor].

Richard Waitt: The devastion maps to 234 square miles, ten Manhattans. I fly and hike about the giant ruin, recording deposits, abraded timber, blasted vehicles. Felled trees show the direction the surge swept each place. The same deposits lie atop big downed logs as on the ground. So trees fell at the surge front, then its sand and silt settled.

A sharp line rings the hills above Spirit Lake. Trees above lie where felled; below they're gone. Rocky hummocks in Bear Cove show a landslide tongue rode through the lake. Its ejected water swept off timber 860 feet above the former lake.

30 May 1980

North Fork below Elk Rock

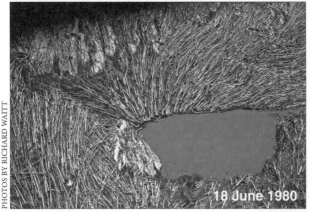

PHOTOS BY RICHARD WAITT

18 June 1980

Grizzly Lake

Metal, plastic, paint, and glass of battered cars and logging equipment divulge the surge's speed and heat. A helicopter lands me by a pickup and horse trailer at the edge of devastation 12½ miles northeast of Mount St. Helens. Glass windows remain, but plastic has sagged.

East of Castle Creek I climb over felled trees to a dented GMC pickup, its glass gone, a wood splinter impaling the seatback, an eight-inch rock in the bed where the boy had lain *{Wedding}*. For all the violence and death here, only 3½ inches of ash cover the ground. Near Meta Lake a battered Pontiac [Don & Natalie Parker] had blown

onto downed firs, a skinny trunk rammed under the hood like a jouster's lance. The glass is gone, paint, upholstery, and plastic burned, but on the ground only three inches of ash. On middle Coldwater ridge lies a crumpled log yarder, its steel tower folded flat, nearby a bruised bulldozer. A water truck lies bottom-up fifty yards downslope.

The glass is out of a green GMC pickup, tail lenses melted, but the body intact [Bill and Jean Parker]. Here nine miles out, an eleven-inch boulder had plunged *down* into the cab. We circle Fawn and Hanaford Lakes. The surge mowed the forest down northwestward, but in the back 200 yards of each cirque big firs fell southeast *toward* the volcano. The surge had eddied behind cliffs as gigantic hot-ash whirlpools. We land

June 1980

Pontiac near Meta Lake

PHOTOS BY RICHARD WAITT

18 June 1980

Flow from volcano (large arrow) circulated as a giant eddy behind bluff in Hanaford Lake basin (small arrows), some trees down toward volcano

June 1980

Bulldozer, middle Coldwater ridge

high on Elk Rock by an overturned Dodge pickup [Edwards], paint sand-blasted but plastic lenses barely sagged. Granular sand overlies both the ground and the truck's underside: the pickup had flipped at surge's front.

On road 3000 by Spud Mountain a sandblasted pickup faces the volcano [Selby].[27] An explosion splayed the bed, burned off the camper, and in the cab burned uphol-stery, gauges, and plastic. Abraded snags show the ash swept through here deeper than forty feet, yet only 1½ inch of granular sand covers the ground. The flow had been mostly hot gas. Just west a Datsun B210 hatch-back faces the mountain [Fitzgerald]. The plastic grill had melted, paint abraded, windows smashed, seats burned, but tail lenses away from the volcano didn't melt. Scorching had been brief and directional.

August 1980

Yarding equipment, middle Coldwater ridge

August 1980

August 1980

RICHARD WAITT

Pickup high on Elk Rock, 10 miles out

And so the deposits, felled forests, and battered cars and logging machines hint how hot, fast, and dense the great surge ran out.

Others

Dwight Reber: Ralph Perry and I recovered the east camera Reid Blackburn had fired by radio. Channel 2 then hired our Hughes to re-enact. I landed Fred Stocker on a ridge steeper than the real site and he replanted the camera. He roped to the helicopter to make it look dangerous. It wasn't. He dug, 'discovered' the camera, and feigned rapture. His girlfriend filmed it from a news helicopter. KATU televised this fake as news.

June 17 I flew Perry and a reporter to Coldwater I. We dug out the Volvo's seat and trunk and found cameras and melted film. Later I flew *Columbian* photographers Perry and Dave Olson to dig more. I'd promised Donna Parker to reach her brother's pickup on a ridge to the north. Their friend helped at Coldwater I. Then I flew him to the Parker truck to recover things.

Dave Olson, Columbian: Reber flew three of us July 1. We dug around Blackburn's Volvo. Even in the trunk, Reid's radio had sagged and warped. Plastic calculator, ballpoint pen, and filterholder had drooped together as if a Dali painting. Doughnuts had baked to charcoal, the sugar glaze still smooth. Digging by the car, we found the radio transmitter. Under its lid lay a notebook, Reid's record of transmissions, the last three May 18.

Jeff Renner: In June I visited David Johnston's parents in Illinois. "Dave had studied journalism at University of Illinois," Tom Johnston said. "He took geology as an elective, wanted to pursue it, but worried about math. As an engineer I told him, 'if you want this you'll conquer the math.' Since he got killed I'm slightly sorry I encouraged him. But I couldn't have done otherwise."

George Wedding: In summer a letter came from Mrs. Barbara Karr. She'd visit the Bay area and wanted to meet. In a quiet spot among trees at Stanford University we talked of families and the media's role in disasters, of privacy and people's rights. It was all quiet and respectful, one of the memorable moments of life. For 1½ hour she held a manila folder. At last she said, "I don't want your photograph in your mind your whole life as the only image of my son." She pulled out school photos of Andy Karr. Despite her great loss she'd thought of me. I fought back tears.

Dwight Reber: In late summer I flew John Marshall to photograph plants bursting through the ash. In April I'd landed him and Michael Lawton to photograph from 1800 feet above Spirit Lake. I flew Lawton there in August. *National Geographic* ran his before and after panoramas.[28]

USGS

Don Swanson: The eruption having erased monitoring targets and instrument sites, we set a new network. From Harrys Ridge above Spirit Lake we laser-ranged the crater floor's swelling, and so forecast an October eruption. Measuring widening crater cracks in December, we forecast that eruption. We climbed the new dome, set targets, then measured its growth closely.

19 August 1980

RICHARD WAITT

Spirit Lake and Mount St. Helens afterwards. Site of Truman's place underwater below the date mark.

Richard Waitt: We land at Bear Cove on Spirit Lake's west arm. The landslide rode the lake bottom to emerge here on the north. Atop it lies a sandblasted strip of planed fir with a patina of red paint, dacite grains shot into it. Mount St. Helens lodged in Mount St. Helens Lodge.

A landslide lump juts into the south shore, close as I can stand to where months ago I'd sipped beer with Truman. "It's heavily timbered through here," he'd said. "Me and my cats are okay." Now no tree stands in miles, his fifty acres underwater. "I'll stay till hell freezes over." The lake won't freeze soon, not steaming and stinking of sulfur, this lifeless evil-spirit lake.

A mile west dozens of cabins had nestled in a forest. Now they lie shredded 400 feet down, beneath gigantic rocky mounds. The landslide speeding through here overrode the ridge just north. We geologists have eyed this place for weeks, but still it still seems a fantasy that rock could run so high.

Costs

Millions of trees leveled. A million and a half animals and birds dead, half a million salmon, steelhead, and trout; thousands of deer, elk, bear, and goat; five dozen people.

Weyerhaeuser Company

Camp Baker and 19-Mile Camp lay deep in muddy sand, 12-Road Camp smashed too. A hundred trucks, rail cars, and crew buses crushed among logs, nineteen company bridges, sixteen miles of railroad gone, 650 miles of road. Fifteen thousand logs washed downvalley. At Camp Baker only six oversize trucks remain out of 28. Through summer, truck foreman Joe Melton finds shredded fenders, a frame, a pretzeled axel, a crushed cab.[29]

The eruption leveled 100 square miles of company forest, most remaining old-growth. A race is on against burrowing insects. Thousands of loggers cut and haul the timber.

Lawsuits

By the eruption's first anniversary, Washington State defended against two lawsuits. One complained the state restricted an unreasonably large zone. Customers had been kept from businesses and the state should compensate them. The other suit complained the state and Weyerhaeuser Company conspired on an unreasonably small restricted zone and are responsible for injuries and deaths outside. Plaintiffs won neither.[30]

Rediscovered Sites

After a quarter century, thirty-foot alders and firs blur 1980s landmarks. Searching for Coldwater I, I find a steel I-beam 55 feet long, one end wrapped like a pretzel. The girder had held the highway over Coldwater Creek. The surge had ripped out the bridge and hurled these ten tons of steel a mile west and 800 feet up. Eventually I spot the tip of a boulder that had guarded the logging platform now deep in ash.

September 2005

September 2005

PHOTOS BY RICHARD WAITT

Digging, I find weathered shreds of tent, twisted scrap of Volvo. This had been Coldwater I.

Keith Ross and I drive road 3900 up Shultz Creek and hike an aldered spur to rusting cables that had guyed his 1980 tower. Here stood the yarder, he points, there a loader, yonder a bulldozer. Ten miles out across mountains, the surge had clobbered them all. He spots a certain collapsing

Undercut made by Wally Bowers or Tom Gadwa into tall cedar 18 May 1980 about 8:35, just before surge burst over south skyline

cedar. Wally Bowers or Tom Gadwa had sawed an undercut into it 25 years earlier. Halfway through marks when an angry gray cloud burst over the southeast ridge. Later at Fawn Lake we study stumps washed out three feet below the level they'd grown. The surge had blown much of Fawn Lake down this gully.

A mysterious eruption photo shows an immense gray cloud about to overrun distant Coldwater Peak. I search along roads where twenty-foot firs now block 1980s views. Finally a roadcurve and hillslope align with Coldwater Peak. Here the photo had been snapped two minutes into the eruption. Racing west, Ron and Barbara Seibold and two children perished as hot ash engulfed their Blazer.

West of Meta Lake a Forest Service geologist and I scramble up a precipice to Black Rock adit, its tip pile bright compared to the aldered workings of a century ago. Eruption-battered powder box, rails, pipe, and cables lie about. Down by Florence Creek we find the rotting plywood floor of the chalet. Bursting from Spirit Lake, the hot surge turned with topography, smashing trees and chalet. Downslope lie twisted toolbox, rusty bed springs, crushed chair, dented pots, rotting raincoat. Natalie and Don Parker had lain in this debris, cousin Rick toward the adit.

High in the South Fork I fight up through forty-foot firs to a logging road dense in alder. But ahead aluminum juts from the ash, beyond a twisted length of chrome, a shredded cable. Here Robert Landsburg had camped a quarter century ago.

Last Account

A fearful black cloud was rent. Soon afterwards the cloud sank down to earth and blotted out C__ and hid the promontory from sight. Ashes were falling, not as yet very thickly. I looked round: a dense black cloud was coming behind us, spreading over the earth like a flood. "Let us leave the road while we can still see," I said. We had scarcely sat down when darkness fell, not the dark of a moonless or cloudy night, but as if the lamp had been put out in a closed room.

A gleam of light returned, then darkness came once more and ashes fell again, this time in heavy showers. We rose from time to time and shook them off. The whole world was dying. . . and I with it.

At last the darkness thinned and dispersed into smoke or cloud, and the sun actually shown, but yellowish as it is during an eclipse. We were terrified to see everything changed, buried deep in the ashes like snowdrifts.

This memory parallels our others—ashy column, falling dark cloud obscures the land, dense ashfall and darkness, a letup, more ashfall, and fuzzy light reveals a drab and foreign landscape. But this isn't of Mount St. Helens or 1980. A teenager named Pliny penned it nineteen centuries earlier not far from a town called Pompeii.[31] The account lies in retrospective letters to historian Cornelius Tacitus. One letter ends:

Of course these details are not important enough for history. If they seem scarcely worth putting in a letter, you have only yourself to blame for asking for them.

Details do matter—all the more so with Tacitus's history lost. If our Mount St. Helens stories matter, it'll be in their details.

Appendix I
Cast of Characters (Chapters 1–6)

Skamania County
William ("Bill") Closner (Sheriff)
George Barker (deputy for Spirit Lake)

Cowlitz County
Les Nelson (Sheriff)
Bill Stuart (Undersheriff)
Gary Waddell (sergeant)
Ben Bena (deputy)
Bob Dieter (reserve deputy)

Gifford Pinchot National Forest (U.S. Forest Service)
Robert ("Bob") Tokarczyk (Forest Supervisor)
Ed Osmond (coordinator)
Paul Stenkamp (Fire Staff)
George Theisen (acting Fire Staff)
Jim Unterwegner (spokesman)
Ken Johnson (Ranger, St. Helens District)
Dave Seesholtz (St. Helens District)
Chuck Tonn (Recreation Assistant, St. Helens District)
Jim Nieland (St. Helens District, assistant to Tonn)
Sharon Burchard (winter guard at Spirit Lake; Nieland's assistant)
Karen Jacobsen (back-country ranger)
Roland Emetaz (snow-avalanche expert)
Eugene Sloniker (surveyor and mapmaker)

U.S. Geological Survey (USGS)
Donal (Don) Mullineaux (official spokesman)
Dwight (Rocky) Crandell (hazards coordinator through May 2)
Dan Miller (hazards coordinator after May 2)
Robert ("Chris") Christiansen (coordinator of monitoring and research)
Robert Decker (geologist; and in early May subbing for Christiansen)
Robert (Bob) I. Tilling (Office Chief; coordinator of Volcano Hazards Program)
David Johnston (geologist)
Harry Glicken (geologic assistant to Johnston)
Don Swanson (geologist)
Peter Lipman (geologist)

Jim Moore (geologist)
Norm Banks (geologist)
Arnold Okamura (geophysicist)
Richard ("Rick") Hoblitt (geologist)
H. William Menard (Director of USGS)
Austin Post (aerial photographer)
Sue Kieffer (geologist)
Hugh Kieffer (geologist)
David Frank (geophysicist)
Dan Dzurisin (geophysicist)
Joe Rosenbaum (geophysicist)
Jim Vallance (assistant to Hoblitt)
Melinda ("Mindy") Brugman (hydrologist)
Carolyn Driedger (hydrologist)
Richard Waitt (geologist)

Associated with USGS
Larry Malinconico (Dartmouth College)
Barry Voight (Pennsylvania State University)
Lon Stickney (helicopter pilot, Aerocopters, Seattle)
Peter Douglass and Mark Utting (University of Washington)
Gerhard Wörner (visiting student from Germany)

University of Washington (UW) and USGS (Seismology laboratory at Seattle)
Steve Malone (UW)
Linda Noson (UW)
Norm Rasmussen (UW)
Craig Weaver (USGS)
Elliot Endo (USGS, and UW grad student)
Dave Harlow (USGS, visiting)
(Dept. of Geological Sciences)
Lee Fairchild (UW graduate student)

State of Washington (Executive)
Dixy Lee Ray (Governor)
Lou Guzzo (Advisor)
Gerry Hanna (Legal counsel and Legislative liason)
Wilbur 'Web' Hallauer (Head, Department of Ecology)

Department of Emergency Services (DES)
Edward Chow Jr. (Director)
Patrick ('Rick') LaValla (Chief of Operations and Deputy Director)
Terry Simmonds (Operations)
Fay Chu (DES staff and attorney)
Jim Thomas (Chief of Planning, and an Assistant Director)
Jim Hall (Chief of Training, and an Assistant Director)

Washington State Patrol (WSP)
Col. Robert ("Bob") Landon (Chief of WSP)
Sgt. Ron Walcker (Olympia, security for the Governor)
Capt. Dick Bullock, (Southwest Regional Director [Vancouver])
Lt. Harvey Thacker (Vancouver)
Lt. Don Mason (Chehalis)
Sgt. W.C. ('Wick') Elder (Kelso)
Sgt. Bob Johnson (Vancouver)
Trooper Russ Cavens (Kelso)
Trooper Ron Spahman (Kelso)
Trooper Danny O'Neill (Kelso)
Capt. Dick Swier (chief of air operations)
Trooper Dave Gardner (pilot)
Trooper Bob Cory (pilot)

Department of Transportation (DOT)
Dick Carroll (Southwest Regional Administrator [Vancouver])
Joe Gallow (Kid Valley shed)

Department of Natural Resources (DNR)
Bert Cole (Commissioner of Public Lands)
Ralph Beswick (Supervisor of DNR)
John DeMeyer (Southwest District DNR [state timber])
Vaughan ("Ted") Livingston Jr. (Washington State Geologist)

Department of Game
Keith O'Neill (Manager, Southwest Regional Office)

Department of Commerce and Economic Development
Don Richardson (tourism)

Weyerhaeuser Company
Dick Ford (District Forester at Camp Baker)
George Steig (Forester; Safety Coordinator)

Jack Schoening (Woods Manager)
Jim Rombach (Forest Engineer and safety officer)
Dick Nesbit (Supervisor of Camp Baker)
Ralph Killian (logging foreman)
John Killian (logger)
John Keatley (Regional Forester)
Bob Booth (bull buck)
Jim Pluard (bull buck)
Jim Nugent (timber faller)
Ed Nugent (hook tender for yarder)
Bill LeMonds (timber faller)
Louis Fanony (timber faller)
Hugh McCully (choker setter)
Bud Tippery (saw mechanic at Camp Baker)

News Media
Mike Beard (KGW radio, Portland)
Mike Erickson (KGW radio)
Donna duBeth (reporter, *Daily News*, Longview)
Roger Werth (photographer, *Daily News*)
Rick Siefert (reporter, *Daily News*)
Brian Drake (photographer, *Daily News*)
Reid Blackburn (photographer, *Columbian*, Vancouver)
Fay Blackburn (*Columbian*)
Ralph Perry (photographer, *Columbian*)
Steve Small (photo editor, *Columbian*)
Bill Stewart (reporter, *Columbian*)
Thomas Ryll (reporter, *Columbian*)
Bill Dietrich (reporter, *Columbian*)
Les Blumenthal (*Associated Press*, Seattle)
Sue Hobart (reporter, *Oregonian*, Portland)
Les Zaitz (reporter, *Oregonian*)
Tim Jewett (photographer, *Oregonian*)
Don Hamilton (reporter, *Oregon Journal*, Portland)
Steve Nehl (photographer, *Oregon Journal*)
Robert Bach (photographer, *Oregon Journal*)
Hill Williams (science reporter, *Seattle Times*)
Jeff Renner (reporter, KING-TV, Seattle)
Mark Anderson (cameraman, KING-TV)
Bob Wright (helicopter pilot for KING-TV)
Brooks Burford (reporter, KIRO-TV, Seattle)
Steve Baxter (cameraman, KIRO-TV)
Chuck Sicotte (helicopter pilot for KIRO-TV)

***National Geographic* magazine**
Rowe Findley (assistant editor)
Bob Gilka (photo editor)
Jim Sugar (freelance photographer)

John Marshall (freelance photographer)
Dwight Reber (Columbia Helicopters, pilot)
Fred Stocker (impromptu freelancer)
Jim McWhirter (Stocker's impromptu driver)

Portland State University
Leonard Palmer (Professor of geology)
John Elliot Allen (Professor of geology)
Paul Hammond (Professor of geology)

Tektronix Radio Amateur Club (TERAC)
Roger McCoy
Tom Hill
Dave Livesay

Valley residents
Harry Truman (Mount St. Helens Lodge on Spirit Lake)
Rob Smith and Kathy Paulson (Spirit Lake Lodge, west of Spirit Lake)
Dave and Laura Berry, and Duncan and Melonie Berry (Harmony Falls Lodge on Spirit Lake)
Harold and Mary Whitney (cabin near Spirit Lake Lodge)
Bob Kaseweter (cabin near Spirit Lake Lodge)
Ray and Linda King (cabin near Spirit Lake Lodge)
Roy and Sandy Ford (cabin near Spirit Lake Lodge)
Jim and Pauline Lund (cabin near Spirit Lake Lodge)
Chuck and Pat Long (cabin near Spirit Lake Lodge)
Chuck Williams (cabin near Spirit Lake Lodge)
Stan and Josephine Lee (Kid Valley merchants)
Jim Nugent (Kid Valley)

Keith Ross (Toutle, independent logger)
Greg Drew (Drew's store, Toutle)
N.B. Gardner (Toutle)
Gary Roggenback (Toutle)
Carl Berg (Kid Valley)

Air Force Reserve 304th Squadron, Portland
Bill Hewes

Black Rock miners
Martin Remmen
Tim Grose
Jay, Don, Natalie, and Rick Parker
Lindsay Thomas
Jim Smith

YMCA and Boy Scouts
Paul Hathaway
Jack Wolff
Duane Rhodes
Jim Lematta (Columbia Helicopters)
Dwight Reber (Columbia Helicopters)
Jerry Koschnick (Columbia Helicopters)

Visitors and Climbers
Brad Backstrom and Don Selby
Bea and Barry Johnston, and Jim Fitzgerald
Ty and Marianna Kearney (radio amateurs affiliated with RACES)
Gerry Martin (radio amateur affiliated with RACES)
Fred Miller
Dr. Peter Reagan and Ancil Nance
Otto Sieber (documentary filmmaker)
Robert Rogers (and with Portland State May 9)
John Williams

Appendix II

Sources and Methods

I keep six honest serving men
(They taught me all I knew);
Their names are What and Why and When
And How and Where and Who.
                    —Rudyard Kipling, *The Elephant's Child*

This story of Mount St. Helens' eruption began as a few eyewitness accounts to aid geologic studies in 1980.[1] Years later while recording other accounts and acquiring eruption photographs, I found the 1980 accounts incomplete and harboring discrepancies. I saw how earlier decades swayed behavior throughout spring 1980 and how that in turn influenced people just before and during the eruption. This book's natural borders mapped out only after years. The research and writing took on traits of science, history, journalism, storytelling—but none of these alone.

Data through Eyewitnesses

Memory is notoriously selective. Primo Levi recounting Auschwitz after four decades: "The memories within us not only tend to become erased as the years go by, but they often change, or even grow, by incorporating extraneous features."[2]

Or Milan Kundera: "After all, what can memory do, the poor thing? It is only capable of retaining a paltry scrap of the past, and who knows why just this scrap and not some other, since in each of us the choice occurs mysteriously."[3]

Yet Michael Mooney reconstructed the last flight of the *Hindenburg*, and J.K. Zawodny a 1940 massacre in Katyn Forest and 1944 Warsaw uprising, considerably from witnesses interviewed two and three decades later.[4]

Most of my Mount St. Helens' interviews occurred two and three decades after the adventures. Recounting one, a witness links clearly remembered facts with ill-remembered parts. The listener records it all only later to find fact alternating with fiction. But most witnesses will reexamine in light of newfound logbooks, photographs, diaries, and other memories. And so we eventually approach accuracy.

We piece together one event or phenomenon by the accounts of many people in different places. But stories happening all at once can be told only in sequence.

I specify some places by township-and-range land grid that locate a site within 200 yards, even should 1980 cultural landmarks eventually disappear. Roads numbers are as in 1980, not as some were later renumbered. Recent Weyerhaeuser maps retain the 1980 road numbers.

The mind can retain visual images for decades, but sense of timing soon fades. To people burned or blinded by darkness, reading a watch was no priority. And remembered time can be hours off. Yet we must reconstruct time to know the sequence of events or the pace of one. Personal diaries, geologists' field notes, radio logs, or a deputy's log of mileage and duty hours anchor some times. A newspaper story saying 'yesterday afternoon' limits time. Sun shadows on a photograph may pin an outdoor scene within an hour. Logs of aerial operations of the Air Force Reserve, National Guard, Forest Service, USGS, and Weyerhaeuser Company time some events.

PRIMARY SOURCES

During the crisis a Forest Service contract aircraft often circled Mount St. Helens and radioed observations to Vancouver where recorded to a logbook. Flights usually included a USGS geologist photographing and recording phenomena: time, altitude, azimuth, color, odor, speed. Historians may bemoan the subjectivity of eyewitnesses, but written records too are selective and few—many lost, diaries and letters self-serving, reports 'spun.'

Science is based in published data that can be reexamined or reacquired by later investigators. A laboratory defines procedures so tightly another lab can reproduce a result. A fossiliferous outcrop is pinpointed so others can restudy the same trilobites. A tenet of science is openness of data.[5] Yet some primary sources of data disappear: the receding walls of a quarry, outcrops drowned behind a dam, roadcuts by concrete, volcanic debris by a new eruption.

An eyewitness account isn't truly repeatable. An interviewer's question can influence the answer. In a later telling the witness may change an earlier one. Witnesses die: reexamination ceases. Yet the existing data from Mount St. Helens' 1980 witnesses shall be archived—interview records, acquired documents from agencies, logbooks, fieldnotes, maps, diaries, photographs.

HISTORICAL METHOD

This work is partly human history. Historiography isn't so different from scholarship on written documents in researching geology and other science.[6] J.K. Zawodny discussed with me his methods recording World War II events based partly on interviews of participants.

Henry Steele Commager writes:

> The record which has come down to us is fragmentary, selective, [and] biased. No two stories of a family quarrel are ever alike; how should we expect that accounts of the Battle of Gettysburg should be alike? History comes to us filtered through the mind. With almost a single voice historians say that there are no facts that can be relied upon. Agreed-on assumptions we call facts so we can get on with the job.[7]

From my Mount St. Helens witnesses I seek descriptions of physical phenomena anchored in time and place. Some witnesses I interview time and again. And so discrepancies among witnesses are eventually resolved.

Oral conversation is full of repetition, flashback, ambiguity, jargon. Almost everyone speaks in passive voice and static verbs. This book is a written record. I may re-order stories into proper time but alter no data. For iterative interviews, I combine from different interviews, delete the repetitious and superfluous, clarify syntax, pare to essence. Like maple sugaring, pails of pale sap distill to pints of amber.

William Zinsser writes:

> Your ethical duty to the person being interviewed is to present his position accurately. After that your duty is to the reader. He or she deserves the tightest package. If you find [late in] your notes a comment that perfectly amplifies a point earlier in the interview, you do everyone a favor if you link the two thoughts, letting the second sentence illustrate the first. This may violate the truth of how the interview actually progressed, but you will be true to the intent of what was said. Just make sure the play is fair. If the speaker's language is so tangled it would embarrass him, the writer has no choice but to to clean up the English and provide the missing links.[8]

Written Accounts

Earthquake logs

Earthquakes at Mount St. Helens in spring 1980 as recorded in catalogue of Pacific Northwest Seismic Network (PNSN) http://pnsn.org. Printoffs of the catalogue consulted throughout research and writing. See Chap 1, note 1 and details in other notes.

Logbooks, radio tapes, and reports

Coldwater logbook kept by different people at the post March 30 to May 18, each observation logged by hour and minute. In bad weather the post sometimes went unstaffed hours or days. Late May 2 it moved to a higher site called Coldwater II, the earlier site then called Coldwater I. Coldwater notebooks A and B rotated, one to Vancouver for photocopying. Book A, lost with David Johnston May 18, had been photocopied. Logbook B includes evening May 17. Missing only are Johnston's entries after 9 PM May 17.

Gifford Pinchot National Forest dispatch-radio "Xray-2" log at Vancouver late March through summer 1980. Original seems lost. Photocopy is in Forest Service's Mount St. Helens files at the National Archives, Pacific Alaska Region (NARA) in Seattle, parts missing. But my photocopy includes some of the missing.

USGS logbook kept from same radio reports as National Forest "X-2" log. Book I, March 28 to April 1; Book II, April 1 to 10; Book III, April 11 to 13; Book IV, May 9 to 18 at 7:00 AM; Book V, May 18 at 8:41 AM to May 25.

USGS radio communications through a National Forest repeater from 16 to 26 May 1980 taped by a ham-radio operator. The voice-activated recorder omits time between transmissions. Time of day rarely mentioned, but some data correspond to timed entries in the written logbooks or geologists' field notes. These analog tapes converted to digital, and some tapes transcribed. To be archived.

Handwritten map by the Washington State Patrol, probably southwest Washington district, noting dates and positions of 1980 roadblocks on highways 503 and 504 March 26 to May 18. Supplied by the Patrol's 1980 Chief, Robert Landon.

Photocopy of dispatch log for Air Force Reserve 304th Rescue and Recovery Squadron, Portland, May 18–20.

Photocopy of partial handwritten dispatch log for Washington Army National Guard aerial operations at Toutle, Kelso, and Toledo, May 18–22.

Photocopy of dispatch log for Weyerhaeuser Company, Longview, May 18–19, and diary of Jack Schoening, May 18.

Taped dispatch communications of Cowlitz County sheriff's office, morning May 18. Summary transcription of this log May 18–19 by John E. Cummans (USGS) dated 17 June 1980.

Field notes late March through May 1980 of USGS geologists Don Swanson, James Moore, Peter Lipman, Robert Christiansen, Rocky Crandell, Harry Glicken (extract), Richard Hoblitt, Richard Waitt, C. Dan Miller, Sue Kieffer (extract), Norman Banks (extract), and others.

Personal flight logs of a few military search-and-rescue flight crew.

Personal logs of some Forest Service staff and sheriff's deputies.

USGS and University of Washington "Monthly Report: Volcanic and Seismic Activity at Mount St. Helens" for March–April 1980 and for May 1980. Unreviewed, distributed informally.

On the Mountain's Brink—A Forest Service History of the 1980 Mount St. Helens Volcanic Emergency, Gifford Pinchot National Forest, probably late 1981.[9]

Newspaper and television reports

The stories of many 1980 news reporters and photographers derive from my interviews with them in 1990s–2000s. Most of them consulted 1980 clip files. Media news derived mostly from the *Daily News* (Longview, Wash.), the *Columbian* (Vancouver, Wash.), the *Oregonian* and *Oregon Journal* (Portland, Oreg.), and the *Seattle Times* and *Seattle Post-Intelligencer*. Years later people may remember some details of a meeting but not date. News stories about such meetings specify date and perhaps time. Earthquakes, eruptions, bulging, and other geologic phenomena are most accurate from USGS sources. Yet part of story is how data disseminate. Inaccurate or misunderstood happenings reported in the media do influence people's behavior. Of television and radio news, difficult and expensive to research, I mention only fragments.

Publications

A USGS piece by Foxworthy and Hill[10] has an immediacy to spring 1980 not contained in the scientists' technical reports. Yet it includes inaccuracies. Many souvenir booklets printed spring–summer 1980 reveal by photographs but most of the brief texts are naive about natural events. Of several 1980 retrospectives by newspapers, the standout for thoroughness and accuracy is the *Oregonian*'s "A Terrible Beauty."[11] Even it contains small errors.

Several of my witnesses and others had been deposed under oath in 1984–85 for *Karr et al. vs. State of Washington and Weyerhaeuser Company*. Though tedious, some depositions reveal logging sites and location of a staffer at a certain time not known from other sources.

Many hundreds of geologic articles have been published about the 1980 eruptions. Only a few of them appear in the reference list.

Interview History and Acknowlegements

Interviews in 1980 by Waitt and by J.G. Rosenbaum summarized in Rosenbaum and Waitt (1981). I interviewed on occasion through the 1980s. In 1980 seismologist Steve Malone (University of Washington) had matched eruptive and timed seismic data to many eyewitnesses' photographs. In 1988–1990 Elizabeth Nielsen transcribed Rosenbaum's 1980 interview tapes and acquired and organized hundreds of witnesses' photographs. In 1998 Kristin Waitt helped select from hundreds of photographs, and in 1999 Mary McKinney and Leah Bjerklund aided some interviews and re-located early interviewees. In 2000–2009 I reinterviewed most 1980s' witnesses—elaborating details, correcting errors, resolving discrepancies. Newly interviewed 1999–2012 were numerous witnesses from federal, state, and local agencies, Weyerhaeuser Company, military fliers, 1980 governor's affiliates, loggers, Toutle valley residents, and media reporters and photographers. Appendix III summarizes interviews 1980 to 2014.

Otto Sieber kindly opened his files of transcripts of many witnesses deposed 1984–85 for *Karr et al.* trial and a few of his 1981–83 interviews when memories were fairly fresh.

Shirley Rosen kindly allowed me her summer-1980 taped interviews with N.B. Gardner and Ken Macdonald, and Carl Berg's taped interview with Harry Truman in mid-May 1980. And she supplied the photo of Truman's lodge under construction.

Former KGW-radio newsman Mike Beard allowed my use of 1980 tapes: a broadcast March 27, interview with Harry Truman May 16, and interview with President Jimmy Carter May 22.

Timing of the many eruption photographs stems from a nearly 50-foot timeline hung with xeroxed photos by Steve Malone and colleagues in University of Washington seismology laboratory in summer 1980.

About 15 colleagues from the USGS and two universities read early drafts of all chapters. Their comments and suggestions improved the manuscripts. They shall go unnamed, but know who they are. I ardently thank my wife Cynthia who for too many years has endured untaken holidays, untraveled vacations, books piled about the house, and what have you.

APPENDIX III
Summary of Interviews 1980–2014

Witness	Date range	No.	Methods*	Who†
Airis, William	Dec.00	2	Pn,Tn	W
Alexander, William	Jun.01–Feb.04	4	Pn,Tn,W	W
Altom, Kerri	Feb.03–Dec.08	2	Pn,Tn	W
Anders, Trixy (Bea Johnston in 1980)	Feb.04–Sep.12	10	Pn,Tn,E,L,W	W
Anderson, Kathy	May.80–Jan.08	4	W,Pt,Pn,Tn	W,R
Anderson, Mark	Jun.01–Aug.11	11	Pn,Tn,W	W
Bacon, Bill	Nov.02–Jan.03	2	Tn,W	W
Backstrom, Brad	Apr.03–Sep.03	4	Pn,Tn,W	W
Bailey, Lt. Darrell	Mar.08	2	Tn	W
Baker, Gil & Baker (O'Keefe), Kathy	Jun.80	1	Pn	W
Bakke, Kit	Oct.05	2	Tn,W	W
Balch, Dan & Thomas, Brian	Jul.80	1	Pt	R
Balch, Dan	Mar.01–Apr.01	2	Pn,Tn,W	W
Banks, Norm	Jul.01–Jul.09	8	Pn,Tn	W
Barker, George	Mar.01–Oct.10	18	Pn,Tn,W	W
Beard, Mike	Apr.10–Jul.01	3	Pn,Tn,Ta	W
Bena, Ben	Aug.01–May.13	21	Pn,Tn,W	W
Berg, Carl	May.80	1	Ta	SR
Bernard, Julia	Dec.06	1	Tn	W
Berry, Dave	Aug.02–Dec.10	10	Pn,Tn,W	W
Berry, Duncan	Feb.03–Jul.03	3	Tn,W	W
Beswick, Ralph	Apr.03–May.03	2	Tn	W
Bioren, Bob	May.07–Jun.07	3	Tn	W
Blackburn, Fay	Aug.04–May.05	7	Pn,Tn,W	W
Blaisdell, Ray	Jun.01	1	Pn	W
Blumenthal, Les	Mar.02	2	Tn	W
Boccia, Conrad & Sandie	Nov.05–Mar.08	3	Tn	W
Bodine, Dave	Aug.01–Jan.07	2	Tn	W
Bowers, Glen	May.07–Jun.07	4	Tn	W
Brugman, Mindy	Mar.00–Jul.04	3	Pn,Tn	W
Bullock, Dick	Jun.01–Jan.08	20	Pn,Tn,W	W
Burford, Brooks	Nov.04–May.10	4	Pn,Tn	W
Bynum, Ardis	Apr.06–Aug.06	3	Tn	W
Cameron, Ken	Jun.04	1	Tn	W
Carlson, Zilda	Nov.05–Dec.05	2	Tn	W
Carroll, Dick	Jan.08	1	Pn	W
Casadevall, Tom	May.02–Jun.09	~8	Pn,E	W
Cavens, Russel M.	Aug.04–Aug.05	3	Pn,Tn	W
Chamberlin, Jim	Nov.01–Sep.05	2	Pn,Tn,F	W
Charnley, Donn	Mar.04–Apr.04	2	Pn,Tn	W
Chausee, Bernadette	May.80–Feb.82	2	Pt,Pn	R,W
Christiansen, John	May.80–May.12	2	Pt,Tn	R,W
Christiansen, Robert	Oct.02–Mar.10	4	Pn,Tn,W	W
Closner, Bill	Mar.01–Feb.08	11	Pn,Tn	W
Cole, Brian	Aug.80	1	Pt	R

Witness	Date range	No.	Methods*	Who†
Coleman, Bob	Feb.03	1	Tn	W
Cooney, Michael "Mike"	Sep.99–Aug.13	~14	Pt, Pn,Tn,W	W,M
Core, Dick	Feb.04	1	Tn	W
Cowlitz County Emergency Services	Jul.04	2	Wn	W
Crandell, Dwight "Rocky"	Mar.01–Jul.05	6	Pn,Tn,W	W
Cranford, Robin	Jan.11	1	Tn	W
Crockett, David	Jun.80	1	Pn,Ta	W
Dardarian, Suki	Jan.09	1	Tn	W
Davidson, James M. "Jim"	Jan.07–Jan.09	4	Pn,Tn	W
Davis, Leslie & Dale (and Brooks, Al)	May.80–Jan.00	6	Pn,Tn,W	W,R
Decker, Bob	Jun.01–Apr.03	2	Tn	W
DeMeyer, John	Nov.01–Jan.08	7	Pn,Tn	W
Dergan, Venus	July.80–May.00	4	Pn,Tn,L	W
Devine, Jim	Feb.03	1	Tn	W
Dieter, Bob	Dec.03–Sep.05	10	Pn,Tn	W
Dietrich, Bill	Apr.05–Jun.07	2	Tn	W
Dinehart, Randy	May.02–Jul.05	3	Pn,Tn	W
Doran, Jeffry	Sep.08–Mar.13	2	Tn,W	W
Downing, John	Aug.80	1	Pt	R
Douglass, Peter	Jul.04–Jan.07	2	Tn	W
Doyle, Jack	Jul.05	2	Tn	W
Drew, Greg	May.05–Aug.05	2	Pn	W
Driedger, Carolyn	Nov.02	1	Pn	W
duBeth Gardiner, Donna	Apr.01–Feb.07	6	Tn,W	W
Dzurisin, Dan	Mar.03–Jun.09	3	Pn	W
Edelbrock, Mark	Dec.99–Mar.07	28	Pn,Tn,E,W	W
Eichelberger, John	Dec.04–Nov.07	2	Pn,Tn	W
Eisele, Dr.	Feb.04	1	Tn	W
Ek, Charlie	Oct.99	1	Pt,Pn	W,M
Elder, Wick	Apr.03–Jul.09	6	Pn,Tn,W	W
Emetaz, Roland	Feb.01–Jan.08	2	Pn	W
Erdelbrock, Dale	Dec.04–Jan.12	5	Pn,Tn	W
Erickson, John	Apr.01–Jul.01	2	Pn,Tn	W
Evans, William C.	Feb.09	1	Tn	W
Fabik, Dave	Jan.07	2	Tn	W
Fairchild, Lee	Jan.07	3	Tn	W
Fanony, Louie (& Lavelle)	Aug.03	1	Pn	W
Filson, John	Jan.03	1	Tn	W
Ford, Dick	Dec.01–Jan.12	5	Pn,Tn,W,L	W
Ford, Roy & Sandy	Feb.06–Feb.09	3	Pn,Tn	W
Frank, David	Oct.02	1	Tn	W
Frishman, Rich	Jun.09–Sep.11	3	Tn	W
Furukawa, Bruce	Dec.01	1	Tn	W
Gadwa, Thorald & Vernice	May.04–Feb.05	2	Tn	W
Gallant, Peter	Dec.00–Dec.01	2	Tn	W
Gardner, David	Nov.04–Mar.12	5	Tn	W
Gaston, Bob	Dec.07–May.09	3	Tn	W
Gianopoulos, George	Jun.05	1	Tn	W
Giesbrecht, Roland	Dec.99–Apr.05	3	Pn,Tn	W
Gilka, Robert "Bob"	Dec.04	1	Tn	W
Glicken, Harry	May.80–1987	~3	Pm,W	W

Witness	Date range	No.	Methods*	Who†
Gould, Alan	Aug.80–Jan.04	2	Pt,Pn	R,W
Graaff, Keith	Oct.03–Nov.05	2	Tn	W
Graham, Ross	Apr.07	1	Tn	W
Grose, Tim	Aug.02	1	Tn	W
Guild, Irving (w/ Wishart)	Aug.80–Feb.82	2	Pn,Tn	W
Guthrie, Steve	Jan.08–Aug.10	4	Tn	W
Guze, Ken	May.03–Nov.03	2	Pn	W
Guzzo, Lou	Jun.01–Feb.07	8	Pn,Tn,W	W
Hagerman, Jess	Nov.99–May.05	7	Pt,Pn,Tn,L	W
Haderly, Joyce & Floyd	Sep.05–May.06	3	Pn,Tn,F	W
Hallauer, Wilbur "Web"	May.04	1	Tn	W
Halliday, William	Jul.80	1	W	
Hamilton, Don	Feb.07	5	Pn,Tn	W
Hammond, Paul	Jun.04–Jul.05	3	Tn	W
Hanks, Dale	Aug.80	1	Tn	W
Hanley, Donald	Nov.05	2	Pn,Tn	W
Hanna, Harold "Jerry"	Jun.01–Apr.04	3	Pn,Tn	W
Harlow, Dave	Mar.01–Nov.02	4	Tn	W
Harris, Stephen	Nov.11	1	Tn	W
Harvey, Joel	Jun.–Jul.95	2	Pn, Tn	W
Hathaway, Paul L.	Jun.01–Feb.09	5	Pn,Tn,W	W
Hazlett, Rich	Sep.04	1	Tn	W
Hembree, Joel	Apr.03	1	Pn	W
Henderson, Paul	Apr.09–Dec.10	2	Tn	W
Herrington, Gregg	Apr.05	1	Tn	W
Hewes, Bill	Sep.05	1	Pn	W
Hickson, Catherine & Paul	Oct.80	2	Pt,W	MR,W
Hickson, Catherine	Oct.80–Feb.08	3	W,L,Tn	W
Hickson, Paul	Jan.06	1	Tn	W
Hill, Jim	May.08–Aug.10	3	Pn,Tn	W
Hill, Greg	Aug.10–Sep.10	3	Tn,W	W
Hill, Richard	Feb.03	1	Tn	W
Hill, Tom	Dec.04–Feb.05	3	Pn,Tn,W	W
Hobart, Sue	Dec.06–Jan.07	2	Pn,Tn	W
Hoblitt, Richard "Rick"	Mar.01–Nov.07	14	Pn,Tn,E	W
Hodgson, Vern	May.80–Jan.08	3	Pt,Pn,Tn	R,W
Hoger, Ernst & Putrow, Vern	July.80–Mar.82	2	Pt,Pn	R,W
Holtsclaw, Michael	Sep.11	1	Tn	W
Hubbard, Mike	Jun.00–Feb.06	3	Tn	W
Hurliman, Ben	Jun.04–Jan.07	3	Tn	W
Jewett, Jim	Dec.06	1	Tn	W
Johnson, Bob	Aug.04–Feb.09	4	Pn,Tn	W
Johnson, Bruce	Jun.10	1	Tn	W
Johnson, Ken	Mar.01–Nov.01	2	Tn	W
Johnson, Wendell & Lou	1980	2	W	
Wendell	Jul.80–Feb.00	4	Pt,Tn	R,W
Johnston, Barry	Feb.04–Jul.04	4	Tn	W
Johnston, Bea (see Trixie Anders)				
Johnston, Billie	Dec.05	1	Tn,W	W
Johnston, David	Apr.80	several	Pm	W
Johnston, Monte	Jan.08	1	Pn	W

Witness	Date range	No.	Methods*	Who†
Jones, Betty	Nov.05–Feb.08	4	Tn	W
Jones, Wayne	Oct.05	1	Tn	W
Joyce, Jack & Audrey	Jan.89	1	Pt,W	N
Judson, Bruce E.	Jan.01–Dec.04	2	Tn	W
Kaseweter (see Pullen)				
Kearney, Ty & Marianna	Aug.80–Jul.82	2	Pt,Pn,F	R,W
Kearney, Marianna	Apr.02–Aug.13	8	L,Pn,Tn,W,F	W
Keatley, John	Nov.11–Dec.11	2	Tn	W
Keith, John	Feb.03–May.10	3	Pn,Tn	W
Keller Bill	Apr.04–Dec.06	4	Tn	W
Keough, Pat	May.12	1	Tn	W
Kern, Dave	Apr.05–May.05	2	Pn,Tn	W
Kieffer, Hugh	Jun.04	1	Tn	W
Kieffer, Sue	Mar.04–Jul.04	3	Tn	W
Kienle, Rick	Jul.05	2	Pn,Tn	W
Killian, Jeanette	Sep.11–Dec.11	3	Pn,Tn	W
Killian, Ralph	Aug.07	1	Pn	W
Kilpatrick, Kran	May.80–Jun.80	2	Pt,W	R
King, Linda	Feb.06–Jan.07	2	Pn,Tn	W
King, Ray	Jan.07	2	Tn	W
King, Shawn	Sep.12–Mar.13	2	Tn	W
Kiver, Eugene	Nov.05–Dec.05	4	Tn	W
Koehler, Alice & Peter	Dec.06	1	Tn	W
Koenniger, Tom	Oct.05	1	Tn	W
Kohn, Allen	Sep.01	1	Tn	W
Kolb, Harold R.	Dec.99–Mar.01	3	Pn,Tn	W
Koon, Carol	Jan.01–Dec.03	2	Pn,Tn	W
Koschnick, Jerry	Aug.04	1	Tn	W
Kratch, Bill	May.06–Jan.10	10	Pn,Tn	W
Kropf, Joan & Purdum, Ronald	May.80–Mar.90	2	W,Tn	N
Lalla, Doug	Nov.02	2	Tn	W
Landon, Robert	Mar.01–Dec.07	17	Pn,Tn,W	W
LaPlaunt, Don	Aug.80	1	Pt	R
Latimer, Dick	Dec.99–May.02	2	Pn,Tn	W
LaValla, Rick	Apr.03–Apr.10	16	Pn,Tn	W
Leighley, Terry	Dec.04–Sep.07	2	Tn	W
Lefevre, Andy	Nov.05	1	Tn	W
Lekse, Joey	May.02	1	Pn	W
Lematta, Jim	Aug.04	1	Tn	W
LeMonds, Bill	Dec.01–Aug.03	4	Pn,Tn	W
Lindeman, Glen	May.06	2	Tn	W
Lineau, Michael	Dec.10–Jan.11	2	Tn	W
Lipman, Peter	Jul.01–Apr.07	4	Pn,Tn	W
Lievsay, Dave	Dec.04–Jan.05	2	Pn,Tn	W
Lloyd, Darryl	Dec.07–Feb.08	2	Pn,Tn	W
Long, Chuck & Pat	Feb.06–Jan.07	2	Pn,Tn	W
Lowry, Ed	1980	1	Pt	SR
Lowry, Mike	Jul.05–Jan.07	2	Tn	W
Ludvig, Paul	Mar.09–Apr.09	4	Tn	W
Lund, Don	Jul.12–Jun.14	2	Tn,E,W	W
Madden, Bob	Dec.04–Jul.05	4	Tn	W

Witness	Date range	No.	Methods*	Who†
Major, Jon	Mar.13	1	Pn	W
Malinconico, Lawrence	Dec.02	1	Tn	W
Malone, Steve	Apr.01–Feb.08	6	Pn,Tn	W
Manasse, Geoff	Feb.09–Mar.09	3	Tn	W
Mansfield, Roxanne (née Edwards)	Sep.04–Jun.10	2	Tn	W
Marshall, John	May.03–May.06	7	Pn,Tn	W
Martin, Gerry	May.80	1	HRT	
Mason, Don	Sep.07–Nov.07	2	Tn	W
Mathes, Joseph	Jun.80–Dec.00	3	Pn,Tn	W
May, Bud	May.03–Aug.03	2	Pn,Tn	W
McCarty, John	Nov.05	1	Tn	W
McClintock, John	Nov.06	1	Pn	W
McClure, Rick	Sep.01–Feb.12	4	Pn,Tn,L	W
McCoy, Roger	Dec.04	4	Pn,Tn,W	W
McCoy, Mary & Whitney, Harold	Apr.03	1	Pn	W
McCully, Hugh	May.02–May.03	2	Pn	W
McCulley, Larry & Findley, Joe	Aug.80	1	Pt	R
McElfrish, Bruce	Dec.04	2	Tn	W
McNerney, Charlie	Jun.80–Dec.99	4	Pn,Tn	W
Melton, Joe	Feb.07–Dec.11	4	Pn,Tn	W
Merzoian, Charlene (née Killian)	Nov.11–Dec.11	2	Pn,Tn	W
Merzoian, Dave	Dec.11–Sep.14	2	Pn,Tn	W
Miller, Dan	Oct.02–Nov.10	20	Pn,Tn,W,L	W
Miller, David	Mar.08	1	Pn	W
Moore, Jim	Mar.01–May.03	9	Pn,Tn,W	W
Moore, Mike & Lu	Jul.80	1	Pt,W	R
Moore, Mike	Aug.98–May.05	5	Pn,Tn,L	W
Moran, Seth	Sep.11	1	Pn	W
Morgan, Ben	Feb.03–Jul.03	2	Tn	W
Mullen, Dave	Mar.05–Mar.08	3	Pn,Tn	W
Mullineaux, Donal "Don"	May.00–Sep.08	15	Pn,Tn,W,L	W
Myers, Rick	Nov.05–Feb.08	3	Tn	W
Nance, Ancel	Oct.04	2	Pn,Tn,W	W
Nehl, Steve	Feb.07–Mar.07	2	Tn	W
Nelson, Bruce & Ruff, Sue	Jun.80	1	Pt	R
Nelson, Bruce	Dec.99–Feb.09	6	Pn,Tn,F,L	W
Nelson, Les	Dec.80–Feb.01	2	L,Pn,W	W
Nelson, Mark	Jun.04	1	Tn	W
Nelson, Susan (1980 Tilton)	Jun.10	2	Tn	W
Nichols, Mike	Jun.04–May.13	3	Tn,E	W
Nieland, Jim	Mar.01–Apr.05	6	Pn,Tn,W	W
Nolan, Tom	Nov.99–Apr.02	3	Pt,Pn,Tn	W,M
Nole, Charles "Chuck"	Jan.01–Sep.10	8	Pn,Tn	W
Norris, Bob	Jul.01	1	Tn	W
Nugent, Al	May.03	1	Pn	W
Nugent, Ed	May.03	2	Tn	W
Nugent, Jim	May.03–Oct.04	5	Pn,Tn	W
Okamura, Arnold	Jul.01–Apr.14	4	Tn	W
O'Keefe, Kathleen	Jun.80–Sep.03	3	Pn,Tn	W
Olson, Dave	Jul.04–Nov.06	6	Pn,Tn	W
Olson, Erik	May.06	1	Pn,F	W

Witness	Date range	No.	Methods*	Who†
Olson, Roger	Apr.06–May.06	2	Pn,F	W
O'Neill, Danny	Apr.05–Aug.05	3	Pn,Tn	W
O'Neill, Judy (née Killian)	Jan.07	2	Pn,Tn	W
O'Neil, Keith	Jan.05–Aug.05	2	Pn	W
O'Shea, Dennis and Carol	Jun.10–Jul.10	2	Tn	W
Osmond, Ed	Feb.08	1	Tn	W
Palmer, Gene & Kathy	Jul.80–Feb.82	2	Pt,Pn	R,W
Parker, Donna	Nov.04–May.13	6	Pn,Tn,F,W	W
Patterson, Rick	Mar.08	1	Tn	W
Paulson, Kathy	Dec.01–Sep.07	8	Pn,Tn	W
Payne, Bob	Aug.98–Feb.06	5	Pn,Tn	W,K
Peck, Dallas	Feb.02	1	Tn	W
Peden, Bill	Jan.00–Feb.04	2	Tn	W
Perry, Rick	Sep.11	2	Tn	W
Peters, Mike	Mar.01–Jul.13	7	Pn,Tn	W
Plamondson II, Martin	Jun.03	1	Pn	W
Pleasant, Ray	Nov.99–Mar.05	4	Pn,Tn	W
Prest, Donald W.	Mar.01	1	Tn	W
Pullen, Connie (née Kaseweter)	Jul.05–Aug.05	5	Pn,Tn,W	W
Purcell, David	Nov.05	1	Tn	W
Ray, Ella	Dec.01–Oct.05	6	Pn,Tn,W	W
Reber, Dwight	Aug.04-2008	~10	W,Pt,Pn	W
Reese, Bill	Oct.02–Jan.08	3	Pn,Tn	W
Reitan, Roald	Jul.80–May.00	3	Pn,Tn,L	W
Renner, Jeff	Jun.01–Sep.10	6	Pn,Tn	W
Rodeback, David	Jan.08–Aug.10	3	Pn	W
Rogers, Robert	Jun.82–May.14	12	Pn,Tn,F,W	W
Roggenback, Gary & Brenda	Jun.04	1	Pn	W
Roggenback, Gary	Aug.05–Jan.07	4	Pn,Tn	W
Rombach, Jim	May.03–Aug.03	2	Pn,Tn	W
Ronholm, Keith	Aug.80–May.05	3	Pt,Pn,Tn,W,L	R,W
Rooth, Guy	Apr.89–Apr.05	4	Pn,Tn,W	W,N
Rosen, Shirley	Jan.04–Feb.04	4	Pn,Tn,W	W
Rosenbaum, Joe	Oct.02–Nov.03	2	Pn,Tn	W
Rosenfeld, Charles "Chuck"	Dec.88–Aug.12	6	Tn,W	W,N
Rosenquist, Gary	Jul.80–Apr.12	3	Pt,Pn,Tn,W,L	R,W
Ross, Keith	Feb.04–Sep.05	3	Pn,Tn,F	W
Ruff-Nelson, Sue	Sep.05–Feb.09	4	Pn,Tn,E	W
Russ, Phil & Betty Dee	Oct.05	2	Tn	W†
Ryan, Richard ("Rich")	May.07–Aug.07	4	Pn,Tn	W
Rylee, Stan	Aug.80	1	Pt	R
Salsman, Dexter	Dec.11–Mar.12	2	Pn,Tn	W
Sarna-Wojcicki, Andrei	Mar.03	1	Tn	W
Schaefer, Don	Apr.02–May.12	2	Pn	W
Schoening, Jack	May.03–Jul.13	6	Pn,Tn,W	W
Schroeder, Deon	Mar.01	1	Pn	W
Scott, Kevin	Feb.03–Dec.08	3	Pn	W
Scymanky, James	Oct.80–Sep.01	8	Pn,Tn,F,L	W
Seesholtz, Dave	Apr.05–Jan.07	2	Tn	W
Seibold, Glenn	Oct.05	2	Tn	W
Seifert, Rick	Aug.04–Sep.04	2	Tn	W

Witness	Date range	No.	Methods*	Who†
Sicotte, Chuck	Oct.04–Aug.10	4	Tn	W
Sieber, Otto	Jun.04–Feb.07	6	Pn,Tn,W	W
Sieber's 1980 film "Keeper of the Fire"	Oct.11		View	W
Siebert, Ken	Mar.82	1	Pn,W	W
Simmonds, Terry	Jun.05–Jan.08	7	Tn	W
Small, Steve	Feb.05–Feb.09	4	Pn,Tn	W
Smith, Dennis	Aug.14	2	Tn,Pn,W	W
Smith, Dorian	Nov.01–Apr.03	2	Tn,W	W
Smith, Edward "Buzz"	Jul.80–Sep.11	5	Pt,Tn	R,W
Smith, Jim	Oct.05	1	Tn	W
Smith, Miriam	May.00	1	Pn	W
Smith, Mark	Aug.05	1	Pn	W
Smith, Rob	Jul.01–Apr.04	4	Pn,Tn	W
Snell, John	Nov.05	1	Tn	W
Sorby, Sharon (née Burchard)	Nov.01–Feb.07	9	Pn,Tn	W
Spahman, Ron	Apr.05–Aug.05	3	Pn,Tn	W
Stebner, Darald	Dec.99–Jun.09	3	Tn	W
Stearns, Richard	Oct.05	1	Tn	W
Steig, George	May.03–Sep.07	4	Pn,Tn	W
Stenkamp, Paul R.	Dec.02	1	Tn	W
Stepankowski, Andrei	Feb.01–Aug.11	4	Pn,Tn	W
Stewart, Bill	Feb.03–Aug.04	2	Tn	W
Stickney, Lon	Jun.04–Jan.05	4	Tn	W
Stoffel, Keith & Dorothy	May.80–Sep.07	7	W,Pn,Tn	W,N
Stoker, Bruce	Sep.11	2	Pn,Tn	W
Stovel, Fred	Dec.01–Mar.08	8	Pn,Tn	W
Strachen, Glen	May.05	1	Pn	W
Sugar, Jim	Nov.04	2	Tn	W
Sugarman, Ken	Mar.08	1	Tn	W
Sullivan, Joe & Annie and Dahl, Mark	May.80–Apr.12	6	W,Pn,Tn,L,E	W
Swanson, Donald	Mar.82–Sep.11	16	W,Tn	W
Swier, Dick	May.03–Aug.11	9	Tn	W
Terrill, Steve	Oct.09	1	Tn	W
Thacker, Harvey	Aug.04–Sep.04	2	Tn	W
Theisen, George	Dec.02–Feb.09	11	Pn,Tn	W
Thomas, Brian	Jul.80–May.00	3	Pt,Pn,Tn	R,W
Thomas, Jim	July.05–Mar.08	4	Tn	W
Thomas, Larry	May.09	1	Pn	W
Thomas, Lindsey	Oct.02–Oct.05	2	Tn	W
Tilling, Robert	Nov.02–Jan.11	7	Tn,W	W
Tilton, Susan (see Nelson)				
Tokarczyk, Bob	Feb.01–Dec.10	2	Pn,Tn	W
Tonn, Chuck	Mar.01–Feb.07	3	Tn	W
Treat, Gary	May.80–Aug.80	1	Tn,W	W
Truman, Harry	Apr.80–May.80	2	Pm,T	W,B
Turgeson, Joel	Jan.11	2	Tn	W
Twedt, Steve	Jan.05	1	Tn	W
Twigg, George	Dec.05	3	Tn	W
Untewegner, Jim	Apr.03	1	Pn	W
Valenzuela, Francisco	Apr.82–Apr.04	2	Pn,Tn	W
Vallance, Jim	Nov.07	2	Pn	W

Witness	Date range	No.	Methods*	Who†
Voight, Barry	Apr.80–Sep.06	~12	Pn,Tn,W,E	W
von Michalofski, Olaf	Jan.81–Feb.90	2	W,Tn	N
Waitt, Richard	Mar.80–2014	many	W,F	W
Walcker, Ron	Nov.04–Feb.13	7	Tn	W
Walters, Tom	Oct.02–Jan.11	7	Tn	W
Ward, Dave	Oct.99–Feb.07	7	Pt,Tn	W,M
Ward, Kyle	Dec.99	2	Tn	W
Warren, George	Aug.04–Feb.09	4	Pn,Tn	W
Weaver, Craig	Oct.02–Nov.02	2	Tn	W
Wedding, George	Mar.05–Jun.09	3	Tn,W	W
Weed, Robert "Bob"	Sep.99–Apr.02	3	Pt,Pn,Tn	W,M
Weidman, Charles "Bud"	Mar.08	1	Tn	W
Wend, Duane	Aug.03	1	Tn	W
Wendt, Dave	Mar.01–May.05	5	Pn,Tn,L	W
Werth, Roger	Apr.01–Feb.07	6	Pn,Tn	W
Wesson, Robert	Jan.03	2	Tn	W
Whiteley, Art	Sep.01–Aug.03	2	Tn	W
Whitlock, Jack & Doreen	18.vii.80	1	Pt	R
Williams, Garvin	Nov.07–Jul.13	3	Pn,Tn	W
Williams, John	Dec..06	3	Tn,E	W
Williamson, Mike	Feb.08	1	Tn	W
Wilson, Larry	May.03–Jul.04	4	Pn,Tn	W
Wishart, Larry (w/ Guild)	Mar.82–Jan.89	2	Pn	D,N
Wolff, Jack & Joann	Jun.01–Dec.12	9	Pn,Tn,W,E	W
Wörner, Gerhard	Jun.04	1	Tn	W
Wright, Bob	Jun.01–Aug.11	7	Pn,Tn,E	W
Wynn, Jeff	May.03	1	Pn	W
Young, Tom	May.10	1	Pn	W
Zais, Richard	May.00	1	Tn	W
Zaitz, Les	Nov.01	2	Pn,Tn	W
Zawodny, Jay	Feb.02	2	Pn,Tn	W
Zink, Joe	Apr.02	1	Pn	W

Key:

* Methods		† By whom	
P =	In person	W =	Richard Waitt
T =	Telephone	R =	Joe Rosenbaum 1980 (transcribed by
E =	Email		E. Nielsen 1990)
L =	Lecture or talk	N =	Elizabeth Nielsen
W =	1980 written account by witness or other	M =	Mary McKinney
	written material and/or photographs	K =	Kristin Waitt
HRT =	ham-radio tape	SR =	Shirley Rosen
F =	field visit with witness	MR =	Norman Macleod and Peter Rowley
t =	Interview taped	D =	Jeanette Dodge
n =	Written notes of interview	B =	Carl Berg, tape supplied by Shirley
m =	By memory		Rosen
e.g., Pn = In-person interview recorded in notes			

Notes

Stick

1. S.E. Ambrose, *Citizen Soldiers,* New York: Simon & Schuster (1997).
2. Mostly from the *Daily News* (Longview, Wash.), the *Columbian* (Vancouver, Wash.), the *Oregonian* (Portland, Oreg.), and the *Oregon Journal* (Portland), but occasionally the *Seattle Times* and *Seattle Post-Intelligencer.*
3. Sabbagh (1999) details a botanical fraud in Scotland in the 1940s, the clue to mischief being the nonrepeatability of published results.
4. Thucydides, *History of the Peloponnesian War,* translation by Rex Warner [Book I, sec. 22], London, Penguin Books (1954).

Chapter 1

1. Earthquake magnitudes measured by duration of seismic trace from onset to where dwindled to twice background, a duration called 'coda' (Endo and others, 1981). Coda magnitudes are calibrated to correspond to Richter magnitudes calculated from a signal's peak amplitude by special seismometers.

   A magnitude 2 would be usually unfelt. A magnitude 4, especially if shallow, would be obvious to someone standing over it, but probably unfelt in a moving automobile. The earthquake that demolished San Francisco in 1906 was a magnitude 8.3—some 20,000 times the energy of a magnitude 4.

   Magnitudes of earthquakes in this book from the catalogue of Pacific Northwest Seismic Network (PNSN) http://pnsn.org. Provisional 1980 magnitudes were later adjusted—typically higher. Many sizable earthquakes not in the catalogue but in a 'count' file for station SHW appear in some 1980 news stories.
2. A seismic station comprises a sensor (seismometer), antenna, batteries, cabling, a housing. Each station is given a letter code. CPW means Capitol Peak West, SHW St. Helens West. A seismometer translates ground velocity into electrical voltage and to an FM tone transmitted by telephone wire or telemetered antenna to a laboratory, here the University of Washington.

3. An oscillograph for displaying seismic signals, the Develocorder was made by Teledyne Co. It records 24 hours of data from 16 stations on a roll of 16-mm film changed daily. At UW three of the signals also played out to rotating drums called helicorders.
4. Pacific Standard Time through April 26, Pacific Daylight Time starting April 27.
5. 'Timberline' on the south flank of Mount Hood near upper limit of trees, since the 1930s the site of a magnificent ski lodge. 'Timberline' also since the 1920s the upper limit of trees on the north flank of Mount St. Helens.
6. 88 Stat. 143 (P.L. 93-288, popularly 'Stafford Act').

Chapter 2

1. Many scientific papers and several textbooks summarize eruptions, for instance Bullard (1962, 1976), Macdonald (1972), Sigurdsson (1999). Siebert and others (2010) catalogue eruptions around the world in the past 10,000 years. Blong (1984) elaborates costs in life and property.
2. Sigurdsson (1999) summarizes evidence of this eruption from literature, archeology, and geology. Castelden (1998) explores Bronze-age (Minoan) Crete and Santorini and their likeness to Plato's description of Atlantis. Sigurdsson and others (2006) greatly increase the volume of ejected magma from previous estimates. Eruptions date between 1500 and 1650 BCE, perhaps 1628 BCE (Castelden, 1998; Grudd and others, 2000).
3. Pliny, in Radice (1963, Book II, letters 16 and 20); Sigurdsson and others, 1985; Sigurdsson, 1999, p. 51–70.
4. Strothers (1984), Self and others (1984), Harrington (1992).
5. Simkin and Fiske (1983), Winchester (2003).
6. Gorshkov (1959).
7. Taylor (1958).
8. Scarth (2002).
9. Slightly rearranged from Bullard (1962).
10. Day and Allen (1925), Clynne and others (2000).

11. Hunn (1990).
12. McClure and Mack (1999).
13. Lamb (1984).
14. Simplified from Gibbs (1855).
15. Firs near Mount Hood grew half a 1781 growth ring before damage or death (Pringle and others, 2010).
16. Wilkes (1845 [IV] 439).
17. Firs at Mount St. Helens had begun an 1800 ring before damage (Yamaguchi [1983] 1993; Yamaguchi and others [1990]). Majors (1980a,b,c) relates native accounts of the 1800 eruption.
18. Peak is indeed Mount St. Helens (9677 feet). But "highest pinnacle above common level" confuses with Mount Adams (12,276 feet) that they mistook for Mount St. Helens. (Moulton, ed. [1988] 301, 304, 307; [1990] 16, 18; [1991] 33–34).
19. Belyea, ed. (1994).
20. Fur companies and explorers: Terrell (1963), Newman (1998), Nisbet (2005).
21. For exploration of westward land routes, Goetzmann (1986), Meinig (1993).
22. Unruh (1993) 118–120.
23. Parker (1942), Majors (1981) [for Gairdner].
24. Frémont (1845) 193–194.
25. Accounts of 1831–57 eruptions in: Frémont (1845), Wilkes (1845, v. 4, 440), Holmes (1955), Majors (1980b,c). Frémont's journal for 14 November 1843 mentions a Mount St. Helens eruption ashing The Dalles 25 November 1842.
26. Major-Frégeau (1976). Lt. Warre spied on Americans for the British Army. After the peaceful boundary settlement, Warre (1848) published his drawings and watercolors.
27. Kane (1859, 1968). Two Kane oil paintings of Mount St. Helens hang at the Stark Museum of Art in Orange, Texas. A studio oil and watercolor sketch hang at the Royal Ontario Museum in Toronto.
28. White (2001).
29. For history of cadastral land survey in the United States, White (1983, 1996).
30. Stevens, I. (1855), Stevens, H. (1900), Richards (1993).
31. Dryer, 1853. This and accounts of many observers of 1842–57 eruptions (notes 23–27) show 19th century near-summit vents (above 9200 feet) and two midlevel north vents (6800–7200 feet): Goat Rocks, and Floating Island lava flow.
32. Account by Loo-Wit Lat-Cla [pseudonym] (1861) of summit ascent 28 September 1860 tells that Klickitat Indians climbed only as high as south-flank huckleberries (~4000 feet).
33. Marino (1990, fig. 1); Fisher (2010, chap 2).
34. Washington State timber lands discussed in 2001 by Dorian Smith, Washington DNR.
35. Some early history of lower Toutle Valley summarized by Jackson and Howarth (1995).
36. Williamson and Donaldson (1880).
37. Sandburg (1954).
38. Railroad and land-claim history from Holbrook (1947), Martin (1976), Lewty (1995), Malone (1996), Strouse (1999). Railroad-grant patents from records of cadastral land-survey and of land withdrawals from the public domain (U.S. Bureau of Land Management at Portland, Oregon).
39. 13 Stat. 356. 16 Stat. 378. The 1870s railroad from Portland to Puget Sound and the road from Wallula to Puget Sound via Stampede Pass in 1887 qualified for land subsidy.
40. Details of 1901 raid on Northern Pacific stock by Edward Harriman, who controlled the Union Pacific and Southern Pacific, in Strouse (1999) 418–427.
41. Weyerhaeuser history from railroad sources (note 38) and from Hidy and others (1963), Jones (1974), Weyerhaeuser Company (1974, 1989), Twinning (1985), Sensel (1999), LeMonds (2001). In 2002 Weyerhaeuser archivist Megan Moholt culled from company records details of mills 1929–1989 and losses in the 1980 eruption. Memories of retired Weyerhaeuser men, particularly George Steig and Jim Nugent, helped with history of the expanding Weyerhaeuser road system 1940s to 1970s. Jones (1974) mines the memories of old-timers back to 1920s' operations at Longview.
42. Felt (1977).
43. Jones (1974).
44. Powell and origin of the USGS from Stegner (1954), Rabbitt (1969, 1979, 1980, 1989), Domick (2001), Worster (2001).
45. McClure and Mack (1999). By the 1970s Gifford Pinchot National Forest held many square miles north of Mount St. Helens that had been granted to the Northern Pacific. The National Forest and Weyerhaeuser traded lands that their holdings be more continuous.

46. For the early Forest Service and great 1910 north Idaho fire, Egan (2009).

47. Al Robbins's remembrance in the *Columbian*, Bob Beck's column, 12 May 1980.

48. By Loo-Wit Lat-Kla's (1861) witty account of early gold hunting in upper Lewis valley, many returned from prospecting valuable diggings vowing to return, but none hastened back. He advises farmers of Lewis River bottoms as if Voltaire's Candide: "I have discovered mines near your own homes that will pay if only the labor be expended upon them which gold placers require to make them profitable. Your farms contain these mines. Cultivate them assiduously and intelligently, and then look for the gold!!"

49. Dr. Henry Waldo Coe (1857–1927), doctor of mental illness, opened a sanitarium in Portland in 1889 and taught medicine at Willamette University. His larger sanitarium became Morningside Hospital in 1915. He founded four banks. He donated copper from Sweden Mine for bronze *Sacajewea* by Alice Cooper. In 1905 it stood atop the grand staircase of Portland's Lewis and Clark Centennial Exhibition in 1905, since then in Washington Park. (*Oregon Historical Quarterly* [2002, 471] shows 1905 venue.) (Lockerly, 1928.)

50. Mining patents—land withdrawn from the U.S. Public Domain—accessible via U.S. Bureau of Land Management, Portland, Oregon.

51. A Coe company proposed a railroad up the Toutle to Spirit Lake to be electrified by a power dam. The project wasn't built. (*Kelsonian* 13 October 1906, 19 January 1907, 20 April 1907.)

52. Zapffe (1912), Winchell (1912), unpublished reports about Norway and Sweden mines of Consolidated Mining Company dated 1910, ~1944, 1955, Moen (1977), McClure (1984). Unpublished mine records from Washington Department of Natural Resources. Winchell writes, "The prospector of judgment and experience . . . could not fail to see on every hand evidences of disappointing results and general barrenness."

53. First summit register of Mount St. Helens archived at Mazamas club, Portland, Oregon.

54. Portrait of the 1910s to 1970s drawn from several maps; from personal vignettes and historical sketches published 1945 to 2008 in *Cowlitz Historical Quarterly, Oregon Historical Quarterly*, and *Mazama*; from reprinted historical newspaper vignettes in the *Daily News* (Longview) and the *Advocate* (Castle Rock); from interviews with former visitors or residents of upper Toutle valley including Joann and Jack Wolff, John Platt, Peter and Alice Koehler, Julia Bernard, Rob Smith, Miriam Smith, Mark Smith, Shirley Rosen, Bill Reese, Leonard Reese, Mary and Harold Whitney, Mac McClintock, and a few others who'd attended YMCA, Boy Scout, or Girl Scout camps; from unpublished October 1980 reminiscence by Portland-YMCA oldtimer Owen Cramer; from books including Rosen (1981, 1992), Guggenheim (1986), Hoy (1993), Jackson and Howarth (1995), Colasurdo (1997), McClure and Mack (1999); and from Shirley Rosen's taped 1980 conversations with N.B. Gardner and Ken Macdonald.

55. Letters and court documents 1907 to 1915 about Lange's property from Washington state surveyor-general's office.

56. Details of Truman 1910s–1920s in Rosen (1981, 1992). Nelson's business items appear in the *Advocate* (Castle Rock) late 1920s.

57. Photographs collected in folios: Atkeson and Gohs (1969), Atkeson and Williams (1980).

58. Story in Rosen (1981, 1992). In spring 1980 a framed Douglas letter hung in Mount St. Helens Lodge.

59. Rosen (1981, 1992) details the poignant scene.

60. Jones (1974), Sensel (1999).

61. Jones (1974) 73–75.

62. Weyerhaeuser operations in the 1970s to Spring 1980 partly from Dick Ford, George Steig, Jack Schoening, Jim Rombach, John Keatley, Joe Melton, Dexter Salsman, Jim Nugent, Ed Nugent, Bill LeMonds, Louis Fanony, Hugh McCully.

63. Diller (1899), Jillson (1917).

64. Verhoogen (1937).

65. Lawrence (1938, 1939, 1941, 1954), Lawrence and Lawrence (1959).

66. Crandell and Waldron (1956), Crandell (1963).

67. Crandell and others (1962), Crandell (1969, 1971), Crandell and Mullineaux (1967), Mullineaux (1974).

68. Hyde and Crandell (1978), Crandell (1980), Miller (1980), Begét (1982).

69. Mullineaux and Crandell (1962), my interviews with them 2000–2008, their vignettes in *Cowlitz Historical Quarterly* December 2000, Crandell's unpublished autobiography.

70. Crandell and others (1975), Crandell and Mullineaux (1978), Hoblitt and others (1980), Mullineaux and Crandell (1981), Yamaguchi (1985), D.R. Mullineaux (pers. commun., 2008).

71. Crandell's unpublished autobiography, and *Cowlitz County Quarterly* 42 [4](2000) 12–13.

72. St. Lawrence and others (1980).

73. Portrait of Dixy Lee Ray from Weckworth and McVay (1977), Guzzo (1980), Scott (2002, chap 5), my interviews 2001–04 with Dr. Ray's 1940s–1960s UW colleagues of the zoology department and Friday Harbor Labs (Allen Kohn, Art Whiteley, Bob Paine, Dennis Willows), my interviews 2001–09 with governor's affiliates Lou Guzzo, Jerry Hanna, Robert Landon (WSP), Rick LaValla (DES), Wilbur "Web"Hallauer (Dept. of Ecology), Ralph Beswick (DNR), and former state legislator Donn Charnley (D - King Co.). Guzzo's book is an account by a loyal insider, Scott's chapter by a legislator of opposing party.

74. Scott (2002) Section II and Appendix I, Stehr and Ellwanger (2004).

75. Washington State Legislative Budget Committee (1980) 102–108.

Chapter 3

1. Endo and others (1981) summarize Mount St. Helens' spring-1980 earthquakes. PNSN catalogue (Chap 1, note 1) lists quakes magnitude 2 and larger recorded clearly by at least four stations.

2. By Simmonds and Bena, and Simmonds' October 1984 deposition for *Karr et al.* trial.

3. Rosen (1981, 1992) gives an authentic historical portrait of Harry Truman.

4. In 2005 *Cowlitz Historical Quarterly* duBeth dates this episode to March 24. But my earlier interviews with her and internal evidence ("Truman said Tuesday") in 1980 *Daily News* stories show interview was Tuesday, March 25. Don Hamilton interviewed Truman just after duBeth and insists on the 25th. Donna duBeth-Gardiner agreed in 2006.

5. Sources in Appendices II and III, mostly interviews with named characters. A few details culled from newpaper reports, mainly *Daily News* (Longview), *Columbian* (Vancouver), and the *Oregonian* and *Oregon Journal* (Portland).

6. Valley residents learned mostly from the media, little directly from the USGS or Forest Service (Perry and others, 1980).

7. An Air Force C-54 and its crew of six vanished in a storm 22 November 1949 when Mount St. Helens lay deep in snow. Tokarczyk climbed 15 August 1950 and discovered the wreck at 8000 feet on the southwest flank.

8. Some geologists reserve "eruption" for big bursts of molten magma, a small steam burst being an "explosion." Some discouraged "eruption" on grounds it might sow panic, and that's the rhetorical squabble here. But a black cloud shooting from a volcano is "eruption" in popular lingo and to most geologists.

9. Paulson says a big earthquake [evidently magnitude 4.7 at 2:00] hit while they sat in the kitchen with Truman. Hamilton says he experienced a big quake with Truman out on the porch and talked with Paulson or Smith. A magnitude 3.6 earthquake at 2:11 (shows in SHW count file) must be the one Hamilton endures.

10. KING-TV supplied a tape only of a televised clip incorrectly dated March 28, the date of a second clip of Johnston on the tape. Newspaper stories capture more of Johnston's words—especially Donna duBeth in the *Daily News*. Six reporters and cameramen recall phrases. Johnston later inked "~16:00" on Kodachromes he shot before landing.

11. All morning deputies staffed the 504 roadblock at mile 40 where State Patrol Capt. Bullock found it just before noon. The trooper stopped the *Daily News* reporters at Maple Flats (mile 20) about 2:15. Reporters slip past while the deputies move the block down.

12. The non-eruption and evacuation at Guadaloupe in summer 1976 from Tazieff, 1977;

several editorials and letters in *Journal of Volcanology and Geothermal Research* 1978–79; Fiske, 1984; and 2004 correspondence from Patrick Allard, one of Tazieff's team in July 1976.

13. Details of hundreds of small bursts before May 18 from unpublished report *Premagmatic Eruptive Activity, 27 March to 18 May 1980* by Waitt compiled from radio and Coldwater logbooks, geologists' fieldnotes, and seismic records.

14. In 2001–2002 geologist Doug Lalla and filmmaker William Bacon related their 1976 stranding on Augustine. I'd heard about it from David Johnston in 1980, Jürgen Kienle in 1988–90, and Robert Forbes in 1997. Bill Bacon's Kodachromes show demolished helicopter, ripped-open hut, and burned objects inside. Eruption details and timing from Kienle and Shaw (1979), Kamata, Johnston, and Waitt (1991), and Johnston's cryptic fieldnotes.

15. Sulfur dioxide measured by correlation spectrometer (COSPEC), in 1980 made by Barringer Research Ltd. It measures solar ultraviolet light absorbed by sulfur dioxide in a plume compared to an internal standard (Casadevall and others, 1981, 1987). Used into the 2000s (Sutton, et al., 2001).

16. Magnitude 4.6 in PNSN catalogue.

17. Chap 1, note 2. CPW is Capitol Peak West 13 miles southwest of Olympia. MBW is Mount Baker West.

18. Declaration by Governor Ray 3 April 1980. Most of document is boilerplate mimicking declarations that a disaster exists from rain and tides (17 December 1979) and from snowfall and blizzard (11 January 1980).

19. Memo 2 April 1980 signed by Governor Ray.

20. Few photos exist in Vancouver to compare changes at the volcano. Most geologists shot Kodachrome—sharp images, warm rock colors—but K-14 dye-transfer developing cost a week in a Kodak lab. By 1990 geologists shot Ektachrome or Fujichrome whose E-6 dye-coupler process develops quickly. By the late 1990s digital cameras gave timely images.

21. Two Ralph Perry photos in *National Geographic* (Jan. 1981, p. 16) I date to April 3 by snow on the lodge's west roof only slightly thinner than in David Johnston's March 27 photos, by ash that fell at Spirit Lake April 3 but not as heavily as April 4–6, and by one of Perry's shots in the *Columbian* April 4.

22. A mysterious man assembled through many who dealt with him: Tom Hill and Roger McCoy (Tektronix); Bob Christiansen, Rick Hoblitt, and Dan Miller (USGS); Bruce McElfresh, Robert Gilka, and Bob Madden (*National Geographic*); Steve Small, Dave Olson, Fay Blackburn, and Jerry Coughlan (*Columbian*); and Dwight Reber (Columbia Helicopters). Stocker's $10,000 in unpaid bills explored in three-part "Reid's Story" by Steve Twedt in the *Daily News* 18–20 August 1981.

23. Details of system—Palmer's original map, extant decoder & receiver, eruption-bruised transmitter, photos of construction—shown by Hill and McCoy, December 2004.

24. Executive Orders and Proclamations authorizing use of the Washington National Guard in civil emergencies at Washington State Archives in Olympia, Governors' Daily Record Book (v. 11 for Gov. Ray). And http://www.governor.wa.gov/exorders/archive.asp.

25. News release 4 April 1980, Washington Army National Guard, Camp Murray.

26. Duncan Berry in *Cowlitz Historical Quarterly* v. 42, no. 4, p. 27–33 (2000).

27. A Tazieff gas eruption. During the 1973 Heimay eruption in Iceland, he came to pronounce the town doomed. The town survived, and the new lava improved the harbor's natural breakwater. He guessed right at La Soufrière in 1976. Articulate in English and French, he mixes data, ire, and humor to persuade, as in his La Soufrière piece (Tazieff, 1977).

28. Tazieff's language from reporter Hill Williams in the *Seattle Times* April 6 and Sue Hobart in the *Oregonian* April 6. Remarks of Baker and Mahood from Donna DuBeth, the *Daily News* April 8.

29. Lipman and others (1981) 145.

30. Meeting notes by Capt. Dick Bullock, Washington State Patrol.

31. Notes from two meetings, Lt. Harvey Thacker, WSP.

32. George Theisen interview April 2007; his deposition 15 April 1985.

33. In 1980 a fax took minutes to deliver one blurry page.

34. Chief of Staff Paul Bender's typed note of Livingston's April 9 phone call, bearing Governor Ray's reply in a secretary's hand is among exhibits of 1985 trial *Karr et al. v. State of Washington and Weyerhaeuser Co.*

Chapter 4

1. Chap 1, note 1. Recalculated earthquake in PNSN catalogue is magnitude 5.0.
2. Truman mentioned the cave to many in spring 1980, perhaps an old mine adit. Forest rangers in the 1960s saw its meat hooks but didn't catch him with a poached deer.
3. For detailed portrait of Truman, see book by niece Shirley Rosen (1981, 1992). Family and friends called him "Truman." Voight and I don't know this and call him "Harry."
4. Lawton's panorama in *National Geographic* (January 1981, p. 12–13) paired with one he shoots in August 1980. Marshall's shots illuminate *National Geographic*'s 20th-anniversary piece (May 2000, p. 113).
5. Bursts from March 27 to May 17—times, heights, wind drift, etc.—compiled in unpublished report (Chap 3, note 13). This burst photographed close by Nance shows a minute later in Lawton's and Marshall's photos, plume drifting northeast.
6. Sieber, Witt, and Sterne tell their story in film *Keeper of the Fire* (1981).
7. The eruption filmed evening the 12th began 6:48 and lasted 5 minutes. In morning one began 7:03 and lasted unsteadily 33 minutes. This one began 9:26 and lasted unsteadily 16 minutes.
8. Meeting notes 14 April 1980 by Dan Miller (USGS), Capt. Dick Bullock (Washington State Patrol), and Lt. Harvey Thacker (WSP).
9. UW's telephoned notes had most earthquakes ⅔ to 1½ mile down. But depths of shallow quakes can't be calculated well, and many were later deemed shallower. Had field geologists known quakes were up *in* the cone, sense of risk would have been higher.
10. Johnston's April 30 crater-pond samples mislabeled April 23 and so published (Barnes and others, 1981). But Johnston's April 23 photos are from The Boot, none *in* the crater. Any such venture would have been foolhardy before it's clear eruptions have ceased. In May with Hill Williams (note 22) and with Harry Glicken (chap 5), Johnston speaks of just one crater descent.
11. Kinoshita and others (1974) detail swelling before and subsidence during Hawaiian eruptions.
12. Magnitude 4.2 at 3:08.
13. DuBeth's Truman report in the *Daily News* April 26. Her interviews at Timberline and with Truman were afternoon April 24, *not* May 13 as by *Cowlitz Historical Quarterly* v. 47, no. 3, p. 21–22 (2005).
14. Much of Crandell's language from duBeth's April 26 report in the *Daily News*. She interviews the oracles of potential violence and reports possible havoc. For such unvarnished writing, *The Daily News*, a small newspaper, wins a Pulitzer Prize for its Mount St. Helens coverage.

    George Theisen (Forest Service), Dick Bullock (WSP), and Dave Berry (Harmony Falls Lodge) add meeting details, Bullock's supported by notes. See duBeth's comment in *Cowlitz Historical Quarterly*, v. 47, no. 3, p. 21 (2005).
15. Revised Code of Washington 38.52.050(1).
16. Bill Stewart (in 1980 *Columbian*), Bill Dietrich (in 1980 *Columbian*), Don Hamilton (in 1980 *Oregon Journal*), Richard Hill (*Oregonian*), Erik Robinson (*Columbian*), Andre Stepankowsky (*Daily News*), Craig Welsh (*Seattle Times*).
17. Deposition by Edmond Osmond November 1984 for *Karr et al.* trial.
18. Awakened by a magnitude 4.5 earthquake at 00:42. In early 2005 Williams had webposted a narrative of a climb the 28th. Photos prove his climb, but the date discords with details of storm and no flying the 28th. The full moon suggested his climb was instead the 30th. When the narrative is shifted two days ahead, all known data on weather, earthquakes, and summit helicopters fall into place. In 2007 Williams concurred with this date. The early-morning helicopter the 30th carries PSU's Leonard Palmer and *Oregonian* newsfolk. The late-morning and postnoon helicopter carries USGS scientists. Williams worries about being caught, but no one in either ship saw him or cared.
19. Cascade Commercial Helicopters, later renamed Transwestern Helicopters.
20. This earthquake, absent from the catalogue, shows in SHW 'count' file. From

coda length 190 seconds, magnitude calculates to 4.0. This one rocks the ridge a mile south where John Williams climbs.

21. SO$_2$ emissions from Kilauea declined from 150 t/d in summer 1979 to 100 t/d in spring 1980 (Casadevall and others, 1987, fig. 29.2). But when eruption began spring 1983, SO$_2$ jumped to 300 t/d. Measured by different methods, Kilauea's SO$_2$ rates 1980–1998 ranged up to 5000 t/d (Sutton and others, 2001). Mount St. Helens's spring 1980 SO$_2$ emissions seemed puny beside other volcanoes near eruption.

22. Hoblitt and fieldnotes, Johnston's photographs, and Hill Williams' *Seattle Times* piece 11 May 1980. Neither PNSN catalogue nor SHW count file show earthquakes these two hours. They must have been below magnitude 3.2 or too clustered to distinguish. Shaking would amplify where Johnston stands above a shallow source. About to descend to the vent, he'd note small quakes that might herald eruption. Water samples mislabeled to April 23 (note 10).

23. In 1984 former Governor Ray says she reviewed only what DES presented. Rick LaValla says DES acted quickly in unfamiliar territory—restricting land as never before. Parroting the Forest Service was all there was time for. Weyerhaeuser published Theisen's map at first opportunity, as if unopposed (*Southwesterner* May 1980).

24. sw¼se¼S21T9R4.

25. Like Pete Lipman's idea from Questa mine. The Chelean pattern known to landslide specialists had been published in a 1969 mining journal and 1970 symposium volume, the time-creep curve republished (Voight and Kennedy, 1979). Jim Moore explains this idea for Mount St. Helens' bulge to reporter Hill Williams (*Seattle Times* 11 May 1980).

26. From four participants and the pilot. Paul Hammond's report in *Mazama* (1980, no.13, p. 31–44) includes three May 4 photographs from the crater. A color shot of Palmer on a rope posing for NBC appears in 1980 photo-essay booklet *The Volcano Explodes* by KOIN-TV.

27. Macdonald (1972); Mimatsu (1995).

28. Highway log trucks—Kenworth, Peterbilt, Mack—8 feet wide, weigh 26,000 pounds empty and gross 77,000 pounds.

Weyerhaeuser's off-highway trucks on their roads are 10-foot-wide Kenworths and a few Macks. Empty they weigh 46,000 pounds and with a full load of oldgrowth logs can gross 250,000 pounds.

29. From Rombach and Jack Schoning. And Claire Jones' typed notes with sign-in sheet in Dixy Lee Ray papers at the Hoover Institution, Stanford University.

30. 1980 *Columbian* photographers Jerry Coughlan and Dave Olson, photo editor Steve Small, reporter Bill Dietrich.

31. Reber revealed site of east camera north of Spirit Lake on the flank of Mount Margaret, altitude 5200 feet. Photographs by Tom Hill and Roger McCoy confirm the site. Reber's May 7 photo of McCoy setting this camera covers radio-amateur *QST* magazine, August 1980.

32. Mullineaux's talk recalled by him; by residents N.B. Gardner (2nd hand), Greg Drew, Gary Roggenback, Floyd Haderly, and Mark Smith; by Sheriff Les Nelson and deputy Ben Bena; and reported in the *Daily News* 19 May. "No worse than spring freshet" will be off the mark, but much of Mullineaux's forecast happens May 18.

33. Text summarized from Rosen (1981).

34. Truman excerpted from Findley's sanitized *National Geographic* piece, Jan. 1981, p. 20, 25.

35. PNSN catalogue has since 1980 listed this earthquake as magnitude 4.3. This seemed small to be felt so strongly and trigger huge snow avalanche. In 2001 seismologist Robert Norris remeasured the paper records. He pegs the quake almost thirty times larger by energy, a magnitude 5.2—large as accompanied the first colossal landslide May 18.

36. From George Barker, and a May 13 piece in the *Daily News*.

37. Meeting through Theisen (USFS), Mullineaux and Miller (USGS), Schoening (Weyerhaeuser), Mason (State Patrol), Simmonds and from behind scenes Rick LaValla (DES). Mullineaux, Schoening, and Mason have meeting notes.

38. In interviews by Otto Sieber in spring 1981 and in deposition in 1984, former Gov. Ray claimed she'd often consulted Rocky Crandell. But Crandell says before May 18 he briefed her in person only April 10 and once by telephone two weeks later.

39. nw¼S17T8R4.

40. Perry's shot of this high hover in Reber's sidebar in *Rotor and Wing International* (February 1981, p. 60–61.)

41. Excerpted from tape by Carl Berg supplied by Shirley Rosen (Rosen, 1981). Truman saying "two or three days before the weekend" and Berg saying retrospectively this was a few days before the eruption show the date Tuesday May 13. May 14 or later seems unlikely, for Truman doesn't mention his exotic helicopter flight.

    Tape clarifies Truman's remarks to reporters and sheriffs. He'd spoken of protection by an upslope ridge, but no ridge separates Timberline from Spirit Lake. Here Truman clearly means Windy Ridge. A high avalanche would indeed flow down east of it, or come north down Dry Gulch—Truman's "draw to the west." Here he's oblivious to an avalanche so large as to overwhelm Spirit Lake and for weeks has worried authorities and been reported in the *Daily News*.

42. Miller misunderstands this gathering. The seven are Blackburn; Reber with Findley and Small; Stocker and McWhirter (drove in); and maybe Ralph Perry (drove in).

43. Details of airlift from Lematta, Reber, Koschnick, Hathaway, and Wolff; from photographs held by Jack and Joann Wolff; from tapes of Portland's KGW and KATU broadcasts; and from an *Oregonian* piece May 16. Hathaway supplied the authorizing letter, an inventory and weights of items from the camps, and the schedule. A summary with photos appeared summer 1980 in *F.Y.I.* bulletin of YMCA of Columbia-Willamette, Portland. A brief with photos appeared in Columbia Helicopters' *Intercompany News* July 1980.

44. Details from former Cowlitz deputy Ben Bena. Former Skamania sheriff Bill Closner confirmed boundaries. Details supported by Otto Sieber's April 1981 interview with Cowlitz sheriff Les Nelson and by several 1984–1985 depositions for *Karr et al.* trial.

45. The report didn't aid the crisis. But seeing Voight's cross section after May 18, Bob Decker thought it prescient.

46. PNSN catalogue lists it magnitude 4.7, largest in four days.

Chapter 5

1. McCully, augmented by *Karr et al.* deposition February 1985 by Ren Broomhead, superintendent of 12-Road Camp.

2. Landon had okayed a telephone request from Portland Boy Scout council for a helicopter flight. Yet the airlift arranged by press secretary Ray Walters had been authorized in a May 14 letter signed by the governor. The governor here pretends not to know of it. But the letter lies among the governor's documents in state archives. It and a provisional May 13 letter Walters to Gov. Ray is among Dixy Lee Ray's papers at the Hoover Institution.

3. Faddis details from friend Bruce Johnson; from his sister and her husband (Carol and Dennis O'Shea); from Faddis's boss 'Bunny' Mason via the O'Sheas and Johnson; and from Susan Nelson, 1980 married name Tilton. Faddis had told co-workers his intent to hike to Spirit Lake. From here he can proceed upvalley only by returning to the roadgate. But many law officers and police cars are about until nearly 8 PM. An upvalley Faddis venture must await morning.

4. Capt. Bullock checking people through roadgate. The lone cruiser means McNerney came after 2:20 when the convoy is upvalley.

5. se¼S5T10R5.

6. Photos and route of Mazamas climb 24 June 1945 in *Mazama* (1945, no. 13, p. 72–73).

7. Gerald Martin's 26-foot Dodge Superior.

8. From Otto Sieber interview of Glicken in April 1981 and Glicken's handwritten comments. But Johnston had already spilled the crater-pond exploit: Hill Williams' *Seattle Times* piece 11 May 1980.

9. Kaseweter, a geologist, knows silicic lava is sluggish. He seems oblivious to talk at Vancouver—reported in newspapers—that a large rock-ice avalanche or hot-ash hurricane may descend on Spirit Lake swiftly.

10. Yet forcing out a resident who violates no statute would be illegal.

11. From Otto Sieber interview with Glicken April 1981 and Glicken's written comments.

12. In 1980 most geologists shot Kodachrome that took a week to develop. Newsmen shot quickly developable Ektachrome.

13. Details of scene from logbooks, radio tapes, Glicken's remembrances, and my interviews with Brugman, Driedger, Swanson, Wörner, and Stickney. Johnston's one visit to Coldwater II begins today about 3:30. Brugman and Driedger come about six. There's no time for Johnston and Glicken to analyze roadcuts, and Glicken later says nothing about it. Johnston knew 5½ miles from an explosive silicic vent—closer than St. Pierre to Mont Pelée—isn't wholly safe. Yet had he imagined what lay in store for tomorrow, neither he nor Glicken would be here now.

14. This guess overstates. PNSN catalogue lists earthquake magnitude 4.3. In 2003 seismologist Bob Norris confirmed this value about right.

15. Even Johnston didn't know of the armored personnel carriers.

Chapter 6

1. Arlene and Jolene Edwards didn't know the roads, but soon threaded the labyrinth to high Elk Rock—as if a passenger knew the way. Bruce Faddis had some time late Saturday with people who knew the roads. Later at the Cowlitz County coroner's, Roxann Edwards saw among items from the pickup an unfamiliar backpack whose male clothing weren't her mother's or sister's.

2. nw¼ne¼S24T10R4.

3. Mysterious vehicle. Jim Pluard's was a yellow Weyerhaeuser rig; Dorothy Stoffel insists on red. This party may be uncounted among the dead.

4. Note 1, chap 1. The PNSN catalogue lists 558 *located* earthquakes magnitude 2 and larger. The actual number is twenty times that, says Steve Malone. Only cleanly recorded quakes are sufficiently located to admit to the catalogue. Many others can be counted. The "count" file of close station SHW lists about 3500 quakes magnitude 2 and larger. But during a swarm, the swiggles overlie one another too much to count. The catalogue probably contains all earthquakes magnitude 4 and larger. Hundreds of magnitude 3, thousands of magnitude 2, and tens of thousands of earthquakes smaller than magnitude 2 are neither located nor counted.

18 May 1980

1. Endo and others, 1981; Lipman and others, 1981; Voight, 1981; Waitt and Dzurisin, 1981; Moore and Sisson, 1981; Sarna-Wojcicki and others, 1981; Harris and others, 1981; Voight and others, 1983; Kanamori and others, 1984; Waitt, 1981, 1989; Sparks and others, 1986; Hoblitt, 2000.

Chapter 7

1. The Stoffels' summarized their story in *Washington Division of Earth Resources Information Circular* 71, June 1980, 5–6, and *Geotimes*, Oct. 1980, 16–17.

2. Sizable quakes triggered ice cascades. This one marks the magnitude 5.1 at 8:32:11.

3. From indicated (instrument) airspeed, actual airspeed increases 2% for every 1000 feet altitude gained. Below 15,000 feet light winds crossed the flight path: groundspeed is close to actual airspeed.

4. Eruption began 8:32:53, but initial small plumes wouldn't be seen at a distance. By Voight's (1981, fig. 30) timing of Gary Rosenquist's photographs, I judge Davidson noticed the eruption clouds around the summit about 8:33:15.

5. Mathes' estimates of altitudes and growth rates of the plume are close to reconstruction by Sparks and others (1986) who from satellite data estimate column began its rise about 8:36. By 8:47 it had formed a giant mushroom cap 16 miles high and 44 miles across. Satellite data have the mushroom's base at 33,000 feet. Flying at that level, Mathes estimates its base at 49,000 feet.

6. Kropf and Purdum published stories in the *Albany Democrat-Herald* 19 May 1980, used here (combined and shortened) by permission.

7. Brief piece by Mike Murphey of Gary Treat's flight appeared in the *Yakima Herald-Republic* 19 May 1980.

8. Werth says just after 9 o'clock; Stepankowski says much later.

9. Artistic photo by Werth in the *Daily News* 19 and 24 May 1980 and on cover of *Cowlitz Historical Quarterly* September 2005 compare to clouds at about 10:30–40 in USGS's Don Swanson's long sequence of timed photos.

10. Meeting the governor indicates *Daily News* flight landed about 1:40 PM. She's been

briefed by Air Force Reserve Maj. Peters [1:30–1:40] about devastation and about a coming flood (chap 16).

11. Rosenfeld summarized in *Oregon Geology* (1980), *American Scientist* (1980), and *Earthfire* (1982).

12. National Weather Service radar at Portland measured plume at 11:30 up to 52,600 feet (Harris, 1981, fig. 190). Timing of ashflow from *{Swanson}* chap 16.

13. Cummans (1981, p. 6, table 2) reports Cowlitz County communications reporting flooding at 12 Road camp 10:03 to 10:07, peaking 10:10.

14. Site identified by Leonard Palmer's photographs from Portland's KOIN-TV helicopter in *Mount St. Helens—The Volcano Explodes!* (1980). A high shot (p. 70) shows the log flood dividing into channels four miles above Tower bridge [se¼S10T10R1W]. A low shot (p. 71) shows Wright's white-and-blue Hughes 500 over massed logs in south channel. By Cummans' (1981) timing, and Jack Schoening's diary *{Pleasant & Schoening}*, KING5 filmed the flood here about 11:25.

15. Timing of flood reaching Cowlitz confluence judged from Cummans (1981, table 2).

16. Timing by Weyerhaeuser radio log and Schoening's diary. Corresponds with Cowlitz sheriff radio log.

17. S10–12T10R1W

18. S28T9R4

19. Rosenfeld sees effects in the upper South Fork before and after Swanson. Capt. Airis saw flows descending the west flank about 8:40. David Crockett (chap 10) encountered peak flow some minutes later.

Chapter 8

1. Some of von Michalofski's story in *Signpost* [Puget Sound hiking magazine] January 1981, used here (edited) with permission.

2. Retired physician Halliday was a speleologist and authored a book about caves including those in glaciers on volcanoes (*Depths of the Earth*: Harper & Row, 1976). Some material in this account was published in the *Geological Newsletter* of the Geological Society of the Oregon Country (Portland, Oreg.). Used here (edited) with permission.

3. Donald L. Lund was an engineer for Washington DOT and had worked with Ron

Seibold (a MSH victim) at DOT. Both were members of the Olympia chapter of the Mountaineers.

4. Photographs by Christiansen and others of this party widely shown in the 1980s. Two appear in *National Geographic* (January 1981, 24–25).

Chapter 9

1. sw¼ne¼S7T9R5.

2. nw¼ne¼S6T9R5.

3. Conversation trimmed. The repeater seems to cut out twice, maybe interference by Ty Kearney transmitting over Martin's signal (chap 10, note 2).

4. No one familiar with this volcano expected a lava flow.

5. se¼S35T9R4.

6. Times based on a timeline hung with photos, built summer 1980 by Steve Malone and colleagues at University of Washington seismology laboratory. *National Geographic* (January 1981, p. 26–27) published four of Landsburg's eruption shots.

7. ne¼ne¼S21T9R4.

8. Colleagues from the *Columbian* dug out Reid Blackburn's car and tent at Coldwater I (chap 20). Photographs of last two pages of Blackburn's notebook in the *Columbian* July 2.

9. nw¼ne¼S32T10R3.

10. Described as a 'thump' from the northeast (*{Hodgson}* chap 12).

11. Motorhome the Johnstons encountered moments earlier.

12. Unidentified man. Training hunting dogs, he'd have been on a logging road. The ash and dead dogs tell he was within the edge of the hot cloud, likely two or three miles above Camp Baker, maybe road 2700.

13. The Baker & O'Keefe account full of speed in a Toronado on pavement discords with the next account that starts much farther upvalley yet runs much slower in a Honda on gravel. McNerney stopped twice on pavement where O'Keefe and Baker's race begins. In reinterviews, both parties stick to their stories and elaborate consistent details.

14. nw¼nw¼S11T9R4.

15. nw¼S26T10R3.

16. ne¼ne¼S33.

17. Parshley and others (1982) detail medical conditions of the three patients.

18. Dale Davis died September 1997, Al Brooks January 1998. A few of Brooks' comments excerpted from interview in the [Morton] *Journal* 21 August 1980 (used by permission). Some Leslie Davis comments from her written account 20 May 1980.
19. ne¼S9T10R4.
20. w¼sw¼S3T10R3.
21. No evidence of hueys in Green River until 3:30 (chap 16).
22. sw¼S17T11R3.
23. se¼S31T11R5.
24. sw¼ne¼S2T10R4.
25. nw¼se¼se¼S5T10R5.
26. ne¼ne¼S1T10R3.

Chapter 10

1. Synopsis by Marianna Kearney "One Sunday in May" in *Mazama* (1980, no. 13, p. 46–52). Much later she published a small book of photographs and art, story as poem (Kearney, 2011).
2. Ty Kearney's radio calls (he says) about the earthquake didn't record. During Martin's report the radio repeater cuts out—maybe Kearney's signal competing with Martin's.
3. sw¼ne¼S16T8R4.
4. nw¼nw¼S17T8R4.
5. The *Daily News* (19 May 1980 by Steve Twedt) reports this party {Smith} offered a ride but wouldn't risk time to tow out a stuck car.
6. Perhaps fir cones swept up by the surge and updraft, now falling.
7. Dwight Reber trying to reach Reid Blackburn ({Reber} chap 7).
8. Change in the column began before 12:17 ({Swanson} chap 7). Earlier it had jetted up, no flows onto the flanks.
9. sw¼sw¼S10T8R4: two miles closer than the Kearneys, Rogers, and Valenzuela.
10. nw¼S31T9R4.
11. Deer reacting to the earthquake at 8:32:11. People driving on gravel wouldn't feel it.
12. nw¼se¼S29T9R3.
13. I reviewed geography near Crockett's car in June 1980. The cloud lofting over the ridge northwest of him shows he lingered at his first site more than two minutes.
14. This site 6¼ miles west of summit [sw¼nw¼S4T8R4]. The South Fork lahar peaked here about ten minutes after eruption's start. Waitt (1989) details effects of flood upvalley.

15. Aerial view of 12-Road Camp in *National Geographic*, February 1981, p. 34.

Chapter 11

1. nw¼sw¼S33T11R5.
2. se¼S18T11R4.
3. An earthquake travels the 17 miles in 7 seconds. Cutting with a chain saw, Merzoian didn't feel it. Since the cloud front had already passed Fawn Lake, this couldn't be the magnitude 5 at 08:32:11. The logs must have rolled in the second magnitude 5 two minutes later.
4. Sound travels the 18 miles from Mount St. Helens in 1⅓ minute.
5. S34T11R3.
6. Compare with Gary Treat in chap 7.
7. s½S21T11R4.
8. Ash from the Palmers' Jeep I examined in 1982 was gray silt. It held a few gray spheres as large as 3 mm that when squeezed turned to loose silt (like layer A3 of Waitt and Dzurisin, 1981).
9. S35T11R5.
10. Center S29T11R5. LaPlaunts' campsite, apparently along road 2645 or 2600, judged by their photographs looking south up Miners Creek. Less than half a mile northeast lay the pass north. On road 2150 they'd have wound more than 15 miles to the bridge east of Riffe Lake.
11. *National Geographic* (Jan 1981, p. 14–15) published a Jack Joyce photograph showing a lightning bolt from a dark cloud that drops heavy curtains of ash.

Chapter 12

1. se¼se¼S27T10R6. Since 1980 called 'Bear Meadow viewpoint.' Bear Meadow—partly a swamp and former horse camp—lies in a vale 120 feet lower half a mile southeast in land section 35.
2. Rosenquist's photo sequence of landslide and initial explosions, morphed into a moving sequence, widely shown on television and at USFS Johnston Ridge Observatory. Stills oft-published: *National Geographic* (Jan 1981, p. 4–8); Voight (1981, fig 38, p. 72–76).
3. In the 1980s Ronnholm sold thousands of his photograph sets.
4. I later examined one of the rocks: medium-gray fresh dacite.

4.   5. Casual witnesses overestimate ash thickness. At 2:40 AM May 19 at Randle I measured dry ash at 17 mm (⅔ inch).

6.   ne¼ne¼S5T10R7.

7.   Described as a 'whoom' from eleven miles northwest of the mountain (chap 7 {Wilson}). Perhaps the surge striking the ridge north of the Toutle (in 1982 named Johnston Ridge). Sound travels to Hodgson's site in 1⅓ minute.

Chapter 13

1.   They summarized their photographs (Hickson and Hickson, 1980). Cathie Hickson later published a brief analysis (Hickson, 1990) and a book (Hickson, 2005).

2.   sw¼sw¼S7T8R7.

3.   nw¼nw¼S8T7R7.

4.   se¼S34T10R10.

5.   The *Columbian* 19 May 1980.

Chapter 14

1.   These witnesses each soon wrote a summary. Two have the second site in section 32. But over maps Kathy Anderson puts it in the southeast of section 36. Witnesses' road descriptions and their escape route would make no sense were the second site farther west in section 32.

2.   se¼S34T8R5.

3.   sw¼se¼S36.

4.   Ken Siebert's photographs from twenty miles south-southeast show two wide columns rising from separate areas miles north-northeast and northwest of the cone. The gap between two columns showed from the northwest {O'Keefe and Baker} and from sixty miles southeast {Guthrie and Rodeback}.

5.   sw¼sw¼S1T7R5.

6.   sw¼se¼S29T6R4.

Chapter 15

1.   Dewey (1985) analyzes sound from Mount St. Helens arcing up, refracting off the stratosphere, and reflecting back to surface beyond 60 miles. At 536 mi/hr (Dewey, fig. 7), sound from the mountain 150 miles south would enter Walker valley in 17.8 minutes.

2.   Excerpted from Cowlitz County Sheriff's tape.

Chapter 16

1.   In 2005 McChord Air Force Base could say only a C-141 flew one Mount St. Helens sortie for 2.9 hours. By Air Force Reserve 304th log, it wasn't airborne by 2:30. It must be the aircraft Ray Pleasant radios about 7:20.

2.   A west breeze gradually clears the air. This flight and the next can see northwest of the volcano as earlier flights could not.

3.   In 1980 Rooth published two summaries: in the Salem *Statesman-Journal* Sunday supplement *Oregon Territory* special edition "The Mountain Speaks" 1 June 1980, p. 6–7; and in *Oregon Geology*, v. 42, p. 141–144 (August 1980).

4.   A photo of this scene in *National Geographic* January 1981, p. 34.

5.   In *Cowlitz Historical Quarterly* (v. 25, no. 3, p. 30–33) duBeth begins flight much too early. I-5 wasn't blocked until nearly noon (South Fork flood). Werth's morning flight ended early afternoon, then he returned to newsroom before helicopter flight. Early in this flight he photographs breakup of Alder Creek bridge, around 3:00 (note 6).

6.   Highway bridge about 3:00 {Pleasant}; Cummans (1981, table); and J.E. Cummans summary, 17 June 1980 of sheriff's 18 May log.

7.   Timing of helicopters 28W and 62W from Weyerhaeuser radio log, from diary of Jack Schoening, from Cowlitz County sheriff's radio log, and from summary compilation of sheriff's log for May 18 & 19 by John E. Cummans (USGS). Details of Schoening's May 18 flight notes, elaborated May 19–20, were deemed accurate then by pilots Pleasant and Erdelbrock.

8.   S28T9R3.

9.   Pleasant says "C-130" but radios an Air Force C-141 (note 1). The C-130 arrived in Portland late evening and began Mount St. Helens flights early the 19th.

10. Helicopter can only be Air Force Reserve Save 80 landing for jumpers. Glicken says Save 82 landed at Toutle about 1:00, so Save 80 and 82 shouldn't still be upvalley at this time. Perhaps some Weyerhaeuser entries were radioed in well after the observation and enter the logbook late.

11. Times suggested by men in Save 80 and 82 were as much as 2½ hours earlier than

recorded here. All but passenger Harry Glicken's were from memory 19½ years later. The 304th squadron's logbook specifies Save 80 and 82 left base at 11:10. Glicken's 19 noted times concord with the logbook. Surveyor and PJ Cooney plotted first sortie by the usual speed of a huey. Cooney's theoretical times early in sortie correspond within a couple minutes to times in Glicken's summary. Glicken's times are consistent with the Forest Service log when occasionally a 304th huey radios Forest aircraft. Adjusted times in these 304th accounts agree with objective times as in the Forest Service log of communications with surveillance aircraft and with other aircraft timed by logbooks *{Reber; Pleasant; Erdelbrock & Schoening}*.

12. se¼sw¼S29T10R3.

13. Spirit Lake is flyable 12:15–12:20 but won't be after 12:30 when a hot flow arrives *{Swanson}*.

14. "Road Runner" probably Joel Colten's seen at mile 33¼ as landslide and eruption began *{O'Keefe & Baker}*. "Peugeot" probably Klaus Zimmerman's.

15. On aerial photographs of July 1980, I found the site [se¼se¼S33T10R3], the most upvalley remaining trace of the highway. It was obliterated after sediment dam N-1 built two miles downvalley in summer 1980 backed up debris by 1981.

16. se¼S25T10R3.

17. Cooney had suggested 12:20 for this. His plotted route of sortie is timed by speed 100 kts from Pearson at Vancouver starting 11:28. These times are minimal, for aircraft speed can be slower at times, and deviations go unremembered. Compared to Glicken's notes and a Weyerhaeuser encounter, Cooney's times seem a few minutes ahead early in this sortie and as much as 35 minutes ahead here late in sortie.

18. Apparently gyppo loggers after Weyerhaeuser men had moved company trucks to high ground *{Keatley}*.

19. Later photos show the back cargo door ajar from its hinges, bashed by a falling tree. The gap a few feet long admitted heat and ash.

20. Having flown *National Geographic* for weeks, Dwight Reber is on his own rescue mission.

21. These dead and injured elk probably the herd Sharon Burchard encountered not far upvalley two months earlier (chap 1).

22. Glicken recorded specific times in field notes. His summary written twelve hours after these flights contains 19 specific times between 11:28 AM and 5:45 PM. At this point (1:15) he claims to fly upvalley. But Save 82 and Save 80 are low on fuel. By the accounts of eight others in these ships, both helicopters fly downvalley to Kelso to refuel. The 304th logbook records a telephone call from Kelso from *each* crew (1:30–2:02). So the timing in Glicken's summary from 1:15 to 2:30 is confused. His valid descriptions I move to 2:40–3:20—clearly the second upvalley sortie for Save 80 and 82.

23. So Maj. Peters thinks and affects behavior (but it was Reber). Soon the National Guard tries to bring the Air Force Reserve under its control *{Edelbrock}*.

24. Dave Ward reports similarly, but National Guard operations *{Edelbrock}* claim they controlled the 304th. The Guard also flew the North Fork. All fliers say they freelanced May 18 and the Guard held little control before the 19th.

25. Save 81, paired with Save 79. Harder died in 1996 before my interviews.

26. Probably the KOMO car stranded on an island-like high surrounded by mudflows *{Crockett}*. The site is 15 miles farther upvalley than Save 81 flew.

27. Forest Service's radio log records at 3:08 a dual message relayed by surveillance aircraft 5GM: "33F + MAST — confirmed Spirit Lake now all boiling ash + gas." 33F is the Hughes flown by Reber. The only military helicopter near at this time is Save 81 of the AFR 304th. Observations could precede logbook entry by a minute or two.

28. Forest Service log records relayed "MAST" radio reports from east of Camp Baker at 12:05, 12:13, and 12:31 about deploying pararescue jumpers (PJs). These reports can only be from the Air Force Reserve 304th. Their log records at 12:20 a call relayed from Save 80: "2 PJs on ground." The high hover seen by Reber must be second attempt to deploy PJs by cable, about 12:10.

29. Forest Service X-2 log records a radio call at 2:28 from helicopter 33F [Reber] reporting an overturned bulldozer.
30. In Forest Service log a call from 33F at 2:59 at Coldwater I reports "four feet of debris."
31. From near here a white billowy plume rose intermittently a few thousand feet—from a cauldron later called Pumice Pond. Either that huge plume lay beyond Reber's view and he describes a much smaller feature, or this is the Pumice Pond plume temporarily subsided.
32. Reber's former chief pilot at Columbia Helicopters, George Warren, says (24 years later) Reber would indeed run such calculations in his head while flying.
   Hot ash flows started down Mount St. Helens's north flank at 12:30. Spirit Lake is surrounded by steep ridges except the south. A hot ash cloud would spread across the basin. One flow at perhaps 1500°F entered the southeast of Spirit Lake at 3:01 {Rosenbaum}. Reber measuring 140°F air temperature a mile away at 3:07 is consistent.
33. See note 27, this chapter. Over the next two days the fliers realize Spirit Lake remains though 200 feet higher. Through May 18's ashfog, the great log raft covered by ash seemed a fill.
34. Times of Hagerman's landings and takeoffs in aircraft 20404 quoted in 2007 from flight form-12 by Capt. Mark Edelbrock (Ret.), National Guard operations. From memory Hagerman had times much earlier.
35. Forest Service aircraft may have spotted vehicles on road 3000 or 4100. None could move. Or maybe they're Rogers and Valenzuela (chap 10) thought by Reber (chap 7) to be stranded.
36. ne¼S33T10R3.
37. Perhaps an illegal alien. His real name is José Dias.
38. Handwritten National Guard 'Toutle' log shows huey G-196 landed 5:40 PM.
39. National Guard 'Kelso' log shows G-196 there 9:50 to 10:30.
40. {Hoblitt} records a radio call at 9:35 about three bodies.
41. Note 2, this chapter. Forest Service X-2 radio log records call from aircraft 004 [Stickney] relayed through surveillance aircraft at 6:32.
42. Forest Service log records three relayed calls from aircraft 004 at 7:02, 7:20, and 7:35.

Chapter 17

1. Governor Ray's stop by DES from Lyle Burt's piece in *Seattle Times* 19 May 1980. She intends Edward Bullwer's 1834 *The Last Days of Pompeii.*
2. In *Cowlitz Historical Quarterly* v. 25, no. 3, p. 30–33, duBeth speeds up time by hours. The sheriff didn't block I-5 for the South Fork flood until 11:45 or later (note 5, chap 16).

Chapter 18

1. A piece appeared in the *Seattle Post-Intellingencer* 20 May 1980. In 2005 Bakke had posted some of her story to a web page.
2. Cover photograph of *National Geographic* January 1981 shows the sagged bottom of the cloud near Ephrata.
3. Some details anchored in Mel Carlson's diary.
4. In June 1980 Ardis and Julie recorded May 18–19 details to audio tape.
5. Chap 15, note 1. At 536 mi/hr (least-squares fit to barometric data (Dewey, 1985)), sound from Mount St. Helens arrives at Cheney in about 26 minutes, or 8:59.
6. Pilot recalls encountering a sulfurous cloud far east, maybe near Pierre. But all reports, satellite images, and numerical models with 18 May 1980 winds allow windsteam from Mount St. Helens no closer than several hundred miles southwest of Pierre. Pilot insists on May 18.

Chapter 19

1. se¼S9T10R2.
2. Henderson's piece and Manasse's photograph in *Seattle Times* 19 May 1980.
3. nw¼S14T10R1.
4. Second vehicle Reed loses to this mudflow—having left a company car when rescued by the Air Force 304th {Cooney; Weed et al; Peters et al; Ward and Williams} chap 16.
5. The USGS gauge a few hundred feet below Coal Bank bridge transmitted at 6:00 but not 6:15. Soon after the bridge released the mud and logs they hit the gauge.

6. Source unknown but possibly—misheard—David Johnston's hurried second transmission.

7. A Roger Werth photo shows the Haderly's drowned house and buried acres (*National Geographic*, January 1981, p. 46–47).

8. ne¼ne¼se¼S19T10R1W.

9. sw¼sw¼S26T10R2W.

10. Two hours earlier the South Fork flood had backed up the lower North Fork.

11. Air Force Reserve 304th huey—Save 80 or Save 82—near the end of first sortie (chap 16).

12. Cummans (1981, table 2) has average velocity at flood's peak as 7–12 feet/second (5-8 mph). Velocity in the center exceeds average—velocity at the banks being nearly nil.

Chapter 20

1. Cummans (1981); Haeni (1983).

2. S26T9R6.

3. Richard Harder died in 1998 before my interviews with the 304th. In disasters like an Air Force C-141 crash in the Olympic Mountains he recovered dozens of bodies before getting a live rescue. It earned him the nickname Bagger.

4. S19–20T10R4.

5. Ralph Perry's photos in *National Geographic* (January 1981, p. 32–33) and in "Mount St. Helens Holocaust" (*Columbian* photo booklet, 1980, p. 26).

6. se¼S31T11R5.

7. *National Geographic,* January 1981, p. 39.

8. Photograph also ran May 21 on the *Oregonian* front page.

9. Times here from handwritten National Guard log of helicopters departing Kelso airfield. Nole's huey is tailnumber 374, the gunship 495.

10. Forest road 1203, nw¼S16T10R6.

11. Eric Nalder piece in *Seattle Post-Intelligencer*, 21 May 1980.

12. Details of the President's visit from several witnesses and from stories in the *Columbian* 22 May 1980. Timing partly from President's official diary online via Carter Presidential Library.

13. The briefcase nicknamed the "football" contains codes by which the President can launch nuclear war.

14. Three days later Mount St. Helens bursts before the USGS announces it. Pumice, ash, and dense darkness envelop where President Carter had flown in rain beneath low clouds.

15. Transcribed from Beard's audio tape, 22 May 1980.

16. Medical conditions of Scymanky, Skorohodoff, and Dias in Parshley and others (1982). Scymanky stays free of bacterial infection. Skorohodoff and Dias arrive with lung damage and soon develop *Staphylococcus* and *Streptococcus* infections in burns and lungs. They die of "adult respiratory distress syndrome."

17. Responsibility had been divided—logistics to Lewis County Sheriff, search-and-rescue to Cowlitz County sheriff, dead and missing persons to Skamania County sheriff, flying to the Army, National Guard, and Air Force Reserve. "Whoever's in charge" rings ambiguously.

18. Probably second car Reed lost to mud *{Henderson & Manasse}*.

19. Eisele and others (1981).

20. Roger Werth photographs Roggenback salvaging from his drowned house (*National Geographic*, January 1981, p. 47).

21. They looked into North Coldwater Creek that then held no lake. Spirit Lake lay miles east behind a higher ridge. The water in Sieber's film *Keeper of the Fire* is Hanaford Lake.

22. ~sw¼S35T10R4.

23. Trial documents, *Transamerica Airlines v. United States*, No. C82-112C, US District Court, Western District of Washington, 1982.

24. Malone and others (1981).

25. *National Geographic* January 1981, p. 26–27.

26. Doran (1980). Fresh memories and photos in Jeffry Doran, *Search on Mount St. Helens*, Bellevue, Wash., Imagesmith (1980).

27. May 28 photo shows truck on its side (Doran, p. 48, in note 25). Later searchers righted it. Oxygen tanks in the back must have exploded, burning camper and cab. A small blackened mass was identified as human by an imbedded gold necklace.

28. January 1981, p. 12–13.

29. Three dozen photographs of destroyed Weyerhaeuser camps, roads, railroad, and logging equipment appear in company *The Southwesterner*, June 1980.

30. *Cougar Business Owners Association v. State. Karr et al. v. State* (State Superior

Court for King County, 81-2-07109-1). See Huffman (1986).

31. Pliny the Younger (Radice, 1963), Book 6, excerpted from Letters 16 and 20.

Appendix II: Sources

1. Rosenbaum and Waitt (1981).
2. Simplified from Primo Levi, *The Drowned and the Saved.* English translation from the Italian by Raymond Rosenthal. New York: Summit Books (Simon & Schuster) (1988), 23–24.
3. Simplified from Milan Kundera, *Ignorance (a novel)*, New York: HarperCollins (2002), 123.
4. Michael Macdonald Mooney, *The Hindenburg* New York: Dodd, Mead & Company (1972); J.K. Zawodny, *Death in the Forest—The Story of the Katyn Forest Massacre*, Notre Dame, Ind.: University of Notre Dame Press (1962); J.K. Zawodny, *Nothing but Honour—The Story of the Warsaw Uprising, 1944,* Stanford, Calif.: Hoover Institution Press (1979).
5. Science philosopher Robert Pennock writes: "the scientific method of investigation is itself inherently public. Scientific knowledge is not validated by appeals to authority, rather by appeal to evidence."

Robert T. Pennock, *Tower of Babel—The Evidence against the New Creationism*, Cambridge, Mass.: MIT Press (1999), 325.
6. For methods of historical research, e.g.: Henry Steele Commager, *The Nature and the Study of History*, Columbus, Ohio: Charles Merrill (1965), 1–71; Barbara A. Tuchman, *Practicing History—Selected Essays*, New York: Ballentine Books (1982), 13–50; William Zinsser, *On Writing Well—The Classic Guide to Writing Nonfiction*, 6th ed., New York: HarperCollins, (1998), 100–115.
7. Condensed from Commager (1965) 5 and 48.
8. Condensed from Zinsser (1998), 108–109.
9. H.K. Beals, S. Cline, and J.M. Koler, *On the Mountain's Brink—A Forest Service History of the 1980 Mount St. Helens Volcanic Emergency,.* Gifford Pinchot National Forest (1981?). Unedited and uncorrected, this work is a source of errors on USGS activity.
10. Bruce L. Foxworthy and Mary Hill, *Volcanic Eruptions of 1980 at Mount St. Helens—The First 100 Days*, U.S. Geological Survey Professional Paper 1249, 1981.
11. A.K. Ota, J. Snell, and L.L. Zaitz, "A Terrible Beauty—Mount St. Helens Special Report," *The Oregonian*, October 27, 1980.

References

Books and Articles

Atkeson, Ray, and Gohs, Carl. *Washington.* Portland, Ore.: Graphic Arts Center (Charles Belding), 1969.

Atkeson, Ray, and Williams, Chuck. *Mount St. Helens.* Portland, Ore.: Graphic Arts Center, 1980.

Barnes, I., Johnston, D.A., Evans, W.C., Presser, T.S., Mariner, R.H., and White, L.D. "Properties of Gases and Waters of Deep Origin near Mount St. Helens." *U.S. Geological Survey Professional Paper 1250* (1981) 233–237.

Begét, J.E. *Postglacial Volcanic Deposits at Glacier Peak, Washington, and Potential Hazards from Future Eruptions.* U.S. Geological Survey Open-File Report 82-830, 1982.

Belyea, Barbara, ed. *Columbia Journals—David Thompson.* Montreal: McGill-Queen's University Press, 1994.

Berry, Duncan. "A Harrowing Trip Across Melting Ice." *Cowlitz Historical Quarterly* 42 (2000) 27–33.

Blong, R.J. *Volcanic Hazards—A Sourcebook on the Effects of Eruptions.* Sydney, Australia: Academic Press, 1984.

Bullard, Fred M. *Volcanoes—in History, in Theory, in Eruption.* Austin: University of Texas Press, 1962, 1976.

Casadevall, T.J., Johnston, D.A., Harris, D.M., Rose, W.I., Malinconico, L.L., Stoiber, R.E., Bornhorst, T.J., Williams, S.N., Woodruff, L, and Thompson, J.M. "SO_2 Emission Rates at Mount St. Helens from March 29 through December 1980." In *U.S. Geological Survey Professional Paper* 1250 (1981) 193–207.

Casadevall, T.J., Stokes, J.B., Greenland, P.L., Malinconico, L.L., Casadevall, J.R., and Furukawa, B.T. "SO_2 and CO_2 Emission Rates at Kilauea Volcano, 1970–1984." *U.S. Geological Survey Professional Paper* 1350 (1987) 771–780.

Castleden, Rodney. *Atlantis Destroyed.* London and New York, Rutledge, 1998.

Clynne, M.A., Christiansen, R.L., Miller, C.D., Stauffer, P.H., and Hendley, J.W. "Volcanic Hazards of the Lassen Volcanic National Park Area, California." *U.S. Geological Survey Fact Sheet* 022-00, 2000.

Colasurdo, Christine. *Return to Spirit Lake—Journey Through a Lost Landscape.* Seattle. Sasquatch Books, 1997.

Crandell, D.R. *Surficial Geology and Geomorphology of the Lake Tapps Quadrangle, Washington.* U.S. Geological Survey Professional Paper 388-A, 1963b.

_____. *Surficial Geology of Mount Rainier National Park, Washington.* U.S. Geological Survey Bulletin 1288, 1969.

_____. *Postglacial Lahars from Mount Rainier Volcano, Washington.* U.S. Geological Survey Professional Paper 677, 1971.

_____. *Recent Eruptive History of Mount Hood, Oregon, and Potential Hazards from Future Eruptions.* U.S. Geological Survey Bulletin 1492, 1980.

Crandell, D.R. and Mullineaux, D.R. *Volcanic Hazards at Mount Rainier, Washington.* U.S. Geological Survey Bulletin 1238, 1967.

_____. *Potential Hazards from Future Eruptions of Mount St. Helens Volcano, Washington.* U.S. Geological Survey Bulletin 1383–C, 1978.

Crandell, D.R., Mullineaux, D.R., Miller, R.D., and Meyer, Rubin. "Pyroclastic Deposits of Recent Age at Mount Rainier, Washington." *U.S. Geological Survey Professional Paper* 450-D (1962) 64–68.

Crandell, D.R., Mullineaux, D.R., and Rubin, M. "Mount St. Helens Volcano—Recent and Future Behavior." *Science* 187 (1975) 438–441.

Crandell, D.R. and Waldron, H.H. "A Recent Volcanic Mudflow of Exceptional Dimensions from Mt. Rainier, Washington." *American Journal of Science* 254 (1956) 349–362.

Cummans, John. *Mudflows Resulting from the May 18, 1980, Eruption of Mount St. Helens, Washington.* U.S. Geological Survey Circular 850-B, 1981.

Day, A.L., and Allen, E.T. "The Volcanic Activity and Hot Springs of Lassen Peak." *Carnegie Institute of Washington.* Publication 190, 1925.

Dewey, J.M. "The Propagation of Sound from the Eruption of Mt. St. Helens on 18 May 1980." *Northwest Science* 59 (1985) 79–92.

Diller, J.S. "Latest Volcanic Eruptions of the Pacific Coast." *Science*, n.s. 9 (1899) 639–640.

Domick, Edward. *Down the Great Unknown—John Wesley Powell's 1869 Journey of Discovery and Tragedy through the Grand Canyon*. New York: HarperCollins, 2001.

Dryer, T.J. (edited by H.M. Majors) "First Ascent of Mount St. Helens." *Northwest Discovery* 1 (1980) 164–180 [from *The Morning Oregonian*, 1853].

Egan, Timothy. *The Big Burn—Teddy Roosevelt and the Fire that Saved America*. New York: Houghton Mifflin Harcourt, 2009.

Eisele, J.W., O'Halloran, R.L., Reay, D.T., Lindholm, G.R., Lewman, L.V., and Brady, W.J. "Deaths During the May 18, 1980 Eruption of Mount St. Helens." *New England Journal of Medicine* 305 (1981) 931–936.

Endo, E.T., Malone, S.D., Noson, L.L., and Weaver, C.S. "Locations, Magnitudes, and Statistics of the March 20–May 18 Earthquake Sequence," in Lipman and Mullineaux, *USGS Professional Paper* 1250 (1981) 93–108.

Felt, M.E. *Yacolt! The Forest that Would Not Die*. Olympia: Washington Department of Natural Resources, 1977.

Fisher, A.H. *Shadow Tribe—The Making of Columbia River Indian Identity*. University of Washington Press, 2010.

Fiske, R.S. "Volcanologists, Journalists, and the Concerned Local Public—A Tale of Two Cities in the Eastern Caribbean." *Explosive Volcanism—Inception, Evolution, and Hazards*. Washington, D.C.: National Academy Press, (1984) 170–176.

Frémont, John Charles. *Report of the Exploring Expedition to the Rocky Mountains in the Year 1842, and to Oregon and North California in the Years 1843–44*. Washington: Gales and Seaton, 1845.

Gibbs, George. "Report upon the Geology of the Central Portion of the Washington Territory." In *Reports of Explorations and Surveys to Ascertain the Most Practical and Economical Route for a Railroad from the Missippi River to the Pacific Ocean*. Washington: Executive Document No. 78, 2nd Session, 33rd Congress, 1853–1854 I (1855) 474–486.

Goetzmann, W.H., *New Lands, New Men—America and the Second Great Age of Discovery*. New York, Viking Penguin, 1986.

Gorshkov, G.S. "Gigantic Eruption of the Volcano Bezymianny." *Bulletin Volcanologique* 20 (1959) 77–109.

Grudd, H., Briffa, K.R., Gunnarson, B.E., and Linderholm, H.W. "Swedish Tree Rings Provide New Evidence in Support of a Major, Widespread Environmental Disruption in 1628 BC." *Geophysical Research Letters* 27 (2000) 2957–2960.

Guggenheim, Alan. *Spirit Lake People—Memories of Mount St. Helens*. Gresham, Oreg.: Salem Press, 1986.

Guzzo, Louis R. *Is it True What They Say about Dixy?—A Biography of Dixy Lee Ray*. Mercer Island, WA: The Writing Works, Inc., 1980.

Haeni, F.P. *Sediment Deposition in the Columbia and Lower Cowlitz Rivers, Washington, Caused by the May 18, 1980, Eruption of Mount St. Helens*. U.S. Geological Survey Circular 850-k, 1983.

Harington, C.R., ed. *The Year Without Summer? World Climate in 1816*. Ottawa: Canadian Museum of Science, 1992.

Harris, D.M., Rose, W.I., Roe, R., and Thompson, M.R. "Radar Observations of Ash Eruptions." *U.S. Geological Survey Professional Paper* 1250 (1981) 323–333.

Hickson, Paul, and Hickson, Cathie. "We Watched Mount St. Helens Blow its Top." *Canadian Geographic* 100 [5] (1980) 54–59.

Hickson, C.J. "The May 18, 1980, Eruption of Mount St. Helens, Washington State—A Synopsis of Events and Review of Phase I from an Eyewitness Perspective." *Geoscience Canada* 17 (1990) 127–131.

Hickson, Catherine. *Mt. St. Helens—Surviving the Stone Wind*. Vancouver, Canada: Tricouni Press, 2005.

Hidy, Ralph W., Hill, Frank E., and Nevins, Allen. *Timber and Men—The Weyerhaeuser Story*. New York: Macmillan Co., 1963.

Hoblitt, R.P. "Was the 18 May 1980 Lateral Blast at Mt St Helens the Product of Two Explosions?" *Philosophical Transactions of the Royal Society of London* 358 (2000) 1639–1661.

Hoblitt, R.P., Crandell, D.R., and Mullineaux, D.R. "Mount St. Helens Eruptive Behavior During the Past 1,500 Years." *Geology* 8 (1980) 555–559.

Holbrook, S.H. *The Story of American Railroads*. New York: Bonanza Books, 1947.

Holmes, K.L. "Mount St. Helens' Recent Eruptions." *Oregon Historical Quarterly* 56 (1955; 3) 196–210.

Hoy, Dale. *Mt. St. Helens & the Toutle Valley—The Early Years.* Longview, Wash.: V.O. Printers, 1993.

Hunn, E.S., *Nch'i-Wana "The Big River"—Mid-Columbia Indians and Their Land.* Seattle, University of Washington Press, 1990.

Hyde, J.H., and Crandell, D.R. *Postglacial Volcanic Deposits at Mount Baker, Washington, and Potential Hazards from Future Eruptions.* U.S. Geological Survey Professional Paper 1022-C (1978).

Jackson, Leland, with Howarth, Trudy. *An Early History of Spirit Lake & the Toutle River Valley.* Red Apple Publishing, Gig Harbor, WA, 1995.

Jillson, Willard R. "New Evidence of a Recent Volcanic Eruption of Mt. St. Helens, Washington." *American Journal of Science* 44 (1917) 59–62.

Jones, Alden H. *From Jamestown to Coffin Rock—A History of Weyerhaeuser Operations in Southwest Washington.* Tacoma: Weyerhaeuser Corporation, 1974.

Kamata, H., Johnson, D.A., and Waitt, R.B. "Stratigraphy, Chronology, and Character of the 1976 Pyroclastic Eruption of Augustine Volcano, Alaska." *Bulletin of Volcanology* 53 (1991) 407–419.

Kanamori, H., Given, J.W., and Lay, T. "Analysis of Seismic Body Waves Excited by the Mount St. Helens Eruption of May 18, 1980." *Journal of Geophysical Research* 89 (1984) 1856–1866.

Kane, Paul. *Wanderings of an Artist—Among the Indians of North America—from Canada to Vancouver's Island and Oregon Through the Hudson's Bay Company's Territory and Back Again.* Rutland, VT: Charles E. Tuttle Co., 1968 (First edition, Toronto, 1859).

Kearney, Marianna. *One Road Out—Survivor of the 1980 Eruption of Mt. St. Helens.* Blurb, Inc. (www.blurb.com), 2011.

Kienle, J. and Shaw, G.E. "Plume Dynamics, Thermal Energy, and Long-Distance Transport of Vulcanian Eruption Clouds from Augustine Volcano, Alaska." *Journal of Volcanology and Geothermal Research* 6 (1979) 139–164.

Kinoshita, W.T., Swanson, D.A., and Jackson, D.B. "The Measurement of Crustal Deformation Related to Volcanic Activity at Kilauea Volcano, Hawaii" in Cicetta, L., Gasparini, P., Luongo, G., and Rapolla, A., eds., *Physical Volcanology.* New York: Elsevier (1974) 87–115.

Lamb, W.K., ed. *A Voyage of Discovery to the North Pacific Ocean and Round the World 1791-1795, vol. II [1792].* London: The Hakluyt Society, 1984.

Lawrence, D.B. "Trees on the March—Notes on the Recent Volcanic and Vegetational History of Mount St. Helens." *Mazama* 20 (1938) 49–54.

_____. "Continuing Research on the Flora of Mount St. Helens." *Mazama* 21 (1939;12) 49–54.

_____. "The 'Floating Island' Lava Flow of Mount St. Helens." *Mazama* 23 (1941;12) 56–60.

_____. "Diagrammatic History of the Northeast Slope of Mount St. Helens, Washington." *Mazama* 36 (1954;13) 41–44.

Lawrence, D.B. and Lawrence, E.G. "Radiocarbon Dating of Some Events on Mount Hood and Mount St. Helens." *Mazama* 40 (1959;14) 10–18.

LeMonds, James. *Deadfall—Generations of Logging in the Pacific Northwest.* Missoula, MT: Mountain Publishing, 2001.

Lewty, P.J. *Across the Columbia Plain—Railroad Expansion in the Interior Northwest, 1885-1893.* Pullman: Washington State Univ. Press, 1995.

Lipman, P.W., and Mullineaux, D.R., eds. *The 1980 Eruptions of Mount St. Helens, Washington.* U.S. Geological Survey Professional Paper 1250, 1981.

Lipman, P.W., Moore, J.G., and Swanson, D.A. "Bulging of the North Flank Before the May 18 Eruption—Geodetic Data." In "The 1980 Eruptions of Mount St. Helens, Washington." *U.S. Geological Survey Professional Paper* 1250 (1981) 143–155.

Lockerly, Fred *History of the Columbia River Valley from The Dalles to the Sea.* Chicago: S.J. Clarke Publ. Co, v. II, 1928.

Loo-Wit Lat-Kla. *Gold Hunting in the Cascade Mountains.* New Haven, CT, Yale Univ. Press, 1957. (facsimile of: Vancouver, Washington Territory, The Chronicle, 1861).

Macdonald, Gordon A. *Volcanoes.* Englewood Cliffs: Prentice Hall. 1972.

Major-Frégeau, M. *Overland to Oregon in 1845—Impressions of a Journey Across North America by H.J. Warre.* Ottawa: Archives of Canada, 1976.

Majors, H.M. "The Great Tephra Eruption of circa 1802." *Northwest Discovery* 1 (1980a) 13–24.

———. "Mount St. Helens—the 1842–44 Eruptions." *Northwest Discovery* 1 (1980b) 68–90.

———. "Remarks on the 1842–44 Eruptions." *Northwest Discovery* 1 (1980c) 91–105.

———. "Mount St. Helens, the 1831 and 1835 Eruptions." *Northwest Discovery* 2 (1981) 534–540.

Malone, Michael P. *James J. Hill—Empire Builder of the Northwest.* Norman, OK: University of Oklahoma Press, 1996.

Malone, S.D., Endo, E.T., Weaver, C.S., and Ramey, J.W. "Seismic Monitoring for Eruption Prediction." *U.S. Geological Survey Professional Paper* 1250 (1981) 803–813.

Marino, Cesare. "History of Western Washington Since 1846." *Handbook of North American Indians, Northwest Coast* (Wayne Suttles, ed.). Washington, D.C.: Smithsonian Institution 7 (1990) 169–179.

Martin, Albro. *James J. Hill and the Opening of the Northwest.* New York: Oxford University Press, 1976.

McClure, Rick. "The St. Helens Mining District—A Condensed History." *Skamania County Heritage,* 13 [2], (1984) 3–8.

McClure, Rick, and Mack, Cheryl. *"For the Greatest Good"—Early History of Gifford Pinchot National Forest.* Seattle, WA: Northwest Interpretive Association, 1999.

Meinig, D.W., *The Shaping of America—A Geographical Perspective on 500 Years of History, v. 2, Continental America 1800–1867.* New Haven, Conn., Yale University Press, 1993.

Miller, C.D. *Potential Hazards from Future Eruptions in the Vicinity of Mount Shasta Volcano, Northern California.* U.S. Geological Survey Bulletin 1503, 1980.

Mimatsu, Masao. *Showa-Shinzan Diary (Expanded Reprint)—Complete Records of the Observations of the Process of the Birth of Showa-Shinzan.* Sapporo, Japan. Suda Seihan Co. (1995).

Moen, Wayne S. *St. Helens and Washougal Mining Districts of the Southern Cascades of Washington.* Washington Division of Geology and Earth Resources, Information Circular 60, 1977.

Moore, J.G., and Sisson, T.W. "Deposits and Effects of the May 18 Pyroclastic Surge." *U.S. Geological Survey Professional Paper* 1250 (1981) 421–438.

Moulton, Gary E. *The Journals of the Lewis and Clark Expedition, v. 5, July 28–November 1, 1805.* Lincoln: University of Nebraska Press, 1988.

———. *The Journals of the Lewis and Clark Expedition, v. 6, November 2, 1805–March 22, 1806.* Lincoln: University of Nebraska Press, 1990.

———. *The Journals of the Lewis and Clark Expedition, v. 7, March 23–June 9, 1806.* Lincoln: University of Nebraska Press, 1991.

Mullineaux, D.R. *Pumice and Other Pyroclastic Deposits in Mount Rainier National Park, Washington.* U.S. Geological Survey Bulletin 1326, 1974.

———. *Pre-1980 Tephra-Fall Deposits Erupted from Mount St. Helens, Washington.* U.S. Geological Survey, Professional Paper 1563, 1996.

Mullineaux, D.R. and Crandell, D.R. "Recent Lahars from Mount St. Helens, Washington." *Geological Society of America Bulletin* 73 (1962) 855–870.

———. "The Eruptive History of Mount St. Helens." *U.S. Geological Survey Professional Paper* 1250 (1981) 3–15.

Newman, P.C., *Empire by the Bay—The Company of Adventurers that Seized a Continent.* New York: Penguin Putnam, 1998.

Nisbet, Jack. *Sources of the River—Tracking David Thompson across Western North America.* Seattle: Sasquatch Books, 1994.

Parker, Rev. Samuel. *Journal of an Exploring Expedition Beyond the Rocky Mountains [in 1835].* Moscow: University of Idaho Press, 1990 (reprint of 3rd edition of 1842; 1st ed. 1838.)

Parshley, P.F., Liessling, P.J., Antonius, J.A., Connell, R.S., Miller, S.H., and Green, F.H.Y. "Pyroclastic flow injury—Mount St. Helens, May 18, 1980." *American Journal of Surgery* 143 (1982) 565–568.

Perry, R.W., Greene, M.R., and Lindell, M.K. *Human Response to Volcanic Eruption—Mount St. Helens, May 18, 1980.* Seattle: Batelle Human Affairs Research Center, 1980.

Pringle, P.T., Pierson, T.C., Cameron, K.A., and Sheppard, P.R. "Late Eighteenth Century Old Maid Eruption and Lahars at Mount Hood, Oregon (USA) Dated with Tree Rings and Historical Observations." *Tree Rings and Natural Hazards—A State-of-the-Art.* Springer (2010) 487–491.

Rabbitt, M.C., "John Wesley Powell—Pioneer Statesman of Federal Science." U.S. Geological Survey Professional Paper 669-A (1969) 1–21.

_____. *Minerals, Lands, and Geology for the Common Defense and General Welfare, vol. 1, Before 1879.* Washington, D.C.: U.S. Government Printing Office, 1979.

_____. *Minerals, Lands, and Geology for the Common Defense and General Welfare, vol. 2, 1879–1904.* Washington, D.C.: U.S. Government Printing Office, 1980.

_____. *The United States Geological Survey—1879–1989.* U.S. Geological Survey Circular 1050, 1989.

Radice, Betty (translator). *The Letters of the Younger Pliny.* London, Penguin, 1963.

Richards, K.D. *Isaac I. Stevens—Young Man in a Hurry.* Pullman: Washington State University Press, 1993.

Rosen, Shirley. *Truman of St. Helens—The Man and His Mountain.* Bothell, WA: Rosebud Publishing, 1981, 1992.

Rosenbaum, J.G., and Waitt, R.B. "Summary of Eyewitness Accounts of the May 18 Eruption." *U.S. Geological Survey Professional Paper* 1250 (1981) 53–68.

Sabbagh, Karl. *A Rum Affair—A True Story of Botanical Fraud.* New York: Farrah Staus, and Giroux, 1999.

Sandburg, Carl. *Abraham Lincoln—The War Years.* New York: Harcourt Brace Jovanovich, 1939.

Sarna-Wojcicki, A.M., Waitt, R.B., Woodward, M.J., Shipley, S., and Rivera, J. "Premagmatic Ash Erupted from March 27 Through May 14—Extent, Mass, Volume, and Composition," *The 1980 Eruptions of Mount St. Helens, Washington.* U.S. Geological Survey Professional Paper 1250 (1981) 569–575.

Scarth, Alwyn. *La Catastrophe—The Eruption of Mount Pelée, the Worst Volcanic Disaster of the 20th Century.* Oxford University Press, 2002.

Scott, G.W. *A Majority of One—Legislative Life.* Seattle, Civitas Press, 2002.

Self, S., Rampino, M.R., Newton, M.S., and Wolf, J.A. "Volcanological Study of the Great Tambora Eruption of 1815." *Geology* 12 (1984) 659–663.

Sensel, Joni. *Traditions through the Trees—Weyerhaeuser's First 100 Years.* Seattle: Documentary Book Publishers, 1999.

Siebert, L., Simkin, T., and Kimberly, P. *Volcanoes of the World, 3rd ed.* Berkeley: University of California Press, 2010.

Sigurdsson, Haraldur. *Melting the Earth—The History of Ideas on Volcanic Eruptions.* New York, Oxford University Press, 1999.

Sigurdsson, H., Carey, S., Cornell, W., and Pescatore, T. "The Eruption of Vesuvius in A.D. 79." *National Geographic Research* 1 (1985) 332–387.

Sigurdsson, H. and 13 others. "Marine Investigations of Greece's Santorini Volcanic Field." *EOS, Transactions American Geophysical Union* 87 (2006) 337–342.

Simkin, T., and Fiske, R.S. *Krakatau 1883—The Volcanic Eruption and Its Effects.* Washington, D.C.: Smithsonian Institution Press, 1983.

Sparks, S.J., Moore, J.G., and Rice, C.J. "The Initial Giant Umbrella Cloud of the May 18th, 1980 Explosive Eruption of Mount St. Helens." *Journal of Volcanology and Geothermal Research* 28 (1986) 257–274.

Stegner, Wallace. *Beyond the Hundredth Meridian—John Wesley Powell and the Second Opening of the West.* Boston: Houghton Mifflin, 1954.

Stehr, S.D. and Ellwanger S.J. "The Executive Branch in Washington Government." *Washington State Government and Politics.* Pullman: Washington State University Press (2004) 131–147.

Stevens, Isaac I. *Report for a Route for the Pacific Railroad near the Forty-Seventh and Forty-Ninth Parallels of North America from St. Paul to Puget Sound.* (vol I of *Reports of Explorations and Surveys to Ascertain the Most Practical and Economical Route for a Railroad from the Mississippi River to the Pacific Ocean.*) Washington: Executive Document No. 78, 2nd Session, 33rd Congress, 1855.

Stevens, Hazard, *Life of Isaac Ingalls Stevens.* Boston: Houghton Mifflin, 1900.

St. Lawrence, W., Qamar, A., Moore, J., and Kendrick, G. "A Comparison of Thermal Observations of Mount St. Helens

Before and During the First Week of the Initial 1980 Eruption." *Science* 209 (1980) 1526-1527.

Strothers, R.B. "The Great Tambora Eruption in 1815 and Its Aftermath." *Science* 224 (1984) 1191-1198.

Strouse, Jean. *Morgan—American Financier*. New York, Random House, 1999.

Sutton, A.J., Elias, T., Gerlach, T.M., and Stokes, J.B. "Implications for Eruptive Processes as Indicated by Sulphur Dioxide Emissions from Kilauea Volcano, Hawaii, 1979–1997." *Journal of Volcanology and Geothermal Research* 108 (2001) 283-302.

Taylor, G.A.M. *The 1951 Eruption of Mount Lamington, Papua*. Australian Bureau of Mineral Resources, Geology, & Geophysics Bulletin 38, 1958.

Tazieff, Haroun. "La Soufrière, Volcanology and Forecasting." *Nature* 269 (1977) 96-97.

Terrell, J.U., *Furs by Astor*. New York: William Morrow & Co., 1963.

Twinning, Charles E. *Phil Weyerhaeuser—Lumberman*. Seattle: University of Washington Press, 1985.

Unruh, J.D., Jr. *The Plains Across—The Overland Emigrants and the Trans-Mississippi West, 1840-60*. University of Illinois Press, 1993.

Verhoogan, Jean ('John'). "Mount St. Helens—A Recent Cascade Volcano." *Bulletin of Department of Geological Sciences, University of California* 24 (1937; 9) 263-302.

Voight, B. "Time Scale for the First Moments of the May 18 Eruption." In *The 1980 Eruptions of Mount St. Helens, Washington*. U.S. Geological Survey Professional Paper 1250 (1981) 69-86.

Voight, B., and Kennedy, B.A. "Slope Failure of 1967-1969, Chuquicamata Mine, Chile." In Voight, B., (ed.), *Rockslides and Avalanches, 2*. New York: Elsevier, 1979, 595-632.

Voight, B., Janda, R. J., Glicken, H.X., and Douglass, P.M. "Nature and Mechanics of the Mount St. Helens Rockslide-Avalanche of 18 May 1980." *Geotechnique* 33 (1983) 243-273.

Waitt, R.B. "Devastating Pyroclastic Density Flow and Attendant Air Fall of May 18— Stratigraphy and Sedimentology of Deposits." *The 1980 Eruptions of Mount St. Helens, Washington*. U.S. Geological Survey Professional Paper 1250 (1981) 439-458.

_____. "Swift snowmelt and floods (lahars) caused by great pyroclastic surge at Mount St. Helens volcano, Washington, 18 May 1980." *Bulletin of Volcanology* 52 (1989) 138-157.

Waitt, R.B., and Dzurisin, D. "Proximal Air-Fall Deposits from the May 18 eruption—Stratigraphy and Field Sedimentology." *The 1980 Eruptions of Mount St. Helens, Washington*. U.S. Geological Survey Professional Paper 1250 (1981) 601-616.

Warre, H.J. *Sketches in North America and the Oregton Territory*. London: Dickenson & Co., 1848.

Weckworth, Trudy and McVay, Al, eds. *Dixy—1977—Her First Year as Governor of Washington*. Seattle: Grange Printing Co., 1977.

Weyerhaeuser Company. *Weyerhaeuser Company History*. Tacoma, Washington, c.1974.

_____. *Where the Future Grows—A History of Weyerhaeuser Company*. Tacoma, Washington, 1989.

White, C. Albert. *A History of the Rectangular Survey System*. U.S. Department of the Interior, Bureau of Land Management, 1983.

_____. *Initial Points of the Rectangular Survey System*. Westminster, Colo.: The Publishing House, 1996.

_____. *A Casebook of Oregon Donation Land Claims*. Oregon City, Oreg.: LLM Publications, 2001.

Wilkes, Charles. *Narrative of the United States Exploring Expedition During the Years 1838, 1839, 1840, 1841, 1842*. Philadelphia: Lea and Blanchard, 1845.

Williamson, J.A., and Donaldson, T. *The Public Domain—Its History, with Statistics*. US Government Printing Office. 1880.

Winchell, H.V. "The St. Helens Mining District." *Transactions of the American Institute of Mining Engineers* 44 (1912) 580-587.

Winchester, Simon. *Krakatoa—The Day the World Exploded—August 27, 1883*. New York: HarperCollins, 2003.

Worster, Donald. *A River Running West—The Life of John Wesley Powell*. New York: Oxford University Press, 2001.

Yamaguchi, D.K. "Forest History, Mount St. Helens—Old-growth Development after Mount St. Helens' 1480 Eruption." *National Geographic Research & Exploration* 9 (1993) 294-325.

_____. "New Tree-Ring Dates for Eruptions of Mount St. Helens." *Quaternary Research* 20 (1983) 246-250.

_____. "Tree-Ring Evidence for a Two-Year Interval Between Recent Prehistoric Explosive Eruptions of Mount St. Helens." *Geology* 13 (1985) 554–557.

Yamaguchi, D.K., Hoblitt, R.P., and Lawrence, D.B. "A New Tree-Ring Date for the 'Floating Island' Lava Flow, Mount St. Helens, Washington." *Bulletin of Volcanology* 52 (1990) 545–550.

Zapffe, Carl. "The Geology of the St. Helens Mining District of Washington." *Economic Geology* 7 (1912) 340–350.

Maps (not specifically cited)

Northern Pacific Railroad. *Northern Pacific Railroad, its Branches, and Allied Lines*, (Map) 1883 (on file at Oregon Historical Society, Portland).

Northern Pacific Railroad, Land Department. *Map of Clarke County, Washington*, 1902 (on file at Oregon Historical Society, Portland).

U.S. Forest Service. Gifford Pinchot National Forest. Columbia National Forest, 1920.

_____. [several historical maps of 1900s to 1930s]

_____. *Gifford Pinchot National Forest*, 1958, 1961, 1979.

_____. *Gifford Pinchot National Forest, Recreation Guide, Spirit Lake & Mount St. Helens, 1963.*

_____. *Mt. St. Helens—Spirit Lake* (Gifford Pinchot National Forest), 1968, 1973.

_____. *Gifford Pinchot National Forest, St. Helens Ranger District, Fireman Map*, 1978.

U.S. Geological Survey. 30-minute series (topographic) of Washington: *Mt. St. Helens* (1919) [surveyed 1913–16].

_____. *Plan and Profile of Toutle River, including North Fork, Washington.* (1939) [surveyed 1935].

_____. 15-minute series (topographic) of Washington at 1:62,500 (1 inch = 1 mile) maps: *Castle Rock* (1953); *Cougar* (1953); *Elk Rock* (1953); *Mount St. Helens* (1958); *Spirit Lake* (1957); *Toutle* (1953).

_____. 7.5-minute series (topographic) of Washington: 50 contiguous detailed maps (1:24,000 scale) of Mount St. Helens area including Green, Toutle, Cowlitz, and Lewis valleys published between 1965 and 1993.

Washington Department of Natural Resources. *Major Public Lands*, 2000.

Weyerhaeuser Company. *Unpublished air-photo sheets showing land boundaries, land sections, and numbered roads*, 1978.

_____. *Longview, Southwest Washington.* Tacoma, Washington, 1991.

_____. *St. Helens Tree Farm—Weyerhaeuser Forest Management.* Tacoma, Washington, 1995.

Weyerhaeuser Company (and others). *Sportsman's Maps* [years 1966 to 1982].

Weyerhaeuser Company (proprietary). *St. Helens Tree Farm, Photos & Maps.* 2002.

Index

Aero–Copters, 24, 27, 290, 293. *See also* Stickney
Air Force. *See* US Air Force
Air Force Reserve. *See* US Air Force Reserve
Airis, William, 126-127, 251, 388n7.19
Alder Creek, 3
Alexander, Bill, 341
Allen, John, permits committee, 71
Altom, Kerri, 239
Amateur (ham) radio. *See* Radio amateurs
Anderson, Mark, 41-43, 93, 133-34, 254, 287, 387n.14
Anderson, Kathy (and Kran Kilpatrick, Valerie Sigfridson, Kate Brennan, John Morris), 108, 114, 234-39, 321, 390n14.1
Ape Cave, 25
Apgar, Reade, 114, 151, 153
Astoria, Oreg., 287-88
Augustine, Mount or Island (Alaska), 8, 42-43, 109

Backstrom, Brad, 51, 70, 74-75, 96, 112, 309-10, 321
Bacon, Bill, 43-44
Bailey, Darryl, 342
Baker, Gil. *See* O'Keefe, Kathie
Baker, Mount, 13, 42
Bakke, Kit, 295-96
Balch, Dan, 96, 114, 175-76, 178-81, 184-86, 285, 340
Bandai–san, Japan, 88
Banks, Norman "Norm," 78, 82, 85, 244
Barker, George (Skamania deputy), 34-35, 38-40, 42, 44-46, 52, 80, 82, 106-08, 244, 309, 311, 347, 392n19.5
Baxter, Steve, 62-63
Bear Meadows overlook, 101, 114, 213-19
Beard, Mike, 37, 92, 336
Bena, Ben (Cowlitz deputy), 35, 64, 79, 86-87, 93, 291, 328, 331-32, 339-40
Berg, Carl, 84, 134, 386n41
Berry, Dave and Laura, 24, 52-53, 69, 339
Berry, Duncan and–or Malonie, 4, 52-53
Bezymianny (USSR) eruption 1955-56, 12, 57, 64, 76
Big Lake, Wash., 241
Billings, Mont., 307
Bioren, Bob. *See* Ryan, Rich
Black Rock mine, 36, 55-56, 65, 80-81, 87, 358

Blackburn, Reid (and Fay), 7, 76-78, 80, 85, 87, 92, 100, 108-09, 112, 135-36, 155, 244, 278, 291-92, 355, 358, 388n9.8
Blast. *See* eruption phenomena: initial explosions, and surge
Blue zone. *See* Volcanic hazard zones
Blumenthal, Les, 40, 42
Boccia, Conrad and Sandie, 299-300, 342
Booth, Bob, 89
Bowers, Glen. *See* Ryan, Rich
Bowers, Wally (and Tom Gadwa), 113-14, 258, 358
Boy Scout camps. *See* Scout camps
Brennan, Kate. *See* Anderson, Kathy
Brooks, Oreg., 84-85
Broomhead, Ren, 256, 258-59
Brugman, Melinda "Mindy," 91-92, 109, 111
Bulge. *See* Mount St. Helens
Bullock, Capt. Dick, 50-51, 65, 69, 71, 73-74, 91, 97, 106, 114-15, 243, 386n4
Burchard, Sharon, 3-5, 7, 33, 98, 109, 391n21
Burford, Brooks, 62-63
Burlington Northern Railroad, 36, 67. *See also* Great Northern Railroad, Northern Pacific Railroad
Burrington, David, 75, 338
Bynum, Ardis and Julia, 303, 343

Camp Baker. *See* Weyerhaeuser Company
Camp Muray. *See* Washington Army National Guard, Gray Army Airfield
Carlson, Zilda and Melvin, 302, 343
Carlson, Chris, 95
Carter, Jimmy, 332-36, 393n14
Casadevall, 244
Castle Rock (town), 17, 259, 316-18
Castle Creek or valley, 100, 163, 251, 353
Cavens, Russ, 97, 105, 160
CBS news. *See* Cronkite
Chausee, Bernadette. *See* Hodgson
Cheney, Wash., 305, 344
Chow, Edward, 30, 40, 73-74, 100, 242
Christiansen, John "Jack," 147-49
Christiansen, Robert "Bob," 45, 67, 71, 76, 88, 111, 249-50, 333, 390n16.2
Christiansen, Grant, 177, 286
Cispus Center, 295
Cispus River and road, 218, 221, 295-96

Clear Creek, 108

Closner, Bill (Skamania Co. Sheriff), 34, 42, 48, 55, 64, 69, 79-80, 82-84, 94, 98-100, 106-07, 331, 333-34

Coal Bank highway bridge (above Toutle), 160, 255, 257, 259, 289-90, 309, 311-12, 316-17, 392n19.5

Coast Guard. *See* US Coast Guard

Coe, Dr. Henry, 19-21, 23

Coldwater Creeks or valleys, 81, 90-91, 93, 167, 275-76, 357

Coldwater ridges & Coldwater Peak, 74, 81-82, 90-91, 101-103, 114, 151-53, 155, 258, 353, 358. *See also*, Coldwater observations posts, Coldwater II, and Martin

Coldwater observation posts: Coldwater I, 47-48, 50, 67, 74, 77, 80-81, 85, 100, 108-09, 112, 135, 155, 272, 274, 291, 329, 355, 357-58; Coldwater II, 74-75, 77-78, 80, 82, 85, 88-90, 94-95, 101-02, 108-11, 114, 137, 151-53, 250, 272, 275, 277-78, 290, 293, 312, 329, 341, 350

Cole, Brian, 210

Collins, Bob, 331

Colten, Joel, 160, 391n14-15

Columbia River or valley, 14, 18, 114, 128, 252, 260, 287, 321, 334-35

Columbia Helicopters, 86-87, 135-36, 277-79, 292, 328-29

Columbian (Vancouver newspaper), 33, 40, 51, 62, 67, 76, 98, 108-09, 155, 244, 278, 291, 355, 388n9.8

Columbus Day storm (1962), 25, 182

Conner, Ron, 352

Consolidated Mining Company, 19-23, 36

Cooney, Mike, 81, 254, 261-67, 269, 271, 277, 348, 391n13, 391n15, 391n17

Cougar (town), 49, 51, 53, 67, 72, 77, 87, 237. *See also* Lewis valley

Cowlitz County, 44, 57, 74, 341. *See also* Medical examiners

Cowlitz County sheriff's office, 256, 266, 271, 287, 291, 313, 328, 331-32, 338, 345, 351-52. *See also* Les Nelson and Ben Bena

Cowlitz River or valley & tributaries, 3, 17, 131, 133-34, 169, 172, 212, 251, 260, 287, 316-18, 328, 334-35, 341, 347; dredging, 347

Crall, Terry (and Karen Varner), 94, 96, 114, 172, 174-75, 180, 338-39

Crandell, Dwight "Rocky," ix, 6, 8, 26-28, 30-31, 36, 44, 48, 50-51, 53, 56, 61, 63, 67-70, 74, 88, 292, 328, 333, 350

Crater. *See* Mount St. Helens

Crockett, David, 111, 196-98, 286-89, 388n7.19, 389nn10.13-14

Croft, Clyde (and Alan Handy), 101, 331, 341

Cronkite, Walter (CBS news), 35

Dahl, Mark. *See* Sullivan

Daily News (Longview newspaper), 27-28, 33, 40, 68, 79, 87, 94, 103, 105, 128-29, 254-55, 292, 384n14

Dardarian, Suki, 99

Dartmouth College, 57

Davidson, Jim, 124-25, 387n7.4

Davis, Dale (and Leslie and Al Brooks), 114, 167-69, 337

Deadman Lake, 201

Deadman's curve, 103

Decker, Bob, 81-82, 92, 111, 244, 333

Deitrich, Bill, 291

DeMeyer, John, 35, 76, 86

Dergan, Venus, 198-201, 256, 258, 340-41. *See also* Reitan

Dias, José, 281, 283-84, 393n16. *See also* Scymanky

Dieter, Bob, 62, 275-76, 311, 325-27, 331, 337, 351-52, 392n19.5

Dinehard, Randall. *See* Doyle

Dollars Corner (Lingle Hill), 239

Doran, Jeffry, 352, 393n27

Downing, John (and Mike Williamson), 141-42

Doyle, Jack (and Randall Dinehart), 316-18, 393n19.10

Dreidger, Carloyn, 109

Drew, Greg, 311, 392n19.5

Dry Gulch (at MSH), ix,

duBeth, Donna, 31, 33, 40, 42, 44, 68-69, 79, 94, 254-55, 292, 384n14, 390n16.5

Dzurisin, Dan, 48

Earthquakes magnitude, 379n1.1

Earthquakes (volcanic, non-eruptive, at Mount St. Helens), 4-9, 31, 33-34, 37, 40-41, 43, 48-49, 53-54, 57, 59-60, 67-69, 72, 74-75, 78, 81-82, 89, 102, 110, 115, 119, 333, 384n9, 387n6.4, 387n7.2; after 19 May, 349, 384n18, 384-85n20, 385n22, 385n35. *See also* Earthquake magnitude; Eruption phenomena, seismic signals; Seismic station

Eastern Washington University (Cheney), 305-06

Edelbrock, Mark, 279-80, 326, 331

Edwards, Arlene and Jolene, 113, 352, 354-55, 387n6.1

Eisele, John, 341-42

Ek, Charlie, 261-64, 325-27

Elder, "Wick," 97, 105-08, 243

Elk Rock, 4, 72, 89-90, 109, 113, 156, 158, 160, 206, 280, 327, 349-50, 354-55

Ellensburg, Wash., 296-97, 342-43

Emetaz, Roland, 7-8, 61-62

Endo, Elliot, 5, 7-9, 31, 33

Erdelbrock, Dale, 201, 256-60

Eruption phenomena (18-19 May 1980) [in rough time order]; animal behavior, 176, 184, 194-95, 205, 201, 225, 227-28, 231, 239, 297, 299-301, 304, 310, 314, 389n10.11; initial earthquakes felt, 119, 153, 174, 187, 189, 206, 211, 235, 243; seismic signals, 241-42, 379n1.3; landslides (or avalanche) and deposit, 119-20, 122-23, 130, 153, 160, 162, 165, 187, 190-91, 193, 213-17, 219, 222, 225-27, 249-51, 254, 262, 264-65, 272-79, 285, 290, 323, 329, 331, 335-36, 341, 352, 357; initial explosions & cloud (seen), 119, 122-23, 125, 141, 148, 150, 153-54, 160, 162, 187, 190-91, 193-94, 196, 206, 208, 211, 213-17, 219-22, 225-27, 235-36, 238-39, 242, 333, 341; surge cloud (forest-felling hot flow) & deposit, 119-20, 123, 125-26, 128, 141-48, 150, 153-65, 167-70, 172-73, 178-79, 182-83; 187-89, 193-96, 203, 206-11, 214-17, 219-22, 227-28, 231, 236, 238-39, 243, 278-79, 288, 290, 329, 339, 342, 351-55, 357-58, 388n9.12; 389n10.13; burning or scorching (of surge), 164-65, 167-68, 170, 173, 179, 183, 352-55; downed trees or forest, 130, 133, 136-37, 140, 164-66, 168-71, 173-76, 178-84, 204-06, 231, 250-51; 257-58, 260-62, 264-65, 268-70, 272-73, 275-77, 280-82, 285, 290, 292, 321, 324-27, 329-30, 333, 338-39, 349-55, 357-58, 389n10.6; water blown (by surge) from lakes, 257, 352, 358; ashfall from surge, 123, 133, 164, 167-68, 170, 173, 178-79; 183-85, 261-75, 277, 330, 342; burned and wounded people or animals, 175-76, 179-81, 184-85, 262, 273, 323, 337, 340, 342, 388n9.12; wrecked vehicles and logging equipment, 257, 261-62, 264-65, 268-71, 274-77, 281, 288, 323-26, 329-31, 350-55, 358; people dead, 251, 257-58, 262, 264, 266, 270, 272-73, 275-76, 285, 288, 290, 292, 321, 323-24, 326, 329-31, 333, 337-39, 341-42, 350-58, 387n6.3;

valley clouds or haze, 130, 133, 136-37, 142-43, 149, 228, 247, 254, 257, 260, 265-66, 274, 276-79, 280-82, 290; mushroom cloud & column & east 'anvil,' 120, 123, 128-30, 133-34, 141-44, 146-50, 153, 157-59, 161, 163, 170-71, 183, 189, 192, 195, 197-98, 203, 207-12, 216-19, 222, 228-32, 236-39, 242, 244-45, 282, 295, 309, 312-13, 387n7.5; fall of ash, rocks, mud, and tree litter from mushroom (& deposits), 120, 134-36, 141-45, 148-50, 161, 165-66, 168, 170-71, 174-78, 180-86, 192-93, 197-98, 204, 207-08, 210-12, 216, 218-23, 229-33, 243-45, 261-64, 268-75, 277-78, 280-82, 285-89, 294-307, 323-27, 330-31, 338-39, 341-45, 347-50, 352-55; daytime darkness, 120, 142-44, 147-49, 164-65, 167-68, 170-71, 173-74, 178-80, 183-84, 192-93, 197-98, 203-04, 207-12, 216, 218-23, 265, 276-80, 282, 295-307; central–vent column or plume, 129-30, 136-40, 193, 239, 247-52, 256, 258, 260, 272, 276-77, 280, 286, 290, 292-93, 315-17, 321, 323-25, 388n7.12; backwind to mushroom and central–column plumes, 148, 170, 192, 207-08, 210, 212, 228, 231, 249, 256; fall of ash and pumice from central–vent plume (& deposits), 120, 130, 229-31, 341-45; distant ash plumes and falls, 279, 282, 284-85, 292, 294-307, 329, 336, 340, 342-45; ash–worn vehicles and machinery, 301-02, 342-44, 349; ashflows (pyroclastic flows), 120, 131, 140, 247-53, 339, 350; upper North Fork plumes & geysers & fumaroles, 137, 250, 262, 272, 276, 278, 285, 290, 317, 324, 336; North Fork river stopped, 258, 262, 264, 268, 272-73, 311, 332; explosions & shaking after surge, 169, 171, 174, 176, 185, 193, 204, 208, 210, 220, 227, 229-30, 267-68, 272; lightning (electrical) and–or thunder, 126-29, 134, 136-37, 141-44, 148, 150, 163, 170, 174, 189, 192, 195, 197, 204, 206-08, 210-12, 217-21, 223, 228, 237-38, 252, 272, 277-79, 296-301, 303, 309, 312-13, 316, 351; Spirit Lake giant wave, 352; Spirit Lake filling and log raft, 253, 262, 265, 276, 278-79, 323, 325, 329, 331, 352; South Fork Toutle AM-PM mudflow (lahar) & logs & jams, 120, 126-27, 129-31, 133-37, 193; 196-201, 233, 251-52, 256, 258, 260, 280, 286, 288, 291-92, 311-14, 316, 341, 388n7.13, 389n10.14; South Fork Toutle new PM mudflows, 250, 288; Muddy River and Pine Creek

mudflows (lahars), 229-32, 253, 325; North Fork Toutle mudflow (lahar) & logs & jams, 166, 186, 251, 253-57, 259-60, 262-67, 269, 271-77, 279-86, 289-90, 292, 309-18, 321, 328, 335, 338, 341, 345-47, 351; buildings lost to mudflow, 312-18, 328, 335, 345-47; initial explosions (heard at distance), 241, 305-06, 390n15.1; summit gone, new crater & north breach, 119, 129, 137, 140, 195, 228, 238, 247-51, 252, 272, 290, 292, 323-24, 327, 331, 333, 339; fires in downed trees, 137, 192, 251-52, 273, 292, 321, 336; ash as fertilizer, 342. *See also* Mount St. Helens
Eruptions (magmatic) and ashfalls after 19 May, 347-49, 356, 393n14
Eruptions (phreatic, nonmagmatic), 37-38, 41, 43-45, 47-48, 53, 55, 62-64, 68, 78, 81, 119, 383n13, 384n7, 387n7.4
Etna, Mount, 11
Everett Herald (newspaper), 284-85

Fabik, Dave, 72
Faddis, Bruce, 96, 113, 386n3, 387n6.1
Fairchild, Lee, 62-63, 81
Fairchild Air Force Base, 306
Fanony, Louie, 90
Fawn Lake, 96, 167, 208, 257, 351-54, 358
Federal Avation Administration (FAA), 40, 55, 332
Federal Communications Commission (FCC), 67, 76
Findley, Rowe, 51, 81, 84, 87, 92, 135, 292, 329
Findley, Joe. *See* McCulley, Larry
Fire lookouts, 19, 25, 342
Fitzgerald, Jim, 97, 112, 154-55, 158, 323-24, 352, 354
Florence Creek, 20, 36, 56, 65, 80, 108, 358
Fontz, Randy, 280-82, 326
Ford, Roy and–or Sandy, 98-99, 103
Forest Service. *See* US Forest Service
Fosterman, 239
Frank, David, 74
Frenchman Hills, Wash., 300
Frishman, Rich, 186, 284-85

Gadwa, Tom. *See* Bowers, Wally
Gallant, Peter, 127-28
Gardner, Dave (and Bob Cory), 100, 133, 289-90
Gasses (vented), 11, 45, 55, 57, 73, 102, 383n15, 384n10, 385n21
Gaston, Bob, 292

Geodetic monitoring. *See* Mount St. Helens, measuring bulge, posteruption monitoring
George, Wash., 300-301, 342
Giesbrecht, Roland. *See* Rooth
Gifford Pinchot National Forest, 35-38, 42. *See also* US Forest Service
Gilbert Ridge (lookout), 100, 113, 145, 155
Gilka, Bob, 51
Girl Scout camps, *See* Scout camps
Glicken, Harry, 74, 78, 80, 82, 85, 88, 90, 94-95, 101-02, 109-10, 264, 266, 268, 271-75, 293, 341, 387n13, 391n17, 391nn21-22
Goat Mountain, 101
Gorshkov, G.S., report of, 64
Gould, Alan "Whoop," 205-08, 389n11.4
Graff, Keith, 300-301, 342
Gray Army airfield, 280, 282, 284-87, 326, 331. *See also* Washington Army National Guard
Great Northern Railroad, 17
Green River, 20, 91, 93, 96, 100-101, 114, 167-86, 172-86; Soda Spring, 181-82, 184, 203-08, 210-11, 257-58, 280-82, 285-86, 288, 324-27, 337-39, 347-50. *See also* Florence Creek
Green Mountain, 19, 22, 26, 51, 54, 313
Grose, Tim, 55-56, 80-81, 87
Guild, Irving. *See* Wishart
Guthrie, Steve (and Dave Rodeback), 150
Guzzo, Lou, 28-29, 242
Haderly, Joyce and Floyd, 311-12, 345
Hagerman, Jess, 166, 178, 280-82, 325-27, 331, 338-41, 351
Halicki, Ray, 97
Hall, Jim, 98, 108
Halliday, William, 143
Hamilton, Don, 33-34, 39-40, 103-04, 106
Hammond, Paul, 75
Hanaford Lake, 101, 167, 347, 352-53
Hanks, Dale, 148-49
Hanley, Donald, 304-05, 344
Harder, Richard "Bagger," 325, 327, 391n25, 393n20.3
Harmonic tremor (earthquake), 49, 57, 333
Harmony Falls (or Park or Lodge), ix, 4, 20-24, 52-53, 69, 265, 329
Harris, Steve, 81
Harrys Ridge, 356
Harvey, Joel and Linda. *See* Rosenquist
Hathaway, Paul, 86-87
Hauser (cadaver dog), 351-52
Hembree, Joel, 89
Henderson, Paul (and Geoff Manasse), 310

Herrington, Greg, 244, 291

Hewes, Bill, 88

Hibok–Hibok, 12

Hickson, Cathie and Paul, 94, 101, 114, 225-31

Hill, James J., 17

Hill, Tom, 51, 67, 77, 385n31

Hill, Jim and Greg, 132-44

Hobart, Sue, 54, 72

Hoblitt, Rick, ix, 39, 47-48, 50, 67, 73-74, 85, 250-51, 288, 292, 390n16.2

Hodgson, Vern (and Bernadette Chausee), 220-23, 341

Hoffstadt Mountain, 43, 254

Hoffstadt Creek, 163-66, 251, 257-58, 280, 326, 331

Hoger, Ernst (and Vern Putrow), 238

Holtsclaw, Mike, 352

Hospitals, 166, 172, 181, 186, 201, 281-82, 284, 287, 289, 337, 340

Hubbard, Mike, 169-72, 337. *See also* Payne

Hurliman, Ben, 75

Illinois Central Railroad, 17

Independence Mine, 100, 203

Interstate–5 bridge (Toutle River), 260, 280, 290-92

Iron Creek (Forest road 125), 216, 218-23

Jackson Creek, 4, 277

Johnson, Bob, 100, 105, 107-08

Johnson, Ken (FS Ranger), 5, 7-8, 38

Johnson, Wendell and Viola, 101, 216, 219-21

Johnston, David, 7, 41-44, 53, 57, 64, 68, 71-73, 76, 81, 85, 88, 92, 95, 101-02, 107-11, 114, 137, 151, 244, 247, 261, 264-65, 272, 275, 290, 293, 312, 323, 329, 355-56, 384n10, 387n13, 387n15

Johnston, Bea and Barry, 74, 97, 113, 155-58

Johnston, Billie, 295-96

Johnston, Tom, 355-56

Jones, Wayne and Betty (and Ken Sugerman), 298-99

Judson, Bruce. *See* Stoffel

Kalama River or valley (and Merrill Lake), 26, 135, 194-96, 256

Karr family, 112, 324, 330, 353, 356

Karr, Barbara, 330, 356

Kaseweter, Robert (and Bev Wetherald), 51, 71, 94-95, 97-98, 103-04, 108, 386n9

KATU TV, 355

Kearney, Marianna and Ty, 84, 101, 108, 112, 114, 151-53, 187-91

Keatley, John, 256-57, 347

Kelso, 54, 243-44, 291, 328-29, 336. *See also* Longview, and Kelso–Longview airport

Kelso-Longview airport or airfield, 129, 135, 276-77, 280-82, 284-85, 289, 310, 315, 326, 331, 335-36

KGAR radio, 106, 336

KGW radio, 37, 92

Kid Valley (village), 3, 34-35, 44, 65, 93, 113, 157, 161, 163, 243-44, 263-64, 267, 272, 275, 309

Kieffer, Sue (and Hugh), 47-48

Kienle, Rick, 97

Kilauea, 11

Killian, Jeanette, 351. *See also* Ralph Killian, John Killian

Killian, John and Christy, 90, 96, 114, 206, 257, 351-52

Killian, Ralph, 52, 351

Kilpatrick, Kran. *See* Anderson, Kathy

King, Ray and-or Linda, 46, 98-99, 103

King, Shawn. *See* Wilson

KING TV, 41-43, 93, 98, 108, 133-34, 254, 287, 388n7.14

KIRO TV, 62-64, 99-100, 134-35

Kittitas Valley, 296-97, 342

Kiver, Eugene, 305-06, 344, 392n18.5

Koenniger, Tom, 291

KOIN TV, 103, 198, 287, 289

Kolb, Harold "Hal" (and Bob Bryant), 185, 284-85

KOMO Radio, 266, 270-71, 310, 340

KOMO TV, 111, 196, 286-89

Koon, Carol, 198, 289

Krakatau, 12

Kratch, Bill, 330-32, 340

Kropf, Joan. *See* Purdum

La Soufrière (Guadaloupe), 43

Lafever, Andy, 344

Lahar. *See* Mount St. Helens, mudflows

Lamington, Mount, 12, 75-76

Land survey, cadastral, 15-16, 21

Landon, Robert, 49, 56, 94, 97-98, 100, 105-07, 242, 386n2

Landsburg, Robert, 93, 101, 112, 153-54, 193, 350-51, 358

Lange, Robert and Minnie, 19-21, 115

LaPlaunt, Don, 211-212

Lassen Peak, 13, 27

Lava flows, 11

LaValla, Rick, 55, 73, 93

Lawton, Michael, 62, 356

Lee, Stan and–or Josephine, 34, 36, 44, 52, 65

Leighley, Terry, 51

Lematta, Jim, 86

LeMonds, Bill, 89-90, 349-50

Leske, Joey, 307

Leveling. *See* Tilt

Lewis County and sheriff, 331, 338, 351-52.

Lewis River or valley (and highway 503), 15, 20-21, 230. *See also* Swift Dam and Reservior, Yale Lake

Lewis and Clark (expedition), 14

Lincoln, Abraham, 17

Lindeman, Glen, 303-304, 344

Lineau, Michael, 347-48, 393n21

Lipman, Peter, 53, 70, 75

Livingston, Ted, 56

Lloyd, Darryl, 149-50, 349

Long, Chuck and Pat, 103

Longview and Kelso, 3, 19, 25, 89, 243, 292, 329. *See also* Weyerhaeuser, mills; Kelso-Longview airport

Ludwig, Paul, 307, 392n18.6

Lund, Pauline, 99, 103

Lund, Don, 145-47, 388n8.3

Lynds, Robert, 352

Macdonald, Ken, 342

McCarty, John, 297-98, 342

McChord Air Force Base, 125, 349

McClellan, George (Capt.), 15

McCoy, Roger, 51, 67, 77, 385n31

McCulley, Hugh, 89, 349

McCulley, Larry (and Joe Findley), 108, 229-32

McNerney, Charles (and John Smart), 100, 162-63, 388n9.13

Magnusson, Warren, 334-35

Malone, Steve, 5, 7, 31, 41, 45, 49, 71, 79, 82, 108, 241, 323, 349

Manasse, Geoff. *See* Henderson

Manastash Ridge, 296

Maple Flats (village), 42, 79, 93, 244, 255-56, 309, 382n11

Maratta Creek or valley, 47-48, 50, 108, 251, 264-65, 278

Marble Mountain and Swift Creek, 234-37

Marshall, John, 62, 292, 356

Martin, Gerry, 98-99, 101, 109, 102, 112, 114, 151, 153, 187-88, 191

Mason, Don, 106

Matthes, Joseph, 126, 387n7.5

Mazamas, 21, 101

Medical examiners & offices, 341-42

Meetings, volcano (and press conferences), 34-35, 37, 42-45, 48-50, 69, 82-83

Melton, Joe, 357

Menard, H.W., 61

Meredith, Steve, 106

Merzoian, Dave, 205-08, 257, 389n11.3

Meta Lake, 56, 353, 358

Miller, Dan, 53, 75, 80, 83, 85, 88, 92, 108, 110-11, 237, 244, 290

Miller, Fred, 50

Miners Creek, 100, 182-83, 205, 349

Mining near Mount St. Helens, 19-21, 36, 381n48-52. *See also* Black Rock mine

Missoula, Mont., 306-07, 344

Moore, Jerome and Shirley, 351

Moore, Mike and Lu, 100, 203-05, 325-27

Moore, Keith, 169, 337. *See also* Payne

Moore, James "Jim," 45, 50, 53, 59-61, 68, 75-76, 78, 81-82, 88, 92

Morris, John. *See* Anderson, Kathy

Morton (town), 219, 223, 293

Moscow, Id., 304-05, 344

Moses Lake, Wash., 301-02, 343-45

Mount Adams, 114, 125, 128, 130, 142, 147-50, 195, 267

Mount Baker, 27-28

Mount Hood, 114, 150, 264, 325; Timberline Lodge, 6, 14

Mount Margaret, 77, 92, 206

Mount Rainier, 26, 114, 141-47, 187, 190

Mount St. Helens, ix-359; prehistoric eruptions, 26-28, 34-35, 43, 67, 76, 380n17; blister or bulge, 54, 59, 61, 63, 68-71, 81, 91-93, 108-110, 114, 118-19, 121, 225; measuring bulge (& heat), 70, 72, 75, 82, 88-89, 91, 93, 106, 109-11, 129-30; Butte Camp, 95; crater, 37, 40-42, 45, 50, 54, 59, 62-63, 68, 75, 95, 115, 118-19, 121-22; Dogs Head, 4, 50, 70; fissures or fractures or cracks, 40-41, 59, 63, 69, 108, 119, 121; Goat Rocks, ix, 50, 61, 70, 72, 75, 82, 91-92, 95, 106, 109-11, 118, 121, 129-30, 187; landslides and avalanches and forecasts of, 62-64, 68-69, 82, 86-87, 92, 109; magmatic eruption forecast, 48-50, 53-54, 56, 63, 109; mudflows (lahars) or floods forecast, 34, 36, 48, 50, 56, 63-64, 68-69, 78-79, 82; daytime darkness forecast, 48, 69; ashfall forecast, 34, 48, 50, 69; Plains of Abraham, 8, 78, 249; Sheep Canyon, 111, 189; Shoestring Glacier or notch, 91-92,

108, 111, 225, 249, 252; Sugarbowl, 82, 121; Smith Creek & Muddy River & tributaries, 227-32; Sugarbowl dome blast, 76; summit, 62-63, 68, 72, 109, 115, 118; The Boot, 68, 102, 109-10, 187; wetness (water oozing), 121; posteruption monitoring, 356. *See also* Eruptions, Eruption phenomena; Marble Mountain and Swift Creek; Timberline

Mount St. Helens Contingency Plan, 56

Mount St. Helens Lodge (Truman's), 21-23, 33, 39, 53, 59-61, 67-68, 80, 82, 84, 86, 92, 100, 104, 106-08, 121, 278, 329, 339, 357

Mount St. Helens Watch Group. *See* Ray, Dixie Lee

Muddy River (and Smith Creek and Clear Creek), 120, 325

Mullen, Dave, 272-76, 323-24, 350

Mullineaux, Donal "Don," ix, 6, 8, 26-28, 30-31, 34-37, 42-44, 53-54, 61-62, 64, 71, 76, 78-79, 82-84, 88, 312-13, 350

Murphy, Ed and Eleanor, 106, 113, 158-60

Myers, Rick, 306, 343

Nance, Ancil, 62

National Geographic Magazine, 51, 62, 67, 76, 81, 84, 87, 92, 135, 244, 261, 292, 328-30, 355-56

National Guard. *See* Washington Army National Guard, Oregon National Guard

Natt, Ted, 292

NBC and Today show, 75, 108, 338

Nehl, Steve, 33

Nelson, Les (Cowlitz Co. Sheriff), 34-35, 44, 55, 57, 64, 69, 71, 75, 79-80, 83, 85-86, 91, 93-94, 98-99, 291, 312-13, 331, 334, 345

Nelson, Jack, 21, 23

Nelson, Bruce, 94, 96, 114, 172-78, 180, 184-86, 338-39

Nesbit, Dick, ix, 86-87, 89-90, 259-60

Nieland, Jim, ix, 37-39

Nolan, Tom. *See* Weed

Nole, Charles "Chuck," 286-89, 331, 334-35

North Fork. *See* Toutle River

Northern Pacific Railroad (or Railway) and land grants, 17-18

Northwest Airlines, 115, 124-25, 307

Noson, Linda, 5-6, 8

Nugent, Jim, 25-26, 91, 350

Nugent, Ed, 81-82, 90-91

O'Keefe, Kathie and Gil Baker, 160-63, 388n9.13

O'Neill, Danny, 97-98, 159-60

O'Neill, Keith, 83

Okamura, Arnold, 88, 333

Olson, Roger and Erik, 315-16, 346

Olson, Dave, 355

Olympia (and Lacey), Wash., 133, 242-43, 289, 291. *See also* Dixy Lee Ray, Washington State Patrol, Washington State (executuve departments)

Oregon Alpine Club, 21

Oregon National Guard, 129-31, 253, 333

Oregon Journal (newspaper), 33-34, 39, 49, 104

Oregon Donation Act of 1850, 15

Oregonian (newspaper), 45, 54, 72, 87, 103, 245, 276, 292

Osmond, Ed, 35, 37

Pacific Highway bridge, 135, 260, 315-18, 341

Pacific Power & Light, 36, 267

Palmer, Gene and Kathy, 208-09, 389n11.8

Palmer, Leonard, 34-35, 51-52, 72-73, 76, 79

Parker, Bill and Jean, 101, 326, 353, 355, 358

Parker, Jay, 36, 65, 80-81

Parker, Rick, 55, 87, 108, 358

Parker, Don and Natalie, 87, 108, 353

Paulson, Kathy, 38-39, 103, 107, 382n9. *See also* Smith, Rob

Payne, Robert (and Mike Hubbard and Keith Moore), 114, 169-72, 337

Pearson Airpark. *See* Vancouver.

Peden, Bill, 276-77, 330, 350

Pelée, Mont, 12, 43

Perry, Ralph, 51, 76-78, 81, 84, 92, 328-29, 355

Peters, Mike, 260, 266-68, 271-76, 277, 323-24, 330-31, 391n21, 391n23

Peterson, Ole, 21

Pierre, S.D., 307

Pine Creek, 325

Pleasant, Ray, 136, 201, 256-59, 324

Pliny the Younger, 304, 358. *See also* Pompeii, Vesuvius

Pluard, Jim and Kathleen, 90, 114, 258

Polar Star Mine, 101

Pole Patch, 220-22

Pompeii, 12, 218, 223, 291, 292n17.1. *See also* Vesuvius, Pliny

Portland, Oreg., 245, 292, 321, 333, 336. See also *Oregonian, Oregon Journal,* Oregon National Guard.

Portland State University, 51

Portland General Electric, 51, 97

Post, Austin, 61

Potlach, Id., 305

Powell, John Wesley, 19
Pullen, Connie, 98, 103-04
Pullman, Wash., 303-04, 344
Purcell, Dave, 87
Purdum, Ronald (and Joan Kropf), 128
Putrow, Vern and Harold. *See* Hogar

Quincy, Wash., 342-43

Radio Amateur Civil Emergency Service (RACES), 84, 114, 151, 153, 187
Radio Amateurs (hams) and clubs, 51-52, 67, 76, 80, 114, 187-89, 355. *See also* Blackburn, Kearney, Martin
Randle (town), 217, 219-21, 223, 233, 293, 341
Ray, Dixy Lee (Washington governor), 28-30, 40, 48, 56, 74, 80, 93-94, 100, 110, 129, 242-43, 260, 273, 291, 321, 328-29, 332-35, 337, 351, 385n23, 385n38, 387-88n7.10, 392n17.1; emergency declarations or orders, 49, 73, 93; governor's office, 75, 242; Mount St. Helens Watch Group, 49, 56, 83; Ray Walters (press secretary), 86, 386n2
Reagan, Ronald, 333
Reagan, Peter, 62, 67
Reber, Dwight, 62, 77, 81, 84-87, 92, 135-36, 193, 272, 274, 277-79, 287, 291-92, 326, 328-29, 355-56, 385n31, 391nn27-28, 392nn29-33
Red zone. *See* Volcanic hazard zones
Red Cross, 332
Reed, Jim, 266, 270-71, 310, 340
Reitan, Roald (and Venus Dergan), 101, 198-201, 256, 258, 340-41
Remmen, Martin, 36, 55-56, 65, 80-81, 87
Renner, Jeff, 41-43, 98, 133-34, 254, 287, 355-56
Riffe Lake, 207, 211-12
Ring of Fire, 11
Ritzville, Wash., 302-03, 343-44
Roadblocks (or roadgates), 35, 38, 40, 42, 44-45, 50-51, 64-65, 68, 93-100, 106-09, 113, 158, 160, 339, 382n11
Rodeback, Dave. *See* Guthrie
Rogers, Robert, 68-69, 75, 101, 111-12, 135, 187, 189-93, 350-51
Roggenback, Gary and Brenda, 54, 312-13, 346
Rollins, Fred and Margery, 160, 391n19
Rombach, Jim, 75, 114, 324
Ronnholm, Keith, 101, 114, 215, 217-19
Rooth, Guy (and Roland Giesbrecht), 251-52
Rosenbaum, Joe, 85, 241, 247, 263, 267
Rosenfeld, Chuck, 129-31, 253, 388n7.19

Rosenquist, Gary (and Joel and Linda Harvey, and William Dilly), 101, 114, 213-17
Ross, Keith, 100, 358
Ruff, Sue, 94, 96, 114, 172-78, 180, 184-86, 338
Russ, Betty Dee and Phil, 306-07, 344
Ryan, Rich (and Glen Bowers and Bob Bioren), 124-25
Ryan Lake, 101, 353

Salem, Oreg. (and *Statesman Journal* newspaper), 245, 251-53
Salsman, Dexter, 87
San Jose Mercury, San Jose News (newspapers), 282, 327, 330
Santorini, 12
Sarna–Wojckcki, Andrei. 45, 51
Schaefer, Don, 268, 272-75
Schmidt, Paul, 352
Schoening, Jack, 83-86, 136, 201, 256, 350
Schrag (I-90 rest area), Wash., 302, 343
Schroeder, Deon, 261, 264, 272
Schultz Creek, 100, 113-14, 167-68, 206-07, 358
Scout camps (on Spirit Lake), 23, 25, 86, 106
Scymanky, Jim (and Leonty Skorohodoff, Evlanty Sharipoff, and José Dias), 91, 95, 113, 163-66, 280-83, 337, 351, 393n16. *See also* Dias and Sharipoff
Search and rescue (posteruption), 256-90, 324-31
Seattle Times (newspaper), 99, 285-86, 310
Seismic station, 379n1.2
Selby, Don, 74-75, 96, 112, 189, 309, 321, 352, 354
Sharipoff, Evlanty, 351. *See also* Scymanky
Showa-Shin-zan (Usu), Japan, 75, 93
Sicotte, Chuck, 62-63, 134-35
Sieber, Otto, 63, 67, 81, 93, 347-48, 384n6, 385n38, 393n21
Siebert, Ken, 239, 390n14.4
Siebold, Ron and Barbara, 113, 145, 155, 288, 326, 331, 358
Siefert, Rick, 94, 103
Sigfridson, Valerie. *See* Anderson, Kathy
Silver Lake (lake or town), 3, 17, 97, 312-13
Simmonds, Terry, 31, 65, 82-83, 87, 242
Skamania County and sheriff, 57, 338 341. *See also* Closner, Medical examiners
Skorohodoff, Leonty. *See* Scymanky
Slonicker, Eugene, 65-67, 72
Small, Steve, 67, 76, 85, 87, 92, 108-09, 244, 291
Smart, John. See McNerney
Smith Creek. *See* Muddy River

Smith, Edward "Buzz," 100, 181, 182-86, 205, 285, 346

Smith, Rob, 38-39, 67, 78, 103, 107, 382n9. *See also* Paulson

Smith, Mark, 103

Smith, Dave and Mariam, 24

Smith, Dennis, 193-94

Snell, John, 297, 342

South Fork. *See* Toutle River

Spahman, Ron, ix, 78, 94-95, 97

Spirit Lake, ix, 3, 7, 19, 23-27, 39, 62-63, 68, 83-84, 89, 94, 103-08, 114, 121-22, 262, 265, 278-79, 323, 325, 339, 352, 356-58; measured for tilt, 45, 54; forecast of damming and giant wave, 63, 69, 79; Bear Cove, 106, 352, 357. *See also* Scout camps, Duck Bay, Harmony Falls, Harmony Falls Lodge, Mount St. Helens Lodge, Spirit Lake Lodge, YMCA camps

Spirit Lake highway (state highway 504), ix, 3, 33, 78, 121, 155-63, 244, 258, 265, 308-10; highway bridge above Alder Creek, 3, 98, 255-57, 266-67, 275. *See also* Coal Bank bridge

Spirit Lake Lodge (the Smith's), 22, 38-39, 51, 61, 69-70, 78, 103, 107, 278

Spokane, Wash., 305-06, 336, 342-43

Spud Mountain, 51, 60, 74-75, 93, 96-97, 112, 155, 189, 309, 321-23, 352, 354

St. Helens Mining District, 19-21, 36, 381n48-52

St. Joe National Forest, Id., 304-05

St. Pierre, Martinique, 12-13

Stearns, Richard, 296-97

Stebner, Darald (and Frank Shipton), 281-84, 327, 329-30

Steele, Bill, 305-06

Steig, George, 89

Stenkamp, Paul, 36, 56, 71, 93

Stepankowsky, Andre, 128-29, 292

Stevens, Isaac (Wash. Territorial governor), 15-17

Stewart, Bill, 33, 109

Stickney, Lon (and Aero–Copters), 48, 59-60, 69, 75, 78, 85, 92, 95, 97, 101-02, 106, 109, 250, 290, 321, 323, 392nn41-42

Stocker, Fred, 51, 67, 76, 84, 87, 108, 135, 355

Stoffel, Keith and Dorothy (and Bruce Judson), 115, 118, 121-24

Stoker, Bruce, 241

Stovel, Fred, 275-76, 292

Sugar, Jim, 51, 330

Sugarman, Ken. *See* Wayne Jones

Sullivan, Annie and Joe (and Mark Dahl), 194-96

Swanson, Don, 45, 50, 53-54, 56, 59-61, 70, 88, 92, 95, 97, 102, 106, 109-11, 137-40, 241, 247, 290, 293, 321, 323, 352, 356

Swier, Dick, 242-43, 260, 291, 333, 335-36. *See also* Washington State Patrol

Swift Dam or Reservoir, 36, 237, 267. *See also* Lewis River

Tacitus, Cornelius, 358

Tambora, 12

Tazieff, Haroun, 53

Tektronix (and TERAC radio club), 51, 67, 80

Terrill, Steve, 238-39

The Dalles, Oreg., 307

Theisen, George, 31, 35, 50, 56, 65, 69, 72-73, 75, 79, 82-83, 93

Thomas, Brian, 96, 114, 175-82, 184, 281-82, 340

Thomas, Jim, 76

Thompson, David, 14

Three Mile Island, Pa. (nuclear plant), 35, 333

Tieton, Wash., 299

Tilling, Robert "Bob," 8, 43

Tilt (or swelling) of land surface, 45, 56-57, 333

Tilton, Bill and Susan, 96, 386n3

Timberline (Mount St. Helens), 7, 33, 37-38, 40, 59, 70, 82, 92, 102, 106, 109, 379n1.5

Tippery, Bud, 92-93

Tokarczyk, Robert "Bob,", 8, 31, 36, 56, 64, 88, 111, 334-35, 382n7

Toledo (airfield and town), 161, 332, 338, 348

Tonn, Chuck, ix, 6-7, 33, 38, 61

Toutle Lake High School (and fields), 78, 98, 201, 254, 257-59, 271, 273, 275, 280, 285-88, 326

Toutle River or valley, 3, 17, 19, 131, 134, 136, 186, 252, 260, 272, 277, 287, 309-18, 308-09, 311-18, 328, 334, 345-46; North Fork, 3, 19, 21, 25, 68, 72, 101-02, 120, 133, 136, 155-63, 194-95, 205, 250-51, 253-54, 256-81, 285-87, 289-90, 308-13, 325, 328, 345; South Fork, 25, 50, 70, 89, 93, 101, 111-12, 114, 120, 130, 133, 135-36, 187-201, 250-52, 256, 258, 275, 280, 282-84, 286-89, 311-13, 324, 346, 350, 353, 358. *See also* Castle Creek, Coal Bank bridge, Coldwater Creeks, Hoffstadt Creek, Interstate–5 bridge, Maratta Creek, Pacific Highway bridge, Weyerhaeuser Company

Toutle (town), 19, 35, 78, 155, 159, 163

Tradedollar Lake, 351

Treat, Gary, 128

Tremor. *See* Harmonic tremor

Tripp, Ernest, 349

Trojan nuclear plant, 97

Truman, Harry (and Eddie), ix, 21-24, 33-34, 36, 39, 44, 48, 51, 53, 59-61, 67-68, 80-82, 84-86, 92, 94-95, 98-99, 104-07, 135, 278-79, 292, 329, 339, 357, 384n2, 386n41

Turgeson, Joel, 347-48, 393n21

Twigg, George, 301-02, 343-45

United Airlines, 115, 126-28, 251

US Air Force, 247, 257, 287, 306, 333-34, 336, 382n7, 390n16.1. *See also* US Air Force Reserve

US Air Force Reserve 303rd squadron (C-130 & command jeep), 324, 329-32, 340. *See also* Kratch, Weidman

US Air Force Reserve 304th squadron (hueys), 81, 88, 95-96, 244, 259-77, 280, 292-93, 323, 324-28, 330-31, 339, 348, 350, 390-91n16.11, 391nn27-28

US Army, 332-35, 338-41, 347, 351

US Coast Guard, 254, 258, 273, 277, 280, 286-89

US Forest Service, 19, 31, 49-50, 64, 79, 296; Columbia National Forest, 19, 21; Gifford Pinchot National Forest, 8, 26, 31, 65-67, 69, 71, 73, 75-76, 79, 81-84, 87, 93, 108, 111, 114, 135, 137, 140, 235-38, 241, 244, 247-51, 254, 263, 267, 275, 290, 321, 332-34, 341, 350, 352, 358; Spirit Lake visitor's center (hut), campground, and docks, 3-6, 24-25, 33, 39, 97. *See also* Fire lookouts

US Geological Survey (USGS), 7-8, 19, 31, 36, 41-43, 45, 48, 50, 53-54, 56-57, 62, 64, 67, 69, 71-72, 74-76, 78-79, 81-85, 92, 94-95, 101-03, 106-11, 137-40, 237-38, 241, 244, 247-51, 267, 278, 290, 292-93, 303, 312-13, 316-18, 321, 329, 333-34, 341, 344-45, 350, 352-56

US Marine Corps (for President Carter), 333-36

University of Washington (UW, in Seattle), 28; seismology laboratory or seismologists, 5-8, 31, 43, 48-49, 54, 56, 62, 64, 72, 81, 94, 108, 241, 323

University of Oregon, 53

Unterwegner, Jim, 37, 42

Valenzuela, Francisco, 101, 111-12, 135, 187, 189-94, 350, 389n10.6

Vallance, Jim, ix,

Vancouver, Fort, 14-15

Vancouver, George, 13

Vancouver, Wash. 241, 244, 293, 333-34; Pearson Airpark, 261, 264, 268, 272, 275, 279, 290-93. *See also* US Forest Service, US Geological Survey

Vanson Peak, 201

Varner, Karen. *See* Crall

Varnes, David, 75

Vesuvius, Mount, 12, 43, 304, 358. *See also* Pompeii, Pliny

Voight, Barry, 59-60, 63, 87-88

Volcanic hazard zones and maps, 45-47, 65-67, 71-74, 82-83, 85-87, 93-94, 111-12, 295, 321, 350

von Michalofski, Olaf, 142

Waitt, Richard, 45, 51, 59-60, 65, 317-18, 329, 341, 352-55, 357-58, 393n19.12, 393n27

Walcker, Ron, 40, 242

Walters, Tom, 251, 254, 258, 277, 286-89

Ward, Kyle, 313-15, 346

Ward, Dave, 261, 265-73, 277, 325, 391n19

Washington Army National Guard, 52-53, 64, 70, 95, 110, 166, 177-78, 181-82, 185-86, 254, 256-57, 263-64, 271, 273, 276-77, 279-88, 309-10, 325-32, 334-35, 338-40

Washington state: constitution, 29; Commerce Department, 83-84; Department of Natural Resources (DNR), 29-30, 35, 50, 69, 75-76, 82-83; Game Department (or Commission), 30, 55, 76, 83; Department of Ecology, 65; Department of Emergency Services, 30-31, 55-56, 69, 72, 74-76, 82-83, 87, 93, 98, 108, 111, 242-43, 280, 291, 385n23; Department of Labor & Industries, 55; Legislative (state capitol) building, 56, 242; State Geologist, 56, 76; Posteruption lawsuits, 357. *See also* Dixy Lee Ray

Washington State Patrol, 31, 34, 40, 51, 55, 69, 78, 83, 93, 98-100, 104-08, 114-15, 133, 159-60, 242-44, 289-91, 301-02, 306, 316, 328, 333, 335-36, 340, 342-45, 386n4

Washington state timber lands, 26

Washington State University (Pullman), 303, 344. *See also* Lindeman

Washington Post (newspaper), 44

Weaver, Craig, 5-7, 31, 36, 54

Wedding, George, 281-85, 326-30, 352, 356

Weed, Bob (and Tom Nolan), 261-67, 271, 391n13

Weidman, Charles "Bud," 324, 330

Wendt, Dave, 324-25, 327

Werth, Roger, 33, 44, 48, 68, 98-99, 103, 105-06, 128-29, 254-55, 292, 387n7.9, 387-88 n7.10, 392n19.5

Weyerhaeuser, Frederick, 18

Weyerhaeuser Company (or Weyerhaeuser Timber Company), 18-19, 52, 57, 62, 69, 74-75, 79, 81, 83, 85-87, 89-93, 99, 114, 136, 256-60, 275, 280, 324, 345, 357; cutting and logging and thinning operations, 89-91, 95, 113-14, 345; off-highway log trucks, 75, 357, 385n25; railroad, 19, 25, 199, 252, 349-50, 357; road system, 25-26, 40, 98, 309, 357; Camp Baker, ix, 3, 25, 86, 88-92, 113, 130, 133, 155, 158, 163, 256-60, 263-64, 266, 271, 275, 277, 285, 290, 349-50, 357; 12–Road Camp, 25, 129-30, 133, 136, 198, 252, 312, 357, 388n7.13; 19–Mile Camp, 3, 256-60, 267-68, 357; helicopters, 201, 256-60; mills 19, 25-26, 345; eruption–smashed camps and equipment, 357; leveled company forest, 357. *See also* Longview

Wheeler, Jerry, 220-21, 340

Wheeler, Melvin, 312-13

White House communications, 332. *See also* Carter, Jimmy

Whitlock, Jack and Doreen, 208-09

Whitney, Mary and Harold, 115

Wiley City, Wash., 297-98, 342

Wilkes, Charles (United States Exploring Expedition), 13-14

Willamette Valley, Oreg., 15

Williams, John, 72, 384n18, 384-85n20

Williams, Garvin, 261, 265-73, 323-24, 348

Williamson, Mike. *See* Downing

Wilson, Larry (and Shawn King), 155-59

Winters Mountain, 167, 208

Wishart, Larry (and Irving Guild), 232-33

Wolfe, Chuck, 97

Wolff, Jack and Joann, 86, 339

Wörner, Gerhard, 92, 95, 102, 106, 109

Wright, Bob, 41-42, 133-34, 254, 287, 388n7.14

Yacolt Burn (& backwind), 18

Yakima, 115, 121, 298-301, 340, 342

Yakima Firing Center, 279, 282, 285–86

Yale Lake, 238, 330. *See also* Lewis River, Swift Dam

YMCA camps (on Spirit Lake), 21-23, 25, 62, 86, 339

Zaitz, Les, 103, 245, 276, 292

Zimmerman, Klaus, 391n14-15

Zink, Joe, 261-64, 266, 271